PRINCE'S DICTIONARY OF LEGAL CITATIONS

A Reference Guide for Attorneys, Legal Secretaries, Paralegals, and Law Students

Seventh Edition

by

Mary Miles Prince

William S. Hein & Co., Inc.
Buffalo, New York
2006

Library of Congress Cataloging-In-Publication Data

Prince, Mary Miles.
    Prince's dictionary of legal citations : a reference guide
for attorneys, legal secretaries, paralegals, and law students. —
7th ed. / by Mary Miles Prince.

    p. cm.
    Rev. ed. of: Prince's Bieber dictionary of legal citations. 6th ed.
by Mary Miles Prince. 2001.
    ISBN 0-8377-3607-2 (cloth : alk. paper)
    1. Law—United States—Abbreviations. 2. Citation of legal
authorities—United States. I. Prince, Mary Miles. Prince's Bieber
dictionary of legal citations. II. Title. III. Title: Dictionary of
legal citations.
    KF246.P73 2006
    349.73'0148—dc22   2006043448

Printed in the United States of America

∞

This volume is printed on acid-free paper.

Dedicated to

Doris Meiyen Bieber Bowers
with admiration and appreciation

Table of Contents

Preface

I wish to express my indebtedness to Doris Meiyen Bieber Bowers, whose vision, intelligence, and hard work created this reference work in 1981, first published as <u>Dictionary of Current American Legal Citations</u>, followed by <u>Current American Legal Citations with 2100 Examples</u>, in 1983. Meiyen, my mentor and former boss, then entrusted the work to me in 1986, my first effort being entitled <u>Bieber's Current American Legal Citations</u>, Second Edition. All who may have been assisted by this publication are also indebted to Meiyen, who realized the usefulness of a reference work which translates citation rules into easy-to-use examples.

<u>Prince's Dictionary of Legal Citations</u>, Seventh Edition, is intended to assist the legal profession in citing legal authorities according to the rules given in <u>The Bluebook: A Uniform System of Citation</u>, Eighteenth Edition (2005). <u>Prince's Dictionary</u> is designed to be a companion to <u>The Bluebook</u>, not a replacement, and applies <u>Bluebook</u> rules to a representative collection of common legal authorities. The citations included in <u>Prince's</u> are based on <u>Bluebook</u> rules, and the abbreviations are those found in <u>The Bluebook</u> or derived from its guidelines.

Although <u>The Bluebook</u> strives to establish uniformity in citation form for court documents, the practitioner should remember that citation rules contained in local rules, state supreme court rules, rules of trial or appellate procedure, and statutes supersede <u>Bluebook</u> rules. <u>Prince's</u> includes both references to state rules for citing cases and statutes, and examples of how to cite cases according to those rules.

Besides adding many additional state court rule references and examples, this edition has been updated to reflect Eighteenth Edition <u>Bluebook</u> revisions. This edition also contains numerous edition and title changes for entries found in the previous edition and many altogether new and revised entries, including additional books and periodicals, expanded treatment of state regulatory compilations and registers, expanded treatment of state session law services, additional foreign and international examples, examples for some foreign law sources with neutral citation, and examples of numerous court documents, including affidavits, answers, briefs, complaints, counterclaims, cross-claims, depositions, hearing transcripts, interrogatories, judgments, memoranda, motions, orders, records, responses, stipulations, and trial transcripts. The book includes a myriad of other new examples, including those for citing depublished cases, I.R.S. Private Letter Rulings, PLI course handbooks, prefaces to books, working papers, letters to the editor and editorials, and articles designated as dedications, commentaries, in memoriams, responses, and tributes. The section concerning electronic media has also been revised and now has examples for citing blogs and websites. Public domain information has been updated and includes additional domestic jurisdictions which now employ this form of citation.

This edition also contains additional information contributed by Bernard J. Sussman, Law Librarian, United States Court of Appeals for Veterans Claims, updating Table 3, which relates for each year the Congress and session number, the volume numbers for the <u>Congressional Record</u>, the <u>United States Statutes at Large</u>, and the <u>Federal Register</u>, and information concerning the numbering systems for federal legislation. His new Table 5 provides information about the various annotated versions of the United States Code, and new Table 6 is his historical discourse on the reporting of United States Supreme Court decisions.

Typeface conventions in this book's examples are those prescribed by The Bluebook for practitioners submitting briefs and court documents. Therefore, ordinary type and underscoring are used in this book rather than, as in law review articles, ordinary roman type, italics, and large and small capitals. The running footnote information concerning typeface conventions for law review articles has also been updated.

The user should bear in mind that some publications, particularly foreign, frequently give only the authors' initials and not first names and, therefore, cannot be cited precisely according to current Bluebook rules.

The legal abbreviations listed are those found in The Bluebook or derived from its guidelines. For extensive lists of general legal abbreviations, consult Bieber's Dictionary of Legal Abbreviations, Fifth Edition, and World Dictionary of Legal Abbreviations.

I wish to thank Martin Cerjan, Assistant Dean and Law Library Director, Vanderbilt University Law School, for his support, Bernard J. Sussman for his suggestions and contributions to this reference work, Stephen M. Jackson for his unfailing good cheer and the proficiency of his typing, Cara Huwieler for her assistance with periodical examples, and Raymond Graham Prince for his assistance with the overall production of the Seventh Edition.

I appreciate your e-mailing suggestions concerning this publication to me at mary.miles.prince@law.vanderbilt.edu.

Mary Miles Prince

PRINCE'S
DICTIONARY OF
LEGAL CITATIONS

A

ABA
See American Bar Association publications.

ABA Journal
See American Bar Association Journal.

ABF
See American Bar Foundation publications.

abridged
    Ab.:   abr.

Accord

    –"'Accord' is commonly used when two or more sources state or clearly support the proposition but the text quotes or refers to only one; the other sources are then introduced by 'accord.'" Bluebook rule 1.2(a).

    Ex.:   Usery v. Kennecott Copper Corp., 577 F.2d 1113 (10th Cir. 1977); accord, Marshall v. Union Oil Co., 616 F.2d 1113 (9th Cir. 1980).

    "Furthermore, conclusory allegations unsupported by any factual assertions will not withstand a motion to dismiss. Briscoe v. LaHue, 663 F.2d 713, 723 (7th Cir. 1981). Accord Hiland Dairy, Inc. v. Kroger Co., 402 F.2d 968, 973 (8th Cir. 1968), cert. denied, 395 U.S. 961, 89 S. Ct. 2096, 23 L. Ed. 2d 748 (1969) (In testing the legal sufficiency of the complaint, conclusions of law and unreasonable inference or unwarranted deductions of fact are not admitted.)"
    –Taken from 675 F.2d 881 (1982).

Accountancy Law Reports (Commerce Clearing House)
    Ab.:   Accountancy L. Rep. (CCH)

Accounting Standards, Generally Accepted
    Ex.:   Accounting for the Costs of Computer Software to be Sold, Leased or Otherwise Marketed, Statement of Financial Accounting Standards No. 86, § 16 (Financial Accounting Standards Bd. 1985).

Acts and Joint Resolutions, South Carolina
    Ab.:   year S.C. Acts page no.
    Ex.:   South Carolina Bed and Breakfast Act, ch. 4, 1998 S.C. Acts 1929.
    –Citation to an entire session law with a popular name.

In law review footnotes, the titles of books and the names of cases, except for procedural phrases, are not underlined. See Bluebook rule 2.1(a) & (b). Further, the following are in large and small capitals: codes, restatements, standards, constitutions, periodicals, authors of books, titles of books, the abbreviated names of codes, most legislative materials except for bills and resolutions, codified ordinances, model codes, court rules, and sentencing guidelines. Refer to The Bluebook.

South Carolina Bed and Breakfast Act, ch. 4, sec. 45-4-30-(A), 1998 S.C. Acts 1929, 1930. –Citation to a section of a session law.

–See Bluebook rule 12.4.

Acts and Resolves of Massachusetts

Ab.:   year Mass. Acts page no.

Ex.:   Act of Apr. 25, 1997, ch. 9, 1997 Mass. Acts 38. –Citation to an entire session law.

Act of Apr. 25, 1997, ch. 9, sec. 1, 1997 Mass. Acts 38, 38. –Citation to a section of a session law.

–See Bluebook rule 12.4.

Acts and Resolves of Rhode Island and Providence Plantations

Ab.:   year R.I. Acts & Resolves page no.

–"Cite to R.I. Pub. Laws, if therein." Bluebook table T.1, p. 230.

–See Bluebook rule 12.4.

Acts and Resolves of Vermont

Ab.:   year Vt. Acts and Resolves page no.

Ex.:   Act of Jan. 24, 1996, No. 65, 1996 Vt. Acts and Resolves 2 (relating to tracking and killing of injured wildlife). –Citation to an entire session law.

Act of Feb. 1, 1996, No. 67, sec. 1, § 801(a), 1996 Vt. Acts and Resolves 3 (relating to motor vehicle financial responsibility). –Citation to a section of a session law amending a prior act.

–See Bluebook rule 12.4.

Acts, Indiana

Ab.:   year Ind. Acts page no.

Ex.:   Act of Mar. 11, 1996, Pub. L. No. 15-1996, 1996 Ind. Acts 1029. –Citation to an entire session law.

Act of Mar. 11, 1996, Pub. L. No. 15-1996, § 2, 1996 Ind. Acts 1029, 1030-33. –Citation to a section of a session law.

–See Bluebook rule 12.4.

Acts of Arkansas

Ab.:   year Ark. Acts page no.

Ex.:   Act of Aug. 26, 1994, No. 62, 1995 Ark. Acts 333. –Citation to an entire session law.

Act of Aug. 26, 1994, No. 62, Sec. 3, § 16-13-326, 1995 Ark. Acts 333, 340. –Citation to a section of session law amending a prior act.

–See Bluebook rule 12.4.

In citing cases in law review footnotes, abbreviate any word listed in table T.6; the names of "states, countries, and other geographical units" unless they are named parties; and any other words of eight or more letters "if substantial space is thereby saved and the result is unambiguous." Bluebook rule 10.2.2. On the other hand, in citing cases in text, abbreviate only widely known acronyms and the following words: "&," "Ass'n," "Bros.," "Co.," "Corp.," "Inc.," "Ltd.," and "No." Bluebook rule 10.2.1(c).

Acts of Congress
See entries herein for private laws and public laws.

Acts of Kentucky
Ab.:   year Ky. Acts page no.

Ex.:   Act of Apr. 11, 1996, ch. 369, 1996 Ky. Acts 1787. –Citation to an entire session law.

Act of Apr. 11, 1996, ch. 369, sec. 2, § 42.066, 1996 Ky. Acts 1787, 1788. –Citation to a section of a session law amending a prior act.
–See Bluebook rule 12.4.

Acts of the General Assembly of the Commonwealth of Virginia
Ab.:   year Va. Acts page no.

Ex.:   Act of Apr. 6, 1995, ch. 824, 1995 Va. Acts 1693 (relating to stalking). –Citation to an entire session law.

Act of Apr. 6, 1995, ch. 824, sec. 1, § 18.2-60.3, 1995 Va. Acts 1693, 1693 (penalty for stalking). –Citation to a section of a session law amending a prior act.

–See Bluebook rule 12.4.

Acts of the Legislature of West Virginia
Ab.:   year W. Va. Acts page no.

Ex.:   Act of Mar. 11, 1995, ch. 166, 1995 W. Va. Acts 1251. –Citation to an entire session law.

Act of Mar. 11, 1995, ch. 166, art. 1 § 9-1-2, 1995 W. Va. Acts 1251, 1152-54. –Citation to a section of a session law.
–See Bluebook rule 12.4.

Acts of the Parliaments of Scotland, The
Ab.:   Scot. Parl. Acts

Acts of the Parliament of South Australia
Ab.:   S. Austl. Acts

Acts of the State of Iowa
Ab.:   year Iowa Acts page no.

Ex.:   Act of Mar. 4, 1998, ch. 1010, 1999 Iowa Acts 7 (relating to the creation of a dental hygiene committee). –Citation to an entire session law.

Act of Mar. 4, 1998, ch. 1010, sec. 1, § 147.14, 1999 Iowa Acts 7, 7. –Citation to a section of a session law amending a prior act.

See Bluebook rule 12.4.

Acts, Resolves and Constitutional Resolutions of the State of Maine
Ab.:   year Me. Acts page no.

In law review footnotes, the titles of books and the names of cases, except for procedural phrases, are not underlined. See Bluebook rule 2.1(a) & (b). Further, the following are in large and small capitals: codes, restatements, standards, constitutions, periodicals, authors of books, titles of books, the abbreviated names of codes, most legislative materials except for bills and resolutions, codified ordinances, model codes, court rules, and sentencing guidelines. Refer to The Bluebook.

–"Cite to Me. Laws, if therein." <u>Bluebook</u> table T.1, p. 212.

–See <u>Bluebook</u> rule 12.4.

addenda
    Ab.:   add.

–See <u>Bluebook</u> rule 3.4.

Adelaide Law Review
    Ab.:   Adel. L. Rev.

    Ex.:   Keith Bennetts, <u>Bankruptcy: Its Consequences for Family Property</u>, 11 Adel. L. Rev. 413 (1988). –Article Citation.

          Keith Bennetts, <u>Bankruptcy: Its Consequences for Family Property</u>, 11 Adel. L. Rev. 413, 426-27 (1988). –Page Citation.

Administrative Adjudications and Arbitrations
See <u>Bluebook</u> rule 14.3

Administrative Decisions Under Immigration and Nationality Laws (1940 – date)
    Ab.:   I. & N. Dec.

    Ex.:   <u>TEE</u>, 20 I. & N. Dec. 949 (B.I.A. 1995).

          <u>Hector Ponce De Leon-Ruiz</u>, Interim Decision No. 3261 (B.I.A. Jan. 3, 1996). –Citation to current unbound material.

Administrative Law, by Bernard Schwartz
    –Do not abbreviate the title.

    Ex.:   Bernard Schwartz, <u>Administrative Law</u> § 6.9 (3d ed. 1991). –Section Citation.

          Bernard Schwartz, <u>Administrative Law</u> § 6.9, at 317 (3d ed. 1991). –Page Citation.

          Bernard Schwartz, <u>Administrative Law</u> § 6.9, at 317 n.10 (3d ed. 1991). –Footnote Citation.

Administrative Law Journal
    Ab.:   Admin. L.J.

    Ex.:   Marshall Breger, <u>Comments on Bernard Schwartz' Essay</u>, 5 Admin. L.J. 347 (1991). –Article Citation.

          Marshall Breger, <u>Comments on Bernard Schwartz' Essay</u>, 5 Admin. L.J. 347, 351-52 (1991). –Page Citation.

Administrative Law Journal of American University
    Ab.:   Admin. L. J. Am. U.

Administrative Law Judge
    Ab.:   A.L.J.

In citing cases in law review footnotes, abbreviate any word listed in table T.6; the names of "states, countries, and other geographical units" unless they are named parties; and any other words of eight or more letters "if <u>substantial</u> space is thereby saved and the result is unambiguous." <u>Bluebook</u> rule 10.2.2. On the other hand, in citing cases in text, abbreviate only widely known acronyms and the following words: "&," "Ass'n," "Bros.," "Co.," "Corp.," "Inc.," "Ltd.," and "No." <u>Bluebook</u> rule 10.2.1(c).

Administrative Law Review
Ab.: Admin. L. Rev.

Ex.: Sidney A. Shapiro, <u>Reflections on Teaching Administrative Law: Time for a Sequel</u>, 43 Admin. L. Rev. 501 (1991). –Article Citation.

Sidney A. Shapiro, <u>Reflections on Teaching Administrative Law: Time for a Sequel</u>, 43 Admin. L. Rev. 501, 503-504 (1991). –Page Citation.

Administrative Law, Third Series (Pike & Fischer)
Ab.: Admin. L.3d (P & F)

Ex.: <u>Vulcan Arber Hill Corp. v. Reich</u>, [Decisions 10] Admin. L.3d (P&F) 306 (D.C. Cir. April 19, 1996). –Citation to looseleaf material.

<u>United States v. White</u>, 67 Admin. L.3d (P&F) 376 (2d Cir. 1988). –Citation to bound material.

–The above examples are proper if the case is not yet available in, or is not reported in, an official or West reporter, a public domain citation, or in a widely used computer database.

<u>River Parishes Co. v. Ornet Primoy Aluminum Corp.</u>, [10 Decisions] Admin. L.3d (P&F) 944 (F.M.C. Aug. 15, 1996). –Citation to administrative looseleaf material.

Administrative Law Treatise, by Richard S. Pierce, Jr.
–Do not abbreviate the title.

Ex.: 2 Richard S. Pierce, Jr., <u>Administrative Law Treatise</u> § 9.11 (4th ed. 2002). –Section Citation.

2 Richard S. Pierce, Jr., <u>Administrative Law Treatise</u> § 9.11, at 703 (4th ed. 2002). –Page Citation.

Richard S. Pierce, Jr., <u>Administrative Law Treatise</u> § 4.2 (4th ed. Cum. Supp. 2005). –Supplement Citation.

Administrative Register of Kentucky
Ab.: vol. no. Ky. Admin. Reg. page no. (month year)

Ex.: 31 Ky. Admin. Reg. 47 (Jan. 2004)

Administrative Rules & Regulations of the Government of Guam
Ab.: x Guam Admin. R. & Regs. § x (year)

Ex.: 26 Guam Admin. R. & Regs. § 4809 (1997)

Administrative Rules of Montana
Ab.: Mont. Admin. R. x.x.x (year).

Ex.: Mont. Admin. R. 2.43.604 (2001).

Administrative Rules of South Dakota
Ab.: S.D. Admin. R. x:x:x:x (year)

In law review footnotes, the titles of books and the names of cases, except for procedural phrases, are not underlined. <u>See</u> <u>Bluebook</u> rule 2.1(a) & (b). Further, the following are in large and small capitals: codes, restatements, standards, constitutions, periodicals, authors of books, titles of books, the abbreviated names of codes, most legislative materials except for bills and resolutions, codified ordinances, model codes, court rules, and sentencing guidelines. Refer to <u>The Bluebook</u>.

Ex.:   S.D. Admin. R. 20:04:15:152 (2000).

Admiralty [Court, Division]
Ab.:   Adm.

Admiralty and Maritime Law
–Do not abbreviate the title.

Ex.:   Thomas J. Schoenbaum, Admiralty and Maritime Law § 16-1 (3d ed. 2001). –Section Citation.

Thomas J. Schoenbaum, Admiralty and Maritime Law § 16-1, at 879 (3d ed. 2001). –Page Citation.

Advisory Opinions
See Bluebook rule 14.4.

Advocacy
Ab.:   Advoc.

Affidavit, citation to
Ab.:   Aff.

Ex.:   (Scott Summ. J. Aff. ¶ 6).

See Bluebook rule B10 and table BT.1.

Note: See Bluebook rule 10.8.3 for citing litigation materials from another case.

Affirmative Action Compliance Manual for Federal Contractors (Bureau of National Affairs)
Ab.:   Aff. Action Compl. Man. (BNA)

Ex.:   Causal Agents and Theories of Discrimination, 2 Aff. Action Compl. Man. (BNA) ¶ 7003 (March 1995).

affirmed
Ab.:   aff'd

Ex.:   Cuppy v. Ward, 187 A.D. 625, 176 N.Y.S. 233, aff'd, 227 N.Y. 603, 125 N.E. 915 (1919).

68th St. Apts., Inc. v. Lauricella, 142 N.J. Super. 546, 362 A.2d 78 (Law Div. 1976), aff'd per curiam, 150 N.J. Super. 47, 374 A.2d 1222 (App. Div. 1977).

See Bluebook rule 10.7 and table T.8.

Agriculture Decisions (U.S.) (1942-date)
Ab.:   Agric. Dec.

Ex.:   Berriman Live Poultry Corp., 1 Agric. Dec. 53 (1942).

Victor Fruit Growers, Inc., 1 Agric. Dec. 108 (1942).

George Blades, 40 Agric. Dec. 1725 (1981). –Citation to current unbound material.

In citing cases in law review footnotes, abbreviate any word listed in table T.6; the names of "states, countries, and other geographical units" unless they are named parties; and any other words of eight or more letters "if substantial space is thereby saved and the result is unambiguous." Bluebook rule 10.2.2. On the other hand, in citing cases in text, abbreviate only widely known acronyms and the following words: "&," "Ass'n," "Bros.," "Co.," "Corp.," "Inc.," "Ltd.," and "No." Bluebook rule 10.2.1(c).

Agriculture
Ab.:   Agric.

AIDS Law & Litigation Reporter
Ab.:   AIDS L. & Litig. Rep. (Univ. Pub. Group)

Ex.:   Weeks v. Scott, 3 AIDS L. & Litig. Rep. (Univ. Pub. Group) 416 (5th Cir. June 23, 1995).

–This example is proper if the case is not yet available in, or is not reported in, an official or West reporter, a public domain citation, or in a widely used computer database.

Air and Space Lawyer
Ab.:   Air & Space Law.

Ex.:   Rudolph V. Pino, Jr. & Frank A. Silane, Civil Liability in Commercial Space Ventures Under United States Law, Air & Space Law., Fall 1991, at 5. —Article Citation.

Rudolph V. Pino, Jr. & Frank A. Silane, Civil Liability in Commercial Space Ventures Under United States Law, Air & Space Law., Fall 1991, at 5, 6-7. —Page Citation.

Air Force Law Review
Ab.:   A.F. L. Rev.

Ex.:   Jessica W. Julian, Noriega: The Capture of a State Leader and Its Implications on Domestic Law, 34 A.F. L. Rev. 153 (1991). –Article Citation.

Jessica W. Julian, Noriega: The Capture of a State Leader and Its Implications on Domestic Law, 34 A.F. L. Rev. 153, 155-58 (1991). –Page Citation.

Air Law
Ab.:   Air L.

Ex.:   Yi Lu, Legal Issues on Aircraft Finance in China, Air L., 1991, at 2. –Article Citation.

Yi Lu, Legal Issues on Aircraft Finance in China, Air L., 1991, at 2, 7-8. –Page Citation.

Note Air Law:

1975 vol. 1 - 1982 vol. 7 –Consecutively paginated.

1983 vol. 8 - 1991 vol. 16 –Nonconsecutively paginated.

Akron Law Review
Ab.:   Akron L. Rev.

In law review footnotes, the titles of books and the names of cases, except for procedural phrases, are not underlined. See Bluebook rule 2.1(a) & (b). Further, the following are in large and small capitals: codes, restatements, standards, constitutions, periodicals, authors of books, titles of books, the abbreviated names of codes, most legislative materials except for bills and resolutions, codified ordinances, model codes, court rules, and sentencing guidelines. Refer to The Bluebook.

Ex.:   Frank P. Darr, <u>Deregulation of Telephone Services in Ohio</u>, 24 Akron L. Rev. 229 (1990). –Article Citation.

Frank P. Darr, <u>Deregulation of Telephone Services in Ohio</u>, 24 Akron L. Rev. 229, 250-51 (1990). –Page Citation.

Akron Tax Journal
    Ab.:   Akron Tax J.
    Ex.:   Nicola Preston, <u>The Interpretation of Taxing Statutes: The English Perspective</u>, 7 Akron Tax J. 43 (1990). –Article Citation.

Nicola Preston, <u>The Interpretation of Taxing Statutes: The English Perspective</u>, 7 Akron Tax J. 43, 55-59 (1990). –Page Citation.

Alabama Acts
    See Alabama Laws.

Alabama Administrative Code
    Ab.:   Ala. Admin. Code r. x-x-x.x (year)
    Ex.:   Ala. Admin. Code r. 70-X-1.04 (1992).

Alabama Administrative Monthly
    Ab.:   volume no. Ala. Admin. Monthly page no. (month day, year)
    Ex.:   22 Ala. Admin. Monthly 12 (Dec. 31, 2003)

Alabama Appellate Court Reports
    Ab.:   Ala. App.
    –Discontinued after 57 Ala. App. 740 (1975).
    –Cite to So. or So. 2d, if therein; otherwise, cite to Ala. App.
    –Give parallel citations, if at all, only in documents submitted to Alabama state courts. <u>See</u> Bluebook rules 10.3.1 & B5.1.3; see also Ala. R. App. P. 28(a)(10), which prescribes citing cases according to <u>The Bluebook</u>, the <u>ALWD Citation Manual</u>, or to the style employed in Alabama Supreme Court opinions, which give parallel citation where available.

    Ex.:

    –Before 45 Ala. App. 1 (1969) cite as follows:
    In documents submitted to Alabama state courts:
        <u>Rivers v. Johnston</u>, 44 Ala. App. 398, 210 So. 2d 707 (Ct. App. 1968).
        –Case citation.
        <u>Rivers v. Johnston</u>, 44 Ala. App. 398, 400, 210 So. 2d 707, 709 (Ct. App. 1968). –Page citation.
    In all other documents:
        <u>Rivers v. Johnston</u>, 210 So. 2d 707 (Ala. Ct. App. 1968). –Case Citation.

In citing cases in law review footnotes, abbreviate any word listed in table T.6; the names of "states, countries, and other geographical units" unless they are named parties; and any other words of eight or more letters "if <u>substantial</u> space is thereby saved and the result is unambiguous." <u>Bluebook</u> rule 10.2.2. On the other hand, in citing cases in text, abbreviate only widely known acronyms and the following words: "&," "Ass'n," "Bros.," "Co.," "Corp.," "Inc.," "Ltd.," and "No." <u>Bluebook</u> rule 10.2.1(c).

Rivers v. Johnston, 210 So. 2d 707, 709 (Ala. Ct. App. 1968).
–Page Citation.

–After 45 Ala. App. 1 (1969) and through 57 Ala. App. 740 (1975), cite as follows:

In documents submitted to Alabama state courts:

Holsombeck v. Pate, 47 Ala. App. 39, 249 So. 2d 861 (Civ. App. 1971). –Case Citation.

Holsombeck v. Pate, 47 Ala. App. 39, 42, 249 So. 2d 861, 864 (Civ. App. 1971). –Page Citation.

Hood v. State, 47 Ala. App. 192, 252 So. 2d 117 (Crim. App. 1971). –Case Citation.

Hood v. State, 47 Ala. App. 192, 197, 252 So. 2d 117, 120 (Crim. App. 1971). –Page Citation.

In all other documents:

Holsombeck v. Pate, 249 So. 2d 861 (Ala. Civ. App. 1971). –Case Citation.

Holsombeck v. Pate, 249 So. 2d 861, 864 (Ala. Civ. App. 1971). –Page Citation.

Hood v. State, 252 So. 2d 117 (Ala. Crim. App. 1971). –Case Citation.

Hood v. State, 252 So. 2d 117, 120 (Ala. Crim. App. 1971). –Page Citation.

After 57 Ala. App. 740 (1975), cite as follows:

In all documents:

Poole v. State, 667 So. 2d 740 (Ala. Crim. App. 1995). –Case Citation.

Poole v. State, 667 So. 2d 740, 742 (Ala. Crim. App. 1995). –Page Citation.

Williams v. Ward, 667 So. 2d 1375 (Ala. Civ. App. 1995). –Case Citation.

Williams v. Ward, 667 So. 2d 1375, 1378 (Ala. Civ. App. 1995). –Page Citation.

Alabama Code
See Code of Alabama & Michie's Alabama Code.

Alabama Constitution
Ab.:   Ala. Const. art.   , §   .

In law review footnotes, the titles of books and the names of cases, except for procedural phrases, are not underlined. See Bluebook rule 2.1(a) & (b). Further, the following are in large and small capitals: codes, restatements, standards, constitutions, periodicals, authors of books, titles of books, the abbreviated names of codes, most legislative materials except for bills and resolutions, codified ordinances, model codes, court rules, and sentencing guidelines. Refer to The Bluebook.

Ex.:   Ala. Const. art. XVI, § 279. –"Cite constitutional provisions currently in force without a date." Bluebook rule 11.

Ala. Const. amend. 55 (repealed 1955).
Ala. Const. amend. 55, repealed by Ala. Const. amend. 223. –"If the cited provision has been repealed, either indicate parenthetically the fact and date of repeal or cite the repealing provision in full." Bluebook rule 11.

Ala. Const. art. IV, § 74 (amended 1939)
Ala. Const. art. IV, § 74, amended by Ala. Const. amend. 40. –"When citing a provision that has been subsequently amended, either indicate parenthetically the fact and date of amendment or cite the amending provision in full." Bluebook rule 11.

Ala. Const. of 1875, art. I, § 5 (1901). –"Cite constitutions that have been totally superseded by year of adoption; if the specific provision cited was adopted in a different year, give that year parenthetically." Bluebook rule 11.

Alabama Law Review
Ab.:   Ala. L. Rev.

Ex.:   Fred H. Miller, U.C.C. Articles 3, 4 and 4A: A Study in Process and Scope, 42 Ala. L. Rev. 405 (1991). –Article Citation.

Fred H. Miller, U.C.C. Articles 3, 4 and 4A: A Study in Process and Scope, 42 Ala. L. Rev. 405, 410-11 (1991). –Page Citation.

Alabama Laws
Ab.:   year Ala. Laws page no.

Ex.:   Act of June 20, 2003, no. 356, 2003 Ala. Laws 976 (relating to franchise agreement in the farm equipment business).

-Citation to an entire session law.

Act of June 20, 2003, no. 356, 2003 Ala. Laws 976, 979 (relating to franchise agreement in the farm equipment business.)

-Citation to a section of a session law.

-See Bluebook rule 12.4.

Alabama Lawyer
Ab.:   Ala. Law.

Ex.:   Andrew P. Campbell, Litigating Minority Shareholder Rights and the New Tort of Oppression, 53 Ala. Law. 108 (1992). –Article Citation.

Andrew P. Campbell, Litigating Minority Shareholder Rights and the New Tort of Oppression, 53 Ala. Law. 108, 110 (1992).
–Page Citation.

Alabama Reports
Ab.:   Ala.

In citing cases in law review footnotes, abbreviate any word listed in table T.6; the names of "states, countries, and other geographical units" unless they are named parties; and any other words of eight or more letters "if substantial space is thereby saved and the result is unambiguous." Bluebook rule 10.2.2. On the other hand, in citing cases in text, abbreviate only widely known acronyms and the following words: "&," "Ass'n," "Bros.," "Co.," "Corp.," "Inc.," "Ltd.," and "No." Bluebook rule 10.2.1(c).

–Discontinued after 295 Ala. 388 (1976).

–Cite to So. or So. 2d, if therein; otherwise, cite to Ala.

–Give parallel citations, if at all, only in documents submitted to Alabama state courts. See Bluebook rules 10.3.1 & B5.1.3; see also Ala. R. App. P. 28(a)(10), which prescribes citing cases according to The Bluebook, the ALWD Citation Manual, or to the style employed in Alabama Supreme Court opinions, which give parallel citation where available.

–Through 295 Ala. 388 (1976), cite as follows:

In documents submitted to Alabama state courts:

Johnson v. Ala. Pub. Serv. Comm'n, 287 Ala. 417, 252 So. 2d 75 (1971). –Case Citation.

Johnson v. Ala. Pub. Serv. Comm'n, 287 Ala. 417, 422, 252 So. 2d 75, 79 (1971). –Page Citation.

In all other documents:

Johnson v. Ala. Pub. Serv. Comm'n, 252 So. 2d 75 (Ala. 1971). –Case Citation.

Johnson v. Ala. Pub. Serv. Comm'n, 252 So. 2d 75, 79 (Ala. 1971). –Page Citation.

–After 295 Ala. 388 (1976), cite as follows:

In all documents:

Pilcher Land Corp. v. Johns, 677 So. 2d 746 (Ala. 1996). –Case Citation.

Pilcher Land Corp. v. Johns, 677 So. 2d 746, 747 (Ala. 1996). –Page Citation.

Alabama Session Laws

See Alabama Laws.

Alaska Administrative Code (LexisNexis)

Ab.: Alaska Admin. Code tit. x, § x.x (year)

Ex.: Alaska Admin. Code tit. 2, § 06.010 (1991).

Alaska Advance Legislative Service (LexisNexis)

Ab.: year-pamph. no. Alaska Adv. Legis. Serv. page no. (LexisNexis)

Ex.: Act effective June 24, 2004, ch. 96, 2004-1 Alaska Adv. Legis. Serv. 376 (LexisNexis) (relating to insurance regulation). –Citation to an entire session law.

Act effective June 24, 2004, ch. 96, sec. 13, § 21.12.020(a), 2004-1 Alaska Adv. Legis. Serv. 376, 380 (LexisNexis) (relating to insurance regulation). –Citation to a section of a session law amending prior act.

–See Bluebook rule 12.4.

–"Cite to Alaska Sess. Laws, if therein." Bluebook table T.1, p. 199.

In law review footnotes, the titles of books and the names of cases, except for procedural phrases, are not underlined. See Bluebook rule 2.1(a) & (b). Further, the following are in large and small capitals: codes, restatements, standards, constitutions, periodicals, authors of books, titles of books, the abbreviated names of codes, most legislative materials except for bills and resolutions, codified ordinances, model codes, court rules, and sentencing guidelines. Refer to The Bluebook.

Alaska Constitution
Ab.:   Alaska Const. art. , §   .

Ex.:   Alaska Const. art. VIII, § 8. –"Cite constitutional provisions currently
         in force without a date." <u>Bluebook</u> rule 11.

         Alaska Const. art. IX, § 17 (amended 1990). –"When citing a provision
         that has been subsequently amended, either indicate parenthetically the
         fact and date of amendment or cite the amending provision in full."
         <u>Bluebook</u> rule 11.

         "If the cited provision has been repealed, either indicate parenthetically
         the fact and date or cite the repealing provision in full. Cite
         constitutions that have been totally superseded by year of adoption; if
         the specific provision cited was adopted in a different year, give that
         year parenthetically." <u>Bluebook</u> rule 11.

Alaska Law Review
Ab.:   Alaska L. Rev.

Ex.:   David C. Crosby, <u>The Constitutionality of Sobriety Checkpoints in
         Alaska</u>, 8 Alaska L. Rev. 227 (1991). –Article Citation.

         David C. Crosby, <u>The Constitutionality of Sobriety Checkpoints in
         Alaska</u>, 8 Alaska L. Rev. 227, 230-33 (1991). –Page Citation.

Alaska Reports
Ab.:   Alaska

         –Discontinued after 17 Alaska 779 (1959). Thereafter, cite only to
         P.2d or P.3d.

         –District Court of Alaska had local jurisdiction from 1884-1959; cite to
         F. Supp., F., or F.2d, if therein; otherwise, cite to Alaska.

Ex.   <u>O'Dey v. Matson</u>, 17 Alaska 763 (D. Alaska 1958). –Case Citation.

         <u>O'Dey v. Matson</u>, 17 Alaska 763, 765 (D. Alaska 1958).
         –Page Citation.

         <u>Boone v. Gipson</u>, 920 P.2d 746 (Alaska 1996). –Case Citation.

         <u>Boone v. Gipson</u>, 920 P.2d 746, 749 (Alaska 1996). –Page Citation.

Alaska Session Laws
         See Session Laws of Alaska.

Alaska Statutes (LexisNexis)
Ab.:   Alaska Stat. § x.x.x (year)

Ex.:   Alaska Stat. § 10.15.115 (2004).

         Alaska Stat. § 42.05.712 (Supp. 2005).

         –For proper citation form in papers submitted to Alaska courts, see
         Alaska Stat. § 01.05.011 (2002).

In citing cases in law review footnotes, abbreviate any word listed in table T.6;
the names of "states, countries, and other geographical units" unless they are named parties;
and any other words of eight or more letters "if <u>substantial</u> space is thereby saved and the
result is unambiguous." <u>Bluebook</u> rule 10.2.2. On the other hand, in citing cases in text,
abbreviate only widely known acronyms and the following words: "&," "Ass'n," "Bros.,"
"Co.," "Corp.," "Inc.," "Ltd.," and "No." <u>Bluebook</u> rule 10.2.1(c).

Albany Law Journal of Science & Technology
Ab.: Alb. L.J. Sci. & Tech.

Ex.: Kenneth R. Adamo, <u>Attorney Disqualification in Patent Litigation</u>, 1 Alb. L.J. Sci. & Tech. 177 (1991). –Article Citation.

Kenneth R. Adamo, <u>Attorney Disqualification in Patent Litigation</u>, 1 Alb. L.J. Sci. & Tech. 177, 196 (1991). –Page Citation.

Albany Law Review
Ab.: Alb. L. Rev.

Ex.: Robert A. Prentice, <u>Section 12(2): A Remedy for Wrongs in the Secondary Market?</u>, 55 Alb. L. Rev. 97 (1991). –Article Citation.

Robert A. Prentice, <u>Section 12(2): A Remedy for Wrongs in the Secondary Market?</u>, 55 Alb. L. Rev. 97, 122-24 (1991). –Page Citation.

Alberta Gazette

Ab.: A. Gaz.

Alberta Law Reports
Ab.: Alta. L.R., Alta. L.R.2d., or Alta. L.R.3d

Ex.: <u>Whitney v. MacLean</u>, [1931] 26 Alta. L.R. 209 (App. Div. Can.). –Case Citation.

See <u>Bluebook</u> table T.2.

Alberta Law Review
Ab.: Alta. L. Rev.

Ex.: Jacob S. Ziegel, <u>The New Personal Property Security Regimes -- Have We Gone Too Far?</u>, 28 Alta. L. Rev. 739 (1990). –Article Citation.

Jacob S. Ziegel, <u>The New Personal Property Security Regimes -- Have We Gone Too Far?</u>, 28 Alta. L. Rev. 739, 752-59 (1990). –Page Citation.

ALI
See American Law Institute publications.

ALI-ABA Course Materials Journal
Ab.: ALI-ABA Course Materials J.

Ex.: David B. Farer, <u>Underground Storage Tank Law</u>, ALI-ABA Course Materials J., June 1991, at 19. –Article Citation.

David B. Farer, <u>Underground Storage Tank Law</u>, ALI-ABA Course Materials J., June 1991, at 19, 21-22. –Page Citation.

In law review footnotes, the titles of books and the names of cases, except for procedural phrases, are not underlined. See <u>Bluebook</u> rule 2.1(a) & (b). Further, the following are in large and small capitals: codes, restatements, standards, constitutions, periodicals, authors of books, titles of books, the abbreviated names of codes, most legislative materials except for bills and resolutions, codified ordinances, model codes, court rules, and sentencing guidelines. Refer to <u>The Bluebook</u>.

All England Law Reports (1936-date)

Ab.:   All E.R.

Ex.:   Davitt v. Titcumb, [1989] 3 All E.R. 417 (Ch. 1989) (Eng.).
–Case Citation.

White v. White, [2001] UKHL 9, [2001] 2 All E.R. 43 (Eng.). –Case with neutral citation.

See Bluebook table T.2.

All States Tax Guide (Research Institute of America)

Ab.:   All St. Tax Guide (RIA)

Ex.:   Richard v. Jefferson County, 1 All States Tax Guide (RIA) ¶ 985.42 (U.S. June 10, 1996). –Citation to looseleaf material.

–This example is proper if the case is not yet available in, or is not reported in, an official or West reporter, a public domain citation, or in a widely used computer database.

ALR

See American Law Reports.

Alternative Dispute Resolution, by Nancy Atlas, Steven Huber, and Wendy Trachte-Huber

–Do not abbreviate the title.

Ex.:   Nancy Atlas et. al, Alternative Dispute Resolution, 25 (2000). –Page Citation.

Nancy Atlas et. al, Alternative Dispute Resolution, 25 n.2 (2000). –Footnote Citation.

amendment(s)

Ab.:   amend., amends.

American Bankruptcy Institute Law Review

Ab: Am. Bankr. Inst. L. Rev.

Ex: Adam Feibelman, Defining the Social Insurance Function of Consumer Bankruptcy, 13 Am. Bankr. Inst. L. Rev. 129 (2005). –Article Citation.

Adam Feibelman, Defining the Social Insurance Function of Consumer Bankruptcy, 13 Am. Bankr. Inst. L. Rev. 129, 135-36 (2005). –Page Citation.

American Bankruptcy Law Journal

Ab.:   Am. Bankr. L.J.

In citing cases in law review footnotes, abbreviate any word listed in table T.6; the names of "states, countries, and other geographical units" unless they are named parties; and any other words of eight or more letters "if substantial space is thereby saved and the result is unambiguous." Bluebook rule 10.2.2. On the other hand, in citing cases in text, abbreviate only widely known acronyms and the following words: "&," "Ass'n," "Bros.," "Co.," "Corp.," "Inc.," "Ltd.," and "No." Bluebook rule 10.2.1(c).

Ex.:   Margaret Howard, <u>Stripping Down Liens: Section 506(d) and the Theory of Bankruptcy</u>, 65 Am. Bankr. L.J. 373 (1991). –Article Citation.

Margaret Howard, <u>Stripping Down Liens: Section 506(d) and the Theory of Bankruptcy</u>, 65 Am. Bankr. L.J. 373, 384-87 (1991). –Page Citation.

American Bar Association Code of Professional Responsibility
See American Bar Association Model Code of Professional Responsibility.

American Bar Association Committee on Ethics and Professional Responsibility, Formal Opinion
Ab.:   ABA Comm. on Ethics and Professional Responsibility, Formal Op. (year)

Ex.:   ABA Comm. on Ethics and Professional Responsibility, Formal Op. 402 (1996).

ABA Comm. on Ethics and Professional Responsibility, Formal Op. 401 (1996) (lawyers practicing in limited liability partnerships). –Citation with a parenthetical reference to subject matter.

American Bar Association Committee on Ethics and Professional Responsibility, Informal Opinion
Ab.:   ABA Comm. on Ethics and Professional Responsibility, Informal Op. (year)

Ex.:   ABA Comm. on Ethics and Professional Responsibility, Informal Op. E-94-6 (1995).

American Bar Association Journal
Ab.:   A.B.A. J.

Ex.:   John Gibeaut, <u>Taking Aim</u>, A.B.A. J., Nov. 1996, at 50. Article Citation.

John Gibeaut, <u>Taking Aim</u>, A.B.A. J., Nov. 1996, at 50, 53. –Page Citation.

American Bar Association Model Code of Judicial Conduct
Ab.:   Model Code of Judicial Conduct [provision] (year)

Ex.:   Model Code of Judicial Conduct Canon 3 (2000)

American Bar Association Model Code of Professional Responsibility
Ab.:   Model Code of Prof'l Responsibility [provision] (year)

Ex.:   Model Code of Prof'l Responsibility Canon 9 (1980).

Model Code of Prof'l Responsibility DR 4-101 (1980).

Model Code of Prof'l Responsibility EC 2-20 (1980).

American Bar Association Model Rules of Professional Conduct
Ab.:   Model Rules of Prof'l Conduct R. (status if necessary, year)

In law review footnotes, the titles of books and the names of cases, except for procedural phrases, are not underlined. <u>See</u> Bluebook rule 2.1(a) & (b). Further, the following are in large and small capitals: codes, restatements, standards, constitutions, periodicals, authors of books, titles of books, the abbreviated names of codes, most legislative materials except for bills and resolutions, codified ordinances, model codes, court rules, and sentencing guidelines. Refer to <u>The Bluebook</u>.

Ex.:   Model Rules of Prof'l Conduct R. 3.4 (2000).

American Bar Association Reports
Ab.:   A.B.A. Rep.
Ex.:   Report of the Commission on Standards of Judicial Administration, 97 A.B.A. Rep. 345 (1972).

American Bar Association Revised Model Business Corporation Act
Ab.:   Revised Model Business Corp. Act
Ex.:   Revised Model Business Corp. Act § 3.02 (1984).

American Bar Foundation Code of Professional Responsibility, Annotated
Ab.:   Annot. Code of Prof'l Responsibility
Ex.:   Annot. Code of Prof'l Responsibility DR 4-101(c)(4) cmt. at 182 (Am. Bar Found. 1979).

American Bar Foundation Research Journal
Ab.:   Am. B. Found. Res. J.
Ex.:   Frederick Schauer, <u>Causation Theory and the Causes of Sexual Violence</u>, 4 Am. B. Found. Res. J. 737 (1987). −Article Citation.
            Frederick Schauer, <u>Causation Theory and the Causes of Sexual Violence</u>, 4 Am. B. Found. Res. J. 737, 742-46 (1987). −Page Citation.

American Business Law Journal
Ab.:   Am. Bus. L.J.
Ex.:   Michael J. Phillips, <u>The Substantive Due Process Rights of College and University Faculty</u>, 28 Am. Bus. L.J. 567 (1991). −Article Citation.
            Michael J. Phillips, <u>The Substantive Due Process Rights of College and University Faculty</u>, 28 Am. Bus. L.J. 567, 591-93 (1991). −Page Citation.

American Constitutional Law, 3d ed., by Louis Fisher
            Louis Fisher, <u>American Constitutional Law</u> 155 (3d. ed. 2000). −Page Citation.

American Constitutional Law, by Laurence H. Tribe
      −Do not abbreviate the title.
Ex.:   Laurence H. Tribe, <u>American Constitutional Law</u> § 5-4 (3d ed. 2000). −Section Citation.
            Laurence H. Tribe, <u>American Constitutional Law</u> § 5-4, at 819 (3d ed. 2000). −Page Citation.
            Laurence H. Tribe, <u>American Constitutional Law</u> § 5-4, at 819 n.48 (3d ed. 2000). −Footnote Citation.

American Criminal Law Review
Ab.:   Am. Crim. L. Rev.

In citing cases in law review footnotes, abbreviate any word listed in table T.6; the names of "states, countries, and other geographical units" unless they are named parties; and any other words of eight or more letters "if <u>substantial</u> space is thereby saved and the result is unambiguous." <u>Bluebook</u> rule 10.2.2. On the other hand, in citing cases in text, abbreviate only widely known acronyms and the following words: "&," "Ass'n," "Bros.," "Co.," "Corp.," "Inc.," "Ltd.," and "No." <u>Bluebook</u> rule 10.2.1(c).

Ex.:   Donald J. Hall, <u>Victims' Voices in Criminal Court: The Need for Restraint</u>, 28 Am. Crim. L. Rev. 233 (1991). –Article Citation.

Donald J. Hall, <u>Victims' Voices in Criminal Court: The Need for Restraint</u>, 28 Am. Crim. L. Rev. 233, 236-38 (1991). –Page Citation.

American Federal Tax Reports, Second Series (Research Institute of America)
Ab.:   A.F.T.R.2d (RIA)

Ex.:   <u>United States v. Clements</u>, 77 A.F.T.R.2d (RIA) 648 (5th Cir. 1996).

–This example is proper if the case is not yet available in, or is not reported in, an official or West reporter, a public domain citation, or in a widely used computer database.

American Indian Law Review
Ab.:   Am. Indian L. Rev.

Ex.:   Dean B. Suagee, <u>The Application of the National Environmental Policy Act to "Development" in Indian Country</u>, 16 Am. Indian L. Rev. 377 (1991). –Article Citation.

Dean B. Suagee, <u>The Application of the National Environmental Policy Act to "Development" in Indian Country</u>, 16 Am. Indian L. Rev. 377, 380-81 (1991). –Page Citation.

American Institute for Certified Public Accountants -- Professional Standards (Commerce Clearing House)
Ab.:   AICPA – Prof. Standards

American Journal of Comparative Law, The
Ab.:   Am. J. Comp. L.

Ex.:   John Quigley, <u>The Soviet Presidency</u>, 39 Am. J. Comp. L. 67 (1991). –Article Citation.

John Quigley, <u>The Soviet Presidency</u>, 39 Am. J. Comp. L. 67, 75-76 (1991). –Page Citation.

American Journal of Criminal Law
Ab.:   Am. J. Crim. L.

Ex.:   Henry Dahl, <u>The Influence and Application of the Standard Penal Code for Latin America</u>, 17 Am. J. Crim. L. 235 (1990). –Article Citation.

Henry Dahl, <u>The Influence and Application of the Standard Penal Code for Latin America</u>, 17 Am. J. Crim. L. 235, 258-59 (1990). –Page Citation.

American Journal of International Law
Ab.:   Am. J. Int'l L.

In law review footnotes, the titles of books and the names of cases, except for procedural phrases, are not underlined. <u>See</u> Bluebook rule 2.1(a) & (b). Further, the following are in large and small capitals: codes, restatements, standards, constitutions, periodicals, authors of books, titles of books, the abbreviated names of codes, most legislative materials except for bills and resolutions, codified ordinances, model codes, court rules, and sentencing guidelines. Refer to <u>The Bluebook</u>.

Ex.:   George H. Aldrich, <u>Prospects for United States Ratification of Additional Protocol I to the Geneva Conventions</u>, 85 Am. J. Int'l L. 1 (1991). –Article Citation.

George H. Aldrich, <u>Prospects for United States Ratification of Additional Protocol I to the Geneva Conventions</u>, 85 Am. J. Int'l L. 1, 5-7 (1991). –Page Citation.

American Journal of Jurisprudence, The
Ab.:   Am. J. Juris.

Ex.:   Troy Harris-Abbott, <u>On Law and Theology</u>, 35 Am. J. Juris. 105 (1990). –Article Citation.

Troy Harris-Abbott, <u>On Law and Theology</u>, 35 Am. J. Juris. 105, 114-15 (1990). –Page Citation.

American Journal of Law & Medicine
Ab.:   Am. J.L. & Med.

Ex.:   Bernard Friedland & Richard W. Valachovic, <u>The Regulation of Dental Licensing: The Dark Ages?</u>, 17 Am. J.L. & Med. 249 (1991). –Article Citation.

Bernard Friedland & Richard W. Valachovic, <u>The Regulation of Dental Licensing: The Dark Ages?</u>, 17 Am. J.L. & Med. 249, 251-52 (1991). –Page Citation.

American Journal of Legal History
Ab.:   Am. J. Legal Hist.

Ex.:   Andrew J. King, <u>The Law of Slander in Early Antebellum America</u>, 35 Am. J. Legal Hist. 1 (1991). –Article Citation.

Andrew J. King, <u>The Law of Slander in Early Antebellum America</u>, 35 Am. J. Legal Hist. 1, 14-17 (1991). –Page Citation.

American Journal of Tax Policy, The
Ab.:   Am. J. Tax Pol'y

Ex.:   H. David Rosenbloom, <u>Toward a New Tax Treaty Policy for a New Decade</u>, 9 Am. J. Tax Pol'y 77 (1991). –Article Citation.

H. David Rosenbloom, <u>Toward a New Tax Treaty Policy for a New Decade</u>, 9 Am. J. Tax Pol'y 77, 85-89 (1991). –Page Citation.

American Journal of Trial Advocacy
Ab.:   Am. J. Trial Advoc.

Ex.:   Morton G. Rosen, <u>RICO Claims by Celebrities Against the Tabloid Media for Publication of Purloined Material</u>, 15 Am. J. Trial Advoc. 47 (1991). –Article Citation.

Morton G. Rosen, <u>RICO Claims by Celebrities Against the Tabloid Media for Publication of Purloined Material</u>, 15 Am. J. Trial Advoc. 47, 51-53 (1991). –Page Citation.

In citing cases in law review footnotes, abbreviate any word listed in table T.6; the names of "states, countries, and other geographical units" unless they are named parties; and any other words of eight or more letters "if <u>substantial</u> space is thereby saved and the result is unambiguous." <u>Bluebook</u> rule 10.2.2. On the other hand, in citing cases in text, abbreviate only widely known acronyms and the following words: "&," "Ass'n," "Bros.," "Co.," "Corp.," "Inc.," "Ltd.," and "No." <u>Bluebook</u> rule 10.2.1(c).

American Jurisprudence
Ab.:   Am. Jur. 2d §   (year)
Ex.:   9 Am. Jur. 2d <u>Bankruptcy</u> § 417 (1999). –Section Citation .
         1 Am. Jur. 2d <u>Abduction and Kidnapping</u> § 6 (Supp. 2000).
         –Supplement Citation.
         20 Am. Jur. 2d <u>Costs</u> § 54, at 49 n.68 (1995). –Footnote Citation.

American Land Planning Law, by Norman Williams, Jr. and John M. Taylor.
See Williams and Taylor American Land Planning Law.

American Law Institute Complex Litigation Project
Ab.:   ALI Complex Litig. Project §   (status if necessary, year)
Ex.:   ALI Complex Litig. Project § 601 (Tentative Draft No. 3, 1992)
         ALI Complex Litig. Project § 3.07 (Proposed Final Draft, 1993)

American Law Institute Federal Estate and Gift Taxation
Ab.:   ALI Fed. Estate and Gift Taxation §   (year)
Ex.:   ALI Fed. Estate and Gift Taxation § EX 10 (1968).

American Law Institute Federal Income Tax Project
Ab.:   ALI Fed. Income Tax Project at   (status if necessary, year)
Ex.:   ALI Fed. Income Tax Project at 20 (Tent. Draft No. 16, 1991).

American Law Institute Federal Securities Code
Ab.:   ALI Fed. Sec. Code § (year)
Ex.:   ALI Fed. Sec. Code § 202 (1978).

American Law Institute Model Code of Evidence
Ab.:   Model Code of Evidence R. (year)
Ex.:   Model Code of Evidence R. 310 (1942).

American Law Institute Model Land Development Code
Ab.:   Model Land Dev. Code § (status if necessary, year)
Ex.:   Model Land Dev. Code § 4-101 (1975).

American Law Institute Model Penal Code
Ab.:   Model Penal Code § (status if necessary, year)
Ex.:   Model Penal Code § 210.2 (Proposed Official Draft 1962).
         Model Penal Code § 210.2, note on status of section (Proposed Official
         Draft 1962). –Citation to auxiliary material.

**American Law Institute Principles of Corporate Governance: Analysis and
   Recommendations**
Ab.:   ALI Principles of Corporate Governance: Analysis and
         Recommendations §   (status if necessary, year)

In law review footnotes, the titles of books and the names of cases, except for procedural
phrases, are not underlined. <u>See</u> <u>Bluebook</u> rule 2.1(a) & (b). Further, the following are in
large and small capitals: codes, restatements, standards, constitutions, periodicals, authors of
books, titles of books, the abbreviated names of codes, most legislative materials except for
bills and resolutions, codified ordinances, model codes, court rules, and sentencing guidelines.
Refer to <u>The Bluebook</u>.

Ex.:   ALI Principles of Corporate Governance: Analysis and Recommendations § 7.11 (1992).

ALI Principles of Corporate Governance: Analysis and Recommendations § 7.17 cmt. g (1992).

American Law Institute Proceedings
Ab.:   A.L.I. Proc.

Ex.:   Bennett Boskey, Report of the Treasurer, 66 A.L.I. Proc. 15 (1989).

American Law Institute Restatements
See various Restatement entries.

American Law of Torts, The, by Stuart M. Speiser, Charles F. Krause, and Alfred W. Gans
–Do not abbreviate the title.

Ex.:   8 Stuart M. Speiser et al., The American Law of Torts § 34:7 (1993). –Section Citation.

8 Stuart M. Speiser et al., The American Law of Torts § 34:7, at 35 (1993). –Page Citation.

8 Stuart M. Speiser et al., The American Law of Torts § 34:7, at 35 n.48 (1993). –Footnote Citation.

American Law of Zoning, by Robert M. Anderson
–Do not abbreviate the title.

Ex.:   2 Robert M. Anderson, American Law of Zoning § 9.44 (3d ed. 1986). –Section Citation.

2 Robert M. Anderson, American Law of Zoning § 9.44, at 237 (3d ed. 1986). –Page Citation.

2 Robert M. Anderson, American Law of Zoning § 9.44, at 237 n.40 (3d ed. 1986). –Footnote Citation.

2 Kenneth H. Young, Anderson's American Law of Zoning § 10.18 (4th ed. 1996). –Citation to Fourth Edition.

2 Kenneth H. Young, Anderson's American Law of Zoning § 10.18, at 429 (4th ed. 1996). –Page Citation to Fourth Edition.

2 Kenneth H. Young, Anderson's American Law of Zoning § 10.18, at 429 n.11 (4th ed. 1996). –Footnote Citation to Fourth Edition.

American Law Reports
Ab.:   A.L.R., A.L.R.2d, A.L.R.3d, A.L.R.4th, A.L.R.5th

Ex.:   A.W. Gans, Annotation, Fee Simple Conditional, 114 A.L.R. 602 (1938). –Citation to annotation.

R.D. Hursh, Annotation, Liability of Operator of Flight Training School for Injury or Death of Trainee, 17 A.L.R.2d 557 (1951). –Citation to annotation.

In citing cases in law review footnotes, abbreviate any word listed in table T.6; the names of "states, countries, and other geographical units" unless they are named parties; and any other words of eight or more letters "if substantial space is thereby saved and the result is unambiguous." Bluebook rule 10.2.2. On the other hand, in citing cases in text, abbreviate only widely known acronyms and the following words: "&," "Ass'n," "Bros.," "Co.," "Corp.," "Inc.," "Ltd.," and "No." Bluebook rule 10.2.1(c).

Alan R. Gilbert, Annotation, <u>Proceedings For Injunction or Restraining Order as Basis of Malicious Prosecution Action</u>, 70 A.L.R.3d 536 (1976). –Citation to annotation.

Joe E. Smith, Annotation, <u>Applicability of Double Jeopardy to Juvenile Court Proceedings</u>, 5 A.L.R.4th 234 (1981). –Citation to annotation.

Linda A. Sharp, Annotation, <u>Medical Malpractice in Connection with Diagnosis, Care, or Treatment of Diabetes</u>, 43 A.L.R.5th 87 (1996). –Citation to annotation.

American Law Reports, Federal
Ab.:   A.L.R. Fed.

Ex.:   Martha M. Cleary, Annotation, <u>Conduct of Union Officer Which Violates § 501 (a) of Landrum-Griffin Act (29 USCS § 501 (a))</u>, 107 A.L.R. Fed. 448 (1992). –Citation to annotation.

American Lawyer
Ab.:   Am. Law.

Ex.:   Roger Parloff, <u>Maybe the Jury Was Right</u>, Am. Law., June 1992, at 7. –Article Citation.

American Review of International Arbitration, The
Ab.:   Am. Rev. Int'l Arb.

Ex.:   Hans Smit, <u>Provisional Relief in International Arbitration: The ICC and Other Proposed Rules</u>, 1 Am. Rev. Int'l Arb. 388 (1990). –Article Citation.

Hans Smit, <u>Provisional Relief in International Arbitration: The ICC and Other Proposed Rules</u>, 1 Am. Rev. Int'l Arb. 388, 391-92 (1990). –Page Citation.

American Samoa Administrative Code
Ab.:   Am. Samoa Admin. Code § x (year)

Ex.:   Am. Samoa Admin. Code § 4.1205 (1985).

American Samoa Code Annotated
Ab.:   Am. Samoa Code Ann. § x (year)

Ex.:   Am. Samoa Code Ann. § 16.0101 (1981).

American Society of International Law Proceedings
Ab.:   Am. Soc'y Int'l L. Proc.

Ex.:   David A. Jones, <u>Diplomatic Immunity: Recent Developments in Law and Practice</u>, 1991 Am. Soc'y Int'l L. Proc. 261. –Article Citation.

David A. Jones, <u>Diplomatic Immunity: Recent Developments in Law and Practice</u>, 1991 Am. Soc'y Int'l L. Proc. 261, 265. –Page Citation.

In law review footnotes, the titles of books and the names of cases, except for procedural phrases, are not underlined. <u>See</u> <u>Bluebook</u> rule 2.1(a) & (b). Further, the following are in large and small capitals: codes, restatements, standards, constitutions, periodicals, authors of books, titles of books, the abbreviated names of codes, most legislative materials except for bills and resolutions, codified ordinances, model codes, court rules, and sentencing guidelines. Refer to <u>The Bluebook</u>.

–This periodical also contains many speeches delivered at the Annual Meeting of the American Society of International Law. Cite speeches according to <u>Bluebook</u> rule 17.1.5.

American State Papers
    Ab.:   Am. St. Papers

American University International Law Review
    Ab: Am. U. Int'l L. Rev.
    Ex: Dwight G. Newman, <u>The Rome Statute, Some Reservations Concerning Amnesties, and a Distributive Problem</u>, 20 Am. U. Int'l L. Rev. 293 (2005). –Article Citation.
           Dwight G. Newman, <u>The Rome Statute, Some Reservations Concerning Amnesties, and a Distributive Problem</u>, 20 Am. U. Int'l L. Rev. 293, 334-35 (2005). –Page Citation.

American University Journal of Gender, Social Policy & the Law
    Ab: Am. U. J. Gender Soc. Pol'y & L.
    Ex: Prentice L. White, <u>You May Never See Your Child Again: Adjusting the Batterer's Visitation Rights to Protect Children From Future Abuse</u>, 13 Am. U. J. Gender Soc. Pol'y & L. 327 (2005). –Article Citation.
           Prentice L. White, <u>You May Never See Your Child Again: Adjusting the Batterer's Visitation Rights to Protect Children From Future Abuse</u>, 13 Am. U. J. Gender Soc. Pol'y & L. 327, 344-47 (2005). –Page Citation.

American University Journal of International Law and Policy, The
    Ab.:   Am. U. J. Int'l L. & Pol'y
    Ex.:   M.C. Jozana, <u>Proposed South African Bill of Rights: A Prescription for Equality or Neo-Apartheid?</u>, 7 Am. U. J. Int'l L. & Pol'y 45 (1991). –Article Citation.
           M.C. Jozana, <u>Proposed South African Bill of Rights: A Prescription for Equality or Neo-Apartheid?</u>, 7 Am. U. J. Int'l L. & Pol'y 45, 49-51 (1991). –Page Citation.

American University Law Review
    Ab.:   Am. U. L. Rev.
    Ex.:   Daniel J. Meador, <u>Origin of the Federal Circuit: A Personal Account</u>, 41 Am. U. L. Rev. 581 (1992). –Article Citation.
           Daniel J. Meador, <u>Origin of the Federal Circuit: A Personal Account</u>, 41 Am. U. L. Rev. 581, 596-604 (1992). –Page Citation.

Am. Jur. 2d
    See American Jurisprudence, Second Edition.

In citing cases in law review footnotes, abbreviate any word listed in table T.6; the names of "states, countries, and other geographical units" unless they are named parties; and any other words of eight or more letters "if <u>substantial</u> space is thereby saved and the result is unambiguous." <u>Bluebook</u> rule 10.2.2. On the other hand, in citing cases in text, abbreviate only widely known acronyms and the following words: "&," "Ass'n," "Bros.," "Co.," "Corp.," "Inc.," "Ltd.," and "No." <u>Bluebook</u> rule 10.2.1(c).

Anderson's American Law of Zoning, by Kenneth H. Young
Ex.:   4 Kenneth H. Young, <u>Anderson's American Law of Zoning</u> § 22.19
         (4th ed. 1997). –Section Citation.

         4 Kenneth H. Young, <u>Anderson's American Law of Zoning</u> § 22.19, at
         52 (4th ed. 1997). –Page Citation.

         4 Kenneth H. Young, <u>Anderson's American Law of Zoning</u> § 22.19, at
         52 n.29 (4th ed. 1997). –Footnote Citation.

Anglo-American Law Review
Ab.:   Anglo-Am. L. Rev.

Ex.:   Timothy H. Jones, <u>Regulatory Policy and Rule-Making</u>, 20 Anglo-Am.
         L. Rev. 131 (1991). –Article Citation.

         Timothy H. Jones, <u>Regulatory Policy and Rule-Making</u>, 20 Anglo-Am.
         L. Rev. 131, 140-45 (1991). –Page Citation.

Annals of the American Academy of Political and Social Science, The
Ab.:   Annals Am. Acad. Pol. & Soc. Sci.

Ex.:   Richard D. Lamm, <u>The Future of the Environment</u>, Annals Am. Acad.
         Pol. & Soc. Sci., July 1992, at 57. –Article Citation.

         Richard D. Lamm, <u>The Future of the Environment</u>, Annals Am. Acad.
         Pol. & Soc. Sci., July 1992, at 57, 62-64. –Page Citation.

Annotated Code of Maryland
See Annotated Code of Maryland (1957), Michie's Annotated Code of Maryland
(LexisNexis), and West's Annotated Code of Maryland.

Annotated Code of Maryland (1957)
Ab.:   Md. Ann. Code art. x, § x (year)

Ex.:   Md. Ann. Code art. 101 § 39A (1957)

Annotated Code of Professional Responsibility (ABF)
See American Bar Foundation Code of Professional Responsibility, Annotated.

Annotated Laws of Massachusetts (LexisNexis)
Ab.:   Mass. Ann. Laws ch. x, § x (LexisNexis year)

Ex.:   Mass. Ann. Laws ch. 68, § 5 (LexisNexis 1998).

         Mass. Ann. Laws ch. 66, § 18 (LexisNexis Supp. 1999).

         –"Cite to Mass. Gen. Laws, if therein." <u>Bluebook</u> table T.1, p. 214.

         For proper citation form in papers submitted to Massachusetts courts,
         see Mass. R. App. P. 16(g) and Mass. Dist. & Mun. App. Div. R. 16(g).

Annotated Model Rules of Professional Conduct (ABA)
Ab.:   Ann. Model Rules of Prof'l Conduct R.   , page (date)

In law review footnotes, the titles of books and the names of cases, except for procedural
phrases, are not underlined. <u>See</u> <u>Bluebook</u> rule 2.1(a) & (b). Further, the following are in
large and small capitals: codes, restatements, standards, constitutions, periodicals, authors of
books, titles of books, the abbreviated names of codes, most legislative materials except for
bills and resolutions, codified ordinances, model codes, court rules, and sentencing guidelines.
Refer to <u>The Bluebook</u>.

Ex.: Ann. Model Rules of Prof'l Conduct R. 1.7, 110 (1991).
–Citation to an annotation.

–Citation to the Model Rules of Professional Conduct is preferred when citing Rules or Comments.

Annotated Revised Code of Washington (LexisNexis)
Ab.: Wash. Rev. Code Ann. § x.x.x (LexisNexis year)

Ex.: Wash. Rev. Code Ann. § 86.15.165 (LexisNexis 2005)

"Cite to Wash. Rev. Code, if therein." <u>Bluebook</u> table T.1, p. 238.

Annotated Tax Cases (Eng.)
Ab.: Ann. Tax Cas.

Annotation
Ex.: John L. Isham, Annotation, <u>Parking Facility Proprietor's Liability for Criminal Attack on Patron</u>, 49 A.L.R.4th 1257 (1986). –Annotation Citation.

Sonja A. Soehnel, Annotation, <u>Sex Discrimination in Employment Against Female Attorney in Violation of Federal Civil Rights Laws –Federal Cases</u>, 81 L. Ed. 2d 894 (1986). –Annotation Citation.

Sonja A. Soehnel, Annotation, <u>Sex Discrimination in Employment Against Female Attorney in Violation of Federal Civil Rights Laws– Federal Cases</u>, 81 L. Ed. 2d 894, 897 (1986). –Page Citation.

Annuaire Français de Droit International
Ab.: Do not abbreviate title.

Ex.: Julio A. Barberis, <u>Reflexions Sur La Coutume Internationale</u>, Annuaire Français de Droit International, 1990, at 8. –Article Citation.

Julio A. Barberis, <u>Reflexions Sur La Coutume Internationale</u>, Annuaire Français de Droit International, 1990, at 8, 22-23. –Page Citation.

Annual Institute on Estate Planning (University of Miami Law Center)
Ab.: Inst. on Est. Plan.

Ex.: Jeffrey A. Schoenblum, <u>Working With the Unified Credit</u>, 15 Inst. on Est. Plan. ¶ 1400 (1981). –Article Citation.

Jeffrey A. Schoenblum, <u>Working With the Unified Credit</u>, 15 Inst. on Est. Plan. ¶ 1400, ¶ 1404.2 (1981). –Paragraph Citation.

Annual Report and Official Opinions of the Attorney General of Indiana
Ab.: Ind. Att'y Gen. Ann. Rep. & Official Op.

Annual Report and Official Opinions of the Attorney General of Maryland
Ab.: Md. Att'y Gen. Ann. Rep. & Official Op.

Annual Report of the Attorney General for the State of South Carolina to the General Assembly
Ab.: S.C. Att'y Gen. Ann. Rep.

In citing cases in law review footnotes, abbreviate any word listed in table T.6; the names of "states, countries, and other geographical units" unless they are named parties; and any other words of eight or more letters "if <u>substantial</u> space is thereby saved and the result is unambiguous." <u>Bluebook</u> rule 10.2.2. On the other hand, in citing cases in text, abbreviate only widely known acronyms and the following words: "&," "Ass'n," "Bros.," "Co.," "Corp.," "Inc.," "Ltd.," and "No." <u>Bluebook</u> rule 10.2.1(c).

Annual Report of the Attorney General, State of Florida
    Ab.:   Fla. Att'y Gen. Ann. Rep.

Annual Review of Banking & Financial Law
    Ab: Ann. Rev. Banking & Fin. L.

    Ex: V. Gerard Comizio, Emerging Federal Regulation of Thrift Cross-Border Activities, 23 Ann. Rev. Banking & Fin. L. 637 (2004). –Article Citation.

            V. Gerard Comizio, Emerging Federal Regulation of Thrift Cross-Border Activities, 23 Ann. Rev. Banking & Fin. L. 637, 641-42 (2004). –Page Citation.

Annual Survey of American Law
    Ab.:   Ann. Surv. Am. L.

    Ex.:   George S. Tolley III, The Freedom of Information Act: Competing Interests in the Supreme Court, 1990 Ann. Surv. Am. L. 497. –Article Citation.

            George S. Tolley III, The Freedom of Information Act: Competing Interests in the Supreme Court, 1990 Ann. Surv. Am. L. 497, 525-30. –Page Citation.

anonymous
    Ab.:   anon.

Answer, citation to
    Ab.:   Answer

    Ex.:   (Answer ¶ 10).

See Bluebook rule B10 and table BT.1.

Note: See Bluebook rule 10.8.3 for citing litigation materials from another case.

Antieau on Local Government Law
    –Do not abbreviate this title.

    Ex.:   6 Sandra M. Stevenson, Antieau Local Government Law § 82.09[5] (2d ed. 2005). –Section Citation.

            6 Sandra M. Stevenson, Antieau Local Government Law § 82.09[5], at 82-95 (2d ed. 2005). –Page Citation.

Antitrust Bulletin
    Ab.:   Antitrust Bull.

    Ex.:   Robert L. Steiner, Intraband Competition–Stepchild of Antitrust, 36 Antitrust Bull. 155 (1991). –Article Citation.

            Robert L. Steiner, Intraband Competition–Stepchild of Antitrust, 36 Antitrust Bull. 155, 160-61 (1991). –Page Citation.

In law review footnotes, the titles of books and the names of cases, except for procedural phrases, are not underlined. See Bluebook rule 2.1(a) & (b). Further, the following are in large and small capitals: codes, restatements, standards, constitutions, periodicals, authors of books, titles of books, the abbreviated names of codes, most legislative materials except for bills and resolutions, codified ordinances, model codes, court rules, and sentencing guidelines. Refer to The Bluebook.

Antitrust Law, by Phillip E. Areeda, Robert D. Blair, & Herbert Hovenkamp
–Do not abbreviate the title.

Ex.:   2 Phillip E. Areeda et al., <u>Antitrust Law</u> § 306d (2d ed. 2000). –Section Citation.

2 Phillip E. Areeda et al., <u>Antitrust Law</u> § 306d, at 62 (2d ed. 2000). –Page Citation.

2 Phillip E. Areeda et al., <u>Antitrust Law</u> § 306d, at 62 n.17 (2d ed. 2000). –Footnote Citation.

Antitrust Law Journal
Ab.:   Antitrust L.J.

Ex.:   Harry M. Reasoner, <u>The State of Antitrust</u>, 59 Antitrust L.J. 63 (1990). –Article Citation.

Harry M. Reasoner, <u>The State of Antitrust</u>, 59 Antitrust L.J. 63, 69-70 (1990). –Page Citation.

Appeal Cases, District of Columbia (1893-1941)
Ab.:   App. D.C.
     –Cite to F. or F.2d, if therein; otherwise, cite to App. D.C.

Ex.:   <u>Army & Navy Club v. District of Columbia</u>, 8 App. D.C. 544 (1896). –Case Citation.

<u>Army & Navy Club v. District of Columbia</u>, 8 App. D.C. 544, 550 (1896). –Page Citation.

Appellate Court Administration Review
Ab.:   App. Ct. Admin. Rev.

Appellate Department
Ab.:   App. Dep't

Appellate Division
Ab.:   App. Div.

appended materials
–Explained and illustrated in <u>Bluebook</u> rule 3.4.

appendix; appendices
Ab.:   app., apps.
     –Explained and illustrated in <u>Bluebook</u> rule 3.4.

Ex.:   Robert J. Hopperton, <u>Teaching the Rule Against Perpetuities in First Year Property</u>, 31 U. Tol. L. Rev. 55 app.II, at 71 (1999).

Appleman on Insurance, 2d,
See Holmes' Appleman on Insurance, 2d, by Eric Mills Holmes and L. Anthony Sutin.

In citing cases in law review footnotes, abbreviate any word listed in table T.6; the names of "states, countries, and other geographical units" unless they are named parties; and any other words of eight or more letters "if <u>substantial</u> space is thereby saved and the result is unambiguous." <u>Bluebook</u> rule 10.2.2. On the other hand, in citing cases in text, abbreviate only widely known acronyms and the following words: "&," "Ass'n," "Bros.," "Co.," "Corp.," "Inc.," "Ltd.," and "No." <u>Bluebook</u> rule 10.2.1(c).

Arbitration Journal
Ab.:   Arb. J.

Ex.:   Donald L. Carper, <u>Remedies in Business Arbitration</u>, Arb. J.,
         Sept. 1991, at 49. –Article Citation.

         Donald L. Carper, <u>Remedies in Business Arbitration</u>, Arb. J.,
         Sept. 1991, at 49, 50-52. –Page Citation.

Arbitration Materials
Ab.:   Arb. Mat'l

Arbitrator
Ab.:   Arb.

Areeda & Turner on Antitrust Law
See Antitrust Law, by Phillip Areeda & Donald F. Turner.

Arizona Administrative Code
Ab.:   Ariz. Admin. Code § x-x-x (year)

Ex.:   Ariz. Admin. Code § R2-2-204 (2000)

Arizona Administrative Register
Ab.:   vol. no. Ariz. Admin. Reg. page no. (month day, year)

Ex.:   10 Ariz. Admin. Reg. 510 (Feb. 13, 2004)

Arizona Appeals Reports
Ab.:   Ariz. App.

         –Discontinued after 27 Ariz. App. 797 (1976); cases thereafter found in
          Arizona Reports.

         –Cite to P., P.2d, or P.3d, if therein; otherwise, cite to Ariz. App. or
          Ariz.

         –Give parallel citations only in documents submitted to Arizona state
          courts. <u>See</u> Bluebook rules 10.3.1 and B5.1.3; see also Ariz. R. Civ.
          App. P.13(a)(6), which requires a parallel citation.

         –Through 27 Ariz. App. 797 (1976), cite as follows:

         In documents submitted to Arizona state courts:

              <u>Comm. for Neighborhood Pres. v. Graham</u>, 14 Ariz. App. 457, 484
              P.2d 226 (1971). –Case Citation.

              <u>Comm. for Neighborhood Pres. v. Graham</u>, 14 Ariz. App. 457,
              460, 484 P.2d 226, 228 (1971). –Page Citation.

         In all other documents:

              <u>Comm. for Neighborhood Pres. v. Graham</u>, 484 P.2d 226 (Ariz. Ct.
              App. 1971). –Case Citation.

              <u>Comm. for Neighborhood Pres. v. Graham</u>, 484 P.2d 226, 228
              (Ariz. Ct. App. 1971). –Page Citation.

In law review footnotes, the titles of books and the names of cases, except for procedural
phrases, are not underlined. <u>See</u> Bluebook rule 2.1(a) & (b). Further, the following are in
large and small capitals: codes, restatements, standards, constitutions, periodicals, authors of
books, titles of books, the abbreviated names of codes, most legislative materials except for
bills and resolutions, codified ordinances, model codes, court rules, and sentencing guidelines.
Refer to <u>The Bluebook</u>.

—After 27 Ariz. App. 797 (1976), cite as follows:

In documents submitted to Arizona state courts:

> State v. Valdez, 182 Ariz. 165, 894 P.2d 708 (Ct. App. 1994).
> —Case Citation.
>
> State v. Valdez, 182 Ariz. 165, 172, 894 P.2d 708, 713
> (Ct. App. 1994). —Page Citation.

In all other documents:

> State v. Valdez, 894 P.2d 708 (Ariz. Ct. App. 1994).
> —Case Citation.
>
> State v. Valdez, 894 P.2d 708, 713 (Ariz. Ct. App. 1994).
> —Page Citation.

Arizona Attorney
Ab.: Ariz. Att'y

Ex.: Roxana Bacon, Supreme Court Adopts Sweeping Changes in Attorney Discipline, Ariz. Att'y, Feb. 1992, at 10. —Article Citation.

Roxana Bacon, Supreme Court Adopts Sweeping Changes in Attorney Discipline, Ariz. Att'y, Feb. 1992, at 10, 11. —Page Citation.

Arizona Constitution
Ab.: Ariz. Const. art.   , pt.   , §   .

—Not all articles are subdivided into parts.

Ex.: Ariz. Const. art. VIII, pt. 2, § 1.
Ariz. Const. art. II, § 4. —"Cite constitutional provisions currently in force without a date." Bluebook rule 11.

Ariz. Const. art. XXIV (repealed 1932). —"If the cited provision has been repealed, either indicate parenthetically the fact and date of repeal or cite the repealing provision in full." Bluebook rule 11.

Ariz. Const. art. XXVIII, § 1 (amended 1988). —"When citing a provision that has been subsequently amended, either indicate parenthetically the fact and date of amendment or cite the amending provision in full." Bluebook rule 11.

Arizona Journal of International and Comparative Law
Ab: Ariz. J. Int'l & Comp. L.

Ex: Robert Kossick, The Rule of Law and Development in Mexico, 21 Ariz. J. Int'l & Comp. L. 715 (2004). —Article Citation.

Robert Kossick, The Rule of Law and Development in Mexico, 21 Ariz. J. Int'l & Comp. L. 715, 762 (2004). —Page Citation.

Arizona Law Review
Ab.: Ariz. L. Rev.

In citing cases in law review footnotes, abbreviate any word listed in table T.6; the names of "states, countries, and other geographical units" unless they are named parties; and any other words of eight or more letters "if substantial space is thereby saved and the result is unambiguous." Bluebook rule 10.2.2. On the other hand, in citing cases in text, abbreviate only widely known acronyms and the following words: "&," "Ass'n," "Bros.," "Co.," "Corp.," "Inc.," "Ltd.," and "No." Bluebook rule 10.2.1(c).

Ex.: Michael H. LeRoy, <u>Strike Crossovers and Striker Replacements: An Empirical Test of the NLRB's No-Presumption Policy</u>, 33 Ariz. L. Rev. 291 (1991). –Article Citation.

Michael H. LeRoy, <u>Strike Crossovers and Striker Replacements: An Empirical Test of the NLRB's No-Presumption Policy</u>, 33 Ariz. L. Rev. 291, 295-97 (1991). –Page Citation.

Arizona Legislative Service (West)

Ab.: year Ariz. Legis. Serv. page no. (West)

Ex.: Act of Apr. 23, 1996, ch. 250, 1996 Ariz. Legis. Serv. 1464 (West) (relating to emergency medical services). –Citation to an entire act.

Act of Apr. 23, 1996, ch. 250, sec. 1, § 36-2201, 1996 Ariz. Legis. Serv. 1464, 1464-66 (West) (relating to emergency medical services). –Citation to a session law amending a prior act.

–<u>See</u> <u>Bluebook</u> rule 12.4.

–"Cite to Ariz. Sess. Laws, if therein." <u>Bluebook</u> table T.1, p. 199.

Arizona Reports

Ab.: Ariz.

–Cite to P., P.2d, or P.3d, if therein; otherwise, cite to Ariz.

–Give parallel citations only in documents submitted to Arizona state courts. <u>See</u> <u>Bluebook</u> rules 10.3.1 and B5.1.3; see also Ariz. R. Civ. App. P.13(a)(6), which requires a parallel citation.

In documents submitted to Arizona state courts:

<u>Zamora v. Reinstein</u>, 185 Ariz. 272, 915 P.2d 1227 (1996). –Case Citation.

<u>Zamora v. Reinstein</u>, 185 Ariz. 272, 273, 915 P.2d 1227, 1228 (1996). –Page Citation.

In all other documents, cite as follows:

<u>Zamora v. Reinstein</u>, 915 P.2d 1227 (Ariz. 1996). –Case Citation.

<u>Zamora v. Reinstein</u>, 915 P.2d 1227, 1228 (Ariz. 1996). –Page Citation.

Arizona Revised Statutes (LexisNexis)

Ab.: Ariz. Rev. Stat. § x-x (LexisNexis year)

Ex.: Ariz. Rev. Stat. § 3-1371 (LexisNexis 2004)

Ariz. Rev. Stat. § 2-1415 (LexisNexis Supp. 2005)

"Cite to Ariz. Rev. Stat. (published by West), if therein." <u>Bluebook</u> table T.1, p. 199

–For proper citation form in papers submitted to Arizona courts, see Ariz. Rev. Stat. Ann. § 1-101 (2002).

Arizona Revised Statutes Annotated (West)

Ab.: Ariz. Rev. Stat. Ann. § x-x (year)

In law review footnotes, the titles of books and the names of cases, except for procedural phrases, are not underlined. <u>See</u> <u>Bluebook</u> rule 2.1(a) & (b). Further, the following are in large and small capitals: codes, restatements, standards, constitutions, periodicals, authors of books, titles of books, the abbreviated names of codes, most legislative materials except for bills and resolutions, codified ordinances, model codes, court rules, and sentencing guidelines. Refer to <u>The Bluebook</u>.

Ex.:   Ariz. Rev. Stat. Ann. § 23-1382 (2005).

Ariz. Rev. Stat. Ann. § 49-550 (Supp. 2005).

–For proper citation form in papers submitted to Arizona courts, see Ariz. Rev. Stat. Ann. § 1-101 (2002).

Arizona Session Laws
See Session Laws, Arizona.

Arizona State Law Journal
Ab.:   Ariz. St. L.J.

Ex.:   Russell L. Weaver, <u>Challenging Regulatory Interpretations</u>, 23 Ariz. St. L.J. 109 (1991). –Article Citation.

Russell L. Weaver, <u>Challenging Regulatory Interpretations</u>, 23 Ariz. St. L.J. 109, 144-48 (1991). –Page Citation.

Arkansas Advance Legislative Service (LexisNexis)
Ab.:   year-pamph. no. Ark. Adv. Legis. Serv. page no. (LexisNexis)

Ex.:   Act of Mar. 9, 2005, No. 839, 2005-4 Ark. Adv. Legis. Serv. 93 (LexisNexis) (concerning appropriations). –Citation to an entire session law.

Act of Mar. 9, 2005, No. 839, sec. 3, 2005-4 Ark. Adv. Legis. Serv. 93, 95 (LexisNexis) (concerning appropriations). –Citation to a section of a session law.

–<u>See</u> <u>Bluebook</u> rule 12.4.

–"Cite to Ark. Acts, if therein." <u>Bluebook</u> table T.1, p. 200.

Arkansas Appellate Reports
Ab.:   Ark. App.

–Bound with Arkansas Reports.

–Cite to S.W., S.W.2d, or S.W.3d, if therein; otherwise, cite to Ark. App.

–Give parallel citations only in documents submitted to Arkansas state courts. <u>See</u> <u>Bluebook</u> rules 10.3.1 and B5.1.3; see also Ark. Sup. Ct. R. 4-2(a)(7), which requires a parallel citation.

In documents submitted to Arkansas state courts, cite as follows:

<u>Jessie v. Jessie</u>, 53 Ark. App. 188, 920 S.W.2d 874 (1996).
–Case Citation.

<u>Jessie v. Jessie</u>, 53 Ark. App. 188, 189, 920 S.W.2d 874, 875 (1996).
–Page Citation.

In all other documents, cite as follows:

<u>Jessie v. Jessie</u>, 920 S.W.2d 874 (Ark. Ct. App. 1996). –Case Citation.

<u>Jessie v. Jessie</u>, 920 S.W.2d 874, 875 (Ark. Ct. App. 1996).
–Page Citation.

In citing cases in law review footnotes, abbreviate any word listed in table T.6; the names of "states, countries, and other geographical units" unless they are named parties; and any other words of eight or more letters "if <u>substantial</u> space is thereby saved and the result is unambiguous." <u>Bluebook</u> rule 10.2.2. On the other hand, in citing cases in text, abbreviate only widely known acronyms and the following words: "&," "Ass'n," "Bros.," "Co.," "Corp.," "Inc.," "Ltd.," and "No." <u>Bluebook</u> rule 10.2.1(c).

Arkansas Code of 1987 Annotated (LexisNexis)
Ab.:   Ark. Code Ann. §   (year)

Ex.:   Ark. Code Ann. § 19-4-1801 (1998).

Ark. Code. Ann. § 28-70-401 (Supp. 1999).

–For proper citation form in papers submitted to Arkansas courts, see Ark. Code Ann. § 1-2-113(c) (1996).

Arkansas Constitution
Ab.:   Ark. Const. art. , §   .

Ex.:   Ark. Const. art. XIV, § 2.–"Cite constitutional provisions currently in force without a date." Bluebook rule 11.

Ark. Const. art. III, § 3 (repealed in part 1963).

Ark. Const. art. III, § 3, repealed by Ark. Const. amend. L, § 1. –"If the cited provision has been repealed, either indicate parenthetically the fact and date of repeal or cite the repealing provision in full." Bluebook rule 11.

Ark. Const. art. XIV, § 3 (amended 1948).

Ark. Const. art. XIV, § 3, amended by Ark. Const. amend. XL. –"When citing a provision that has been subsequently amended, either indicate parenthetically the fact and date of amendment or cite the amending provision in full." Bluebook rule 11.

Ark. Const. of 1868, art. III, § 2 (1873). –"Cite constitutions that have been totally superseded by year of adoption; if the specific provision cited was adopted in a different year, give that year parenthetically." Bluebook rule 11.

Arkansas Law Notes
Ab.:   Ark. L. Notes

Ex.:   Howard W. Brill, Punitive Damages in Arkansas -- Expanded? Restricted?, 1990 Ark. L. Notes 25. –Article Citation.

Howard W. Brill, Punitive Damages in Arkansas -- Expanded? Restricted?, 1990 Ark. L. Notes 25, 27-28. –Page Citation.

Arkansas Law Review
Ab.:   Ark. L. Rev.

Ex.:   Mark R. Gillett, Perfecting the Special Use Election: Congress Giveth and the Service Taketh Away, 45 Ark. L. Rev. 171 (1992). –Article Citation.

Mark R. Gillett, Perfecting the Special Use Election: Congress Giveth and the Service Taketh Away, 45 Ark. L. Rev. 171, 185-89 (1992). –Page Citation.

Arkansas Lawyer, The
Ab.:   Ark. Law.

Ex.:   Richard F. Hatfield, Significant Developments in Probate & Trusts in the Past 25 Years, Ark. Law., Jan. 1992, at 29. –Article Citation.

In law review footnotes, the titles of books and the names of cases, except for procedural phrases, are not underlined. See Bluebook rule 2.1(a) & (b). Further, the following are in large and small capitals: codes, restatements, standards, constitutions, periodicals, authors of books, titles of books, the abbreviated names of codes, most legislative materials except for bills and resolutions, codified ordinances, model codes, court rules, and sentencing guidelines. Refer to The Bluebook.

Richard F. Hatfield, <u>Significant Developments in Probate & Trusts in the Past 25 Years</u>, Ark. Law., Jan. 1992, at 29, 32. –Page Citation.

Arkansas Legislative Service (West)

Ab.: year Ark. Legis. Serv. page no. (West)

Ex.: Act of Apr. 13, 2005, No. 2214, sec. 1, § 6-82-1002(1)(a), 2005 Ark. Legis. Serv. 1309 (West) –Citation to a section of a session law amending prior act.

–See <u>Bluebook</u> rule 12.4.

–"Cite to Ark. Acts, if therein." <u>Bluebook</u> table T.1, p. 200.

Arkansas Register

Ab.: vol. no. Ark. Reg. page no. (month year)

Ex.: 28 Ark. Reg. 12 (Apr. 2005)

Arkansas Reports

Ab.: Ark.

–Cite to S.W., S.W.2d, or S.W.3d, if therein; otherwise, cite to Ark.

–Give parallel citations only in documents submitted to Arkansas state courts. See <u>Bluebook</u> rules 10.3.1 and B5.1.3; see also Ark. Sup. Ct. R. 4-2(a)(7), which requires a parallel citation.

In documents submitted to Arkansas state courts, cite as follows:

<u>Pledger v. Halvorson</u>, 324 Ark. 302, 921 S.W.2d 576 (1996). –Case Citation.

<u>Pledger v. Halvorson</u>, 324 Ark. 302, 304, 921 S.W.2d 576, 578 (1996). –Page Citation.

In all other documents, cite as follows:

<u>Pledger v. Halvorson</u>, 921 S.W.2d 576 (Ark. 1996). –Case Citation.

<u>Pledger v. Halvorson</u>, 921 S.W.2d 576, 578 (Ark. 1996). –Page Citation.

Arkansas Session Laws

See Acts of Arkansas.

Arkansas Statutes Annotated

See Arkansas Code of 1987 Annotated.

Army Lawyer, The

Ab.: Army Law.

Ex.: Thomas K. Emswiller, <u>Security Assistance and Operations Law</u>, Army Law., Nov. 1991, at 10. –Article Citation.

Thomas K. Emswiller, <u>Security Assistance and Operations Law</u>, Army Law., Nov. 1991, at 10, 13-15. –Page Citation.

Arrêts du Tribunal Fédéral Suisse (Switzerland)

Ab.: ATF

In citing cases in law review footnotes, abbreviate any word listed in table T.6; the names of "states, countries, and other geographical units" unless they are named parties; and any other words of eight or more letters "if <u>substantial</u> space is thereby saved and the result is unambiguous." <u>Bluebook</u> rule 10.2.2. On the other hand, in citing cases in text, abbreviate only widely known acronyms and the following words: "&," "Ass'n," "Bros.," "Co.," "Corp.," "Inc.," "Ltd.," and "No." <u>Bluebook</u> rule 10.2.1(c).

Constitutional cases	ATF I
Administrative and international law cases	ATF II
Civil and Bankruptcy cases	ATF III
Criminal cases	ATF IV
Social security cases	ATF V

See Bluebook table T.2, p. 314.

article(s)
Ab.:   art., arts.

as reprinted in
Ex.:   H.R. Rep. No. 104-311, at 96 (1995), as reprinted in 1995 U.S.C.C.A.N. 793, 808.

Note: "As reprinted in" indicates an excerpt rather than a full reprinting, which is indicated by "reprinted in." See Bluebook rule 1.6(a)(iii) (3d prtg. 2006).

ASILS International Law Journal
Ab.:   ASILS Int'l L.J.

Ex.:   Johanna M. Klema, Note, Strategic Defense Initiative and the New Interpretation of the ABM Treaty, 10 ASILS Int'l L.J. 149 (1986). –Note Citation.

Johanna M. Klema, Note, Strategic Defense Initiative and the New Interpretation of the ABM Treaty, 10 ASILS Int'l L.J. 149, 161-63 (1986). –Page Citation.

–A designation of the piece should appear before the title of the work to indicate that it is student written. See Bluebook rule 16.6.2(a).

Assembl[yman, ywoman]
Ab.:   Assemb.

Atlantic Reporter
–Do not give a parallel citation unless required by local rule. See Bluebook rules 10.3.1 and B5.1.3. See also the various state court and state reporter entries herein for local rule parallel citation requirements.

Ab.:   A.

Ex.:

Connecticut:
Valente v. Hopper, 126 A. 706 (Conn. 1924). –Case Citation.
Valente v. Hopper, 126 A. 706, 708 (Conn. 1924). –Page Citation.
Delaware:

In law review footnotes, the titles of books and the names of cases, except for procedural phrases, are not underlined. See Bluebook rule 2.1(a) & (b). Further, the following are in large and small capitals: codes, restatements, standards, constitutions, periodicals, authors of books, titles of books, the abbreviated names of codes, most legislative materials except for bills and resolutions, codified ordinances, model codes, court rules, and sentencing guidelines. Refer to The Bluebook.

Charles Tire Co. v. Owens, 186 A. 737 (Del. Super. Ct. 1936).
–Case Citation.
Charles Tire Co. v. Owens, 186 A. 737, 738 (Del. Super. Ct. 1936).
–Page Citation.

Maine:
Pelletier v. Cent. Me. Power Co., 126 A. 836 (Me. 1924). –Case
Citation.
Pelletier v. Cent. Me. Power Co., 126 A. 836, 838 (Me. 1924).
–Page Citation.

Maryland:
Frey & Son, Inc. v. Magness, 157 A. 400 (Md. 1931). –Case Citation.
Frey & Son, Inc. v. Magness, 157 A. 400, 402 (Md. 1931).
–Page Citation.

New Hampshire:
Sarkise v. Boston & M.R.R., 186 A. 332 (N.H. 1936). –Case Citation.
Sarkise v. Boston & M.R.R., 186 A. 332, 335 (N.H. 1936).
–Page Citation.

New Jersey:
Paletz v. Camden Safe Deposit & Trust Co., 157 A. 456 (N.J. Ch.
1931). –Case Citation.
Paletz v. Camden Safe Deposit & Trust Co., 157 A. 456, 458 (N.J. Ch.
1931). –Page Citation.

Pennsylvania:
Davis v. Hillman, 126 A. 246 (Pa. 1924). –Case Citation.
Davis v. Hillman, 126 A. 246, 247 (Pa. 1924). –Page Citation.

Rhode Island:
Gorham v. Robinson, 186 A. 832 (R.I. 1936). –Case Citation.
Gorham v. Robinson, 186 A. 832, 839 (R.I. 1936). –Page Citation.

Vermont:
Pennock v. Goodrich, 157 A. 922 (Vt. 1932). –Case Citation.
Pennock v. Goodrich, 157 A. 922, 924 (Vt. 1932). –Page Citation.

Atlantic Reporter, Second Series

–Do not give a parallel citation unless required by local rule or unless the
particular state has a public domain format. See Bluebook rules 10.3.1,
10.3.3, and B5.1.3. See also the various state court and state reporter entries
herein for public domain information and local rule parallel citation
requirements.
–With volume 532 (1988), Atlantic Reporter, Second Series, became West's
Atlantic Reporter, Second Series. Citation form is not affected by this title
change.

Ab.:   A.2d
Ex.:

In citing cases in law review footnotes, abbreviate any word listed in table T.6;
the names of "states, countries, and other geographical units" unless they are named parties;
and any other words of eight or more letters "if substantial space is thereby saved and the
result is unambiguous." Bluebook rule 10.2.2. On the other hand, in citing cases in text,
abbreviate only widely known acronyms and the following words: "&," "Ass'n," "Bros.,"
"Co.," "Corp.," "Inc.," "Ltd.," and "No." Bluebook rule 10.2.1(c).

Connecticut:

State v. Robinson, 676 A.2d 384 (Conn. 1996). –Case Citation.

State v. Robinson, 676 A.2d 384, 388 (Conn. 1996). –Page Citation.

Delaware:

Acierno v. Worthy Bros. Pipeline Corp., 656 A.2d 1085 (Del. Super. Ct. 1995). –Case Citation.

Acierno v. Worthy Bros. Pipeline Corp., 656 A.2d 1085, 1090 (Del. Super. Ct. 1995). –Page Citation.

District of Columbia:

Davis v. Henderson, 652 A.2d 634 (D.C. 1995). –Case Citation.

Davis v. Henderson, 652 A.2d 634, 636 (D.C. 1995). –Page Citation.

Maine:

Dutil v. Burns, 674 A.2d 910 (Me. 1996). –Case Citation.

Dutil v. Burns, 674 A.2d 910, 911 (Me. 1996). –Page Citation.

Maryland:

Mangrum v. State, 676 A.2d 80 (Md. 1996). –Case Citation.

Mangrum v. State, 676 A.2d 80, 84 (Md. 1996). –Page Citation.

New Hampshire:

State v. Vandebogart, 652 A.2d 671 (N.H. 1994). –Case Citation.

State v. Vandebogart, 652 A.2d 671, 679 (N.H. 1994). –Page Citation.

New Jersey:

Anderson v. Piccotti, 676 A.2d 127 (N.J. 1996). –Case Citation.

Anderson v. Piccotti, 676 A.2d 127, 136 (N.J. 1996). –Page Citation.

Pennsylvania:

Commonwealth v. Brown, 676 A.2d 1178 (Pa. 1996). –Case Citation.

Commonwealth v. Brown, 676 A.2d 1178, 1183 (Pa. 1996). –Page Citation.

Rhode Island:

Bruzzese v. Wood, 674 A.2d 390 (R.I. 1996). –Case Citation.

Bruzzese v. Wood, 674 A.2d 390, 394 (R.I. 1996). –Page Citation.

Vermont:

State v. Quinn, 675 A.2d 1336 (Vt. 1996). –Case Citation.

State v. Quinn, 675 A.2d 1336, 1338 (Vt. 1996). –Page Citation.

Atomic Energy Commission Reports (U.S.) (1956-1975)

Ab.:   A.E.C.

Ex.:   S. Cal. Edison Co., 7 A.E.C. 410 (1974).

         T.V.A. (Watts Bar Nuclear Plant, Units 1 and 2), 6 A.E.C. 37 (1973).

Attorney General

Ab.:   Att'y Gen.

In law review footnotes, the titles of books and the names of cases, except for procedural phrases, are not underlined. See Bluebook rule 2.1(a) & (b). Further, the following are in large and small capitals: codes, restatements, standards, constitutions, periodicals, authors of books, titles of books, the abbreviated names of codes, most legislative materials except for bills and resolutions, codified ordinances, model codes, court rules, and sentencing guidelines. Refer to The Bluebook.

Attorney General's Annual Report
Ab.: Att'y Gen. Ann. Rep.
Ex.: 1956 Att'y Gen. Ann. Rep. 118.

Attorney General's Opinions, generally
See Bluebook rule 14.4.

Attorney General's Opinions (State)
See Opinions of the Attorney General, as titled by the individual state.

Attorney General's Opinions (U.S.)
See Opinions of the Attorney General (U.S.) (1789-date).

Auckland University Law Review
Ab.: Auckland U. L. Rev.
Ex.: Ian Narev, Unjust Enrichment and De Facto Relationships, 6 Auckland U. L. Rev. 504 (1991). −Article Citation.
Ian Narev, Unjust Enrichment and De Facto Relationships, 6 Auckland U. L. Rev. 504, 511-12 (1991). −Page Citation.

Audio Recordings
See Electronic media and other nonprint sources.

Auditing Standards, Generally Accepted
Ex.: Report on Audited Financial Statements, Statement on Auditing Standards No. 2, § 509 (Am. Inst. of Certified Pub. Accountants 1974).

Australia Treaty Series
Ab.: year Austl. T.S. No. .
Ex.: Treaty Between the Government of Australia and the Government of the United Kingdom of Great Britain and Northern Ireland Concerning the Investigation of Drug Trafficking and Confiscation of the Proceeds of Drug Trafficking, Austl.- Gr. Brit.- N. Ir., Aug. 3, 1988, art. 8, 1990 Austl. T.S. No. 33.

Australian Argus Law Reports
Ab.: A.A.L.R.
Ex.: Morris v. Morris, (1972) 1972-73 A.A.L.R. 893 (Austl.).

Australian Business Law Review
Ab.: Austl. Bus. L. Rev.
Ex.: Andrew Keay, The Parameters of Bankruptcy Examinations, 22 Austl. Bus. L. Rev. 75 (1994). −Article Citation.
Andrew Keay, The Parameters of Bankruptcy Examinations, 22 Austl. Bus. L. Rev. 75, 79-81 (1994). −Page Citation.

Australian Law Journal, The
Ab.: Austl. L.J.

In citing cases in law review footnotes, abbreviate any word listed in table T.6; the names of "states, countries, and other geographical units" unless they are named parties; and any other words of eight or more letters "if substantial space is thereby saved and the result is unambiguous." Bluebook rule 10.2.2. On the other hand, in citing cases in text, abbreviate only widely known acronyms and the following words: "&," "Ass'n," "Bros.," "Co.," "Corp.," "Inc.," "Ltd.," and "No." Bluebook rule 10.2.1(c).

Ex.:   Laurence Claus, Implication and the Concept of a Constitution, 69 Austl. L.J. 887 (1995). –Article Citation.

Laurence Claus, Implication and the Concept of a Constitution, 69 Austl. L.J. 887, 890-96 (1995). –Page Citation.

Australian Law Reports
Ab.:   A.L.R.
Ex.:   Commonwealth & Another v. Esber, (1991) 101 A.L.R. 35 (Fed. Ct.) (Austl.). –Case Citation.

Commonwealth & Another v. Esber, (1991) 101 A.L.R. 35, 38 (Fed. Ct.) (Austl.). –Page Citation.

Birdseye v. Sheahan [2005] FCAFC 60; (2005) 216 A.L.R. 176 (Austl.). –Case with medium-neutral citation.

Note: For explanation of Australia's medium-neutral citation, see L.T. Olsson, Guide to Uniform Production of Judgments (2d ed. 1999), available at http://www.aija.org.au/online/judguide.htm.

Australian Yearbook of International Law, The
Ab.:   Austl. Y.B. Int'l L.
Ex.:   Yash Chai, Human Rights and Governance: The Asia Debate, 15 Austl. Y.B. Int'l L. 1 (1994). –Article Citation.

Yash Chai, Human Rights and Governance: The Asia Debate, 15 Austl. Y.B. Int'l L. 1, 11 (1994). –Page Citation.

author(s)
See various title entries in this work and Bluebook rules 15.1 and 16.1.

Ex.:   Jeffrey M. Hertzfeld, Negotiating East-West Deals: Case Studies for Lawyers in Current Legal Aspects of Doing Business With Sino-Soviet Nations 8 (James T. Haight ed., 1973).

Jenia Iontcheva, Jury Sentencing as Democratic Practice, 89 Va. L. Rev. 311, 318 (2003).

authorities, order of authorities within each signal
See Bluebook rule 1.4.

Automobile Liability Insurance, by Irvin E. Schermer
          –Do not abbreviate the title.
Ex.:   1 Irvin F. Schermer, Automobile Liability Insurance § 4.01[1] (3d ed. 1995). –Section Citation.

1 Irvin F. Schermer, Automobile Liability Insurance § 4.01[1], at 4-4 (3d ed. 1995). –Page Citation.

1 Irvin F. Schermer, Automobile Liability Insurance § 4.01[1], at 4-4 n.15 (3d ed. 1995). –Footnote Citation.

Aviation Law Reports (Commerce Clearing House)
Ab.:   Av. L. Rep. (CCH) [looseleaf]
          Av. Cas. (CCH) [bound]

In law review footnotes, the titles of books and the names of cases, except for procedural phrases, are not underlined. See Bluebook rule 2.1(a) & (b). Further, the following are in large and small capitals: codes, restatements, standards, constitutions, periodicals, authors of books, titles of books, the abbreviated names of codes, most legislative materials except for bills and resolutions, codified ordinances, model codes, court rules, and sentencing guidelines. Refer to The Bluebook.

B

Bail Court
    Ab.:   Bail Ct.

Baldwin's Kentucky Revised Statutes Annotated (West)
    Ab.:   Ky. Rev. Stat. Ann. § x.x (West year)
    Ex.:   Ky. Rev. Stat. Ann. § 123.120 (West 1998).
             Ky. Rev. Stat. Ann. § 92.560 (West Supp. 1999).
             –For proper citation form in papers submitted to Kentucky courts, see Ky. R. Civ. P. 76.12(4)(g).

Baldwin's Ohio Administrative Code (West)
    Ab.:   Baldwin's Ohio Admin. Code x:x-x (year)
    Ex.:   Baldwin's Ohio Admin. Code 109:5-1-01 (2000).

Baldwin's Ohio Legislative Service Annotated (West)
    Ab.:   year Ohio Legis. Serv. Ann. page no. (West)
    Ex.:   Act of Sept. 11, 1996, No. 351, 1996 Ohio Legis. Serv. Ann. 3343 (West) (concerning peace officer training council). –Citation to an entire session law.
             Act of Sept. 11, 1996, No. 351, sec. 1, §109.71, 1996 Ohio Legis. Serv. 3343-44, (West) (concerning definition of peace officer).
             –Citation to a session law amending a prior act.
             –See Bluebook rule 12.4.
             –"Cite to Ohio Laws, if therein." Bluebook table T.1, p. 227.

Baldwin's Ohio Revised Code Annotated (West)
    Ab.:   Ohio Rev. Code Ann. § x.x (West year)
    Ex.:   Ohio Rev. Code Ann. § 4511.452 (West 1999).
             Ohio Rev. Code Ann. § 3111.12 (West Supp. 2000).

    –For proper citation form in papers submitted to Ohio state courts, see Interim Edition to the Manual of the Forms of Citation used in the Ohio Official Reports, 88 Ohio App. 3d XXVI, XLIV (1992), available at http://www.sconet.state.oh.us/rod/pdf/MANCITEmain.pdf.

Ballentine's Law Dictionary
    Ab.:   Ballentine's Law Dictionary page (ed. year)
    Ex.:   Ballentine's Law Dictionary 98 (3d ed. 1969).

Banking Law Journal, The
Ab.:   Banking L.J.

In law review footnotes, the titles of books and the names of cases, except for procedural phrases, are not underlined. See Bluebook rule 2.1(a) & (b). Further, the following are in large and small capitals: codes, restatements, standards, constitutions, periodicals, authors of books, titles of books, the abbreviated names of codes, most legislative materials except for bills and resolutions, codified ordinances, model codes, court rules, and sentencing guidelines. Refer to The Bluebook.

Ex.:   Katrina Grider, <u>Employer Liability Under FIRREA</u>, 109 Banking L.J. 129 (1992). –Article Citation.

            Katrina Grider, <u>Employer Liability Under FIRREA</u>, 109 Banking L.J. 129, 131-36 (1992). –Page Citation.

Bankruptcy Appellate Panel
Ab.:   B.A.P.

Ex.:   <u>Hal, Inc. v. United States</u> (<u>In re Hal, Inc.</u>), 196 B.R. 159 (B.A.P. 9th Cir. 1996).

Bankruptcy Cases
Ex.:   <u>Chase Lumber & Fuel Co. v. Koch</u> (<u>In re Koch</u>), 197 B.R. 654 (Bankr. W.D. Wis. 1996)

            <u>Nunez v. Nunez</u> (<u>In re Nunez</u>), 196 B.R. 150 (B.A.P. 9th Cir. 1996).

            –If both the adversary and nonadversary name appear at the beginning of the opinion, cite as above, giving the adversary name first followed in parenthesis by the nonadversary name.

            –If only the nonadversary or adversary name appear at the beginning of the opinion, cite as follows:

                 <u>In re Calore Express Co.</u>, 199 B.R. 424 (Bankr. D. Mass. 1996).

                 <u>Bell v. Alden Owners, Inc.</u>, 199 B.R. 451 (S.D.N.Y. 1996).

Bankruptcy Court
Ab.:   Bankr.

Ex.:   <u>In re Masegian</u>, 134 B.R. 402, 403 (Bankr. E.D. Cal. 1991).

Bankruptcy Court Decisions
Ab.:   Bankr. Ct. Dec. (CRR)

Bankruptcy Court Rules
Ab.:   Bankr. R.

Ex.:   Bankr. R. 3002(c)(5).

Bankruptcy Law Reports (Commerce Clearing House) (formerly reporter)
Ab.:   Bankr. L. Rep. (CCH)

Ex.:   <u>In re Fernandez</u>, 3 Bankr. L. Rep. (CCH) ¶ 74,279 (Bankr. D. Kan. Sept. 30, 1991). –Citation to looseleaf material.

            <u>In re Goodwin</u>, [1985-1986 Transfer Binder] Bankr. L. Rep. (CCH) ¶ 71,025 (Bankr. D. Me. 1986).

            <u>In re Citadel Properties, Inc.</u>, [1987-1989 Transfer Binder] Bankr. L. Rep. (CCH) ¶ 72,301 (Bankr. M.D. Fla. 1988). –Citations to transfer binder.

            –The above examples are proper if the case is not yet available in, or is not reported in, an official or West reporter, a public domain citation, or in a widely used computer database.

In citing cases in law review footnotes, abbreviate any word listed in table T.6; the names of "states, countries, and other geographical units" unless they are named parties; and any other words of eight or more letters "if <u>substantial</u> space is thereby saved and the result is unambiguous." <u>Bluebook</u> rule 10.2.2. On the other hand, in citing cases in text, abbreviate only widely known acronyms and the following words: "&," "Ass'n," "Bros.," "Co.," "Corp.," "Inc.," "Ltd.," and "No." <u>Bluebook</u> rule 10.2.1(c).

Bankruptcy Law and Practice, by Daniel R. Cowans, Mark C. Ellenberg, Elizabeth Van Horn, & Russell W. Savory
–Do not abbreviate the title.
Ex.: 3 Daniel R. Cowans et al., <u>Bankruptcy Law and Practice</u> § 11.1 (7th ed. 1998). –Section Citation.

3 Daniel R. Cowans et al., <u>Bankruptcy Law and Practice</u> § 11.1, at 3 (7th ed. 1998). –Page Citation.

3 Daniel R. Cowans et al., <u>Bankruptcy Law and Practice</u> § 11.1, at 3 n.1 (7th ed. 1998). –Footnote citation.

Bankruptcy Reporter
Ab.: B.R.
Ex.: <u>In re Masegian</u>, 134 B.R. 402, 403 (Bankr. E.D. Cal. 1991).

Bar Bulletin: State Bar of New Mexico
Ab.: B. Bull. St. B. N.M.
Section A–nonconsecutively paginated
Ex.: Matthew E. Cohen, <u>Income Tax Aspects of Lawsuits</u>, B. Bull. St. B. N.M., Dec. 19, 1991, at 6. –Article Citation.

Matthew E. Cohen, <u>Income Tax Aspects of Lawsuits</u>, B. Bull. St. B. N.M., Dec. 19, 1991, at 6, 8. –Page Citation.
Section B–consecutively paginated
Ex.: <u>Proposed Amendments of Bar Commission Rules</u>, 30 B. Bull. St. B. N.M. 1055 (1991). –Article Citation.

Baron
Ab.: B.

Basic Text on Labor Law, by Robert A. Gorman and Matthew W. Finkin
–Do not abbreviate the title.
Ex.: Robert A. Gorman & Matthew W. Finkin, <u>Basic Text on Labor Law</u> § 19.7 (2d ed. 2004). –Section Citation.

Robert A. Gorman & Matthew W. Finkin, <u>Basic Text on Labor Law</u> § 19.7, at 529 (2d ed. 2004). –Page Citation.

Baylor Law Review
Ab.: Baylor L. Rev.
Ex.: Kevin F. Risley, <u>Why Texas Courts Should Not Retain the Inherent Power to Impose Sanctions</u>, 44 Baylor L. Rev. 253 (1992). –Article Citation.

Kevin F. Risley, <u>Why Texas Courts Should Not Retain the Inherent Power to Impose Sanctions</u>, 44 Baylor L. Rev. 253, 262-65 (1992). –Page Citation.

Behavioral Sciences and the Law
Ab.: Behav. Sci. & L.

In law review footnotes, the titles of books and the names of cases, except for procedural phrases, are not underlined. <u>See</u> <u>Bluebook</u> rule 2.1(a) & (b). Further, the following are in large and small capitals: codes, restatements, standards, constitutions, periodicals, authors of books, titles of books, the abbreviated names of codes, most legislative materials except for bills and resolutions, codified ordinances, model codes, court rules, and sentencing guidelines. Refer to <u>The Bluebook</u>.

Ex.: Michael Perlin, <u>Dignity Was the First to Leave: Godinez v. Moran, Colin Ferguson, and the Trial of Mentally Disabled Criminal Defendants</u>, 14 Behav. Sci. & L. 81 (1996). –Article Citation.

Michael Perlin, <u>Dignity Was the First to Leave: Godinez v. Moran, Colin Ferguson, and the Trial of Mentally Disabled Criminal Defendants</u>, 14 Behav. Sci. & L. 81, 86 (1996). –Page Citation.

Bench and Bar of Minnesota
Ab.: Bench & B. Minn.

Ex.: Marshall H. Tanick & Edwin Cheeseboro, <u>Football Law in Minnesota: From Antitrust to Zebras</u>, Bench & B. Minn., Jan. 1992, at 18. –Article Citation.

Marshall H. Tanick & Edwin Cheeseboro, <u>Football Law in Minnesota: From Antitrust to Zebras</u>, Bench & B. Minn., Jan. 1992, at 18, 19. –Page Citation.

Benedict on Admiralty
–Do not abbreviate this title.

Ex.: 1 Steven R. Friedell, <u>Benedict on Admiralty</u> § 123, at 8-9. (7th rev. ed. 2005). –Page Citation.

2A Richard Ziade, <u>Benedict on Admiralty</u> § 35, at 19 (7th ed. cum. supp. Mar. 2005). –Supplement Citation.

Benefits Law Journal
Ab.: Benefits L.J.

Ex.: Eric L. Smithback & Steven T. Idelson, <u>Municipal Retiree Benefits: Many Plans but No Prefunding –Yet</u>, 3 Benefits L.J. 477 (1990-91). –Article Citation.

Eric L. Smithback & Steven T. Idelson, <u>Municipal Retiree Benefits: Many Plans but No Prefunding –Yet</u>, 3 Benefits L.J. 477, 478 (1990-91). –Page Citation.

Bergin on Estates in Land and Future Interests
See Preface to Estates in Land and Future Interests, by Thomas F. Bergin & Paul G. Haskell.

Berkeley Journal of Employment and Labor Law
Ab: Berkeley J. Emp. & Lab. L.

Ex: Matthew A. Edwards, <u>The Law and Social Norms of Pay Secrecy</u>, 26 Berkeley J. Emp. & Lab. L. 41 (2005). –Article Citation.

Matthew A. Edwards, <u>The Law and Social Norms of Pay Secrecy</u>, 26 Berkeley J. Emp. & Lab. L. 41, 53-60 (2005).–Page Citation.

Berkeley Journal of International Law
Ab: Berkeley J. Int'l L.

In citing cases in law review footnotes, abbreviate any word listed in table T.6; the names of "states, countries, and other geographical units" unless they are named parties; and any other words of eight or more letters "if <u>substantial</u> space is thereby saved and the result is unambiguous." <u>Bluebook</u> rule 10.2.2. On the other hand, in citing cases in text, abbreviate only widely known acronyms and the following words: "&," "Ass'n," "Bros.," "Co.," "Corp.," "Inc.," "Ltd.," and "No." <u>Bluebook</u> rule 10.2.1(c).

Ex: Haider Ala Hamoudi, <u>Toward a Rule of Law Society in Iraq:</u> <u>Introducing Clinical Legal Education into Iraqi Law Schools</u>, 23 Berkeley J. Int'l L. 112 (2005). –Article Citation.

Haider Ala Hamoudi, <u>Toward a Rule of Law Society in Iraq:</u> <u>Introducing Clinical Legal Education into Iraqi Law Schools</u>, 23 Berkeley J. Int'l L. 112, 122 (2005). –Page Citation.

Berkeley Technology Law Journal
Ab: Berkeley Tech. L.J.

Ex: Eugene Choo, <u>Going Dutch: The Google IPO</u>, 20 Berkeley Tech. L.J. 405 (2005). –Article Citation.

Eugene Choo, <u>Going Dutch: The Google IPO</u>, 20 Berkeley Tech. L.J. 405, 411 (2005). –Page Citation.

Berkeley Women's Law Journal
Ab.: Berkeley Women's L.J.

Ex.: Judy Scales-Trent, <u>Using Literature in Law School: The Importance of</u> <u>Reading and Telling Tales</u>, 7 Berkeley Women's L.J. 90 (1992). –Article Citation.

Judy Scales-Trent, <u>Using Literature in Law School: The Importance of</u> <u>Reading and Telling Tales</u>, 7 Berkeley Women's L.J. 90, 98 (1992). –Page Citation.

Biennial Report and Official Opinions of the Attorney General of the State of West Virginia
Ab.: Op. W. Va. Att'y Gen.

See Opinions of the Attorney General of West Virginia.

Biennial Report of the Attorney General of the State of South Dakota
See Opinions of the Attorney General of South Dakota.

Biennial Report of the Attorney General of the State of Iowa
See Opinions of the Attorney General of Iowa.

Biennial Report of the Attorney General of the State of Michigan
See Opinions of the Attorney General of Michigan.

Bill of Rights Journal, The
Ab.: Bill Rts. J.

Ex.: David L. Sobel, <u>Free Speech and National Security</u>, Bill Rts. J., Dec. 1987, at 5. –Article Citation.

David L. Sobel, <u>Free Speech and National Security</u>, Bill Rts. J., Dec. 1987, at 5, 7. –Page Citation.

Bills, Congressional
See Congressional Bills.

In law review footnotes, the titles of books and the names of cases, except for procedural phrases, are not underlined. <u>See</u> <u>Bluebook</u> rule 2.1(a) & (b). Further, the following are in large and small capitals: codes, restatements, standards, constitutions, periodicals, authors of books, titles of books, the abbreviated names of codes, most legislative materials except for bills and resolutions, codified ordinances, model codes, court rules, and sentencing guidelines. Refer to <u>The Bluebook</u>.

Bittker and Eustice on Federal Income Taxation of Corporations and Shareholders

See Federal Income Taxation of Corporations and Shareholders, by Boris I. Bittker & James S. Eustice.

Black (United States Reports)

See United States Reports.

Black's Law Dictionary

    Ab.:   Black's Law Dictionary (ed. year)

    Ex.:   Black's Law Dictionary 1123 (8th ed. 2004).

Blashfield Automobile Law and Practice, by Patrick D. Kelly

    –Do not abbreviate the title.

    Ex.:   11 Patrick D. Kelly, Blashfield Automobile Law and Practice § 421.2 (rev. 3d ed. 1987). –Section Citation.

            11 Patrick D. Kelly, Blashfield Automobile Law and Practice § 421.2, at 279 (rev. 3d ed. 1987). –Page Citation.

            7 Lance W. LeFevre, Blashfield Automobile Law and Practice § 291.9 (rev. 3d ed. Supp. 2004). –Citation to Supplement.

Blue Sky Law Reports (Commerce Clearing House)

    Ab.:   Blue Sky L. Rep. (CCH)

    Ex.:   Carney v. Mantuano, 3 Blue Sky L. Rep. (CCH) ¶ 74,122 (Wis. Ct. App. Sept. 25, 1996). –Citation to looseleaf material.

            Gohler v. Wood, [1993-1994 Decisions Tansfer Binder] Blue Sky L. Rep. (CCH) ¶ 73,269 (S.D. Utah Apr. 29, 1994). –Citation to transfer binder material.

            –The above examples are proper if the case is not yet available in, or is not reported in, an official or West reporter, a public domain citation, or in a widely used computer database.

(The) Bluebook: A Uniform System of Citation

    Ab.:   The Bluebook

            Bluebook

    Ex.:   The Bluebook: A Uniform System of Citation R. 15.8(c)(v), at 136 (Columbia Law Review Ass'n et al. eds., 18th ed. 2005).

            The Bluebook: A Uniform System of Citation 310 tbl.T.10 (Columbia Law Review Ass'n et al. eds., 17th ed. 2d prtg. 2000).

Board of Contract Appeals

See Contract Appeals Decisions.

Board of Tax Appeals

See Reports of the United States Board of Tax Appeals.

In citing cases in law review footnotes, abbreviate any word listed in table T.6; the names of "states, countries, and other geographical units" unless they are named parties; and any other words of eight or more letters "if substantial space is thereby saved and the result is unambiguous." Bluebook rule 10.2.2. On the other hand, in citing cases in text, abbreviate only widely known acronyms and the following words: "&," "Ass'n," "Bros.," "Co.," "Corp.," "Inc.," "Ltd.," and "No." Bluebook rule 10.2.1(c).

Book Review
> –Non-Student-Written Book Reviews. See <u>Bluebook</u> rule 16.6.1.

Ex.:   Jason S. Johnston, <u>Not So Cold an Eye: Richard Posner's Pragmatism</u>, 44 Vand. L. Rev. 741 (1991) (reviewing Richard A. Posner, <u>The Problems of Jurisprudence</u> (1990)). –"Include a second parenthetical after the date parenthetical indicating, if relevant to the purpose of the citation and if not clear from the surrounding discussion, the author, title, and publication date of the book reviewed." <u>Bluebook</u> rule 16.6.1

> Jason S. Johnston, <u>Not So Cold an Eye: Richard Posner's Pragmatism</u>, 44 Vand. L. Rev. 741 (1991) (book review). –"If it is unnecessary to identify the book under review, simply include the words 'book review' in the second parenthetical." <u>Bluebook</u> rule 16.6.1

> –Student-Written Book Reviews. See <u>Bluebook</u> rule 16.6.2(c).

Ex.:   Thomas C. Grey, Book Note, 106 Yale L.J. 493 (1996) (reviewing Neil Duxbury, <u>Patterns of American Jurisprudence</u> (1995)).

> –Signed, student-written, untitled book review.

> Geoffrey C. Rupp, Book Note, <u>DNA's Dark Side</u>, 110 Yale L. J. 163 (2000) (reviewing Jim Duyer, Peter Neufeld & Barry Scheck, <u>Actual Innocence: Five Days to Execution and Other Dispatches from the Wrongly Convicted</u> (2000)) –Signed, student-written, titled book review.

> Book Note, <u>Translating Truth</u>, 114 Harv. L. Rev. 640 (2000) (reviewing Peter Brooks, <u>Troubling Confessions: Speaking Guilt in Law and Literature</u> (2000)). –Unsigned, student-written book review.

Boston Bar Journal
Ab.:   Boston B.J.

Ex.:   Paul J. Liacos, <u>The Origins of the Massachusetts Supreme Judicial Court</u>, Boston B.J., Mar.-Apr. 1992, at 4. –Article Citation.

> Paul J. Liacos, <u>The Origins of the Massachusetts Supreme Judicial Court</u>, Boston B.J., Mar.-Apr. 1992, at 4, 6. –Page Citation.

Boston College Environmental Affairs Law Review
Ab.:   B.C. Envtl. Aff. L. Rev.

Ex.:   James P. Boggs, <u>NEPA in the Domain of Federal Indian Policy: Social Knowledge and the Negotiation of Meaning</u>, 19 B.C. Envtl. Aff. L. Rev. 31 (1991). –Article Citation.

> James P. Boggs, <u>NEPA in the Domain of Federal Indian Policy: Social Knowledge and the Negotiation of Meaning</u>, 19 B.C. Envtl. Aff. L. Rev. 31, 35-39 (1991). –Page Citation.

Boston College International and Comparative Law Review
Ab.:   B.C. Int'l & Comp. L. Rev.

In law review footnotes, the titles of books and the names of cases, except for procedural phrases, are not underlined. See <u>Bluebook</u> rule 2.1(a) & (b). Further, the following are in large and small capitals: codes, restatements, standards, constitutions, periodicals, authors of books, titles of books, the abbreviated names of codes, most legislative materials except for bills and resolutions, codified ordinances, model codes, court rules, and sentencing guidelines. Refer to <u>The Bluebook</u>.

Ex.:   Clyde H. Crockett, <u>The Role of Federal Common Law in Alien Tort Statute Cases,</u> 14 B.C. Int'l & Comp. L. Rev. 29 (1991). –Article Citation.

Clyde H. Crockett, <u>The Role of Federal Common Law in Alien Tort Statute Cases,</u> 14 B.C. Int'l & Comp. L. Rev. 29, 42-46 (1991). –Page Citation.

Boston College Law Review
Ab.:   B.C. L. Rev.

Ex.:   Dean M. Hashimoto, <u>Justice Brennan's Use of Scientific and Empirical Evidence in Constitutional and Administrative Law,</u> 32 B.C. L. Rev. 739 (1991). –Article Citation.

Dean M. Hashimoto, <u>Justice Brennan's Use of Scientific and Empirical Evidence in Constitutional and Administrative Law,</u> 32 B.C. L. Rev. 739, 752-55 (1991). –Page Citation.

Boston College Third World Law Journal
Ab.:   B.C. Third World L.J.

Ex.:   Louis W. Sullivan & Ronald W. Roskens, <u>Child Survival and AIDS in Sub-Saharan Africa: Findings and Recommendations of the Presidential Mission to Africa,</u> 11 B.C. Third World L.J. 227 (1991). –Article Citation.

Louis W. Sullivan & Ronald W. Roskens, <u>Child Survival and AIDS in Sub-Saharan Africa: Findings and Recommendations of the Presidential Mission to Africa,</u> 11 B.C. Third World L.J. 227, 240-41 (1991). –Page Citation.

Boston University International Law Journal
Ab.:   B.U. Int'l L.J.

Ex.:   Dennis S. Karjala, <u>The Closely Held Enterprise Under Japanese Law,</u> 7 B.U. Int'l L.J. 229 (1989). –Article Citation.

Dennis S. Karjala, <u>The Closely Held Enterprise Under Japanese Law,</u> 7 B.U. Int'l L.J. 229, 230 (1989). –Page Citation.

Boston University Journal of Science & Technology Law
Ab.:   B.U. J. Sci. & Tech. L.

Ex.:   Susan W. Brenner, <u>Toward a Criminal Law for Cyberspace: Distributed Security,</u> 10 B.U. J. Sci. & Tech. 1 (2004). –Article Citation.

Susan W. Brenner, <u>Toward a Criminal Law for Cyberspace: Distributed Security,</u> 10 B.U. J. Sci. & Tech. 1, 65 (2004). –Page Citation.

Boston University Journal of Tax Law
Ab.:   B.U. J. Tax L.

In citing cases in law review footnotes, abbreviate any word listed in table T.6; the names of "states, countries, and other geographical units" unless they are named parties; and any other words of eight or more letters "if <u>substantial</u> space is thereby saved and the result is unambiguous." <u>Bluebook</u> rule 10.2.2. On the other hand, in citing cases in text, abbreviate only widely known acronyms and the following words: "&," "Ass'n," "Bros.," "Co.," "Corp.," "Inc.," "Ltd.," and "No." <u>Bluebook</u> rule 10.2.1(c).

Ex.:   Stewart G. Thomsen, <u>Irrevocable Life Insurance Trust Planning Into the Nineties</u>, 7 B.U. J. Tax L. 109 (1991). –Article Citation.

Stewart G. Thomsen, <u>Irrevocable Life Insurance Trust Planning Into the Nineties</u>, 7 B.U. J. Tax L. 109, 119-20 (1991). –Page Citation.

Boston University Law Review
Ab.:   B.U. L. Rev.

Ex.:   Erwin Chemerinsky, <u>Ending the Parity Debate</u>, 71 B.U. L. Rev. 593 (1991). –Article Citation.

Erwin Chemerinsky, <u>Ending the Parity Debate</u>, 71 B.U. L. Rev. 593, 598-600 (1991). –Page Citation.

Boston University Public Interest Law Journal
Ab.:   B.U. Pub. Int. L.J.

Ex.:   Gerry Singsen, <u>The Role of Competition in Making Grants for the Provision of Legal Services to the Poor</u>, 1 B.U. Pub. Int. L.J. 57 (1991). –Article Citation.

Gerry Singsen, <u>The Role of Competition in Making Grants for the Provision of Legal Services to the Poor</u>, 1 B.U. Pub. Int. L.J. 57, 69 (1991). –Page Citation.

Bracton Law Journal
Ab.:   Bracton L.J.

Ex.:   Nicholas Grief, <u>Legal Aspects of Nuclear Testing</u>, 23 Bracton L.J. 25 (1991). –Article Citation.

Nicholas Grief, <u>Legal Aspects of Nuclear Testing</u>, 23 Bracton L.J. 25, 33-35 (1991). –Page Citation.

Brandeis Law Journal
Ab: Brandeis L.J.

Ex: Royce de R. Barondes, <u>Rejecting the Marie Antoinette Paradigm of Prejudgment Interest</u>, 43 Brandeis L.J. 1 (2004). –Article Citation.

Royce de R. Barondes, <u>Rejecting the Marie Antoinette Paradigm of Prejudgment Interest</u>, 43 Brandeis L.J. 1, 22 (2004). –Page Citation.

Brief, citation to
Ab.:   Br.

Ex.:   (Pl.'s Br. Summ. J. 45-48).

See <u>Bluebook</u> rule B10 and table BT.1.

Note: See <u>Bluebook</u> rule 10.8.3 for citing litigation materials from another case.

briefs, typeface conventions for briefs
See <u>Bluebook</u> rule B13.

In law review footnotes, the titles of books and the names of cases, except for procedural phrases, are not underlined. See <u>Bluebook</u> rule 2.1(a) & (b). Further, the following are in large and small capitals: codes, restatements, standards, constitutions, periodicals, authors of books, titles of books, the abbreviated names of codes, most legislative materials except for bills and resolutions, codified ordinances, model codes, court rules, and sentencing guidelines. Refer to <u>The Bluebook</u>.

Brigham Young University Education and Law Journal
Ab: BYU Educ. & L.J.

Ex: Ashley McDonald Delja, Across Four Aprils: School Finance Litigation in Virginia, 2004 BYU Educ. & L.J. 191. -Article Citation.

Ashley McDonald Delja, Across Four Aprils: School Finance Litigation in Virginia, 2004 BYU Educ. & L.J. 191, 245-46.-Page Citation.

Brigham Young University Journal of Public Law
Ab.:   B.Y.U. J. Pub. L.

Ex.:   Robert E. Riggs & Michael R. Moss, Supreme Court Voting Behavior: 1987 Term, 3 B.Y.U. J. Pub. L. 1 (1989). −Article Citation.

Robert E. Riggs & Michael R. Moss, Supreme Court Voting Behavior: 1987 Term, 3 B.Y.U. J. Pub. L. 1, 4-5 (1989). −Page Citation.

Brigham Young University Law Review
Ab.:   B.Y.U. L. Rev.

Ex.:   Arthur Austin, The Waste Land, 1991 B.Y.U. L. Rev. 1229. −Article Citation.

Arthur Austin, The Waste Land, 1991 B.Y.U. L. Rev. 1229, 1233-35. −Page Citation.

British Columbia Gazette
Ab.:   B.C. Gaz.

British Columbia Statutes
Ab.:   S.B.C.

Ex.:   International Financial Business Act, ch. 16, 1988 S.B.C. 105 (Can.). −Citation to an entire act.

International Financial Business Act, ch. 16, § 9, 1988 S.B.C. 105, 109 (Can.). −Citation to a section of an act.

British Journal of Criminology
Ab.:   Brit. J. Criminology

Ex.:   Roy D. King & Kathleen McDermott, British Prisons 1970-1987, 29 Brit. J. Criminology 107 (1989). −Article Citation.

Roy D. King & Kathleen McDermott, British Prisons 1970-1987, 29 Brit. J. Criminology 107, 114 (1989). −Page Citation.

British Tax Review
Ab.:   Brit. Tax Rev.

       B.T.R. [U.K.]

Ex.:   Peter Sundgren, Interpretation of Tax Treaties--A Case Study, 1990 Brit. Tax Rev. 286. −Article Citation.

Peter Sundgren, Interpretation of Tax Treaties--A Case Study, 1990 Brit. Tax Rev. 286, 289-90. −Page Citation.

In citing cases in law review footnotes, abbreviate any word listed in table T.6; the names of "states, countries, and other geographical units" unless they are named parties; and any other words of eight or more letters "if substantial space is thereby saved and the result is unambiguous." Bluebook rule 10.2.2. On the other hand, in citing cases in text, abbreviate only widely known acronyms and the following words: "&," "Ass'n," "Bros.," "Co.," "Corp.," "Inc.," "Ltd.," and "No." Bluebook rule 10.2.1(c).

British Yearbook of International Law
    Ab.:   Brit. Y.B. Int'l L.

    Ex.:   Campbell McLachlan, <u>Splitting the Proper Law in Private International Law</u>, 61 Brit. Y.B. Int'l L. 311 (1990). –Article Citation.

            Campbell McLachlan, <u>Splitting the Proper Law in Private International Law</u>, 61 Brit. Y.B. Int'l L. 311, 315-17 (1990). –Page Citation.

Bromberg and Lowenfels on Securities Fraud & Commodities Fraud, by Alan R. Bromberg and Lewis D. Lowenfels
        –Do not abbreviate the title.

    Ex.:   4 Alan R. Bromberg & Lewis D. Lowenfels, <u>Bromberg and Lowenfels on Securities Fraud & Commodities Fraud</u> § 15.07(230) (2d ed. 2000). –Section Citation.

            4 Alan R. Bromberg & Lewis D. Lowenfels, <u>Bromberg and Lowenfels on Securities Fraud & Commodities Fraud</u> § 15.07(230), at 15:169 (2d ed. 2000). –Page Citation.

Brooklyn Journal of International Law
    Ab.:   Brook. J. Int'l L.

    Ex.:   Jacob S. Ziegel, <u>Canadian Perspectives on Transborder Insolvencies</u>, 17 Brook. J. Int'l L. 539 (1991). –Article Citation.

            Jacob S. Ziegel, <u>Canadian Perspectives on Transborder Insolvencies</u>, 17 Brook. J. Int'l L. 539, 551-53 (1991). –Page Citation.

Brooklyn Law Review
    Ab.:   Brook. L. Rev.

    Ex.:   Thomas J. Meskill, <u>Caseload Growth: Struggling to Keep Pace</u>, 57 Brook. L. Rev. 299 (1991). –Article Citation.

            Thomas J. Meskill, <u>Caseload Growth: Struggling to Keep Pace</u>, 57 Brook. L. Rev. 299, 299-301 (1991). –Page Citation.

Buffalo Criminal Law Review
    Ab: Buff. Crim. L. Rev.

    Ex: Stefan D. Cassella, <u>The Forfeiture of Property Involved in Money Laundering Offenses</u>, 7 Buff. Crim. L. Rev. 583 (2004). –Article Citation.

          Stefan D. Cassella, <u>The Forfeiture of Property Involved in Money Laundering Offenses</u>, 7 Buff. Crim. L. Rev. 583, 593 (2004). –Page Citation.

Buffalo Law Review
    Ab.:   Buff. L. Rev.

In law review footnotes, the titles of books and the names of cases, except for procedural phrases, are not underlined. <u>See</u> <u>Bluebook</u> rule 2.1(a) & (b). Further, the following are in large and small capitals: codes, restatements, standards, constitutions, periodicals, authors of books, titles of books, the abbreviated names of codes, most legislative materials except for bills and resolutions, codified ordinances, model codes, court rules, and sentencing guidelines. Refer to <u>The Bluebook</u>.

Ex.: Michael Ariens, <u>Evidence of Religion and the Religion of Evidence</u>, 40 Buff. L. Rev. 65 (1992). –Article Citation.

Michael Ariens, <u>Evidence of Religion and the Religion of Evidence</u>, 40 Buff. L. Rev. 65, 78-81 (1992). –Page Citation.

Bulletin of the European Communities
Ab.: Bull. Eur. Commmunities

Ex.: <u>Role of the Community in the World</u>, Bull. Eur. Communities, June 1991, at 43. –Article Citation.

<u>Role of the Community in the World</u>, Bull. Eur. Communities, June 1991, at 43, 45-46. –Page Citation.

BundesGerichts Entscheidungen Suisse (Switzerland)
Ab.: BGE

Constitutional cases	BGE I
Administrative and international law cases	BGE II
Civil and Bankruptcy cases	BGE II
Criminal cases	BGE IV
Social security cases	BGE V

<u>See</u> <u>Bluebook</u> table T.2, p. 314.

Bureau of National Affairs
Ab.: BNA

Bürgerliches Gesetzbuch (Civil Code) (F.R.G.)
Ab.: BGB

Ex.: Bürgerliches Gesetzbuch [BGB] [Civil Code] Aug. 18, 1896, Reichsgesetzblatt [RGBl] 318, § 2116, ¶ 6, sentence 1. (F.R.G.).

<u>See</u> <u>Bluebook</u> rules 20.2.3 and 20.5.2 and table T.2, p. 270.

Burns Indiana Statutes Annotated (LexisNexis)
Ab.: Ind. Code Ann. § x-x-x-x (LexisNexis year)

Ex.: Ind. Code Ann. § 6-7-1-16 (LexisNexis 2005)

Ind. Code Ann. § 6-1.1-12-285 (LexisNexis Supp. 2004)

–"Cite to Ind. Code, if therein." <u>Bluebook</u> table T.1, p. 208.

–For proper citation form in papers submitted to Indiana courts, see Ind. Code § 1-1-1-1(2002) and Ind. R. App. P. 22.

Burns Indiana Statutes Annotated Advance Legislative Service (LexisNexis)
Ab.: year-pamph. no. Ind. Stat. Ann. Adv. Legis. Serv. page no. (LexisNexis)

In citing cases in law review footnotes, abbreviate any word listed in table T.6; the names of "states, countries, and other geographical units" unless they are named parties; and any other words of eight or more letters "if <u>substantial</u> space is thereby saved and the result is unambiguous." <u>Bluebook</u> rule 10.2.2. On the other hand, in citing cases in text, abbreviate only widely known acronyms and the following words: "&," "Ass'n," "Bros.," "Co.," "Corp.," "Inc.," "Ltd.," and "No." <u>Bluebook</u> rule 10.2.1(c).

Ex.: Act effective July 1, 2005, No. 1032, 2005-1 Ind. Stat. Ann. Adv. Legis. Serv. 213 (LexisNexis) (concerning state offices and administration). –Citation to an entire session law.

Act effective July 1, 2005, No. 1032, Sec. 1, § 5-22-5-8, Ind. Stat. Ann. Adv. Legis. Serv. 213, 213 (LexisNexis) (concerning state offices and administration). –Citation to a section of a session law amending prior act.

–"Cite to Ind. Acts, if therein." Bluebook table T.1, p. 208.

–See Bluebook rule 12.4.

Business America
Ab.: Bus. Am.

Ex.: Jean H. Grier, Legal Obligations to Remove Trade Barriers in New U.S. Trade Agreements With Japan, Bus. Am., Feb. 11, 1991, at 5. –Article Citation.

Jean H. Grier, Legal Obligations to Remove Trade Barriers in New U.S. Trade Agreements With Japan, Bus. Am., Feb. 11, 1991, at 5, 7-9. –Page Citation.

Business Law Journal
Ab.: Bus. L.J.

Ex.: Daniel L. Goelzer & Susan Nash, Expanding Disclosure in Control Transactions: The Proposed Significant Equity Participant Regulations and the Co-Bidder Cases, 1 Bus. L.J. 1 (1990). –Article Citation.

Daniel L. Goelzer & Susan Nash, Expanding Disclosure in Control Transactions: The Proposed Significant Equity Participant Regulations and the Co-Bidder Cases, 1 Bus. L.J. 1, 3-4 (1990). –Page Citation.

Business Lawyer
Ab.: Bus. Law.

Ex.: Victor Futter, An Answer to the Public Perception of Corporations: A Corporate Ombudsperson?, 46 Bus. Law. 29 (1990). –Article Citation.

Victor Futter, An Answer to the Public Perception of Corporations: A Corporate Ombudsperson?, 46 Bus. Law. 29, 35-38 (1990). –Page Citation.

Business Week
Ab.: Bus. Wk.

Ex.: Christopher Farrell, The Recovery: Why So Slow?, Bus. Wk., July 20, 1992, at 60. –Article Citation.

Christopher Farrell, The Recovery: Why So Slow?, Bus. Wk., July 20, 1992, at 60, 63. –Page Citation.

In law review footnotes, the titles of books and the names of cases, except for procedural phrases, are not underlined. See Bluebook rule 2.1(a) & (b). Further, the following are in large and small capitals: codes, restatements, standards, constitutions, periodicals, authors of books, titles of books, the abbreviated names of codes, most legislative materials except for bills and resolutions, codified ordinances, model codes, court rules, and sentencing guidelines. Refer to The Bluebook.

But cf.

    –"But cf." is used when the "[c]ited authority supports a proposition analagous to the contrary of the main proposition." <u>Bluebook</u> rule 1.2(c).

Ex.:   "In <u>Brown</u> there was evidence that the corporation's agents had misled the plaintiff about the name of the corporation they represented. <u>Id.</u> at 1409 n.3. <u>But cf.</u> <u>Hofferman v. Westinghouse Elec. Corp.</u>, 653 F.Supp. 423, 429 (D.D.C. 1986) (holding rule 15(c) relation back proper where defendants conduct partly responsible for plaintiff's mistake in naming wrong party)." –Taken from 952 F.2d 1008, 1012 (8th Cir. 1991).

But see

    –"But see" is used when the "[c]ited authority clearly supports a proposition contrary to the main proposition. 'But see' is used where 'see' would be used for support. " <u>Bluebook</u> rule 1.2(c).

Ex.:   "After <u>Hughey</u>, any other conclusion seems unsupportable. <u>But see</u> <u>United States v. Hurt</u>, 940 F.2d 130, 131 (5th Cir. 1991); <u>United States v. Duvall</u>, 926 F.2d 875, 876-77 (9th Cir. 1991)." –Taken from 952 F.2d 1262, 1264 n.3 (10th Cir. 1991).

In citing cases in law review footnotes, abbreviate any word listed in table T.6; the names of "states, countries, and other geographical units" unless they are named parties; and any other words of eight or more letters "if <u>substantial</u> space is thereby saved and the result is unambiguous." <u>Bluebook</u> rule 10.2.2. On the other hand, in citing cases in text, abbreviate only widely known acronyms and the following words: "&," "Ass'n," "Bros.," "Co.," "Corp.," "Inc.," "Ltd.," and "No." <u>Bluebook</u> rule 10.2.1(c).

C

(Les) Cahiers de Droit
    Ab.:   C. de D.

    Ex.:   Dominique Goubau, <u>L'adoption d'un enfant contre la volunté de ses parents</u>, 35 C. de D. 151 (1994). –Article Citation.

            Dominique Goubau, <u>L'adoption d'un enfant contre la volunté de ses parents</u>, 35 C. de D. 151, 155 (1994). –Page Citation.

            –The original-language title may be followed by a translation or a shortened name in English in brackets in the same typeface as the original. <u>See</u> <u>Bluebook</u> rule 20.2.2

Cahiers de Droit Fiscal International (International Fiscal Association)
    Ab.:   C. de D. Fisc. Int'l

    Ex.:   Dr. Guillermo H. Fernández, <u>General Aspects of the Deduction of Interest and other Financing Expenses</u>, 79 Cahiers de Droit Fiscal International [C. de D. Fisc. Int'l] 23 (1994). –Article Citation.

            Dr. Guillermo H. Fernández, <u>General Aspects of the Deduction of Interest and other Financing Expenses</u>, 79 C. de D. Fisc. Int'l 23, 26 (1994). –Page Citation.

Calamari and Perillo on Contracts, by Joseph M. Perillo
    –Do not abbreviate the title.

    Ex.:   Joseph M. Perillo, <u>Calamari and Perillo on Contracts</u> § 13.12 (5th ed. 2003). –Section Citation.

            Joseph M. Perillo, <u>Calamari and Perillo on Contracts</u> § 13.12, at 537 (5th ed. 2003). –Page Citation.

            Joseph M. Perillo, <u>Calamari and Perillo on Contracts</u> § 13.12, at 537 n.7 (5th ed. 2003). –Footnote Citation.

California Advance Legislative Service (Deering)
    See Deering's California Advance Legislative Service (LexisNexis).

California Annotated and Unannotated Code (Deering)
    See Deering's California Codes, Annotated.

California Appellate Reports
    Ab.:   Cal. App., Cal. App. 2d, Cal. App. 3d, Cal. App. 4th

            –In documents submitted to California state courts, cite to Cal. App., Cal. App. 2d, Cal. App. 3d, or Cal. App. 4th, if therein. In all other documents, cite only to P. or P.2d (before 1960) or to Cal Rptr. or

---

In law review footnotes, the titles of books and the names of cases, except for procedural phrases, are not underlined. <u>See</u> <u>Bluebook</u> rule 2.1(a) & (b). Further, the following are in large and small capitals: codes, restatements, standards, constitutions, periodicals, authors of books, titles of books, the abbreviated names of codes, most legislative materials except for bills and resolutions, codified ordinances, model codes, court rules, and sentencing guidelines. Refer to <u>The Bluebook</u>.

Cal. Rptr. 2d (after 1959), if therein; otherwise, cite to a California Appellate Report.

—Give parallel citations, if at all, only in documents submitted to California state courts. See Bluebook rules 10.3.1 and B5.1.3; see also Cal. R. Ct. 313(c), which requires citation only to Cal. App., Cal. App. 2d, Cal. App. 3d, or Cal. App. 4th, Cal. R. Ct. 313(g), which requires adherence to either The Bluebook or to the California Style Manual, and the California Style Manual § 1.12 (4th ed. 2000), which encourages one or more parallel citations.

In documents submitted to California state courts, cite as follows:

VanDerHoof v. Chambon, 121 Cal. App. 118, 8 P.2d 925(1932). —Case Citation.

VanDerHoof v. Chambon, 121 Cal. App. 118, 8 P.2d 925, 930 (1932). —Page Citation.

Brantley v. Pisaro, 42 Cal. App. 4th 1591, 50 Cal. Rptr. 431 (1996). —Case Citation.

Brantley v. Pisaro, 42 Cal. App. 4th 1591, 1593, 50 Cal. Rptr. 431, 433 (1996). —Page Citation.

In all other documents, cite as follows:

VanDerHoof v. Chambon, 8 P.2d 925 (Cal. Dist. Ct. App. 1932). —Case Citation.

VanDerHoof v. Chambon, 8 P.2d 925, 930 (Cal. Dist. Ct. App. 1932). —Page Citation.

Brantley v. Pisaro, 50 Cal. Rptr. 2d 431 (Ct. App. 1996). —Case Citation.

Brantley v. Pisaro, 50 Cal. Rptr. 2d 431, 433 (Ct. App. 1996). —Page Citation.

California Appellate Reports Supplement
Ab.: Cal. App. Supp.

Cal. App. 2d Supp.

Cal. App. 3d Supp.

Cal. App. 4th Supp.

—In documents submitted to California state courts, cite to Cal. App. Supp., Cal. App. 2d Supp., Cal. App. 3d Supp., or Cal. App. 4th Supp., if therein. In all other documents, cite only to P. or P.2d (before 1960) or to Cal Rptr. or Cal. Rptr. 2d (after 1959), if therein; otherwise, cite to a California Appellate Report Supplement.

—Bound with Cal. App.

In citing cases in law review footnotes, abbreviate any word listed in table T.6; the names of "states, countries, and other geographical units" unless they are named parties; and any other words of eight or more letters "if substantial space is thereby saved and the result is unambiguous." Bluebook rule 10.2.2. On the other hand, in citing cases in text, abbreviate only widely known acronyms and the following words: "&," "Ass'n," "Bros.," "Co.," "Corp.," "Inc.," "Ltd.," and "No." Bluebook rule 10.2.1(c).

–Give parallel citations, if at all, only in documents submitted to California state courts. <u>See</u> <u>Bluebook</u> rules 10.3.1 and B5.1.3; see also Cal. R. Ct. 313(c), which requires citation only to Cal. App. Supp., Cal. App. 2d Supp., Cal. App. 3d Supp., or Cal. App. 4th Supp., Cal. R. Ct. 313(g), which requires adherence to either <u>The Bluebook</u> or to the <u>California Style Manual</u>, and <u>California Style Manual</u> § 1.12 (4th ed. 2000), which encourages one or more parallel citations.

In documents submitted to California state courts, cite as follows:

<u>People v. Studley</u>, 44 Cal. App. 4th Supp. 1, 52 Cal Rptr. 2d 461 (App. Dep't Super. Ct. 1996). –Case Citation.

<u>People v. Studley</u>, 44 Cal. App. 4th Supp. 1, 52 Cal. Rptr. 2d 461, 463 (App. Dep't Super. Ct. 1996). –Page Citation.

In all other documents, cite as follows:

<u>People v. Studley</u>, 52 Cal. Rptr. 2d 461 (App. Dep't Super. Ct. 1996). –Case Citation.

<u>People v. Studley</u>, 52 Cal. Rptr. 2d 461, 463 (App. Dep't Super. Ct. 1996). –Page Citation.

California Attorney General Opinions
See Opinions of the Attorney General of California.

California Bankruptcy Journal
Ab.:   Cal. Bankr. J.

California Code Annotated (West)
See West's Annotated California Code.

California Code of Regulations
Ab.:   Cal. Code Regs. tit. x, § x (year)

Ex.:   Cal. Code Regs. tit. 11, § 2 (1978).

California Constitution
Ab.:   Cal. Const. art.   , §   .

Ex.:   Cal. Const. art. I, § 6. –"Cite constitutional provisions currently in force without a date." <u>Bluebook</u> rule 11.

Cal. Const. art. IV, § 27 (repealed 1980). –"If the cited provision has been repealed, either indicate parenthetically the fact and date of repeal or cite the repealing provision in full." <u>Bluebook</u> rule 11.

Cal. Const. art. IV, § 2 (amended 1990). –"When citing a provision that has been subsequently amended, either indicate parenthetically the fact and date of amendment or cite the amending provision in full." <u>Bluebook</u> rule 11.

In law review footnotes, the titles of books and the names of cases, except for procedural phrases, are not underlined. <u>See</u> <u>Bluebook</u> rule 2.1(a) & (b). Further, the following are in large and small capitals: codes, restatements, standards, constitutions, periodicals, authors of books, titles of books, the abbreviated names of codes, most legislative materials except for bills and resolutions, codified ordinances, model codes, court rules, and sentencing guidelines. Refer to <u>The Bluebook</u>.

Cal. Const. of 1849, art. I, § 1 (1879). –"Cite constitutions that have been totally superseded by year of adoption; if the specific provision cited was adopted in a different year, give that year parenthetically." Bluebook rule 11.

California Jurisprudence, third edition

See West's California Jurisprudence, third edition.

California Law Review

Ab.: Cal. L. Rev.

Ex.: Richard L. Roe, Valuing Student Speech: The Work of the Schools as Conceptual Development, 79 Cal. L. Rev. 1269 (1991). –Article Citation.

Richard L. Roe, Valuing Student Speech: The Work of the Schools as Conceptual Development, 79 Cal. L. Rev. 1269, 1277-78 (1991). –Page Citation.

California Lawyer

Ab.: Cal. Law.

Ex.: Gregory Tordahl, Making the Workplace Safe for Computer Users, Cal. Law., Feb. 1992, at 51. –Article Citation.

Gregory Tordahl, Making the Workplace Safe for Computer Users, Cal. Law., Feb. 1992, at 51, 58. –Page Citation.

California Legislative Service (West)

Ab.: year Cal. Legis. Serv. (West)

Ex.: Act of Sept. 11, 1996, ch. 418, 1996 Cal. Legis. Serv. 2228 (West) (relating to economic development). –Citation to an entire session law.

Act of Sept. 21, 1996, ch. 694 sec. 3, § 8020(a), 1996 Cal. Legis. Serv. 3125, 3125-26, (West) (relating to shorthand reporters). –Citation to a session law amending a prior act.

–See Bluebook rule 12.4.

–"Cite to Cal. Stat., if therein." Bluebook table T.1, p. 201.

California Regulatory Law Reporter

Ab.: Cal. Reg. L. Rep.

California Regulatory Notice Register

Ab.: issue no. Cal. Regulatory Notice Reg. page no. (month day, year)

Ex.: 5-Z Cal. Regulatory Notice Reg. 121 (Jan. 30, 2004)

California Reporter, West's

See West's California Reporter.

In citing cases in law review footnotes, abbreviate any word listed in table T.6; the names of "states, countries, and other geographical units" unless they are named parties; and any other words of eight or more letters "if substantial space is thereby saved and the result is unambiguous." Bluebook rule 10.2.2. On the other hand, in citing cases in text, abbreviate only widely known acronyms and the following words: "&," "Ass'n," "Bros.," "Co.," "Corp.," "Inc.," "Ltd.," and "No." Bluebook rule 10.2.1(c).

California Reports

Ab.: Cal., Cal. 2d, Cal. 3d, Cal. 4th

–In documents submitted to California state courts, cite to Cal., Cal. 2d, Cal. 3d, or Cal. 4th, if therein. In all other documents, cite to P., P.2d, or P.3d, if therein; otherwise, cite to Cal., Cal. 2d, Cal. 3d, or Cal. 4th or to Cal. Rptr. or Cal. Rptr. 2d.

–Give parallel citations, if at all, only in documents submitted to California state courts. See Bluebook rules 10.3.1 and B5.1.3; see also Cal. R. Ct. 313(c), which requires citation only to Cal., Cal. 2d, Cal. 3d, or Cal. 4th, Cal. R. Ct. 313(g), which requires adherence to either The Bluebook or to the California Style Manual, and the California Style Manual § 1.12 (4th ed. 2000), which encourages one or more parallel citations.

In documents submitted to California state courts, cite as follows:

Mangini v. Aerojet-General Corp., 12 Cal. 4th 1087, 912 P.2d 1220, 51 Cal. Rptr. 2d 272 (1996). –Case Citation.

Mangini v. Aerojet-General Corp., 12 Cal. 4th 1087, 1088, 912 P.2d 1220, 1222, 51 Cal. Rptr. 2d 272, 273 (1996). –Page Citation.

In all other documents, cite as follows:

Mangini v. Aerojet-General Corp., 912 P.2d 1220 (Cal. 1996). –Case Citation.

Mangini v. Aerojet-General Corp., 912 P.2d 1220, 1222 (Cal. 1996). –Page Citation.

California Session Laws

See California Legislative Service (West) and Statutes of California.

California Unreported Cases

Ab.: Cal. Unrep.

Ex.: Ganahl v. Soher, 2 Cal. Unrep. 415 (Super. Ct. 1884). –Case Citation.

Ganahl v. Soher, 2 Cal. Unrep. 415, 416 (Super Ct. 1884). –Page Citation.

California Western International Law Journal

Ab.: Cal. W. Int'l L.J.

Ex.: Mark Gibney, Compensation for Civilians Harmed in the Pursuit of Foreign Policy Goals: Recent Litigation in U.S. Courts, 22 Cal. W. Int'l L.J. 59 (1991). –Article Citation.

Mark Gibney, Compensation for Civilians Harmed in the Pursuit of Foreign Policy Goals: Recent Litigation in U.S. Courts, 22 Cal. W. Int'l L.J. 59, 72-74 (1991). –Page Citation.

In law review footnotes, the titles of books and the names of cases, except for procedural phrases, are not underlined. See Bluebook rule 2.1(a) & (b). Further, the following are in large and small capitals: codes, restatements, standards, constitutions, periodicals, authors of books, titles of books, the abbreviated names of codes, most legislative materials except for bills and resolutions, codified ordinances, model codes, court rules, and sentencing guidelines. Refer to The Bluebook.

California Western Law Review
Ab.:   Cal. W. L. Rev.

Ex.:   Michael Ariens, <u>On the Road of Good Intentions: Justice Brennan and the Religion Clauses</u>, 27 Cal. W. L. Rev. 311 (1991). –Article Citation.

        Michael Ariens, <u>On the Road of Good Intentions: Justice Brennan and the Religion Clauses</u>, 27 Cal. W. L. Rev. 311, 314-17 (1991). –Page Citation.

Cambrian Law Review, The
Ab.:   Cambrian L. Rev.

Ex.:   John Hughes, <u>Legal and Ethical Implications of Clinical Research on Human Subjects</u>, 22 Cambrian L. Rev. 5 (1991). –Article Citation.

        John Hughes, <u>Legal and Ethical Implications of Clinical Research on Human Subjects</u>, 22 Cambrian L. Rev. 5, 22-24 (1991). –Page Citation.

Cambridge Law Journal
Ab.:   Cambridge L.J.

Ex.:   P.P. Craig, <u>The Common Law, Reasons and Administrative Justice</u>, 53 Cambridge L.J. 282 (1994). –Article Citation.

        P.P. Craig, <u>The Common Law, Reasons and Administrative Justice</u>, 53 Cambridge L.J. 282, 285 (1994). –Page Citation.

Campaigns and the Court: The U.S. Supreme Court in Presidential Elections, by Donald Grier Stephenson, Jr.
    –Do not abbreviate the title.

Ex.:   Donald Grier Stephenson, Jr., <u>Campaigns and the Court: The U.S. Supreme Court in Presidential Elections</u> 185 (1999). –Page Citation.

        Donald Grier Stephenson, Jr., <u>Campaigns and the Court: The U.S. Supreme Court in Presidential Elections</u> 185, n.124 (1999). –Footnote Citation.

Campbell Law Review
Ab.:   Campbell L. Rev.

Ex.:   Anthony M. Brannon, <u>Successful Shadowboxing: The Art of Impeaching Hearsay Declarants</u>, 13 Campbell L. Rev. 157 (1991). –Article Citation.

        Anthony M. Brannon, <u>Successful Shadowboxing: The Art of Impeaching Hearsay Declarants</u>, 13 Campbell L. Rev. 157, 160-67 (1991). –Page Citation.

Canada Gazette
Ab.:   C. Gaz.

In citing cases in law review footnotes, abbreviate any word listed in table T.6; the names of "states, countries, and other geographical units" unless they are named parties; and any other words of eight or more letters "if <u>substantial</u> space is thereby saved and the result is unambiguous." <u>Bluebook</u> rule 10.2.2. On the other hand, in citing cases in text, abbreviate only widely known acronyms and the following words: "&," "Ass'n," "Bros.," "Co.," "Corp.," "Inc.," "Ltd.," and "No." <u>Bluebook</u> rule 10.2.1(c).

Ex.:   An Act to Implement the North American Free Trade Agreement, 16 C. Gaz. Part III 374 (1994 Can.).

Canada: Supreme Court Reports (1876-date)

–"Cite to S.C.R., if therein; otherwise, cite to D.L.R." Bluebook table T.2, p. 254.

Ab.:   S.C.R.

Ex.:   Leiriao v. Town of Val-Bélair, [1991] 3 S.C.R. 349 (Can.). –Case Citation.

–Provide neutral citation, if available. See Bluebook table T.2, p. 254 (3d prtg. 2006).

R. v. Sazant, [2004] 3 S.C.R. 635, 2004 SCC 77 (Can.).

Note: For information on Canada's neutral citation, see A Neutral Citation Standard for Case Law (2000), available at

http://www.lexum.umontreal.ca/ccc-ccr/neutr/neutr.jur_en.html.

Canada Treaty Series

Ab.:   year Can. T.S. No. x

Ex.:   Vienna Convention on Diplomatic Relations, 1996 Can. T.S. No. 29.

Canada-United States Law Journal

Ab.:   Can.-U.S. L.J.

Ex.:   Malcom E. Wheeler, Comparative Aspects of Dispute Resolution in Particular Subject Areas: Product Liability, 17 Can.-U.S. L.J. 359 (1991). –Article Citation.

Malcom E. Wheeler, Comparative Aspects of Dispute Resolution in Particular Subject Areas: Product Liability, 17 Can.-U.S. L.J. 359, 360-61 (1991). –Page Citation.

Canada-U.S. Business Law Review

Ab.:   Can.-U.S. Bus. L. Rev.

Ex.:   Guy Dionne, Entering the EEC to Provide Services: The Case of Insurance, 4 Can.-U.S. Bus. L. Rev. 113 (1990-1991). –Article Citation.

Guy Dionne, Entering the EEC to Provide Services: The Case of Insurance, 4 Can.-U.S. Bus. L. Rev. 113, 122 (1990-1991). –Page Citation.

Canadian-American Law Journal

Ab.:   Can.-Am. L.J.

In law review footnotes, the titles of books and the names of cases, except for procedural phrases, are not underlined. See Bluebook rule 2.1(a) & (b). Further, the following are in large and small capitals: codes, restatements, standards, constitutions, periodicals, authors of books, titles of books, the abbreviated names of codes, most legislative materials except for bills and resolutions, codified ordinances, model codes, court rules, and sentencing guidelines. Refer to The Bluebook.

Ex.:   Alan L. Schechter, <u>United States - Canadian Bankruptcy Litigation: Is the Treaty the Way to Go?</u>, 4 Can.-Am. L.J. 1 (1988). –Article Citation.

Alan L. Schechter, <u>United States - Canadian Bankruptcy Litigation: Is the Treaty the Way to Go?</u>, 4 Can.-Am. L.J. 1, 21 (1988). –Page Citation.

Canadian Bar Review
Ab.:   Can. B. Rev.

Ex.:   John J. Chapman, <u>Judicial Scrutiny of Domestic Commercial Arbitral Awards</u>, 74 Can. B. Rev. 401 (1995). –Article Citation.

John J. Chapman, <u>Judicial Scrutiny of Domestic Commercial Arbitral Awards</u>, 74 Can. B. Rev. 401, 410-411 (1995). –Page Citation.

Canadian Constitution
See <u>Bluebook</u> table T.2, p. 254.

Canadian Tax Journal
Ab.:   Can. Tax J.

Ex.:   Al Katiya, <u>Proposed Changes to the SR and ED Program Under the Income Tax Act</u>, 42 Can. Tax J. 309 (1994). –Article Citation.

Al Katiya, <u>Proposed Changes to the SR and ED Program Under the Income Tax Act</u>, 42 Can. Tax J. 309, 311-12 (1994). –Page Citation.

Canadian Tax Reports (Commerce Clearing House)
Ab.:   Can. Tax Rep. (CCH)

Canadian Yearbook of International Law
Ab.:   Can. Y.B. Int'l L.

Ex.:   William A. Schabas, <u>Reservations to Human Rights Treaties: Time for Innovation and Reform</u>, 32 Can. Y.B. Int'l L. 39 (1994). –Article Citation.

William A. Schabas, <u>Reservations to Human Rights Treaties: Time for Innovation and Reform</u>, 32 Can. Y.B. Int'l L. 39, 45-46 (1994). –Page Citation.

Canal Zone Code
Ab.:   C.Z. Code tit. x, § x (year)

Ex.:   C.Z. Code tit. 6, § 1191(b) (1963). –Section Citation.

Capital Defense Digest
Ab.:   Cap. Def. Dig.

Capital University Law Review
Ab.:   Cap. U. L. Rev.

In citing cases in law review footnotes, abbreviate any word listed in table T.6; the names of "states, countries, and other geographical units" unless they are named parties; and any other words of eight or more letters "if <u>substantial</u> space is thereby saved and the result is unambiguous." <u>Bluebook</u> rule 10.2.2. On the other hand, in citing cases in text, abbreviate only widely known acronyms and the following words: "&," "Ass'n," "Bros.," "Co.," "Corp.," "Inc.," "Ltd.," and "No." <u>Bluebook</u> rule 10.2.1(c).

Ex.: Gregory M. Travalio, <u>Values and Schizophrenia in Intercollegiate Athletics</u>, 20 Cap. U. L. Rev. 587 (1991). –Article Citation.

Gregory M. Travalio, <u>Values and Schizophrenia in Intercollegiate Athletics</u>, 20 Cap. U. L. Rev. 587, 593-95 (1991). –Page Citation.

Cardozo Arts & Entertainment Law Journal
Ab.: Cardozo Arts & Ent. L.J.

Ex.: Sherri L. Burr, <u>Artistic Parody: A Theoretical Construct</u>, 14 Cardozo Arts & Ent. L.J. 65 (1996). –Article Citation.

Sherri L. Burr, <u>Artistic Parody: A Theoretical Construct</u>, 14 Cardozo Arts & Ent. L.J. 65, 67 (1996). –Page Citation.

Cardozo Law Review
Ab.: Cardozo L. Rev.

Ex.: Matthew P. Bergman, <u>Status, Contract, and History: A Dialectical View</u>, 13 Cardozo L. Rev. 171 (1991). –Article Citation.

Matthew P. Bergman, <u>Status, Contract, and History: A Dialectical View</u>, 13 Cardozo L. Rev. 171, 181-87 (1991). –Page Citation.

Case citations
See <u>Bluebook</u> rule 10.1 for samples of basic case citations in law reviews, briefs, and legal memoranda. Sample citations are provided for each stage in the course of litigation and alternative citations are provided when the case is available in alternative sources (i.e., a final decision by a federal district court available in an electronic database, service, newspaper, or as a slip opinion).

Case names
–In text: Give the last name of an individual and the full name of an institution, political entity, or corporation without abbreviation except as provided in <u>Bluebook</u> rule 10.2.1.

–In citations: In addition to the rules for a case name in text, abbreviate according to rule 10.2.2 and table T.6.

–Basic citation forms: See various title entries in this work. See also <u>Bluebook</u> rules 10.1, 10.2, 10.6 (parenthetical information regarding cases), 10.7 (prior and subsequent history), and 10.8 (special citation forms).

–In law review footnotes: See the guidelines and illustrations on pp. 79-99 of <u>The Bluebook</u>.

In law review footnotes, the titles of books and the names of cases, except for procedural phrases, are not underlined. <u>See</u> <u>Bluebook</u> rule 2.1(a) & (b). Further, the following are in large and small capitals: codes, restatements, standards, constitutions, periodicals, authors of books, titles of books, the abbreviated names of codes, most legislative materials except for bills and resolutions, codified ordinances, model codes, court rules, and sentencing guidelines. Refer to <u>The Bluebook</u>.

Case overruled

See Bluebook rule 10.7(c)(i).

Case superseded by statute

See Bluebook rule 10.7(c)(iii).

Case Western Reserve Journal of International Law

Ab.: Case W. Res. J. Int'l L.

Ex.: Michael I. Kraus, The Perils of Rural Land Use Planning: The Case of Canada, 23 Case W. Res. J. Int'l L. 65 (1991). –Article Citation.

Michael I. Kraus, The Perils of Rural Land Use Planning: The Case of Canada, 23 Case W. Res. J. Int'l L. 65, 71-74 (1991). –Page Citation.

Case Western Reserve Law Review

Ab.: Case W. Res. L. Rev.

Ex.: Michael P. Healy, Direct Liability for Hazardous Substance Cleanups Under CERCLA: A Comprehensive Approach, 42 Case W. Res. L. Rev. 65 (1992). –Article Citation.

Michael P. Healy, Direct Liability for Hazardous Substance Cleanups Under CERCLA: A Comprehensive Approach, 42 Case W. Res. L. Rev. 65, 77-80 (1992). –Page Citation.

cases, basic citation forms

See various title entries in this work. See also Bluebook rule 10.

cases, subsequent citation to

See subsequent citations to cases, statutes, and prior citations.

Casner on Estate Planning

See Estate Planning, by A. James Casner and Jeffrey N. Pennell.

Catholic Lawyer, The

Ab.: Cath. Law.

Ex.: Angela C. Carmella, Landmark Preservation of Church Property, 34 Cath. Law. 41 (1991). –Article Citation.

Angela C. Carmella, Landmark Preservation of Church Property, 34 Cath. Law. 41, 50-53 (1991). –Page Citation.

Catholic University Law Review

Ab.: Cath. U. L. Rev.

Ex.: David M. Cohen, Claims for Money in the Claims Court, 40 Cath. U. L. Rev. 533 (1991). –Article Citation.

David M. Cohen, Claims for Money in the Claims Court, 40 Cath. U. L. Rev. 533, 534-38 (1991). –Page Citation.

CBA Record

Ab.: CBA Rec.

In citing cases in law review footnotes, abbreviate any word listed in table T.6; the names of "states, countries, and other geographical units" unless they are named parties; and any other words of eight or more letters "if substantial space is thereby saved and the result is unambiguous." Bluebook rule 10.2.2. On the other hand, in citing cases in text, abbreviate only widely known acronyms and the following words: "&," "Ass'n," "Bros.," "Co.," "Corp.," "Inc.," "Ltd.," and "No." Bluebook rule 10.2.1(c).

Ex.:   Sherwin J. Malkin, <u>Beware the Lost Volume Seller</u>, CBA Rec., May 1992, at 20. –Article Citation.

Sherwin J. Malkin, <u>Beware the Lost Volume Seller</u>, CBA Rec., May 1992, at 20, 23. –Page Citation.

CD-ROM

"Information found on CD-ROM usually is available in print form, and citation to the print form is preferred where available. If the information is accessed on CD-ROM, it should be cited to CD-ROM. When citing cases on CD-ROM, the possibility exists that a case published near the date of the CD-ROM itself may have been included in slip opinion form, and (like a decision in an advance sheet) may have been edited or otherwise changed before the case was published in final form.

When citing CD-ROM media, include the title of the material, the publisher of the CD-ROM, the version searched, and the date of the material, if available, or the date of the version searched. The information may be provided in a source-date parenthetical or, if the information is voluminous, as related authority (rule 1.6)."
–<u>Bluebook</u> rule 18.3.

Ex.   <u>Taylor v. Heldman</u>, No. M1999-00729-COA-R3-CV, (Tenn. Ct. App. 2000) (Tennessee Unpublished Decisions, 1985-2000, West CD-ROM Libraries, current through Nov. 1, 2000).

5 C.F.R. § 630.101 (West LawDesk Code of Federal Regulations CD-ROM, current through Sept. 2000).

1 Lee R. Russ & Thomas F. Segalla, <u>Couch on Insurance</u> §1.4 (Couch on Insurance West LawDesk CD-ROM, July 2000).

certiorari denied
Ab.:   cert. denied

Ex.:   <u>Bernhard v. Harrah's Club</u>, 16 Cal. 3d 313, 546 P.2d 719, 128 Cal. Rptr. 215, <u>cert. denied</u>, 429 U.S. 859 (1976).

certiorari granted
Ab.:   cert. granted

Ex.:   <u>Walker v. Armco Steel Corp.</u>, 592 F.2d 1133 (10th Cir. 1979), <u>cert. granted</u>, No. 78-1862, 48 U.S.L.W. 3186 (Oct. 1, 1979).

Cf.

–"<u>Cf.</u>" is used when the "[c]ited authority supports a proposition different from the main proposition but sufficiently analogous to lend support." <u>Bluebook</u> rule 1.2(a).

In law review footnotes, the titles of books and the names of cases, except for procedural phrases, are not underlined. <u>See</u> <u>Bluebook</u> rule 2.1(a) & (b). Further, the following are in large and small capitals: codes, restatements, standards, constitutions, periodicals, authors of books, titles of books, the abbreviated names of codes, most legislative materials except for bills and resolutions, codified ordinances, model codes, court rules, and sentencing guidelines. Refer to <u>The Bluebook</u>.

Ex.: "The St. John testimony was not so extremely inflammatory and repetitive that it could not be cured by an admonition to the jury. <u>Cf.</u> <u>United States v. Gillespie</u>, 852 F.2d 475, 479 (9th Cir. 1988) (extreme prejudice from admission of improper evidence of defendant's homosexuality could not be cured by admonition to jury)." —Taken from 941 F.2d 761, 765 (9th Cir. 1991).

Chancellor
Ab.: C.

Chancery
Ab.: Ch.

Chancery Court
Ab.: Ch.

Chancery Division
Ab.: Ch.

chapter(s)
Ab.: ch., chs.

Charter of the United Nations
Ab.: U.N. Charter

Ex.: U.N. Charter art. 33, para. 1.

Chartered Life Underwriters
Ab.: C.L.U.

Chemical Regulation Reporter (Bureau of National Affairs)
Ab.: Chem. Reg. Rep. (BNA)

Chicago Board Options Exchange (Commerce Clearing House)
Ab.: Chicago Bd. Options Ex. (CCH)

Chicago Journal of International Law
Ab: Chi. J. Int'l L.

Ex: Roger B. Myerson, <u>The Empirical and Theoretical Underpinnings of</u> <u>the Law Merchant: Justice, Institutions, and Multiple Equilibria</u>, 5 Chi. J. Int'l L. 91 (2004). —Article Citation.

Roger B. Myerson, <u>The Empirical and Theoretical Underpinnings</u> <u>of the Law Merchant: Justice, Institutions, and Multiple Equilibria</u>, 5 Chi. J. Int'l L. 91, 94 (2004). —Page Citation.

Chicago-Kent Law Review
Ab.: Chi.-Kent L. Rev.

In citing cases in law review footnotes, abbreviate any word listed in table T.6; the names of "states, countries, and other geographical units" unless they are named parties; and any other words of eight or more letters "if <u>substantial</u> space is thereby saved and the result is unambiguous." <u>Bluebook</u> rule 10.2.2. On the other hand, in citing cases in text, abbreviate only widely known acronyms and the following words: "&," "Ass'n," "Bros.," "Co.," "Corp.," "Inc.," "Ltd.," and "No." <u>Bluebook</u> rule 10.2.1(c).

Ex.:   Gordon S. Wood, <u>Classical Republicanism and the American Revolution</u>, 66 Chi.-Kent L. Rev. 13 (1990). −Article Citation.

Gordon S. Wood, <u>Classical Republicanism and the American Revolution</u>, 66 Chi.-Kent L. Rev. 13, 14-15 (1990). −Page Citation.

Chicago Tribune
Ab.:   Chi. Trib.

Chicano Law Review
Ab.:   Chicano L. Rev.

Ex.:   Adela de la Torre & Refugio Rochin, <u>Hispanic Poor and the Effects of Immigration Reform</u>, 10 Chicano L. Rev. 1 (1990). −Article Citation.

Adela de la Torre & Refugio Rochin, <u>Hispanic Poor and the Effects of Immigration Reform</u>, 10 Chicano L. Rev. 1, 3-6 (1990). −Page Citation.

Chief Baron
Ab.:   C.B.

Chief Judge
Ab.:   C.J.

Chief Justice
Ab.:   C.J.

Children's Court
Ab.:   Child. Ct.

Children's Legal Rights Journal
Ab.:   Child. Legal Rts. J.

Ex.:   David W. Lloyd, <u>Ritual Child Abuse: Where Do We Go From Here?</u>, Child. Legal Rts. J. Winter 1991, at 12. −Article Citation.

David W. Lloyd, <u>Ritual Child Abuse: Where Do We Go From Here?</u>, Child. Legal Rts. J. Winter 1991, at 12, 13-15. −Page Citation.

China Law Reporter (ABA Section of International Law)
Ab.:   P.R.C. L. Rep.

Ex.:   Zhengdong Huang, <u>Negotiation in China: Cultural and Practical Characteristics</u>, 6 P.R.C. L. Rep. 139 (1990). −Article Citation.

Zhengdong Huang, <u>Negotiation in China: Cultural and Practical Characteristics</u>, 6 P.R.C. L. Rep. 139, 142-43 (1990). −Page Citation.

Chommie on Federal Income Taxation
See Law of Federal Income Taxation, by Michael D. Rose and John C. Chommie.

Chronicle
Ab.:   Chron.

In law review footnotes, the titles of books and the names of cases, except for procedural phrases, are not underlined. <u>See</u> Bluebook rule 2.1(a) & (b). Further, the following are in large and small capitals: codes, restatements, standards, constitutions, periodicals, authors of books, titles of books, the abbreviated names of codes, most legislative materials except for bills and resolutions, codified ordinances, model codes, court rules, and sentencing guidelines. Refer to <u>The Bluebook</u>.

Cincinnati Bar Association Journal
 Ab.: Cincinnati B.A. J.

Circuit Court (old federal)
 Ab.: C.C.

Circuit Court (state)
 Ab.: Cir. Ct.

Circuit Court of Appeal(s) (state)
 Ab.: Cir. Ct. App.

Circuit Court of Appeals (federal)
 See U.S. Court of Appeals.

Cited in
 Ex.: Unif. Probate Code §§ 2-102, 2-103 (1969), cited in Wellman, The Uniform Probate Code: A Possible Answer to Probate Avoidance, 44 Ind. L.J. 191, 200 (1969).
 See Bluebook rule 1.6 for proper use of cited in.

City Court
 Ab.: [name city] City Ct.

Civil Aeronautics Board Reports (U.S.) (1940-1984) (vol. 1 by C.A.A.)
 Ab.: C.A.B.
 Ex.: Pandair Freight Ltd., Foreign Indirect Permit, 60 C.A.B. 205 (1972).
 Braniff Airways, 1 C.A.B. 291 (1939). –Citation to the first volume of the series, published by the Civil Aeronautics Authority.

Civil Appeals
 Ab.: Civ. App.

Civil Court of Record
 Ab.: Civ. Ct. Rec.

Civil Procedure, by Fleming James, Jr., Geoffrey C. Hazard, Jr., and John Leubsdorf
 –Do not abbreviate the title.
 Ex.: Fleming James, Jr. et al., Civil Procedure § 9.4 (5th ed. 2001).
 –Section Citation.
 Fleming James, Jr. et al., Civil Procedure § 9.4, at 552 (5th ed. 2001).
 –Page Citation.
 Fleming James, Jr. et al., Civil Procedure § 9.4, at 552 n.4 (5th ed. 2001). –Footnote Citation.

Civil Procedure, by Jack H. Friedenthal, Mary Kay Kane, and Arthur R. Miller
 –Do not abbreviate the title.

In citing cases in law review footnotes, abbreviate any word listed in table T.6; the names of "states, countries, and other geographical units" unless they are named parties; and any other words of eight or more letters "if substantial space is thereby saved and the result is unambiguous." Bluebook rule 10.2.2. On the other hand, in citing cases in text, abbreviate only widely known acronyms and the following words: "&," "Ass'n," "Bros.," "Co.," "Corp.," "Inc.," "Ltd.," and "No." Bluebook rule 10.2.1(c).

Ex.:   Jack H. Friedenthal et al., Civil Procedure § 14.10 (5th ed. 2005).
           –Section Citation.

           Jack H. Friedenthal et al., Civil Procedure § 14.10, at 707 (5th ed.
           2005). –Page Citation.

           Jack H. Friedenthal et al., Civil Procedure § 14.10, at 707, n.51 (5th ed.
           2001). –Footnote Citation.

Civil Rights Digest
Ab.:   Civ. Rts. Dig.

C.J.S.
See Corpus Juris Secundum.

Claims Court
Ab.:   Cl. Ct.
           –Created 1982, successor to the Court of Claims (Ct. Cl.). In 1992,
           succeeded by the United States Court of Federal Claims (Fed. Cl.).
           –Cite to F. Supp. or F.2d, if therein; otherwise to United States Claims
           Court Reporter.

Claims Court Reporter
Ab.:   Cl. Ct.
Ex.:   Mobley v. United States, 8 Cl. Ct. 767 (1985).

clause(s)
Ab.:   cl., cls.

Clearinghouse Review
Ab.:   Clearinghouse Rev.
Ex.:   Paula Roberts, Child Support Enforcement in 1991, 25 Clearinghouse
           Rev. 1098 (1992). –Article Citation.

           Paula Roberts, Child Support Enforcement in 1991, 25 Clearinghouse
           Rev. 1098, 1102-03 (1992). –Page Citation.

           –If the author of the article is an institutional author, cite according to
           Bluebook rule 15.1(c).

Cleveland State Law Review
Ab.:   Clev. St. L. Rev.
Ex.:   Himanshu S. Amin, The Lack of Protection Afforded Software Under
           the Current Intellectual Property Laws, 43 Clev. St. L. Rev. 19 (1995).
           –Article Citation.

           Himanshu S. Amin, The Lack of Protection Afforded Software Under
           the Current Intellectual Property Laws, 43 Clev. St. L. Rev. 19, 25
           (1995). –Page Citation.

Close Corporations, by F. Hodge O'Neal & Robert B. Thompson
See O'Neal and Thompson's Close Corporations and LLCs, by Robert B.
Thompson.

In law review footnotes, the titles of books and the names of cases, except for procedural
phrases, are not underlined. See Bluebook rule 2.1(a) & (b). Further, the following are in
large and small capitals: codes, restatements, standards, constitutions, periodicals, authors of
books, titles of books, the abbreviated names of codes, most legislative materials except for
bills and resolutions, codified ordinances, model codes, court rules, and sentencing guidelines.
Refer to The Bluebook.

Code administratif (France)
 Ab.: C. adm.
 Ex.: Code administratif [C. adm.] art. 60 (Fr.).
    C. adm. art. 60. –Subsequent abbreviated citation.
 See Bluebook rules 20.2.3 and 20.5.2 and table T.2, p. 267.

Code civil (France)
 Ab.: C. civ.
 Ex.: Code civil [C. civ.] art. 1165 (Fr.).
    C. civ. art. 1165. –Subsequent abbreviated citation.
 See Bluebook rules 20.2.3 and 20.5.2 and table T.2, p. 267.

Code de commerce (France)
 Ab.: C. com.
 Ex.: Code de commerce [C. com.] art. 632 (Fr.).
    C. com. art. 632. –Subsequent abbreviated citation.
 See Bluebook rules 20.2.3 and 20.5.2 and table T.2., p. 267.

Code de procédure pénale
 Ab.: C. pr. pén.
 See Bluebook rules 20.2.3 and 20.5.2 and table T.2, p. 267.

Code du travail
 Ab.: C. trav.
 Ex.: Code du travail [C. trav.] art. L. 434-7 (Fr.).
    C. trav. art. L. 434-7. –Subsequent abbreviated citation.
 See Bluebook rules 20.2.3 and 20.5.2 and table T.2, p. 267

Code of Alabama, 1975 (West)
 Ab.: Ala. Code § (year)
 Ex.: Ala. Code § 2-15-27 (2005).
    Ala. Code § 40-14-40 (Supp. 2005).

Code of Arkansas Rules (Weil)
 Ab.: x-x-x Ark. Code R. § x (Weil year)
 Ex.: 168-02-005 Ark. Code R. § II.A. (Weil 2004).

Code of Colorado Regulations (Weil)
 Ab.: vol. no. Colo. Code Regs. § x-x (year)
 Ex.: 3 Colo. Code Regs. § 301-58 (2005).

Code of Delaware Regulations (Weil)
 Ab.: x-x-x Del. Code Regs. § x (Weil year)
 Ex.: 9-100-104 Del. Code Regs. § 2.4 (Weil 2003).

Code of District of Columbia Municipal Regulations (Weil)
 Ab.: D.C. Mun. Regs. tit. x, § x (Weil year)

In citing cases in law review footnotes, abbreviate any word listed in table T.6;
the names of "states, countries, and other geographical units" unless they are named parties;
and any other words of eight or more letters "if substantial space is thereby saved and the
result is unambiguous." Bluebook rule 10.2.2. On the other hand, in citing cases in text,
abbreviate only widely known acronyms and the following words: "&," "Ass'n," "Bros.,"
"Co.," "Corp.," "Inc.," "Ltd.," and "No." Bluebook rule 10.2.1(c).

Ex.:   D.C. Mun. Regs. tit. 9, § 472.1 (Weil 2004).

Code of Federal Regulations
Ab.:   C.F.R.

Ex.:   23 C.F.R. § 750.308 (1996).

Regulation D, 12 C.F.R. § 204 (1996). —Cite to a regulation with a popular name.

—For citations to the Federal Register, see the entry under Federal Register.

Code of Georgia Annotated, Official (LexisNexis)
See Official Code of Georgia Annotated (LexisNexis).

Code of Illinois Rules (Weil)
Ab.:   x Ill. Code R. x.x (Weil year)

Ex.:   77 Ill. Code R. 750.1140 (Weil 2004).

Code of Iowa
Ab.:   Iowa Code § x.x (year)

Ex.:   Iowa Code § 633.273 (1979).

Code of Laws of South Carolina 1976 Annotated: Code of Regulations (West)
Ab.:   S.C. Code Ann. Regs. x-x (year)

Ex.:   S.C. Code Ann. Regs. 69-2 (2000).

Code of Laws of South Carolina 1976 Annotated (West)
Ab.:   S.C. Code Ann. § x-x-x (year)

Ex.:   S.C. Code Ann. § 40-5-20 (2000).

—For proper citation form in papers submitted to South Carolina courts, see S.C. App. Ct. R. 239 (b).

Code of Maine Rules (Weil)
Ab.:   x-x-x Me. Code R. § x (Weil year)

Ex.:   10-144-201 Me. Code R. § 1.2.B (Weil 2004).

Code of Maryland Regulations
Ab.:   Md. Regs. Code x.x.x.x (year)

Ex.:   Md. Regs. Code 17.05.01.01 (2000).

Code of Massachusetts Regulations
Ab.:   x Mass. Code Regs. x.x (year)

Ex.:   104 Mass. Code Regs. 29.15 (2000).

Code of Mississippi Rules (Weil)
Ab.:   x-x-x Miss. Code R. § x (Weil year)

Ex.:   08-013-003 Miss. Code R. § 111 (Weil 2004).

Code of Nebraska Rules (Weil)
Ab.:   x Neb. Code R. § x-x (Weil year)

In law review footnotes, the titles of books and the names of cases, except for procedural phrases, are not underlined. See Bluebook rule 2.1(a) & (b). Further, the following are in large and small capitals: codes, restatements, standards, constitutions, periodicals, authors of books, titles of books, the abbreviated names of codes, most legislative materials except for bills and resolutions, codified ordinances, model codes, court rules, and sentencing guidelines. Refer to The Bluebook.

Ex.: 23 Neb. Code R. § 3-001 (Weil 2004).

Code of New Hampshire Rules (Weil)
Ab.: N.H. Code R. [department name as abbreviated in rules] x.x (Weil year)
Ex.: N.H. Code R. He-P 830.13 (Weil 2004).

Code of New Mexico Rules (Weil)
Ab.: N.M. Code R. § x.x.x.x (Weil year)
Ex.: N.M. Code R. § 7.6.2.7 (Weil 2004).

Code of Professional Responsibility ABA
See American Bar Association Model Code of Professional Responsibility.

Code of Professional Responsibility Annotated (ABF)
See American Bar Foundation Code of Professional Responsibility, Annotated.

Code of Rhode Island Rules (Weil)
Ab.: x-x-x R.I. Code R. § x (Weil year)
Ex.: 43-000-003 R.I. Code R. § 12 (Weil 2002).

Code of U.S. Virgin Islands Rules (Weil)
Ab.: x-x V.I. Code R. § x-x (Weil year)
Ex.: 20-33 V.I. Code R. § 332(c)-22 (Weil 2004).

Code of Vermont Rules (Weil)
Ab.: x-x-x Vt. Code R. § x (year)
Ex.: 10-060-001 Vt. Code R. § 1.9741(25) 5 (2004).

Code of Virginia 1950 Annotated (LexisNexis)
Ab.: Va. Code Ann. § x-x (year)
Ex.: Va. Code Ann. § 55-66.01 (2003)
Va. Code Ann. § 15.2-2293 (Supp. 2005).

Code pénal (Fr.)
Ab.: C. pén.
Ex.: Code pénal [C. pén.] art. 418 (Fr.)
C. pén. art. 418. –Subsequent abbreviated citation.
See Bluebook rules 20.2.3 and 20.5.2 and table T.2, p. 267.

Código Civil Federal (Mexico)
Ab.: C.C.F.
Ex.: Código Civil Federal [C.C.F.] [Federal Civil Code], as amended, art. 1118, Diario Oficial de la Federación [D.O.], 16 de Diciembre de 2001 (Mex.).
C.C.F. art. 1118. –Subsequent abbreviated citation.
–See Bluebook rules 20.2.3, 20.5.2, and table T.2, p. 294.

In citing cases in law review footnotes, abbreviate any word listed in table T.6; the names of "states, countries, and other geographical units" unless they are named parties; and any other words of eight or more letters "if substantial space is thereby saved and the result is unambiguous." Bluebook rule 10.2.2. On the other hand, in citing cases in text, abbreviate only widely known acronyms and the following words: "&," "Ass'n," "Bros.," "Co.," "Corp.," "Inc.," "Ltd.," and "No." Bluebook rule 10.2.1(c).

Código de Comercio (Mexico)
    Ab.:   Cód.Com.
    Ex.:   Código de Comercio [Cód.Com.] [Commercial Code], <u>as amended</u>, art. 94, Diario Oficial de la Federación [D.O.], 13 de Agosto de 1972 (Mex.).
           Cód.Com. art. 94. –Subsequent abbreviated citation.
           –<u>See</u> <u>Bluebook</u> rules 20.2.3, 20.5.2, and table T.2, p. 294.

Código Penal Federal (Mexico)
    Ab.:   C.P.F.
    Ex.:   Código Penal para el Distrito Federal [C.P.F.] [Federal Criminal Code], art. 387, Diario Oficial de la Federación [D.O.], 6 de Febrero de 2004 (Mex.).
           C.P.F. art. 387. –Subsequent abbreviated citation.
           –<u>See</u> <u>Bluebook</u> rules 20.2.3, 20.5.2, and table T.2, p. 294.

Collections of Decisions of the European Commission of Human Rights
    Ab.:   Eur. Comm'n H.R. Dec. & Rep. <u>See</u> <u>Bluebook</u> rule 21.5.3 and table T.3.
    Ex.:   <u>Farragut v. France</u>, App. No. 10103/82, 42 Eur. Comm'n H.R. Dec. & Rep. 77, 83 (1982). –Page Citation.

Collective Bargaining Negotiations & Contracts (Bureau of National Affairs)
    Ab.:   Collective Bargaining Negot. & Cont. (BNA)

College Law Digest
    Ab.:   College L. Dig. (Nat'l Ass'n College & Univ. Att'ys)

Collier Bankruptcy Manual
           –Do not abbreviate the title.
    Ex.:   2 <u>Collier Bankruptcy Manual</u> ¶ 523.05[2] (Lawrence P. King ed., 3d ed. 1990). –Paragraph Citation.
           2 <u>Collier Bankruptcy Manual</u> ¶ 523.05[2], at 523-21 (Lawrence P. King ed., 3d ed. 1990). –Page Citation.
           2 <u>Collier Bankruptcy Manual</u> ¶ 523.05[2], at 523-21 n.51b (Lawrence P. King ed., 3d ed. 1990). –Footnote Citation.

Collier Bankruptcy Practice Guide
           –Do not abbreviate the title.
    Ex.:   5 <u>Collier Bankruptcy Practice Guide</u> ¶ 85.08 (Asa S. Herzog & Lawrence P. King eds., 2000). –Paragraph Citation.
           5 <u>Collier Bankruptcy Practice Guide</u> ¶ 85.08, at 85-18 (Asa S. Herzog & Lawrence P. King eds., 2000). –Page Citation.
           5 <u>Collier Bankruptcy Practice Guide</u> ¶ 88.08, at 85-18 n.1 (Asa S. Herzog & Lawrence P. King eds., 2000). –Footnote Citation.

In law review footnotes, the titles of books and the names of cases, except for procedural phrases, are not underlined. <u>See</u> <u>Bluebook</u> rule 2.1(a) & (b). Further, the following are in large and small capitals: codes, restatements, standards, constitutions, periodicals, authors of books, titles of books, the abbreviated names of codes, most legislative materials except for bills and resolutions, codified ordinances, model codes, court rules, and sentencing guidelines. Refer to <u>The Bluebook</u>.

Collier on Bankruptcy
–Do not abbreviate the title.

Ex.: 5 <u>Collier on Bankruptcy</u> ¶ 544.08 (Lawrence P. King ed., 15th ed. 2000). –Paragraph Citation.

5 <u>Collier on Bankruptcy</u> ¶ 544.08, at 544-15 (Lawrence P. King ed., 15th ed. 2000). –Page Citation.

5 <u>Collier on Bankruptcy</u> ¶ 544.08, at 544-15 n.3 (Lawrence P. King ed., 15th ed. 2000). –Footnote Citation.

Colonial Lawyer, The
Ab.: Colonial Law.

Ex.: Keith Finch, Note, <u>Virginia's New Rule 11 "Clone" -- An Empirical Study</u>, 19 Colonial Law. 1 (1990). –Article Citation.

Keith Finch, Note, <u>Virginia's New Rule 11 "Clone" -- An Empirical Study</u>, 19 Colonial Law. 1, 9-12 (1990). –Page Citation.

–A designation of the piece should appear before the title of the work to indicate that it is student written. <u>See</u> <u>Bluebook</u> rule 16.5.1(a).

Colorado
Ab.: Colo.

Colorado Bar Association
Ab.: Colo. B.A.

Colorado Code of Regulations
See Code of Colorado Regulations.

Colorado Constitution
Ab.: Colo. Const. art.　, §　.

Ex.: Colo. Const. art. II, § 7. –"Cite constitutional provisions currently in force without a date." <u>Bluebook</u> rule 11.

Colo. Const. art. V, § 37 (repealed 1974). –"If the cited provision has been repealed, either indicate parenthetically the fact and date of repeal or cite the repealing provision in full." <u>Bluebook</u> rule 11.

Colo. Const. art. IV, § 18 (amended 1990). –"When citing a provision that has been subsequently amended, either indicate parenthetically the fact and date of amendment or cite the amending provision in full." <u>Bluebook</u> rule 11.

Colorado Court of Appeals Reports
Ab.: Colo. App.

–Discontinued after 44 Colo. App. 561 (1980).

–Cite to P., P.2d, or P.3d, if therein; otherwise, cite to Colo. App.

–Give parallel citations, if at all, only in documents submitted to Colorado state courts. <u>See</u> <u>Bluebook</u> rules 10.3.1 and B5.1.3

In citing cases in law review footnotes, abbreviate any word listed in table T.6; the names of "states, countries, and other geographical units" unless they are named parties; and any other words of eight or more letters "if <u>substantial</u> space is thereby saved and the result is unambiguous." <u>Bluebook</u> rule 10.2.2. On the other hand, in citing cases in text, abbreviate only widely known acronyms and the following words: "&," "Ass'n," "Bros.," "Co.," "Corp.," "Inc.," "Ltd.," and "No." <u>Bluebook</u> rule 10.2.1(c).

Because Colorado Supreme Court opinions provide parallel citations to Colorado decisions where they exist, we advise giving a parallel citation in documents submitted to Colorado state courts.

Through 44 Colo. App. 561 (1980), cite as follows:

In documents submitted to Colorado state courts, cite as follows:

Alley v. Kal, 44 Colo. App. 561, 610 P.2d 191 (1980).
–Case Citation.

Alley v. Kal, 44 Colo. App. 561, 564, 610 P.2d 191, 193 (1980).
–Page Citation.

In all other documents, cite as follows:

Alley v. Kal, 610 P.2d 191 (Colo. Ct. App. 1980). –Case Citation.

Alley v. Kal, 610 P.2d 191, 193 (Colo. Ct. App. 1980). –Page Citation.

–After 44 Colo. App. 561 (1980), cite as follows:

In all documents:

Dewey v. Hardy, 917 P.2d 305 (Colo. Ct. App. 1996). –Case Citation.

Dewey v. Hardy, 917 P.2d 305, 311 (Colo. Ct. App. 1996). –Page Citation.

Colorado Journal of International & Environmental Law and Policy
Ab.:   Colo. J. Int'l Envtl. L. & Pol'y

Ex.:   M. Wray Witten, Institutional Failure in the Water and Sanitation Decade, 2 Colo. J. Int'l Envtl. L. & Pol'y 277 (1991). –Article Citation.

M. Wray Witten, Institutional Failure in the Water and Sanitation Decade, 2 Colo. J. Int'l Envtl. L. & Pol'y 277, 293-294 (1991). –Page Citation.

Colorado Lawyer
Ab.:   Colo. Law.

Ex.:   Cassandra G. Sasso, Liability of Fiduciaries under ERISA, 21 Colo. Law. 197 (1991). –Article Citation.

Cassandra G. Sasso, Liability of Fiduciaries under ERISA, 21 Colo. Law. 197, 198 (1991). –Page Citation.

Colorado Legislative Service (West)
Ab.:   year Colo. Legis Serv. page no. (West)

Ex.:   Act of Apr. 16, 1996, No. 97, Sec. 3, § 30-15-402(1), 1996 Colo. Legis. Serv. 403, 403 (West) (concerning ordinance violations punishable by fines). –Citation to a session law amending prior act.

Act of Apr. 16, 1996, No. 97, § 3, 1996 Colo. Legis. Serv. 403 (West) (concerning ordinance violations punishable by fines). –Citation to an entire session law.

In law review footnotes, the titles of books and the names of cases, except for procedural phrases, are not underlined. See Bluebook rule 2.1(a) & (b). Further, the following are in large and small capitals: codes, restatements, standards, constitutions, periodicals, authors of books, titles of books, the abbreviated names of codes, most legislative materials except for bills and resolutions, codified ordinances, model codes, court rules, and sentencing guidelines. Refer to The Bluebook.

–<u>See</u> <u>Bluebook</u> rule 12.4.

–"Cite to Colo. Sess. Laws, if therein." <u>Bluebook</u> table T.1, p. 202.

Colorado Register
> Ab.: Colo. Reg.

Colorado Reports
> Ab.: Colo.

–Discontinued after 200 Colo. 549 (1980).

–Cite to P., P.2d or P.3d, if therein; otherwise, cite to Colo.

–Give parallel citations, if at all, only in documents submitted to Colorado state courts. <u>See</u> <u>Bluebook</u> rules 10.3.1 and B5.1.3. Because Colorado Supreme Court opinions provide parallel citations to Colorado decisions where they exist, we advise giving a parallel citation in documents submitted to Colorado state courts.

–Through 200 Colo. 549 (1980), cite as follows:

In documents submitted to Colorado state courts:
> <u>Mishek v. Stanton</u>, 200 Colo. 514, 616 P.2d 135 (1980). –Case Citation.
> <u>Mishek v. Stanton</u>, 200 Colo. 514, 515, 616 P.2d 135, 136 (1980). –Page Citation.

In all other documents:
> <u>Mishek v. Stanton</u>, 616 P.2d 135 (Colo. 1980). –Case Citation.
> <u>Mishek v. Stanton</u>, 616 P.2d 135, 136 (Colo. 1980). –Page Citation.

–After 200 Colo. 549 (1980), cite as follows:

In all documents:
> <u>Boyer v. Karakehian</u>, 915 P.2d 1295 (Colo. 1996). –Case Citation.
> <u>Boyer v. Karakehian</u>, 915 P.2d 1295, 1296-97 (Colo. 1996). –Page Citation.

Colorado Revised Statutes (LexisNexis)
> Ab.: Colo. Rev. Stat. § x-x-x (year)
> Ex.: Colo. Rev. Stat. § 25-5-504 (2003)
> Colo. Rev. Stat. § 12-3-402 (Supp. 2005)

Colorado Revised Statutes Annotated (West)
> See West's Colorado Revised Statutes Annotated.

Colorado Session Laws
> See Session Laws of Colorado and Colorado Legislative Service (West).

In citing cases in law review footnotes, abbreviate any word listed in table T.6; the names of "states, countries, and other geographical units" unless they are named parties; and any other words of eight or more letters "if <u>substantial</u> space is thereby saved and the result is unambiguous." <u>Bluebook</u> rule 10.2.2. On the other hand, in citing cases in text, abbreviate only widely known acronyms and the following words: "&," "Ass'n," "Bros.," "Co.," "Corp.," "Inc.," "Ltd.," and "No." <u>Bluebook</u> rule 10.2.1(c).

Columbia Business Law Review
Ab.: Colum. Bus. L. Rev.

Ex.: Marc I. Steinberg, <u>Attorney Liability for Client Fraud</u>, 1991 Colum. Bus. L. Rev. 1. –Article Citation.

Marc I. Steinberg, <u>Attorney Liability for Client Fraud</u>, 1991 Colum. Bus. L. Rev. 1, 3-7. –Page Citation.

Columbia Human Rights Law Review
Ab.: Colum. Hum. Rts. L. Rev.

Ex.: Mark Parts, <u>The Eighth Amendment and the Requirement of Active Measures to Prevent the Spread of AIDS in Prison</u>, 22 Colum. Hum. Rts. L. Rev. 217 (1991). –Article Citation.

Mark Parts, <u>The Eighth Amendment and the Requirement of Active Measures to Prevent the Spread of AIDS in Prison</u>, 22 Colum. Hum. Rts. L. Rev. 217, 225-27 (1991). –Page Citation.

Columbia Journal of Asian Law
Ab.: Colum. J. Asian L.

Ex.: Richard Cullen & Pinky D. W. Choy, <u>The Internet in China</u>, 13 Colum. J. Asian L. 99 (1999). –Article Citation.

Richard Cullen & Pinky D. W. Choy, <u>The Internet in China</u>, 13 Colum. J. Asian L. 99, 103 (1999). –Page Citation.

Columbia Journal of Environmental Law
Ab.: Colum. J. Envtl. L.

Ex.: Robert Abrams, <u>The Maturing Discipline of Environmental Prosecution</u>, 16 Colum. J. Envtl. L. 279 (1991). –Article Citation.

Robert Abrams, <u>The Maturing Discipline of Environmental Prosecution</u>, 16 Colum. J. Envtl. L. 279, 280-85 (1991). –Page Citation.

Columbia Journal of Gender & Law
Ab.: Colum. J. Gender & L.

Ex.: Angela L. Padilla & Jennifer J. Winrich, <u>Christianity, Feminism, and the Law</u>, 1 Colum. J. Gender & L. 67 (1991). –Article Citation.

Angela L. Padilla & Jennifer J. Winrich, <u>Christianity, Feminism, and the Law</u>, 1 Colum. J. Gender & L. 67, 73 (1991). –Page Citation.

Columbia Journal of Law and Social Problems
Ab.: Colum. J.L. & Soc. Probs.

Ex.: Matthew T. Golden, Note, <u>On Replacing the Replacement Worker Doctrine</u>, 25 Colum. J.L. & Soc. Probs. 51 (1991). –Article Citation.

Matthew T. Golden, Note, <u>On Replacing the Replacement Worker Doctrine</u>, 25 Colum. J.L. & Soc. Probs. 51, 58-60 (1991). –Page Citation.

In law review footnotes, the titles of books and the names of cases, except for procedural phrases, are not underlined. <u>See</u> <u>Bluebook</u> rule 2.1(a) & (b). Further, the following are in large and small capitals: codes, restatements, standards, constitutions, periodicals, authors of books, titles of books, the abbreviated names of codes, most legislative materials except for bills and resolutions, codified ordinances, model codes, court rules, and sentencing guidelines. Refer to <u>The Bluebook</u>.

–A designation of the piece should appear before the title of the work to indicate that it is student written. <u>See</u> <u>Bluebook</u> rule 16.6.2.

Columbia Journal of Law & the Arts
Ab: Colum. J.L. & Arts

Ex: Naomi Mezey and Mark C. Niles, <u>Screening the Law: Ideology and Law In American Popular Culture</u>, 28 Colum. J.L. & Arts 91 (2005). –Article Citation.

Naomi Mezey and Mark C. Niles, <u>Screening the Law: Ideology and Law In American Popular Culture</u>, 28 Colum. J.L. & Arts 91, 95-96 (2005). –Page Citation.

Columbia Journal of Transnational Law
Ab.:   Colum. J. Transnat'l L.

Ex.:   Louis Henkin, <u>The Invasion of Panama Under International Law: A Gross Violation</u>, 29 Colum. J. Transnat'l L. 293 (1991). –Article Citation.

Louis Henkin, <u>The Invasion of Panama Under International Law: A Gross Violation</u>, 29 Colum. J. Transnat'l L. 293, 312-15 (1991). –Page Citation.

Columbia Journal of World Business
Ab.:   Colum. J. World Bus.

Ex.:   Roberto E. Batres, <u>A Mexican View of the North American Free Trade Agreement</u>, Colum. J. World Bus., Summer 1991, at 78. –Article Citation.

Roberto E. Batres, <u>A Mexican View of the North American Free Trade Agreement</u>, Colum. J. World Bus., Summer 1991, at 78, 81. –Page Citation.

Columbia Law Review
Ab.:   Colum. L. Rev.

Ex.:   David Yassky, <u>Eras of the First Amendment</u>, 91 Colum. L. Rev. 1699 (1991). –Article Citation.

David Yassky, <u>Eras of the First Amendment</u>, 91 Colum. L. Rev. 1699, 1717-20 (1991). –Page Citation.

Columbia-VLA Journal of Law & the Arts
Ab.:   Colum.-VLA J.L. & Arts

Ex.:   Leo J. Raskind, <u>The Continuing Process of Refining and Adapting Copyright Principles</u>, 14 Colum.-VLA J.L. & Arts 125 (1990). –Article Citation.

Leo J. Raskind, <u>The Continuing Process of Refining and Adapting Copyright Principles</u>, 14 Colum.-VLA J.L. & Arts 125, 126 (1990). –Page Citation.

In citing cases in law review footnotes, abbreviate any word listed in table T.6; the names of "states, countries, and other geographical units" unless they are named parties; and any other words of eight or more letters "if <u>substantial</u> space is thereby saved and the result is unambiguous." <u>Bluebook</u> rule 10.2.2. On the other hand, in citing cases in text, abbreviate only widely known acronyms and the following words: "&," "Ass'n," "Bros.," "Co.," "Corp.," "Inc.," "Ltd.," and "No." <u>Bluebook</u> rule 10.2.1(c).

COM documents
Ab.: COM

Ex.: Communication from the Commission to the Council and the European Parliament: Modernising Company Law and Enhancing Corporate Governance in the European Union—A Plan to Move Forward, at 13, COM (2003) 284 final (May 21, 2003).

COMM/ENT
See Hastings Communication and Entertainment Law Journal.

Command Papers
Ab.: Cm. (6th series, 1986-date)

Ex.: Ministry of Defence, Delivering Security in a Changing World, 2003, Cm. 6040, at 3.

See Bluebook table T.2, p. 322.

Commentary (article designation)
Ex.: Pierre Schlag, Commentary, The Aesthetics of American Law, 115 Harv. L. Rev. 1047 (2002).

See Bluebook rule 16.6.4.

CommLaw Conspectus: Journal of Communications Law & Policy
Ab: Commlaw Conspectus

Ex: Shannon M. Heim, Signaling System Seven: A Case Study in Local Telephone Competition, 13 Commlaw Conspectus 51 (2004).

–Article Citation.

Shannon M. Heim, Signaling System Seven: A Case Study in Local Telephone Competition, 13 Commlaw Conspectus 51, 80 (2004).

–Page Citation.

Commentaries, by William Blackstone
Ex.: 1 William Blackstone, Commentaries, *35. –The asterisk denotes the page number in the original edition. See Bluebook rule 15.8(b).

Commerce Clearing House
Ab.: CCH

Commerce Court
Ab.: Comm. Ct.

Commercial Law Journal
Ab.: Com. L.J.

Ex.: Rhett Frimet, The Birth of Bankruptcy in the United States, 96 Com. L.J. 160 (1991). –Article Citation.

Rhett Frimet, The Birth of Bankruptcy in the United States, 96 Com. L.J. 160, 164-66 (1991). –Page Citation.

In law review footnotes, the titles of books and the names of cases, except for procedural phrases, are not underlined. See Bluebook rule 2.1(a) & (b). Further, the following are in large and small capitals: codes, restatements, standards, constitutions, periodicals, authors of books, titles of books, the abbreviated names of codes, most legislative materials except for bills and resolutions, codified ordinances, model codes, court rules, and sentencing guidelines. Refer to The Bluebook.

Commissioner
Ab.: Comm'r

Committee prints, Congressional
See Congressional Committee Prints.

Commodity Futures Law Reports (Commerce Clearing House)
Ab.: Comm. Fut. L. Rep. (CCH)

Ex.: Schroeder v. Indorsky, 2 Comm. Fut. L. Rep. (CCH) ¶ 26,698 (S.D.N.Y. Apr. 24, 1996). –Citation to looseleaf material.

Buckwalter v. Global Futures Holdings, Inc., 2 Comm. Fut. L. Rep. (CCH) ¶ 26,309 (Comm. Fut. Trading Comm'n Feb. 17, 1995). –Citation to looseleaf administative material.

Aamot v. Kassel, [1993-1994 Decisions Transfer Binder] Comm. Fut. L. Rep. (CCH) ¶ 25,815 (6th Cir. Aug 6, 1993). –Citation to transfer binder material.

–The above examples are proper if the case is not yet available in, or is not reported in, an official or West reporter, a public domain citation, or in a widely used computer database.

Bosley v. Cecil, 2 Comm. Fut. L. Rep. (CCH) ¶ 25,128 (Comm. Fut. Trading Comm'n Sept. 10, 1991). –Citation to looseleaf administrative material.

Ferruggia v. Shearson Lehman Hutton, Inc., [1992-1994 Decisions Transfer Binder] Comm. Fut. L. Rep. (CCH) ¶ 25,653 (Comm. Fut. Trading Comm'n Jan. 26, 1993). –Citation to transfer binder administrative material.

Common Extravagants (Catholic Church) (1261-1484)
Ab.: Extrav. Com.

Common Market Law Reports (European Community)
–Cite the Court of Justice of the European Communities and the Court of First Instance to E.C.R., if therein. Otherwise, cite to C.M.L.R., Common Mkt. Rep. (CCH) or CEC (CCH), if therein, in that order of preference. See Bluebook rule 21.5.2 and table T.3.

Ab.: C.M.L.R.

Ex.: Case 98/86, Centros Ltd. v. Erhverys-og Selskabsstyrelen, 1999 E.C.R. I-1459, 2 C.M.L.R. 551.

Common Market Law Review
Ab.: Common Mkt. L. Rev.

Ex.: Gaudencio Esteban, The Reform of Company Law in Spain, 28 Common Mkt. L. Rev. 935 (1991). –Article Citation.

Gaudencio Esteban, The Reform of Company Law in Spain, 28 Common Mkt. L. Rev. 935, 938-41 (1991). –Page Citation.

In citing cases in law review footnotes, abbreviate any word listed in table T.6; the names of "states, countries, and other geographical units" unless they are named parties; and any other words of eight or more letters "if substantial space is thereby saved and the result is unambiguous." Bluebook rule 10.2.2. On the other hand, in citing cases in text, abbreviate only widely known acronyms and the following words: "&," "Ass'n," "Bros.," "Co.," "Corp.," "Inc.," "Ltd.," and "No." Bluebook rule 10.2.1(c).

Common Market Reports (Commerce Clearing House)
Ab.: Common Mkt. Rep. (CCH)

Ex.: Case 57/43, <u>Regina v. Kirk</u>, [1983-1985 Transfer Binder] Common Mkt. Rep. (CCH) ¶ 14,070 (1984). –Citation to transfer binder.

Common Pleas
Ab.: C.P. "[When appropriate, name county or similar subdivision]" <u>Bluebook</u> table T.7.

Commonwealth
Ab.: Commw.

Commonwealth Court
Ab.: Commw. Ct.

Commonwealth Law Reports (Austl.)
Ab.: C.L.R.

Ex.: <u>Jago v. District Court (N.S.W.)</u>, (1990) 168 C.L.R. 23 (Austl.). –Case Citation.

<u>Purvis v. State</u> [2003] HCA 62; (2003) 217 C.L.R. 92 (Austl.). –Case with medium-neutral citation.

Note: For explanation of Australia's medium-neutral citation, see L.T. Olsson, <u>Guide to Uniform Production of Judgments</u> (2d ed. 1999), available at http://www.aija.org.au/online/judguide.htm.

Communication(s)
Ab.: Comm.

Comparative Juridical Review
Ab.: Comp. Jurid. Rev.

Ex.: Lajos Schmidt, <u>Legal Aspects of Doing Business With and In Hungary</u>, 26 Comp. Jurid. Rev. 127 (1989). –Article Citation.

Lajos Schmidt, <u>Legal Aspects of Doing Business With and In Hungary</u>, 26 Comp. Jurid. Rev. 127, 137-40 (1989). –Page Citation.

Comparative Labor Law Journal
Ab.: Comp. Lab. L.J.

Ex.: Manfred Weiss, <u>The Transition of Labor Law and Industrial Relations: The Case of German Unification -- A Preliminary Perspective</u>, 13 Comp. Lab. L.J. 1 (1991). –Article Citation.

Manfred Weiss, <u>The Transition of Labor Law and Industrial Relations: The Case of German Unification -- A Preliminary Perspective</u>, 13 Comp. Lab. L.J. 1, 8-9 (1991). –Page Citation.

Comparative Law
Ab.: Comp. L.

In law review footnotes, the titles of books and the names of cases, except for procedural phrases, are not underlined. <u>See</u> <u>Bluebook</u> rule 2.1(a) & (b). Further, the following are in large and small capitals: codes, restatements, standards, constitutions, periodicals, authors of books, titles of books, the abbreviated names of codes, most legislative materials except for bills and resolutions, codified ordinances, model codes, court rules, and sentencing guidelines. Refer to <u>The Bluebook</u>.

Ex.:   Allan D. Smith, <u>Recruit Cosmos: The Viewpoint From U.S. Law</u>,
        7 Comp. L. 67 (1990). –Article Citation.

        Allan D. Smith, <u>Recruit Cosmos: The Viewpoint From U.S. Law</u>,
        7 Comp. L. 67, 73-75 (1990). –Page Citation.

Compare [and] with

–"<u>Compare</u>"and "<u>with</u>" are used when a "[c]omparison of the
authorities cited will offer support for or illustrate the proposition."
<u>Bluebook</u> rule 1.2(b).

Ex.:   "The district court's order of restitution in the amount of $23,208
        exceeds its statutory authority and is therefore an abuse of discretion.
        <u>Compare</u> <u>Jalilian</u>, 896 F.2d at 448-49, <u>with</u> <u>United States v. Jack</u>, 868
        F.2d 1186, 1188-89 (10th Cir.) (probation order of district court
        expressly authorized by FPA), <u>cert. denied</u>, 490 U.S. 1112, 109 S. Ct.
        3171, 104 L. Ed. 2d 1032 (1989)." –Taken from 952 F.2d 1262, 1266
        (10th Cir. 1991).

compilation
Ab.:   comp.

compiled
Ab.:   comp.

compiled statutes
Ab.:   comp. stat.

Complaint, citation to

Ab.:   Compl.

Ex.:   (Pl.'s Compl. ¶ 8).

<u>See</u> <u>Bluebook</u> rule B10 and table BT.1.

Note: See <u>Bluebook</u> rule 10.8.3 for citing litigation materials from another case.

Comptroller General
Ab.:   Comp. Gen.

Computer/Law Journal
Ab.:   Computer/L.J.

Ex.:   George S. Cole, <u>Tort Liability for Artificial Intelligence and Expert</u>
        <u>Systems</u>, 10 Computer/L.J. 127 (1990). –Article Citation.

        George S. Cole, <u>Tort Liability for Artificial Intelligence and Expert</u>
        <u>Systems</u>, 10 Computer/L.J. 127, 145-49 (1990). –Page Citation.

Congress
Ab.:   Cong.

In citing cases in law review footnotes, abbreviate any word listed in table T.6;
the names of "states, countries, and other geographical units" unless they are named parties;
and any other words of eight or more letters "if <u>substantial</u> space is thereby saved and the
result is unambiguous." <u>Bluebook</u> rule 10.2.2. On the other hand, in citing cases in text,
abbreviate only widely known acronyms and the following words: "&," "Ass'n," "Bros.,"
"Co.," "Corp.," "Inc.," "Ltd.," and "No." <u>Bluebook</u> rule 10.2.1(c).

Congressional Bills

–Pre-enactment and post-enactment when used to document legislative history.

House of Representatives:

Ab.: H.R.

Ex.: H.R. 44, 101st Cong. (1990).

H.R. 44, 101st Cong., § 1 (1990). –Citation to a section of a bill.

H.R. 44, 101st Cong., 136 Cong. Rec. 9704 (1990).–Citation if the bill is printed in the Congressional Record.

H.R. 4111, 102d Cong. (1991) (enacted). –Citation to House Bill without parallel citation to Statutes at Large.

H.R. 4111, 102d Cong., 106 Stat. 986 (1991). –Citation with parallel reference to Statutes at Large.

Senate:

Ab.: S.

Ex.: S. 1045, 101st Cong. (1990).

S. 1045, 101st Cong., § 1 (1990). –Citation to a section of a bill.

S. 1045, 101st Cong., 136 Cong. Rec. 16438 (1990). –Citation if the bill is printed in the Congressional Record.

Congressional Committee Prints

Ab.: Comm. Print

Ex.: Staff of Subcomm. on Select Revenue Measures of the House Comm. on Ways and Means, 103d Cong., 1st Sess., Description of Miscellaneous Revenue Proposals 5 (Comm. Print 1993).

–See Bluebook rule 13.4(c).

Congressional Debates

Ex.: 126 Cong. Rec. H2061 (daily ed. Mar. 24, 1980) (remark of Rep. Duncan). –Unbound.

122 Cong. Rec. 5447-48 (1976). –Bound.

Congressional Digest

Ab.: Cong. Dig.

Congressional Documents

House Document:

Ab.: H.R. Doc.

In law review footnotes, the titles of books and the names of cases, except for procedural phrases, are not underlined. See Bluebook rule 2.1(a) & (b). Further, the following are in large and small capitals: codes, restatements, standards, constitutions, periodicals, authors of books, titles of books, the abbreviated names of codes, most legislative materials except for bills and resolutions, codified ordinances, model codes, court rules, and sentencing guidelines. Refer to The Bluebook.

Ex.: H.R. Doc. No. 104-159 (1996).

Board of Trustees, Federal Old-Age and Survivors Insurance and Disability Insurance Trust Funds, <u>1995 Annual Report of the Board of Trustees of the Federal Old Age and Survivors Insurance and Disability Insurance Trust Funds</u>, H.R. Doc. No. 104-159, at 4 (1996). –Citation if the title and author are to be given.

–"When possible (and particularly for documents published after 1974), give parallel citation to the permanent edition of <u>United States Code Congressional and Administrative News</u>." <u>Bluebook</u> rule 13.4(a).

Senate Document:

Ab.: S. Doc.

Ex.: S. Doc. No. 104-4 (1996).

Bipartisan Task Force on Funding Disaster Relief, <u>Federal Disaster Assistance: Report of the Senate Task Force on Funding Disaster Relief</u>, S. Doc. No. 104-4, at 15 (1995). –Citation if the title and author are to be given.

–"When possible (and particularly for documents published after 1974), give parallel citation to the permanent edition of <u>United States Code Congressional and Administrative News</u>." <u>Bluebook</u> rule 13.4(a).

Congressional Hearings
–Use full title.

Ex.: <u>Reproductive Hazards and Miliary Service: What are the Risks of Radiation, Agent Orange, and Gulf War Exposures?: Hearing Before the Senate Comm. on Veterans' Affairs</u>, 103d Cong. 140 (1994) (statement of Jackie C. Maxwell, Director of Atomic Parents, National Association of Radiation Survivors).

<u>Evidence Against a Higher Minimum Wage: Hearing Before the Joint Economic Committee</u>, 104th Cong. 88 (1995) (statement of Sen. Connie Mack).

Congressional Index (Commerce Clearing House)
Ab.: Cong. Index (CCH)

Congressional Record (U.S.)
Ab.: Cong. Rec.

Ex.: 95 Cong. Rec. 7441 (1949).

130 Cong. Rec. H7758 (daily ed. July 25, 1984) (statement of Rep. Dingell)

131 Cong. Rec. 29,292 (1984). –Citation to permanent edition.

<u>See</u> <u>Bluebook</u> rule 13.5.

Congressional Reports
House of Representatives Reports:

Ab.: H.R. Rep.

In citing cases in law review footnotes, abbreviate any word listed in table T.6; the names of "states, countries, and other geographical units" unless they are named parties; and any other words of eight or more letters "if <u>substantial</u> space is thereby saved and the result is unambiguous." <u>Bluebook</u> rule 10.2.2. On the other hand, in citing cases in text, abbreviate only widely known acronyms and the following words: "&," "Ass'n," "Bros.," "Co.," "Corp.," "Inc.," "Ltd.," and "No." <u>Bluebook</u> rule 10.2.1(c).

Ex.: H.R. Rep. No. 103-403, at 21 (1994).

H.R. Rep. No. 103-403 (1994), as reprinted in 1994 U.S.C.C.A.N. 3598, 3599. –Citation when a parallel citation to the permanent edition of United States Code Congressional and Administrative News exists.

Senate Reports:

Ab.: S. Rep.

Ex.: S. Rep. No. 103-300, at 7 (1994).

S. Rep. No. 103-300 (1994), as reprinted in 1994 U.S.C.C.A.N. 3683, 3687. –Citation when a parallel citation to the permanent edition of United States Code Congressional and Administrative News exists.

See Bluebook rule 13.4(a).

Congressional Resolutions

House of Representatives Simple Resolutions:

–A parallel citation to the Congressional Record may be provided if of assistance to the reader in locating an unenacted or enacted resolution. See Bluebook rule 13.2(a) & (b).

Ab.: H.R. Res.

Ex.: H.R. Res. 510, 104th Cong. (1996). –Unenacted.

H.R. Res. 531, 104th Cong., 142 Cong. Rec. H10,971 (daily ed. Sept. 24, 1996). –When the unenacted resolution is printed in the Congressional Record.

H.R. Res. 525, 104th Cong., 142 Cong. Rec. H10,927 (daily ed. Sept. 24, 1996) (enacted).

–When the resolution has been enacted.

House of Representatives Concurrent Resolutions:

–A parallel citation to Statutes at Large may be provided if of assistance to the reader in locating an enacted concurrent resolution. No parenthetical noting enactment is necessary if parallel citation is given to Statutes at Large. See Bluebook rule 13.2(b).

Ab.: H.R. Con. Res.

Ex.: H.R. Con. Res. 21, 104th Cong. (1996). –Unenacted.

H.R. Con. Res. 230, 104th Cong. (1996) (enacted). –Enacted.

H.R. Con. Res. 145, 104th Cong., 142 Cong. Rec. II11,239 (daily ed. Sept. 26, 1996).

–When the unenacted resolution is printed in the Congressional Record.

H.R. Con. Res. 237, 103d Cong., 108 Stat. 5075 (1994). –When the resolution has been enacted and appears in Statutes at Large (if it has yet to appear, cite to the Congressional Record with parenthetical noting enactment).

House of Representatives Joint Resolutions:

In law review footnotes, the titles of books and the names of cases, except for procedural phrases, are not underlined. See Bluebook rule 2.1(a) & (b). Further, the following are in large and small capitals: codes, restatements, standards, constitutions, periodicals, authors of books, titles of books, the abbreviated names of codes, most legislative materials except for bills and resolutions, codified ordinances, model codes, court rules, and sentencing guidelines. Refer to The Bluebook.

Ab.:   H.R.J. Res.

Ex.:   H.R.J. Res. 70, 104th Cong. (1996). –Unenacted.

H.R.J. Res. 191, 104th Cong. (1996) (enacted). –Enacted.

H.R.J. Res. 197, 104th Cong., 121 Cong. Rec. H11,636 (daily ed. Sept. 28, 1996) (enacted). –When the text of the enacted resolution can be found in the Congressional Record.

–Cite enacted Joint Resolutions as statutes except when used to document legislative history, in which case the format for unenacted bills should be used. Only enacted resolutions appear in the Statutes at Large. See Bluebook rule 13.2.

H.R.J. Res. 208, 92d Cong., 86 Stat. 1523 (1972).

Senate Simple Resolutions:

Ab.:   S. Res.

Ex.:   S. Res. 296, 104th Cong. (1996). –Unenacted.

S. Res. 301, 104th Cong., 142 Cong. Rec. S11,435 (daily ed. Sept. 26, 1996). –When the text of the unenacted resolution can be found in the Congressional Record.

S. Res. 275, 104th Cong., 142 Cong. Rec. S11,201 (daily ed. Sept. 24, 1996) (enacted).

–When the resolution has been enacted.

Senate Concurrent Resolutions:

Ab.:   S. Con. Res.

Ex.:   S. Con. Res. 74, 104th Cong. (1996). –Unenacted.

S. Con. Res. 47, 104th Cong., 142 Cong. Rec. S12,292 (Oct. 3, 1996) (enacted). –When a printing of the unenacted resolution can be found in the Congressional Record and has not yet appeared in Statutes at Large.

Senate Joint Resolutions:

Ab.:   S.J. Res.

Ex.:   S.J. Res. 60, 104th Cong. (1996). –Unenacted.

S.J. Res. 65, 104th Cong., 142 Cong. Rec. S11,999 (1994). –When a printing of the unenacted resolution can be found in the Congressional Record.

–Cite enacted Joint Resolutions as statutes except when used to document legislative history, in which case the format for unenacted bills should be used. Only enacted resolutions appear in the Statutes at Large. See Bluebook rule 13.2.

Connecticut

Ab.:   Conn.

In citing cases in law review footnotes, abbreviate any word listed in table T.6; the names of "states, countries, and other geographical units" unless they are named parties; and any other words of eight or more letters "if substantial space is thereby saved and the result is unambiguous." Bluebook rule 10.2.2. On the other hand, in citing cases in text, abbreviate only widely known acronyms and the following words: "&," "Ass'n," "Bros.," "Co.," "Corp.," "Inc.," "Ltd.," and "No." Bluebook rule 10.2.1(c).

Connecticut Appellate Reports

Ab.: Conn. App.

–Cite to A. or A.2d, if therein; otherwise, cite to Conn. App.

–Give parallel citations only in documents submitted to Connecticut state courts. See Bluebook rules 10.3.1 and B5.1.3; see also Conn. R. App. P. § 67-11, which requires in the table of authorities, but not in the argument portion of a brief, a parallel citation to the regional reporter.

In documents submitted to Connecticut state courts, cite as follows:

Dunbar v. Lindbolm, 41 Conn. App. 903, 673 A.2d 1184 (1996). –Case Citation.

Dunbar v. Lindbolm, 41 Conn. App. 903, 906, 673 A.2d 1184, 1187 (1996). –Page Citation.

In all other documents, cite as follows:

Dunbar v. Lindbolm, 673 A.2d 1184 (Conn. App. Ct. 1996). –Case Citation.

Dunbar v. Lindbolm, 673 A.2d 1184, 1187 (Conn. App. Ct. 1996). –Page Citation.

Connecticut Bar Journal

Ab.: Conn. B.J.

Ex.: Arthur E. Balbiner & Gaetano Ferro, Survey of 1991 Developments in Connecticut Family Law, 66 Conn. B.J. 40 (1992). –Article Citation.

Arthur E. Balbiner & Gaetano Ferro, Survey of 1991 Developments in Connecticut Family Law, 66 Conn. B.J. 40, 44-45 (1992). –Page Citation.

Connecticut Circuit Court Reports

Ab.: Conn. Cir. Ct.

–Discontinued after 6 Conn. Cir. Ct. 751 (1974). Thereafter, cite only to A.2d.

–Give parallel citations only in documents submitted to Connecticut state courts. See Bluebook rules 10.3.1 and B5.1.3; see also Conn. R. App. P. § 67-11, which requires in the table of authorities, but not in the argument portion of a brief, a parallel citation to the regional reporter.

In documents submitted to Connecticut state courts, cite as follows:

LeClair v. Woodward, 6 Conn. Cir. Ct. 727, 316 A.2d 791 (1970). –Case Citation.

LeClair v. Woodward, 6 Conn. Cir. Ct. 727, 730, 316 A.2d 791, 793 (1970). –Page Citation.

In all other documents, cite as follows:

In law review footnotes, the titles of books and the names of cases, except for procedural phrases, are not underlined. See Bluebook rule 2.1(a) & (b). Further, the following are in large and small capitals: codes, restatements, standards, constitutions, periodicals, authors of books, titles of books, the abbreviated names of codes, most legislative materials except for bills and resolutions, codified ordinances, model codes, court rules, and sentencing guidelines. Refer to The Bluebook.

LeClair v. Woodward, 316 A.2d 791 (Conn. Cir. Ct. 1970).
–Case Citation.
LeClair v. Woodward, 316 A.2d 791, 793 (Conn. Cir. Ct. 1970).
–Page Citation.

Connecticut Constitution
Ab.:   Conn. Const. art.   , §   .
Ex.:   Conn. Const. art. IV, § 15. –"Cite constitutional provisions currently in
        force without a date." Bluebook rule 11.

        Conn. Const. art. VI, § 9 (repealed 1980). Conn. Const. art. VI, § 9,
        repealed by Conn. Const. amend. XIII. –"If the cited provision has been
        repealed, either indicate parenthetically the fact and date of repeal or
        cite the repealing provision in full." Bluebook rule 1.

        Conn. Const. art. I, § 8 (amended 1982).

        Conn. Const. art. I, § 8, amended by Conn. Const. amend. XVII.
        –"When citing a provision that has been subsequently amended, either
        indicate parenthetically the fact and date of amendment or cite the
        amending provision in full." Bluebook rule 11.

        Conn. Const. of 1818, art. VI, § 8. –"Cite constitutions that have been
        totally superseded by year of adoption; if the specific provision cited
        was adopted in a different year, give that year parenthetically."
        Bluebook rule 11.

Connecticut General Statutes
See General Statutes of Connecticut.

Connecticut General Statutes Annotated (West)
Ab.:   Conn. Gen. Stat. Ann. §   (West year).
Ex.:   Conn. Gen. Stat. Ann. § 26-91 (West 1999).

        Conn. Gen. Stat. Ann. § 54-82h (West Supp. 2000).

        –"Cite to Conn. Gen. Stat., if therein." Bluebook table T.1, p. 203.

Connecticut Journal of International Law
Ab.:   Conn. J. Int'l L.
Ex.:   Matthew Lippman, Nuremberg: Forty Five Years Later, 7 Conn. J. Int'l
        L. 1 (1991). –Article Citation.

        Matthew Lippman, Nuremberg: Forty Five Years Later, 7 Conn. J. Int'l
        L. 1, 7 (1991). –Page Citation.

Connecticut Law Journal
Ab.:   Conn. L. J.
Ex.:   Ralph Gregory Elliot, Public Trust Is a Fragile Bond, 77 Conn. L.J. 41
        (2003). –Article Citation.

        Ralph Gregory Elliot, Public Trust Is a Fragile Bond, 77 Conn. L.J. 41,
        44 (2003). –Page Citation.

In citing cases in law review footnotes, abbreviate any word listed in table T.6;
the names of "states, countries, and other geographical units" unless they are named parties;
and any other words of eight or more letters "if substantial space is thereby saved and the
result is unambiguous." Bluebook rule 10.2.2. On the other hand, in citing cases in text,
abbreviate only widely known acronyms and the following words: "&," "Ass'n," "Bros.,"
"Co.," "Corp.," "Inc.," "Ltd.," and "No." Bluebook rule 10.2.1(c).

Connecticut Law Review
Ab.:   Conn. L. Rev.

Ex.:   Richard Briffault, The Role of Local Control in School Finance Reform, 24 Conn. L. Rev. 773 (1992). –Article Citation.

Richard Briffault, The Role of Local Control in School Finance Reform, 24 Conn. L. Rev. 773, 775 (1992). –Page Citation.

Connecticut Legislative Service (West)
Ab.:   year Conn. Legis. Serv. page no. (West)

Ex.:   Act of June 12, 1996, P.A. 92-266, 1996 Conn. Legis. Serv. 984 (West) (concerning local telephone service). –Citation to an entire session law.

Act of June 12, 1996, P.A. 92-266, sec. 2, § 16-256c, 1996 Conn. Legis. Serv. 984, 984 (West) (concerning local telephone service). –Citation to a session law amending prior act.

–See Bluebook rule 12.4.

–"Cite to Conn. Acts, Conn. Pub. Acts, or Conn. Spec. Acts, if therein." Bluebook table T.1, p. 203.

Connecticut Probate Law Journal, The
Ab.:   Conn. Prob. L.J.

Ex.:   Koreen Labrecque, Note, Grandparent Visitation After Stepparent Adoption, 6 Conn. Prob. L.J. 61 (1991). –Article Citation.

Koreen Labrecque, Note, Grandparent Visitation After Stepparent Adoption, 6 Conn. Prob. L.J. 61, 78-79 (1991). –Page Citation.

–These examples indicate the article was written by a student. See Bluebook rule 16.6.2.

Connecticut Public Acts
Ab.:   year Conn. Pub. Acts

–Used for years 1650-1971. See Bluebook table T.1, p. 203.

Connecticut Public & Special Acts
Ab.:   year Conn. Acts   (Reg. [Spec.] Sess.)

Ex.:   Act of July 6, 1995, No. 95-281, 1995 Conn. Acts 1317 (concerning hawkers and peddlers). –Citation to an entire session law.

Act of July 6, 1995, No. 95-281, sec. 2, § 21-38, 1995 Conn. Acts 1317, 1318. –Citation to a section of a session law amending a prior act.

–See Bluebook rule 12.4.

–Used for years 1972-date. See Bluebook table T.1, p. 203.

Connecticut Regulations of State Agencies
See Regulations of Connecticut State Agencies.

In law review footnotes, the titles of books and the names of cases, except for procedural phrases, are not underlined. See Bluebook rule 2.1(a) & (b). Further, the following are in large and small capitals: codes, restatements, standards, constitutions, periodicals, authors of books, titles of books, the abbreviated names of codes, most legislative materials except for bills and resolutions, codified ordinances, model codes, court rules, and sentencing guidelines. Refer to The Bluebook.

Connecticut Reports
Ab.:   Conn.

    –Cite to A. or A.2d, if therein; otherwise, cite to Conn.

    –Give parallel citations only in documents submitted to Connecticut state courts. See Bluebook rules 10.3.1 and B5.1.3; see also Conn. R. App. P. § 67-11, which requires in the table of authorities, but not in the argument position of a brief, a parallel citation to the regional reporter.

    In documents submitted to Connecticut state courts, cite as follows:

        Westerson v. Coccoli, 237 Conn. 907, 674 A.2d 1334 (1996). –Case Citation.

        Westerson v. Coccoli, 237 Conn. 907, 908, 674 A.2d 1334, 1335 (1996). –Page Citation.

    In all other documents, cite as follows:

        Westerson v. Coccoli, 674 A.2d 1334 (Conn. 1996). –Case Citation.

        Westerson v. Coccoli, 674 A.2d 1334, 1335 (Conn. 1996). –Page Citation.

Connecticut Session Laws
    See Connecticut Public Acts, Connecticut Public and Special Acts, Connecticut Special Acts, and Connecticut Legislative Service (West).

Connecticut Special Acts
Ab.:   year Conn. Spec. Acts

    –Used for years 1789-1971. See Bluebook table T.1, p. 203.

Connecticut Supplement
    –Cite to A. or A.2d, if therein; otherwise, cite to Conn. Supp.

    –Give parallel citations only in documents submitted to Connecticut state courts. See Bluebook rules 10.3.1 and B5.1.3; see also Conn. R. App. P. § 67-11, which requires in the table of authorities, but not in the argument portion of a brief, a parallel citation to the regional reporter.

Ab.:   Conn. Supp.

    In documents submitted to Connecticut state courts, cite as follows:

        Brown v. Ellis, 40 Conn. Supp. 165, 484 A.2d 944 (Super. Ct. 1984). –Case Citation.

        Brown v. Ellis, 40 Conn. Supp. 165, 170, 484 A.2d 944, 947 (Super. Ct. 1984). –Page Citation.

        Gulash v. Stylarama, 33 Conn. Supp. 108, 364 A.2d 1221 (C.P. 1975). –Case Citation.

        Gulash v. Stylarama, 33 Conn. Supp. 108, 111, 364 A.2d 1221, 1222 (C.P. 1975). –Page Citation.

In citing cases in law review footnotes, abbreviate any word listed in table T.6; the names of "states, countries, and other geographical units" unless they are named parties; and any other words of eight or more letters "if substantial space is thereby saved and the result is unambiguous." Bluebook rule 10.2.2. On the other hand, in citing cases in text, abbreviate only widely known acronyms and the following words: "&," "Ass'n," "Bros.," "Co.," "Corp.," "Inc.," "Ltd.," and "No." Bluebook rule 10.2.1(c).

In all other documents, cite as follows:

Brown v. Ellis, 484 A.2d 944 (Conn. Super. Ct. 1984). –Case Citation.

Brown v. Ellis, 484 A.2d 944, 947 (Conn. Super. Ct. 1984). –Page Citation.

Gulash v. Stylarama, 364 A.2d 1221 (Conn. C.P. 1975). –Case Citation.

Gulash v. Stylarama, 364 A.2d 1221, 1222 (Conn. C.P. 1975). –Page Citation.

Consolidated Laws Service (Statutory Compilation)
Ab.: N.Y. [subject] Law § x (Consol. year)
See Bluebook table T.1, pp. 222-23, for the abbreviation of each subject and entry herein for New York Consolidated Law Service (LexisNexis).

Consolidated Laws Service (Uncompiled Laws) (New York)
See Bluebook table T.1, p. 224, for abbreviation of Acts.

Consolidated Regulations of Canada
Ab.: C.R.C.

Consolidated Treaty Series (a.k.a. Parry's Consolidated Treaty Series)
Ab.: Consol. T.S.
Ex.: Exchange of Declarations for the Provisional Regulation of Commercial Relations, Fr.–Rom., Nov. 5, 1876, 151 Consol. T.S. 121.

constitution
Ab.: const.

Constitution of the United States
See United States Constitution.

constitutional
Ab.: const.

Constitutional Commentary
Ab.: Const. Commentary
Ex.: Daniel O. Conkle, Compromising on Abortion, 8 Const. Commentary 353 (1991). –Article Citation.

Daniel O. Conkle, Compromising on Abortion, 8 Const. Commentary 353, 354-55 (1991). –Page Citation.

Constitutional Law Journal (Seton Hall Law School)
Ab.: Const. L.J.

In law review footnotes, the titles of books and the names of cases, except for procedural phrases, are not underlined. See Bluebook rule 2.1(a) & (b). Further, the following are in large and small capitals: codes, restatements, standards, constitutions, periodicals, authors of books, titles of books, the abbreviated names of codes, most legislative materials except for bills and resolutions, codified ordinances, model codes, court rules, and sentencing guidelines. Refer to The Bluebook.

Ex.:   Ronald K. Chen, <u>Once More Into the Breach: Fact Versus Opinion Revisited After Mikovich v. Lorain Journal Co.</u>, 1 Const. L.J. 331 (1991).–Article Citation.

Ronald K. Chen, <u>Once More Into the Breach: Fact Versus Opinion Revisited After Mikovich v. Lorain Journal Co.</u>, 1 Const. L.J. 331, 340 (1991).–Page Citation.

<u>construed in</u>

Ex.:   Congressional Budget and Impoundment Control Act § 402, 31 U.S.C. § 1352 (1974), <u>construed in</u> Muskie, <u>Sunset Legislation: Restoring Public Confidence in Government</u>, 4 J. Legis. 11, 13 (1977).

See <u>Bluebook</u> rule 1.6(a)(iii) for proper use of <u>construed in</u>.

Consumer Credit Guide (Commerce Clearing House)

Ab.:   Consumer Cred. Guide (CCH)

Ex.:   <u>Lee v. Nationwide Cassel, L.P.</u>, 6 Consumer Cred. Guide (CCH) ¶ 95,260 (Ill. App. Ct. Dec. 22, 1995). –Citation to looseleaf material.

<u>Atkinson v. Gen. Elec. Credit Corp.</u>, [1980-1989 Decisions Transfer Binder] Consumer Cred. Guide (CCH) ¶ 95,809 (11th Cir. Feb. 21, 1989). –Citation to transfer binder material.

–The above examples are proper if the case is not yet available in, or is not reported in, an official or West reporter, a public domain citation, or in a widely used computer database.

Consumer Product Safety Guide (Commerce Clearing House)

Ab.:   Consumer Prod. Safety Guide (CCH)

Ex.:   <u>United States v. ILLCO Toy Co.</u>, 3 Consumer Prod. Safety Guide (CCH) ¶ 75,455 (S.D.N.Y. Jan. 17, 1991). –Citation to looseleaf material.

<u>United States v. Salem Carpet Mills, Inc.</u>, [1977-1979 Developments Transfer Binder] Consumer Prod. Safety Guide (CCH) ¶ 75,212 (N.D. Ga. 1978). –Citation to transfer binder material.

–The above examples are proper if the case is not yet available in, or is not reported in, an official or West reporter, a public domain citation, or in a widely used computer database.

<u>contra</u>

"<u>Contra</u>" is used when the "[c]ited authority directly states the contrary of the proposition. '<u>Contra</u>' is used where '[no signal]' would be used for support. " <u>Bluebook</u> rule 1.2(c).

In citing cases in law review footnotes, abbreviate any word listed in table T.6; the names of "states, countries, and other geographical units" unless they are named parties; and any other words of eight or more letters "if <u>substantial</u> space is thereby saved and the result is unambiguous." <u>Bluebook</u> rule 10.2.2. On the other hand, in citing cases in text, abbreviate only widely known acronyms and the following words: "&," "Ass'n," "Bros.," "Co.," "Corp.," "Inc.," "Ltd.," and "No." <u>Bluebook</u> rule 10.2.1(c).

Ex.: "... <u>Harman v. United States</u>, 199 F.2d 34, 36 (4th Cir. 1952) ("when the witness testified that the statement was true it became a part of his testimony, and not a mere matter of impeachment"). <u>Contra</u> <u>United States v. Check</u>, 582 F.2d 688, 680, 3 Fed. R. Evid. Serv. 685 (2d Cir. 1978) (the admission of prior consistent statements is error unless offered to rebut a charge of fabrication or improper motive)." –Taken from 946 F.2d 147, 153 (1st Cir. 1991).

Contract Appeals Decisions (bound as Board of Contract Appeals Decisions) (Commerce Clearing House)

Ab.: Cont. App. Dec. (CCH)

Ab.: B.C.A. (CCH) (bound)

Contracts and Conveyances of Real Property, by Milton R. Friedman

–Do not abbreviate the title.

Ex.: 1 Milton R. Friedman, <u>Contracts and Conveyances of Real Property</u> § 1.2(f) (6th ed. 1998). –Section Citation.

1 Milton R. Friedman, <u>Contracts and Conveyances of Real Property</u> § 1.2(f), at 108 (6th ed. 1998). –Page Citation.

1 Milton R. Friedman, <u>Contracts and Conveyances of Real Property</u> § 1.2(f), at 108 n.2 (6th ed. 1998). –Footnote Citation.

Contracts Cases, Federal

See Government Contracts Reports.

Conveyancer and Property Lawyer, The (new series)

Ab.: Conv. & Prop. Law. (n.s.)

Ex.: Alan Prichard, <u>New Jurisdictions for Rent Assessment Committees?</u>, 1991 Conv. & Prop. Law. (n.s.) 447. –Article Citation.

Alan Prichard, <u>New Jurisdictions for Rent Assessment Committees?</u>, 1991 Conv. & Prop. Law. (n.s.) 447, 448-49. –Page Citation.

Cooley Law Review

Ab.: Cooley L. Rev.

Ex.: Timothy A. Boughman, <u>Michigan's "Uncommon Law" of Homicide</u>, 7 Cooley L. Rev. 1 (1990). –Article Citation.

Timothy A. Boughman, <u>Michigan's "Uncommon Law" of Homicide</u>, 7 Cooley L. Rev. 1, 15-17 (1990). –Page Citation.

–In 1991 this publication changed its name to Thomas M. Cooley Law Review.

Cooper's Tennessee Chancery Reports

Ab.: Coop. Tenn. Ch.

Copyright, by Paul Goldstein

–Do not abbreviate the title.

In law review footnotes, the titles of books and the names of cases, except for procedural phrases, are not underlined. <u>See</u> <u>Bluebook</u> rule 2.1(a) & (b). Further, the following are in large and small capitals: codes, restatements, standards, constitutions, periodicals, authors of books, titles of books, the abbreviated names of codes, most legislative materials except for bills and resolutions, codified ordinances, model codes, court rules, and sentencing guidelines. Refer to <u>The Bluebook</u>.

Ex.:   2 Paul Goldstein, <u>Copyright</u> § 11.4.2.2 (2d ed. 1996). –Section Citation.

2 Paul Goldstein, <u>Copyright</u> § 11.4.2.2, at 11:61 (2d ed. 1996). –Page Citation.

2 Paul Goldstein, <u>Copyright</u> § 11.4.2.2, at 11:61 n.58 (2d ed. 1996). –Footnote Citation.

Copyright Decisions (1909-1985) (U.S.)

Ab.:   Copy. Dec.

Ex.:   <u>Jackson v. Stone & Simon Adver., Inc.</u>, 40 Copy. Dec. 693 (E.D. Mich. 1974).

Copyright Law Decisions (Commerce Clearing House)

Ab.:   Copyright L. Dec. (CCH)

Ex.:   <u>Rano v. Sipa Press, Inc.</u>, 1992-1994 Copyright L. Dec. (CCH) ¶ 27,067 (9th Cir. Mar. 2, 1993). –Citation to bound material.

–This example is proper if the case is not yet available in, or is not reported in, an official or West reporter, a public domain citation, or in a widely used computer database.

Copyright Law Reporter (Commerce Clearing House)

Ab.:   Copyright L. Rep. (CCH)

Ex.:   <u>Adler v. World Bazaars, Inc.</u>, 2 Copyright L. Rep. (CCH) ¶ 27,524 (S.D.N.Y. Aug. 16, 1995). –Citation to looseleaf material.

<u>Pillsbury Co. v. Milky Way Prods.</u>, 1978-1981 Copyright L. Dec. (CCH) ¶ 25,139 (N.D. Ga. 1978). –Citation to bound material.

–The above examples are proper if the case is not yet available in an official or West reporter, or is not reported in an official or West reporter.

Copyright Law Symposium (American Society of Composers, Authors, & Publishers)

Ab.:   Copyright L. Symp. (ASCAP)

Ex.:   Jack B. Hicks, <u>Copyright and Computer Databases: Is Traditional Compilation Law Adequate?</u>, 37 Copyright L. Symp. (ASCAP) 85 (1990). –Article Citation.

Jack B. Hicks, <u>Copyright and Computer Databases: Is Traditional Compilation Law Adequate?</u>, 37 Copyright L. Symp. (ASCAP) 85, 87-89 (1990). –Page Citation.

Corbin on Contracts, by Arthur Linton Corbin

–Do not abbreviate the title.

In citing cases in law review footnotes, abbreviate any word listed in table T.6; the names of "states, countries, and other geographical units" unless they are named parties; and any other words of eight or more letters "if <u>substantial</u> space is thereby saved and the result is unambiguous." <u>Bluebook</u> rule 10.2.2. On the other hand, in citing cases in text, abbreviate only widely known acronyms and the following words: "&," "Ass'n," "Bros.," "Co.," "Corp.," "Inc.," "Ltd.," and "No." <u>Bluebook</u> rule 10.2.1(c).

Ex.:   3A Arthur Linton Corbin, <u>Corbin on Contracts</u> § 644, at 81 (1960).
        –Page Citation.

        6A Arthur Linton Corbin, <u>Corbin on Contracts</u> § 1375 (1962).
        –Section Citation.

        3 Eric Mills Holmes, <u>Corbin on Contracts</u> § 9.20 (Joseph M. Perillo
        ed., rev. ed. 1996). –Section Citation to Revised Edition.

        3 Eric Mills Holmes, <u>Corbin on Contracts</u> § 9.20, at 299 (Joseph M.
        Perillo ed., rev. ed. 1996). –Page Citation to Revised Edition.

        5 Margaret N. Kniffen, <u>Corbin on Contracts</u>, § 24.5 (Joseph M. Perillo
        ed., rev. ed. 1998). –Section Citation.

        13 John E. Murray, Jr. & Timothy Murray, <u>Corbin on Contracts</u> § 70.2,
        at 12 (Cum. Supp. Spring 2005). –Supplement Citation.

Cornell International Law Journal
Ab.:   Cornell Int'l L.J.

Ex.:   Michael E. Solimine, <u>Forum-Selection Clauses and the Privatization of
        Procedure</u>, 25 Cornell Int'l L.J. 51 (1992). –Article Citation.

        Michael E. Solimine, <u>Forum-Selection Clauses and the Privatization of
        Procedure</u>, 25 Cornell Int'l L.J. 51, 77 (1992). –Page Citation.

Cornell Law Review
Ab.:   Cornell L. Rev.

Ex.:   Dennis Patterson, <u>Postmodernism/Feminism/Law</u>, 77 Cornell L. Rev.
        254 (1992). –Article Citation.

        Dennis Patterson, <u>Postmodernism/Feminism/Law</u>, 77 Cornell L. Rev.
        254, 262-67 (1992). –Page Citation.

Corporate Counsel Weekly (Bureau of National Affairs)
Ab.:   Corp. Couns. Wkly. (BNA)

Corporate Income Taxation, by Douglas A. Kahn and Jeffrey S. Lehman
        –Do not abbreviate the title.

Ex.:   Douglas A. Kahn & Jeffrey S. Lehman, <u>Corporate Income Taxation</u> §
        6.19.4 (5th ed. 2001). –Section Citation.

        Douglas A. Kahn & Jeffrey S. Lehman, <u>Corporate Income Taxation</u> §
        6.19.4, at 550 (5th ed. 2001). –Page Citation.

Corporate Law and Practice, by Larry D. Soderquist, Linda O. Smiddy, A.A. Sommer, Jr. and Pat K. Chew
        –Do not abbreviate the title.

Ex.:   Larry D. Soderquist et. al, <u>Corporate Law and Practice</u> § 2.2.4 (2d ed.
        1999). –Section Citation.

        Larry D. Soderquist et. al, <u>Corporate Law and Practice</u> § 2.2.4, at 23
        (2d ed. 1999). –Page Citation.

In law review footnotes, the titles of books and the names of cases, except for procedural
phrases, are not underlined. <u>See</u> <u>Bluebook</u> rule 2.1(a) & (b). Further, the following are in
large and small capitals: codes, restatements, standards, constitutions, periodicals, authors of
books, titles of books, the abbreviated names of codes, most legislative materials except for
bills and resolutions, codified ordinances, model codes, court rules, and sentencing guidelines.
Refer to <u>The Bluebook</u>.

Larry D. Soderquist et. al, <u>Corporate Law and Practice</u> § 2.2.4, at 23 n.29 (2d ed. 1999). –Footnote Citation.

Corporate Law of Banks, The, by Michael P. Malloy
    –Do not abbreviate the title.

    Ex.:   2 Michael P. Malloy, <u>The Corporate Law of Banks</u> § 8.2.5 (1988). –Section Citation.

           2 Michael P. Malloy, <u>The Corporate Law of Banks</u> § 8.2.5, at 741 (1988). –Page Citation.

           2 Michael P. Malloy, <u>The Corporate Law of Banks</u> § 8.2.5, at 741 n.104 (1988). –Footnote Citation.

Corporate Secretary's Guide (Commerce Clearing House)
    Ab.:   Corp. Secretary's Guide (CCH)

    Ex.:   <u>Study Paints Favorable Picture of Corporate Boards</u>, 3 Corp. Secretary's Guide (CCH) ¶ 48,017 (May 1988). –Citation to unsigned looseleaf commentary.

Corpus Juris Secundum
    Ab.:   C.J.S.

    Ex.:   47A C.J.S. <u>Internal Revenue</u> § 68 (2000).

           44 C.J.S. <u>Insurance</u> § 9 (Supp. 2000). –Supplement Citation.

           77 C.J.S. <u>Insurance</u> § 33, at 104 n.34.5 (Supp. 2000). –Footnote Citation.

Cost Accounting Standards Guide (Commerce Clearing House)
    Ab.:   Cost Accounting Stand. Guide (CCH)

Couch on Insurance, by Lee R. Russ & Thomas F. Segalla
    –Do not abbreviate the title.

    Ex.:   14 Lee R. Russ & Thomas F. Segalla, <u>Couch on Insurance</u> § 199:4 (3d ed. 1999). –Section Citation.

           14 Lee R. Russ & Thomas F. Segalla, <u>Couch on Insurance</u> § 199:4, at 199-13 (3d ed. 1999). –Page Citation.

           14 Lee R. Russ & Thomas F. Segalla, <u>Couch on Insurance</u> § 199:4, at 199-13 n.14 (3d ed. 1999). –Footnote Citation.

Counterclaim, citation to

    Ab.:   Countercl.

    Ex.:   (Countercl. ¶ 4).

<u>See</u> <u>Bluebook</u> rule B10 and table BT.1

Note: See <u>Bluebook</u> rule 10.8.3 for citing litigation materials from another case.

County Court
    Ab.:   [name of county] County Ct.

In citing cases in law review footnotes, abbreviate any word listed in table T.6; the names of "states, countries, and other geographical units" unless they are named parties; and any other words of eight or more letters "if <u>substantial</u> space is thereby saved and the result is unambiguous." <u>Bluebook</u> rule 10.2.2. On the other hand, in citing cases in text, abbreviate only widely known acronyms and the following words: "&," "Ass'n," "Bros.," "Co.," "Corp.," "Inc.," "Ltd.," and "No." <u>Bluebook</u> rule 10.2.1(c).

Court Administrative Orders
See Bluebook rule 14.8

Court Management Journal
Ab.:   Ct. Mgmt. J.

Court Martial Reports (1951-1975) (U.S.)
Ab.:   C.M.R.
Ex.:   United States v. Burwell, 50 C.M.R. 192 (1975). –Case Citation.
          United States v. Burwell, 50 C.M.R. 192, 193 (1975). –Page Citation.

Court of Appeal (England)
Ab.:   C.A.

Court of Appeal(s) (state)
Ab.:   Ct. App.

Court of Appeal for East Africa Digest of Decisions of the Court
Ab.:   E. Afr. Ct. App. Dig.

See Bluebook rule 21.5.5 and table T.3.

Court of Appeals (federal)
Ab.:   Cir.

Court of Claims
Ab.:   Ct. Cl.
          –Succeeded in 1982 by the United States Claims Court (Cl. Ct.).
          –Cite to Federal Reporter series or Federal Supplement series, if
            therein; otherwise to Court of Claims Reports.

Court of Claims Reports
Ab.:   Ct. Cl.
          –Cite to Federal Reporter series or Federal Supplement series, if
            therein; otherwise, cite to the Reports as follows:
Ex.:   Kay Mfg. v. United States, 230 Ct. Cl. 83 (1982).
          –After 231 Ct. Cl. 105 (1982), title became Claims Court Reporter (Cl.
            Ct.).

Court of Claims Rules (rules of the Court of Claims of the United States)
Ab.:   Ct. Cl. R.
Ex.:   Ct. Cl. R. 176.

Court of Criminal Appeals
Ab.:   Crim. App.

Court of Customs and Patent Appeals Reports
Ab.:   C.C.P.A.
          –Cite to Federal Reporter Series, if therein; otherwise, cite as follows:

In law review footnotes, the titles of books and the names of cases, except for procedural
phrases, are not underlined. See Bluebook rule 2.1(a) & (b). Further, the following are in
large and small capitals: codes, restatements, standards, constitutions, periodicals, authors of
books, titles of books, the abbreviated names of codes, most legislative materials except for
bills and resolutions, codified ordinances, model codes, court rules, and sentencing guidelines.
Refer to The Bluebook.

Ex.: Krupp Int'l, Inc. v. United States Int'l Trade Comm'n, 67 C.C.P.A. 166 (1980).

Court of Customs Appeals
Ab.: Ct. Cust. App.

Court of Customs Appeals Reports
Ab.: Ct. Cust.
–Cite to Federal Reporter Series, if therein; otherwise, cite as follows:
Ex.: Wells Fargo & Co. v. United States, 7 Ct. Cust. 346 (1916).
–Becomes C.C.P.A after volume 16.

Court of Errors and Appeals
Ab.: Ct. Err. & App.

Court of International Trade Reports
Ab.: Ct. Int'l Trade
Ex.: Torrington Co. v. United States, 21 Ct. Int'l Trade 491 (1997).

**Court of Justice of the European Communities
(Common Market cases)**
Ab.: E.C.J (court)
E.C.R. (Reports)
Ex.: Case C-158/96, Kohll v. Union des Caisses d Maladie,
1998 E.C.R. I-1931, ¶ 33. –Case before the Court after 1989.
See Bluebook rule 21.5.2 and table T.3.

Court of Military Appeals
Ab.: C.M.A.

Court of Military Review
Ab.: C.M.R.

Court of [General, Special] Sessions
Ab.: Ct. Gen. Sess.
Ct. Spec. Sess.

Court rules (Federal and State)
See Rules of Evidence and Procedure.

Courts, Health Science and the Law
Ab.: Cts. Health Sci. & L.
Ex.: David Rosenberg, Damage Scheduling in Mass Exposure Cases, 1 Cts. Health Sci. & L. 335 (1991).–Article Citation.
David Rosenberg, Damage Scheduling in Mass Exposure Cases, 1 Cts. Health Sci. & L. 335, 343-45 (1991).–Page Citation.

Cranch (United States Reports)
See United States Reports.

In citing cases in law review footnotes, abbreviate any word listed in table T.6; the names of "states, countries, and other geographical units" unless they are named parties; and any other words of eight or more letters "if substantial space is thereby saved and the result is unambiguous." Bluebook rule 10.2.2. On the other hand, in citing cases in text, abbreviate only widely known acronyms and the following words: "&," "Ass'n," "Bros.," "Co.," "Corp.," "Inc.," "Ltd.," and "No." Bluebook rule 10.2.1(c).

Creighton Law Review
  Ab.: Creighton L. Rev.

  Ex.: Wayne A. Kalkwarf, <u>The Jurisdictional Dilemma in Reopening Social Security Decisions</u>, 23 Creighton L. Rev. 545 (1990). –Article Citation.

  Wayne A. Kalkwarf, <u>The Jurisdictional Dilemma in Reopening Social Security Decisions</u>, 23 Creighton L. Rev. 545, 551-53 (1990). –Page Citation.

Crime and Delinquency
  Ab.: Crime & Delinq.

  Ex.: Barry C. Feld, <u>The Punitive Juvenile Court and the Quality of Procedural Justice: Distinctions Between Rhetoric and Reality</u>, 36 Crime & Delinq. 443 (1990). –Article Citation.

  Barry C. Feld, <u>The Punitive Juvenile Court and the Quality of Procedural Justice: Distinctions Between Rhetoric and Reality</u>, 36 Crime & Delinq. 443, 459-62 (1990). –Page Citation.

Crime and Justice
  Ab.: Crime & Just.

  Ex.: Jack Katz, <u>The Motivation of the Persistent Robber</u>, Crime & Just., 1991, at 277. –Article Citation.

  Jack Katz, <u>The Motivation of the Persistent Robber</u>, Crime & Just., 1991, at 277, 289-91. –Page Citation.

Criminal Appeals Reports (Eng.) (1908-date)
  See <u>Bluebook</u> table T.2.

  Ab.: Crim. App. R.

  Ex.: <u>Cruttenden</u>, 93 Crim. App. R. 119 (1991) (Eng.). –Case Citation.

  <u>Sheldrake v. Dir. of Pub. Prosecutions</u>, [2005] UKHL 43, [2005] 1 Cr. App. R. 28 (Eng.). –Case with neutral citation.

Criminal Law, by Paul H. Robinson
  –Do not abbreviate the title.

  Ex.: Paul H. Robinson, <u>Criminal Law</u> § 6.4, (1997). –Section Citation.

  Paul H. Robinson, <u>Criminal Law</u> § 6.4, at 357 (1997). –Page Citation.

Criminal Law Bulletin
  Ab.: Crim. L. Bull.

  Ex.: Richard A. Powers III, <u>Anticipatory Search Warrants: Future Probable Cause</u>, 28 Crim. L. Bull. 59 (1992). –Article Citation.

  Richard A. Powers III, <u>Anticipatory Search Warrants: Future Probable Cause</u>, 28 Crim. L. Bull. 59, 61-63 (1992). –Page Citation.

In law review footnotes, the titles of books and the names of cases, except for procedural phrases, are not underlined. <u>See</u> <u>Bluebook</u> rule 2.1(a) & (b). Further, the following are in large and small capitals: codes, restatements, standards, constitutions, periodicals, authors of books, titles of books, the abbreviated names of codes, most legislative materials except for bills and resolutions, codified ordinances, model codes, court rules, and sentencing guidelines. Refer to <u>The Bluebook</u>.

Criminal Law Forum
Ab.: Crim. L.F.

Ex.: Friedrich-Christian Schroeder, The Rise and Fall of the Criminal Law of the German Democratic Republic, 2 Crim. L.F. 217 (1991). –Article Citation.

Friedrich-Christian Schroeder, The Rise and Fall of the Criminal Law of the German Democratic Republic, 2 Crim. L.F. 217, 222-24 (1991). –Page Citation.

Criminal Law Reporter (Bureau of National Affairs)
Ab.: Crim. L. Rep. (BNA)

Ex.: Albernaz v. U.S., [General] Crim. L. Rep. (BNA) 1015 (U.S. Sept. 23, 1996). –Citation to looseleaf material.

Batson v. Kentucky, 59 Crim. L. Rep. (BNA) 1007 (U.S. 1986). –Citation to bound material.

–The above examples are proper if the case is not yet available in, or is not reported in, an official or West reporter, a public domain citation, or in a widely used computer database.

Criminal Law Review, The
Ab.: Crim. L. Rev.

Ex.: C.J. Miller, Some Problems of Contempt, 1992 Crim. L. Rev. 107. –Article Citation.

C.J. Miller, Some Problems of Contempt, 1992 Crim. L. Rev. 107, 110-11. –Page Citation.

Criminal Procedure, by Wayne R. LaFave, Jerold H. Israel, and Nancy J. King
–Do not abbreviate the title.

Ex.: Wayne R. LaFave, Jerold H. Israel, & Nancy J. King, Criminal Procedure § 11.9 (3d ed. 2000). –Section Citation.

Wayne R. LaFave, Jerold H. Israel, & Nancy J. King, Criminal Procedure § 11.9, at 624 (3d ed. 2000). –Page Citation.

Wayne R. LaFave, Jerold H. Israel, & Nancy J. King, Criminal Procedure § 11.9, at 624 n.17 (3d ed. 2000). –Footnote Citation.

Cross-claim, citation to
Ab.: Cross-cl.

Ex.: (Cross-cl. ¶ 13).

See Bluebook rule B10 and table BT.1.

Note: See Bluebook rule 10.8.3 for citing litigation materials from another case.

Cumberland Law Review
Ab.: Cumb. L. Rev.

In citing cases in law review footnotes, abbreviate any word listed in table T.6; the names of "states, countries, and other geographical units" unless they are named parties; and any other words of eight or more letters "if substantial space is thereby saved and the result is unambiguous." Bluebook rule 10.2.2. On the other hand, in citing cases in text, abbreviate only widely known acronyms and the following words: "&," "Ass'n," "Bros.," "Co.," "Corp.," "Inc.," "Ltd.," and "No." Bluebook rule 10.2.1(c).

Ex.: Andrew W. Austin, <u>Faith and the Constitutional Definition of Religion</u>, 22 Cumb. L. Rev. 1 (1991). –Article Citation.

Andrew W. Austin, <u>Faith and the Constitutional Definition of Religion</u>, 22 Cumb. L. Rev. 1, 17-19 (1991). –Page Citation.

Cumulative Bulletin (U.S.) (1919-date)

Ab.: C.B.

Ex.: (1919-1921) T.B.R. 39, 1 C.B. 45 (1919). –Citation to volumes of the Cumulative Bulletin from 1919-1921 are by volume number.

(1921-1936) I.T. 2258, 5-1 C.B. 10 (1926). –Citation to volumes of the Cumulative Bulletin from 1921-1936 are by volume and part numbers.

(1937-date) Rev. Rul. 95-44, 1995-1 C.B. 3. –Citation to volumes of the Cumulative Bulletin from 1937 to date are by year and part numbers.

Rev. Rul. 82-4, 1982-1 I.R.B. 14. –Citation to the material found in the Cumulative Bulletin before a bound volume is issued is to the Internal Revenue Bulletin.

Current Legal Problems

Ab.: Current Legal Probs.

C.L.P. [U.K.]

Ex.: James J. Fawcett, <u>The Interrelationship of Jurisdiction and Choice of Law in Private International Law</u>, 1991 Current Legal Probs. 39. –Article Citation.

James J. Fawcett, <u>The Interrelationship of Jurisdiction and Choice of Law in Private International Law</u>, 1991 Current Legal Probs. 39, 49. –Page Citation.

Customs Bulletin and Decisions (U.S.) (1967-date)

Ab.: Cust. B. & Dec.

Ex.: T.D. 67-1, 1 Cust. B. & Dec. 1 (1967).

C.S.D. 79-4, 13 Cust. B. & Dec. 998 (1978).

T.D. 96-64, 30 Cust. B. & Dec. No. 37/38, at 1 (Aug. 17, 1996). –Citation to current, unbound material.

Customs Court Reports (1938-1980)

Ab.: Cust. Ct.

–Cite to Federal Reporter series or Federal Supplement series, if therein; otherwise, cite to the Reports as follows:

Ex.: <u>T.D. Downing Co. v. United States</u>, 60 Cust. Ct. 345 (1968). –Case Citation.

<u>T.D. Downing Co. v. United States</u>, 60 Cust. Ct. 345, 347 (1968). –Page Citation.

In law review footnotes, the titles of books and the names of cases, except for procedural phrases, are not underlined. <u>See</u> <u>Bluebook</u> rule 2.1(a) & (b). Further, the following are in large and small capitals: codes, restatements, standards, constitutions, periodicals, authors of books, titles of books, the abbreviated names of codes, most legislative materials except for bills and resolutions, codified ordinances, model codes, court rules, and sentencing guidelines. Refer to <u>The Bluebook</u>.

Customs Court Rules (rules of the United States Customs Court)
    Ab.:   Cust. Ct. R.

    Ex.:   Cust. Ct. R. 11.1.

Cyclopedia of Trial Practice, by Syndey C. Schweitzer
          –Do not abbreviate the title.

    Ex.:   4 Sydney C. Schweitzer, <u>Cyclopedia of Trial Practice</u> § 731 (3d ed. 1985). –Section Citation.

          4 Sydney C. Schweitzer, <u>Cyclopedia of Trial Practice</u> § 731, at 499 (3d ed. 1985). –Page Citation.

          4 Sydney C. Schweitzer, <u>Cyclopedia of Trial Practice</u> § 731, at 499 n.2 (3d ed. 1985). –Footnote Citation.

          4 Sydney C. Schweitzer, <u>Cyclopedia of Trial Practice</u> § 740 (3d ed. Supp. 1995). –Section Citation to Supplement.

In citing cases in law review footnotes, abbreviate any word listed in table T.6; the names of "states, countries, and other geographical units" unless they are named parties; and any other words of eight or more letters "if <u>substantial</u> space is thereby saved and the result is unambiguous." <u>Bluebook</u> rule 10.2.2. On the other hand, in citing cases in text, abbreviate only widely known acronyms and the following words: "&," "Ass'n," "Bros.," "Co.," "Corp.," "Inc.," "Ltd.," and "No." <u>Bluebook</u> rule 10.2.1(c).

D

Dalhousie Law Journal
  Ab.:   Dalhousie L.J.
  Ex.:   Dawn Russell, <u>Paedophilia: The Criminal Responsibility of Canada's Churches</u>, 15 Dalhousie L.J. 380 (1992). –Article Citation.
            Dawn Russell, <u>Paedophilia: The Criminal Responsibility of Canada's Churches</u>, 15 Dalhousie L.J. 380, 389-93 (1992). –Page Citation.

Dallas (United States Reports)
  See United States Reports.

Dalloz (France)
  See Recueil Dalloz.

Debates, Congressional
  See Congressional Debates.

Decisiones de Puerto Rico
  Ab.:   P.R. Dec.

Decisioni del Tribunale Federale Suisse (Switzerland)
  Ab.:   DTF

Constitutional cases	DTF I
Administrative and	
international law cases	DTF II
Civil and Bankruptcy cases	DTF III
Criminal cases	DTF IV
Social security cases	DTF V

  <u>See</u> <u>Bluebook</u> table T.2 p. 314.

Decisions and Orders of the National Labor Relations Board (U.S.) (1935-date)
  Ab.:   N.L.R.B.
  Ex.:   <u>Maramount Corp.</u>, 317 N.L.R.B. 1035 (1995). –Citation to official reporter.
            <u>Wis. Steel Indus., Inc.</u>, 321 N.L.R.B. No. 175 (Aug. 27, 1996). –Slip opinion.
            <u>Alanis Airport Serv., Inc.</u>, 316 N.L.R.B. No 185, [5 Labor Relations] Lab. L. Rep. (CCH) (1995-1996 NLRB Dec.) ¶ 15,769 (April 14, 1995). –Slip opinion when reported in looseleaf unofficial case service.

In law review footnotes, the titles of books and the names of cases, except for procedural phrases, are not underlined. <u>See</u> <u>Bluebook</u> rule 2.1(a) & (b). Further, the following are in large and small capitals: codes, restatements, standards, constitutions, periodicals, authors of books, titles of books, the abbreviated names of codes, most legislative materials except for bills and resolutions, codified ordinances, model codes, court rules, and sentencing guidelines. Refer to <u>The Bluebook</u>.

Inland Container Corp., 275 N.L.R.B. No. 60, 1985-1986 NLRB Dec. (CCH) ¶ 17,343 (May 7, 1985). –Slip opinion when reported in bound unofficial case service.

Decisions of the Commissioner of Patents (1869-1968)
Ab.:   Dec. Comm'r Pat.

Decisions of the Comptroller General of the United States (1921-1994)
Ab.:   Comp. Gen.

Ex.:   In re Ostrom Painting & Sandblasting, Inc., 72 Comp. Gen. 207 (1993).
Decision of the Comptroller General B-261166 (July 18, 1995). –Citation to unpublished decisions. (Note: Unpublished decisions in the Digest of the Comptroller General of the United States ceased publication July-Sept. 1995).

Decisions of the Employees' Compensation Appeals Board (1946-date)
Ab.:   Emp. Comp. App. Bd.

Ex.:   In re Zerega, 45 Empl. Comp. App. Bd. 860 (1994).

Decisions of the Federal Labor Relations Authority (1979-date)
Ab.:   F.L.R.A.

Ex.:   Overseas Educ. Ass'n, 51 F.L.R.A. 1246 (1996). –Case Citation.
Overseas Educ. Ass'n, 51 F.L.R.A. 1246, 1251 (1996). –Page Citation.

Decisions of the Federal Maritime Commission
Ab.:   F.M.C.

Ex.:   Proctor & Schwartz, Inc., 24 F.M.C. 133 (1982). –Case Citation.

Decisions of the Judicial Committee of the Privy Council re the British North American Act, 1867, and the Canadian Constitution (Canada)
Ab.:   Olms.

Decisions of the United States Department of the Interior (1881-date)
Ab.:   Pub. Lands Dec. –Citation for vols. 1-52.
Interior Dec. –Citation for vol. 53 onward.

Ex.:   Union Pacific Ry. Co., 25 Pub. Lands Dec. 540 (1897).
Amoco Prod. Co., 101 Interior Dec. 39 (1994).

Decisions of the United States Maritime Commission (U.S.) (1919-1947)
Ab.:   Dec. U.S. Mar. Comm'n

In citing cases in law review footnotes, abbreviate any word listed in table T.6; the names of "states, countries, and other geographical units" unless they are named parties; and any other words of eight or more letters "if substantial space is thereby saved and the result is unambiguous." Bluebook rule 10.2.2. On the other hand, in citing cases in text, abbreviate only widely known acronyms and the following words: "&," "Ass'n," "Bros.," "Co.," "Corp.," "Inc.," "Ltd.," and "No." Bluebook rule 10.2.1(c).

Ex.:   Acme Novelty Co., 2 Dec. U.S. Mar. Comm'n 412 (1940).

Dedication (article designation)
Ex.:   Ellen P. Goodman, Dedication, Tender Justice: Judge Norma Levy Shapiro's Hard-Headed Humanity, 152 U. Pa. L. Rev. 25 (2003).

–See Bluebook rule 16.6.4.

Deering's California Advance Legislative Service (LexisNexis)
Ab.:   year-pamph. no. Cal. Adv. Legis. Serv. page no. (Deering)

Ex.:   Act of Aug. 30, 2005, ch. 150, sec. 5, § 125050, 2005-6 Cal. Adv. Legis. Serv. 190 (Deering) (concerning the Public Utilities Code).

–Citation to a section of a session law amending prior act.

–See Bluebook rule 12.4.

–"Cite to Cal Stat., if therein." Bluebook table T.1, p. 201.

Deering's California Codes Annotated
Ab.:   Cal. [subject] Code § (Deering year)

See Bluebook table T.1, pp. 192-93, for the abbreviation of each subject.

Ex.:   Cal. Corp. Code § 317 (Deering Supp. 2004).

–"Cite to either the West or the Deering subject-matter code, if therein." Bluebook table T.1, p. 201.

Defense Counsel Journal
Ab.:   Def. Couns. J.

Ex.:   Harry Downs, Strategic Management of Complex Litigation: Reaching Objectives, 59 Def. Couns. J. 86 (1992). –Article Citation.

Harry Downs, Strategic Management of Complex Litigation: Reaching Objectives, 59 Def. Couns. J. 86, 90-91 (1992). –Page Citation.

Defense Law Journal
Ab.:   Def. L.J.

Ex.:   Kent D. Syverud, The Duty to Settle, 40 Def. L.J. 155 (1991).
–Article Citation.

Kent D. Syverud, The Duty to Settle, 40 Def. L.J. 155, 161-65 (1991).
–Page Citation.

Delaware
Ab.:   Del.

Delaware Chancery Reports
Ab.:   Del. Ch.

–Discontinued after 43 Del. Ch. 534 (1968).

In law review footnotes, the titles of books and the names of cases, except for procedural phrases, are not underlined. See Bluebook rule 2.1(a) & (b). Further, the following are in large and small capitals: codes, restatements, standards, constitutions, periodicals, authors of books, titles of books, the abbreviated names of codes, most legislative materials except for bills and resolutions, codified ordinances, model codes, court rules, and sentencing guidelines. Refer to The Bluebook.

–Cite to A. or A.2d, if therein; otherwise, cite to Del. Ch.

–Parallel citations are not required either in documents submitted to Delaware state courts or in any other documents. See Bluebook rules 10.3.1 and B5.1.3; see also Del. Ch. Ct. R. 171(g), Del. Sup. Ct. R. 14(g), Del. Super. Ct. Civ. R. 107(c)(4), Del. Ct. C.P. Civ. R. 107(c)(4), and Del. Fam. Ct. Civ. R. 107(c)(5).

In documents submitted to Delaware Chancery Court, Court of Common Pleas, and Family Court, cite as follows:

> Mayer v. Mayer, Del. Ch., 132 A.2d 617 (1957). –Case Citation.
>
> Mayer v. Mayer, Del. Ch., 132 A.2d 617, 619 (1957). –Page Citation.

In all other documents, cite as follows:

> Mayer v. Mayer, 132 A.2d 617 (Del. Ch. 1957). –Case Citation.
>
> Mayer v. Mayer, 132 A.2d 617, 619 (Del. Ch. 1957). –Page Citation.

Delaware Code Annotated (LexisNexis)

Ab.:   Del. Code Ann. tit.   , §   (year)

Ex.:   Del. Code Ann. tit. 18, § 314 (2001).

–For proper citation form in papers submitted to Delaware courts, see Del. Code Ann. tit. 1 § 101(b) (2001).

Delaware Code Annotated Advance Legislative Service (LexisNexis)

Ab.:   year-pamph. Del. Code Ann. Adv. Legis. Serv. page no. (LexisNexis)

Ex.:   Act of July 19, 2004, ch. 376, 2004-3 Del. Code Ann. Adv. Legis. Serv. 35 (LexisNexis). –Citation to an entire session law.

Act of July 19, 2004, ch. 376, sec. 4, § 2603, 2004-3 Del. Code Ann. Adv. Legis. Serv. 35, 36 (LexisNexis). –Citation to a section of a session law amending prior act.

–See Bluebook rule 12.4.

–"Cite to Del. Laws, if therein." Bluebook table T.1, p. 204.

Delaware Constitution

Ab.:   Del. Const. art.   , §   .

Ex.:   Del. Const. art. II, § 3. –"Cite constitutional provisions currently in force without a date." Bluebook rule 11.

Del. Const. art. IV, § 25 repealed by 51 Del. Laws, c. 78. –"If the cited provision has been repealed, either indicate parenthetically the fact and date of repeal or cite the repealing provision in full." Bluebook rule 11.

In citing cases in law review footnotes, abbreviate any word listed in table T.6; the names of "states, countries, and other geographical units" unless they are named parties; and any other words of eight or more letters "if substantial space is thereby saved and the result is unambiguous." Bluebook rule 10.2.2. On the other hand, in citing cases in text, abbreviate only widely known acronyms and the following words: "&," "Ass'n," "Bros.," "Co.," "Corp.," "Inc.," "Ltd.," and "No." Bluebook rule 10.2.1(c).

Del. Const. art. I, § 20 (amended 1986). –"When citing a provision that has been subsequently amended, either indicate parenthetically the fact and date of amendment or cite the amending provision in full." Bluebook rule 11.

Del. Const. of 1792, art. I, § 19. –"Cite constitutions that have been totally superseded by year of adoption; if the specific provision cited was adopted in a different year, give that year parenthetically." Bluebook rule 11.

Delaware Government Register (Weil)
Ab.:   issue no. Del. Gov't Reg. page no. (Weil month year)

Delaware Journal of Corporate Law
Ab.:   Del. J. Corp. L.

Ex.:   Lyman Johnson, Sovereignty Over Corporate Stock, 16 Del. J. Corp. L. 485 (1991). –Article Citation.

Lyman Johnson, Sovereignty Over Corporate Stock, 16 Del. J. Corp. L. 485. 490 (1991). –Page Citation.

Delaware Law Review
Ab: Del. L. Rev.

Ex: E. Norman Veasey, Musings From the Center of the Corporate Universe, 7 Del. L. Rev. 163 (2004). –Article Citation.

E. Norman Veasey, Musings From the Center of the Corporate Universe, 7 Del. L. Rev. 163, 172 (2004). –Page Citation.

Delaware Lawyer
Ab.:   Del. Law.

Ex.:   William Pricket, Scull & Heap, Del. Law., Fall 1991, at 31. –Article Citation.

William Pricket, Scull & Heap, Del. Law., Fall 1991, at 31, 31-32. –Page Citation.

Delaware Register of Regulations
Ab.:   vol. no. Del. Reg. Regs. page no. (month day, year)

Ex.:   9 Del. Reg. Regs. 17 (Aug. 1, 2004)

Delaware Reports (1920-1966)
Ab.:   Del.

–Discontinued after 59 Del. 302 (1966).

–Cite to A. or A.2d, if therein; otherwise, cite to Del.

In law review footnotes, the titles of books and the names of cases, except for procedural phrases, are not underlined. See Bluebook rule 2.1(a) & (b). Further, the following are in large and small capitals: codes, restatements, standards, constitutions, periodicals, authors of books, titles of books, the abbreviated names of codes, most legislative materials except for bills and resolutions, codified ordinances, model codes, court rules, and sentencing guidelines. Refer to The Bluebook.

–Parallel citations are not required either in documents submitted to Delaware state courts or in any other document. See Bluebook rules 10.3.1 and B5.1.3; see also Del. Ch. Ct. R. 171(g), Del. Sup. Ct. R. 14(g), Del. Super. Ct. Civ. R. 107(c)(4), Del. Ct. C.P. Civ. R. 107(c)(4), and Del. Fam. Ct. Civ. R. 107(c)(5).

In documents submitted to Delaware Chancery Court, Court of Common Pleas, and Family Court, cite as follows:

Carey v. Bryan & Rollins, Del. Supr., 105 A.2d 201 (1954). –Case Citation.

Carey v. Bryan & Rollins, Del. Supr., 105 A.2d 201, 202 (1954). –Page Citation.

In all other documents, cite as follows:

Carey v. Bryan & Rollins, 105 A.2d 201 (Del. 1954). –Case Citation.

Carey v. Bryan & Rollins, 105 A.2d 201, 202 (Del. 1954). –Page Citation.

Delaware Session Laws
See Laws of Delaware.

Denver Journal of International Law and Policy
Ab.:   Denv. J. Int'l L. & Pol'y

Ex.:   Kevin Ryan, Rights, Intervention, and Self-Determination, 20 Denv. J. Int'l L. & Pol'y 55 (1991). –Article Citation.

Kevin Ryan, Rights, Intervention, and Self-Determination, 20 Denv. J. Int'l L. & Pol'y 55, 61-66 (1991). –Page Citation.

Denver Law Journal
Ab.:   Denv. L.J.

Ex.:   John A. Martin & Elizabeth A. Prescott, The Problem of Delay in the Colorado Court of Appeals, 58 Denver L.J. 1 (1980). –Article Citation.

John A. Martin & Elizabeth A. Prescott, The Problem of Delay in the Colorado Court of Appeals, 58 Denver L.J. 1, 2-6 (1980). –Page Citation.

–In 1985, this publication changed its name to Denver University Law Review.

Denver University Law Review
Ab.:   Denv. U. L. Rev.

Ex.:   Ben A. Rich, The Assault on Privacy in Healthcare Decisionmaking, 68 Denv. U. L. Rev. 1 (1991). –Article Citation.

Ben A. Rich, The Assault on Privacy in Healthcare Decisionmaking, 68 Denv. U. L. Rev. 1, 21-27 (1991). –Page Citation.

In citing cases in law review footnotes, abbreviate any word listed in table T.6; the names of "states, countries, and other geographical units" unless they are named parties; and any other words of eight or more letters "if substantial space is thereby saved and the result is unambiguous." Bluebook rule 10.2.2. On the other hand, in citing cases in text, abbreviate only widely known acronyms and the following words: "&," "Ass'n," "Bros.," "Co.," "Corp.," "Inc.," "Ltd.," and "No." Bluebook rule 10.2.1(c).

–In 1985, Denver Law Journal changed its name to Denver University Law Review.

Department of State Bulletin
Ab.: Dep't St. Bull.

Ex.: James A. Baker, <u>Power for Good: American Foreign Policy in the New Era</u>, Address Before the American Society of Newspaper Editors (ASNE) (Apr. 14, 1989), <u>in</u> Dep't St. Bull., June 1989, at 8, 11. –Address Citation.

Department of State Dispatch
Ab.: Dep't St. Dispatch

Ex.: Alan Larson, <u>U.S. Perspective on the WTO Ministerial Meeting</u>, Dep't St. Dispatch, Dec. 1999, at 7, 8.

DePaul Business Law Journal
Ab.: DePaul Bus. L.J.

Ex.: David Ackerman, <u>Planning for Ownership Succession in the Closely Held Business</u>, 3 DePaul Bus. L.J. 245 (1991). –Article Citation.

David Ackerman, <u>Planning for Ownership Succession in the Closely Held Business</u>, 3 DePaul Bus. L.J. 245, 254 (1991). –Page Citation.

DePaul Law Review
Ab.: DePaul L. Rev.

Ex.: Steven R. Greenberger, <u>Democracy and Congressional Tenure</u>, 41 DePaul L. Rev. 37 (1991). –Article Citation.

Steven R. Greenberger, <u>Democracy and Congressional Tenure</u>, 41 DePaul L. Rev. 37, 38-40 (1991). –Page Citation.

Deposition, citation to

Ab.: Dep.

Ex.: (Fucci Dep. 3:12, June 11, 2005).

<u>See</u> <u>Bluebook</u> rule B10 and table BT.1.

Note: See <u>Bluebook</u> rule 10.8.3 for citing litigation materials from another case.

Depublished cases

Ex.: <u>Forrest v. Gump</u>, 237 Cal. Rptr. 311 (Ct. App. 1987) (depublished).

"If the order depublishing a case <u>is</u> reported, the order should be indicated as subsequent history pursuant to rule 10.7, introduced with the explanatory phrase '<u>depublished by</u>.'" <u>Bluebook</u> rule 10.8.1(d).

Detroit College of Law Review
Ab.: Det. C.L. Rev.

In law review footnotes, the titles of books and the names of cases, except for procedural phrases, are not underlined. <u>See</u> <u>Bluebook</u> rule 2.1(a) & (b). Further, the following are in large and small capitals: codes, restatements, standards, constitutions, periodicals, authors of books, titles of books, the abbreviated names of codes, most legislative materials except for bills and resolutions, codified ordinances, model codes, court rules, and sentencing guidelines. Refer to <u>The Bluebook</u>.

Ex.:   John E. Sanchez, <u>Religious Affirmative Action in Employment: Fearful Symmetry</u>, 3 Det. C.L. Rev. 1019 (1991). –Article Citation.

John E. Sanchez, <u>Religious Affirmative Action in Employment: Fearful Symmetry</u>, 3 Det. C.L. Rev. 1019, 1019 (1991). –Page Citation.

Developing Labor Law, The
–Do not abbreviate the title.

Ex.:   2 <u>The Developing Labor Law</u> § 8(e) (Patrick Hardin ed., 3rd ed. 1992). –Section Citation.

2 <u>The Developing Labor Law</u> § 8(e), at 1359 (Patrick Hardin ed., 3rd ed. 1992). –Page Citation.

2 <u>The Developing Labor Law</u> § 8(e), at 1361 n.219 (Patrick Hardin ed., 3rd ed. 1992). –Footnote Citation.

Dickinson Law Review
Ab.:   Dick. L. Rev.

Ex.:   Thomas Grexa, <u>Title VII Tenure Litigation in the Academy and Academic Freedom --A Current Appraisal</u>, 96 Dick. L. Rev. 11 (1991). –Article Citation.

Thomas Grexa, <u>Title VII Tenure Litigation in the Academy and Academic Freedom --A Current Appraisal</u>, 96 Dick. L. Rev. 11, 26-27 (1991). –Page Citation.

Digest and Decisions of the Employees' Compensation Appeals Board (U.S.) (1946-date)
(v. 1-35 titled Decisions of the Employees' Compensation Appeals Board; v.36-present-current title)

Ab.:   Dig. & Dec. Empl. Comp. App. Bd.

Ex.:   <u>Gary L. Whitmore</u>, 43 Dig. & Dec. Empl. Comp. App. Bd. 441 (1992).

Digest of International Law, by Green Haywood Hackworth
Ab.:   Hackworth Digest

Ex.:   Prisoners of War, 6 <u>Hackworth Digest</u> § 576, at 274.

–Include the title of the section, volume number, editor's name, the word Digest, section number, and page reference as necessary. <u>See</u> <u>Bluebook</u> rule 21.11(b).

Digest of International Law, by John B. Moore
–Do not abbreviate the title.

Ex.:   4 John B. Moore, <u>A Digest of International Law</u> § 590 (1906). –Section Citation.

4 John B. Moore, <u>A Digest of International Law</u> § 590, at 272 (1906). –Page Citation.

In citing cases in law review footnotes, abbreviate any word listed in table T.6; the names of "states, countries, and other geographical units" unless they are named parties; and any other words of eight or more letters "if <u>substantial</u> space is thereby saved and the result is unambiguous." <u>Bluebook</u> rule 10.2.2. On the other hand, in citing cases in text, abbreviate only widely known acronyms and the following words: "&," "Ass'n," "Bros.," "Co.," "Corp.," "Inc.," "Ltd.," and "No." <u>Bluebook</u> rule 10.2.1(c).

Digest of International Law, by Marjorie M. Whiteman
Ab.: Whiteman Digest
Ex.: Capture, 11 <u>Whiteman Digest</u> § 7, at 55.
–Include the title of the section, volume number, editor's name, the word Digest, section number, and page references as necessary. <u>See</u> <u>Bluebook</u> rule 21.11(b).

Digest of United States Practice in International Law
Ab.: Digest
Ex.: Sovereign Immunity: Foreign Sovereign Immunities Act: Assassination Within the United States, 1980 <u>Digest</u> § 7, at 546.

dissenting opinion
Ex.: <u>Roe v. Wade</u>, 410 U.S. 113, 171 (1973) (Rehnquist, J., dissenting).
<u>See</u> <u>Bluebook</u> rule 10.6(a).

District Court (federal)
Ab.: D.

District Court (state)
Ab.: Dist. Ct.

District Court of Appeal(s)
Ab.: Dist. Ct. App.

District of Columbia Appeals Cases (1893-1941)
See Appeal Cases, District of Columbia (1893-1941).

District of Columbia Code Encyclopedia
Ab.: D.C. Code Encycl. § (West year)

District of Columbia Court of Appeals
Ab.: D.C.
–1943-date, cite to A.2d.
Ex.: <u>Sayyad v. Fawzi</u>, 674 A.2d 905 (D.C. 1996). –Article Citation.
<u>Sayyad v. Fawzi</u>, 674 A.2d 905, 906 (D.C. 1996). –Page Citation.

District of Columbia, Laws in Statutes at Large relating to
Ab.: volume Stat. (year)

District of Columbia Law Review
Ab.: D.C. L. Rev.
Ex.: Margaret Beyer, <u>Juvenile Detention to 'Protect' Children from Neglect</u>, 3 D.C. L. Rev. 213 (1995). –Article Citation.
Margaret Beyer, <u>Juvenile Detention to 'Protect' Children from Neglect</u>, 3 D.C. L. Rev. 213, 215 (1995). –Page Citation.

In law review footnotes, the titles of books and the names of cases, except for procedural phrases, are not underlined. <u>See</u> <u>Bluebook</u> rule 2.1(a) & (b). Further, the following are in large and small capitals: codes, restatements, standards, constitutions, periodicals, authors of books, titles of books, the abbreviated names of codes, most legislative materials except for bills and resolutions, codified ordinances, model codes, court rules, and sentencing guidelines. Refer to <u>The Bluebook</u>.

District of Columbia Municipal Regulations
    Ab.:   D.C. Mun. Regs. tit. x, § x (year)
    Ex.:   D.C. Mun. Regs. tit. 14, § 803.3 (2004)

District of Columbia Official Code (West)
    Ab.:   D.C. Code § x-x (year)
    Ex.:   D.C. Code § 47-410 (2001)
            D.C. Code § 46-308 (Supp. 2004)

District of Columbia Register
    Ab.:   vol. no. D.C. Reg. page no. (month day, year)
            "Cite to Stat, if therein." Bluebook table T.1, p. 205.
            See Bluebook rule 12.4.

District of Columbia Session Law Service (West)
    Ab.:   year D.C. Sess. Law Serv. page no. (West)
    Ex.:   Act of Mar. 17, 2005, No. 16-56, 2005 D.C. Sess. Law Serv. 100 (West) (relating to premature release of mentally incompetent defendants). –Citation to an entire session law.
            Act of Mar. 17, 2005, No. 16-56, sec. 2, § 21-541, 2005-1 D.C. Sess. Law Serv. 100, 101 (West) (relating to premature release of mentally incompetent defendants). –Citation to a section of a session law amending prior act.
            See Bluebook rule 12.4.
            "Cite to Stat., if therein." Bluebook table T.1, p. 205.

District of Columbia Session Laws
    See District of Columbia Register, Lexis District of Columbia Code Advance Legislative Service, and District of Columbia Session Law Service (West).

Divisional Court
    Ab.:   Div. Ct.

Dobbs Law of Remedies, by Dan B. Dobbs
    –Do not abbreviate the title.
    Ex.:   Dan B. Dobbs, Dobbs Law of Remedies § 6.5(2) (2d ed. 1993). –Section Citation.
            Dan B. Dobbs, Dobbs Law of Remedies § 6.5(2), at 123 (2d ed. 1993). –Page Citation.
            Dan B. Dobbs, Dobbs Law of Remedies § 6.5(2), at 123 n.40 (2d ed. 1993). –Footnote Citation.

In citing cases in law review footnotes, abbreviate any word listed in table T.6; the names of "states, countries, and other geographical units" unless they are named parties; and any other words of eight or more letters "if substantial space is thereby saved and the result is unambiguous." Bluebook rule 10.2.2. On the other hand, in citing cases in text, abbreviate only widely known acronyms and the following words: "&," "Ass'n," "Bros.," "Co.," "Corp.," "Inc.," "Ltd.," and "No." Bluebook rule 10.2.1(c).

Documents, Congressional
See Congressional Documents.

Documents of the United Nations Conference on International Organization
Ab.:   U.N.C.I.O. Docs.

Domestic Relations Court
Ab.:   Dom. Rel. Ct.

Dominion Law Reports (Canada) (1912-date)
–Cite to Canada: Supreme Court Reports (S.C.R.), otherwise cite to D.L.R. See Bluebook table T.2.

Ab.:   D.L.R.

Ex.:   Bateman v. Toronto Dominion Bank, [1991] 86 D.L.R.4th 354, 359 (Can.). –Page Citation.

–Provide neutral citation, if available. See Bluebook table T.2, p. 254 (3d prtg. 2006).

Berry v. Hart, [2003] 233 D.L.R.4th 1, [2003] BCCA 659 (Can.).
–Case with neutral citation.

Note: For information on Canada's neutral citation, see A Neutral Citation Standard for Case Law (2000), available at http://www.lexum.umontreal.ca/ccc-ccr/neutr/neutr.jur_en.html.

Drake Journal of Agricultural Law
Ab: Drake J. Agric. L.

Ex: Bernard O'Connor, Sui Generis Protection of Geographical Indications, 9 Drake J. Agric. L. 359 (2004). –Article Citation.

Bernard O'Connor, Sui Generis Protection of Geographical Indications, 9 Drake J. Agric. L. 359, 380-82 (2004). –Page Citation.

Drake Law Review
Ab.:   Drake L. Rev.

Ex.:   Frona M. Powell, Mistake of Fact in the Sale of Real Property, 40 Drake L. Rev. 91 (1991). –Article Citation.

Frona M. Powell, Mistake of Fact in the Sale of Real Property, 40 Drake L. Rev. 91, 113-15 (1991). –Page Citation.

Duke Environmental Law & Policy Forum
Ab: Duke Envtl. L. & Pol'y F.

Ex: Jennifer S. Hendricks, Preemption of Common Law Claims and the Prospect for FIFRA: Justice Stevens Puts the Genie Back in the Bottle, 15 Duke Envtl. L. & Pol'y F. 65 (2004). –Article Citation.

Jennifer S. Hendricks, Preemption of Common Law Claims and the Prospect for FIFRA: Justice Stevens Puts the Genie Back in the Bottle, 15 Duke Envtl. L. & Pol'y F. 65, 83-84 (2004).–Page Citation.

In law review footnotes, the titles of books and the names of cases, except for procedural phrases, are not underlined. See Bluebook rule 2.1(a) & (b). Further, the following are in large and small capitals: codes, restatements, standards, constitutions, periodicals, authors of books, titles of books, the abbreviated names of codes, most legislative materials except for bills and resolutions, codified ordinances, model codes, court rules, and sentencing guidelines. Refer to The Bluebook.

Duke Journal of Comparative & International Law
Ab.:   Duke J. Comp. & Int'l L.

Ex.:   Michael P. Scharf, <u>The Jury is Still Out on the Need for an International Criminal Court</u>, 1991 Duke J. Comp. & Int'l L. 135 (1991). –Article Citation.

Michael P. Scharf, <u>The Jury is Still Out on the Need for an International Criminal Court</u>, 1991 Duke J. Comp. & Int'l L. 135, 154-55 (1991). –Page Citation.

Duke Journal of Gender Law & Policy
Ab: Duke J. Gender L. & Pol'y

Ex: Jane M. Gaines, <u>Sexual Semiosis</u>, 11 Duke J. Gender L. & Pol'y 55 (2004). –Article Citation.

Jane M. Gaines, <u>Sexual Semiosis</u>, 11 Duke J. Gender L. & Pol'y 55, 59-63 (2004). –Page Citation.

Duke Law Journal
Ab.:   Duke L.J.

Ex.:   Mark H. Grunewald, <u>The NLRB's First Rulemaking: An Exercise in Pragmatism</u>, 41 Duke L.J. 274 (1991). –Article Citation.

Mark H. Grunewald, <u>The NLRB's First Rulemaking: An Exercise in Pragmatism</u>, 41 Duke L.J. 274, 281-82 (1991). –Page Citation.

Duquesne Law Review
Ab.:   Duq. L. Rev.

Ex.:   David E. Seidelson, <u>The Appropriate Judicial Response to Evidence of the Violation of a Criminal Statute in a Negligence Action</u>, 30 Duq. L. Rev. 1 (1991). –Article Citation.

David E. Seidelson, <u>The Appropriate Judicial Response to Evidence of the Violation of a Criminal Statute in a Negligence Action</u>, 30 Duq. L. Rev. 1, 11-15 (1991). –Page Citation.

In citing cases in law review footnotes, abbreviate any word listed in table T.6; the names of "states, countries, and other geographical units" unless they are named parties; and any other words of eight or more letters "if <u>substantial</u> space is thereby saved and the result is unambiguous." <u>Bluebook</u> rule 10.2.2. On the other hand, in citing cases in text, abbreviate only widely known acronyms and the following words: "&," "Ass'n," "Bros.," "Co.," "Corp.," "Inc.," "Ltd.," and "No." <u>Bluebook</u> rule 10.2.1(c).

E

East African Law Reports
    Ab.:   E. Afr. L. Rep
    Ex.:   Esiroyo v. Esiroyo, 1973 E. Afr. L. Rep. 388 (Kenya).

EEOC Compliance Manual (Bureau of National Affairs)
    Ab.:   EEOC Compl. Man. (BNA)

EEOC Compliance Manual (Commerce Clearing House)
    Ab.:   EEOC Compl. Man. (CCH)

    Ex.:   St. Mary's Honor Ctr. v. Hicks, EEOC Compl. Man. (CCH) ¶ 2099
        (EEOC Apr. 12, 1994). –Citation to looseleaf material.

Ecclesiastical
    Ab.:   Eccl.

Ecclesiastical Court
    Ab.:   Eccl. Ct.

Ecclesiastical Law Journal
    Ab.:   Ecclesiastical L.J.

    Ex.:   Rupert Bursell, The Parson's Freehold, 2 Ecclesiastical L.J. 259 (1992).
        –Article Citation.

        Rupert Bursell, The Parson's Freehold, 2 Ecclesiastical L.J. 259, 264
        (1992). –Page Citation.

Ecology Law Quarterly
    Ab.:   Ecology L.Q.

    Ex.:   David J. Bederman, International Control of Marine "Pollution" by
        Exotic Species, 18 Ecology L.Q. 677 (1991). –Article Citation.

        David J. Bederman, International Control of Marine "Pollution" by
        Exotic Species, 18 Ecology L.Q. 677, 690-95 (1991). –Page Citation.

Economic Analysis of Law, by Richard A. Posner
        –Do not abbreviate the title.

    Ex.   Richard A. Posner, Economic Analysis of Law § 14.7 (6th ed. 2003).
        –Section Citation.

        Richard A. Posner, Economic Analysis of Law § 14.7, at 428 (6th ed.
        2003). –Page Citation.

edition
    Ab.:   ed.

In law review footnotes, the titles of books and the names of cases, except for procedural
phrases, are not underlined. See Bluebook rule 2.1(a) & (b). Further, the following are in
large and small capitals: codes, restatements, standards, constitutions, periodicals, authors of
books, titles of books, the abbreviated names of codes, most legislative materials except for
bills and resolutions, codified ordinances, model codes, court rules, and sentencing guidelines.
Refer to The Bluebook.

editor
  Ab.:   ed.

Editorial (newspaper)
  Ex.:   Editorial, <u>Inside Wal-Mart, a Larger Debate</u>, N.Y. Times, Oct. 28, 2005, at A24.
  –<u>See</u> <u>Bluebook</u> rule 16.5.

Education Law Reporter (West)
  Ab.:   Educ. L. Rep.

E.g.

  –"<u>E.g.</u>" is used when the "[c]ited authority states the proposition; other authorities also state the proposition, but citation to them would not be helpful or is not necessary. '<u>E.g.</u>' may also be used in combination with other signals, preceded by a comma ...." <u>Bluebook</u> rule 1.2(a).

  Ex.:   "It is well settled that a speaker's rights are not lost merely because compensation is received; a speaker is no less a speaker because he or she is paid to speak. <u>E.g.</u>, <u>N. Y. Times Co. v. Sullivan</u>, 376 U.S. at 265-66." -- Taken from 487 U.S. 781, 801 (1987).

Electronic media and other nonprint sources
  –<u>See</u> <u>Bluebook</u> rule 18.

  "This rule covers citation of information found in electronic media and other nonprint resources: widely used commercial databases such as Westlaw and LEXIS (rule 18.1); the Internet (rule 18.2); CD-ROMS (rule 18.3); microforms (rule 18.4); films, broadcasts, and noncommercial videotapes (rule 18.5); and audio recordings (rule 18.6).

  Sources in these media pose special problems because they often lack the permanence and authoritativeness of traditional printed material. Therefore, <u>The Bluebook</u> **requires the use and citation of traditional printed sources** unless (1) the information cited is unavailable in a traditional printed source; or (2) a copy of the source cannot be located because it is so obscure that it is practically unavailable. Only in these two cases should citation be made to the electronic source alone.

  Even if a printed source can be found, a parallel citation to an electronic source as related authority (rule 1.6) may be provided if it will substantially improve access to the relevant information. In this case, citation should be made first to the printed source and then separately to the electronic source, introduced with the explanatory phrase '<u>available at</u>.' In such cases, the content of the electronic source must be identical to that of the printed version.

In citing cases in law review footnotes, abbreviate any word listed in table T.6; the names of "states, countries, and other geographical units" unless they are named parties; and any other words of eight or more letters "if <u>substantial</u> space is thereby saved and the result is unambiguous." <u>Bluebook</u> rule 10.2.2. On the other hand, in citing cases in text, abbreviate only widely known acronyms and the following words: "&," "Ass'n," "Bros.," "Co.," "Corp.," "Inc.," "Ltd.," and "No." <u>Bluebook</u> rule 10.2.1(c).

In general using and citing those electronic sources that will maximize the authoritativeness, permanence, and accessibility of the citation is preferred." –Bluebook rule 18.

Commercial Electronic Databases.

–Cases.

"When a case is unreported but available on a widely used electronic database, it may be cited to that database. Provide the case name, docket number, database identifier, court name, and full date of the most recent major disposition of the case. If the database contains codes or numbers that uniquely identify the case (as do LEXIS and Westlaw), these must be given. Screen or page numbers, if assigned, should be preceded by an asterisk; paragraph numbers, if assigned, should be preceded by a paragraph symbol.... If the name of the database is not clear from the database identifier, include it parenthetically at the end of the citation.... Citations to cases that have not been assigned unique database identifiers should include all relevant information, such as the specific collection within the database in which the case can be found." –Bluebook rule 18.1.1.

Ex.:

Williams v. East Coast Truck Lines, No. 98-1903, 1999 U.S. App. LEXIS 16773, at *2 (4th Cir. July 19, 1999).

Ashley v. ITT Hartford, No. C 97-3226 TEH, 1999 U.S. Dist. LEXIS 1228, at *3 (N.D. Cal. Jan. 20, 1998).

Jackson v. Samedan Oil Corp., No. Civ.A.98-0472, 2000 WL 343361, at *6 (E.D. La. Mar. 31, 2000).

Reed v. Hamilton, No. W1999-00440-COA-R3-CV, 2000 WL 558613, at *4 (Tenn. Ct. App. May 4, 2000).

Hoffmann Elec. Co. v. Undlin, 2000 WL 1869556, at *4 (Minn. Ct. App. Dec. 26, 2000) (WESTLAW MC-CS).

"Citation to cases that have not been assigned unique database identifiers should include all relevant information." –Bluebook rule 18.1.1.

–Constitutions and Statutes

In law review footnotes, the titles of books and the names of cases, except for procedural phrases, are not underlined. See Bluebook rule 2.1(a) & (b). Further, the following are in large and small capitals: codes, restatements, standards, constitutions, periodicals, authors of books, titles of books, the abbreviated names of codes, most legislative materials except for bills and resolutions, codified ordinances, model codes, court rules, and sentencing guidelines. Refer to The Bluebook.

"Cite codes and session laws according to rules 12.3 and 12.4. In addition, when citing a code contained in an electronic database, give parenthetically the name of the database and information regarding the currency of the database as provided by the database itself (rather than the year of the code according to rule 12.3.2). In accordance with rule 12.3.1(d), also give the name of the publisher, editor, or compiler unless the code is published, edited, compiled by, or under the supervision of, federal or state officials." –Bluebook rule 18.1.2.
Ex.:

> Tenn Const. art. 3, § 10 (West, Westlaw through 2005 Sess.).
>
> Mich. Comp. Laws Ann. § 431.316 (West, Westlaw through No. 225 of 2000 Reg. Sess.)
>
> Cal. Prob. Code § 6110 (Matthew Bender, LEXIS through 2000 Sess.)

–Legislative, Administrative and Executive Materials

"Cite legislative, administrative, and executive materials according to rules 13 and 14. In addition, when citing materials contained in a commercial electronic database, give the name of the database and any identifying codes or numbers that uniquely identify the material. If the name of the database is not clear from the database identifier, include it parenthetically at the end of the citation." –Bluebook rule 18.1.3.

–federal bill (unenacted)
Ex.:

> H.R. 1390, 106th Cong. § 3(c) (1999), 1999 CONG US HR 1390 (Westlaw).

–federal report
Ex.:

> H.R. Rep. No. 106-556 (2000), 2000 WL 347371.
>
> H.R. Rep. No. 100-946(I) (1988), reprinted in 1988 U.S.C.C.A.N. 3636, 1988 WL 170033.

–congressional debate
Ex.:

> 147 Cong. Rec. S1105 (daily ed. Feb. 7, 2001) (statement of Sen. Sarbanes), 147 Cong Rec S 1104, at *S1105 (LEXIS).

–federal regulation cited to Code of Federal Regulations
Ex.:

> Regulation D, 12 C.F.R. § 204.1 (2000), WL 12 CFR s 204.1

In citing cases in law review footnotes, abbreviate any word listed in table T.6; the names of "states, countries, and other geographical units" unless they are named parties; and any other words of eight or more letters "if substantial space is thereby saved and the result is unambiguous." Bluebook rule 10.2.2. On the other hand, in citing cases in text, abbreviate only widely known acronyms and the following words: "&," "Ass'n," "Bros.," "Co.," "Corp.," "Inc.," "Ltd.," and "No." Bluebook rule 10.2.1(c).

–administrative adjudication

Ex.:

> In re Tomy Corp., 99 F.T.C. 1 (1982), 1982 WL 608299..

–formal advisory opinion

Ex.:

> 41 Op. Att'y Gen. 88 (1951), 1951 US AG LEXIS 1.

–revenue ruling

Ex.:

> Rev. Rul. 99-14, 1999-1 C.B. 835, 1999 IRB LEXIS 132.

–Books, Periodicals, and Other Secondary Materials

"When citing secondary materials to a database, provide a complete citation to the document according to rules 15-17 and a citation to the database. If the database assigns a unique identifier or code to each document within the database, include that identifier or code to assist the reader in locating the document cited.

Some sources are available in two forms, electronic and paper. To increase availability of the source, it is permissible to include a parallel citation to a commercial electronic database using 'available at.'" – Bluebook rule 18.1.4.

–newspaper

Ex.:

> Beth Daley, Global Warming: What Lies Ahead?, Boston Globe, Jan. 29, 2001, at B6, available at 2001 WLNR 2238880.

–newswire

Ex.:

> Study: Car Exhaust Polluting Puget Sound, AP Newswires, Aug 17, 2005, available at 08/17/07 APWIRES 00:54:42 (Westlaw).

–periodical

Ex.:

> Jennifer Cannon and Michelle Haas, Recent Development, The Human Cloning Prohibition Act: Did Congress Go Too Far?, 35 Harv. J. Legis. 637 (1998), available at 35 HVJL 637 (Westlaw).

–press release

Ex.:

In law review footnotes, the titles of books and the names of cases, except for procedural phrases, are not underlined. See Bluebook rule 2.1(a) & (b). Further, the following are in large and small capitals: codes, restatements, standards, constitutions, periodicals, authors of books, titles of books, the abbreviated names of codes, most legislative materials except for bills and resolutions, codified ordinances, model codes, court rules, and sentencing guidelines. Refer to The Bluebook.

Analysis: What's the Future of U.S. National Defense?, UPI, Dec. 18, 2000, available at LEXIS, News & Business >News > U.S. Newspapers and Wires.

The Internet

For a detailed discussion of basic citation principles, including the Uniform Resource Locator, multiple URLs, document format options, date of Internet citations, parenthetical information, direct and parallel citations, sources without a printed analogue, and preservation of information, see Bluebook rules 18.2.1, 18.2.2, and 18.2.3

"When information is available in a traditional printed source or on a widely available commercial database, it should be cited to that source rather than to the Internet (rule 18). An Internet citation should only be provided when (1) the source is unavailable in a traditional printed format or on a widely available commercial database; or (2) the source is available in a traditional printed format, but the content of the Internet source is identical to that of the printed version and a parallel citation to the Internet (introduced by the explanatory phrase 'available at') will substantially improve access to the source cited." Bluebook rule 18.2.

Primary Authority

–Cases

Ex.:

Kuwait Airways Corp. v. Iraqi Airways Co. (H.L. Feb. 8, 2001), available at http://www.parliament.the-stationery-office.co.uk/pa/ldjudgmt/ldjudgmt.htm.

State v. Hodge, No. E2000-00040-CCA-R3-CD (Tenn. Crim. App. Feb. 9, 2001), available at http://www.tsc.state.tn.us/PDF/tcca/011/HodgeTR.pdf at 3.

"If a document is available both in HTML format and in a widely used format that preserves pagination and other attributes of printed work (such as Adobe's portable document format, or 'PDF'), the latter should always be cited in lieu of an HTML document." –Bluebook rule 18.2.1(c).

Ex.:

Troxel v. Granville, 530 U.S. 57 (2000), available at Cornell Legal Info. Inst., http://supct.law.cornell.edu/supct/pdf/99-138P.ZO, aff'g 940 P.2d 698 (Wash. 1997).

–Constitutions & Statutes

In citing cases in law review footnotes, abbreviate any word listed in table T.6; the names of "states, countries, and other geographical units" unless they are named parties; and any other words of eight or more letters "if substantial space is thereby saved and the result is unambiguous." Bluebook rule 10.2.2. On the other hand, in citing cases in text, abbreviate only widely known acronyms and the following words: "&," "Ass'n," "Bros.," "Co.," "Corp.," "Inc.," "Ltd.," and "No." Bluebook rule 10.2.1(c).

Ex.:

>Cal. Const. art. I, § 2(b), <u>available at</u>
>http://www.leginfo.ca.gov/.const/.article_1.

>Ky. Rev. Stat. § 5.031 (1996), <u>available at</u>
>http://162.114.4.13/KRS/005-00/031.PDF

>Beaverton Code ch. 4.01.100 (1989), <u>available at</u>
>http://www.ci.beaverton.or.us/departments/attorney/docs/chapter4/
>pdf

–Legislative Material

–pending federal legislation

Ex.:

>Drug Importer Death Penalty Act, H.R. 213, 107th Cong. § 2
>(2001), <u>available at</u> http://thomas.loc.gov/cgi-
>bin/query/z?c107:H.R.213:

–congressional debate

Ex.:

>147 Cong. Rec. S1206 (daily ed. Feb. 8, 2001) (statement of Sen.
>Wellstone), <u>available at</u>
>http://www.gpoaccess.gov/crecord/index/html

>–recently enacted state public act

Ex.:

>Act of June 28, 2000, ch. 999, 2000 Tenn. Pub. Acts 3 (concerning
>Tennessee Millenium Trust), <u>available at</u>
>http://www.state.tn.us/sos/acts/101pub/pc999/pdf

–pending state bill

Ex.:

>SB 2, 2001 Gen. Assemb., Reg. Sess. (Fla. 2001), <u>available at</u>
>http://www.leg.state.fl.us/data/session/2001/Senate/bills/billtext/pdf
>/s0020.pdf

–Administrative and Executive Materials

–final rules and regulations

Ex.:

>Or. Admin. R. ch. 177-010-0025 (2001), <u>available at</u>
>http://archweb.sos.state.or.us/rules/OARS_100?0AR_177/177_010
>.html

In law review footnotes, the titles of books and the names of cases, except for procedural
phrases, are not underlined. <u>See</u> <u>Bluebook</u> rule 2.1(a) & (b). Further, the following are in
large and small capitals: codes, restatements, standards, constitutions, periodicals, authors of
books, titles of books, the abbreviated names of codes, most legislative materials except for
bills and resolutions, codified ordinances, model codes, court rules, and sentencing guidelines.
Refer to <u>The Bluebook</u>.

–proposed federal regulations

Ex.:

> Airworthiness Directives: Pilatus Aircraft Ltd. Model PC-7
> Airplanes, 66 Fed. Reg. 57, 58 (proposed Dec. 21, 2000) (to be
> codified at 14 C.F.R. pt. 39), GPO Access, available at
> http://www.access.gpo.gov/su_docs/aces/aces140.html

Secondary Materials

–Books, Journals, and Magazines

–traditional print source

Ex.:

> George J. Edwards., Jr., The Grand Jury 12 (1906), available at
> http://www.constitutuion.org/gje/gj_01.htm

–on-line journals

"An Internet source may be cited directly when it does not exist in a
traditional printed format or on a widely available commercial database,
or when a traditional printed source, such as a letter or unpublished
dissertation, exists but cannot be found and is so obscure that it is
practically unavailable. In either case, the title, pagination, and
publication date should be reported as they appear on the Internet. The
Internet URL should then be appended directly to the end of the citation
(i.e., not preceded by 'available at' or 'at.')." –Bluebook rule 18.2.3(a).

Ex.:

> John LaBarre & Xavier Gomez-Velasco, Ready, Set, Mark Your
> Patented Software! 12 Rich. J.L. & Tech. 1, ¶ 14 (Fall 2005),
> http://www.richmond.edu/jolt/v12i1/article3.pdf. –pinpoint
> citation.

–Other Secondary Sources

–speech

Ex.:

> Attorney General Janet Reno, Farewell Address to the Justice Dept.
> Staff (Jan. 11, 2001), available at
> http://www.usdoj.gov/archive/ag/speeches/2001/011101agfarewell.
> htm

–newspaper

Ex.:

In citing cases in law review footnotes, abbreviate any word listed in table T.6;
the names of "states, countries, and other geographical units" unless they are named parties;
and any other words of eight or more letters "if substantial space is thereby saved and the
result is unambiguous." Bluebook rule 10.2.2. On the other hand, in citing cases in text,
abbreviate only widely known acronyms and the following words: "&," "Ass'n," "Bros.,"
"Co.," "Corp.," "Inc.," "Ltd.," and "No." Bluebook rule 10.2.1(c).

Richard W. Stevenson, <u>Greenspan Hints Tax Cut Might Help Weak Economy</u>, N.Y. Times, Jan. 25, 2001, <u>available at</u> http://www.nytimes.com/2001/01/25/business/25CND-GSPAN.html

–news release

Ex.:

News Release, U.S. Dept. of Housing and Urban Dev., <u>Bush Administration Announces $17.1 Billion to Rebuild Gulf Region</u> (Oct. 28, 2005), <u>available at</u> http://www.hud.gov/news/release.cfm?content=pr05-152.cfm

E-mail Correspondence and Online Postings

"In citing personal e-mail messages, analogize to unpublished letters (rule17.1.3).The date of the message and possibly the time-stamp may be needed for specific identification of the message. Archival information may be included parenthetically, and is recommended. The e-mail addresses of the sender and recipient are not required, although they may be included if there is a reason for doing so." –<u>Bluebook</u> rule 18.2.4.

Ex.:

E-mail from Andrew Morton, Bluebook Editor, University of Pennsylvania Law Review, to Kathleen Hartnett, Harvard Law Review (Sept. 1, 1999, 07:16:09 EDT) (on file with author).

"Postings to listservs should follow a similar format, but should include the author's e-mail address and the address of the listserv." –<u>Bluebook</u> rule 18.2.4.

Ex.:

Posting of Maitland Stewart, mstewart@paw.org, to Paramount-Fan@paramount.org (Feb. 16, 2001) (on file with author).

"Postings to discussion forums should also follow a similar format, but should include the URL and should not include the author's e-mail address." –<u>Bluebook</u> rule 18.2.4.

Ex.:

Posting of Hu Dunit to http://forums.lark.com (June 6, 2005, 01:08 CDT)

"Postings to blogs take one of two formats. If there is only one poster to the blog, cite as a Web page, but include the date and time-stamp to indicate the specific posting cited. If there are multiple posters on the blog, cite as a posting to a discussion forum. In both cases, indicate the title of the blog before the URL." <u>Bluebook</u> rule 18.2.4.

In law review footnotes, the titles of books and the names of cases, except for procedural phrases, are not underlined. <u>See</u> Bluebook rule 2.1(a) & (b). Further, the following are in large and small capitals: codes, restatements, standards, constitutions, periodicals, authors of books, titles of books, the abbreviated names of codes, most legislative materials except for bills and resolutions, codified ordinances, model codes, court rules, and sentencing guidelines. Refer to <u>The Bluebook</u>.

Ex.:

> Single poster:
> InstaPundit.com, http://instapundit.com (Nov. 6, 2005, 01:53 MST)

> Multiple posters:
> Posting of John J. Miller to The Corner, http://www.nationalreview.com/thecorner/corner.asp (Nov. 5, 2005, 06:36 PST)

Web pages

"Many web pages, especially those maintained by institutions, do not have 'authors' or 'titles' as conventionally understood. When authorship is not conspicuously attributed at the top of the site, a title alone may be used as long as it clearly identifies the site. But if the site is headed by a bare corporate logo, of if not serviceable title can be discerned, a description of the site may be uses instead." <u>Bluebook</u> rule 18.2.3(c).

> Ex.: NASDAQ Trader, http://www.nasdaqtrader.com/asp/tdMarkSpec.asp (last visited Nov. 11, 2005).

> Vanderbilt University Law School Homepage, http://www.law.vanderbilt.edu (last visited Nov. 6, 2005).

CD-ROM

"Information found on CD-ROM usually is available in print form, and citation to the print form is preferred where available. If the information is accessed on CD-ROM, it should be cited to CD-ROM. When citing cases on CD-ROM, the possibility exists that a case published near the date of the CD-ROM itself may have been included in slip opinion form, and (like a decision in an advance sheet) may have been edited or otherwise changed before the case was published in final form.

When citing CD-ROM media, include the title of the material, the publisher of the CD-ROM, the version searched, and the date of the material, if available, or the date of the version searched. The information may be provided in a source-date parenthetical or, if the information is voluminous, as related authority (rule 1.6)." –<u>Bluebook</u> rule 18.3.

Ex.:

In citing cases in law review footnotes, abbreviate any word listed in table T.6; the names of "states, countries, and other geographical units" unless they are named parties; and any other words of eight or more letters "if <u>substantial</u> space is thereby saved and the result is unambiguous." <u>Bluebook</u> rule 10.2.2. On the other hand, in citing cases in text, abbreviate only widely known acronyms and the following words: "&," "Ass'n," "Bros.," "Co.," "Corp.," "Inc.," "Ltd.," and "No." <u>Bluebook</u> rule 10.2.1(c).

Taylor v. Heldman, No. M1999-00729-COA-R3-CV, (Tenn. Ct. App. 2000) (Tennessee Unpublished Decisions, 1985-2000, West CD-ROM Libraries, current through Nov. 1, 2000).

5 C.F.R. § 630.101 (West LawDesk Code of Federal Regulations CD-ROM, current through Sept. 2000).

1 Lee R. Russ and Thomas F. Segalla, Couch on Insurance §1.4 (Couch on Insurance West LawDesk CD-ROM, July 2000).

Microform

"In general, when a document is reproduced in microform, it is not necessary to indicate this fact unless it would otherwise be difficult for a reader to identify and obtain the source. When citing material as 'microformed on' a service, provide a complete citation to the original document and a citation to the microform in accordance with rule 1.6 regarding citations to related authority. If the mircroform service assigns a unique identifier or code to each document reproduced, include that identifier to assist the reader in locating the document cited. Include the name of the publisher of the microform series in parentheses, abbreviated according to rule 15.1(d)."

–Bluebook rule 18.4.1.

Ex.:

S.2626, 101st Cong. § 4 (1990), microformed on Sup. Docs. Y1.4/1:101-2351 (U.S. Gov't Printing Office).

Turner v. Fouch, 396 U.S. 346 (1969) (No. 71-3120) microformed on U.S. Supreme Court Records and Briefs (Microform, Inc.).

Films, Broadcasts, and Noncommercial Videotapes

Ex.:

To Catch a Thief (Paramount Pictures 1955).

CSI: Crime Scene Investigation: What's Eating Gilbert Grissom? (CBS television broadcast July 20, 2005).

–See Bluebook rule 18.5.

"Cite video materials containing images that have not been commercially displayed or broadcast by the medium of the material, the title of the video or DVD (if any), the name of the person or institution that produced the video, and the year of production." Bluebook rule 18.5.

Ex.:

Videotape: Interview with Dean John Wade (Vanderbilt Law School 1990).

DVD: Updating Your Computer (Shyster Equipment Co. 2004).

In law review footnotes, the titles of books and the names of cases, except for procedural phrases, are not underlined. See Bluebook rule 2.1(a) & (b). Further, the following are in large and small capitals: codes, restatements, standards, constitutions, periodicals, authors of books, titles of books, the abbreviated names of codes, most legislative materials except for bills and resolutions, codified ordinances, model codes, court rules, and sentencing guidelines. Refer to The Bluebook.

Audio Recording

–See <u>Bluebook</u> rule 18.6.1.

Ex.:

> The Rolling Stones, <u>Emotional Rescue</u> (Atlantic Records 1980).
> –Citation to an entire audio recording.

> Marvin Gaye, <u>I Heard It Through the Grapevine,</u> <u>on</u> <u>The Big Chill</u>
> (Motown Record Co. 1983). –Citation to an entire audio recording.

Short Citation Forms

Commercial Electronic Databases

–See <u>Bluebook</u> rule 18.7(a).

Ex.:

> <u>Reed v. Hamilton,</u> No. W1999-00440-COA-R3-CV, 2000 WL
> 558613, at *4 (Tenn. Ct. App. May 4, 2000)
> *becomes*
> <u>Reed,</u> 2000 WL 558613, at *3.

> <u>Ashley v. ITT Hartford,</u> No. C 97-3226 TEH, 1999 U.S. Dist.
> LEXIS 1228, at *3 (N.D. Cal. Jan. 20, 1998)
> *becomes*
> <u>Ashley,</u> 199 U.S. Dist. LEXIS 1228, at *5.

> H.R. 1390, 106th Cong. § 3(c) (1999), 1999 Cong US HR 1390
> (Westlaw)
> *becomes*
> HR 1390 § 3(c), 1999 Cong US HR 1390 (Westlaw)

> Regulation D, 12 C.F.R. § 204.1 (2000), 12 CFR s 204.1
> (Westlaw)
> *becomes*
> 12 C.F.R. § 204.1, 12 CFR s 204.1(Westlaw) *or* 12 CFR s 204.1
> Westlaw)

Internet

"For a source available in a traditional printed format or with a
close print analogue, use the short form appropriate for that type of
printed source. For sources without close print analogues, use a
'<u>supra</u>' form with the last name of the author, if any, or the title or
description of the document. A URL need not be repeated after a
full citation." <u>Bluebook</u> rule 18.7(c).

In citing cases in law review footnotes, abbreviate any word listed in table T.6;
the names of "states, countries, and other geographical units" unless they are named parties;
and any other words of eight or more letters "if <u>substantial</u> space is thereby saved and the
result is unambiguous." <u>Bluebook</u> rule 10.2.2. On the other hand, in citing cases in text,
abbreviate only widely known acronyms and the following words: "&," "Ass'n," "Bros.,"
"Co.," "Corp.," "Inc.," "Ltd.," and "No." <u>Bluebook</u> rule 10.2.1(c).

Ex.: [1] Transocean, Inc., http://www.deepwater.com (last visited Aug. 24, 2005).

[2] Transocean, Inc., supra note 1.

See Bluebook rules 18.7(b), (c), and (d) for instruction on short citation forms for CD-ROM, microform, Internet, films, broadcasts, and audio recordings.

Electronic sources and databases
–See Electronic media and other nonprint sources.

E-mail correspondence and online postings
–See Electronic media and other nonprint sources.

Emory Bankruptcy Developments Journal
Ab: Emory Bankr. Dev. J.

Ex: George W. Kuney, Hijacking Chapter 11, 21 Emory Bankr. Dev. J. 19 (2004). –Article Citation.

George W. Kuney, Hijacking Chapter 11, 21 Emory Bankr. Dev. J. 19, 45-46 (2004). –Page Citation.

Emory International Law Review
Ab.: Emory Int'l L. Rev.

Ex.: Bruce Zagaris & Elizabeth Kingma, Asset Forfeiture International and Foreign Law: An Emergency Regime, 5 Emory Int'l L. Rev. 445 (1991). –Article Citation.

Bruce Zagaris & Elizabeth Kingma, Asset Forfeiture International and Foreign Law: An Emergency Regime, 5 Emory Int'l L. Rev. 445, 449-50 (1991). –Page Citation.

Emory Law Journal
Ab.: Emory L.J.

Ex.: Michael Corrado, Automatism and the Theory of Action, 39 Emory L.J. 1191 (1990). –Article Citation.

Michael Corrado, Automatism and the Theory of Action, 39 Emory L.J. 1191, 1193 (1990). –Page Citation.

Employee Benefits Cases (Bureau of National Affairs)
Ab.: Empl. Benefits Cas. (BNA)

Employee Relations Law Journal
Ab.: Emp. Rel. L.J.

In law review footnotes, the titles of books and the names of cases, except for procedural phrases, are not underlined. See Bluebook rule 2.1(a) & (b). Further, the following are in large and small capitals: codes, restatements, standards, constitutions, periodicals, authors of books, titles of books, the abbreviated names of codes, most legislative materials except for bills and resolutions, codified ordinances, model codes, court rules, and sentencing guidelines. Refer to The Bluebook.

Ex.:   Niall A. Paul, <u>The Civil Rights Act of 1991: What Does It Really Accomplish?</u>, 17 Emp. Rel. L.J. 567 (1992). –Article Citation.

Niall A. Paul, <u>The Civil Rights Act of 1991: What Does It Really Accomplish?</u>, 17 Emp. Rel. L.J. 567, 569-72 (1992). –Page Citation.

Employee Rights and Employment Policy Journal
Ab: Emp. Rts. & Emp. Pol'y J.

Ex: Eliza S. Vanderstar, <u>Workplace Bullying in the Healthcare Professions</u>, 8 Emp. Rts. & Emp. Pol'y J. 455 (2004). –Article Citation.

Eliza S. Vanderstar, <u>Workplace Bullying in the Healthcare Professions</u>, 8 Emp. Rts. & Emp. Pol'y J. 455, 465-66 (2004). –Page Citation.

Employment and Training Reporter (Bureau of National Affairs)
Ab.:   Empl. & Training Rep. (BNA)

Employment Practices Guide (Commerce Clearing House)
         –Bound as Employment Practices Decisions (Commerce Clearing House)

Ab.:   Empl. Prac. Guide (CCH)

         –Bound as Empl. Prac. Dec. (CCH)

Ex.:   <u>Quaratino v. Wright</u>, 67 Empl. Prac. Dec. (CCH) ¶ 43,795 (2nd Cir. Nov. 20, 1995). –Citation to bound material.

<u>Cordova v. West</u>, 4 Empl. Prac. Guide (CCH) (69 Empl. Prac. Dec.) ¶ 44,309 (D. Colo. May 17, 1996). –Citation to looseleaf material.

–The above examples are proper if the case is not yet available in, or is not reported in, an official or West reporter, a public domain citation, or in a widely used computer database.

EEOC Discusses Liability of Labor Organizations under ADEA, [Sept. 1989 - Sept. 1991 New Developments Transfer Binder] ¶ 5271 (EEOC May 11, 1990) –Citation to bound administrative materials.

EEOC Issues Guidance as Workers' Compensation and NADA, 2 Empl. Prac. Guide (CCH) ¶ 5426 (EEOC Sept. 3, 1996). –Citation to looseleaf administrative material.

Employment Safety and Health Guide (Commerce Clearing House)
Ab.:   Empl. Safety & Health Guide (CCH)

en banc
         –Do not abbreviate

Ex.:   <u>United States v. Aguilar</u>, 21 F.3d 1475 (9th Cir. 1994) (en banc).

Encyclopedia of European Community Law
Ab.:   E.E.C.L.

Encyclopedia of Public International Law
         –Do not abbreviate the title.

In citing cases in law review footnotes, abbreviate any word listed in table T.6; the names of "states, countries, and other geographical units" unless they are named parties; and any other words of eight or more letters "if <u>substantial</u> space is thereby saved and the result is unambiguous." <u>Bluebook</u> rule 10.2.2. On the other hand, in citing cases in text, abbreviate only widely known acronyms and the following words: "&," "Ass'n," "Bros.," "Co.," "Corp.," "Inc.," "Ltd.," and "No." <u>Bluebook</u> rule 10.2.1(c).

Ex.:   IV Encyclopedia of Public International Law <u>Slavery</u> 422 (2000).

Endnote(s)
See <u>Bluebook</u> rule 3.2(b) and (c).
See footnotes.

Energy Law Journal
Ab.:   Energy L.J.

Ex.:   Philip M. Marston, <u>Pipeline Restructuring: The Future of Open-Access Transportation</u>, 12 Energy L.J. 53 (1991). –Article Citation.

Philip M. Marston, <u>Pipeline Restructuring: The Future of Open-Access Transportation</u>, 12 Energy L.J. 53, 61-64 (1991). –Page Citation.

Energy Management (Commerce Clearing House)
Ab.:   Energy Mgmt. (CCH)

English Law Reports and other materials
–Explained and illustrated in <u>Bluebook</u> at rule 20.3.1, and table T.2.

English Reports–Full Reprint (U.K.)
Ab.:   Eng. Rep.

Ex.:   <u>Ridgway v. Wharton</u>, 10 Eng. Rep. 1287 (1857). –Case Citation.

<u>Donegani v. Donegani</u>, 12 Eng. Rep. 571 (P.C. 1835) (appeal taken from Lower Can.). –Case Citation.

<u>Leaf v. Coles</u>, 42 Eng. Rep. 517 (Ch. 1851). –Case Citation.

<u>Marston v. Roe</u>, 112 Eng. Rep. 742 (Q.B. 1838). –Case Citation.

<u>Milker v. Seagrave</u>, 125 Eng. Rep. 935 (C.P. 1723). –Case Citation.

See <u>Bluebook</u> table T.2, pages 320 and 324, and rule 20.3.1.

Entertainment and Sports Lawyer
Ab.:   Ent. & Sports Law.

Ex.:   Robert Acosta-Lewis, <u>A Basic Approach to Securing Event Sponsorship Rights</u>, Ent. & Sports Law., Spring 1991, at 1. –Article Citation.

Robert Acosta-Lewis, <u>A Basic Approach to Securing Event Sponsorship Rights</u>, Ent. & Sports Law., Spring 1991, at 1, 19. –Page Citation.

Entscheidungen des Bundegerichtshofes in Strafsachen (Germany)
Ab.:   BGHSt; <u>see</u> <u>Bluebook</u> rule 20.3.2 and table T.2.

Entscheidungen des Bundegerichtshofes in Zivilsachen (Germany)
Ab.:   BGHZ, <u>see</u> <u>Bluebook</u> rule 20.3.2 and table T.2.

Entscheidungen des Bundesverfassungsgerichts (Germany)
Ab.:   BVerfGE; <u>see</u> <u>Bluebook</u> rule 20.3.2 and table T.2.

In law review footnotes, the titles of books and the names of cases, except for procedural phrases, are not underlined. See <u>Bluebook</u> rule 2.1(a) & (b). Further, the following are in large and small capitals: codes, restatements, standards, constitutions, periodicals, authors of books, titles of books, the abbreviated names of codes, most legislative materials except for bills and resolutions, codified ordinances, model codes, court rules, and sentencing guidelines. Refer to <u>The Bluebook</u>.

Entscheidungen des Bundesverwaltungsgericht (Germany)
    Ab.:   BVerwGE; see Bluebook rule 20.3.2 and table T.2.

Environmental Law
    Ab.:   Envtl. L.

    Ex.:   Laksham Guruswamy, Integrated Environmental Control: The Expanding Matrix, 22 Envtl. L. 77 (1991). –Article Citation.

             Laksham Guruswamy, Integrated Environmental Control: The Expanding Matrix, 22 Envtl. L. 77, 83-87 (1991). –Page Citation.

Environmental Law Reporter (Environmental Law Institute)
    Ab.:   Envtl. L. Rep. (Envtl. L. Inst.)

    Ex.:   Alabama Power Co. v. Gorsuch, 12 Envtl. L. Rep. (Envtl. L. Inst.) 20218 (D.C. Cir. Feb. 5, 1982). –Citation to looseleaf material.

             Comm. for Charter Prot. for Parks v. Brown, 10 Envtl. L. Rep. (Envtl. L. Inst.) 20,246 (S.D. Cal. 1980). –Citation to non-current looseleaf material.

             Arizona v. Nucar Corp., 26 Envtl. L. Rep. (Envtl. L. Inst.) 20,061 (9th Cir. Sept. 15, 1995).

             –The above examples are proper if the case is not yet available in an official or West reporter, or is not reported in an official or West reporter.

             Trauberman, Dunwoody & Horne, Compensation for Toxic Substances Pollution: Michigan Case Study, 10 Envtl. L. Rep. (Envtl. L. Inst.) 50,021 (Sept. 1980).

             –Citation to current or non-current looseleaf material. The citation is to an article or monograph written by the named contributors.

             Nuclear Weapons and "Secret" Impact Statements: High Court Applies FOIA Exemptions to EIS Disclosure Rules, 12 Envtl. L. Rep. (Envtl. L. Inst.) 10,007 (Feb. 1982). –Citation to current or non-current looseleaf material; this citation is to an editorial comment written by the publisher's staff.

Environment Regulation Handbook
    Ab.:   Env't Reg. Handbook (Env't Information Center)

Environment Reporter (Bureau of National Affairs)
             –Bound as Environment Reporter Cases (Bureau of National Affairs)

    Ab.:   Env't Rep. (BNA)

             –Bound as Env't Rep. Cas. (BNA)

In citing cases in law review footnotes, abbreviate any word listed in table T.6; the names of "states, countries, and other geographical units" unless they are named parties; and any other words of eight or more letters "if substantial space is thereby saved and the result is unambiguous." Bluebook rule 10.2.2. On the other hand, in citing cases in text, abbreviate only widely known acronyms and the following words: "&," "Ass'n," "Bros.," "Co.," "Corp.," "Inc.," "Ltd.," and "No." Bluebook rule 10.2.1(c).

Ex.:   City of Albuquerque v. EPA, [Decisions] Env't Rep. (BNA) (43 Env't
           Rep. Cas.) 1276 (10th Cir. Oct. 7, 1996). –Citation to looseleaf
           material.

           Papas v. Upjohn Co., 32 Env't Rep. Cas. (BNA) 1815 (11th Cir. 1991).
           –Citation to bound material.

           –The above examples are proper if the case is not yet available in, or is
           not reported in, an official or West reporter, a public domain citation,
           or in a widely used computer database.

Statutes

           Nuclear Regulatory Commission Standards for Protection Against
           Radiation, [8 Rederal Regulations] Env't Rep. (BNA) 151:0101 (June
           17, 1996). –Citation to looseleaf statutes.

Equal Employment Compliance Manual
           Ab.:   Eq. Empl. Compl. Man. (CBC)

equity
           Ab.:   eq.

Equity Court or Division
           Ab.:   Eq.

Estate Planning, by A. James Casner & Jeffrey N. Pennell
           –Do not abbreviate the title.

Ex.:   3 A. James Casner & Jeffrey N. Pennell, Estate Planning § 7.2.2.3 (6th
           ed. 1999). –Section Citation.

           3 A. James Casner & Jeffrey N. Pennell, Estate Planning § 7.2.2.3, at
           7.204 (6th ed. 1999). –Page Citation.

           3 A. James Casner & Jeffrey N. Pennell, Estate Planning § 7.2.2.3, at
           7.204 n.62 (6th ed. 1999). –Footnote Citation.

et al.

           –If a book, pamphlet or other nonperiodic material has more than two
           authors, either use the first author's name followed by "et al." or list
           all of the authors' names. See Bluebook rule 15.1(b).

           –Do not use "et al." to indicate multiple parties in cases, but use name
           of first party only. See Bluebook rule 10.2.1(a).

et seq.

           –Should not be used when citing consecutive sections or subsections.
           Always use inclusive numbers. See Bluebook rule 3.3(b).

In law review footnotes, the titles of books and the names of cases, except for procedural
phrases, are not underlined. See Bluebook rule 2.1(a) & (b). Further, the following are in
large and small capitals: codes, restatements, standards, constitutions, periodicals, authors of
books, titles of books, the abbreviated names of codes, most legislative materials except for
bills and resolutions, codified ordinances, model codes, court rules, and sentencing guidelines.
Refer to The Bluebook.

European Community Cases (CCH) (Beginning 1989; Common Mkt. Rep. through 1988)
Ab.:   CEC (CCH)
Ex.:   Case 341/87, <u>EMJ Electrola v. Patricia</u>, 1990-1 CEC (CCH) 322, 333.
        –Page Citation.

European Consultative Assembly Debates
Ab.:   Eur. Consult. Ass. Deb. <u>See</u> <u>Bluebook</u> rule 21.8.3.

European Court of Human Rights
Ab.:   Eur. Ct. H.R.
        –"Cite cases before the European Court to <u>European Court of Human Rights, Reports of Judgments and Decisions</u> (Eur. Ct. H.R.)."
        –<u>Bluebook</u> rule 21.5.3.
Ex.:   <u>Laino v. Italy</u>, 1999-I Eur. Ct. H.R. 3611, 366.
        <u>Fischer v. Austria</u>, 312 Eur. Ct. H.R. (ser. A) at 23 (1995).
        –"Older decisions may also be cited to <u>Publications of the European Court of Human Rights</u>, which was issued in multiple Series (e.g., Eur. Ct. H.R. (ser. A)) or <u>Yearbook of the European Convention on Human Rights</u> (Y.B. Eur. Conv. on H.R.)." –<u>Bluebook</u> rule 21.5.3.

European Human Rights Reports
Ab.:   Eur. H.R. Rep.
Ex.:   <u>Cossey v. United Kingdom</u>, App. No. 10843/84, 13 Eur. H.R. Rep. 662 (1991). –Case Citation.
        –If case does not appear in Eur. Comm'n H.R. Dec. & Rep. or Y.B. Eur. Conv. on H.R., then it is permissible to use Eur. H.R. Rep. <u>See</u> <u>Bluebook</u> rule 21.5.3.

European Law Review
Ab.:   Eur. L. Rev.
Ex.:   Scott Crosby, <u>The Single Market and the Rule of Law</u>, 16 Eur. L. Rev. 451 (1991). –Article Citation.
        Scott Crosby, <u>The Single Market and the Rule of Law</u>, 16 Eur. L. Rev. 451, 461-64 (1991). –Page Citation.

European Parliament Session Documents
Ab.:   Eur. Parl. Doc.
Ex.:   Community Legislation and Regulations, Eur. Parl. Doc. (COM No. A2-133/87) 5 (1987).

European Treaty Series (1948 - date)
Ab.:   Europ. T.S. No.

In citing cases in law review footnotes, abbreviate any word listed in table T.6; the names of "states, countries, and other geographical units" unless they are named parties; and any other words of eight or more letters "if <u>substantial</u> space is thereby saved and the result is unambiguous." <u>Bluebook</u> rule 10.2.2. On the other hand, in citing cases in text, abbreviate only widely known acronyms and the following words: "&," "Ass'n," "Bros.," "Co.," "Corp.," "Inc.," "Ltd.," and "No." <u>Bluebook</u> rule 10.2.1(c).

Ex.:   European Convention for the Protection of Human Rights, art. 2, Sept. 16, 1963, Europ. T.S. 2.

–See Bluebook rule 21.4.5(a)(ii).

European Yearbook
Ab.:   Eur. Y.B.

Ex.:   Daniel Tarschys, The Council of Europe Heading Towards the Year 2000, 42 Eur. Y.B. 53 (1994). –Article Citation.

Executive Agreement Series (U.S. Dep't State) (1922-1945)
Ab.:   E.A.S. No.

Ex.:   Arrangement on Air Navigation, U.S.- Ger., art. 19, Aug. 8, 1945, E.A.S. No. 472. –Example of agreement between United States and one other party.

Trade Agreement, art. 3, Nov. 15, 1935, E.A.S. No. 91, 143 L.N.T.S. 71. –Multilateral agreement.

Executive Document
Ab.:   Exec. Doc.

Executive Order
Ab.:   Exec. Order

Ex.:   Exec. Order No. 12, 893, 3 C.F.R. 867 (1995), reprinted as amended in 31 U.S.C. § 501 (1996). –Page Citation.

Exempt Organizations Reports (Commerce Clearing House)
Ab.:   Exempt Org. Rep. (CCH)

Ex parte

–Procedural phrases should always be italicized, regardless of whether the rest of the case name is italicized. See Bluebook rule 10.2.1(b).

ex rel.

–Expressions such as "on the relation of," "for the use of," and "on behalf of" should be abbreviated "ex rel." See Bluebook rule 10.2.1(b).

–Procedural phrases should always be italicized, or underlined, even if the rest of the case name may not be. See Bluebook rule 10.2.1(b).

In law review footnotes, the titles of books and the names of cases, except for procedural phrases, are not underlined. See Bluebook rule 2.1(a) & (b). Further, the following are in large and small capitals: codes, restatements, standards, constitutions, periodicals, authors of books, titles of books, the abbreviated names of codes, most legislative materials except for bills and resolutions, codified ordinances, model codes, court rules, and sentencing guidelines. Refer to The Bluebook.

F

Fair Employment Practice Cases (Bureau of National Affairs)
See Labor Relations Reporter.

Family Court
Ab.:   Fam. Ct.

Family Division
Ab.:   Fam. Div.

Family Law Quarterly
Ab.:   Fam. L.Q.

Ex.:   Andrew Schepard, <u>Divorce, Interspousal Torts, and Res Judicata</u>,
           24 Fam. L.Q. 127 (1990). –Article Citation.

           Andrew Schepard, <u>Divorce, Interspousal Torts, and Res Judicata</u>,
           24 Fam. L.Q. 127, 133-35 (1990). –Page Citation.

Family Law Reporter (Bureau of National Affairs)
Ab.:   Fam. L. Rep. (BNA)

Ex.:   <u>DuJack v. DuJack</u>, [Current Developments] Fam. L. Rep. (BNA) (22
           Fam. L. Rep.) 1024 (N.Y. App. Div. Nov. 2, 1995). –Citation to
           looseleaf material.

           <u>Speer v. Dealy</u>, 19 Fam. L. Rep. (BNA) 1222 (Neb. Feb. 26, 1993).
           –Citation to bound material.

           –The above examples are proper if the case is not yet available in, or is
           not reported in, an official or West reporter, a public domain citation,
           or in a widely used computer database.

           Angela Arkin Byne, <u>Using DNA Evidence to Prove Paternity: What the
           Attorney Needs to Know</u>, 19 Fam. L. Rep. (BNA) 3001 (Dec. 15,
           1992). –Citation to bound article or monograph.

Family Law Tax Guide (Commerce Clearing House)
Ab.:   Fam. L. Tax Guide (CCH)

Farnsworth on Contracts, by E. Allan Farnsworth
–Do not abbreviate the title.

Ex.:   II E. Allan Farnsworth, <u>Farnsworth on Contracts</u> § 6.12 (3d ed. 2004).
           –Section Citation.

           II E. Allan Farnsworth, <u>Farnsworth on Contracts</u> § 6.12, at 212 (3d ed.
           2004). – Page Citation.

In law review footnotes, the titles of books and the names of cases, except for procedural
phrases, are not underlined. <u>See</u> <u>Bluebook</u> rule 2.1(a) & (b). Further, the following are in
large and small capitals: codes, restatements, standards, constitutions, periodicals, authors of
books, titles of books, the abbreviated names of codes, most legislative materials except for
bills and resolutions, codified ordinances, model codes, court rules, and sentencing guidelines.
Refer to <u>The Bluebook</u>.

II E. Allan Farnsworth, <u>Farnsworth on Contracts</u> § 6.12, at 212 n.29 (3d ed. 2004). – Footnote Citation.

Federal Audit Guide (Commerce Clearing House)
     Ab.:   Fed. Audit Guide (CCH)

Federal Banking Law Reporter (Commerce Clearing House)
     Ab.:   Fed. Banking L. Rep. (CCH)

     Ex.:   <u>Rivera v. Fair Chevrolet Geo P'ship</u>, [Current] Fed. Banking L. Rep. (CCH) ¶ 100,101 (D.C. Conn. Mar. 25, 1996). –Citation to looseleaf material.

            <u>RTC v. City Fed.</u>, [1995-1996 Transfer Binder] Fed. Banking L. Rep. (CCH) ¶ 100,026 (3rd Cir. 1995). –Citation to transfer binder material.

            –The above examples are proper if the case is not yet available in, or is not reported in, an official or West reporter, a public domain citation, or in a widely used computer database.

Federal Bar News & Journal
     Ab.:   Fed. B. News & J.

     Ex.:   A. Darby Dickerson, <u>Contractual Jury Waiver Provisions</u>, 39 Fed. B. News & J. 206 (1992). –Article Citation.

            A. Darby Dickerson, <u>Contractual Jury Waiver Provisions</u>, 39 Fed. B. News & J. 206, 209-10 (1992). –Page Citation.

Federal Carriers Reports (Commerce Clearing House)
     Ab.:   Fed. Carr. Rep. (CCH)

            Fed. Carr. Cas. (CCH (bound))

Federal Cases
     Ab.:   F. Cas.

            <u>See</u> <u>Bluebook</u> table T.1, p.194.

     Ex.:   <u>Corfield v. Coryell</u>, 6 F. Cas. 546 (C.C.E.D Pa. 1825) (No. 3230). –Case Citation.

            <u>DeLovio v. Boit</u>, 7 F. Cas. 418 (C.C.D. Mass. 1815) (No. 3776). –Case Citation.

Federal Claims Reporter
     Ab.:   Fed. Cl.

     Ex.:   <u>Davis v. United States</u>, 35 Fed. Cl. 392 (1996).

Federal Communications Commission Record (1986-date)
     Ab.:   F.C.C.R.

     Ex.:   <u>In the Matter of KIDS-TV 6</u>, 14 F.C.C.R. 13351 (1999).

Federal Communications Commission Reports (1934-1986)
     Ab.:   F.C.C., F.C.C.2d

In citing cases in law review footnotes, abbreviate any word listed in table T.6; the names of "states, countries, and other geographical units" unless they are named parties; and any other words of eight or more letters "if <u>substantial</u> space is thereby saved and the result is unambiguous." <u>Bluebook</u> rule 10.2.2. On the other hand, in citing cases in text, abbreviate only widely known acronyms and the following words: "&," "Ass'n," "Bros.," "Co.," "Corp.," "Inc.," "Ltd.," and "No." <u>Bluebook</u> rule 10.2.1(c).

Ex.:   Deregulation of Radio, 73 F.C.C.2d 457 (1979).

A.T. & T. Co., 88 F.C.C.2d 1656 (1982).

Federal Communications Law Journal
Ab.:   Fed. Comm. L.J.

Ex.:   David R. Poe, As the World Turns: Cable Television and the Cycle of Regulation, 43 Fed. Comm. L.J. 141 (1991). −Article Citation.

David R. Poe, As the World Turns: Cable Television and the Cycle of Regulation, 43 Fed. Comm. L.J. 141, 153-55 (1991). −Page Citation.

Federal Contracts Report (Bureau of National Affairs)
Ab.:   Fed. Cont. Rep. (BNA)

Federal Court Reports (Canada) (1971-date)
          −Cite to Federal Court Reports (F.C.) or Exchequer Court Reports (Ex. C.R.), if therein; otherwise, cite to Dominion Law Reports (D.L.R.). See Bluebook table T.2., p. 254.

Ab.:   F.C.

Ex.:   Mileva v. Canada, [1991] 3 F.C. 398, 401 (Can.). −Page Citation.

          −Provide neutral citation, if available. See Bluebook table T.2, p. 254 (3d prtg. 2006).

Duncan v. R. [2003] 2 F.C. 25, 2002 FCA 291 (Can.). −Case with neutral citation.

Note: For information on Canada's neutral citation, see A Neutral Citation Standard for Case Law, available at http://www.lexum.umontreal.ca/ccc-ccr/neutr/neutr.jur_en.html.

Federal Election Campaign Financing Guide (Commerce Clearing House)
Ab.:   Fed. Election Camp. Fin. Guide (CCH)

Federal Energy Regulatory Commission Reports (Commerce Clearing House)
Ab.:   Fed. Energy Reg. Comm'n Rep. (CCH)

Federal Estate and Gift Tax Reporter (Commerce Clearing House)
Ab.:   Fed. Est. & Gift Tax Rep. (CCH)

          −Bound as U.S. Tax Cas. (CCH)

Ex.:   Hall v. United States, 3 Fed. Est. & Gift Tax Rep. (CCH) (92-1 U.S. Tax Cas.) ¶ 60,096 (M.D. Tenn. Nov. 22, 1991). −Citation to looseleaf material.

Estate of Moran v. United States, 96-1 U.S. Tax Cas. (CCH) ¶ 50,141 (9th Cir. 1996). −Citation to bound material.

          −The above examples are proper if the case is not yet available in, or is not reported in, an official or West reporter, a public domain citation, or in a widely used computer database.

In law review footnotes, the titles of books and the names of cases, except for procedural phrases, are not underlined. See Bluebook rule 2.1(a) & (b). Further, the following are in large and small capitals: codes, restatements, standards, constitutions, periodicals, authors of books, titles of books, the abbreviated names of codes, most legislative materials except for bills and resolutions, codified ordinances, model codes, court rules, and sentencing guidelines. Refer to The Bluebook.

Federal Excise Tax Reports (Commerce Clearing House)
> Ab.:   Fed. Ex. Tax Rep. (CCH)
>
>   –Bound as U.S. Tax Cas. (CCH)
>
> Ex.:   Amax Coal Co. v. United States, Fed. Ex. Tax Rep. (CCH) (96-1 U.S. Tax Cas.) ¶ 70,053 (S.D. Ind. Feb. 2, 1996). –Citation to looseleaf material.
>
>   United States v. Miller, 79-2 U.S. Tax Cas. (CCH) ¶ 16,318 (N.D. Tex. 1979). –Citation to bound material.
>
>   –The above examples are proper if the case is not yet available in, or is not reported in, an official or West reporter, a public domain citation, or in a widely used computer database.

Federal Income Gift and Estate Taxation (Matthew Bender)
> Ab.:   Fed. Inc. Gift & Est. Tax'n (MB)

Federal Income Taxation, by Michael D. Rose and John C. Chommie
> –Do not abbreviate the title.
>
> Ex.:   Michael D. Rose & John C. Chommie, Federal Income Taxation § 3.33 (3d ed. 1988). –Section Citation.
>
>   Michael D. Rose & John C. Chommie, Federal Income Taxation § 3.33, at 183 (3d ed. 1988). –Page Citation.
>
>   Michael D. Rose & John C. Chommie, Federal Income Taxation § 3.33, at 183 n.19 (3d ed. 1988). –Footnote Citation.

Federal Income Taxation of Corporations and Shareholders, by Boris I. Bittker and James S. Eustice
> –Do not abbreviate the title.
>
> Ex.:   Boris I. Bittker & James S. Eustice, Federal Income Taxation of Corporations and Shareholders § 357 (7th ed. 2000). –Section Citation.
>
>   Boris I. Bittker & James S. Eustice, Federal Income Taxation of Corporations and Shareholders § 357, at 12-202 (7th ed. 2000). –Page Citation.

Federal Income Taxation of Individuals, by Boris L. Bittker, Martin J. McMahan, Jr., and Lawrence A. Zelenak
> –Do not abbreviate the title.
>
> Ex.:   Boris L. Bittker et al., Federal Income Taxation of Individuals ¶ 15.05 (3rd ed. 2002). –Paragraph Citation.
>
>   Boris L. Bittker et al., Federal Income Taxation of Individuals ¶ 15.05, at 15-20 (3rd ed. 2002). –Page Citation.

In citing cases in law review footnotes, abbreviate any word listed in table T.6; the names of "states, countries, and other geographical units" unless they are named parties; and any other words of eight or more letters "if substantial space is thereby saved and the result is unambiguous." Bluebook rule 10.2.2. On the other hand, in citing cases in text, abbreviate only widely known acronyms and the following words: "&," "Ass'n," "Bros.," "Co.," "Corp.," "Inc.," "Ltd.," and "No." Bluebook rule 10.2.1(c).

Federal Law Reports (Austl.)
Ab.: F.L.R.

Ex.: MNJ v. MEB (No. 2), [2004] FMCAfam 294; (2004) 184 F.L.R. 37 (Austl.).

Note: For explanation of Australia's medium-neutral citation, see L.T. Olsson, Guide to Uniform Production of Judgments (2d ed. 1999), available at http://www.aija.org.au/online/judguide.htm.

Federal Law Review
Ab.: Fed. L. Rev.

Ex.: Lee Aitken, Jurisdiction, Liability and "Double Function" Legislation, 19 Fed. L. Rev. 31 (1990). –Article Citation.

Lee Aitken, Jurisdiction, Liability and "Double Function" Legislation, 19 Fed. L. Rev. 31, 37-39 (1990). –Page Citation.

Federal Maritime Commission Reports (U.S.) (1919-1985)
Ab.: F.M.C.

Ex.: Universal Nolin UMC Indus., 19 F.M.C. 780 (1977).

Federal Mine Safety and Health Review Commission Decisions (1979-date)
Ab.: F.M.S.H.R.C.

Ex.: Local 2274, United Mine Workers, 8 F.M.S.H.R.C. 1310 (1986). –Case Citation.

Local 2274, United Mine Workers, 8 F.M.S.H.R.C. 1310, 1313 (1986). –Page Citation.

Federal Power Commission Reports (U.S.) (1931-1977)
Ab.: F.P.C.

Ex.: N. Natural Gas Co., 58 F.P.C. 1744 (1977). –Case Citation.

Federal Practice and Procedure, by Charles Alan Wright, Arthur R. Miller, and others
–Do not abbreviate the title.

Ex.: 7A Charles A. Wright et al., Federal Practice and Procedure § 1753 (3d ed. 2005). –Section Citation.

7A Charles A. Wright et al., Federal Practice and Procedure § 1753, at 45 (3d ed. 2005). –Page Citation.

15A Charles A. Wright et al., Federal Practice and Procedure § 3914.7, at 253 (2d ed. Supp. 2005). –Supplement Citation.

Federal Probation
Ab.: Fed. Probation

In law review footnotes, the titles of books and the names of cases, except for procedural phrases, are not underlined. See Bluebook rule 2.1(a) & (b). Further, the following are in large and small capitals: codes, restatements, standards, constitutions, periodicals, authors of books, titles of books, the abbreviated names of codes, most legislative materials except for bills and resolutions, codified ordinances, model codes, court rules, and sentencing guidelines. Refer to The Bluebook.

Ex.:   Thomas W. White, <u>Corrections: Out of Balance</u>, Fed. Probation, Dec. 1989, at 31. –Article Citation.

Thomas W. White, <u>Corrections: Out of Balance</u>, Fed. Probation, Dec. 1989, at 31, 34. –Page Citation.

Federal Register

Ab.:   Fed. Reg.

Ex.:   61 Fed. Reg. 56,640 (Oct. 27, 1996).

61 Fed. Reg. 56,746 (Nov. 13, 1996) (to be codified at 29 C.F.R. pt.1910).
–Where Fed. Reg. so indicates.

Comment Request, 61 Fed. Reg. 56,659 (Nov. 5, 1996). –When material is not of a permanent nature.

61 Fed. Reg. 56,656 (proposed Nov. 4, 1996) (to be codified at 49 C.F.R. pt. 1310). –Proposed rule.

Federal Reporter

–With volume 831 (1988), Federal Reporter, Second Series, became West's Federal Reporter, Second Series. Citation form is not affected by this title change.

Ab.:   F., F.2d, F.3d

Ex.:   <u>Pan-Am. Petroleum Transp. Co. v. Robins Dry Dock & Repair Co.</u>, 281 F. 97 (2d Cir. 1922). –Case Citation.

<u>Pan-Am. Petroleum Transp. Co. v. Robins Dry Dock & Repair Co.</u>, 281 F. 97, 98 (2d Cir. 1922). –Page Citation.

<u>Foy v. Donnelly</u>, 959 F.2d. 1307 (7th Cir. 1990). –Case Citation.

<u>Foy v. Donnelly</u>, 959 F.2d. 1307, 1309 (7th Cir. 1990). –Page Citation.

<u>Johnson v. Heffron</u>, 88 F.3d 404 (6th Cir. 1996). –Case Citation.

<u>Johnson v. Heffron</u>, 88 F.3d 404, 406 (6th Cir. 1996). –Page Citation.

Federal Reserve Bulletin (1915-date)

Ab.:   Fed. Res. Bull.

Ex.:   Alan Greenspan, Statement Before the Committee on Banking, Housing and Urban Affairs, U.S. Senate (Apr. 16, 1991), <u>in</u> 77 Fed. Res. Bull. 423 (1991). –Statement Citation.

Federal Rules Decisions

–With volume 117 (1988), Federal Rules Decisions became West's Federal Rules Decisions. Citation form is not affected by this title change.

Ab.:   F.R.D.

In citing cases in law review footnotes, abbreviate any word listed in table T.6; the names of "states, countries, and other geographical units" unless they are named parties; and any other words of eight or more letters "if <u>substantial</u> space is thereby saved and the result is unambiguous." <u>Bluebook</u> rule 10.2.2. On the other hand, in citing cases in text, abbreviate only widely known acronyms and the following words: "&," "Ass'n," "Bros.," "Co.," "Corp.," "Inc.," "Ltd.," and "No." <u>Bluebook</u> rule 10.2.1(c).

Ex.:   <u>Gonzales v. Wing</u>, 167 F.R.D. 352 (N.D. N.Y. 1996).

Federal Rules of Appellate Procedure
Ab.:   Fed. R. App. P.

Ex.:   Fed. R. App. P. 34.

See also Rules of Evidence and Procedure and <u>Bluebook</u> rule 12.8.3.

Federal Rules of Civil Procedure
Ab.:   Fed. R. Civ. P.

Ex.:   Fed. R. Civ. P. 23.

See also Rules of Evidence and Procedure and <u>Bluebook</u> rule 12.8.3.

Federal Rules of Criminal Procedure
Ab.:   Fed. R. Crim. P.

Ex.:   Fed. R. Crim. P. 18.

See also Rules of Evidence and Procedure and <u>Bluebook</u> rule 12.8.3.

Federal Rules of Evidence
Ab.:   Fed. R. Evid.

Ex.:   Fed. R. Evid. 804(b)(4).

See also Rules of Evidence and Procedure and <u>Bluebook</u> rule 12.8.3.

Federal Rules of Evidence Service
Ab.:   Fed. R. Evid. Serv. (West)

Federal Rules of Habeas Procedure
Ab.:   28 U.S.C. § 2254 R. _____ (person in state custody)

28 U.S.C. § 2255 R. _____ (person in federal custody)

Ex.:   28 U.S.C. § 2254 R. 9(b).

28 U.S.C. § 2255 R. 5.

Federal Rules Service, Third Series
Ab.:   Fed. R. Serv. 3d (West)

Ex.:   <u>Gordon v. Gouline</u>, 34 Fed. R. Serv. 3d (West) 967 (D.C. Cir. Apr. 19, 1996). –Citation to bound material.

–The above example is proper if the case is not yet available in, or is not reported in, an official or West reporter, a public domain citation, or in a widely used computer database.

Federal Securities Code (ALI)
See American Law Institute Federal Securities Code.

Federal Securities Law Reports (Commerce Clearing House)
Ab.:   Fed. Sec. L. Rep. (CCH)

In law review footnotes, the titles of books and the names of cases, except for procedural phrases, are not underlined. <u>See</u> <u>Bluebook</u> rule 2.1(a) & (b). Further, the following are in large and small capitals: codes, restatements, standards, constitutions, periodicals, authors of books, titles of books, the abbreviated names of codes, most legislative materials except for bills and resolutions, codified ordinances, model codes, court rules, and sentencing guidelines. Refer to <u>The Bluebook</u>.

Ex.:   <u>Energy Factors, Inc. v. Nueva Energy Co.</u>, [Current] Fed. Sec. L. Rep. (CCH) ¶ 96,446 (S.D.N.Y. Nov. 22, 1991). –Citation to looseleaf material.

           <u>SEC v. Weil</u>, [1980 Transfer Binder] Fed. Sec. L. Rep. (CCH) ¶ 97,541 (M.D. Fla. 1980). –Citation to transfer binder material.

           –The above examples are proper if the case is not yet available in, or is not reported in, an official or West reporter, a public domain citation, or in a widely used computer database.

           <u>Funding Capital Corp.</u>, Exchange Act Release No. 29,425, [1991 Transfer Binder] Fed. Sec. L. Rep. (CCH) ¶ 84,836 (SEC July 10, 1991). –Citation to transfer binder administrative material.

Federal Supplement

           –With volume 671 (1988), Federal Supplement became West's Federal Supplement. Citation form is not affected by this title change.

Ab.:   F. Supp.

Ex.:   <u>Marchwinski v. Oliver Tyrone Corp.</u>, 461 F. Supp. 160 (W.D. Pa. 1978). –Case Citation.

           <u>Marchwinski v. Oliver Tyrone Corp.</u>, 461 F. Supp. 160, 162 (W.D. Pa. 1978). –Page Citation.

Federal Tax Coordinator Second Series (Research Institute of America)

Ab.:   Fed. Tax Coordinator 2d (RIA)

Ex.:   <u>How the Estate Tax Works</u>, 22A. Fed. Tax Coordinator 2d (RIA) ¶ R-100M0, at 46,051 (Apr. 18, 1996). –Citation to section of publication.

Federal Taxation of Income, Estates and Gifts, by Boris I. Bittker and Lawrence Lokken

           –Do not abbreviate the title.

Ex.:   3 Boris I. Bittker & Lawrence Lokken, <u>Federal Taxation of Income, Estates and Gifts</u> § 75.2.6, at 75-29 (2d ed. 1991). –Page Citation.

           1 Boris I. Bittker & Lawrence Lokken, <u>Federal Taxation of Income, Estates, and Gifts</u> ¶ 22.2.2 (3d ed. 1999). –Paragraph Citation.

Federal Trade Commission Decisions (U.S.) (1915-date)

Ab.:   F.T.C.

Ex.:   <u>Mannesmann, A.G.</u>, 115 F.T.C. 412 (1980). –Case Citation.

Federalist, The

Ab.:   The Federalist No. (author)

Ex.:   <u>The Federalist</u> No. 15 (A. Hamilton).

           <u>The Federalist</u> No. 41, at 248 (J. Madison) (H. Lodge ed. 1888).

In citing cases in law review footnotes, abbreviate any word listed in table T.6; the names of "states, countries, and other geographical units" unless they are named parties; and any other words of eight or more letters "if <u>substantial</u> space is thereby saved and the result is unambiguous." <u>Bluebook</u> rule 10.2.2. On the other hand, in citing cases in text, abbreviate only widely known acronyms and the following words: "&," "Ass'n," "Bros.," "Co.," "Corp.," "Inc.," "Ltd.," and "No." <u>Bluebook</u> rule 10.2.1(c).

Films
    Ex.:   To Catch a Thief (Paramount 1955).

Fire & Casualty Cases
    See Insurance Law Reports.

Fleming and Hazard on Civil Procedure
    See Civil Procedure, by James Fleming, Jr., Geoffrey C. Hazard, Jr. and John Leubsdorf

Fletcher Forum of World Affairs, The
    Ab.:   Fletcher F. World Aff.

    Ex.:   Kent Jones, Selectivity and the Changing Structure of Trade Policy, 16 Fletcher F. World Aff. 15 (1992). –Article Citation.

             Kent Jones, Selectivity and the Changing Structure of Trade Policy, 16 Fletcher F. World Aff. 15, 16-20 (1992). –Page Citation.

Fletcher Cyclopedia of the Law of Private Corporations, by William Meade Fletcher
    –Do not abbreviate the title.

    Ex.:   1 William Meade Fletcher et. al., Fletcher Cyclopedia of the Law of Private Corporations § 41.10 (perm ed., rev. vol. 1999 and Cum. Supp. 2000). –Section Citation.

             3A James Solheim & Kenneth Elkins, Fletcher Cyclopedia of the Law of Private Corporations § 1117 (perm. ed., rev. vol. 1994 and Supp. 2000). –Section Citation.

             3A James Solheim & Kenneth Elkins, Fletcher Cyclopedia of the Law of Private Corporation § 1117, at 218 (perm. ed., rev. vol. 1994 and Supp. 2000). –Page Citation.

Florida Administrative Code Annotated (LexisNexis)
    Ab.:   Fla. Admin. Code Ann. r. x-x.x (year)
    Ex.:   Fla. Admin. Code Ann. r. 6-1.0996 (2003)

Florida Administrative Weekly
    Ab.:   vol. no. Fla. Admin. Weekly page no. (month day, year)
    Ex.:   30 Fla. Admin. Weekly 25 (Jan. 2, 2004)

Florida, Annual Report of the Attorney General
    See Annual Report of the Attorney General, State of Florida.

Florida Bar Journal
    Ab.:   Fla. B.J.
    Ex.:   Nicholas J. Watkins & Joel Stewart, Employer Sanctions and the Employer's Response, Fla. B.J., May 1992, at 60. –Article Citation.
             Nicholas J. Watkins & Joel Stewart, Employer Sanctions and the Employer's Response, Fla. B.J., May 1992, at 60, 62. –Page Citation.

In law review footnotes, the titles of books and the names of cases, except for procedural phrases, are not underlined. See Bluebook rule 2.1(a) & (b). Further, the following are in large and small capitals: codes, restatements, standards, constitutions, periodicals, authors of books, titles of books, the abbreviated names of codes, most legislative materials except for bills and resolutions, codified ordinances, model codes, court rules, and sentencing guidelines. Refer to The Bluebook.

Florida Constitution

Ab.: Fla. Const. art. , § .

Ex.: Fla. Const. art. III, § 5. –"Cite constitutional provisions currently in force without a date." Bluebook rule 11.

Fla. Const. art. V (repealed 1973) . –"If the cited provision has been repealed, either indicate parenthetically the fact and date of repeal or cite the repealing provision in full." Bluebook rule 11.

Fla. Const. art. III , § 7 (amended 1980). –"When citing a provision that has been subsequently amended, either indicate parenthetically the fact and date of amendment or cite the amending provision in full." Bluebook rule 11.

Fla. Const. of 1868, art. XII , §§ 7, 8 (1968). –"Cite constitutions that have been totally superseded by year of adoption; if the specific provision cited was adopted in a different year, give that year parenthetically." Bluebook rule 11.

Florida District Court of Appeals

Ab.: Fla. Dist. Ct. App.

–Cite to So. 2d, if therein; otherwise to Fla. L. Weekly.

In documents submitted to Florida state courts, cite as follows:

Oakley v. State, 677 So. 2d 879 (Fla. 2d DCA 1996). –Case Citation.

Oakley v. State, 677 So. 2d 879, 880 (Fla. 2d DCA 1996). –Page Citation.

In all other documents, cite as follows:

Oakley v. State, 677 So. 2d 879 (Fla. Dist. Ct. App. 1996). –Case Citation.

Oakley v. State, 677 So. 2d 879, 880 (Fla. Dist. Ct. App. 1996). –Page Citation.

See Bluebook table T.1, p.205; see also Fla. R. App. P. 9.800.

Florida Journal of International Law

Ab.: Fla. J. Int'l L.

Ex.: Karen Y. Crabbs, The German Abortion Debate: Stumbling Block to Unity, 6 Fla. J. Int'l L. 213 (1991). –Article Citation.

Karen Y. Crabbs, The German Abortion Debate: Stumbling Block to Unity, 6 Fla. J. Int'l L. 213, 217-19 (1991). –Page Citation.

Florida Law Review

Ab.: Fla. L. Rev.

In citing cases in law review footnotes, abbreviate any word listed in table T.6; the names of "states, countries, and other geographical units" unless they are named parties; and any other words of eight or more letters "if substantial space is thereby saved and the result is unambiguous." Bluebook rule 10.2.2. On the other hand, in citing cases in text, abbreviate only widely known acronyms and the following words: "&," "Ass'n," "Bros.," "Co.," "Corp.," "Inc.," "Ltd.," and "No." Bluebook rule 10.2.1(c).

Ex.:   Michael L. Radelet & Glenn L. Pierce, <u>Choosing Those Who Will Die:</u>
<u>Race and the Death Penalty in Florida</u>, 43 Fla. L. Rev. 1 (1991).
–Article Citation.

Michael L. Radelet & Glenn L. Pierce, <u>Choosing Those Who Will Die:</u>
<u>Race and the Death Penalty in Florida</u>, 43 Fla. L. Rev. 1, 7 (1991).
–Page Citation.

Florida Reports
Ab.:   Fla.

–Discontinued after 160 Fla. 974 (1948).

–Cite to So. or So. 2d, if therein; otherwise, cite to Fla.

–Give parallel citations, if at all, only in documents submitted to Florida
state courts. <u>See</u> <u>Bluebook</u> rules 10.3.1 and B5.1.3; see also Fla. R.
App. P. 9.800, which permits a parallel citation.

–Through 160 Fla. 974 (1948), cite as follows:

<u>Winfield v. Truitt</u>, 71 Fla. 38, 70 So. 775 (1916) –Case Citation.

<u>Winfield v. Truitt</u>, 71 Fla. 38, 48, 70 So. 775, 778-79 (1916) –Page
Citation.

In all other documents:

<u>Winfield v. Truitt</u>, 70 So. 775 (Fla. 1916). –Case Citation.

<u>Winfield v. Truitt</u>, 70 So. 775, 778-79 (Fla. 1916). –Page Citation.

–After 60 Fla. 974 (1948), cite as follows:

In all documents:

<u>Florida Bar v. McAtee</u>, 674 So. 2d 734 (Fla. 1996). –Case Citation.

<u>Florida Bar v. McAtee</u>, 674 So. 2d 734, 736 (Fla. 1996). –Page
Citation.

Florida Session Laws
See Florida Session Law Service and Laws of Florida.

Florida Session Law Service (West)
Ab.:   year Fla. Sess. Law Serv. (West)

Ex.:   Act of July 1, 1996, ch. 96-414, 1996 Fla. Sess. Law Serv. 2248 (West)
(relating to driver's licenses). –Citation to an entire session law.

Act of July 1, 1996, ch. 96-414, sec. 4, § 322.16, 1996 Fla. Sess. Law
Serv. 2248, 2250-51 (West) (relating to driver's license restrictions).
–Citation to a session law amending a prior act.

– "Cite to Fla. Laws, if therein." <u>Bluebook</u> table T.1, p. 205.

–For proper citation form in papers submitted to Florida courts, see Fla.
R. App. P. 9.800 (h).

Florida State University Law Review
Ab.:   Fla. St. U. L. Rev.

In law review footnotes, the titles of books and the names of cases, except for procedural
phrases, are not underlined. <u>See</u> <u>Bluebook</u> rule 2.1(a) & (b). Further, the following are in
large and small capitals: codes, restatements, standards, constitutions, periodicals, authors of
books, titles of books, the abbreviated names of codes, most legislative materials except for
bills and resolutions, codified ordinances, model codes, court rules, and sentencing guidelines.
Refer to <u>The Bluebook</u>.

Ex.:   Daniel E. Georges-Abeyie, <u>Law Enforcement and Racial and Ethnic Bias</u>, 19 Fla. St. U. L. Rev. 717 (1992). –Article Citation.

Daniel E. Georges-Abeyie, <u>Law Enforcement and Racial and Ethnic Bias</u>, 19 Fla. St. U. L. Rev. 717, 723-26 (1992). –Page Citation.

Florida Statutes

Ab.:   Fla. Stat. § x.x (year)

Ex.:   Fla. Stat. § 327.461 (2004).

–For proper citation form in papers submitted to Florida courts, see Fla. R. App. P. 9.800(f).

Florida Statutes Annotated (West)

See West's Florida Statutes Annotated.

Florida Statutes Annotated (LexisNexis)

See LexisNexis Florida Statutes Annotated.

Florida Supplement

Ab.:   Fla. Supp.

Fla. Supp. 2d

–Cite Florida Circuit Court (Fla. Cir. Ct.), County Court (e.g. Dade County Ct.), Public Service Commission (Fla. P.S.C.) and other lower courts of record to Fla. Supp. or Fla. Supp. 2d., if therein, otherwise to Fla. L. Weekly Supp. <u>See</u> <u>Bluebook</u> table T.1, p. 205; <u>see also</u> Fla. R. App. P. 9.800.

In documents submitted to Florida state courts, cite as follows:

<u>Peavy v. Boyd</u>, 48 Fla. Supp. 101 (Fla. 11th Cir. Ct. 1977). –Case Citation.

<u>Garcia v. Ruiz</u>, 50 Fla. Supp. 2d 176 (Fla. Dade County Ct. 1991). –Case Citation.

In all other documents, cite as follows:

<u>Peavy v. Boyd</u>, 48 Fla. Supp. 101 (Cir. Ct. 1977). –Case Citation.

<u>Garcia v. Ruiz</u>, 50 Fla. Supp. 2d 176 (County Ct. 1991). –Case Citation.

Food and Drug Law Journal

Ab: Food & Drug L.J.

Ex: John C. Yoo, <u>Takings Issues in the Approval of Generic Biologics</u>, 60 Food & Drug L.J. 33 (2005). –Article Citation.

John C. Yoo, <u>Takings Issues in the Approval of Generic Biologics</u>, 60 Food & Drug L.J. 33, 42 (2005). –Page Citation

Food Drug Cosmetic Law Journal

Ab.:   Food Drug Cosm. L.J.

In citing cases in law review footnotes, abbreviate any word listed in table T.6; the names of "states, countries, and other geographical units" unless they are named parties; and any other words of eight or more letters "if <u>substantial</u> space is thereby saved and the result is unambiguous." <u>Bluebook</u> rule 10.2.2. On the other hand, in citing cases in text, abbreviate only widely known acronyms and the following words: "&," "Ass'n," "Bros.," "Co.," "Corp.," "Inc.," "Ltd.," and "No." <u>Bluebook</u> rule 10.2.1(c).

Ex.:   Hugh Latimer, <u>Whither the FTC on Food Advertising?</u>, 46 Food Drug
Cosm. L.J. 503 (1991). –Article Citation.

Hugh Latimer, <u>Whither the FTC on Food Advertising?</u>, 46 Food Drug
Cosm. L.J. 503, 511-12 (1991). –Page Citation.

Food Drug Cosmetic Law Reports (Commerce Clearing House)
Ab.:   Food Drug Cosm. L. Rep. (CCH)

Ex.:   <u>Moore v. Armour Pharm. Co.</u>, [New Matters] Food Drug Cosm. L. Rep.
(CCH) ¶ 38,188 (M.D. Fla. Aug. 27, 1990). –Citation to looseleaf
material.

<u>DeVito v. HEM, Inc.</u>, [1988-1989 Developments Transfer Binder]
Food Drug Cosm. L. Rep. (CCH) ¶ 38,108 (M.D. Pa. 1988). –Citation
to transfer binder material.

–The above examples are proper if the case is not yet available in, or is
not reported in, an official or West reporter, a public domain citation,
or in a widely used computer database.

footnote(s)
Ab.:   note, notes

n., nn.

Ex.:   <u>supra</u> note 211.

J. William Futrell, <u>The Hidden Crisis in Georgia Land Use</u>, 10 Ga. L.
Rev. 53, 88, n.124 (1975).

J. William Futrell, <u>The Hidden Crisis in Georgia Land Use</u>, 10 Ga. L.
Rev. 53, 89, nn.133-34 (1975).

<u>See</u> <u>Bluebook</u> rules 2.2(b), 3.2(b), & 3.5.

Fordham Environmental Law Journal
Ab.:   Fordham Envtl. L.J.

Ex.:   Peter N. Ching & Brian M. Diglio, Note, <u>Staff Accounting Bulletin 92:</u>
<u>A Paradigmatic Shift in Disclosure Standards</u>, 7 Fordham Envtl. L.J. 75
(1995). –Article Citation.

Peter N. Ching & Brian M. Diglio, Note, <u>Staff Accounting Bulletin 92:</u>
<u>A Paradigmatic Shift in Disclosure Standards</u>, 7 Fordham Envtl. L.J.
75, 78 (1995). –Page Citation.

Fordham Intellectual Property, Media & Entertainment Law Journal
Ab: Fordham Intell. Prop. Media & Ent. L.J.

Ex: John Vukelj, <u>Post No Bills: Can the NBA Prohibit Its Players from</u>
<u>Wearing Tatoo Advertisements?</u>, 15 Fordham Intell. Prop. Media &
Ent. L.J. 507 (2005). –Article Citation.

John Vukelj, <u>Post No Bills: Can the NBA Prohibit Its Players from</u>
<u>Wearing Tatoo Advertisements?</u>, 15 Fordham Intell. Prop. Media &
Ent. L.J. 507, 510 (2005). –Page Citation.

In law review footnotes, the titles of books and the names of cases, except for procedural
phrases, are not underlined. <u>See</u> <u>Bluebook</u> rule 2.1(a) & (b). Further, the following are in
large and small capitals: codes, restatements, standards, constitutions, periodicals, authors of
books, titles of books, the abbreviated names of codes, most legislative materials except for
bills and resolutions, codified ordinances, model codes, court rules, and sentencing guidelines.
Refer to <u>The Bluebook</u>.

Fordham International Law Journal
>   Ab.:   Fordham Int'l L.J.
>
>   Ex.:   Julian M. Joshua, <u>The Right to be Heard in EEC Competition Procedures</u>, 15 Fordham Int'l L.J. 16 (1991-1992). –Article Citation.
>
>   Julian M. Joshua, <u>The Right to be Heard in EEC Competition Procedures</u>, 15 Fordham Int'l L.J. 16, 29-35 (1991-1992). –Page Citation.

Fordham Law Review
>   Ab.:   Fordham L. Rev.
>
>   Ex.:   William E. Kovacic, <u>Reagan's Judicial Appointees and Antitrust in the 1990's</u>, 60 Fordham L. Rev. 49 (1991). –Article Citation.
>
>   William E. Kovacic, <u>Reagan's Judicial Appointees and Antitrust in the 1990's</u>, 60 Fordham L. Rev. 49, 57-59 (1991). –Page Citation.

Fordham Urban Law Journal
>   Ab.:   Fordham Urb. L.J.
>
>   Ex.:   Cyrus Vance, <u>Foreword: Legal Ethics and Government Integrity</u>, 18 Fordham Urb. L.J. 153 (1990-1991). –Article Citation.
>
>   Cyrus Vance, <u>Foreword: Legal Ethics and Government Integrity</u>, 18 Fordham Urb. L.J. 153, 154-55 (1990-1991). –Page Citation.

Foreign Broadcast Information Service
>   Ab.:   F.B.I.S.

forewords, prefaces, and introductions
>   Ex.:   Norman Dorsen, <u>Foreword</u> to William L. Dwyer, <u>The Goldmark Case: An American Libel Trial</u>, at vii, xi (1984). –Citation for a preface, foreword, introduction, or epilogue by someone other than the author.

See <u>Bluebook</u> rule 15.6.

Formal Advisory Opinions
See <u>Bluebook</u> rule 14.4

Forthcoming Publications
>   Ex.:   Brendan A. Thompson, Note, <u>Final Exit: Should the Double Effect Rule Regarding the Legality of Euthenasia in the United Kingdom be Laid to Rest?</u>, 33 Vand. J. Trans. L. (forthcoming Oct. 2000).
>
>   <u>Peacemaking in International Conflict: Methods and Techniques</u> (William Zartman ed., rev. ed. forthcoming Mar. 2006).

See <u>Bluebook</u> rule 17.2.

Franchise Law Journal
>   Ab.:   Franchise L.J.

In citing cases in law review footnotes, abbreviate any word listed in table T.6; the names of "states, countries, and other geographical units" unless they are named parties; and any other words of eight or more letters "if <u>substantial</u> space is thereby saved and the result is unambiguous." <u>Bluebook</u> rule 10.2.2. On the other hand, in citing cases in text, abbreviate only widely known acronyms and the following words: "&," "Ass'n," "Bros.," "Co.," "Corp.," "Inc.," "Ltd.," and "No." <u>Bluebook</u> rule 10.2.1(c).

Ex.:   Jay Conison, <u>Restrictive Lease Covenants and the Law of Monopoly</u>, Franchise L.J., Winter 1990, at 3. –Article Citation.

Jay Conison, <u>Restrictive Lease Covenants and the Law of Monopoly</u>, Franchise L.J., Winter 1990, at 3, 5. –Page Citation.

Fundamentals of Securities Regulation, by Louis Loss and Joel Seligman
–Do not abbreviate the title.

Ex.:   Louis Loss & Joel Seligman, <u>Fundamentals of Securities Regulation</u> 1122 (5th ed. 2004). –Page Citation.

Louis Loss & Joel Seligman, <u>Fundamentals of Securities Regulation</u> 1122 n.3 (5th ed. 2004). –Footnote Citation.

In law review footnotes, the titles of books and the names of cases, except for procedural phrases, are not underlined. <u>See</u> <u>Bluebook</u> rule 2.1(a) & (b). Further, the following are in large and small capitals: codes, restatements, standards, constitutions, periodicals, authors of books, titles of books, the abbreviated names of codes, most legislative materials except for bills and resolutions, codified ordinances, model codes, court rules, and sentencing guidelines. Refer to <u>The Bluebook</u>.

G

GATT - Basic Instruments and Selected Documents
Ab.:   B.I.S.D.
Ex.:   Report of the Working Party, <u>The Free-Trade Agreement between Canada and the United States</u>, ¶ 76, L/6927, (Nov. 12, 1991), GATT B.I.S.D. (35th Supp.) at 118, 125 (1992).

Gavel, The (Milwaukee Bar Association)
Ab.:   Gavel
Ex.:   Russell Eisenberg, <u>Recent Developments in Sales and Secured Transactions Law</u>, Gavel, Fall 1975, at 8. –Article Citation.

Russell Eisenberg, <u>Recent Developments in Sales and Secured Transactions Law</u>, Gavel, Fall 1975, at 8, 9. –Page Citation.

Gavel, The (State Bar Association of North Dakota)
Ab.:   Gavel
Ex.:   Beth Baumstark, <u>U.C.C. Refiling Procedures</u>, Gavel, Dec. 1991-1992, at 15. –Article Citation.

Beth Baumstark, <u>U.C.C. Refiling Procedures</u>, Gavel, Dec. 1991-1992, at 15, 16. –Page Citation.

General Agreement on Tariffs and Trade Documents
Ab.:   GATT
Ex.:   <u>Observers Status of Governments in the Council of Representatives</u>, GATT Doc. L/7286 (July 21, 1993) (communication from the Committee on Trade and Development).

General and Special Laws of the State of Texas
A.:   year Tex. Gen. Laws page no.
Ex.:   Act of June 17, 1995, ch. 1013, 1995 Tex. Gen. Laws 5068 (relating to electric cooperative corporations). –Citation to an entire session law.

Act of June 17, 1995, ch. 1013, sec. 1, § 2.2011, 1995 Tex. Gen. Laws 5068, 5068-71 (relating to electric cooperative corporations exemption from rate regulation). –Citation to a section of a session law amending a prior act.

–See <u>Bluebook</u> rule 12.4.

General Counsel Memoranda
Ab.:   I.R.S. Gen. Couns. Mem. or I.R.S. G.C.M.

In law review footnotes, the titles of books and the names of cases, except for procedural phrases, are not underlined. <u>See Bluebook</u> rule 2.1(a) & (b). Further, the following are in large and small capitals: codes, restatements, standards, constitutions, periodicals, authors of books, titles of books, the abbreviated names of codes, most legislative materials except for bills and resolutions, codified ordinances, model codes, court rules, and sentencing guidelines. Refer to <u>The Bluebook</u>.

Ex.:   I.R.S. Gen. Couns. Mem. 39,862 (Nov. 21, 1991).

General Laws of Massachusetts (Mass. Bar Assoc./West)
Ab.:   Mass. Gen. Laws ch. x, § x (year)
Ex.:   Mass. Gen. Laws ch. 6, 6:12I (1994).

–For proper citation form in papers submitted to Massachusetts courts, see Mass. R. App. P. 16(g) and Mass. Dist. & Mun. App. Div. R. 16(6).

General Laws of Mississippi
Ab.:   year Miss. Laws page no.
Ex.:   Act of Apr. 7, 1995, ch. 570, 1995 Miss. Laws 874. –Citation to an entire session law.

Act of Apr. 7, 1995, ch. 570, sec. 2, § 37-13-107, 1995 Miss. Laws 874, 881. –Citation to a section of a session law amending a prior act.

–See Bluebook rule 12.4.

General Laws of Rhode Island (LexisNexis)
Ab.:   R.I. Gen. Laws § x-x-x (year)
Ex.:   R.I. Gen. Laws § 5-22-26 (1999).

R.I. Gen. Laws § 4-12-8 (Supp. 2004).

General Statutes of Connecticut
Ab.:   Conn. Gen. Stat. §   (year)
Ex.:   Conn. Gen. Stat. § 17a-112(b) (1995).

General Statutes of North Carolina (LexisNexis)
Ab.:   N.C. Gen. Stat. § x-x (year)
Ex.:   N.C. Gen. Stat. § 20-87.1 (2003).

N.C. Gen. Stat. § 96-13 (Supp. 2005).

–For proper citation form in papers submitted to North Carolina courts, see N.C. R. App. P. app. B.

Generally Accepted Accounting Principles
See Accounting Standards, Generally Accepted.

George Mason Law Review
Ab.:   Geo. Mason L. Rev.
Ex.:   Michael J. Phillips, Entry Restrictions in the Lochner Court, 4 Geo. Mason L. Rev. 405 (1996). –Article Citation.

Michael J. Phillips, Entry Restrictions in the Lochner Court, 4 Geo. Mason L. Rev. 405, 410 (1996). –Page Citation.

George Mason University Civil Rights Law Journal
Ab.:   Geo. Mason U. Civ. Rts. L.J.

In citing cases in law review footnotes, abbreviate any word listed in table T.6; the names of "states, countries, and other geographical units" unless they are named parties; and any other words of eight or more letters "if substantial space is thereby saved and the result is unambiguous." Bluebook rule 10.2.2. On the other hand, in citing cases in text, abbreviate only widely known acronyms and the following words: "&," "Ass'n," "Bros.," "Co.," "Corp.," "Inc.," "Ltd.," and "No." Bluebook rule 10.2.1(c).

Ex.: Peter E. Millspaugh, <u>When Self-Organization Includes Racial Harassment: Must the NLRA Yield to Title VII?</u>, 2 Geo. Mason U. Civ. Rts. L.J. 1 (1991). –Article Citation.

Peter E. Millspaugh, <u>When Self-Organization Includes Racial Harassment: Must the NLRA Yield to Title VII?</u>, 2 Geo. Mason U. Civ. Rts. L.J. 1, 1-2 (1991). –Page Citation.

George Mason University Law Review
Ab.: Geo. Mason U. L. Rev.
Ex.: Konrad Bonsack, <u>Damages Assessment, Janis Joplin's Yearbook, and the Pie-Powder Court</u>, 13 Geo. Mason U. L. Rev. 1 (1990). –Article Citation.

Konrad Bonsack, <u>Damages Assessment, Janis Joplin's Yearbook, and the Pie-Powder Court</u>, 13 Geo. Mason U. L. Rev. 1, 11-15 (1990). –Page Citation.

George Washington International Law Review
Ab: Geo. Wash. Int'l L. Rev.
Ex: Christopher J. Borgen, <u>Resolving Treaty Conflicts</u>, 37 Geo. Wash. Int'l L. Rev. 573 (2005). –Article Citation.

Christopher J. Borgen, <u>Resolving Treaty Conflicts</u>, 37 Geo. Wash. Int'l L. Rev. 573, 584-87 (2005). –Page Citation.

George Washington Journal of International Law and Economics, The
Ab.: Geo. Wash. J. Int'l L. & Econ.
Ex.: Charles Lister, <u>Two Cheers for Competition: Spain's New Antitrust and Unfair Competition Acts</u>, 24 Geo. Wash. J. Int'l L. & Econ. 587 (1991). –Article Citation.

Charles Lister, <u>Two Cheers for Competition: Spain's New Antitrust and Unfair Competition Acts</u>, 24 Geo. Wash. J. Int'l L. & Econ. 587, 587-88 (1991). –Page Citation.

George Washington Law Review, The
Ab.: Geo. Wash. L. Rev.
Ex.: Herbert Hovenkamp, <u>Rationality in Law & Economics</u>, 60 Geo. Wash. L. Rev. 293 (1992). –Article Citation.

Herbert Hovenkamp, <u>Rationality in Law & Economics</u>, 60 Geo. Wash. L. Rev. 293, 294-97 (1992). –Page Citation.

Georgetown Immigration Law Journal
Ab.: Geo. Immigr. L.J.

In law review footnotes, the titles of books and the names of cases, except for procedural phrases, are not underlined. <u>See</u> <u>Bluebook</u> rule 2.1(a) & (b). Further, the following are in large and small capitals: codes, restatements, standards, constitutions, periodicals, authors of books, titles of books, the abbreviated names of codes, most legislative materials except for bills and resolutions, codified ordinances, model codes, court rules, and sentencing guidelines. Refer to <u>The Bluebook</u>.

Ex.:   Bruce A. Hake, <u>Dual Representation in Immigration Practice: The Simple Solution is the Wrong Solution</u>, 5 Geo. Immigr. L.J. 581 (1991). –Article Citation.

Bruce A. Hake, <u>Dual Representation in Immigration Practice: The Simple Solution is the Wrong Solution</u>, 5 Geo. Immigr. L.J. 581, 591-93 (1991). –Page Citation.

Georgetown International Environmental Law Review
Ab.:   Geo. Int'l Envtl. L. Rev.

Ex.:   William T. Burke, <u>Regulation of Driftnet Fishing on the High Seas and the New International Law of the Sea</u>, 3 Geo. Int'l Envtl. L. Rev. 265 (1990). –Article Citation.

William T. Burke, <u>Regulation of Driftnet Fishing on the High Seas and the New International Law of the Sea</u>, 3 Geo. Int'l Envtl. L. Rev. 265, 281-82 (1990). –Page Citation.

Georgetown Journal of International Law
Ab: Geo. J. Int'l L.

Ex: John Y. Gotanda, <u>Recovering Lost Profits in International Disputes</u>, 36 Geo. J. Int'l L. 61 (2004). –Article Citation.

John Y. Gotanda, <u>Recovering Lost Profits in International Disputes</u>, 36 Geo. J. Int'l L. 61, 73-79 (2004). –Page Citation.

Georgetown Journal of Legal Ethics, The
Ab.:   Geo. J. Legal Ethics

Ex.:   Roger C. Crampton, <u>The Lawyer as Whistleblower: Confidentiality and the Government Lawyer</u>, 5 Geo. J. Legal Ethics 291 (1991). –Article Citation.

Roger C. Crampton, <u>The Lawyer as Whistleblower: Confidentiality and the Government Lawyer</u>, 5 Geo. J. Legal Ethics 291, 299-300 (1991). –Page Citation.

Georgetown Law Journal, The
Ab.:   Geo. L.J.

Ex.:   Edward L. Rubin, <u>Legislative Methodology: Some Lessons from the Truth-in-Lending Act</u>, 80 Geo. L.J. 233 (1991). –Article Citation.

Edward L. Rubin, <u>Legislative Methodology: Some Lessons from the Truth-in-Lending Act</u>, 80 Geo. L.J. 233, 242-45 (1991). –Page Citation.

Georgia Appeals Reports
Ab.:   Ga. App.

–Cite to S.E. or S.E.2d, if therein; otherwise, cite to Ga. App.

In citing cases in law review footnotes, abbreviate any word listed in table T.6; the names of "states, countries, and other geographical units" unless they are named parties; and any other words of eight or more letters "if <u>substantial</u> space is thereby saved and the result is unambiguous." <u>Bluebook</u> rule 10.2.2. On the other hand, in citing cases in text, abbreviate only widely known acronyms and the following words: "&," "Ass'n," "Bros.," "Co.," "Corp.," "Inc.," "Ltd.," and "No." <u>Bluebook</u> rule 10.2.1(c).

–Give parallel citations, if at all, only in documents submitted to Georgia state courts. See Bluebook rules 10.3.1 and B5.1.3; see also Ga. Sup. Ct. R. 22 and Ga. Ct. App. R. 23(c), which require a citation only to the official reporter.

In documents submitted to Georgia state courts, cite as follows:

Harris v. State, 222 Ga. App. 56, 473 S.E.2d 229 (1996). –Case Citation.

Harris v. State, 222 Ga. App. 56, 59, 473 S.E.2d 229, 230 (1996). –Page Citation.

In all other documents, cite as follows:

Harris v. State, 222 S.E.2d 56 (Ga. Ct. App. 1996). –Case Citation.

Harris v. State, 222 S.E.2d 56, 59 (Ga. Ct. App. 1996). –Page Citation.

Georgia Code
See Official Code of Georgia Annotated (LexisNexis).

Georgia Code Annotated
See West's Code of Georgia Annotated.

Georgia Constitution
Ab.:   Ga. Const. art.   , §   , ¶

Ex.:   Ga. Const. art. I, § I, ¶ XIII. –"Cite constitutional provisions currently in force without a date." Bluebook rule 11.

Ga. Const. art. III, § VIII, ¶ XII (1976, amended 1979). –"Cite provisions which have been repealed or amended by giving the date of the adoption of the particular provision and the date of repeal or amendment." Bluebook rule 11.

Ga. Const. art. VIII , § 1 , ¶ 1 (amended 1990). –"When citing a provision that has been subsequently amended, either indicate parenthetically the fact and date of amendment or cite the amending provision in full." Bluebook rule 11.

Ga. Const. art. I , §   , ¶ 12 (1983). –"Cite constitutions that have been totally superseded by year of adoption; if the specific provision cited was adopted in a different year, give that year parenthetically." Bluebook rule 11.

Georgia Journal of International and Comparative Law
Ab.:   Ga. J. Int'l & Comp. L.

In law review footnotes, the titles of books and the names of cases, except for procedural phrases, are not underlined. See Bluebook rule 2.1(a) & (b). Further, the following are in large and small capitals: codes, restatements, standards, constitutions, periodicals, authors of books, titles of books, the abbreviated names of codes, most legislative materials except for bills and resolutions, codified ordinances, model codes, court rules, and sentencing guidelines. Refer to The Bluebook.

Ex.:   Charles Mwalimu, <u>Police, State Security Forces and Constitutionalism of Human Rights in Zambia</u>, 21 Ga. J. Int'l & Comp. L. 217 (1991). —Article Citation.

Charles Mwalimu, <u>Police, State Security Forces and Constitutionalism of Human Rights in Zambia</u>, 21 Ga. J. Int'l & Comp. L. 217, 223-24 (1991). —Page Citation.

Georgia Journal of Southern Legal History, The
Ab.:   Ga. J.S. Legal Hist.

Ex.:   Thomas D. Russell, <u>Historical Study of Personal Injury Litigation: A Comment on Method</u>, 1 Ga. J.S. Legal Hist. 109 (1991). —Article Citation.

Thomas D. Russell, <u>Historical Study of Personal Injury Litigation: A Comment on Method</u>, 1 Ga. J.S. Legal Hist. 109, 113-15 (1991). —Page Citation.

Georgia Law Review
Ab.:   Ga. L. Rev.

Ex.:   John A. Robertson, <u>Assessing Quality of Life: A Response to Professor Kamisar</u>, 25 Ga. L. Rev. 1243 (1991). —Article Citation.

John A. Robertson, <u>Assessing Quality of Life: A Response to Professor Kamisar</u>, 25 Ga. L. Rev. 1243, 1247-52 (1991). —Page Citation.

Georgia Laws
Ab.:   year Ga. Laws page no.

Ex.:   Act of Apr. 12, 1995, No. 318, 1995 Ga. Laws 569. —Citation to an entire session law.

Act of Apr. 12, 1995, No. 318, sec. 1, § 31-21-44.1, 1995 Ga. Laws 569, 569. —Citation to a section of a session law amending a prior act.

—<u>See</u> Bluebook rule 12.4.

Georgia Official Code
See Official Code of Georgia Annotated (LexisNexis).

Georgia, Opinions of the Attorney General
See Opinions of the Attorney General of Georgia.

Georgia Reports
Ab.:   Ga.

—Cite to S.E. or S.E.2d, if therein; otherwise, cite to Ga.

—Give parallel citations, if at all, only in documents submitted to Georgia state courts. <u>See</u> Bluebook rules 10.3.1 and B5.1.3; see also Ga. Sup. Ct. R. 22 and Ga. Ct. App. R. 23(c), which require a citation only to the official reporter.

In documents submitted to Georgia state courts, cite as follows:

In citing cases in law review footnotes, abbreviate any word listed in table T.6; the names of "states, countries, and other geographical units" unless they are named parties; and any other words of eight or more letters "if <u>substantial</u> space is thereby saved and the result is unambiguous." Bluebook rule 10.2.2. On the other hand, in citing cases in text, abbreviate only widely known acronyms and the following words: "&," "Ass'n," "Bros.," "Co.," "Corp.," "Inc.," "Ltd.," and "No." Bluebook rule 10.2.1(c).

Taylor v. Chitwood, 266 Ga. 793, 471 S.E.2d 511 (1996). –Case Citation.

Taylor v. Chitwood, 266 Ga. 793, 794, 471 S.E.2d 511, 512 (1996). –Page Citation.

In all other documents, cite as follows:

Taylor v. Chitwood, 266 S.E.2d 793 (Ga. 1996). –Case Citation.

Taylor v. Chitwood, 266 S.E.2d 793, 794 (Ga. 1996). –Page Citation.

Georgia Rules and Regulations
See Official Compilation Rules and Regulations of the State of Georgia.

Georgia Session Laws
See Georgia Laws.

Georgia State Bar Journal
Ab.:   Ga. St. B.J.

Ex.:   Marc Treadwell, An Analysis of Georgia's Proposed Rules of Evidence, 26 Ga. St. B.J. 173 (1990). –Article Citation.

Marc Treadwell, An Analysis of Georgia's Proposed Rules of Evidence, 26 Ga. St. B.J. 173, 174-75 (1990). –Page Citation.

Georgia State University Law Review
Ab.:   Ga. St. U. L. Rev.

Ex.:   Byard Q. Clemmans, Personal Liability of the Military Official, 7 Ga. St. U. L. Rev. 417 (1991). –Article Citation.

Byard Q. Clemmans, Personal Liability of the Military Official, 7 Ga. St. U. L. Rev. 417, 423 (1991). –Page Citation.

German Yearbook of International Law
Ab.:   German Y.B. Int'l L.

Ex.:   Albert Bleckmann, General Theory of Obligations Under Public International Law, 38 German Y.B. Int'l L. 26 (1995). –Article Citation.

Albert Bleckmann, General Theory of Obligations Under Public International Law, 38 German Y.B. Int'l L. 26, 28-30 (1995). –Page Citation.

Glendale Law Review
Ab.:   Glendale L. Rev.

Ex.:   Frederick Grab, Photo-Radar: What's Wrong with this Picture?, 10 Glendale L. Rev. 51 (1991). –Article Citation.

Frederick Grab, Photo-Radar: What's Wrong with this Picture?, 10 Glendale L. Rev. 51, 59-61 (1991). –Page Citation.

In law review footnotes, the titles of books and the names of cases, except for procedural phrases, are not underlined. See Bluebook rule 2.1(a) & (b). Further, the following are in large and small capitals: codes, restatements, standards, constitutions, periodicals, authors of books, titles of books, the abbreviated names of codes, most legislative materials except for bills and resolutions, codified ordinances, model codes, court rules, and sentencing guidelines. Refer to The Bluebook.

Golden Gate University Law Review
Ab.:   Golden Gate U. L. Rev.

Ex.:   Allan E. Morgan, <u>ADR: In Search of the Emperor's New Clothes</u>, 21 Golden Gate U. L. Rev. 351 (1991). –Article Citation.

        Allan E. Morgan, <u>ADR: In Search of the Emperor's New Clothes</u>, 21 Golden Gate U. L. Rev. 351, 353-55 (1991). –Page Citation.

Gonzaga Law Review
Ab.:   Gonz. L. Rev.

Ex.:   Charles H. Sheldon, <u>"We Feel Constrained to Hold...." An Inquiry into the Basis for Decision in the Exercise of State Judicial Review</u>, 27 Gonz. L. Rev. 73 (1991-92). –Article Citation.

        Charles H. Sheldon, <u>"We Feel Constrained to Hold...." An Inquiry into the Basis for Decision in the Exercise of State Judicial Review</u>, 27 Gonz. L. Rev. 73, 79-80 (1991-92). –Page Citation.

Gorman on Labor Law
See Basic Text on Labor Law, by Robert A. Gorman and Matthew W. Finkin.

Gould's New York Consolidated Laws Unannotated
Ab.:   N.Y. [subject] Law § x (Consol. year)

Ex.:   N.Y. Ins. Law § 107 (Consol. 2004)

See <u>Bluebook</u> table T.1, pp. 222-24 for subject abbreviations.

        –For proper citation form in papers submitted to New York courts, see <u>New York Law Reports Style Manual</u> § 3.1 (2002), <u>available at</u> http://www.courts.state.ny.us/reporter/2002_style_manual.pdf.

Government Contracts, by John Cosgrove McBride and Thomas J. Touhey
        –Do not abbreviate the title.

Ex.:   8 John C. McBride & Thomas J. Touhey, <u>Government Contracts</u> § 49.40[2] (1992). –Section Citation.

        8 John C. McBride & Thomas J. Touhey, <u>Government Contracts</u> § 49.40[2], at 49-67 (1992). –Page Citation.

Government Contracts Reports (Commerce Clearing House)
        –Bound as Contracts Cases, Federal (Commerce Clearing House)-Cont. Cas. Fed. (CCH)

Ab.:   Gov't Cont. Rep. (CCH)

Ex.:   <u>Kit-San-Azusa v. United States</u>, 8 Gov't Cont. Rep. (CCH) (40 Cont. Cas. Fed.) ¶ 76,732 (Fed. Cl. Jan. 24, 1995). –Citation to looseleaf material.

        <u>Miller Elevator Co. v. United States</u>, 39 Cont. Cas. Fed. (CCH) ¶ 76,635 (Fed. Cl. Feb. 24, 1994). –Citation to bound material.

In citing cases in law review footnotes, abbreviate any word listed in table T.6; the names of "states, countries, and other geographical units" unless they are named parties; and any other words of eight or more letters "if <u>substantial</u> space is thereby saved and the result is unambiguous." <u>Bluebook</u> rule 10.2.2. On the other hand, in citing cases in text, abbreviate only widely known acronyms and the following words: "&," "Ass'n," "Bros.," "Co.," "Corp.," "Inc.," "Ltd.," and "No." <u>Bluebook</u> rule 10.2.1(c).

–The above examples are proper if the case is not yet available in, or is not reported in, an official or West reporter, a public domain citation, or in a widely used computer database.

Government Employee Relations Report (Bureau of National Affairs)
Ab.:   Gov't Empl. Rel. Rep. (BNA)

Ex.:   EEOC v. AFSCME, [Current Reports July-Dec.] Gov't Empl. Rel. Rep. (BNA) 939:34 (N.D.N.Y. June 14, 1996). –Citation to looseleaf material.

EEOC v. Wyoming, [Jan.-June 1981] Gov't Empl. Rel. Rep. (BNA) 916:37 (D. Wyo. 1981). –Citation to bound material.

–The above examples are proper if the case is not yet available in, or is not reported in, an official or West reporter, a public domain citation, or in a widely used computer database.

United States Dep't of Agri., Meat Grading Branch Livestock Div. v. American Fed'n of Gov't Employees, [July-Dec. 1978] Gov't Emp. Rel. Rep. (BNA) 780:45 (1978) (Doyle, Arb.). –Citation to bound administrative material.

Great Britain Treaty Series (1883-date)
Ab.:   year Gr. Brit. T.S. No.   (Cmnd.   )

Green Bag
Ab: Green Bag

Ex: Neal Devins, Better Lucky Than Good, 8 Green Bag 33 (2004). – Article Citation.

Neal Devins, Better Lucky Than Good, 8 Green Bag 33, 40 (2004). – Page Citation.

Guam Civil Code
Ab.:   Guam Civ. Code § (year)

–Guam Code Annotated will eventually replace this statutory compilation.

Guam Code Annotated
Ab.:   Guam Code Ann. tit. x, § x (year)

Ex.:   Guam Code Ann. tit. 3, § 4112 (1995).

Guam Code of Civil Procedure
Ab.:   Guam Civ. P. Code § (year)

–Guam Code Annotated will eventually replace this statutory compilation.

Guam Government Code
Ab.:   Guam Gov't Code § (year)

In law review footnotes, the titles of books and the names of cases, except for procedural phrases, are not underlined. See Bluebook rule 2.1(a) & (b). Further, the following are in large and small capitals: codes, restatements, standards, constitutions, periodicals, authors of books, titles of books, the abbreviated names of codes, most legislative materials except for bills and resolutions, codified ordinances, model codes, court rules, and sentencing guidelines. Refer to The Bluebook.

–Guam Code Annotated will eventually replace this statutory compilation.

Guam Session Laws
Ab.:   year Guam Sess. Laws page no.

Ex.:   Act of May 2, 1995, No. 23-13, 1995-1996 Guam Sess. Laws 112 (concerning a portion of an unused right-of-way). –Citation to an entire session law.

Act of May 2, 1995, No. 23-13, 1995-1996 Guam Sess. Laws 112, 114 (concerning a portion of an unused right-of-way). –Citation to a section of a session law amending prior act.

–See Bluebook rule 12.4.

Guild Practitioner
Ab.:   Guild Prac.

In citing cases in law review footnotes, abbreviate any word listed in table T.6; the names of "states, countries, and other geographical units" unless they are named parties; and any other words of eight or more letters "if substantial space is thereby saved and the result is unambiguous." Bluebook rule 10.2.2. On the other hand, in citing cases in text, abbreviate only widely known acronyms and the following words: "&," "Ass'n," "Bros.," "Co.," "Corp.," "Inc.," "Ltd.," and "No." Bluebook rule 10.2.1(c).

H

Hackworth Digest
   See Digest of International Law, by Green Haywood Hackworth.

Hague Court Reports
   Ab.:   Hague Ct. Rep. (Scott) or Hague Ct. Rep. 2d (Scott)

Hague Yearbook of International Law
   Ab.:   Hague Y.B. Int'l L.

   Ex.:   P.K. Menon, <u>Subjects of Modern International Law</u>, 3 Hague Y.B. Int'l
             L. 30 (1990). –Article Citation.

             P.K. Menon, <u>Subjects of Modern International Law</u>, 3 Hague Y.B. Int'l
             L. 30, 33 (1990). –Page Citation.

Hamline Law Review
   Ab.:   Hamline L. Rev.

   Ex.:   Stephen E. Kalish, <u>The Side-Switching Staff Person in a Law Firm:
             Uncomplimentary Assumptions and an Ethics Curtain</u>, 15 Hamline L.
             Rev. 35 (1991). –Article Citation.

             Stephen E. Kalish, <u>The Side-Switching Staff Person in a Law Firm:
             Uncomplimentary Assumptions and an Ethics Curtain</u>, 15 Hamline L.
             Rev. 35, 41-45 (1991). –Page Citation.

Harvard BlackLetter Law Journal
   Ab: Harv. BlackLetter L.J.

   Ex: Alfred L. Brophy, <u>Norms, Law, and Reparations: The Case of the Ku
             Klux Klan in 1920s Oklahoma</u>, 20 Harv. BlackLetter L.J. 17 (2004).
             –Article Citation.

             Alfred L. Brophy, <u>Norms, Law, and Reparations: The Case of the Ku
             Klux Klan in 1920s Oklahoma</u>, 20 Harv. BlackLetter L.J. 17, 23-24
             (2004). –Page Citation.

Harvard Civil Rights–Civil Liberties Law Review
   Ab.:   Harv. C.R.-C.L. L. Rev.

   Ex.:   Larry Gastin, <u>The Interconnected Epidemics of Drug Dependency and
             AIDS</u>, 26 Harv. C.R.-C.L. L. Rev. 113 (1991). –Article Citation.

             Larry Gastin, <u>The Interconnected Epidemics of Drug Dependency and
             AIDS</u>, 26 Harv. C.R.-C.L. L. Rev. 113, 121-24 (1991). –Page Citation.

In law review footnotes, the titles of books and the names of cases, except for procedural
phrases, are not underlined. <u>See</u> <u>Bluebook</u> rule 2.1(a) & (b). Further, the following are in
large and small capitals: codes, restatements, standards, constitutions, periodicals, authors of
books, titles of books, the abbreviated names of codes, most legislative materials except for
bills and resolutions, codified ordinances, model codes, court rules, and sentencing guidelines.
Refer to <u>The Bluebook</u>.

Harvard Environmental Law Review
Ab.:   Harv. Envtl. L. Rev.

Ex.:   Allson Rieser, <u>Ecological Preservation as a Public Property Right: An Emerging Doctrine in Search of a Theory</u>, 15 Harv. Envtl. L. Rev. 393 (1991). –Article Citation.

        Allson Rieser, <u>Ecological Preservation as a Public Property Right: An Emerging Doctrine in Search of a Theory</u>, 15 Harv. Envtl. L. Rev. 393, 411-12 (1991). –Page Citation.

Harvard Human Rights Journal
Ab.:   Harv. Hum. Rts. J.

Ex.:   Richard B. Lillich, <u>The United States Constitution and International Human Rights Law</u>, 3 Harv. Hum. Rts. J. 53 (1990). –Article Citation.

        Richard B. Lillich, <u>The United States Constitution and International Human Rights Law</u>, 3 Harv. Hum. Rts. J. 53, 54-58 (1990). –Page Citation.

Harvard International Law Journal
Ab.:   Harv. Int'l L.J.

Ex.:   Joel R. Paul, <u>Comity in International Law</u>, 32 Harv. Int'l L.J. 1 (1991). –Article Citation.

        Joel R. Paul, <u>Comity in International Law</u>, 32 Harv. Int'l L.J. 1, 15-23 (1991). –Page Citation.

Harvard Journal of Law & Gender
Ab.:   Harv. J. L. & Gend.

Ex.:   Gillian Lester, <u>A Defense of Paid Family Leave</u>, 28 Harv. J. L. & Gend. 1(2005). –Article Citation.

        Gillian Lester, <u>A Defense of Paid Family Leave</u>, 28 Harv. J. L. & Gend. 1, 25 (2005). –Page Citation.

Harvard Journal of Law and Public Policy
Ab.:   Harv. J.L. & Pub. Pol'y

Ex.:   Herbert R. Northrup, <u>The Railway Labor Act - Time for Repeat?</u>, 13 Harv. J.L. & Pub. Pol'y 441 (1990). –Article Citation.

        Herbert R. Northrup, <u>The Railway Labor Act - Time for Repeat?</u>, 13 Harv. J.L. & Pub. Pol'y 441, 490-92 (1990). –Page Citation.

Harvard Journal of Law & Technology
Ab.:   Harv. J.L. & Tech.

Ex.:   Randolph N. Janakait, <u>Forensic Science: The Need for Regulation</u>, 4 Harv. J.L. & Tech. 109 (1991). –Article Citation.

        Randolph N. Janakait, <u>Forensic Science: The Need for Regulation</u>, 4 Harv. J.L. & Tech. 109, 116-17 (1991). –Page Citation.

In citing cases in law review footnotes, abbreviate any word listed in table T.6; the names of "states, countries, and other geographical units" unless they are named parties; and any other words of eight or more letters "if <u>substantial</u> space is thereby saved and the result is unambiguous." <u>Bluebook</u> rule 10.2.2. On the other hand, in citing cases in text, abbreviate only widely known acronyms and the following words: "&," "Ass'n," "Bros.," "Co.," "Corp.," "Inc.," "Ltd.," and "No." <u>Bluebook</u> rule 10.2.1(c).

Harvard Journal on Legislation
Ab.: Harv. J. on Legis.

Ex.: Thomas E. Baker, <u>Why Congress Should Repeal the Federal Employers' Liability Act of 1908</u>, 29 Harv. J. on Legis. 79 (1992). –Article Citation.

Thomas E. Baker, <u>Why Congress Should Repeal the Federal Employers' Liability Act of 1908</u>, 29 Harv. J. on Legis. 79, 109-10 (1992). –Page Citation.

Harvard Law Review
Ab.: Harv. L. Rev.

Ex.: Elner R. Elhauge, <u>The Scope of Antitrust Process</u>, 104 Harv. L. Rev. 667 (1991). –Article Citation.

Elner R. Elhauge, <u>The Scope of Antitrust Process</u>, 104 Harv. L. Rev. 667, 688-89 (1991). –Page Citation.

Harvard Negotiation Law Review
Ab.: Harv. Negot. L. Rev.

Ex.: John Lande, <u>Failing Faith in Litigation: A survey of Business Lawyers' and Executives' Opinions</u>, Harv. Negot. L. Rev., Spring 1998, at 1, 3. –Page Citation.

Harvard Women's Law Journal
Ab.: Harv. Women's L.J.

Ex.: Naomi R. Cahn, <u>Defining Feminist Litigation</u>, 14 Harv. Women's L.J. 1 (1991). –Article Citation.

Naomi R. Cahn, <u>Defining Feminist Litigation</u>, 14 Harv. Women's L.J. 1, 16-17 (1991). –Page Citation.

Hastings Communications and Entertainment Law Journal
Ab.: Hastings Comm. & Ent. L.J.

Ex.: Leonard D. Duboff, <u>What is Art? Toward a Legal Definition</u>, 12 Hastings Comm. & Ent. L.J. 303 (1990). –Article Citation.

Leonard D. Duboff, <u>What is Art? Toward a Legal Definition</u>, 12 Hastings Comm. & Ent. L.J. 303, 346-49 (1990). –Page Citation.

Hastings Constitutional Law Quarterly
Ab.: Hastings Const. L.Q.

Ex.: Steven A. Blum, <u>Public Executions: Understanding the "Cruel and Unusual Punishments" Clause</u>, 19 Hastings Const. L.Q. 413 (1992). –Article Citation.

Steven A. Blum, <u>Public Executions: Understanding the "Cruel and Unusual Punishments" Clause</u>, 19 Hastings Const. L.Q. 413, 418-20 (1992). –Page Citation.

In law review footnotes, the titles of books and the names of cases, except for procedural phrases, are not underlined. <u>See</u> Bluebook rule 2.1(a) & (b). Further, the following are in large and small capitals: codes, restatements, standards, constitutions, periodicals, authors of books, titles of books, the abbreviated names of codes, most legislative materials except for bills and resolutions, codified ordinances, model codes, court rules, and sentencing guidelines. Refer to <u>The Bluebook</u>.

Hastings International and Comparative Law Review

Ab.: Hastings Int'l & Comp. L. Rev.

Ex.: Lynn Berat, <u>The Future of Customary Law in Nambia: A Call for an Integration Model</u>, 15 Hastings Int'l & Comp. L. Rev. 1 (1991). –Article Citation.

Lynn Berat, <u>The Future of Customary Law in Nambia: A Call for an Integration Model</u>, 15 Hastings Int'l & Comp. L. Rev. 1, 29-30 (1991). –Page Citation.

Hastings Law Journal

Ab.: Hastings L.J.

Ex.: Andrew Kuu, <u>Mistake, Frustration, and the Windfall Principle of Contract Remedies</u>, 43 Hastings L.J. 1 (1991). –Article Citation.

Andrew Kuu, <u>Mistake, Frustration, and the Windfall Principle of Contract Remedies</u>, 43 Hastings L.J. 1, 19-20 (1991). –Page Citation.

Hawaii Administrative Rules Directory

Ab.: Haw. Admin. R. § (year).

Ex.: Haw. Admin. R. § 4-7-3 (1981).

Hawaii Appellate Reports

Ab.: Haw. App.

–Discontinued after 10 Haw. App. 631 (1994). Cases from the Intermediate Court of Appeals (Haw. Ct. App.) are now found in West's Hawaii Reports (Haw.) beginning with vol. 76.

–Cite to P.2d or P.3d, if therein; otherwise, cite to Haw. App.

–Give parallel citations only in documents submitted to Hawaii state courts. <u>See</u> <u>Bluebook</u> rules 10.3.1 and B5.1.3; see also Haw. R. App. P. 28(b)(1), which requires a parallel citation.

–Through 10 Haw. App. 631 (1994), cite as follows:

In documents submitted to Hawaii state courts:

<u>Hong v. Kong</u>, 5 Haw. App. 174, 683 P.2d 833 (1984). –Case Citation.

<u>Hong v. Kong</u>, 5 Haw. App. 174, 177, 683 P.2d 833, 835 (1984). –Page Citation.

In all other documents:

<u>Hong v. Kong</u>, 683 P.2d 833 (Haw. Ct. App. 1984). –Case Citation.

<u>Hong v. Kong</u>, 683 P.2d 833, 835 (Haw. Ct. App. 1984). –Page Citation.

–After 10 Haw. App. 631 (1994), cite as follows:

In documents submitted to Hawaii state courts:

In citing cases in law review footnotes, abbreviate any word listed in table T.6; the names of "states, countries, and other geographical units" unless they are named parties; and any other words of eight or more letters "if <u>substantial</u> space is thereby saved and the result is unambiguous." <u>Bluebook</u> rule 10.2.2. On the other hand, in citing cases in text, abbreviate only widely known acronyms and the following words: "&," "Ass'n," "Bros.," "Co.," "Corp.," "Inc.," "Ltd.," and "No." <u>Bluebook</u> rule 10.2.1(c).

Baldonado v. Liberty Mutual Ins. Co., 81 Haw. 403, 917 P.2d 730 (Ct. App. 1996). –Case Citation.

Baldonado v. Liberty Mutual Ins. Co., 81 Haw. 403, 405, 917 P.2d 730, 732 (Ct. App. 1996). –Page Citation.

In all other documents:

Baldonado v. Liberty Mutual Ins. Co., 917 P.2d 730 (Haw. Ct. App. 1996). –Case Citation.

Baldonado v. Liberty Mutual Ins. Co., 917 P.2d 730, 732 (Haw. Ct. App. 1996). –Page Citation.

Hawaii Attorney General Report
See Opinions of the Attorney General of Hawaii.

Hawaii Bar Journal
Ab.: Haw. B.J.

Ex.: Dana B. Tasdina & Robin L. Filion, The Judicial Improvements Acts of 1990: Historic Changes in Federal Civil Procedure Aimed at Improving the Efficiency of Federal Courts and Reducing the Uncertainty and Cost Associated with Federal Litigation, 23 Haw. B.J. 41 (1991). –Article Citation.

Dana B. Tasdina & Robin L. Filion, The Judicial Improvements Acts of 1990: Historic Changes in Federal Civil Procedure Aimed at Improving the Efficiency of Federal Courts and Reducing the Uncertainty and Cost Associated with Federal Litigation, 23 Haw. B.J. 41, 43 (1991). –Page Citation.

Hawaii Constitution
Ab.: Haw. Const. art.   , §   .

Ex.: Haw. Const. art. I, § 1. –"Cite constitutional provisions currently in force without a date." Bluebook rule 11.

–"If the cited provision has been repealed, either indicate parenthetically the fact and date of repeal or cite the repealing provision in full." Bluebook rule 11.

Haw. Const. art. I, § 12 (amended 1978). –"When citing a provision that has been subsequently amended, either indicate parenthetically the fact and date of amendment or cite the amending provision in full." Bluebook rule 11.

Haw. Const. art. XVII (formerly at art. XV). –Hawaii's constitution was renumbered in 1976; renumbered provisions may be parenthetically noted.

Hawaii Reports, West's
Ab.: Haw.

–Cite to P.2d or P.3d, if therein; otherwise, cite to Haw.

In law review footnotes, the titles of books and the names of cases, except for procedural phrases, are not underlined. See Bluebook rule 2.1(a) & (b). Further, the following are in large and small capitals: codes, restatements, standards, constitutions, periodicals, authors of books, titles of books, the abbreviated names of codes, most legislative materials except for bills and resolutions, codified ordinances, model codes, court rules, and sentencing guidelines. Refer to The Bluebook.

–Give parallel citations only in documents submitted to Hawaii state courts. See Bluebook rules 10.3.1 and B5.1.3; see also Haw. R. App. P. 28(b)(1), which requires a parallel citation.

In documents submitted to Hawaii state courts, cite as follows:

Richard v. Metcalf, 82 Haw. 249, 921 P.2d 169 (1996). –Case Citation.

Richard v. Metcalf, 82 Haw. 249, 251, 921 P.2d 169, 171 (1996). –Page Citation.

In all other documents, cite as follows:

Richard v. Metcalf, 921 P.2d 169 (Haw. 1996). –Case Citation.

Richard v. Metcalf, 921 P.2d 169, 171 (Haw. 1996). –Page Citation.

Hawaii Revised Statutes
Ab.:   Haw. Rev. Stat. § x-x (year)

Ex.:   Haw. Rev. Stat. § 171-58 (2004).

Hawaii Revised Statutes Annotated
See Michie's Hawaii Revised Statutes Annotated.

Hawaii Session Laws
See Session Laws of Hawaii.

Hearings, Congressional
See Congressional hearings.

Hearing Transcript, citation to
Ab.:   TRO Hr'g Tr.

Ex.:   (TRO Hr'g Tr. 6:13-20, May 1, 2005)

See Bluebook rule B10 and table BT.1.

Note: See Bluebook rule 10.8.3 for citing litigation materials from another case.

Hein's United States Treaties and Other International Agreements
See Bluebook rule 21.4.5(c) concerning unofficial treaty sources.

Ab.:   Hein's No. KAV

Ex.:   Swap Agreement, U.S.-Pan., Jan. 30, 1992, Hein's No. KAV 3145.

hereinafter
See Bluebook rule 4.2(b).

Hofstra Labor & Employment Law Journal
Ab: Hofstra Lab. & Emp. L.J.

In citing cases in law review footnotes, abbreviate any word listed in table T.6; the names of "states, countries, and other geographical units" unless they are named parties; and any other words of eight or more letters "if substantial space is thereby saved and the result is unambiguous." Bluebook rule 10.2.2. On the other hand, in citing cases in text, abbreviate only widely known acronyms and the following words: "&," "Ass'n," "Bros.," "Co.," "Corp.," "Inc.," "Ltd.," and "No." Bluebook rule 10.2.1(c).

Ex: Robert Belton, <u>Title VII at Forty: A Brief Look at the Birth, Death, and Resurrection of the Disparate Impact Theory of Discrimination</u>, 22 Hofstra Lab. & Emp. L.J. 431 (2005). –Article Citation.

Robert Belton, <u>Title VII at Forty: A Brief Look at the Birth, Death, and Resurrection of the Disparate Impact Theory of   Discrimination</u>, 22 Hofstra Lab. & Emp. L.J. 431, 442-43 (2005). –Page Citation.

Hofstra Law Review
Ab.: Hofstra L. Rev.
Ex.: Ralph Nader, <u>Leadership and the Law</u>, 19 Hofstra L. Rev. 543 (1991). –Article Citation.

Ralph Nader, <u>Leadership and the Law</u>, 19 Hofstra L. Rev. 543, 559-60 (1991) –Page Citation.

Hofstra Property Law Journal
Ab.: Hofstra Prop. L.J.
Ex.: Anne M. Fealey, <u>Privacy and Publicity, Then and Now</u>, 3 Hofstra Prop. L.J. 15 (1989). –Article Citation.

Anne M. Fealey, <u>Privacy and Publicity, Then and Now</u>, 3 Hofstra Prop. L.J. 15, 19-20 (1989). –Page Citation.

Holmes' Appleman on Insurance, 2d., by Eric Mills Holmes and L. Anthony Sutin.
–Do not abbreviate title.
Ex.: 14 Eric Mills Holmes & L. Anthony Sutin, <u>Holmes' Appleman on Insurance</u> ¶ 107.2 (2d ed. 2000). –Section Citation.

14 Eric Mills Holmes & L. Anthony Sutin, <u>Holmes' Appleman on Insurance</u> ¶ 107.2, at 553 (2d ed. 2000). –Page Citation.

14 Eric Mills Holmes & L. Anthony Sutin, <u>Holmes' Appleman on Insurance</u> ¶ 107.2, at 553 n.97 (2d ed. 2000). –Footnote Citation.

Hong Kong Law Journal
Ab.: H.K. L.J.
Ex.: Michael Wikinson, <u>Taking Other Offences Into Consideration in Hong Kong</u>, 21 H.K. L.J. 19 (1991). –Article Citation.

Michael Wikinson, <u>Taking Other Offences Into Consideration in Hong Kong</u>, 21 H.K. L.J. 19, 19-20 (1991). –Page Citation.

House Bills (U.S. Congress)
See Congressional Bills.

House Concurrent Resolution
See Congressional Resolutions.

House Conference Report
Ab.: H.R. Conf. Rep.
Ex.: H.R. Conf. Rep. No. 99-962, at 7 (1986).

In law review footnotes, the titles of books and the names of cases, except for procedural phrases, are not underlined. <u>See</u> <u>Bluebook</u> rule 2.1(a) & (b). Further, the following are in large and small capitals: codes, restatements, standards, constitutions, periodicals, authors of books, titles of books, the abbreviated names of codes, most legislative materials except for bills and resolutions, codified ordinances, model codes, court rules, and sentencing guidelines. Refer to <u>The Bluebook</u>.

House Joint Resolution
See Congressional Resolutions.

House Resolution
See Congressional Resolutions.

Houston Journal of International Law
Ab.:   Hous. J. Int'l L.

Ex.:   Dean C. Alexander, <u>The North American Free Trade Area: Potential Framework for an Agreement</u>, 14 Hous. J. Int'l L. 85 (1991).
–Article Citation.

Dean C. Alexander, <u>The North American Free Trade Area: Potential Framework for an Agreement</u>, 14 Hous. J. Int'l L. 85, 89-90 (1991).
–Page Citation.

Houston Law Review
Ab.:   Hous. L. Rev.

Ex.:   G. Sidney Buchanan, <u>Women in Combat: An Essay on Ultimate Rights and Responsibilities</u>, 28 Hous. L. Rev. 503 (1991). –Article Citation.

G. Sidney Buchanan, <u>Women in Combat: An Essay on Ultimate Rights and Responsibilities</u>, 28 Hous. L. Rev. 503, 546-47 (1991). –Page Citation.

Howard (United States Reports)
See United States Reports.

Howard Journal of Criminal Justice, The
Ab.:   How. J. Crim. Just.

Ex.:   Peter Raynor, <u>Sentencing With and Without Reports: A Local Study</u>, 30 How. J. Crim. Just. 293 (1991). –Article Citation.

Peter Raynor, <u>Sentencing With and Without Reports: A Local Study</u>, 30 How. J. Crim. Just. 293, 309-10 (1991). –Page Citation.

Howard Law Journal
Ab.:   How. L.J.

Ex.:   Victor Goode, <u>Cultural Racism in Public Education: A Legal Tactic for Black Texans</u>, 33 How. L.J. 321 (1990). –Article Citation.

Victor Goode, <u>Cultural Racism in Public Education: A Legal Tactic for Black Texans</u>, 33 How. L.J. 321, 329-30 (1990). –Page Citation.

Human Life Review, The
Ab.:   Hum. Life Rev.

Ex.:   Joseph Sobran, <u>AIDS and the Tribe</u>, 18 Hum. Life Rev. 18 (1992).
–Article Citation.

Joseph Sobran, <u>AIDS and the Tribe</u>, 18 Hum. Life Rev. 18, 19-20 (1992). –Page Citation.

In citing cases in law review footnotes, abbreviate any word listed in table T.6; the names of "states, countries, and other geographical units" unless they are named parties; and any other words of eight or more letters "if <u>substantial</u> space is thereby saved and the result is unambiguous." <u>Bluebook</u> rule 10.2.2. On the other hand, in citing cases in text, abbreviate only widely known acronyms and the following words: "&," "Ass'n," "Bros.," "Co.," "Corp.," "Inc.," "Ltd.," and "No." <u>Bluebook</u> rule 10.2.1(c).

Human Rights
    Ab.:   Hum. Rts.

Human Rights Quarterly
    Ab.:   Hum. Rts. Q.

    Ex.:   Douglas Sanders, Collective Rights, 13 Hum. Rts. Q. 368 (1991). –Article Citation.

           Douglas Sanders, Collective Rights, 13 Hum. Rts. Q. 368, 379-80 (1991). –Page Citation.

In law review footnotes, the titles of books and the names of cases, except for procedural phrases, are not underlined. See Bluebook rule 2.1(a) & (b). Further, the following are in large and small capitals: codes, restatements, standards, constitutions, periodicals, authors of books, titles of books, the abbreviated names of codes, most legislative materials except for bills and resolutions, codified ordinances, model codes, court rules, and sentencing guidelines. Refer to The Bluebook.

I

ICC Practitioner's Journal
Ab.:   ICC Prac. J.

Ex.:   Charles L. Freed, <u>Current Status of the Keogh Doctrine</u>, 51 ICC Prac. J. 599 (1984). –Article Citation.

       Charles L. Freed, <u>Current Status of the Keogh Doctrine</u>, 51 ICC Prac. J. 599, 604 (1984). –Article Citation.

<u>Id.</u>; <u>id.</u>

– "'<u>Id.</u>' may be used in citation sentences and clauses for any kind of authority except internal cross-references (as described in rule 3.5)." <u>Bluebook</u> rule 4.1. See also <u>Bluebook</u> rules B5.2, B8.2, and 10.9.

Text:

Ex.:   "Similarly, in <u>United States v. Nicholson</u>, 885 F.2d 481 (8th Cir. 1989), the court accepted the race-neutral reason for peremptorily challenging a juror who 'had a relative who was incarcerated.' <u>Id.</u> at 483. . . . On remand, the prosecutor recalled the fact that one juror had an incarcerated relative. <u>Id.</u>" –Taken from <u>United States v. Johnson</u>, 941 F.2d 1102, 1109 (10th Cir. 1991).

footnotes:

Ex.:   123. 414 A.2d 220 (Me. 1980).

       124. <u>Id.</u> at 223.

       125. <u>Id.</u> –Taken from 45 Vand. L. Rev. 161, 180 nn.123-25 (1992).

       209. <u>See</u> <u>Grady</u>, 110 S. Ct. at 2104 (Scalia, J., dissenting).

       210. <u>See</u> <u>id.</u> –Taken from 45 Vand. L. Rev. 273, 302 nn.209-210 (1992).

       256. 445 U.S. 684 (1980).

       257. <u>See</u> <u>id.</u> at 695. –Taken from 45 Vand. L. Rev. 273, 308 nn.256-57 (1992).

Idaho Administrative Bulletin
Ab.:   vol. no. Idaho Admin. Bull. page no. (month day, year)

Ex.:   03-12 Idaho Admin. Bull. 50 (Dec. 3, 2003)

Idaho Administrative Code
Ab.:   Idaho Admin. Code r. x.x.x.x (year)

In law review footnotes, the titles of books and the names of cases, except for procedural phrases, are not underlined. <u>See</u> <u>Bluebook</u> rule 2.1(a) & (b). Further, the following are in large and small capitals: codes, restatements, standards, constitutions, periodicals, authors of books, titles of books, the abbreviated names of codes, most legislative materials except for bills and resolutions, codified ordinances, model codes, court rules, and sentencing guidelines. Refer to <u>The Bluebook</u>.

Ex.:   Idaho Admin. Code r. 6.03.14.550 (2004).

Idaho Attorney General's Annual Report
Ab.:   Idaho Att'y Gen. Ann. Rep.

          See Opinions of the Attorney General of Idaho.

Idaho Code Annotated Advance Legislative Service (LexisNexis)
Ab.:   year-pamph. no. Idaho Code Ann. Adv. Legis. Serv. page no.
          (LexisNexis)

Ex.:   Act effective July 1, 2005, ch. 22, 2005-1 Idaho Code Ann. Adv. Legis.
          Serv. 59 (LexisNexis) (relating to tax collection). –Citation to an entire
          session law.

          Act effective July 1, 2005, ch. 22, sec. 1, § 63-3061A, 2005-1 Idaho
          Code Ann. Adv. Legis. Serv. 59, 59 (LexisNexis) (relating to tax
          collection). –Citation to a section of a session law amending prior act.

          –See Bluebook rule 12.4.

          –"Cite to Idaho Sess. Laws, if therein." Bluebook table T.1, p. 207.

Idaho Code Annotated (LexisNexis)
Ab.:   Idaho Code Ann. § x-x (year)

Ex.:   Idaho Code Ann. § 39-251 (2002)

          Idaho Code Ann. § 15-203 (Supp. 2004)

Idaho Constitution
Ab.:   Idaho Const. art.   , §   .

Ex.:   Idaho Const. art. I, § 13. –"Cite constitutional provisions currently in
          force without a date." Bluebook rule 11.

          Idaho Const. art. X, § 6 (repealed 1931). –"If the cited provision has
          been repealed, either indicate parenthetically the fact and date of repeal
          or cite the repealing provision in full." Bluebook rule 11.

          Idaho Const. art. XX, § 1 (amended 1974). –"When citing a provision
          that has been subsequently amended, either indicate parenthetically the
          fact and date of amendment or cite the amending provision in full."
          Bluebook rule 11.

          Idaho Const. of 1890, art. XIX, §§ 1, 2. –"Cite constitutions that have
          been totally superseded by year of adoption; if the specific provision
          cited was adopted in a different year, give that year parenthetically."
          Bluebook rule 11.

Idaho Court of Appeals
Ab.:   Idaho Ct. App.

          –Cite to P., P.2d, or P.3d, if therein; otherwise, cite to Idaho

---

In citing cases in law review footnotes, abbreviate any word listed in table T.6;
the names of "states, countries, and other geographical units" unless they are named parties;
and any other words of eight or more letters "if substantial space is thereby saved and the
result is unambiguous." Bluebook rule 10.2.2. On the other hand, in citing cases in text,
abbreviate only widely known acronyms and the following words: "&," "Ass'n," "Bros.,"
"Co.," "Corp.," "Inc.," "Ltd.," and "No." Bluebook rule 10.2.1(c).

–Give parallel citations, if at all, only in documents submitted to Idaho state courts. See Bluebook rules 10.3.1 and B5.1.3; see also Idaho Sup. Ct. Internal Operating R. 15(e), which adopts The Bluebook.

In documents submitted to Idaho state courts, cite as follows:

Ohio v. Smith, 127 Idaho 771, 906 P.2d 141 (Ct. App. 1995). –Case Citation.

Ohio v. Smith, 127 Idaho 771, 773, 906 P.2d 141, 143 (Ct. App. 1995). –Page Citation.

In all other documents, cite as follows:

Hines v. Wells, 814 P.2d 437 (Idaho Ct. App. 1991). –Case Citation.

Hines v. Wells, 814 P.2d 437, 438 (Idaho Ct. App. 1991). –Page Citation.

Idaho Law Review

Ab.: Idaho L. Rev.

Ex.: Bruce J. Wilcox, The Constitutionality of Exclusive Cable Franchising, 28 Idaho L. Rev. 33 (1991-1992). –Article Citation.

Bruce J. Wilcox, The Constitutionality of Exclusive Cable Franchising, 28 Idaho L. Rev. 33, 39-40 (1991-1992). –Page Citation.

Idaho Reports

Ab.: Idaho

–Cite to P., P.2d, or P.3d, if therein; otherwise, cite to Idaho.

–Give parallel citations, if at all, only in documents submitted to Idaho state courts. See Bluebook rules 10.3.1 and B5.1.3; see also Idaho Sup. Ct. Internal Operating R. 15(e), which adopts The Bluebook.

In documents submitted to Idaho state courts, cite as follows:

Higginson v. Wadsworth, 128 Idaho 439, 915 P.2d 1 (1996). –Case Citation.

Higginson v. Wadsworth, 128 Idaho 439, 442, 915 P.2d 1, 4 (1996). –Page Citation.

In all other documents, cite as follows:

Higginson v. Wadsworth, 915 P.2d 1 (Idaho 1996). –Case Citation.

Higginson v. Wadsworth, 915 P.2d 1, 4 (Idaho 1996). –Page Citation.

In law review footnotes, the titles of books and the names of cases, except for procedural phrases, are not underlined. See Bluebook rule 2.1(a) & (b). Further, the following are in large and small capitals: codes, restatements, standards, constitutions, periodicals, authors of books, titles of books, the abbreviated names of codes, most legislative materials except for bills and resolutions, codified ordinances, model codes, court rules, and sentencing guidelines. Refer to The Bluebook.

Idaho Session Laws

Ab.:   year Idaho Sess. Laws page no.

Ex.:   Act of Feb. 4, 2003, ch. 2, 2003 Idaho Sess. Laws 3 (relating to the employment security law). –Citation to an entire session law.

Act of Feb. 4, 2003, ch. 2, 2003 Idaho Sess. Laws 3, 4 (relating to the employment security law). –Citation to a section of a session law.

–See <u>Bluebook</u> rule 12.4.

IDEA: The Journal of Law and Technology

Ab.:   IDEA

Ex.:   Scott M. Alter, <u>Trade Secrets and Telecommunications: The Problems with Local Area Networks</u>, 31 IDEA 297 (1991). –Article Citation.

Scott M. Alter, <u>Trade Secrets and Telecommunications: The Problems with Local Area Networks</u>, 31 IDEA 297, 299-300 (1991).

Illinois

Ab.:   Ill. Const. art.   , §   .

Ex.:   Ill. Const. art. II, § 2. –"Cite constitutional provisions currently in force without a date." <u>Bluebook</u> rule 11.

–"If the cited provision has been repealed, either indicate parenthetically the fact and date of repeal or cite the repealing provision in full." <u>Bluebook</u> rule 11.

Ill. Const. art. III, § 1 (amended 1988). –"When citing a provision that has been subsequently amended, either indicate parenthetically the fact and date of amendment or cite the amending provision in full." <u>Bluebook</u> rule 11.

Ill. Const. of 1870, art. V, § 24. –"Cite constitutions that have been totally superseded by year of adoption; if the specific provision cited was adopted in a different year, give that year parenthetically." <u>Bluebook</u> rule 11.

Illinois Administrative Code

Ab.:   Ill. Admin. Code tit. x, § x (year).

Ex.:   Ill. Admin. Code tit. 62, § 240.312 (2000).

Illinois Annotated Statutes, West's Smith-Hurd

See West's Smith-Hurd Illinois Compiled Statutes Annotated.

Illinois Appellate Court Reports

Ab.:   Ill. App., Ill. App. 2d, Ill. App. 3d

–In documents submitted to Illinois state courts, cite to Ill. App., Ill. App. 2d, or Ill. App., if therein; otherwise, cite to N.E. or N.E.2d. In all other documents, cite to N.E. or N.E.2d, if therein; otherwise, cite to Ill. App., Ill. App. 2d, or Ill. App. 3d.

In citing cases in law review footnotes, abbreviate any word listed in table T.6; the names of "states, countries, and other geographical units" unless they are named parties; and any other words of eight or more letters "if <u>substantial</u> space is thereby saved and the result is unambiguous." <u>Bluebook</u> rule 10.2.2. On the other hand, in citing cases in text, abbreviate only widely known acronyms and the following words: "&," "Ass'n," "Bros.," "Co.," "Corp.," "Inc.," "Ltd.," and "No." <u>Bluebook</u> rule 10.2.1(c).

–Give parallel citations only in documents submitted to Illinois state courts. See Bluebook rules 10.3.1 and B5.1.3; see also Ill. Sup. Ct. R.6 and Ill. 2d J. Civ. R. 18, which require citation to Ill., Ill. App. 2d, or Ill. App. 3d and permit a parallel citation to the regional reporter and/or to Ill. Dec.

In documents submitted to Illinois state courts, cite as follows:

First Nat'l Bank v. Strong, 278 Ill. App. 3d 762, 663 N.E.2d 432, 215 Ill. Dec. 421 (1996). –Case Citation.

First Nat'l Bank v. Strong, 278 Ill. App. 3d 762, 765, 663 N.E.2d 432, 434, 215 Ill. Dec. 421, 427 (1996). –Page Citation.

In all other documents, cite as follows:

First Nat'l Bank v. Strong, 663 N.E.2d 432 (Ill. App. Ct. 1996). –Case Citation.

First Nat'l Bank v. Strong, 663 N.E.2d 432, 434 (Ill. App. Ct. 1996). –Page Citation.

Illinois Bar Journal
Ab.: Ill. B.J.

Ex.: John M. Ferguson, Fees -- Their Judgment or Ours?, Ill. B.J., Feb. 1979, at 348. –Article Citation.

John M. Ferguson, Fees -- Their Judgment or Ours?, Ill. B.J., Feb. 1979, at 348, 350. –Page Citation.

Illinois Compiled Statutes
Ab.: x Ill. Comp. Stat. x/x-x (year)

Ex.: 720 Ill. Comp. Stat. 5/12-7.1 (1992).

–For proper citation form in papers submitted to Illinois courts, see Ill. Sup. Ct. R. 6.

Illinois Compiled Statutes Annotated (LexisNexis)
Ab.: x Ill. Comp. Stat. Ann. x/x-x (LexisNexis)

Ex.: 720 Ill. Comp. Stat. Ann. 5/9-1.2 (LexisNexis 2004)

720 Ill. Comp. Stat. Ann. 5/8-3.1 (LexisNexis Supp. 2005)

"Cite to Ill. Comp. Stat., if therein." Bluebook table T.1, p. 208.

–For proper citation form in papers submitted to Illinois courts, see Ill. Sup. Ct. R. 6.

Illinois Compiled Statutes Annotated Advance Legislative Service (LexisNexis)
Ab.: year-pamph. no. Ill. Comp. Stat. Ann. Adv. Legis. Serv. page no. (LexisNexis)

In law review footnotes, the titles of books and the names of cases, except for procedural phrases, are not underlined. See Bluebook rule 2.1(a) & (b). Further, the following are in large and small capitals: codes, restatements, standards, constitutions, periodicals, authors of books, titles of books, the abbreviated names of codes, most legislative materials except for bills and resolutions, codified ordinances, model codes, court rules, and sentencing guidelines. Refer to The Bluebook.

Ex.: Act of Aug. 18, 2005, No. 94-612, sec. 5, § 14-104, 2005-3 Ill. Comp. Stat. Ann. Adv. Legis. Serv. 39 (LexisNexis) (concerning death benefit annuities). –Citation to a section of a session law amending prior act.

–See Bluebook rule 12.4.

–"Cite to Ill. Laws, if therein." Bluebook table T.1, p. 208.

Illinois Court of Claims Reports

Ab.: Ill. Ct. Cl.

Ex.: Maier v. State, 32 Ill. Ct. Cl. 924 (1979). –Case Citation.

Maier v. State, 32 Ill. Ct. Cl. 924, 926-27 (1979). –Page Citation.

Illinois Law Review (1906 - 1951)

Ab.: Ill. L.R.

Ex.: Frances A. Allen, The Wolf Case: Search and Seizure, Federalism, and the Civil Liberties. Ill. L.R., Mar.-Apr. 1950, at 1. –Article Citation.

Frances A. Allen, The Wolf Case: Search and Seizure, Federalism, and the Civil Liberties. Ill. L.R., Mar.-Apr. 1950, at 1, 25-29. –Page Citation.

–In 1952, this publication changed its name to Northwestern University Law Review.

See Northwestern University Law Review.

Illinois Legislative Service (West)

Ab.: year Ill. Legis. Serv. page no. (West)

Ex.: Act of Aug. 9, 1996, No. 89-622, 1996 Ill. Legis. Serv. 2743 (West) (concerning the school code). –Citation to an entire session law.

Act of Aug. 9, 1996, No. 89-622, sec. 5, § 2-3.13a, 1996 Ill. Legis. Serv. 2743, 2743-44 (West) (concerning School Code regarding scholastic records of transferring students). –Citation to a session law amending prior act.

–See Bluebook rule 12.4.

–"Cite to Ill. Laws, if therein." Bluebook table T.1, p. 208.

Illinois Register

Ab.: vol. no. Ill. Reg. page no. (month day, year)

Ex.: 27 Ill. Reg. 19180 (Dec. 26, 2003).

Illinois Reports

Ab.: Ill., Ill. 2d

–In documents submitted to Illinois state courts, cite to Ill. or Ill. 2d, if therein; otherwise, cite to N.E. or N.E.2d. In all other documents, cite N.E. or N.E.2d., if therein; otherwise, cite to Ill. or Ill. 2d.

In citing cases in law review footnotes, abbreviate any word listed in table T.6; the names of "states, countries, and other geographical units" unless they are named parties; and any other words of eight or more letters "if substantial space is thereby saved and the result is unambiguous." Bluebook rule 10.2.2. On the other hand, in citing cases in text, abbreviate only widely known acronyms and the following words: "&," "Ass'n," "Bros.," "Co.," "Corp.," "Inc.," "Ltd.," and "No." Bluebook rule 10.2.1(c).

–Give parallel citations only in documents submitted to Illinois state courts. See Bluebook rules 10.3.1 and B5.1.3; see also Ill. Sup. Ct. R.6 and Ill. 2d J. Civ. R. 18, which require citation to Ill. or Ill. 2d and permit a parallel citation to the regional reporter and/or to Ill. Dec.

In documents submitted to Illinois state courts, cite as follows:

People v. Bounds, 171 Ill. 2d 1, 662 N.E.2d 1168, 215 Ill. Dec. 28 (1995). –Case Citation.

People v. Bounds, 171 Ill. 2d 1, 5, 662 N.E.2d 1168, 1171, 215 Ill. Dec. 28, 35 (1995). –Page Citation.

In all other documents, cite as follows:

People v. Bounds, 662 N.E.2d 1168 (Ill. 1995). –Case Citation.

People v. Bounds, 662 N.E.2d 1168, 1171 (Ill. 1995). –Page Citation.

Illinois Session Laws
See Laws of Illinois and Illinois Legislative Service (West).

ILSA Journal of International & Comparative Law
Ab: ILSA J. Int'l & Comp. L.

Ex: Julie R. Hess, United States and Africa on FGM: Cultural Comparatives, Resolutions, and Rights, 10 ILSA J. Int'l & Comp. L. 581 (2004). –Article Citation.

Julie R. Hess, United States and Africa on FGM: Cultural Comparatives, Resolutions, and Rights, 10 ILSA J. Int'l & Comp. L. 581, 593-94 (2004). –Page Citation.

Immigration Journal
Ab.:   Immigr. J.

Ex.:   Roxana C. Bacon, Estopping the INS, Immigr. J., Jan.-Feb. 1982, at 8. –Article Citation.

Roxana C. Bacon, Estopping the INS, Immigr. J., Jan.-Feb. 1982, at 8, 9. –Page Citation.

in

–Use for citation of shorter works in collection. Bluebook rules 15.5.1 and 1.6(a).

Ex.:   Uriel Gorney, American Precedent in the Supreme Court of Israel, in Comparative Law of Israel and the Middle East 93, 104-05 (Nicholas N. Kittrie ed., 1971).

in banc
–Do not abbreviate.

–See en banc.

In law review footnotes, the titles of books and the names of cases, except for procedural phrases, are not underlined. See Bluebook rule 2.1(a) & (b). Further, the following are in large and small capitals: codes, restatements, standards, constitutions, periodicals, authors of books, titles of books, the abbreviated names of codes, most legislative materials except for bills and resolutions, codified ordinances, model codes, court rules, and sentencing guidelines. Refer to The Bluebook.

In Memoriam (article designation)

Ex.: David A. Anderson, In Memoriam, <u>Page Keeton, Torts Scholar</u>, 77 Tex. L. Rev. 1361 (1999).

–<u>See</u> <u>Bluebook</u> rule 16.6.4.

In the Public Interest

Ab.: In Pub. Interest

Ex.: Brenna Mahoney, <u>Tracking: The End to Equal Educational Opportunity</u>, In Pub. Interest, Spring 1991, at 51. –Article Citation.

Brenna Mahoney, <u>Tracking: The End to Equal Educational Opportunity</u>, In Pub. Interest, Spring 1991, at 51, 54-55. –Page Citation.

Indiana Administrative Code (West)

Ab.: x Ind. Admin. Code x-x-x (year)

Ex.: 410 Ind. Admin. Code 6-2.1-42 (2003).

Indiana, Annual Report and Official Opinions of the Attorney General

See Annual Report and Official Opinions of the Attorney General of Indiana.

Indiana Appellate Court Reports (1890-1971) (continued as Indiana Court of Appeals Reports)

Ab.: Ind. App.

–Cite to N.E. or N.E.2d, if therein; otherwise, cite to Ind. App.

–Give parallel citations only in documents submitted to Indiana state courts. <u>See</u> <u>Bluebook</u> rules 10.3.1 and B5.1.3; see also Ind. R. App. P. 22, which requires a parallel citation.

In documents submitted to Indiana state courts, cite as follows:

<u>Evans v. Enoco Colleries, Inc.</u>, 137 Ind. App. 11, 202 N.E.2d 595 (1964). –Case Citation.

<u>Evans v. Enoco Colleries, Inc.</u>, 137 Ind. App. 11, 13, 202 N.E.2d 595, 596 (1964). –Page Citation.

In all other documents, cite as follows:

<u>Evans v. Enoco Colleries, Inc.</u>, 202 N.E.2d 595 (Ind. App. 1964). –Case Citation.

<u>Evans v. Enoco Colleries, Inc.</u>, 202 N.E.2d 595, 596 (Ind. App. 1964). –Page Citation.

Indiana Code

Ab.: Ind. Code § x-x-x-x (year)

In citing cases in law review footnotes, abbreviate any word listed in table T.6; the names of "states, countries, and other geographical units" unless they are named parties; and any other words of eight or more letters "if <u>substantial</u> space is thereby saved and the result is unambiguous." <u>Bluebook</u> rule 10.2.2. On the other hand, in citing cases in text, abbreviate only widely known acronyms and the following words: "&," "Ass'n," "Bros.," "Co.," "Corp.," "Inc.," "Ltd.," and "No." <u>Bluebook</u> rule 10.2.1(c).

Ex.:   Ind. Code § 32-2-1-1 (1993).

–For proper citation form in papers submitted to Indiana courts, see Ind. Code § 1-1-1-1(2002) and Ind. R. App. P. 22.

Indiana Code Annotated
See West's Annotated Indiana Code.

Indiana Constitution
Ab.:   Ind. Const. art.   , §   .

Ex.:   Ind. Const. art. I, § 19. –"Cite constitutional provisions currently in force without a date." Bluebook rule 11.

Ind. Const. art. II, § 5 (repealed 1881). –"If the cited provision has been repealed, either indicate parenthetically the fact and date of repeal or cite the repealing provision in full." Bluebook rule 11.

Ind. Const. art. V, § 17 (amended 1984). –"When citing a provision that has been subsequently amended, either indicate parenthetically the fact and date of amendment or cite the amending provision in full." Bluebook rule 11.

Ind. Const. art. XII, § 4. –"Cite constitutions that have been totally superseded by year of adoption; if the specific provision cited was adopted in a different year, give that year parenthetically." Bluebook rule 11.

Indiana Court of Appeals Reports
Ab.:   Ind. App.

–Discontinued after 182 Ind. App. 697 (1979).

–Cite to N.E. or N.E.2d, if therein; otherwise, cite to Ind. App.

–Give parallel citations only in documents submitted to Indiana state courts. See Bluebook rules 10.3.1 and B5.1.3; see also Ind. R. App. P. 22, which requires a parallel citation.

–Through 182 Ind. App. 697 (1979), cite as follows:

In documents submitted to Indiana state courts:

Keck v. Kerbs, 182 Ind. App. 530, 395 N.E.2d 845 (1979). –Case Citation.

Keck v. Kerbs, 182 Ind. App. 530, 530, 395 N.E.2d 845, 845 (1979). –Page Citation.

In all other documents:

Keck v. Kerbs, 395 N.E.2d 845 (Ind. Ct. App. 1979). –Case Citation.

Keck v. Kerbs, 395 N.E.2d 845, 845 (Ind. Ct. App. 1979). –Page Citation.

–After 182 Ind. App. 697 (1979), cite as follows:

In all documents:

In law review footnotes, the titles of books and the names of cases, except for procedural phrases, are not underlined. See Bluebook rule 2.1(a) & (b). Further, the following are in large and small capitals: codes, restatements, standards, constitutions, periodicals, authors of books, titles of books, the abbreviated names of codes, most legislative materials except for bills and resolutions, codified ordinances, model codes, court rules, and sentencing guidelines. Refer to The Bluebook.

Cram v. Howell, 662 N.E.2d 678 (Ind. Ct. App. 1996). –Case Citation.

Cram v. Howell, 662 N.E.2d 678, 680 (Ind. Ct. App. 1996). –Page Citation.

Indiana International & Comparative Law Review
Ab.:   Ind. Int'l & Comp. L. Rev.

Ex.:   John Quigley, Apartheid Outside Africa: The Case of Israel, 2 Ind. Int'l & Comp. L. Rev. 221 (1991). –Article Citation.

John Quigley, Apartheid Outside Africa: The Case of Israel, 2 Ind. Int'l & Comp. L. Rev. 221, 239-40 (1991). –Page Citation.

Indiana Journal of Global Legal Studies
Ab: Ind. J. Global Legal Stud.

Ex: Robert F. Arnove, To What Ends: Educational Reform Around the World, Ind. J. Global Legal Stud., Winter 2005, at 79. –Article Citation.

Robert F. Arnove, To What Ends: Educational Reform Around the World, Ind. J. Global Legal Stud., Winter 2005, at 79, 91-94.

–Page Citation.

Indiana Law Journal
Ab.:   Ind. L.J.

Ex.:   Timothy J. Moran, Formal Restrictions on Televised Political Advertising: Elevating Political Debate Without Supressing Free Speech, 67 Ind. L.J. 663 (1992). –Article Citation.

Timothy J. Moran, Formal Restrictions on Televised Political Advertising: Elevating Political Debate Without Supressing Free Speech, 67 Ind. L.J. 663, 669-70 (1992). –Page Citation.

Indiana Law Review
Ab.:   Ind. L. Rev.

Ex.:   Paul H. Brietzke, Urban Development and Human Development, 25 Ind. L. Rev. 741 (1992). –Article Citation.

Paul H. Brietzke, Urban Development and Human Development, 25 Ind. L. Rev. 741, 756-57 (1992). –Page Citation.

Indiana Register
Ab.:   vol. no. Ind. Reg. page no. (month day, year)

Ex.:   27 Ind. Reg. 1621 (Feb. 1, 2004)

Indiana Reports
Ab.:   Ind.

–Discontinued after 275 Ind. 699 (1981).

–Cite to N.E. or N.E.2d, if therein; otherwise, cite to Ind.

In citing cases in law review footnotes, abbreviate any word listed in table T.6; the names of "states, countries, and other geographical units" unless they are named parties; and any other words of eight or more letters "if substantial space is thereby saved and the result is unambiguous." Bluebook rule 10.2.2. On the other hand, in citing cases in text, abbreviate only widely known acronyms and the following words: "&," "Ass'n," "Bros.," "Co.," "Corp.," "Inc.," "Ltd.," and "No." Bluebook rule 10.2.1(c).

–Give parallel citations only in documents submitted to Indiana state courts. See Bluebook rules 10.3.1 and B5.1.3; see also Ind. R. App. P. 22, which requires a parallel citation.

–Through 275 Ind. 699 (1981), cite as follows:

In documents submitted to Indiana state courts:

> Moon v. State, 275 Ind. 651, 419 N.E.2d 740 (1981). –Case Citation.

> Moon v. State, 275 Ind. 651, 655, 419 N.E.2d 740, 743 (1981). –Page Citation.

In all other documents:

> Moon v. State, 419 N.E.2d 740 (Ind. 1981). –Case Citation.

> Moon v. State, 419 N.E.2d 740, 743 (Ind. 1981). –Page Citation.

–After 275 Ind. 699 (1981), cite as follows:

In all documents:

> Humbert v. Smith, 664 N.E.2d 356 (Ind. 1996). –Case Citation.

> Humbert v. Smith, 664 N.E.2d 356, 357 (Ind. 1996). –Page Citation.

Indiana Session Laws
See Acts, Indiana and Burns Indiana Statutes Advance Legislative Service (LexisNexis).

Indiana Statutes Annotated
See Burns Indiana Statutes Annotated.

Industrial and Labor Relations Review
Ab.:   Indus. & Lab. Rel. Rev.

Ex.:   Kevin J. Murphy, Determinants of Contract Duration in Collective Bargaining Agreements, 45 Indus. & Lab. Rel. Rev. 352 (1992). –Article Citation.

Kevin J. Murphy, Determinants of Contract Duration in Collective Bargaining Agreements, 45 Indus. & Lab. Rel. Rev. 352, 355-56 (1992). –Page Citation.

Industrial Law Journal
Ab.:   Indus. L.J.

Ind. Law. J. [U.K.]

Ex.:   Kenneth Miller, Piper Alpha and the Cullen Report, 20 Indus. L.J. 176 (1991). –Article Citation.

Kenneth Miller, Piper Alpha and the Cullen Report, 20 Indus. L.J. 176, 179-80 (1991). –Page Citation.

Industrial Relations
Ab.:   Indus. Rel.

In law review footnotes, the titles of books and the names of cases, except for procedural phrases, are not underlined. See Bluebook rule 2.1(a) & (b). Further, the following are in large and small capitals: codes, restatements, standards, constitutions, periodicals, authors of books, titles of books, the abbreviated names of codes, most legislative materials except for bills and resolutions, codified ordinances, model codes, court rules, and sentencing guidelines. Refer to The Bluebook.

Ex.:   Joseph D. Reid, Jr., <u>Future Unions</u>, 31 Indus. Rel. 122 (1992). –Article
         Citation.

         Joseph D. Reid, Jr., <u>Future Unions</u>, 31 Indus. Rel. 122, 126-27 (1992).
         –Page Citation.

Industrial Relations Law Journal
Ab.:   Indus. Rel. L.J.

Ex.:   Mark Daniels, <u>The Regulation of Severance Plans Under ERISA</u>,
         12 Indus. Rel. L.J. 340 (1990). –Article Citation.

         Mark Daniels, <u>The Regulation of Severance Plans Under ERISA</u>,
         12 Indus. Rel. L.J. 340, 349-50 (1990). –Page Citation.

<u>infra</u>

–"Portions of text, footnotes, and groups of authorities within the piece
may be cited using '<u>supra</u>' or '<u>infra</u>'. Use <u>supra</u> to refer back to
material that has already appeared within the piece. Use <u>infra</u> to refer
to material that appears later in the piece." <u>Bluebook</u> rule 3.5.

Ex.:   See <u>infra</u> notes 198-203 and accompanying text.

Inheritance, Estate & Gift Tax Reports (Commerce Clearing House)
Ab.:   Inher. Est. & Gift Tax Rep. (CCH)

Ex.:   <u>Offret v. DiDomenico</u>, [State Current] Inher. Est. & Gift Tax Rep.
         (CCH) ¶ 21,426 (Ohio May 26, 1993). –Citation to looseleaf material.

         <u>Cranley v. Schirmer</u>, [1965-1973 All State New Matters Transfer
         Binder] Inher. Est. & Gift Tax Rep. (CCH) ¶ 93,913 (Conn. Super. Ct.
         1967). –Citation to transfer binder material.

         –The above examples are proper if the case is not yet available in, or is
         not reported in, an official or West reporter, a public domain citation,
         or in a widely used computer database.

<u>In re</u>

–Expressions such as "in the matter of," "petition of," and "application
of" should be abbreviated "<u>In re</u>". <u>See</u> <u>Bluebook</u> rule 10.2.1(b).

–"Procedural phrases should always be italicized [or underlined],
regardless of whether the rest of the case name is italicized."
<u>Bluebook</u> rule 10.2.1(b).

Ex.:   <u>In re T.J. Ronan Paint Corp.</u>, 98 A.D.2d 413, 419-20 (N.Y. App. Div.
         1984).

Institute on Federal Taxation (New York University)
Ab.:   Inst. on Fed. Tax'n

Ex.:   C. Ellen McNeil, <u>The Limitations on Interest Deductions</u>, 48 Inst. on
         Fed. Tax'n § 5.00 (1990). –Article Citation.

         C. Ellen McNeil, <u>The Limitations on Interest Deductions</u>, 48 Inst. on
         Fed. Tax'n § 5.05[4], at 5-19 (1990). –Page Citation.

In citing cases in law review footnotes, abbreviate any word listed in table T.6;
the names of "states, countries, and other geographical units" unless they are named parties;
and any other words of eight or more letters "if <u>substantial</u> space is thereby saved and the
result is unambiguous." <u>Bluebook</u> rule 10.2.2. On the other hand, in citing cases in text,
abbreviate only widely known acronyms and the following words: "&," "Ass'n," "Bros.,"
"Co.," "Corp.," "Inc.," "Ltd.," and "No." <u>Bluebook</u> rule 10.2.1(c).

Institute on Mineral Law (Louisiana State University)
    Ab.:   Inst. on Min. L.
    Ex.:   Arthur R. Carmondy, Jr., <u>Legal Problems in the Development and Mining of Lignite</u>, 23 Inst. on Min. L. 39 (1977). –Article Citation.

          Arthur R. Carmondy, Jr., <u>Legal Problems in the Development and Mining of Lignite</u>, 23 Inst. on Min. L. 39, 48-51 (1977). –Page Citation.

Institute on Oil and Gas Law and Taxation (Southwestern Legal Foundation)
    Ab.:   Inst. on Oil & Gas L. & Tax'n
    Ex.:   Bruce S. Marks, <u>Commercial Conflict Management and Alternative Dispute Resolution in the Oil and Gas Industry</u>, 41 Inst. on Oil & Gas L. & Tax'n § 9.03 (1990). –Article Citation.

          Bruce S. Marks, <u>Commercial Conflict Management and Alternative Dispute Resolution in the Oil and Gas Industry</u>, 41 Inst. on Oil & Gas L. & Tax'n § 9.03, at 9-41 (1990). –Page Citation.

Institute on Planning, Zoning and Eminent Domain Proceedings (Southwestern Legal Foundation)
    Ab.:   Inst. on Plan. Zoning & Eminent Domain
    Ex.:   Christopher J. Caso, <u>Zoning and the First Amendment</u>, 1991 Inst. on Plan. Zoning & Eminent Domain § 5.0. –Article Citation.

          Christopher J. Caso, <u>Zoning and the First Amendment</u>, 1991 Inst. on Plan. Zoning & Eminent Domain § 5.0, at 5.03[3]. –Page Citation.

Institute on Securities Regulation
    Ab.:   Inst. on Sec. Reg.
    Ex.:   Robert D. Rosenbaum, <u>Proxy Reform</u>, 22 Inst. on Sec. Reg. 77 (1991). –Article Citation.

          Robert D. Rosenbaum, <u>Proxy Reform</u>, 22 Inst. on Sec. Reg. 77, 83 (1991). –Page Citation.

institutional authors
    See authors.

Insurance Counsel Journal
    Ab.:   Ins. Couns. J.
    Ex.:   Ronald Lee Gilman, <u>Dishonesty Alone Does Not Deck a Fidelity Insurer</u>, 51 Ins. Couns. J. 529 (1984). –Article Citation.

          Ronald Lee Gilman, <u>Dishonesty Alone Does Not Deck a Fidelity Insurer</u>, 51 Ins. Couns. J. 529, 530-31 (1984). –Page Citation.

Insurance Law Reports (Commerce Clearing House)
    (formerly Reporter)
    Ab.:   Ins. L. Rep. (CCH)

In law review footnotes, the titles of books and the names of cases, except for procedural phrases, are not underlined. <u>See</u> <u>Bluebook</u> rule 2.1(a) & (b). Further, the following are in large and small capitals: codes, restatements, standards, constitutions, periodicals, authors of books, titles of books, the abbreviated names of codes, most legislative materials except for bills and resolutions, codified ordinances, model codes, court rules, and sentencing guidelines. Refer to <u>The Bluebook</u>.

Intellectual Property Law
Ab.: Intell. Prop. L.

Ex.: Kyung Jae Park, <u>Protection Against Counterfeiting in Korea</u>, 1 Intell. Prop. L. 71 (1991). –Article Citation.

Kyung Jae Park, <u>Protection Against Counterfeiting in Korea</u>, 1 Intell. Prop. L. 71, 73-74 (1991). –Page Citation.

Intellectual Property Law Review
Ab.: Intell. Prop. L. Rev.

Ex.: Alan Lawrence, <u>The Value of Copyright Law as a Deterrent to Discovery Abuse</u>, 23 Intell. Prop. L. Rev. 605 (1991). –Article Citation.

Alan Lawrence, <u>The Value of Copyright Law as a Deterrent to Discovery Abuse</u>, 23 Intell. Prop. L. Rev. 605, 611 (1991). –Page Citation.

Inter-Alia, Journal of the Nevada State Bar
Ab.: Inter-Alia

Ex.: John C. Orenschall & C. Nicholas Pereos, <u>A Primer in Nevada Water Law</u>, Inter-Alia, April 1978, at 7. –Article Citation.

John C. Orenschall & C. Nicholas Pereos, <u>A Primer in Nevada Water Law</u>, Inter-Alia, April 1978, at 7, 9-10. –Page Citation.

Inter-American Court of Human Rights
Ab.: Inter-Am. Ct. H.R.

Internal Revenue Code
Ab.: 26 U.S.C. § (year)

I.R.C. § (year).

–When citing to the Internal Revenue Code, "26 U.S.C." may be replaced with "I.R.C." <u>See</u> <u>Bluebook</u> rule 12.8.1.

Ex.: 26 U.S.C. § 401 (1992).

I.R.C. § 401 (1992).

–When citing to the Internal Revenue Code as it appears in an unofficial code, identify the publisher in the date parenthetical.

Ex.: 26 U.S.C.A. § 401 (West 1996).

I.R.C. § 401 (West 1996).

Internal Revenue Regulations
See Treasury Regulations.

Internal Revenue Rulings
See Revenue Rulings.

In citing cases in law review footnotes, abbreviate any word listed in table T.6; the names of "states, countries, and other geographical units" unless they are named parties; and any other words of eight or more letters "if <u>substantial</u> space is thereby saved and the result is unambiguous." <u>Bluebook</u> rule 10.2.2. On the other hand, in citing cases in text, abbreviate only widely known acronyms and the following words: "&," "Ass'n," "Bros.," "Co.," "Corp.," "Inc.," "Ltd.," and "No." <u>Bluebook</u> rule 10.2.1(c).

Internal Revenue Service Positions (Commerce Clearing House)
Ab.: IRS Pos. (CCH)

International and Comparative Law Quarterly
Ab.: Int'l & Comp. L.Q.

Int. Comp. Law. Q. [U.K.]

Ex.: Geoff Gilbert, The Irish Interpretation of the Poltical Offence Exemption, 41 Int'l & Comp. L.Q. 66 (1991). –Article Citation.

Geoff Gilbert, The Irish Interpretation of the Poltical Offence Exemption, 41 Int'l & Comp. L.Q. 66, 69-70 (1991). –Page Citation.

International Arbitral Awards
Ex.: Argentine-Chile Frontier Case (Arg. v. Chile), 16 R.I.A.A. 109 (1969).

See Bluebook rule 21.6 and table T.5 for frequently cited arbitration reporters.

International Atomic Energy Agency Documents
Ab.: IAEA Doc.

International Centre for Settlement of Investment Disputes (World Bank ICSID)
Ab.: ICSID (W. Bank)

International Chamber of Commerce Arbitration
Ab.: Int'l Comm. Arb.

International Civil Aviation Organization Documents
Ab.: ICAO Doc.

International Court of Justice
Ab.: year I.C.J. xx

year I.C.J. Pleadings xx

year I.C.J. Acts & Docs. xx

–"Cite decisions to I.C.J.; cite separately published pleadings to I.C.J. Pleadings; cite rules and acts to I.C.J. Acts & Docs." Bluebook table T.3, p. 332.

International Court of Justice, Acts and Documents
Ab.: I.C.J. Acts & Docs.

See Bluebook rule 21.5.1(g) and table T.3.

International Court of Justice, Pleadings, Oral Arguments, Documents
Ab.: I.C.J. Pleadings

In law review footnotes, the titles of books and the names of cases, except for procedural phrases, are not underlined. See Bluebook rule 2.1(a) & (b). Further, the following are in large and small capitals: codes, restatements, standards, constitutions, periodicals, authors of books, titles of books, the abbreviated names of codes, most legislative materials except for bills and resolutions, codified ordinances, model codes, court rules, and sentencing guidelines. Refer to The Bluebook.

Ex.:　Canter-Memorial of Libya (Lib. v. Malta), 1991 I.C.J. Pleadings (2 Continental Shelf) 1 (May 23). See Bluebook rule 21.5.1(f) and table T.3.

International Court of Justice, Reports of Judgments, Advisory Opinions, and Orders

Ab.:　I.C.J.

Ex.:　Border and Transborder Armed Actions (Nicar. v. Hond.), 1988 I.C.J. 68 (Dec. 20). –Case Citation.

Applicability of the Obligation to Arbitrate Under Section 21 of the United Nations Headquarters Agreement of 26 June 1947, Advisory Opinion, 1988 I.C.J. 12 (Apr. 26). –Advisory Opinion Citation.

International Court of Justice Yearbook

Ab.:　I.C.J.Y.B.

Ex.:　1988-1989 I.C.J.Y.B. 95 (1989).

International Criminal Tribunal for Rwanda

Ab.:　ICTR

Ex.:　Prosecutor v. Mpambara, Case No. ICTR-2001-65-T, Decision on the Defence's Motion for Judgment of Acquittal, ¶ 2 (Oct. 21, 2005).

International Criminal Tribunal for the Former Yugoslavia

Ab:　IT

Ex.:　Prosecutor v. Delalic, Case No. IT-96-21-A, Appeal Judgment, ¶ 602 (Feb. 20, 2001).

International Digest of Health Legislation

Ab.:　Int'l Dig. Health Legis.

Ex.:　M. Bolis, First Subregional Meeting on Women, Health and Legislation. 42 Int'l Dig. Health Legis. 797 (1991). –Article Citation.

M. Bolis, First Subregional Meeting on Women, Health and Legislation. 42 Int'l Dig. Health Legis. 797, 798-799 (1991). –Page Citation.

International Environment Reporter (Bureau of National Affairs)

Ab.:　Int'l Envt. Rep. (BNA)

Ex.:　Parliament, Commission Inch Closer to Bar on Experts & Hazardous Waste, [Current Reports] Int'l Envt. Rep. (BNA) vol. 19, at 47 (Jan. 24, 1996). –Cite to looseleaf monograph, article, or commentary.

International Financial Law Review

Ab:　Int'l Fin. L. Rev.

Ex.:　Marcus Collins, Reviving Thailand's Securities Market, 11 Int'l Fin. L. Rev. 30 (1992). –Article Citation.

In citing cases in law review footnotes, abbreviate any word listed in table T.6; the names of "states, countries, and other geographical units" unless they are named parties; and any other words of eight or more letters "if substantial space is thereby saved and the result is unambiguous." Bluebook rule 10.2.2. On the other hand, in citing cases in text, abbreviate only widely known acronyms and the following words: "&," "Ass'n," "Bros.," "Co.," "Corp.," "Inc.," "Ltd.," and "No." Bluebook rule 10.2.1(c).

Marcus Collins, <u>Reviving Thailand's Securities Market</u>, 11 Int'l Fin. L. Rev. 30, 31-32 (1992). –Page Citation.

International Journal of Law and Psychiatry
Ab.:   Int'l J.L. & Psychiatry

Ex.:   Jeffrey Rubin, <u>Economic Aspects of Law and Psychiatry</u>, 14 Int'l J.L. & Psychiatry 299 (1991). –Article Citation.

Jeffrey Rubin, <u>Economic Aspects of Law and Psychiatry</u>, 14 Int'l J.L. & Psychiatry 299, 297-98 (1991). –Page Citation.

International Journal of Legal Information
Ab.:   Int'l J. Legal Info.

Ex.:   Ralph Lansky, <u>Law Libraries in Germany: An Introduction</u>, 19 Int'l J. Legal Info. 179 (1991). –Article Citation.

Ralph Lansky, <u>Law Libraries in Germany: An Introduction</u>, 19 Int'l J. Legal Info. 179, 189-90 (1991). –Page Citation.

International Labour Review
Ab.:   Int'l Lab. Rev.

Ex.:   George Psacharopoulos, <u>From Manpower Planning to Labour Market Analysis</u>, 130 Int'l Lab. Rev. 459 (1991). –Article Citation.

George Psacharopoulos, <u>From Manpower Planning to Labour Market Analysis</u>, 130 Int'l Lab. Rev. 459, 464-65 (1991). –Page Citation.

International Law Commission
Ab.:   Int'l L. Comm'n

International Law Commission Yearbook
Ab.:   Y.B. Int'l L. Comm'n

Ex.:   <u>Summary Records of the 1814th Meeting</u>, [1984] 1 Y.B. Int'l L. Comm'n 2, U.N. Doc. A/CN.4/SER.A/1984.

International Law Reports
Ab.:   I.L.R.

       Int'l L. Rep.

Ex.:   <u>S v. Mharapara</u>, 84 I.L.R. 1 (Zimb. S. Ct. 1985). –Case Citation.

<u>S v. Mharapara</u>, 84 I.L.R. 1, 17 (Zimb. S. Ct. 1985). –Page Citation.

International Lawyer, The
Ab.:   Int'l Law.

Ex.:   Hiram E. Chodosh, <u>Swap Centres in The People's Republic of China</u>, 25 Int'l Law. 415 (1991). –Article Citation.

Hiram E. Chodosh, <u>Swap Centres in The People's Republic of China</u>, 25 Int'l Law. 415, 429-30 (1991). –Page Citation.

In law review footnotes, the titles of books and the names of cases, except for procedural phrases, are not underlined. <u>See</u> Bluebook rule 2.1(a) & (b). Further, the following are in large and small capitals: codes, restatements, standards, constitutions, periodicals, authors of books, titles of books, the abbreviated names of codes, most legislative materials except for bills and resolutions, codified ordinances, model codes, court rules, and sentencing guidelines. Refer to <u>The Bluebook</u>.

International Legal Materials
Ab.: I.L.M.

Ex.: International Court of Justice: Judgment in Case concerning the Arbitral Award of 31 July 1989 (Guinea Bissau v. Senegal), 31 I.L.M 32 (1992) –Article Citation.

International Court of Justice: Judgment in Case concerning the Arbitral Award of 31 July 1989 (Guinea Bissau v. Senegal), 31 I.L.M. 32, 33-35 (1992). –Page Citation.

Final Act embodying the Results of the Uruguay Round of Multilateral Trade Negotaions, April 15, 1994, 33 I.L.M. 1125 (1994).
–See Bluebook rule 21.4.5(c).

International Legal Perspectives
Ab.: Int'l Legal Persp.

Ex.: Todd Beard, The Tax Consequences of Conducting Operations Abroad, Int'l Legal Persp., Spring 1992, at 65. –Article Citation.

Todd Beard, The Tax Consequences of Conducting Operations Abroad, Int'l Legal Persp., Spring 1992, at 65, 71. –Page Citation.

International Maritime Organization Assembly Resolutions
Ab.: IMO Assembly Res.

International Organization
Ab.: Int'l Org.

Ex.: Raymond F. Hopkins, Reform in the International Food Aid Regime: The Role of Consensual Knowledge, 46 Int'l Org. 225 (1992). –Article Citation.

Raymond F. Hopkins, Reform in the International Food Aid Regime: The Role of Consensual Knowledge, 46 Int'l Org. 225, 249-50 (1992). –Page Citation.

International Review of Law and Economics
Ab: Int'l Rev. L. & Econ.

Ex: Sara Markowitz, Alcohol, Drugs and Violent Crime, 25 Int'l Rev. L. & Econ. 20 (2005). –Article Citation.

Sara Markowitz, Alcohol, Drugs and Violent Crime, 25 Int'l Rev. L. & Econ. 20, 37-38 (2005). –Page Citation.

International Social Security Review
Ab.: Int'l Soc. Sec. Rev.

Ex.: Alan Borowski, The Economics and Politics of Retirement Incomes Policy in Australia, 44 Int'l Soc. Sec. Rev. 27 (1991). –Article Citation.

Alan Borowski, The Economics and Politics of Retirement Incomes Policy in Australia, 44 Int'l Soc. Sec. Rev. 27, 31-32 (1991). –Page Citation.

In citing cases in law review footnotes, abbreviate any word listed in table T.6; the names of "states, countries, and other geographical units" unless they are named parties; and any other words of eight or more letters "if substantial space is thereby saved and the result is unambiguous." Bluebook rule 10.2.2. On the other hand, in citing cases in text, abbreviate only widely known acronyms and the following words: "&," "Ass'n," "Bros.," "Co.," "Corp.," "Inc.," "Ltd.," and "No." Bluebook rule 10.2.1(c).

International Symposium on Comparative Law
  Ab.:   Int'l Symp. on Comp. L.

International Tax & Business Lawyer
  Ab.:   Int'l Tax & Bus. Law.

  Ex.:   James J. Fisman, <u>Enforcement of Securities Laws Violations in the United Kingdom</u>, Int'l Tax & Bus. Law., Summer 1991, at 131. –Article Citation.

            James J. Fisman, <u>Enforcement of Securities Laws Violations in the United Kingdom</u>, Int'l Tax & Bus. Law., Summer 1991, at 131, 149-50. –Page Citation.

International Tax Journal, The
  Ab.:   Int'l Tax J.

  Ex.:   Walter T. Raineri, <u>Dual Consolidated Losses</u>, 16 Int'l Tax J. 167 (1990). –Article Citation.

            Walter T. Raineri, <u>Dual Consolidated Losses</u>, 16 Int'l Tax J. 167, 170-71 (1990). –Page Citation.

International Tax Planning Manual (Commerce Clearing House)
  Ab.:   Int'l Tax Planning Man. (CCH)

International Trade Law Journal
  Ab.:   Int'l Trade L.J.

  Ex.:   David L. Simon, <u>Legal Developments in U.S.-R.O.C. Trade Since Derecognition</u>, 7 Int'l Trade L.J. 203 (1983). –Article Citation.

            David L. Simon, <u>Legal Developments in U.S.-R.O.C. Trade Since Derecognition</u>, 7 Int'l Trade L.J. 203, 228-29 (1983). –Page Citation.

International Trade Reporter (Bureau of National Affairs)
            –Bound as International Trade Reporter Decisions-Int'l Trade Rep. Dec. (BNA).
  Ab.:   Int'l Trade Rep. (BNA)

  Ex.:   <u>Timken Co. v. United States</u>, [Decisions] Int'l Trade Rep. (BNA) (18 Int'l Trade Rep. Dec.) 1065 (Ct. Int'l Trade Jan. 3, 1996). –Case Citation to looseleaf material.

            <u>Sharp Corp. v. United States</u>, 12 Int'l Trade Rep. Dec. (BNA) 1340 (Ct. Int'l Trade 1990). –Citation to bound material.

            –This example is proper if the case is not yet available in, or is not reported in, an official or West reporter, a public domain citation, or in a widely used computer database.

International Trade Reporter Decisions
  Ab.:   I.T.R.D. (BNA)

In law review footnotes, the titles of books and the names of cases, except for procedural phrases, are not underlined. <u>See</u> <u>Bluebook</u> rule 2.1(a) & (b). Further, the following are in large and small capitals: codes, restatements, standards, constitutions, periodicals, authors of books, titles of books, the abbreviated names of codes, most legislative materials except for bills and resolutions, codified ordinances, model codes, court rules, and sentencing guidelines. Refer to <u>The Bluebook</u>.

Ex.:   Torrington Co. v. United States, 17 I.T.R.D. 1961 (Fed. Cir. 1996).
         –If possible, cite to official reporters.

Internet sources
See Electronic media and other nonprint resources.

Interrogatory, citation to
Ab.:   Interrog.

Ex.:   (Def.'s Interrog. No. 7).

See Bluebook rule B10 and table BT.1.

Note: See Bluebook rule 10.8.3 for citing litigation materials from another case.

Interstate Commerce Commission Reports, Motor Carrier Cases (1936-1986)
Ab.:   M.C.C.

Ex.:   In re Mfrs. Express, Inc., 126 M.C.C. 174 (1976).

Interstate Commerce Commission Reports, Second Series
Ab.:   I.C.C.2d

Ex.:   Del. & Hudson Ry. Co. v. Consol. Rail Corp., 9 I.C.C.2d 989 (1993).

Interviews, unpublished
Ex.:   Interview with Pam Malone, President of the National Association for
         Legal Placement, in Nashville, Tenn. (Dec. 10, 1996). –author
         conducted interview.

         Interview by Stephen Teel with Don Welch, Associate Dean,
         Vanderbilt University Law School, in Nashville, Tenn. (Jan 2, 1997).

         –author did not conduct interview.

See Bluebook rule 17.1.4.

Iowa Administrative Bulletin
Ab.:   vol. no. Iowa Admin. Bull. page no. (month day, year)

Ex.:   26 Iowa Admin. Bull. 1004 (Dec. 10, 2003)

Iowa Administrative Code
Ab.:   Iowa Admin. Code r. x-x.x (year).

Ex.:   Iowa Admin. Code r. 571-101.2(109) (2004).

Iowa, Biennial Report of the Attorney General
See Biennial Report of the Attorney General, State of Iowa.

Iowa Code
See Code of Iowa.

Iowa Code Annotated (West)
See West's Iowa Code Annotated.

In citing cases in law review footnotes, abbreviate any word listed in table T.6;
the names of "states, countries, and other geographical units" unless they are named parties;
and any other words of eight or more letters "if substantial space is thereby saved and the
result is unambiguous." Bluebook rule 10.2.2. On the other hand, in citing cases in text,
abbreviate only widely known acronyms and the following words: "&," "Ass'n," "Bros.,"
"Co.," "Corp.," "Inc.," "Ltd.," and "No." Bluebook rule 10.2.1(c).

Iowa Constitution
Ab.:   Iowa Const. art.   , §   .

Ex.:   Iowa Const. art. I, § 6. –"Cite constitutional provisions currently in force without a date." <u>Bluebook</u> rule 11.

Iowa. Const. art. I, § 5 (repealed 1992). –"If the cited provision has been repealed, either indicate parenthetically the fact and date of repeal or cite the repealing provision in full." <u>Bluebook</u> rule 11.

Iowa. Const. art. III, § 6 (amended 1968). –"When citing a provision that has been subsequently amended, either indicate parenthetically the fact and date of amendment or cite the amending provision in full." <u>Bluebook</u> rule 11.

Iowa Const. of 1846, art. V, § 4. –"Cite constitutions that have been totally superseded by year of adoption; if the specific provision cited was adopted in a different year, give that year parenthetically." <u>Bluebook</u> rule 11.

Iowa Court of Appeals
Ab.:   Iowa Ct. App.

–Cite to N.W.2d

Ex.:   <u>Ames v. Poston</u>, 551 N.W.2d 340 (Iowa Ct. App. 1996). –Case Citation.

<u>Ames v. Poston</u>, 551 N.W.2d 340, 341 (Iowa Ct. App. 1996). –Page Citation.

Iowa Law Review
Ab.:   Iowa L. Rev.

Ex.:   Beryl R. Jones, <u>Copyrights and State Liability</u>, 76 Iowa L. Rev. 701 (1991). –Article Citation.

Beryl R. Jones, <u>Copyrights and State Liability</u>, 76 Iowa L. Rev. 701, 719-20 (1991). –Page Citation.

Iowa Lawyer, The
Ab.:   Iowa Law.

Ex.:   Jennifer J. Rose, <u>Walk Awhile in Your Client's Shoes</u>, Iowa Law., Feb. 1992, at 24. –Article Citation.

Jennifer J. Rose, <u>Walk Awhile in Your Client's Shoes</u>, Iowa Law., Feb. 1992, at 24, 25. –Page Citation.

Iowa Legislative Service (West)
Ab.:   year Iowa Legis. Serv. page no. (West).

In law review footnotes, the titles of books and the names of cases, except for procedural phrases, are not underlined. <u>See</u> <u>Bluebook</u> rule 2.1(a) & (b). Further, the following are in large and small capitals: codes, restatements, standards, constitutions, periodicals, authors of books, titles of books, the abbreviated names of codes, most legislative materials except for bills and resolutions, codified ordinances, model codes, court rules, and sentencing guidelines. Refer to <u>The Bluebook</u>.

Ex.:   Act of May 16, 1996, No. 196, 1996 Iowa Legis. Serv. 526 (West) (speed limit increase). –Citation to an entire session law.

Act of May 16, 1996, No. 196, sec. 1 § 321.285(6), 1996 Iowa Legis. Serv. 526, 527 (West) (speed limit for multi-laned highway). –Citation to a session law amending prior act.

–See Bluebook rule 12.4.

–"Cite to Iowa Acts, if therein." Bluebook table T.1, p. 209.

Iowa Reports
Ab.:   Iowa

–Discontinued after 261 Iowa 1395 (1968).

–Cite to N.W. or N.W.2d, if therein; otherwise, cited to Iowa.

–Give parallel citations only in documents submitted to Iowa state courts. See Bluebook rules 10.3.1 and B5.1.3; see also Iowa R. App. P. 6.14(5), which requires a parallel citation.

–Through 261 Iowa 1395 (1968), cite as follows:

In documents submitted to Iowa state courts:

Burlington & Summit Apts. v. Manolato, 233 Iowa 15, 7 N.W.2d 26 (1943). –Case Citation.

Burlington & Summit Apts. v. Manolato, 233 Iowa 15, 18, 7 N.W.2d 26, 28 (1943). –Page Citation.

In all other documents:

Burlington & Summit Apts. v. Manolato, 7 N.W.2d 26 (Iowa 1943). –Case Citation.

Burlington & Summit Apts. v. Manolato, 7 N.W.2d 26, 28 (Iowa 1943). –Page Citation.

–After 261 Iowa 1395 (1968), cite as follows:

In all documents:

Rokusek v. Jensen, 548 N.W.2d 570 (Iowa 1996). –Case Citation.

Rokusek v. Jensen, 548 N.W.2d 570, 573 (Iowa 1996). –Page Citation.

Iowa Session Laws
See Acts of the State of Iowa and Iowa Legislative Service.

Iran-United States Claims Tribunal Reports
Ab.:   Iran-U.S. Cl. Trib. Rep.

Ex.:   Stewart v. Iran, 24 Iran-U.S. Cl. Trib. Rep. 116 (1991).

Irish Law Times Reports (1866-1980)
Ab.:   I.L.T.R.

In citing cases in law review footnotes, abbreviate any word listed in table T.6; the names of "states, countries, and other geographical units" unless they are named parties; and any other words of eight or more letters "if substantial space is thereby saved and the result is unambiguous." Bluebook rule 10.2.2. On the other hand, in citing cases in text, abbreviate only widely known acronyms and the following words: "&," "Ass'n," "Bros.," "Co.," "Corp.," "Inc.," "Ltd.," and "No." Bluebook rule 10.2.1(c).

Ex.:   Elkinson v. Cassidy, [1975] 110 I.L.T.R. 27 (C.C.) (Ir.).
         —See Bluebook rule 20.3.1 and table T.2.

Irish Reports (1868 - date)
Ab.:   I.R.

Ex.:   Roche v. Peilow, [1985] I.R. 232 (Ir.).

See Bluebook rule 20.3.1; see also table T.2, p. 282, concerning neutral citation.

Israel Law Review
Ab.:   Isr. L. Rev.

Ex.:   Ruth Lapidoth, Jerusalem and the Peace Process, 28 Isr. L. Rev. 402
         (1994). —Article Citation.

         Ruth Lapidoth, Jerusalem and the Peace Process, 28 Isr. L. Rev. 402,
         410-12 (1994). —Page Citation.

Israel Yearbook on Human Rights
Ab.:   Isr. Y.B. on H.R.

Ex.:   Tania Domb, The Gaza and Jericho Autonomy and Human Rights,
         25 Isr. Y.B. on Hum. Rts. 21 (1995). —Article Citation.

         Tania Domb, The Gaza and Jericho Autonomy and Human Rights,   25
         Isr. Y.B. on Hum. Rts. 21, 23-24 (1995). —Page Citation.

Italian Yearbook of International Law, The
Ab.:   Ital. Y.B. Int'l L.

Ex.:   Salvatore Vitale, New Cooperation Treaty Between Italy and
         Argentina, 1987 Ital. Y.B. Int'l L. 163. —Article Citation.

         Salvatore Vitale, New Cooperation Treaty Between Italy and
         Argentina, 1987 Ital. Y.B. Int'l L. 163, 167-68. —Page Citation.

In law review footnotes, the titles of books and the names of cases, except for procedural
phrases, are not underlined. See Bluebook rule 2.1(a) & (b). Further, the following are in
large and small capitals: codes, restatements, standards, constitutions, periodicals, authors of
books, titles of books, the abbreviated names of codes, most legislative materials except for
bills and resolutions, codified ordinances, model codes, court rules, and sentencing guidelines.
Refer to The Bluebook.

J

John Marshall Journal of Computer & Information Law
Ab.:   J. Marshall J. Computer & Info. L.

Ex.: Moritz Keller, <u>Lessons for the Hague: Internet Jurisdiction in Contract and Tort Cases in the European Community and the United States</u>, 23 J. Marshall J. Computer & Info. L. 1 (2004). – Article Citation.

Moritz Keller, <u>Lessons for the Hague: Internet Jurisdiction in Contract and Tort Cases in the European Community and the United States</u>, 23 J. Marshall J. Computer & Info. L. 1, 52-54 (2004). –Page Citation.

John Marshall Law Review, The
Ab.:   J. Marshall L. Rev.

Ex.:   James M. Smith, <u>Legal Issues Confronting Families Affected by HIV</u>, 24 J. Marshall L. Rev. 543 (1991). –Article Citation.

James M. Smith, <u>Legal Issues Confronting Families Affected by HIV</u>, 24 J. Marshall L. Rev. 543, 559-60 (1991). –Page Citation.

Journal of Accountancy
Ab.:   J. Acct.

Ex.:   Paul Caster, <u>The Role of Confirmations as Audit Evidence</u>, J. Acct., Feb. 1992, at 73. –Article Citation.

Paul Caster, <u>The Role of Confirmations as Audit Evidence</u>, J. Acct., Feb. 1992, at 73, 75-76. –Page Citation.

Journal of African Law
Ab.:   J. Afr. L.

Ex.:   Bojosi Otlhogile, <u>Infanticide in Bechuanaland: A Footnote to Schapera</u>, 34 J. Afr. L. 159 (1990). –Article Citation.

Bojosi Otlhogile, <u>Infanticide in Bechuanaland: A Footnote to Schapera</u>, 34 J. Afr. L. 159, 159-60 (1990). –Page Citation.

Journal of Agricultural Taxation & Law
Ab.:   J. Agric. Tax & L.

Ex.:   Gary L. Maydew, <u>Incorporating the Family Farm May Generally Be Done Tax-Free</u>, 14 J. Agric. Tax & L. 53 (1992). –Article Citation.

Gary L. Maydew, <u>Incorporating the Family Farm May Generally Be Done Tax-Free</u>, 14 J. Agric. Tax & L. 53, 59-60 (1992). –Page Citation.

In law review footnotes, the titles of books and the names of cases, except for procedural phrases, are not underlined. See <u>Bluebook</u> rule 2.1(a) & (b). Further, the following are in large and small capitals: codes, restatements, standards, constitutions, periodicals, authors of books, titles of books, the abbreviated names of codes, most legislative materials except for bills and resolutions, codified ordinances, model codes, court rules, and sentencing guidelines. Refer to <u>The Bluebook</u>.

Journal of Air Law and Commerce
Ab.: J. Air L. & Com.

Ex.: Alan B. Rich, Current Issues in Removal Jurisdiction, 57 J. Air L. & Com. 395 (1991). –Article Citation.

Alan B. Rich, Current Issues in Removal Jurisdiction, 57 J. Air L. & Com. 395, 419-20 (1991). –Page Citation.

Journal of Appellate Practice and Process
Ab.: J. App. Prac. & Process

Ex.: Susan Calkins, Ineffective Assistance of Counsel in Parental-Rights Termination Cases: The Challenge for Appellate Courts, 6 J. App. Prac. & Process 179 (2004). –Article Citation.

Susan Calkins, Ineffective Assistance of Counsel in Parental-Rights Termination Cases: The Challenge for Appellate Courts, 6 J. App. Prac. & Process 179, 190-91 (2004). –Page Citation.

Journal of Arts Management and Law
Ab.: J. Arts Mgmt. & L.

Ex.: Harry H. Chartrand, Context and Continuity: Philistines, Pharisees and Art in English Culture, 21 J. Arts Mgmt. & L. 141 (1991). –Article Citation.

Harry H. Chartrand, Context and Continuity: Philistines, Pharisees and Art in English Culture, 21 J. Arts Mgmt. & L. 141, 149-50 (1991). –Page Citation.

Journal of Broadcasting & Electronic Media
Ab.: J. Broadcasting & Electronic Media

Ex.: Donald R. Browne, Local Radio in Switzerland: The Limits of Localism, 35 J. Broadcasting & Electronic Media 449 (1991). –Article Citation.

Donald R. Browne, Local Radio in Switzerland: The Limits of Localism, 35 J. Broadcasting & Electronic Media 449, 459-60 (1991). –Page Citation.

Journal of Business Law, The
Ab.: J. Bus. L.

Ex.: M. G. Bridge, Form, Substance and Innovation in Personal Property Security Law, 36 J. Bus. L. 1 (1992). –Article Citation.

M. G. Bridge, Form, Substance and Innovation in Personal Property Security Law, 36 J. Bus. L. 1, 19-20 (1992). –Page Citation.

In citing cases in law review footnotes, abbreviate any word listed in table T.6; the names of "states, countries, and other geographical units" unless they are named parties; and any other words of eight or more letters "if substantial space is thereby saved and the result is unambiguous." Bluebook rule 10.2.2. On the other hand, in citing cases in text, abbreviate only widely known acronyms and the following words: "&," "Ass'n," "Bros.," "Co.," "Corp.," "Inc.," "Ltd.," and "No." Bluebook rule 10.2.1(c).

Journal of Catholic Legal Studies
Ab.: J. Cath. Legal Stud.

Ex.: Michael J. Broyde, <u>Why Educate?: A Jewish Law Perspective</u>, 44 J. Cath. Legal Stud. 179 (2005). −Article Citation.

Journal of Chinese Law
Ab.: J. Chinese L.

Ex.: Lester Ross, <u>Force Majeure and Related Doctrines of Excuse in Contract Law of the People's Republic of China</u>, 5 J. Chinese L. 1 (1991). −Article Citation.

Lester Ross, <u>Force Majeure and Related Doctrines of Excuse in Contract Law of the People's Republic of China</u>, 5 J. Chinese L. 1, 49-50 (1991). −Page Citation.

Journal of Church and State
Ab.: J. Church & St.

Ex.: Walter Sawatsky, <u>Truth Telling in Eastern Europe: The Liberation and the Burden</u>, 33 J. Church & St. 701 (1991). −Article Citation.

Walter Sawatsky, <u>Truth Telling in Eastern Europe: The Liberation and the Burden</u>, 33 J. Church & St. 701, 715-16 (1991). −Page Citation.

Journal of Collective Negotiations in the Public Sector
Ab.: J. Collective Negot. Pub. Sector

Ex.: Clete Bulach, <u>The Collective Bargaining Potpourri: Is There a Right Way?</u>, 20 J. Collective Negot. Pub. Sector 281 (1991). −Article Citation.

Clete Bulach, <u>The Collective Bargaining Potpourri: Is There a Right Way?</u>, 20 J. Collective Negot. Pub. Sector 281, 289-90 (1991). −Page Citation.

Journal of College and University Law, The
Ab.: J.C. & U.L.

Ex.: Andrew H. Baida, <u>Not All Minority Scholarships Are Created Equal: Why Some May Be More Constitutional Than Others</u>, 18 J.C. & U.L. 333 (1992). −Article Citation.

Andrew H. Baida, <u>Not All Minority Scholarships Are Created Equal: Why Some May Be More Constitutional Than Others</u>, 18 J.C. & U.L. 333, 349-50 (1992). −Page Citation.

Journal of Common Market Studies
Ab.: J. Common Mkt. Stud.

Ex.: Alfred Tovias, <u>EC-Eastern Europe: A Case Study of Hungary</u>, 29 J. Common Mkt. Stud. 291 (1991). −Article Citation.

Alfred Tovias, <u>EC-Eastern Europe: A Case Study of Hungary</u>, 29 J. Common Mkt. Stud. 291, 298-99 (1991). −Page Citation.

In law review footnotes, the titles of books and the names of cases, except for procedural phrases, are not underlined. <u>See</u> Bluebook rule 2.1(a) & (b). Further, the following are in large and small capitals: codes, restatements, standards, constitutions, periodicals, authors of books, titles of books, the abbreviated names of codes, most legislative materials except for bills and resolutions, codified ordinances, model codes, court rules, and sentencing guidelines. Refer to <u>The Bluebook</u>.

Journal of Conflict Resolution, The
Ab.:   J. Conflict Resol.

Ex.:   Chae-han Kim, <u>Third-Party Participation in Wars</u>, 35 J. Conflict Resol. 659 (1991). –Article Citation.

        Chae-han Kim, <u>Third-Party Participation in Wars</u>, 35 J. Conflict Resol. 659, 669-70 (1991). –Page Citation.

Journal of Consumer Affairs, The
Ab.:   J. Consumer Aff.

Ex.:   James D. Reschovsky, <u>The Emergency Food Relief System: An Empirical Study</u>, 25 J. Consumer Aff. 258 (1991). –Article Citation.

        James D. Reschovsky, <u>The Emergency Food Relief System: An Empirical Study</u>, 25 J. Consumer Aff. 258, 269-70 (1991). –Page Citation.

Journal of Contemporary Criminal Justice
Ab.:   J. Contemp. Crim. Just.

Ex.:   Charles H. Rogovin & Frederick T. Martens, <u>The Evil Men Do</u>, 8 J. Contemp. Crim. Just. 62 (1992). –Article Citation.

        Charles H. Rogovin & Frederick T. Martens, <u>The Evil Men Do</u>, 8 J. Contemp. Crim. Just. 62, 74 (1992). –Page Citation.

Journal of Contemporary Health Law and Policy
Ab.:   J. Contemp. Health L. & Pol'y

Ex.:   Charles F. Rice, <u>The Coming Retreat from Roe v. Wade</u>, J. Contemp. Health L. & Pol'y, Spring 1988, at 1. –Article Citation.

        Charles F. Rice, <u>The Coming Retreat from Roe v. Wade</u>, J. Contemp. Health L. & Pol'y, Spring 1988, at 1, 19-20. –Page Citation.

Journal of Contemporary Law
Ab.:   J. Contemp. L.

Ex.:   Edwin B. Firmage, <u>The War Power of Congress and Revision of the War Powers Resolution</u>, 17 J. Contemp. L. 237 (1991). –Article Citation.

        Edwin B. Firmage, <u>The War Power of Congress and Revision of the War Powers Resolution</u>, 17 J. Contemp. L. 237, 249-50 (1991). –Page Citation.

Journal of Contemporary Legal Issues, The
Ab.:   J. Contemp. Legal Issues

In citing cases in law review footnotes, abbreviate any word listed in table T.6; the names of "states, countries, and other geographical units" unless they are named parties; and any other words of eight or more letters "if <u>substantial</u> space is thereby saved and the result is unambiguous." <u>Bluebook</u> rule 10.2.2. On the other hand, in citing cases in text, abbreviate only widely known acronyms and the following words: "&," "Ass'n," "Bros.," "Co.," "Corp.," "Inc.," "Ltd.," and "No." <u>Bluebook</u> rule 10.2.1(c).

Ex.:   David M. Star, <u>The Private-Facts Torts in California and Beyond: Is There Life After Florida Star?</u>, 3 J. Contemp. Legal Issues 199 (1989-1990). −Article Citation.

David M. Star, <u>The Private-Facts Torts in California and Beyond: Is There Life After Florida Star?</u>, 3 J. Contemp. Legal Issues 199, 204-05 (1989-1990). −Page Citation.

Journal of Corporate Taxation, The
Ab.:   J. Corp. Tax'n
Ex.:   Gilbert D. Bloom, <u>Private Letter Rulings</u>, 19 J. Corp. Tax'n 160 (1992). −Article Citation.

Gilbert D. Bloom, <u>Private Letter Rulings</u>, 19 J. Corp. Tax'n 160, 161-62 (1992). −Page Citation.

Journal of Corporation Law, The
Ab.:   J. Corp. L.
Ex.:   Martin Riger, <u>The Trust Indenture as Bargained Contract: The Persistence of Myth</u>, 16 J. Corp. L. 211 (1991). −Article Citation.

Martin Riger, <u>The Trust Indenture as Bargained Contract: The Persistence of Myth</u>, 16 J. Corp. L. 211, 229-30 (1991). −Page Citation.

Journal of Criminal Law
Ab.:   J. Crim. L.
Ex.:   Jennifer A. James, <u>Cut-throat Defenses and Character Evidence</u>, 55 J. Crim. L. 103 (1991). −Article Citation.

Jennifer A. James, <u>Cut-throat Defenses and Character Evidence</u>, 55 J. Crim. L. 103, 115-16 (1991). −Page Citation.

Journal of Criminal Law and Criminology, The
Ab.:   J. Crim. L. & Criminology
Ex.:   Ellen H. Steury, <u>Specifying "Criminalization" of the Mentally Disordered Misdemeanant</u>, 82 J. Crim. L. & Criminology 334 (1991). −Article Citation.

Ellen H. Steury, <u>Specifying "Criminalization" of the Mentally Disordered Misdemeanant</u>, 82 J. Crim. L. & Criminology 334, 339-42 (1991). −Page Citation.

Journal of Dispute Resolution
Ab.:   J. Disp. Resol.

In law review footnotes, the titles of books and the names of cases, except for procedural phrases, are not underlined. <u>See</u> Bluebook rule 2.1(a) & (b). Further, the following are in large and small capitals: codes, restatements, standards, constitutions, periodicals, authors of books, titles of books, the abbreviated names of codes, most legislative materials except for bills and resolutions, codified ordinances, model codes, court rules, and sentencing guidelines. Refer to <u>The Bluebook</u>.

Ex.:   Jeffrey W. Stempel, <u>Reconsidering the Employment Contract Exclusion in Section 1 of the Federal Arbitration Act: Correcting the Judiciary's Failure of Statutory Vision</u>, 1991 J. Disp. Resol. 259 (1991). –Article Citation.

Jeffrey W. Stempel, <u>Reconsidering the Employment Contract Exclusion in Section 1 of the Federal Arbitration Act: Correcting the Judiciary's Failure of Statutory Vision</u>, 1991 J. Disp. Resol. 259, 270-71 (1991). –Page Citation.

Journal of Energy Law and Policy
Ab.:   J. Energy L. & Pol'y
Ex.:   Adrian J. Bradbrook, <u>The Role of the Courts in Advancing the Use of Solar Energy</u>, 9 J. Energy L. & Pol'y 135 (1989). –Article Citation.

Adrian J. Bradbrook, <u>The Role of the Courts in Advancing the Use of Solar Energy</u>, 9 J. Energy L. & Pol'y 135, 137 (1989). –Page Citation.

Journal of Energy, Natural Resources, & Environmental Law
Ab.:   J. Energy Nat. Resources & Envtl. L.

Ex.:   Phillip W. Lear, <u>Accretion, Reliction, Erosion, and Avulsion: A Survey of Riparian and Littoral Title Problems</u>, 11 J. Energy Nat. Resources & Envtl. L. 265 (1991). –Article Citation.

Phillip W. Lear, <u>Accretion, Reliction, Erosion, and Avulsion: A Survey of Riparian and Littoral Title Problems</u>, 11 J. Energy Nat. Resources & Envtl. L. 265, 269-73 (1991). –Page Citation.

Journal of Environmental Law and Litigation
Ab.:   J. Envtl. L. & Litig.

Ex.:   Brian J. Preston, <u>Public Enforcement of Environmental Laws in Australia</u>, 6 J. Envtl. L. & Litig. 39 (1991). –Article Citation.

Brian J. Preston, <u>Public Enforcement of Environmental Laws in Australia</u>, 6 J. Envtl. L. & Litig. 39, 42-46 (1991). –Page Citation.

Journal of Family Law
Ab.:   J. Fam. L.

Ex.:   Elizabeth L. Gibson, <u>Artificial Insemination by Donor: Information, Communication and Regulation</u>, 30 J. Fam. L. 1 (1991-92). –Article Citation.

Elizabeth L. Gibson, <u>Artificial Insemination by Donor: Information, Communication and Regulation</u>, 30 J. Fam. L. 1, 20-25 (1991-92). –Page Citation.

Journal of Forensic Sciences
Ab.:   J. Forensic Sci.

In citing cases in law review footnotes, abbreviate any word listed in table T.6; the names of "states, countries, and other geographical units" unless they are named parties; and any other words of eight or more letters "if <u>substantial</u> space is thereby saved and the result is unambiguous." <u>Bluebook</u> rule 10.2.2. On the other hand, in citing cases in text, abbreviate only widely known acronyms and the following words: "&," "Ass'n," "Bros.," "Co.," "Corp.," "Inc.," "Ltd.," and "No." <u>Bluebook</u> rule 10.2.1(c).

Ex.:   Rena A. Merrill & Edward G. Bartick, <u>Analysis of Ballpoint Pen Inks</u>
<u>by Diffuse Reflectance Infrared Spectometry</u>, 37 J. Forensic Sci. 528
(1992). –Article Citation.

Rena A. Merrill & Edward G. Bartick, <u>Analysis of Ballpoint Pen Inks</u>
<u>by Diffuse Reflectance Infrared Spectometry</u>, 37 J. Forensic Sci. 528,
536-38 (1992). –Page Citation.

Journal of Gender, Race and Justice
Ab.:   J. Gender Race & Just.

Ex.:   Lee Ann Basser, <u>Justice for All? The Challenge of Realizing the Right</u>
<u>to Education for Children with Disabilities</u>, 8 J. Gender Race & Just.
531 (2005). –Article Citation.

Lee Ann Basser, <u>Justice for All? The Challenge of Realizing the Right</u>
<u>to Education for Children with Disabilities</u>, 8 J. Gender Race & Just.
531, 535 (2005). –Page Citation.

Journal of Health Law
Ab.:   J. Health L.

Ex.:   Margaret Gilhooley, <u>Heal the Damage: Prescription Drug Consumer</u>
<u>Advertisements and Relative Choices</u>, 38 J. Health L. 1 (2005).
–Article Citation.

Margaret Gilhooley, <u>Heal the Damage: Prescription Drug Consumer</u>
<u>Advertisements and Relative Choices</u>, 38 J. Health L. 1, 36-37 (2005).
–Page Citation.

Journal of Health, Politics, Policy and Law
Ab.:   J. Health Pol. Pol'y & L.

Ex.:   Harvey M. Sapolsky, <u>Empire and the Business of Health Insurance</u>,
16 J. Health Pol. Pol'y & L. 747 (1991). –Article Citation.

Harvey M. Sapolsky, <u>Empire and the Business of Health Insurance</u>,
16 J. Health Pol. Pol'y & L. 747, 757-58 (1991). –Page Citation.

Journal of Intellectual Property Law
Ab.:   J. Intell. Prop. L.

Ex.: Deborah Tussey, <u>Technology Matters: The Courts, Media</u>
<u>Neutrality, and New Technologies</u>, 12 J. Intell. Prop. L. 427 (2005).
–Article Citation.

Deborah Tussey, <u>Technology Matters: The Courts, Media Neutrality,</u>
<u>and New Technologies</u>, 12 J. Intell. Prop. L. 427, 433 (2005). –Page
Citation.

Journal of International Arbitration
Ab.:   J. Int'l Arb.

In law review footnotes, the titles of books and the names of cases, except for procedural
phrases, are not underlined. <u>See</u> Bluebook rule 2.1(a) & (b). Further, the following are in
large and small capitals: codes, restatements, standards, constitutions, periodicals, authors of
books, titles of books, the abbreviated names of codes, most legislative materials except for
bills and resolutions, codified ordinances, model codes, court rules, and sentencing guidelines.
Refer to <u>The Bluebook</u>.

Ex.:   Alexander C. Hoagland, <u>Modification of Mexican Arbitration Law</u>, J. Int'l Arb., Mar. 1990, at 91. –Article Citation.

Alexander C. Hoagland, <u>Modification of Mexican Arbitration Law</u>, J. Int'l Arb., Mar. 1990, at 91, 99-100. –Page Citation.

Journal of International Law and Practice
Ab.:   J. Int'l L. & Prac.

Ex.:   Alison Matsumoto, Comment, <u>A Place of Considerations of Culture in the American Criminal Justice System: Japanese Law and the Kimura Case</u>, 4 J. Int'l L. & Prac. 507 (1995). –Article Citation.

Alison Matsumoto, Comment, <u>A Place of Considerations of Culture in the American Criminal Justice System: Japanese Law and the Kimura Case</u>, 4 J. Int'l L. & Prac. 507, 511 (1995). –Page Citation.

Journal of International Money and Finance
Ab.:   J. Int'l Money & Fin.

Ex.:   Janet Ceglowski, <u>Intertemporal Substitution in Import Demand</u>, 10 J. Int'l Money & Fin. 118 (1991). –Article Citation.

Janet Ceglowski, <u>Intertemporal Substitution in Import Demand</u>, 10 J. Int'l Money & Fin. 118, 119-21 (1991). –Page Citation.

Journal of Juvenile Law
Ab.:   J. Juv. L.

Ex.:   Patricia A. Andreoni, <u>Juvenile Extradition: Denial of Due Process</u>, 1989 J. Juv. L. 193. –Article Citation.

Patricia A. Andreoni, <u>Juvenile Extradition: Denial of Due Process</u>, 1989 J. Juv. L. 193, 219-20. –Page Citation.

Journal of Labor Research
Ab.:   J. Lab. Res.

Ex.:   Javed Ashraf, <u>Union Wage Premiums in an Instrumental Variables Framework</u>, 13 J. Lab. Res. 231 (1992). –Article Citation.

Javed Ashraf, <u>Union Wage Premiums in an Instrumental Variables Framework</u>, 13 J. Lab. Res. 231, 232-35 (1992). –Page Citation.

Journal of Land Use & Environmental Law
Ab.:   J. Land Use & Envtl. L.

Ex.:   William R. Mitchell, <u>CERCLA: The Problem of Lender Liability</u>, 7 J. Land Use & Envtl. L. 101 (1991). –Article Citation.

William R. Mitchell, <u>CERCLA: The Problem of Lender Liability</u>, 7 J. Land Use & Envtl. L. 101, 109-10 (1991). –Page Citation.

Journal of Law and Commerce, The
Ab.:   J.L. & Com.

In citing cases in law review footnotes, abbreviate any word listed in table T.6; the names of "states, countries, and other geographical units" unless they are named parties; and any other words of eight or more letters "if <u>substantial</u> space is thereby saved and the result is unambiguous." <u>Bluebook</u> rule 10.2.2. On the other hand, in citing cases in text, abbreviate only widely known acronyms and the following words: "&," "Ass'n," "Bros.," "Co.," "Corp.," "Inc.," "Ltd.," and "No." <u>Bluebook</u> rule 10.2.1(c).

Ex.: Mark F. Nowak, <u>Occupational Noise Exposure of Railroad Workers –</u> <u>Which Regulation Applies?</u>, 11 J.L. & Com. 39 (1991). –Article Citation.

Mark F. Nowak, <u>Occupational Noise Exposure of Railroad Workers –</u> <u>Which Regulation Applies?</u>, 11 J.L. & Com. 39, 44-45 (1991). –Page Citation.

Journal of Law & Economics, The
Ab.: J.L. & Econ.

Ex.: Pauline M. Ippolito, <u>Resale Price Maintenance: Empirical Evidence</u> <u>from Litigation</u>, 34 J.L. & Econ. 263 (1991). –Article Citation.

Pauline M. Ippolito, <u>Resale Price Maintenance: Empirical Evidence</u> <u>from Litigation</u>, 34 J.L. & Econ. 263, 273-78 (1991). –Page Citation.

Journal of Law & Education
Ab.: J.L. & Educ.

Ex.: Gretchen Martin, <u>HIV/AIDS and Adolescents: Implications for School</u> <u>Policies</u>, 20 J.L. & Econ. 325 (1991). –Article Citation.

Gretchen Martin, <u>HIV/AIDS and Adolescents: Implications for School</u> <u>Policies</u>, 20 J.L. & Econ. 325, 333-34 (1991). –Page Citation.

Journal of Law and Health
Ab.: J.L. & Health

Ex.: James J. Nocon, <u>Physicians and Maternal - Fetal Conflicts: Duties,</u> <u>Rights and Responsibilities</u>, 5 J.L. & Health 1 (1990-91). –Article Citation.

James J. Nocon, <u>Physicians and Maternal - Fetal Conflicts: Duties,</u> <u>Rights and Responsibilities</u>, 5 J.L. & Health 1, 29-32 (1990-91). –Page Citation.

Journal of Law and Policy
Ab.: J.L. & Pol'y

Ex.: George Smith & Gloria Dabiri, <u>The Judicial Role in the Treatment of</u> <u>Juvenile Delinquents</u>, 3 J.L. & Pol'y 347 (1995). –Article Citation.

George Smith & Gloria Dabiri, <u>The Judicial Role in the Treatment of</u> <u>Juvenile Delinquents</u>, 3 J.L. & Pol'y 347, 350 (1995). –Page Citation.

Journal of Law and Politics
Ab.: J.L. & Pol.

Ex.: Shiela B. Kamerman, <u>Doing Better by Children: Focus on Families</u>, 8 J.L. & Pol. 75 (1990). –Article Citation.

Shiela B. Kamerman, <u>Doing Better by Children: Focus on Families</u>, 8 J.L. & Pol. 75, 79-80 (1990). –Page Citation.

Journal of Law and Society
Ab.: J.L. & Soc'y

In law review footnotes, the titles of books and the names of cases, except for procedural phrases, are not underlined. <u>See</u> <u>Bluebook</u> rule 2.1(a) & (b). Further, the following are in large and small capitals: codes, restatements, standards, constitutions, periodicals, authors of books, titles of books, the abbreviated names of codes, most legislative materials except for bills and resolutions, codified ordinances, model codes, court rules, and sentencing guidelines. Refer to <u>The Bluebook</u>.

J.L.S. [U.K.]

Ex.: Carol Smart, <u>The Legal and Moral Ordering of Child Custody</u>, 18 J.L. & Soc'y 485 (1991). –Article Citation.

Carol Smart, <u>The Legal and Moral Ordering of Child Custody</u>, 18 J.L. & Soc'y 485, 491-93 (1991). –Page Citation.

Journal of Law and Technology
Ab.: J.L. & Tech.
Ex.: S. Neil Hosenball, <u>Financing Space Ventures</u>, J.L. & Tech., Winter 1989, at 15. –Article Citation.

S. Neil Hosenball, <u>Financing Space Ventures</u>, J.L. & Tech., Winter 1989, at 15, 16. –Page Citation.

Journal of Law, Economics, & Organization, The
Ab.: J.L. Econ. & Org.
Ex.: Denis C. Mueller, <u>Constitutional Rights</u>, 7 J.L. Econ. & Org. 313 (1991). –Article Citation.

Denis C. Mueller, <u>Constitutional Rights</u>, 7 J.L. Econ. & Org. 313, 329-31 (1991). –Page Citation.

Journal of Law, Medicine & Ethics
Ab.: J.L. Med. & Ethics
Ex.: David W. Barnes, <u>Imwinkelried's Argument for Normative Ethical Testimony</u>, 33 J.L. Med. & Ethics 234 (2005). –Article Citation.

David W. Barnes, <u>Imwinkelried's Argument for Normative Ethical Testimony</u>, 33 J.L. Med. & Ethics 234, 243-35 (2005). –Page Citation.

Journal of Legal Education
Ab.: J. Legal Educ.
Ex.: Judith S. Kaye, <u>One Judge's View of Academic Law Review Writing</u>, 1989 J. Legal Educ. 313. –Article Citation.

Judith S. Kaye, <u>One Judge's View of Academic Law Review Writing</u>, 1989 J. Legal Educ. 313, 315. –Page Citation.

Journal of Legal History
Ab.: J. Legal Hist.
Ex.: Peter Goodrich, <u>Eating Law: Commons, Common Land, Common Law</u>, 12 J. Legal Hist. 246 (1991). –Article Citation.

Peter Goodrich, <u>Eating Law: Commons, Common Land, Common Law</u>, 12 J. Legal Hist. 246, 249-51 (1991). –Page Citation.

Journal of Legal Medicine
Ab.: J. Legal Med.

In citing cases in law review footnotes, abbreviate any word listed in table T.6; the names of "states, countries, and other geographical units" unless they are named parties; and any other words of eight or more letters "if <u>substantial</u> space is thereby saved and the result is unambiguous." <u>Bluebook</u> rule 10.2.2. On the other hand, in citing cases in text, abbreviate only widely known acronyms and the following words: "&," "Ass'n," "Bros.," "Co.," "Corp.," "Inc.," "Ltd.," and "No." <u>Bluebook</u> rule 10.2.1(c).

Ex.: Howard Smith, <u>A Model for Validating an Expert's Opinion in Medical Negligence Cases</u>, 26 J. Legal Med. 207 (2005). –Article Citation.

Howard Smith, <u>A Model for Validating an Expert's Opinion in Medical Negligence Cases</u>, 26 J. Legal Med. 207, 210-15 (2005). –Page Citation.

Journal of Legal Pluralism
Ab.:   J. Legal Pluralism
Ex.:   Koti E. Agorsah, <u>Women in African Traditional Politics</u>, 1990-91 J. Legal Pluralism 77. –Article Citation.

Koti E. Agorsah, <u>Women in African Traditional Politics</u>, 1990-91 J. Legal Pluralism 77, 79-80. –Page Citation.

Journal of Legal Studies, The
Ab.:   J. Legal Stud.

Ex.:   Lloyd Cohen, <u>Holdouts and Free Rides</u>, 20 J. Legal Stud. 351 (1991). –Article Citation.

Lloyd Cohen, <u>Holdouts and Free Rides</u>, 20 J. Legal Stud. 351, 359-60 (1991). –Page Citation.

Journal of Legislation
Ab.:   J. Legis.

Ex.:   W.H. Moore, <u>U.S. Energy Prospects: 1990's and Beyond</u>, 17 J. Legis. 193 (1991). –Article Citation.

W.H. Moore, <u>U.S. Energy Prospects: 1990's and Beyond</u>, 17 J. Legis. 193, 197-98 (1991). –Page Citation.

Journal of Maritime Law and Commerce
Ab.:   J. Mar. L. & Com.

Ex.:   David J. Sharpe, <u>Removal to Admiralty Revisited</u>, 22 J. Mar. L. & Com. 485 (1991). –Article Citation.

David J. Sharpe, <u>Removal to Admiralty Revisited</u>, 22 J. Mar. L. & Com. 485, 493-95 (1991). –Page Citation.

Journal of Medicine and Philosophy
Ab.:   J. Med. & Phil.

Ex.:   E. Haavi Morreim, <u>Access Without Excess</u>, 17 J. Med. & Phil. 1 (1992). –Article Citation.

E. Haavi Morreim, <u>Access Without Excess</u>, 17 J. Med. & Phil. 1, 6-7 (1992). –Page Citation.

Journal of Mineral Law & Policy
Ab.:   J. Min. L. & Pol'y

In law review footnotes, the titles of books and the names of cases, except for procedural phrases, are not underlined. <u>See</u> <u>Bluebook</u> rule 2.1(a) & (b). Further, the following are in large and small capitals: codes, restatements, standards, constitutions, periodicals, authors of books, titles of books, the abbreviated names of codes, most legislative materials except for bills and resolutions, codified ordinances, model codes, court rules, and sentencing guidelines. Refer to <u>The Bluebook</u>.

Ex.:   John S. Palmore, <u>Kentucky's New Nuisance Statute</u>, 7 J. Min. L. &
          Pol'y 1 (1991-1992). –Article Citation.

          John S. Palmore, <u>Kentucky's New Nuisance Statute</u>, 7 J. Min. L. &
          Pol'y 1, 9-10 (1991-1992). –Page Citation.

Journal of Pension Planning & Compliance
Ab.:   J. Pension Plan. & Compliance

Ex.:   Nicholas P. Damico, <u>Rollovers for AU: Simplification or Riff-OH?</u>,
          18 J. Pension Plan. & Compliance 42 (1992). –Article Citation.

          Nicholas P. Damico, <u>Rollovers for AU: Simplification or Riff-OH?</u>,
          18 J. Pension Plan. & Compliance 42, 49-51 (1992). –Page Citation.

Journal of Police Science and Administration
Ab.:   J. Police Sci. & Admin.

Ex.:   Harvey L. McMurray, <u>Attitudes of Assaulted Police Officers and Their
          Policy Implications</u>, 17 J. Police Sci. & Admin. 44 (1990). –Article
          Citation.

          Harvey L. McMurray, <u>Attitudes of Assaulted Police Officers and Their
          Policy Implications</u>, 17 J. Police Sci. & Admin. 44, 46-48 (1990).
          –Page Citation.

Journal of Products Liability
Ab.:   J. Prod. Liab.

Ex.:   William J. Warfel, <u>State-of-the-Art Evidence in Long-Tall Product
          Liability Litigation: The Transformation of the Tort System into a
          Compensation System</u>, 13 J. Prod. Liab. 183 (1991). –Article Citation.

          William J. Warfel, <u>State-of-the-Art Evidence in Long-Tall Product
          Liability Litigation: The Transformation of the Tort System into a
          Compensation System</u>, 13 J. Prod. Liab. 183, 189-94 (1991). –Page
          Citation.

Journal of Psychiatry & Law
Ab.:   J. Psychiatry & L.

Ex.:   Sana Loue, <u>Homo-Sexuality and Immigration Law: A Reexamination</u>,
          18 J. Psychiatry & L. 109 (1990). –Article Citation.

          Sana Loue, <u>Homo-Sexuality and Immigration Law: A Reexamination</u>,
          18 J. Psychiatry & L. 109, 110-19 (1990). –Page Citation.

Journal of Research in Crime and Delinquency
Ab.:   J. Res. Crime & Delinq.

In citing cases in law review footnotes, abbreviate any word listed in table T.6;
the names of "states, countries, and other geographical units" unless they are named parties;
and any other words of eight or more letters "if <u>substantial</u> space is thereby saved and the
result is unambiguous." <u>Bluebook</u> rule 10.2.2. On the other hand, in citing cases in text,
abbreviate only widely known acronyms and the following words: "&," "Ass'n," "Bros.,"
"Co.," "Corp.," "Inc.," "Ltd.," and "No." <u>Bluebook</u> rule 10.2.1(c).

Ex.: Julie Horney & Tneke Haen-Marshall, <u>An Experimental Comparison of Two Self-Report Methods of Measuring Lambda</u>, 29 J. Res. Crime & Delinq. 102 (1992). –Article Citation.

Julie Horney & Tneke Haen-Marshall, <u>An Experimental Comparison of Two Self-Report Methods of Measuring Lambda</u>, 29 J. Res. Crime & Delinq. 102, 109-10 (1992). –Page Citation.

Journal of Space Law
Ab.: J. Space L.

Ex.: Carl Q. Christol, <u>The Moon and Mars Missions: Can International Law Meet the Challenge?</u>, 19 J. Space L. 123 (1991). –Article Citation.

Carl Q. Christol, <u>The Moon and Mars Missions: Can International Law Meet the Challenge?</u>, 19 J. Space L. 123, 123 (1991). –Page Citation.

Journal of State Government, The
Ab.: J. St. Gov't

Ex.: William A. O'Neil, <u>Meeting the Challenge of Leadership</u>, 63 J. St. Gov't 3 (1990). –Article Citation.

William A. O'Neil, <u>Meeting the Challenge of Leadership</u>, 63 J. St. Gov't 3, 4 (1990). –Page Citation.

Journal of State Taxation
Ab.: J. St. Tax'n

Ex.: Jean Yingst-Sickles, <u>Corporate State Taxation of Federal Safe Harbour Leases</u>, J. St. Tax'n, Winter 1991, at 17. –Article Citation.

Jean Yingst-Sickles, <u>Corporate State Taxation of Federal Safe Harbour Leases</u>, J. St. Tax'n, Winter 1991, at 17, 20. –Page Citation.

Journal of Taxation, The
Ab.: J. Tax'n

Ex.: Jasper L. Cummings, Jr., & Samuel P. Staff, <u>The Impact of New S Corporation Revisions</u>, 85 J. Tax'n 197 (1996). –Article Citation.

Jasper L. Cummings, Jr., & Samuel P. Staff, <u>The Impact of New S Corporation Revisions</u>, 85 J. Tax'n 197, 198-99 (1996). –Page Citation.

Journal of the American Academy of Matrimonial Lawyers
Ab.: J. Am. Acad. Matrim. Law.

Ex.: Reba G. Rasor, <u>The Contingent Fee and Domestic Law</u>, 7 J. Am. Acad. Matrim. Law 43 (1991). –Article Citation.

Reba G. Rasor, <u>The Contingent Fee and Domestic Law</u>, 7 J. Am. Acad. Matrim. Law 43, 59-62 (1991).

Journal of the American Board of Trial Advocates
Ab.: J. Am. Board Trial Advocates

In law review footnotes, the titles of books and the names of cases, except for procedural phrases, are not underlined. <u>See</u> <u>Bluebook</u> rule 2.1(a) & (b). Further, the following are in large and small capitals: codes, restatements, standards, constitutions, periodicals, authors of books, titles of books, the abbreviated names of codes, most legislative materials except for bills and resolutions, codified ordinances, model codes, court rules, and sentencing guidelines. Refer to <u>The Bluebook</u>.

Ex.:   Keith Evans, <u>The Jury and the Democratic Impulse</u>, 1 J. Am. Board
         Trial Advocates 87 (1991). —Article Citation.

         Keith Evans, <u>The Jury and the Democratic Impulse</u>, 1 J. Am. Board
         Trial Advocates 87, 89-94 (1991). —Page Citation.

Journal of the American Medical Association

Ab.:   JAMA

Ex.:   Warren S. Browner et al., <u>In-Hospital and Long-term Mortality in Male
         Veterans Following Noncardiac Surgery</u>, 268 JAMA 228 (1992).
         —Article Citation.

         Warren S. Browner et al., <u>In-Hospital and Long-term Mortality in Male
         Veterans Following Noncardiac Surgery</u>, 268 JAMA 228, 231 (1992).
         —Page Citation.

Journal of the American Society of CLU & ChFC

Ab.:   J. Am. Soc'y CLU & ChFC

Ex.:   Robert W. Cooper & Garry L. Frank, <u>Business Ethics in the Insurance
         Industry</u>, J. Am. Soc'y CLU & ChFC, May 1991, at 74. —Article
         Citation.

         Robert W. Cooper & Garry L. Frank, <u>Business Ethics in the Insurance
         Industry</u>, J. Am. Soc'y CLU & ChFC, May 1991, at 74, 76-77. —Page
         Citation.

Journal of the Copyright Society of the U.S.A.

Ab.:   J. Copyright Soc'y U.S.A.

Ex.:   David B. Wolf, <u>Is There Any Copyright Protection for Maps After
         Feist?</u>, 39 J. Copyright Soc'y U.S.A. 224 (1992). —Article Citation.

         David B. Wolf, <u>Is There Any Copyright Protection for Maps After
         Feist?</u>, 39 J. Copyright Soc'y U.S.A. 224, 229-30 (1992). —Page
         Citation.

Journal of the Indian Law Institute

Ab.:   J. Indian L. Inst.

Ex.:   Chhatrapati Singh, <u>The Concept of Time in Law: Basis of Laws of
         Limitation and Prescription</u>, 32 J. Indian L. Inst. 328 (1990). —Article
         Citation.

         Chhatrapati Singh, <u>The Concept of Time in Law: Basis of Laws of
         Limitation and Prescription</u>, 32 J. Indian L. Inst. 328, 329 (1990).
         —Page Citation.

Journal of the Kansas Bar Association

Ab.:   J. Kan. B.A.

In citing cases in law review footnotes, abbreviate any word listed in table T.6;
the names of "states, countries, and other geographical units" unless they are named parties;
and any other words of eight or more letters "if <u>substantial</u> space is thereby saved and the
result is unambiguous." <u>Bluebook</u> rule 10.2.2. On the other hand, in citing cases in text,
abbreviate only widely known acronyms and the following words: "&," "Ass'n," "Bros.,"
"Co.," "Corp.," "Inc.," "Ltd.," and "No." <u>Bluebook</u> rule 10.2.1(c).

Ex.:   Paul B. Rusor, <u>Commercial Transacting Under the New Bankruptcy Act</u>, J. Kan. B.A., Fall 1979, at 199. –Article Citation.

Paul B. Rusor, <u>Commercial Transacting Under the New Bankruptcy Act</u>, J. Kan. B.A., Fall 1979, at 199, 200-01. –Page Citation.

Journal of the Legal Profession, The
Ab.:   J. Legal Prof.

Ex.:   Glenn S. Kaplan, <u>Chinese Walls: A New Approach</u>, 15 J. Legal Prof. 63 (1990). –Article Citation.

Glenn S. Kaplan, <u>Chinese Walls: A New Approach</u>, 15 J. Legal Prof. 63, 72-74 (1990). –Page Citation.

Journal of the Missouri Bar
Ab.:   J. Mo. B.

Ex.:   Timothy E. Gammon, <u>When Are Acts of an Insured Expected or Intended?</u>, 48 J. Mo. B. 115 (1992). –Article Citation.

Timothy E. Gammon, <u>When Are Acts of an Insured Expected or Intended?</u>, 48 J. Mo. B. 115, 116 (1992). –Page Citation.

Journal of the Patent and Trademark Office Society
Ab.:   J. Pat. & Trademark Off. Soc'y

Ex.:   Jerome Rosenstook, <u>Appeals Practice</u>, 73 J. Pat. & Trademark Off. Soc'y 565 (1991). –Article Citation.

Jcrome Rosenstook, <u>Appeals Practice</u>, 73 J. Pat. & Trademark Off. Soc'y 565, 569-72 (1991). –Page Citation.

Journal of World Trade
Ab.:   J. World Trade

Ex.:   Steven M. Hoffer, <u>May Exchange Rate Volatility Cause Dumping Injury?</u>, J. World Trade, June 1992, at 61. –Articlc Citation.

Steven M. Hoffer, <u>May Exchange Rate Volatility Cause Dumping Injury?</u>, J. World Trade, June 1992, at 61, 68-70. –Page Citation.

–Formerly J. of World Trade Law (vol. 1 1967 - vol. 21 1987).

–Nonconsecutively paginated from 1987-date.

Journal Officiel Des Communautés Européenes
Ab.:   J.O.

See <u>Bluebook</u> table T.3, rule 21.8.2, and entry herein for Official Journal of the European Community.

Judge
Ab.:   J.

Judges
Ab.:   JJ.

In law review footnotes, the titles of books and the names of cases, except for procedural phrases, are not underlined. See <u>Bluebook</u> rule 2.1(a) & (b). Further, the following are in large and small capitals: codes, restatements, standards, constitutions, periodicals, authors of books, titles of books, the abbreviated names of codes, most legislative materials except for bills and resolutions, codified ordinances, model codes, court rules, and sentencing guidelines. Refer to <u>The Bluebook</u>.

Judgment, citation to
> Ab.:   J.
>
> Ex.:   (J. for Def., Oct. 26, 1998).
>
> See Bluebook rule B10 and table BT.1.
>
> Note: See Bluebook rule 10.8.3 for citing litigation materials from another case.

Judicial Panel on Multidistrict Litigation
> Ab.:   J.P.M.L.

Judicature
> Ab.:   Do not abbreviate title.
>
> Ex.:   Nancy J. King, Jury Research and Reform: An Introduction,
>   79 Judicature 214 (1996). –Article Citation.
>
>   Nancy J. King, Jury Research and Reform: An Introduction,
>   79 Judicature 214, 214 (1996). –Page Citation.

Juridical Review
> Ab.:   Jurid. Rev.
>
> Ex.:   Paul Robertshaw, Regional Jury Verdicts in Scotland, Jurid. Rev., Oct.
>   1991, at 222. –Article Citation.
>
>   Paul Robertshaw, Regional Jury Verdicts in Scotland, Jurid. Rev., Oct.
>   1991, at 222, 224. –Page Citation.

Jurimetrics: Journal of Law, Science, and Technology
> Ab.:   Jurimetrics J.
>
> Ex.:   Evan L. Rosenfield, The Strict Products Liability Crisis and Beyond: Is
>   There Hope for an AIDS Vaccine?, 31 Jurimetrics J. 187 (1991).
>   –Article Citation.
>
>   Evan L. Rosenfield, The Strict Products Liability Crisis and Beyond: Is
>   There Hope for an AIDS Vaccine?, 31 Jurimetrics J. 187, 192 (1991).
>   –Page Citation.

Jurisprudencia de la Suprema Corte (Mexico)
> Ab.:   J.S.C.
>
> See Bluebook table T.2.

Jurisprudencia del Tribunal Supremo (Spain)
> Ab.:   J.T.S.
>
> See Bluebook table T.2.

Jurist, The
> Ab.:   Jurist

In citing cases in law review footnotes, abbreviate any word listed in table T.6;
the names of "states, countries, and other geographical units" unless they are named parties;
and any other words of eight or more letters "if substantial space is thereby saved and the
result is unambiguous." Bluebook rule 10.2.2. On the other hand, in citing cases in text,
abbreviate only widely known acronyms and the following words: "&," "Ass'n," "Bros.,"
"Co.," "Corp.," "Inc.," "Ltd.," and "No." Bluebook rule 10.2.1(c).

Ex.: James A. Coriden, <u>The Canonical Doctrine of Reception</u>, 50 Jurist 58 (1990). –Article Citation.

James A. Coriden, <u>The Canonical Doctrine of Reception</u>, 50 Jurist 58, 59-62 (1990). –Page Citation.

Justice
Ab.: J.

Justice of the Peace Reports and Local Government Review Reports (England) (1837-date)
Ab.: J.P.R.
Ex.: <u>Vandyk v. Oliver</u>, 140 J.P.R. 180 (H.L. 1976) (Eng.). –Case Citation.
–For information concerning neutral citation for cases decided after 2001, see <u>Bluebook</u> table T.2.

Justice System Journal, The
Ab.: Just. Sys. J.
Ex.: Mark A. Zaflarano, <u>A Call to Leadership</u>, 15/2 Just. Sys. J. 628 (1991). –Article Citation.

Mark A. Zaflarano, <u>A Call to Leadership</u>, 15/2 Just. Sys. J. 628, 635-38 (1991). –Page Citation.

Justices
Ab.: J.J.

Juvenile Court
Ab.: Juv. Ct.

In law review footnotes, the titles of books and the names of cases, except for procedural phrases, are not underlined. <u>See</u> <u>Bluebook</u> rule 2.1(a) & (b). Further, the following are in large and small capitals: codes, restatements, standards, constitutions, periodicals, authors of books, titles of books, the abbreviated names of codes, most legislative materials except for bills and resolutions, codified ordinances, model codes, court rules, and sentencing guidelines. Refer to <u>The Bluebook</u>.

K

Kansas Administrative Regulations
Ab.:   Kan. Admin. Regs. § x-x-x (year)

Ex.:   Kan. Admin. Regs. § 91-8-26 (1999).

Kansas Bar Association Journal
Ab.:   Kan. B. Ass'n J.

Kansas City Law Review
See UMKC Law Review.

Kansas Constitution
Ab.:   Kan. Const. art   , §   .

Ex.:   Kan. Const. art. 11, § 2. –"Cite constitutional provisions currently in force without a date." Bluebook rule 11.

Kan. Const. art. 10, § 3 (repealed 1972). –"If the cited provision has been repealed, either indicate parenthetically the fact and date of repeal or cite the repealing provision in full." Bluebook rule 11.

Kan. Const. art. 12, § 2 (amended 1906). –"When citing a provision that has been subsequently amended, either indicate parenthetically the fact and date of amendment or cite the amending provision in full." Bluebook rule 11.

Kansas Court of Appeals Reports
Ab.:   Kan. App., Kan. App. 2d

–Cite to P., P.2d, or P.3d, if therein; otherwise, cite to Kan. App. or Kan. App. 2d

–Give parallel citations only in documents submitted to Kansas state courts. See Bluebook rules 10.3.1 and B5.1.3; see also Kan. Sup. Ct. R. 6.08, which requires a parallel citation.

In documents submitted to Kansas state courts, cite as follows:

Lonning v. Anderson, 22 Kan. App. 2d 474, 921 P.2d 813 (1996). –Case Citation.

Lonning v. Anderson, 22 Kan. App. 2d 474, 476, 921 P.2d 813, 815 (1996). –Page Citation.

In all other documents, cite as follows:

Lonning v. Anderson, 921 P.2d 813 (Kan. Ct. App. 1996). –Case Citation.

In law review footnotes, the titles of books and the names of cases, except for procedural phrases, are not underlined. See Bluebook rule 2.1(a) & (b). Further, the following are in large and small capitals: codes, restatements, standards, constitutions, periodicals, authors of books, titles of books, the abbreviated names of codes, most legislative materials except for bills and resolutions, codified ordinances, model codes, court rules, and sentencing guidelines. Refer to The Bluebook.

Lonning v. Anderson, 921 P.2d 813, 815 (Kan. Ct. App. 1996).
–Page Citation.

Kansas Journal of Law & Public Policy
Ab.:   Kan. J.L. & Pub. Pol'y
Ex.:   Wilma Mankiller, Public Perception as a Sovereignty Protection
        Issue, 14 Kan. J.L. & Pub. Pol'y 639 (2005). –Article Citation.
        Wilma Mankiller, Public Perception as a Sovereignty Protection
        Issue, 14 Kan. J.L. & Pub. Pol'y 639, 640 (2005). –Page Citation.

Kansas Law Review
See University of Kansas Law Review.

Kansas, Opinions of the Attorney General
See Opinions of the Attorney General of Kansas.

Kansas Register
Ab.:   vol. no. Kan. Reg. page no. (month day, year)
Ex.:   23 Kan. Reg. 720 (Mar. 1, 2004)

Kansas Reports
Ab.:   Kan.
        –Cite to P., P.2d, or P.3d, if therein; otherwise, cite to Kan.
        –Give parallel citations only in documents submitted to Kansas state
        courts. See Bluebook rules 10.3.1 and B5.1.3; see also Kan. Sup. Ct.
        R. 6.08, which requires a parallel citation.
        In documents submitted to Kansas state courts, cite as follows:
        Degollado v. Gallegos, 260 Kan. 169, 917 P.2d 823 (1996). –Case
        Citation.
        Degollado v. Gallegos, 260 Kan. 169, 170, 917 P.2d 823, 824
        (1996). –Page Citation.
        In all other documents, cite as follows:
        Degollado v. Gallegos, 917 P.2d 823 (Kan. 1996). –Case Citation.
        Degollado v. Gallegos, 917 P.2d 823, 824 (Kan. 1996). –Page
        Citation.

Kansas Session Laws
See Session Laws of Kansas.

Kansas Statutes Annotated
Ab.:   Kan. Stat. Ann. § x-x (year)
Ex.:   Kan. Stat. Ann. § 79-1444 (1997).
        Kan. Stat. Ann. § 80-1903 (Supp. 1999).
        –For proper citation form in papers submitted to Kansas courts, see
        title pages to Kan. Stat. Ann. volumes.

In citing cases in law review footnotes, abbreviate any word listed in table T.6;
the names of "states, countries, and other geographical units" unless they are named parties;
and any other words of eight or more letters "if substantial space is thereby saved and the
result is unambiguous." Bluebook rule 10.2.2. On the other hand, in citing cases in text,
abbreviate only widely known acronyms and the following words: "&," "Ass'n," "Bros.,"
"Co.," "Corp.," "Inc.," "Ltd.," and "No." Bluebook rule 10.2.1(c).

Kansas Statutes Annotated, Vernon's
See Vernon's Kansas Statutes Annotated.

Keio Law Review
Ab.: Keio L. Rev.
Ex.: Brian J. Arnold, <u>The New Canadian General Anti-tax Avoidance Rule</u>, 6 Keio L. Rev. 49 (1990). –Article Citation.
Brian J. Arnold, <u>The New Canadian General Anti-tax Avoidance Rule</u>, 6 Keio L. Rev. 49, 59-63 (1990). –Page Citation.

Kentucky Administrative Regulations Service
Ab.: x Ky. Admin. Regs. x:x (year)
Ex.: 30 Ky. Admin. Regs. 3:030 (1994).

Kentucky Bench and Bar
Ab.: Ky. Bench & B.
Ex.: Gerald R. Toner & Ellen Cox Call, <u>Three Cases that Shaped Kentucky's History</u>, Ky. Bench & B., Winter 1992, at 11. –Article Citation.
Gerald R. Toner & Ellen Cox Call, <u>Three Cases that Shaped Kentucky's History</u>, Ky. Bench & B., Winter 1992, at 11, 12. –Page Citation.

Kentucky Constitution
Ab.: Ky. Const. § .
Ex.: Ky. Const. § 6. –"Cite constitutional provisions currently in force without a date." <u>Bluebook</u> rule 11.
Ky. Const. § 31 (repealed 1979). –"If the cited provision has been repealed, either indicate parenthetically the fact and date of repeal or cite the repealing provision in full." <u>Bluebook</u> rule 11.
Ky. Const. § 147 (amended 1945). –"When citing a provision that has been subsequently amended, either indicate parenthetically the fact and date of amendment or cite the amending provision in full." <u>Bluebook</u> rule 11.
Ky. Const. of 1850, art. 11, § 2 (1891). –"Cite constitutions that have been totally superseded by year of adoption; if the specific provision cited was adopted in a different year, give that year parenthetically." <u>Bluebook</u> rule 11.

Kentucky Court of Appeals
Ab.: Ky. Ct. App.
–Prior to 1976, Kentucky Court of Appeals was the highest Kentucky court. See Kentucky Reports.
–Cite to S.W.2d or S.W.3d, if therein; otherwise, cite to Ky. App., Ky. Att'y Memo, or Ky. L. Summ.
In all documents, cite as follows:

In law review footnotes, the titles of books and the names of cases, except for procedural phrases, are not underlined. <u>See</u> <u>Bluebook</u> rule 2.1(a) & (b). Further, the following are in large and small capitals: codes, restatements, standards, constitutions, periodicals, authors of books, titles of books, the abbreviated names of codes, most legislative materials except for bills and resolutions, codified ordinances, model codes, court rules, and sentencing guidelines. Refer to <u>The Bluebook</u>.

Leeco, Inc. v. Agner, 919 S.W.2d 227 (Ky. Ct. App. 1996). –Case Citation.

Leeco, Inc. v. Agner, 919 S.W.2d 227, 228 (Ky. Ct. App. 1996). –Page Citation.

Kentucky Law Journal
Ab.:   Ky. L.J.
Ex.:   Henry H. Perritt, Jr., The Internet Is Changing the Public International Legal System, 88 Ky. L.J. 885 (1999-2000). –Article Citation.

Henry H. Perritt, Jr., The Internet Is Changing the Public International Legal System, 88 Ky. L.J. 885, 889 (1999-2000). –Page Citation.

Kentucky Reports
Ab.:   Ky.

–Discontinued after 314 Ky. 885 (1951).

–Cite to S.W., S.W.2d, or S.W.3d, if therein; otherwise, cite to Ky.

–Give parallel citations only in documents submitted to Kentucky state courts. See Bluebook rules 10.3.1 and B5.1.3; see also Ky. R. Civ. P. 76.12(4)(g), which requires a parallel citation.

–Through 314 Ky. 885 (1951), cite as follows:

In documents submitted to Kentucky state courts:

Wagner v. Wagner's Adm'x, 188 Ky. 692, 223 S.W. 1011 (1920). –Case Citation.

Wagner v. Wagner's Adm'x, 188 Ky. 692, 693, 223 S.W. 1011, 1011-12 (1920). –Page Citation.

In all other documents:

Wagner v. Wagner's Adm'x, 223 S.W. 1011 (Ky. 1920). –Case Citation.

Wagner v. Wagner's Adm'x, 223 S.W. 1011, 1011-12 (Ky. 1920). –Page Citation.

–After 314 Ky. 885 (1951), cite as follows:

In all documents:

Candler v. Blevins, 922 S.W.2d 376 (Ky. 1996). –Case Citation.

Candler v. Blevins, 922 S.W.2d 376, 377 (Ky. 1996). –Page Citation.

Kentucky Revised Statutes and Rules Service (West)
Ab.:   year Ky. Rev. Stat. & R. Serv. page no. (West)
Ex.:   Act of Apr. 2, 2005, ch. 33, sec. 1, § 16.582, 2005 Ky. Rev. Stat. & R. Serv. 1109 (West) (relating to retirement). –Citation to a section of a session law amending prior act.

–See Bluebook rule 12.4.

–"Cite to Ky. Acts, if therein." Bluebook table T.1, p. 210.

In citing cases in law review footnotes, abbreviate any word listed in table T.6; the names of "states, countries, and other geographical units" unless they are named parties; and any other words of eight or more letters "if substantial space is thereby saved and the result is unambiguous." Bluebook rule 10.2.2. On the other hand, in citing cases in text, abbreviate only widely known acronyms and the following words: "&," "Ass'n," "Bros.," "Co.," "Corp.," "Inc.," "Ltd.," and "No." Bluebook rule 10.2.1(c).

Kentucky Revised Statutes Annotated
> See Baldwin's Kentucky Revised Statutes Annotated (West) and Michie's
> Kentucky Revised Statutes Annotated (LexisNexis).

Kentucky Session Laws
> See Kentucky Acts.

Korea and World Affairs: A Quarterly Review
> Ab.:   Korea & World Aff.
> Ex.:   Yong-Sup Han, <u>China's Leverages Over North Korea</u>, 18 Korea &
>   World Aff. 233 (1994). –Article Citation.
>   Yong-Sup Han, <u>China's Leverages Over North Korea</u>, 18 Korea &
>   World Aff. 233, 235-37 (1994). –Page Citation.

Korea Journal of Comparative Law
> Ab.:   Korea J. Comp. L.
> Ex.:   Seong-Ki Kim, <u>Patent Law of China</u>, 18 Korea J. Comp. L. 90 (1990).
>   –Article Citation.
>   Seong-Ki Kim, <u>Patent Law of China</u>, 18 Korea J. Comp. L. 90, 91-95
>   (1990). –Page Citation.

In law review footnotes, the titles of books and the names of cases, except for procedural phrases, are not underlined. <u>See</u> <u>Bluebook</u> rule 2.1(a) & (b). Further, the following are in large and small capitals: codes, restatements, standards, constitutions, periodicals, authors of books, titles of books, the abbreviated names of codes, most legislative materials except for bills and resolutions, codified ordinances, model codes, court rules, and sentencing guidelines. Refer to <u>The Bluebook</u>.

L

Labor Arbitration Awards (Commerce Clearing House)
Ab.:   Lab. Arb. Awards (CCH)

Ex.:   NACCO v. Indep. Builders Union, Lab. Arb. Awards (CCH) (96-2 Lab.
         Arb. Awards) ¶ 6312 (Mar. 25, 1996) (Belshaw, Arb.).
         –Citation to looseleaf administrative material.

         Beta Steel Corp. v. Int'l Longshoremen's Ass'n, Local 2038, 95-1 Lab.
         Arb. Awards (CCH) ¶ 5165 (1995) (Traynor, Arb.).
         –Citation to bound administrative material.

Labor Arbitration Reports (Bureau of National Affairs)
Ab.:   Lab. Arb. Rep. (BNA)

See Labor Relations Reporter (Bureau of National Affairs).

Labor Law Journal
Ab.:   Lab. L.J.

Ex.:   John A. Gray, Preferential Affirmative Action in Employment, 43 Lab.
         L.J. 23 (1992). –Article Citation.

         John A. Gray, Preferential Affirmative Action in Employment, 43 Lab.
         L.J. 23, 25-27 (1992). –Page Citation.

Labor Law Reporter (Commerce Clearing House)
         –Bound as: Labor Cases; NLRB Decisions

Ab.:   Lab. L. Rep. (CCH)

         –Bound as: Lab. Cas (CCH); NLRB Dec. (CCH)

Ex.:   Cox v. Nashe, [3 State Laws] Lab. L. Rep. (CCH) (131 Lab. Cas.)
         ¶ 58,034 (9th Cir. Aug. 23, 1995). –Citation to looseleaf material.

         Stanley v. McDaniel, [2 Wage-Hour] Lab. L. Rep. (CCH) (131 Lab.
         Cas.) ¶ 33,349 (Ohio Ct. App. Feb. 27, 1996). –Citation to looseleaf
         material.

         United States v. Carson, 130 Lab. Cas. (CCH) ¶ 11,313 (S.D.N.Y.
         1995). –Citation to bound material.

         –The above examples are proper if the case is not yet available in, or is
         not reported in, an official or West reporter, a public domain citation,
         or in a widely used computer database.

         Dep't of Labor v. New Way Laundry & Cleaning, [2 Wage-Hour] Lab.
         L. Rep. (CCH) ¶ 32,425 (Wage Appeals Board Mar. 15, 1996).
         –Looseleaf administrative material.

In law review footnotes, the titles of books and the names of cases, except for procedural
phrases, are not underlined. See Bluebook rule 2.1(a) & (b). Further, the following are in
large and small capitals: codes, restatements, standards, constitutions, periodicals, authors of
books, titles of books, the abbreviated names of codes, most legislative materials except for
bills and resolutions, codified ordinances, model codes, court rules, and sentencing guidelines.
Refer to The Bluebook.

Opinion Letter of the Wage-Hour Administrator No. 1546 (WH 493) [Sept. 1978 - Jan. 1981 Transfer Binder, Wages-Hours Administrative Rulings] Lab. L. Rep. (CCH) ¶ 31,281 (Wage Appeals Board 1979).
–Citation to transfer binder administrative material.

Checker Cab Co., 1981-82 NLRB Dec. (CCH) ¶ 18,827 (NLRB 1982).
–Citation to bound administrative material.

Labor Lawyer
Ab.: Lab. Law.

Ex.: Steven H. Winterbauer, Sexual Harassment: The Reasonable Woman Standard, 7 Lab. Law. 811 (1991). –Article Citation.

Steven H. Winterbauer, Sexual Harassment: The Reasonable Woman Standard, 7 Lab. Law. 811, 813-16 (1991). –Page Citation.

Labor Relations Reference Manual (Bureau of National Affairs)
Ab.: L.R.R.M. (BNA)

Labor Relations Reporter (Bureau of National Affairs)
–Bound as: Fair Employment Practices Cases; Labor Arbitration Reports; Labor Relations Reference Manual; Wage and Hour Cases

Ab.: Lab. Rel. Rep. (BNA)

–Bound as: Fair Empl. Prac. Cas. (BNA); Lab. Arb. Rep. (BNA); L.R.R.M. (BNA); Wage & Hour Cas. (BNA)

Ex.: Rich v. Delta Air Lines, 5 Lab. L. Rep. (BNA) (3 Wage & Hour Cas.) 1 (N.D. Ga. Feb. 7, 1996). –Citation to looseleaf material.

Miller v. Butcher, 7 Lab. L. Rep. (BNA) (71 Fair Empl. Prac. Cas.) 641 (5th Cir. July 29, 1996). –Citation to looseleaf material.

Providence and Mercy Hosps. v. NLRB, 2 Lab. L. Rep. (BNA) (153 L.R.R.M). 2097 (1st Cir. Aug. 28, 1996). –Citation to looseleaf material.

IAFF Local 2916 v. PERC, 152 L.R.R.M. (BNA) 2668 (Wash. 1995).
–Citation to bound material.

Vega v. Gasper, 2 Wage & Hour Cas.2d (BNA) 614 (5th Cir. 1994).
–Citation to bound material.

Jones v. Clinton, 70 Fair Empl. Prac. Cas. (BNA) 585 (8th Cir. 1996).
–Citation to bound material.

–The above examples are proper if the case is not yet available in, or is not reported in, an official or West reporter, a public domain citation, or in a widely used computer database.

Tower Auto., 2 Lab. Rel. Rep. (BNA) (153 L.R.R.M.) 1241 (NLRB Nov. 12, 1996).
–Citation to looseleaf administrative material.

In citing cases in law review footnotes, abbreviate any word listed in table T.6; the names of "states, countries, and other geographical units" unless they are named parties; and any other words of eight or more letters "if substantial space is thereby saved and the result is unambiguous." Bluebook rule 10.2.2. On the other hand, in citing cases in text, abbreviate only widely known acronyms and the following words: "&," "Ass'n," "Bros.," "Co.," "Corp.," "Inc.," "Ltd.," and "No." Bluebook rule 10.2.1(c).

Dunlop Tire Corp., 3 Lab. Rel. Rep. (BNA) (107 Lab. Arb. Rep.) 97 (July 5, 1996) (Kindig, Arb.). −Citation to looseleaf administrative material.

Sanderson Plumbing Prods., 106 Lab. Arb. Rep. (BNA) 535 (1996) (Howell, Arb.).

−Citation to bound administrative material.

LaFave & Scott on Criminal Law
See Criminal Law, by Wayne R. LaFave & Austin W. Scott, Jr.

Land and Water Law Review
Ab.: Land & Water L. Rev.

Ex.: Joseph R. Membrino, Indian Reserved Water, Rights, Federalism and the Trust Responsibility, 27 Land & Water L. Rev. 1 (1992). −Article Citation.

Joseph R. Membrino, Indian Reserved Water, Rights, Federalism and the Trust Responsibility, 27 Land & Water L. Rev. 1, 9 (1992). −Page Citation.

Land Use & Environment Law Review
Ab.: Land Use & Env't L. Rev.

Ex.: David L. Callies, Property Rights: Are There Any Left?, 21 Land Use & Env't L. Rev. 181 (1990). −Article Citation.

David L. Callies, Property Rights: Are There Any Left?, 21 Land Use & Env't L. Rev. 181, 189-92 (1990). −Page Citation.

Lane's Goldstein Trial Techniques, by Fred Lane
−Do not abbreviate the title.

Ex.: 2 Fred Lane, Lane's Goldstein Trial Techniques § 13.95 (3d ed. 1985 & Supp. 1991). −Section Citation.

2 Fred Lane, Lane's Goldstein Trial Techniques § 13.95, at 13-170 (3d ed. 1985 & Supp. 1991). −Page Citation.

2 Fred Lane, Lane's Goldstein Trial Techniques § 13.95, at 13-170 n.12 (3d ed. 1985 & Supp. 1991). −Footnote Citation.

Larson on Workmen's Compensation
See Law of Workmen's Compensation, by Arthur Larson.

Larson's Workers' Compensation Law, by Arthur Larson and Lex K. Larson
−Do not abbreviate the title.

Ex.: 2 Arthur Larson & Lex K. Larson, Larson's Workers' Compensation Law § 43.03 (2000). − Section Citation.

2 Arthur Larson & Lex K. Larson, Larson's Workers' Compensation Law § 43.03, at 43-11 (2000). − Page Citation.

In law review footnotes, the titles of books and the names of cases, except for procedural phrases, are not underlined. See Bluebook rule 2.1(a) & (b). Further, the following are in large and small capitals: codes, restatements, standards, constitutions, periodicals, authors of books, titles of books, the abbreviated names of codes, most legislative materials except for bills and resolutions, codified ordinances, model codes, court rules, and sentencing guidelines. Refer to The Bluebook.

2 Arthur Larson & Lex K. Larson, Larson's Workers' Compensation Law § 43.03, at 43-11 n.1 (2000). – Footnote Citation.

Law & Anthropology
Ab.:   Do not abbreviate title.

Ex.:   Maureen Davies, International Developments in Indigenous Rights, 2 Law & Anthropology 29 (1987). –Article Citation.

Maureen Davies, International Developments in Indigenous Rights, 2 Law & Anthropology 29, 30-33 (1987). –Page Citation.

Law and Contemporary Problems
Ab.:   Law & Contemp. Probs.

Ex.:   Peter Huber, Medical Experts and the Ghost of Galileo, Law & Contemp. Probs., Summer 1991, at 119. –Article Citation.

Peter Huber, Medical Experts and the Ghost of Galileo, Law & Contemp. Probs., Summer 1991, at 119, 130-34. –Page Citation.

Law and History Review
Ab.:   Law & Hist. Rev.

Ex.:   David C. Frederick, John Quincy Adams, Slavery and the Disappearance of the Right of Petition, Law & Hist. Rev., Spring 1991, at 113. –Article Citation.

David C. Frederick, John Quincy Adams, Slavery and the Disappearance of the Right of Petition, Law & Hist. Rev., Spring 1991, at 113, 120-22. –Page Citation.

Law and Human Behavior
Ab.:   Law & Hum. Behav.

Ex.:   Virginia Aldigé Hiday, Dangerousness of Civil Commitment Candidates: A Six-Month Follow-Up, 14 Law & Hum. Behav. 551 (1990). –Article Citation.

Virginia Aldigé Hiday, Dangerousness of Civil Commitment Candidates: A Six-Month Follow-Up, 14 Law & Hum. Behav. 551, 552 (1990). –Page Citation.

Law and Inequality
Ab.:   Law & Ineq.

Ex.:   Eila Savela, Homelessness and the Affordable Housing Shortage: What Is to be Done?, 9 Law & Ineq. 279 (1991). –Article Citation.

Eila Savela, Homelessness and the Affordable Housing Shortage: What Is to be Done?, 9 Law & Ineq. 279, 281-82 (1991). –Page Citation.

Law and Philosophy
Ab.:   Law & Phil.

In citing cases in law review footnotes, abbreviate any word listed in table T.6; the names of "states, countries, and other geographical units" unless they are named parties; and any other words of eight or more letters "if substantial space is thereby saved and the result is unambiguous." Bluebook rule 10.2.2. On the other hand, in citing cases in text, abbreviate only widely known acronyms and the following words: "&," "Ass'n," "Bros.," "Co.," "Corp.," "Inc.," "Ltd.," and "No." Bluebook rule 10.2.1(c).

Ex.:   Daniel Brudney, <u>Hypothetical Consent and Moral Force</u>, 10 Law &
         Phil. 235 (1991). –Article Citation.

         Daniel Brudney, <u>Hypothetical Consent and Moral Force</u>, 10 Law &
         Phil. 235, 240-42 (1991). –Page Citation.

Law and Policy
Ab.:   Law & Pol'y
Ex.:   Frank Anechiarico & Stephen L. Lockwood, <u>The Responsibility of the</u>
         <u>Police Command for Street Level Actions</u>, 12 Law & Pol'y 331 (1990).
         –Article Citation.

         Frank Anechiarico & Stephen L. Lockwood, <u>The Responsibility of the</u>
         <u>Police Command for Street Level Actions</u>, 12 Law & Pol'y 331, 333
         (1990). –Page Citation.

Law and Policy in International Business
Ab.:   Law & Pol'y Int'l Bus.
Ex.:   John P. Simpson, <u>Rules of Origin in Transition: A Changing</u>
         <u>Environment and Prospects for Reform</u>, 22 Law & Pol'y Int'l Bus. 665
         (1991). –Article Citation.

         John P. Simpson, <u>Rules of Origin in Transition: A Changing</u>
         <u>Environment and Prospects for Reform</u>, 22 Law & Pol'y Int'l Bus. 665,
         669-70 (1991). –Page Citation.

Law & Psychology Review
Ab.:   Law & Psychol. Rev.
Ex.:   William W. Patton, <u>Opening Student's Eyes: Visual Learning Theory in</u>
         <u>the Socratic Classroom</u>, 15 Law & Psychol. Rev. 1 (1991). –Article
         Citation.

         William W. Patton, <u>Opening Student's Eyes: Visual Learning Theory in</u>
         <u>the Socratic Classroom</u>, 15 Law & Psychol. Rev. 1, 6-10 (1991).
         –Page Citation.

Law & Social Inquiry
Ab.:   Law & Soc. Inquiry
Ex.:   Stephen M. Griffin, <u>Bringing the State into Constitutional Theory:</u>
         <u>Public Authority and the Constitution</u>, 16 Law & Soc. Inquiry 659
         (1991). –Article Citation.

         Stephen M. Griffin, <u>Bringing the State into Constitutional Theory:</u>
         <u>Public Authority and the Constitution</u>, 16 Law & Soc. Inquiry 659, 663
         (1991). –Page Citation.

Law & Society Review
Ab.:   Law & Soc'y Rev.
Ex.:   Janet A. Gilboy, <u>Deciding Who Gets In: Decisionmaking by</u>
         <u>Immigration Inspectors</u>, 25 Law & Soc'y Rev. 571 (1991). –Article
         Citation.

In law review footnotes, the titles of books and the names of cases, except for procedural
phrases, are not underlined. <u>See</u> Bluebook rule 2.1(a) & (b). Further, the following are in
large and small capitals: codes, restatements, standards, constitutions, periodicals, authors of
books, titles of books, the abbreviated names of codes, most legislative materials except for
bills and resolutions, codified ordinances, model codes, court rules, and sentencing guidelines.
Refer to <u>The Bluebook</u>.

Janet A. Gilboy, <u>Deciding Who Gets In: Decisionmaking by Immigration Inspectors</u>, 25 Law & Soc'y Rev. 571, 577-78 (1991). —Page Citation.

Law and State
Ab.:   Law & St.
Ex.:   Hugo J. Hahn, <u>International Loan and Guarantee Agreements</u>, 41 Law & St. 29 (1990). —Article Citation.

Hugo J. Hahn, <u>International Loan and Guarantee Agreements</u>, 41 Law & St. 29, 30-32 (1990). —Page Citation.

Law in Japan: An Annual
Ab.:   Law in Japan
Ex.:   Akio Takeuchi, <u>Legal Control of Commodity Fraud Transactions</u>, 22 Law in Japan 26 (1989). —Article Citation.

Akio Takeuchi, <u>Legal Control of Commodity Fraud Transactions</u>, 22 Law in Japan 26, 27-30 (1989). —Page Citation.

Law Journal Reports (U.K.)
See Table T.2.
Ab.:   L.J.R.
Ex.:   <u>Lipshitz v. Valero</u>, 1948 L.J.R. 625 (P.C. 1947) (Eng.) (taken on appeal from Palestine). —Case Citation.

Law Journal Reports, King's Bench, New Series (U.K.)
See Table T.2.
Ab.:   L.J.K.B.
Ex.:   <u>Price v. Webb</u>, 82 L.J.K.B. 720 (1913) (Eng.). —Case Citation.

Law Journal Reports, King's Bench, Old Series (U.K.)
See Table T.2.
Ab.:   L.J.K.B.O.S.
Ex.:   <u>Marsden v. Stanfield</u>, 6 L.J.K.B.O.S. 159 (1828) (Eng.). —Case Citation.

Law Library Journal
Ab.:   Law Libr. J.
Ex.:   Marsha Trimble, <u>Archives and Manuscripts: New Collecting Areas for Law Libraries</u>, 83 Law Libr. J. 429 (1991). —Article Citation.

Marsha Trimble, <u>Archives and Manuscripts: New Collecting Areas for Law Libraries</u>, 83 Law Libr. J. 429, 431-32 (1991). —Page Citation.

Law, Medicine & Health Care
Ab.:   Law Med. & Health Care
Ex.:   Carol Levine, <u>Children in HIV/AIDS Clinical Trials: Still Vulnerable after All These Years</u>, 19 Law Med. & Health Care 231 (1991). —Article Citation.

In citing cases in law review footnotes, abbreviate any word listed in table T.6; the names of "states, countries, and other geographical units" unless they are named parties; and any other words of eight or more letters "if <u>substantial</u> space is thereby saved and the result is unambiguous." <u>Bluebook</u> rule 10.2.2. On the other hand, in citing cases in text, abbreviate only widely known acronyms and the following words: "&," "Ass'n," "Bros.," "Co.," "Corp.," "Inc.," "Ltd.," and "No." <u>Bluebook</u> rule 10.2.1(c).

Carol Levine, <u>Children in HIV/AIDS Clinical Trials: Still Vulnerable after All These Years</u>, 19 Law Med. & Health Care 231, 235-36 (1991). –Page Citation.

Law of Contracts, The, by John D. Calamari and Joseph M. Perillo
See Calamari and Perillo on Contracts.

Law of Easements and Licenses in Land, The, by Jon W. Bruce and James W. Ely, Jr.
–Do not abbreviate the title.
Ex.: Jon W. Bruce & James W. Ely, Jr., <u>The Law of Easements and Licenses in Land</u> ¶ 5:15 (2001). –Paragraph Citation.

Jon W. Bruce & James W. Ely, Jr., <u>The Law of Easements and Licenses in Land</u> ¶ 5:15, at 5-45 (2001). –Page Citation.

Law of Federal Courts, The, by Charles A. Wright
–Do not abbreviate the title.
Ex.: Charles A. Wright, <u>The Law of Federal Courts</u> § 70 (6th ed. 2002). –Section Citation.

Charles A. Wright, <u>The Law of Federal Courts</u> § 70, at 501 (6th ed. 2002). –Page Citation.

Charles A. Wright, <u>The Law of Federal Courts</u> § 70, at 501 n.49 (6th ed. 2002). –Footnote Citation.

Law of Federal Income Taxation, Second Edition, by Michael D. Rose and John C. Chommie
–Do not abbreviate the title.
Ex.: Michael D. Rose & John C. Chommie, <u>Law of Federal Income Taxation</u> § 10.32 (3d ed. 1988). –Section Citation.

Michael D. Rose & John C. Chommie, <u>Law of Federal Income Taxation</u> § 10.32, at 589 (3d ed. 1988). –Page Citation.

Law of Municipal Corporations, The, by Eugene McQuillin
–Do not abbreviate the title.
Ex.: John H. Silvestri & Mark S. Nelson, 1 <u>Law of Municipal Corporations</u> § 3.28.30 (3d ed., rev. vol. 1999 & Cum. Supp. 2000). –Section Citation to vol. revised by named authors.

Eugene McQuillan, 3 <u>Law of Municipal Corporations</u> § 12.59, at 329 (3d ed., rev. vol. 2001). –Page Citation to vol. revised by editorial staff.

Law of Probation and Parole, The, by Neil P. Cohen
–Do not abbreviate the title.

In law review footnotes, the titles of books and the names of cases, except for procedural phrases, are not underlined. <u>See</u> Bluebook rule 2.1(a) & (b). Further, the following are in large and small capitals: codes, restatements, standards, constitutions, periodicals, authors of books, titles of books, the abbreviated names of codes, most legislative materials except for bills and resolutions, codified ordinances, model codes, court rules, and sentencing guidelines. Refer to <u>The Bluebook</u>.

Ex.: Neil P. Cohen, <u>The Law of Probation and Parole</u> § 7.30 (2d ed. 1999). –Section Citation.

Neil P. Cohen, <u>The Law of Probation and Parole</u> § 7.30, at 7-57 (2d ed. 1999). –Page Citation.

Neil P. Cohen, <u>The Law of Probation and Parole</u> § 7.30, at 7-57 n.3 (2d ed. 1999). –Footnote Citation.

Law of Property, The, by Ralph E. Boyer, Herbert Hovenkamp, and Sheldon F. Kurtz

–Do not abbreviate the title.

Ex.: Ralph E. Boyer et al., <u>The Law of Property</u> § 10.21 (4th ed. 1991). –Section Citation.

Ralph E. Boyer et al., <u>The Law of Property</u> § 10.21, at 321 (4th ed. 1991). –Page Citation.

Law of Property, The, by William B. Stoebuck & Dale A. Whitman

–Do not abbreviate the title.

Ex.: William B. Stoebuck & Dale A. Whitman, <u>The Law of Property</u> § 10.21 (3d ed. 2000). –Section Citation.

William B. Stoebuck & Dale A. Whitman, <u>The Law of Property</u> § 10.21, at 321 (3d ed. 2000). –Page Citation.

Law of Real Property, The, by Richard R. Powell

–Do not abbreviate the title.

Ex.: 2 Richard R. Powell, <u>The Law of Real Property</u> § 15.04[1] (Michael Allan Wolf ed., 2000). –Section Citation.

2 Richard R. Powell, <u>The Law of Real Property</u> § 15.04[1], at 15-61 (Michael Allan Wolf ed., 2000). –Page Citation.

2 Richard R. Powell, <u>The Law of Real Property</u> § 15.04[1], at 15-61 n.20 (Michael Allan Wolf ed., 2000). –Footnote Citation.

Law of Remedies, by Dan B. Dobbs

See Dobbs Law of Remedies.

Law of Restitution, The, by George E. Palmer

–Do not abbreviate the title.

Ex.: 2 George E. Palmer, <u>The Law of Restitution</u> § 9.5 (1978). –Section Citation.

2 George E. Palmer, <u>The Law of Restitution</u> § 9.5, at 267 (1978). –Page Citation.

2 George E. Palmer, <u>The Law of Restitution</u> § 9.5, at 267 n.17 (1978). –Footnote Citation.

Lawrence Kaplan, <u>Palmer's Law of Restitution</u> § 2.2(a), at 50 (Supp. No. 2 1998). –Supplement Citation.

In citing cases in law review footnotes, abbreviate any word listed in table T.6; the names of "states, countries, and other geographical units" unless they are named parties; and any other words of eight or more letters "if <u>substantial</u> space is thereby saved and the result is unambiguous." <u>Bluebook</u> rule 10.2.2. On the other hand, in citing cases in text, abbreviate only widely known acronyms and the following words: "&," "Ass'n," "Bros.," "Co.," "Corp.," "Inc.," "Ltd.," and "No." <u>Bluebook</u> rule 10.2.1(c).

Law of Securities Regulation, The, by Thomas Lee Hazen
–Do not abbreviate the title.

Ex.:   Thomas L. Hazen, <u>The Law of Securities Regulation</u> § 4.27 (3d ed. 1996). –Section Citation.

Thomas L. Hazen, <u>The Law of Securities Regulation</u> § 4.27, at 306 (3d ed. 1996). –Page Citation.

Thomas L. Hazen, <u>The Law of Securities Regulation</u> § 4.27, at 306 n.14 (3d ed. 1996). –Footnote Citation.

Law of Torts, The, by Dan B. Dobbs
–Do not abbreviate the title.

Ex.:   1 Dan B. Dobbs, <u>The Law of Torts</u> § 7 (2001). –Section Citation

1 Dan B. Dobbs, <u>The Law of Torts</u> § 7, at 11 (2001). –Page Citation

1 Dan B. Dobbs, <u>The Law of Torts</u> § 19, at 37 n.3 (2001). –Footnote Citation

Law of Torts, The, by Fowler V. Harper, Fleming James, Jr., and Oscar S. Gray
–Do not abbreviate the title.

Ex.:   4 Fowler V. Harper et al., <u>The Law of Torts</u> § 22.6 (2d ed. 1986). –Section Citation to second edition.

4 Fowler V. Harper et al., <u>The Law of Torts</u> § 22.6, at 303 (2d ed. 1986). –Page Citation to second edition.

4 Fowler V. Harper et al., <u>The Law of Torts</u> § 22.6, at 303 n.19 (2d ed. 1986). –Footnote Citation to second edition.

5 Oscar S. Gray, <u>The Law of Torts</u> § 26.9 (2d ed. Cum. Supp. no. 2 2005). –Section Citation to second edition supplement.

1 Fowler V. Harper et al., <u>The Law of Torts</u> § 1.1 (3d ed. 1996). –Section Citation to third edition.

Law of Trusts and Trustees, The, by Amy Morris Hess, George Gleason Bogert, and George Taylor Bogert
–Do not abbreviate the title.

Ex.   Amy Morris Hess et al., <u>The Law of Trusts and Trustees</u> § 646 (3d ed. 2000). – Section Citation.

Amy Morris Hess et al., <u>The Law of Trusts and Trustees</u> § 646, at 442 (3d ed. 2000). – Page Citation.

Amy Morris Hess et al., <u>The Law of Trusts and Trustees</u> § 646, at 442 n.2 (3d ed. 2000). – Footnote Citation

Law of Workers' Compensation, The, by Arthur Larson and Lex K. Larson
See Larson's Workers' Compensation Law.

Law Office Economics and Management
Ab.:   Law Off. Econ. & Mgmt.

In law review footnotes, the titles of books and the names of cases, except for procedural phrases, are not underlined. <u>See</u> <u>Bluebook</u> rule 2.1(a) & (b). Further, the following are in large and small capitals: codes, restatements, standards, constitutions, periodicals, authors of books, titles of books, the abbreviated names of codes, most legislative materials except for bills and resolutions, codified ordinances, model codes, court rules, and sentencing guidelines. Refer to <u>The Bluebook</u>.

Ex.: James G. Frierson, <u>Does Your Law Office Meet the Requirements of the Americans With Disabilities Act?</u>, 32 Law Off. Econ. & Mgmt. 397 (1992). –Article Citation.

James G. Frierson, <u>Does Your Law Office Meet the Requirements of the Americans With Disabilities Act?</u>, 32 Law Off. Econ. & Mgmt. 397, 401 (1992). –Page Citation.

Law Practice Management
Ab.: L. Prac. Mgmt.
Ex.: Jack Kaufman, <u>The Staff Lawyer</u>, L. Prac. Mgmt., July-Aug. 1990, at 30. –Article Citation.

Jack Kaufman, <u>The Staff Lawyer</u>, L. Prac. Mgmt., July-Aug. 1990, at 30, 31-2. –Page Citation.

Law Quarterly Review, The
Ab.: L.Q. Rev.
L.Q.R. [U.K.]
Ex.: Ruth Deech, <u>Divorce Law and Empirical Studies</u>, 106 L.Q. Rev. 229 (1990). –Article Citation.

Ruth Deech, <u>Divorce Law and Empirical Studies</u>, 106 L.Q. Rev. 229, 239-43 (1990). –Page Citation.

Law Reports: Admiralty and Ecclesiastical Cases (U.K.)
Ab.: L.R.A. & E.
Ex.: <u>Sheppard v. Bennett</u>, 3 L.R.A. & E. 167 (Eccl. 1870) (Eng.). –Case Citation.

<u>The Waverly</u>, 3 L.R.A. & E. 369 (Adm. 1871) (Eng.). –Case Citation.

Law Reports: Appeal Cases (U.K.) (1891-date)
See <u>Bluebook</u> table T.2.
Ab.: A.C.
Ex.: <u>Beckford v. R</u>, [1988] A.C. 130 (P.C. 1987) (appeal taken from Jam.) (Eng.). –Privy Council Case Citation.

<u>Bellinger v. Bellinger</u>, [2003] UKHL 21, [2003] 2 A.C. 467 (appeal taken from Eng.). –Case with neutral citation.

Law Reports: Chancery Division (U.K.)
See <u>Bluebook</u> table T.2.
Ab.: 1891-date: Ch.
1875-1890: Ch.D.
1865-1875: L.R.Ch.
Ex.: <u>Briggs v. Upton</u>, 7 L.R.Ch. 376 (1871) (Eng.). –Case Citation.
<u>Doucet v. Geoghegan</u>, 9 Ch.D. 441 (1877) (Eng.). –Case Citation.

In citing cases in law review footnotes, abbreviate any word listed in table T.6; the names of "states, countries, and other geographical units" unless they are named parties; and any other words of eight or more letters "if <u>substantial</u> space is thereby saved and the result is unambiguous." <u>Bluebook</u> rule 10.2.2. On the other hand, in citing cases in text, abbreviate only widely known acronyms and the following words: "&," "Ass'n," "Bros.," "Co.," "Corp.," "Inc.," "Ltd.," and "No." <u>Bluebook</u> rule 10.2.1(c).

Rignoll Devs., Ltd. v. Halil, 1988 Ch. 190 (1987) (Eng.).
–Case Citation.

Law Reports: Common Pleas (England)
See Bluebook table T.2.
Ab.:   1875-1880: C.P.D.
         1865-1875: L.R.C.P.
Ex.:   Abel v. Lee, 6 L.R.C.P. 365 (1871) (Eng.). –Case Citation.
         Pickard v. Baylis, 5 C.P.D. 235 (1879) (Eng.). –Case Citation.

Law Reports: English & Irish Appeal Cases (U.K.)
See Bluebook table T.2.
Ab.:   L.R.E. & I. App.
Ex.:   Allen v. Bishop of Gloucester, 6 L.R.E. & I. App. 219 (1873) (Eng.).
         –Case Citation.

Law Reports: Exchequer Division (England)
See Bluebook table T.2.
Ab.:   1875-1880: Exch. Div.
         1865-1875: L.R. Exch.
Ex.:   Holker v. Poritt, 8 L.R. Exch. 107 (1873) (Eng.). –Case Citation.
         Gilbertson v. Ferguson, 5 Exch. Div. 57 (1879) (Eng.). –Case Citation.

Law Reports: Family (England) (1872-date)
See Bluebook table T.2.
Ab.:   Fam.
Ex.:   McVeigh v. Beattie, 1988 Fam. 69 (1987) (Eng.). –Case Citation.
         Bellinger v. Bellinger, [2001] EWCA (Civ.) 1140, [2002] Fam. 150
         (Eng.) –Case with neutral citation.
         –See Bluebook table T.2.

Law Reports: Privy Council Appeal Cases (U.K.)
See Bluebook table T.2.
Ab.:   L.R.–P.C.
Ex.:   Richer v. Voyer, 5 L.R.–P.C. 461 (1874) (U.K.). –Case Citation.

Law Reports: Probate and Divorce Cases (England)
See Bluebook table T.2.
Ab.:   L.R.P. & D. (1865-75)
Ex.:   Davies v. Gregory, 3 L.R.P. & D. 28 (1873) (Eng.). –Case Citation.

Law Reports: Probate, Divorce & Admiralty Cases (England)
See Bluebook table T.2.

In law review footnotes, the titles of books and the names of cases, except for procedural phrases, are not underlined. See Bluebook rule 2.1(a) & (b). Further, the following are in large and small capitals: codes, restatements, standards, constitutions, periodicals, authors of books, titles of books, the abbreviated names of codes, most legislative materials except for bills and resolutions, codified ordinances, model codes, court rules, and sentencing guidelines. Refer to The Bluebook.

Ab.: P.D. (1875-90)

Ex.: <u>Scott v. Sebright</u>, 12 P.D. 21 (1886) (Eng.). –Case Citation.

Law Reports: Probate, Divorce & Admiralty Division (England)
See <u>Bluebook</u> table T.2.

Ab.: P. (1891-1971)

Ex.: <u>P. v. P.</u>, 1971 P. 217 (C.A.) (Eng.). –Court of Appeals–Case Citation.

<u>Adams v. Adams</u>, 1971 P. 188 (1970) (Eng.). –Case Citation.

Law Reports: Queen's and King's Bench (England)
See <u>Bluebook</u> table T.2. Indicate the court only if it is the Court of Appeals.

Ab.: 1952-date: Q.B.

1901-1951: K.B.

1891-1900: Q.B.

1875-1890: Q.B.D.

1865-1875: L.R.Q.B.

Ex.: <u>Foster v. Robinson</u>, [1951] 1 K.B. 149 (1950) (Eng. C.A.). –Court of Appeal–Case Citation.

<u>Longden-Griffiths v. Smith</u>, [1951] 1 K.B. 295 (1950) (Eng.). –Case Citation.

<u>F.C. Shepherd & Co. Ltd. v. Jerrom</u>, [1987] 1 Q.B. 301 (1986) (Eng. C.A.). –Court of Appeal–Case Citation.

<u>Coastplace Ltd. v. Hartley</u>, [1987] 1 Q.B. 948 (Eng.). –Case Citation.

<u>Hamilton v. Al Fayed</u> (No. 2) [2002] EWCA (Civ) 665, [2003] 2 Q.B. 1175 (Eng.). –Case with neutral citation.

Law Reports: Scotch & Divorce Appeal Cases (U.K.) (1866-1875)
See <u>Bluebook</u> table T.2.

Ab.: L.R.S. & D. App.

Ex.: <u>Carlton v. Thompson</u>, 1 L.R.S. & D. App. 232 (1867) (Eng.). –Case Citation.

law review
See periodicals.

law review footnotes, typeface conventions for law review footnotes
See <u>Bluebook</u> rules 2.1 and 7. See also the excellent examples on the inside front cover and on the facing page next to the inside front cover of <u>The Bluebook</u>.

law review texts, typeface conventions for law review texts
See <u>Bluebook</u> rules 2.2 and 7.

In citing cases in law review footnotes, abbreviate any word listed in table T.6; the names of "states, countries, and other geographical units" unless they are named parties; and any other words of eight or more letters "if <u>substantial</u> space is thereby saved and the result is unambiguous." <u>Bluebook</u> rule 10.2.2. On the other hand, in citing cases in text, abbreviate only widely known acronyms and the following words: "&," "Ass'n," "Bros.," "Co.," "Corp.," "Inc.," "Ltd.," and "No." <u>Bluebook</u> rule 10.2.1(c).

Law Teacher, The
  Ab.:   Law Tchr.
  Ex.:   Stephen Migdal & Martin Cartwright, <u>Student Based Learning - A Polytechnic's Experience</u>, 25 Law Tchr. 120 (1991). –Article Citation.

            Stephen Migdal & Martin Cartwright, <u>Student Based Learning - A Polytechnic's Experience</u>, 25 Law Tchr. 120, 122 (1991). –Page Citation.

Law/Technology
  Ab.:   Law/Tech.
  Ex.:   Linda Maher, <u>Environmental Concerns: In Domestic and International Regulatory Frameworks for Biotechnology</u>, 1991 Law/Tech. 1. –Article Citation.

            Linda Maher, <u>Environmental Concerns: In Domestic and International Regulatory Frameworks for Biotechnology</u>, 1991 Law/Tech. 1, 5. –Page Citation.

Law Times Reports (England) (1859-1947)
  Ab.:   L.T.
  Ex.:   <u>Glanville v. Sulton and Co.</u>, 138 L.T. 336 (K.B. 1928) (Eng.). –Case Citation.

            <u>See</u> <u>Bluebook</u> table T.2.

Lawasia
  Ab.:   Do not abbreviate title.
  Ex.:   Stanley Yeo, <u>Reforming Duress Under Indian Penal Code</u>, 1987 Lawasia 85. –Article Citation.

            Stanley Yeo, <u>Reforming Duress Under Indian Penal Code</u>, 1987 Lawasia 85, 90-93. –Page Citation.

Laws of Delaware
  Ab.:   vol. Del. Laws page no. (year)
  Ex.:   Act of July 15, 1994, ch. 444, 69 Del. Laws 921 (1994). –Citation to an entire session law.

            Act of July 15, 1994, ch. 444, § 2, 69 Del. Laws 921, 922 (1994). –Citation to a section of a session law.

            –See <u>Bluebook</u> rule 12.4.

Laws of Florida
  Ab.:   year Fla. Laws page no.
  Ex.:   Act of Jan. 22, 2002, ch. 2002-162, 2002 Fla. Laws 1031. –Citation to an entire session law.

            Act of Jan. 22, 2002, ch. 2002-162, sec. 2, § 812.0145, 2002 Fla. Laws 1031, 1031. –Citation to a section of a session law amending prior act.

In law review footnotes, the titles of books and the names of cases, except for procedural phrases, are not underlined. <u>See</u> <u>Bluebook</u> rule 2.1(a) & (b). Further, the following are in large and small capitals: codes, restatements, standards, constitutions, periodicals, authors of books, titles of books, the abbreviated names of codes, most legislative materials except for bills and resolutions, codified ordinances, model codes, court rules, and sentencing guidelines. Refer to <u>The Bluebook</u>.

–For proper citation form in papers submitted to Florida courts, see Fla. R. App. P. 9.800(h).

–See Bluebook rule 12.4.

Laws of Illinois
Ab.: year Ill. Laws page no.

Ex.: Act of June 30, 1995, No. 89-71, 1995 Ill. Laws 1507. –Citation to an entire session law.

Act of June 30, 1995, No. 89-71, sec. 5(a), § 6-106.1, 1995 Ill. Laws 1507, 1507. –Citation to a section of a session law amending a prior act.

–See Bluebook rule 12.4.

Laws of Maryland
Ab.: year Md. Laws page no.

Ex.: Act of Apr. 11, 1995, ch. 98, 1995 Md. Laws 1453 (radiation control - definition of a person). –Citation to an entire session law.

Act of Apr. 11, 1995, ch. 98, § 1, 1995 Md. Laws 1453, 1453-54 (radiation control - definition of a person). –Citation to a section of a session law.

–See Bluebook rule 12.4.

Laws of Minnesota
Ab.: year Minn. Laws page no.

Ex.: Act of Apr. 11, 1996, ch. 442, 1996 Minn. Laws 1176 (relating to driving while intoxicated). –Citation to an entire session law.

Act of Apr. 11, 1996, ch. 442, sec. 2, § 168.024, 1996 Minn. Laws 1176, 1178 (acquiring another vehicle during plate impounding). –Citation to a section of a session law.

–See Bluebook rule 12.4.

Laws of Missouri
Ab.: year Mo. Laws page no.

Ex.: Act of June 27, 1995, 1995 Mo. Laws 826 (concerning licensing of cosmetologists). –Citation to an entire session law.

Act of June 27, 1995, 1995 Mo. Laws 826, 826-27, sec. A(1-4), § 329.010 (licensing of cosmetologists - definitions). –Citation to a section of a session law amending a prior act.

–See Bluebook rule 12.4.

Laws of Montana
Ab.: year Mont. Laws page no.

In citing cases in law review footnotes, abbreviate any word listed in table T.6; the names of "states, countries, and other geographical units" unless they are named parties; and any other words of eight or more letters "if substantial space is thereby saved and the result is unambiguous." Bluebook rule 10.2.2. On the other hand, in citing cases in text, abbreviate only widely known acronyms and the following words: "&," "Ass'n," "Bros.," "Co.," "Corp.," "Inc.," "Ltd.," and "No." Bluebook rule 10.2.1(c).

Ex.:   Act of Apr. 14, 1995, ch. 466, 1995 Mont. Laws 2244. –Citation to an entire session law.

Act of Apr. 14, 1995, ch. 466, sec. 3, § 41-5-521, 1995 Mont. Laws 2244, 2245. –Citation to a section of a session law amending a prior act.

–See Bluebook rule 12.4.

Laws of Nebraska
Ab.:   year Neb. Laws page no.

Ex.:   Act of Mar. 25, 1996, No. 1041, 1995 Neb. Laws 750. –Citation to an entire session law.

Act of Mar. 25, 1996, No. 1041, sec. 7, § 77-2708, 1995 Neb. Laws 750, 756-58. –Citation to a section of a session law amending a prior act.

–See Bluebook rule 12.4.

Laws of New Jersey
Ab.:   year N.J. Laws page no.

Ex.:   Act of Aug. 11, 1994, ch. 95, 1994 N.J. Laws 884 (concerning admissibility of evidence in prosecutions for sex crimes). –Citation to an entire session law.

Act of Aug. 11, 1994, ch. 95, sec. 1, § 2C:14-7, 1994 N.J. Laws 884, 884-85 (sex crimes - victim's previous sexual conduct). –Citation to a section of a session law amending a prior act.

–See Bluebook rule 12.4.

Laws of New York
Ab.:   year N.Y. Laws page no.

Ex.:   Act of Aug. 2, 1995, ch. 389, 1995 N.Y. Laws 3171 (regarding child custody and support). –Citation to an entire session law.

Act of Aug. 2, 1995, ch. 389, sec. 1, § 240(1), 1995 N.Y. Laws 3171, 3171 (orders for child custody and support). –Citation to a section of a session law amending a prior act.

–See Bluebook rule 12.4.

Laws of North Dakota
Ab.:   year N.D. Sess. Laws

Ex.:   Act of Mar. 31, 1999, ch. 394, 1999 N.D. Sess. Laws 1524. –Citation to an entire session law.

Act of Mar. 31, 1999, ch. 394, sec. 5, § 43-40-08, 1999 N.D. Sess. Laws 1524, 1527 (concerning occupational therapist licensing practice). –Citation to a section of a session law amending a prior act.

–See Bluebook rule 12.4.

In law review footnotes, the titles of books and the names of cases, except for procedural phrases, are not underlined. See Bluebook rule 2.1(a) & (b). Further, the following are in large and small capitals: codes, restatements, standards, constitutions, periodicals, authors of books, titles of books, the abbreviated names of codes, most legislative materials except for bills and resolutions, codified ordinances, model codes, court rules, and sentencing guidelines. Refer to The Bluebook.

Laws of Pennsylvania
Ab.:   year Pa. Laws page no.

Ex.:   Act of June 13, 1995, No. 8, 1995 Pa. Laws 52. –Citation to an entire session law.

        Act of June 13, 1995, No. 8, sec. 1(a), § 910, 1995 Pa. Laws 52, 52-53. –Citation to a section of a session law amending a prior act.

        –See Bluebook rule 12.4.

Laws of Puerto Rico
Ab.:   year P.R. Laws page no.

Ex.:   Act of Nov. 28, 1989, No. 5, 1989 P.R. Laws 549. –Citation to an entire session law.

        Act of Nov. 28, 1989, No. 5, sec. 1, § 16-102A, 1989 P.R. Laws 549, 549-50. –Citation to a section of a session law amending a prior act.

        –See Bluebook rule 12.4.

Laws of Puerto Rico Annotated (LexisNexis)
Ab.:   P.R. Laws Ann. tit. x, § x (year)

Ex.:   P.R. Laws Ann. tit. 24, § 4003 (2002)

        P.R. Laws Ann. tit. 24, § 7061 (Supp. 2002)

        –For proper citation form in papers submitted to Puerto Rico courts, see prefatory pages to P.R. Laws Ann. volumes.

Laws of the Republic of Texas
Ab.:   18xx Repub. Tex. Laws page no.

        – See Bluebook rule 12.4.

        – "Cite to Tex. Gen. Laws, if therein." Bluebook table T.1, p. 235

Laws of the State of Maine
Ab.:   year Me. Laws page no.

Ex.:   Act of Mar. 11, 1999, ch. 7, 1999 Me. Laws 29. –Citation to an entire session law.

        Act of Mar. 11, 1999, ch. 7, sec. 7, § 6575, 1999 Me. Laws 29, 30. –Citation to a section of a session law.

        –See Bluebook rule 12.4.

Laws of the State of New Hampshire
Ab.:   year N.H. Laws page no.

Ex.:   Act of June 21, 1995, ch. 280, 1995 N.H. Laws 469. –Citation to an entire session law.

        Act of June 21, 1995, ch. 280, sec. 3, § 510-A8, II, 1995 N.H. Laws 469, 469-70. –Citation to a section of a session law amending a prior act.

In citing cases in law review footnotes, abbreviate any word listed in table T.6; the names of "states, countries, and other geographical units" unless they are named parties; and any other words of eight or more letters "if substantial space is thereby saved and the result is unambiguous." Bluebook rule 10.2.2. On the other hand, in citing cases in text, abbreviate only widely known acronyms and the following words: "&," "Ass'n," "Bros.," "Co.," "Corp.," "Inc.," "Ltd.," and "No." Bluebook rule 10.2.1(c).

–See Bluebook rule 12.4.

Laws of the State of New Mexico
Ab.:   year N.M. Laws

Ex.:   Act of Feb. 15, 2000, ch. 3, 2000 N.M. Laws 24 (relating to unemployment compensation). –Citation to an entire session law.

Act of Feb. 15, 2000, ch. 3, sec. 1, § 51-1-4, 2000 N.M. Laws 24, 24. –Citation to a section of a session law amending a prior act.

–See Bluebook rule 12.4.

Laws of Utah
Ab.:   year Utah Laws page no.

Ex.:   Act of Feb. 17, 1995, ch. 286, 1995 Utah Laws 943. –Citation to an entire session law.

Act of Feb. 17, 1995, ch. 286, sec. 2 § 77-18-15, 1995 Utah Laws 943, 944-45. –Citation to a section of a session law amending a prior act.

–See Bluebook rule 12.4.

Laws of Washington
Ab.:   year Wash. Laws

Ex.:   Act of Feb. 18, 2000, ch. 3, 2000 Wash. Laws 19 (relating to jail booking). –Citation to an entire session law.

Act of Feb. 18, 2000, ch. 3, sec. 1, § 36.28A, 2000 Wash. Laws 19, 20. –Citation to a section of a session law amending a prior act.

–See Bluebook rule 12.4.

Lawyer's Edition, United States Supreme Court Reports
See United States Supreme Court Reports, Lawyer's Edition.

Leader's Product Liability Law and Strategy
Ab.:   Leader's Product Liability L. & Strategy

Ex.:   Mark Shayne, Defending Against Claims For Lost Wages & Profits, Leader's Product Liability L. & Strategy, Dec. 1991, at 1. –Article Citation.

Mark Shayne, Defending Against Claims For Lost Wages & Profits, Leader's Product Liability L. & Strategy, Dec. 1991, at 1, 1. –Page Citation.

League of Nations Covenant
Ex.:   League of Nations Covenant art. 18, para. 2.

See Bluebook rule 21.8.1.

League of Nations Official Journal
Ab.:   League of Nations O.J.

In law review footnotes, the titles of books and the names of cases, except for procedural phrases, are not underlined. See Bluebook rule 2.1(a) & (b). Further, the following are in large and small capitals: codes, restatements, standards, constitutions, periodicals, authors of books, titles of books, the abbreviated names of codes, most legislative materials except for bills and resolutions, codified ordinances, model codes, court rules, and sentencing guidelines. Refer to The Bluebook.

League of Nations Treaty Series
Ab.:   L.N.T.S.

Ex.:   Convention Relating to Upper Silesia, Ger.-Pol., art. 5, May 15, 1922, 9 L.N.T.S. 466.

See <u>Bluebook</u> rule 21.4.5, and table T.3.

Legal Issues of European Integration
Ab.:   Legal Issues Eur. Integration

Ex.:   Nicholas J. Skaelatos, <u>European Lawyers' Right to Transnational Legal Practice in The European Community</u>, 1991 Legal Issues Eur. Integration, at 49. –Article Citation.

Nicholas J. Skaelatos, <u>European Lawyers' Right to Transnational Legal Practice in The European Community</u>, 1991 Legal Issues Eur. Integration, at 49, 52. –Page Citation.

Legal Malpractice, by Ronald E. Mallen and Jeffrey M. Smith
–Do not abbreviate the title.

Ex.:   1 Ronald E. Mallen & Jeffrey M. Smith, <u>Legal Malpractice</u> § 2.6 (5th ed. 2000). –Section Citation.

1 Ronald E. Mallen & Jeffrey M. Smith, <u>Legal Malpractice</u> § 2.6, at 67 (5th ed. 2000). –Page Citation.

1 Ronald E. Mallen & Jeffrey M. Smith, <u>Legal Malpractice</u> § 2.6, at 67 n.2 (5th ed. 2000). –Footnote Citation.

Legal Medicine
Ab.:   Legal Med.

Ex.:   Bernard J. Ficarra, <u>Physicians' Legal and Moral Responsibility to Treat Contagious Disease</u>, 1991 Legal Med. 93. –Article Citation.

Bernard J. Ficarra, <u>Physicians' Legal and Moral Responsibility to Treat Contagious Disease</u>, 1991 Legal Med. 93, 94. –Page Citation.

legal memoranda, basic citation forms
See various title entries of this work. See also examples included on the facing page next to the inside back cover and on the inside back cover of <u>The Bluebook</u>.

legal memoranda, typeface conventions for legal memoranda
See <u>Bluebook</u> rules B13 and 7.

Legal Studies
Ab.:   Legal Stud.

Ex.:   Andrew J. Cunningham, <u>"To the Uttermost Ends of the Earth?" The War Crimes Act and International Law</u>, 11 Legal Stud. 281 (1991). –Article Citation.

Andrew J. Cunningham, <u>"To the Uttermost Ends of the Earth?" The War Crimes Act and International Law</u>, 11 Legal Stud. 281, 286-87 (1991). –Page Citation.

In citing cases in law review footnotes, abbreviate any word listed in table T.6; the names of "states, countries, and other geographical units" unless they are named parties; and any other words of eight or more letters "if <u>substantial</u> space is thereby saved and the result is unambiguous." <u>Bluebook</u> rule 10.2.2. On the other hand, in citing cases in text, abbreviate only widely known acronyms and the following words: "&," "Ass'n," "Bros.," "Co.," "Corp.," "Inc.," "Ltd.," and "No." <u>Bluebook</u> rule 10.2.1(c).

Legal Times
   Ab.:   Legal Times
   Ex.:   John Murawski, Law Faces Budget Ax-Again, Legal Times, Feb. 24, 1992, at 2. –Article Citation.

        –"[G]ive only the first page of the piece and do not indicate the location of specific material." Bluebook rule 16.5.

Legislative History (separately bound)
   Ex.:   H.R. Rep. No. 901, 91st Cong., 2d Sess. 3 (1970), reprinted in 4 Railway Labor Act of 1926: A Legislative History § 5 (Michael H. Campbell & Edward C. Brewer, III eds. 1988).

        H.R. Rep. No. 101-787, at 25 (1990), reprinted in 1 Individuals with Disabilities Education Act: A Legislative History of Public Law 101-476 as Amended by Public Law 102-119, Doc. No. 4 (Bernard D. Reams, Jr., J.D., Ph.D. 1994).

   See Bluebook rule 13.6.

Leiden Journal of International Law
   Ab.:   Leiden J. Int'l L.
   Ex.:   Sam Muller, International Organizations and Their Officials: To Tax or Not to Tax?, 6 Leiden J. Int'l L. 47 (1993). –Article Citation.

        Sam Muller, International Organizations and Their Officials: To Tax or Not to Tax?, 6 Leiden J. Int'l L. 47, 57 (1993). –Page Citation.

Lesotho Law Journal
   Ab.:   Lesotho L.J.
   Ex.:   Kenneth Asamoa Acheampoug, The African Charter and the Equalization of Human Rights, 7 Lesotho L.J. 21 (1991). –Article Citation.

        Kenneth Asamoa Acheampoug, The African Charter and the Equalization of Human Rights, 7 Lesotho L.J. 21, 29-31 (1991). –Page Citation.

Letter to the Editor (newspaper)
   Ex.:   Stephen J. Ubl, Letter to the Editor, Heart Device Saves Lives, N.Y. Times, Oct. 28, 2005, at A24.

   See Bluebook rule 16.5.

Letters, unpublished
   Ex.:   Letter from Kurt Grasinger, Film Critic, The New Yorker, to Jean Winter, Editor, Vanderbilt Law School Brief (Feb. 26, 1996) (on file with author).

Lewis & Clark Law Review
   Ab.:   Lewis & Clark L. Rev.

In law review footnotes, the titles of books and the names of cases, except for procedural phrases, are not underlined. See Bluebook rule 2.1(a) & (b). Further, the following are in large and small capitals: codes, restatements, standards, constitutions, periodicals, authors of books, titles of books, the abbreviated names of codes, most legislative materials except for bills and resolutions, codified ordinances, model codes, court rules, and sentencing guidelines. Refer to The Bluebook.

Ex.:   Carol M. Rose, <u>Environmental Law Grows Up (More or Less), and What Science Can Do to Help</u>, 9 Lewis & Clark L. Rev. 273 (2005). –Article Citation.

Carol M. Rose, <u>Environmental Law Grows Up (More or Less), and What ScienceCan Do to Help</u>, 9 Lewis & Clark L. Rev. 273, 275-78 (2005). –Page Citation.

Lex et Scientia
Ab.:   Lex et Scientia

Ex.:   Mark E. Kalmansohn, Note, <u>Law, Lawyers, and Literature</u>, 12 Lex et Scientia 92 (1976).

Mark E. Kalmansohn, Note, <u>Law, Lawyers, and Literature</u>, 12 Lex et Scientia 92, 105 (1976).

LEXIS
See pending and unreported cases, electronic media and other nonprint resources, and <u>Bluebook</u> rule 18.1.

Lexis District of Columbia Code Advance Legislative Service
Ab.:   year-pamph. no. D.C. Code Adv. Leg. Serv. page no. (LexisNexis)

Ex.:   Act of Jan. 27, 2005, No. 15-757, 2004-2005-3 D.C. Code Adv. Leg. Serv. 422 (LexisNexis) (concerning First Amendment assemblies). –Citation to an entire session law.

Act of Jan. 27, 2005, No.15-757, sec. 105, 2004-2005-3 D.C. Code Adv. Leg. Serv. 422, 424 (LexisNexis) (concerning First Amendment assemblies). –Citation to a section of a session law.

–<u>See</u> <u>Bluebook</u> rule 12.4.

–"Cite to Stat., if therein." <u>Bluebook</u> table T.1, p. 205.

Lexis District of Columbia Code Annotated
Ab.:   D.C. Code Ann. § x-x (LexisNexis year).

Ex.:   D.C. Code Ann. § 46-319 (LexisNexis 2001).

D.C. Code Ann. § 42-105 (LexisNexis Supp. 2004).

– "Cite to D.C. Code, if therein." <u>Bluebook</u> table T.1, p. 205.

Lexis New Hampshire Revised Statutes Annotated
Ab.:   N.H. Rev. Stat. Ann. § x:x (LexisNexis year).

Ex.:   N.H. Rev. Stat. Ann. § 677:7 (LexisNexis 2004).

N.H. Rev. Stat. Ann. § 644:9 (LexisNexis Supp. 2005).

– "Cite to N.H. Rev. Stat. Ann. (published by West), if therein." <u>Bluebook</u> table T.1, p. 218.

Lexis New Hampshire Revised Statutes Annotated Advance Legislative Service
Ab.:   year-pamph. no. N.H. Rev. Stat. Ann. Adv. Legis. Serv. page no. (LexisNexis)

In citing cases in law review footnotes, abbreviate any word listed in table T.6; the names of "states, countries, and other geographical units" unless they are named parties; and any other words of eight or more letters "if <u>substantial</u> space is thereby saved and the result is unambiguous." <u>Bluebook</u> rule 10.2.2. On the other hand, in citing cases in text, abbreviate only widely known acronyms and the following words: "&," "Ass'n," "Bros.," "Co.," "Corp.," "Inc.," "Ltd.," and "No." <u>Bluebook</u> rule 10.2.1(c).

Ex.:   Act effective May 10, 2005, ch. 32, 2005-1 N.H. Rev. Stat. Ann. Adv. Legis. Serv. 76 (LexisNexis) (relative to timber harvesting). –Citation to an entire session law.

Act effective May 10, 2005, ch. 32, sec. 32:1, § 485-A:17, 2005-1 N.H. Rev. Stat. Ann. Adv. Leg. Serv. 76, 76 (LexisNexis). –Citation to a section of a session law amending prior act.

–See Bluebook rule 12.4.

– "Cite to N.H. Laws, if therein." Bluebook table T. 1, p. 219.

LexisNexis Florida Statutes Annotated
Ab.:   Fla. Stat. Ann. § x.x (LexisNexis year).

Ex.:   Fla. Stat. Ann. § 327.461 (LexisNexis 2004).

Fla. Stat. Ann. § 206.119 (Supp. LexisNexis 2004).

– "Cite to Fla. Stat., if therein." Bluebook table T.1, p. 205.

–For proper citation form in papers submitted to Florida courts, see Fla. R. App. P. 9.800(g).

Licensing Law and Business Report
Ab.:   Licensing L. & Bus. Rep.

Life, Health & Accident Insurance Cases
See Insurance Law Reports.

Lincoln Law Review
Ab.:   Lincoln L. Rev.

Ex.:   Robert W. McGee, The "Essence of the Transaction" Test for Computer Software Tangibility and Taxation, 20 Lincoln L. Rev. 21 (1991). –Article Citation.

Robert W. McGee, The "Essence of the Transaction" Test for Computer Software Tangibility and Taxation, 20 Lincoln L. Rev. 21, 23 (1991). –Page Citation.

Lindey on Entertainment, Publishing, and the Arts, by Alexander Lindey and Michael Landau
–Do not abbreviate the title.

Ex.:   1 Alexander Lindey & Michael Landau, Lindey on Entertainment, Publishing, and the Arts § 2:66.50 (3d ed. 2004). –Section Citation.

1 Alexander Lindey & Michael Landau, Lindey on Entertainment, Publishing, and the Arts § 2:66.50, at 2-154.1 (3d ed. 2004). –Page Citation.

Lindey and Parley on Separation Agreements and Ante-Nuptial Contracts, by Alexander Lindey & Louis I. Parley
–Do not abbreviate this title.

In law review footnotes, the titles of books and the names of cases, except for procedural phrases, are not underlined. See Bluebook rule 2.1(a) & (b). Further, the following are in large and small capitals: codes, restatements, standards, constitutions, periodicals, authors of books, titles of books, the abbreviated names of codes, most legislative materials except for bills and resolutions, codified ordinances, model codes, court rules, and sentencing guidelines. Refer to The Bluebook.

Ex.: 2 Alexander Lindey & Louis I. Parley, <u>Lindey and Parley on Separation Agreements and Ante-Nuptial Contracts</u> § 61.35 (2d ed. 2000). –Section Citation.

2 Alexander Lindey & Louis I. Parley, <u>Lindey and Parley on Separation Agreements and Ante-Nuptial Contracts</u> § 61.35, at 61-20 (2d ed. 2000). –Page Citation.

2 Alexander Lindey & Louis I. Parley, <u>Lindey and Parley on Separation Agreements and Ante-Nuptial Contracts</u> § 61.35, at 61-20 n.1 (2d ed. 2000). –Footnote Citation.

Lipscomb's Walker on Patents, by Ernest Lipscomb III
–Do not abbreviate the title.

Ex.: 6 Ernest B. Lipscomb III, <u>Lipscomb's Walker on Patents</u> § 21:7 (3d ed. 1987). –Section Citation.

6 Ernest B. Lipscomb III, <u>Lipscomb's Walker on Patents</u> § 21:7, at 278 (3d ed. 1987). –Page Citation.

6 Ernest B. Lipscomb III, <u>Lipscomb's Walker on Patents</u> § 21:7, at 278 n.11 (3d ed. 1987). –Footnote Citation.

Liquor Control Law Reports (Commerc Clearing House)
Ab.: Liquor Cont. L. Rep. (CCH)

Listserv messages
See Electronic media and other nonprint resources.

Litigation
Ab.: Litig.
Ex.: Michael E. Tigar, <u>Discovering Your Litigator's Voice</u>, Litig., Summer 1990, at 1. –Article Citation.

Michael E. Tigar, <u>Discovering Your Litigator's Voice</u>, Litig., Summer 1990, at 1, 3. –Page Citation.

Lloyd's Law Reports (U.K.) (1968-date)
<u>See</u> <u>Bluebook</u> table T.2.
Ab.: Lloyd's Rep.
Ex.: <u>Vesta v. Butcher</u>, [1989] 1 Lloyd's Rep. 331 (1988) (Eng.). –Case Citation.

<u>Haiti v. Duvalier</u>, [1989] 1 Lloyd's Rep. 111 (C.A. 1988) (Eng.). –Case Citation.

<u>Morris v. KLM Royal Dutch Airlines</u>, [2002] UKHL 7, [2002] 1 Lloyd's Rep. 745 (Eng.). –Case with neutral citation.

–<u>See</u> <u>Bluebook</u> table T.2.

Lloyd's List Law Reports (U.K.) (1919-1967)
<u>See</u> <u>Bluebook</u> table T.2.

In citing cases in law review footnotes, abbreviate any word listed in table T.6; the names of "states, countries, and other geographical units" unless they are named parties; and any other words of eight or more letters "if <u>substantial</u> space is thereby saved and the result is unambiguous." <u>Bluebook</u> rule 10.2.2. On the other hand, in citing cases in text, abbreviate only widely known acronyms and the following words: "&," "Ass'n," "Bros.," "Co.," "Corp.," "Inc.," "Ltd.," and "No." <u>Bluebook</u> rule 10.2.1(c).

Ab.:   Lloyd's List L. Rep.

Ex.:   The "Lucille Bloomfield", [1966] 2 Lloyd's List L. Rep. 239 (Adm. 1966) (Eng.). –Case Citation.

Stoney Stanton Supplies, Ltd. v. Midland Bank, Ltd., [1966] 2 Lloyd's List L. Rep. 373 (C.A. 1966) (Eng.). –Case Citation.

Lloyd's Maritime and Commercial Law Quarterly
Ab.:   Lloyd's Mar. & Com. L.Q.

L.M.C.L.Q. [U.K.]

Ex.:   David Milman, The Courts and the Companies Acts: the Judicial Contribution to Company Law, 1990 Lloyd's Mar. & Com. L.Q. 401 (1990). –Article Citation.

David Milman, The Courts and the Companies Acts: the Judicial Contribution to Company Law, 1990 Lloyd's Mar. & Com. L.Q. 401, 415 (1990). –Page Citation.

looseleaf services
Ex.:

current unbound:

Standard Metals Corp. v. Tomlin, [Current] Fed. Sec. L. Rep. (CCH) ¶ 98,004 (S.D.N.Y. May 20, 1981). –Citation for a case.

Sea-Land Serv., Inc. v. Fed. Mar. Comm'n [Current Materials] Admin. L.2d (P & F) (50 Admin. L.2d) 927 (D.C. Cir. Apr.14, 1981). –Citation for a case for which the bound volume number is known.

transfer binder:

SEC v. Wencke, [1980 Transfer Binder] Fed. Sec. L. Rep. (CCH) ¶ 97,533 (9th Cir. June 9, 1980). –Citation to transfer binder.

bound:

Bartell v. Cohen, 29 Admin. L.2d (P & F) 342 (7th Cir. 1971).

–The above example is proper if the case is not yet available in, or is not reported in, an official or West reporter, a public domain citation, or a widely used computer database.

Lord Justice
Ab.:   L.J.

Los Angeles Bar Bulletin
Ab.:   L.A. B. Bull.

Ex.:   Murray Projector, Valuation of Retirement Benefits in Marriage Dissoultions, 50 L.A. B. Bull. 229 (1975). –Article Citation.

Murray Projector, Valuation of Retirement Benefits in Marriage Dissoultions, 50 L.A. B. Bull. 229, 232 (1975). –Page Citation.

In law review footnotes, the titles of books and the names of cases, except for procedural phrases, are not underlined. See Bluebook rule 2.1(a) & (b). Further, the following are in large and small capitals: codes, restatements, standards, constitutions, periodicals, authors of books, titles of books, the abbreviated names of codes, most legislative materials except for bills and resolutions, codified ordinances, model codes, court rules, and sentencing guidelines. Refer to The Bluebook.

Los Angeles Lawyer
Ab.: L.A. Law.

Ex.: Randall L. Erickson, <u>Mechanics' Lien Actions: New Standing Amendments and Future Trends</u>, L.A. Law., Feb. 1992, at 22. –Article Citation.

Randall L. Erickson, <u>Mechanics' Lien Actions: New Standing Amendments and Future Trends</u>, L.A. Law., Feb. 1992, at 22, 23. –Page Citation.

Louisiana Administrative Code
Ab.: La. Admin. Code tit. x, § x (year)

Ex.: La. Admin. Code tit. 33, § 4301 (2000).

Louisiana Annual Reports
Ab.: La. Ann.

Ex.: <u>State v. Edwards</u>, 34 La. Ann. 1012 (1882). –Case Citation.

<u>State v. Edwards</u>, 34 La. Ann. 1012, 1013 (1882). –Page Citation.

Louisiana Bar Journal
Ab.: La. B.J.

Ex.: William C. Swanson, <u>Stress and the Practice of Law</u>, 37 La. B.J. 7 (1989). –Article Citation.

William C. Swanson, <u>Stress and the Practice of Law</u>, 37 La. B.J. 7, 8 (1989). –Page Citation.

Louisiana Children's Code Annotated
See West's Louisiana Children's Code Annotated.

Louisiana Civil Code Annotated
See West's Louisiana Civil Code Annotated.

Louisiana Code of Civil Procedure Annotated
See West's Louisiana Code of Civil Procedure Annotated.

Louisiana Code of Criminal Procedure Annotated
See West's Louisiana Code of Criminal Procedure Annotated.

Louisiana Code of Evidence Annotated
See West's Louisiana Code of Evidence Annotated.

Louisiana Constitution
Ab.: La. Const. art.   , pt.   , §   .
–Not all articles are subdivided into parts.

In citing cases in law review footnotes, abbreviate any word listed in table T.6; the names of "states, countries, and other geographical units" unless they are named parties; and any other words of eight or more letters "if <u>substantial</u> space is thereby saved and the result is unambiguous." <u>Bluebook</u> rule 10.2.2. On the other hand, in citing cases in text, abbreviate only widely known acronyms and the following words: "&," "Ass'n," "Bros.," "Co.," "Corp.," "Inc.," "Ltd.," and "No." <u>Bluebook</u> rule 10.2.1(c).

Ex.:   La. Const. art. I, § 10. –"Cite constitutional provisions currently in force without a date." Bluebook rule 11.

La. Const. art. XIV, § 29 (repealed 1986). –"If the cited provision has been repealed, either indicate parenthetically the fact and date of repeal or cite the repealing provision in full." Bluebook rule 11.

La. Const. art. XII, § 6 (amended 1990). –"When citing a provision that has been subsequently amended, either indicate parenthetically the fact and date of amendment or cite the amending provision in full." Bluebook rule 11.

La. Const. of 1921, art. I, § 7 (1974). –"Cite constitutions that have been totally superseded by year of adoption; if the specific provision cited was adopted in a different year, give that year parenthetically." Bluebook rule 11.

Louisiana Court of Appeals
Ab.:   La. Ct. App.

–Cite to So. or So. 2d, if therein; in addition, give public domain citation if available.

–Prior to inclusion in So. in 1928, cite as follows:

In all documents:

Hirsch v. Ashford, 5 La. App. 290 (Ct. App. 1927) –Case Citation.

Hirsch v. Ashford, 5 La. App. 290, 292 (Ct. App. 1927) –Page Citation.

–From 1928 until January 1, 1994, when a public domain format was adopted, cite as follows:

In all documents:

Perry v. W.K. Henderson Iron Works & Supply Co., 133 So. 805 (La. Ct. App. 1931). –Case Citation.

Perry v. W.K. Henderson Iron Works & Supply Co., 133 So. 805, 806 (La. Ct. App. 1931). –Page Citation.

–After January 1, 1994, cite as follows:

In all documents:

Taylor v. Sider, 99-2521 (La. App. 4 Cir. 5/31/00); 765 So. 2d 416–Case Citation.

Taylor v. Sider, 99-2521, p. 4 (La. App. 4 Cir. 5/31/00); 765 So. 2d 416, 419 –Page Citation.

See Bluebook rules 10.3.1, 10.3.3, B5.1.3, and table T.1; see also La. Sup. Ct. Gen. Admin. R. Pt. G § 8.

Louisiana Law Review
Ab.:   La. L. Rev.

In law review footnotes, the titles of books and the names of cases, except for procedural phrases, are not underlined. See Bluebook rule 2.1(a) & (b). Further, the following are in large and small capitals: codes, restatements, standards, constitutions, periodicals, authors of books, titles of books, the abbreviated names of codes, most legislative materials except for bills and resolutions, codified ordinances, model codes, court rules, and sentencing guidelines. Refer to The Bluebook.

Ex.:   Walter F. Murphy, <u>Civil Law, Common Law, and Constitutional Democracy</u>, 52 La. L. Rev. 91 (1991). –Article Citation.

Walter F. Murphy, <u>Civil Law, Common Law, and Constitutional Democracy</u>, 52 La. L. Rev. 91, 119 (1991). –Page Citation.

Louisiana, Opinions of the Attorney General
See Opinions of the Attorney General of Louisiana.

Louisiana Register
Ab.:   vol. no. La. Reg. page no. (month year)

Ex.:   30 La. Reg. 1071 (July 2004)

Louisiana Revised Statutes Annotated
See West's Louisiana Revised Statutes Annotated.

Louisiana Session Laws
See State of Louisiana: Acts of the Legislature and Louisiana Session Law Service (West).

Louisiana Session Law Service (West).
Ab.:   year La. Sess. Law Serv. (West)

Ex.:   Act of June 27, 1996, S.B. No. 76, 1996 La. Sess. Law Serv. 218 (West) (capital companies). –Citation to an entire session law.

Act of June 27, 1996, S.B. No. 76, sec. 1, § 22:1068, 1996 La. Sess. Law Serv. 218, 218-19 (West) (capital companies tax reduction). –Citation to a session law amending a prior act.

–"Cite to La. Acts, if therein." <u>Bluebook</u> table T.1, p. 211.

Louisiana Supreme Court
See public domain citations.

Ab.:   La.

–Cite to So. or So. 2d, if therein; otherwise, cite to La. Give public domain citation if available. Otherwise, give parallel citations only in documents submitted to Louisiana state courts.

–Through 263 La. 1111 (1972), when Louisiana Reports were discontinued, cite as follows:

In documents submitted to Louisiana state courts:

     <u>Schmidt v. City of New Orleans</u>, 164 La. 1006, 115 So. 63 (1927). –Case Citation.

     <u>Schmidt v. City of New Orleans</u>, 164 La. 1006, 1008-09, 115 So. 63, 64 (1927). –Page Citation.

In all other documents:

     <u>Schmidt v. City of New Orleans</u>, 115 So. 63 (La. 1927). –Case Citation.

In citing cases in law review footnotes, abbreviate any word listed in table T.6; the names of "states, countries, and other geographical units" unless they are named parties; and any other words of eight or more letters "if <u>substantial</u> space is thereby saved and the result is unambiguous." <u>Bluebook</u> rule 10.2.2. On the other hand, in citing cases in text, abbreviate only widely known acronyms and the following words: "&," "Ass'n," "Bros.," "Co.," "Corp.," "Inc.," "Ltd.," and "No." <u>Bluebook</u> rule 10.2.1(c).

Schmidt v. City of New Orleans, 115 So. 63, 64 (La. 1927). –Page Citation.

–After 263 La. 1111 (1972) and until January 1, 1994, when a public domain format was adopted, cite as follows:

In all documents:

Pendleton v. Barrett, 675 So. 2d 720 (La. 1996). –Case Citation.

Pendleton v. Barrett, 675 So. 2d 720, 722 (La. 1996). –Page Citation.

–After January 1, 1994, cite as follows:

In all documents:

In re Carreras, 2000-1094 (La. 6/16/00); 765 So. 2d 321. –Case Citation.

In re Carreras, 2000-1094, p. 4 (La. 6/16/00); 765 So. 2d 321, 323. –Page Citation.

See Bluebook rules 10.3.1, 10.3.3, B5.1.3, and table T.1; see also La. Sup. Ct. Gen. Admin. R. Pt. G § 8.

Loyola Consumer Law Reporter

Ab.:   Loy. Consumer L. Rep.

Ex.:   Michael N. Petkovich, Consumer Rights Under the Americans With Disabilities Act, 4 Loy. Consumer L. Rep. 44 (1992). –Article Citation.

Michael N. Petkovich, Consumer Rights Under the Americans With Disabilities Act, 4 Loy. Consumer L. Rep. 44, 46 (1992). –Page Citation.

Loyola Law Review

Ab.:   Loy. L. Rev.

Ex.:   Robert J. Aravjo, Legal Education and Jesuit Universities: Mission and Ministry of the Society of Jesus?, 37 Loy. L. Rev. 245 (1991). –Article Citation.

Robert J. Aravjo, Legal Education and Jesuit Universities: Mission and Ministry of the Society of Jesus?, 37 Loy. L. Rev. 245, 249-51 (1991). –Page Citation.

Loyola of Los Angeles Entertainment Law Review

Ab.:   Loy. L.A. Ent. L. Rev.

Ex.:   Joel Anderson, What's Wrong With This Picture? Dead or Alive: Protecting Actors in the Age of Virtual Reanimation, 25 Loy. L.A. Ent. L. Rev. 155 (2004-2005). –Article Citation.

Joel Anderson, What's Wrong With This Picture? Dead or Alive: Protecting Actors in the Age of Virtual Reanimation, 25 Loy. L.A. Ent. L. Rev. 155, 165 (2004-2005). –Page Citation.

In law review footnotes, the titles of books and the names of cases, except for procedural phrases, are not underlined. See Bluebook rule 2.1(a) & (b). Further, the following are in large and small capitals: codes, restatements, standards, constitutions, periodicals, authors of books, titles of books, the abbreviated names of codes, most legislative materials except for bills and resolutions, codified ordinances, model codes, court rules, and sentencing guidelines. Refer to The Bluebook.

Loyola of Los Angeles International & Comparative Law Journal

Ab.: Loy. L.A. Int'l & Comp. L.J.

Ex.: Anne Moebes, Negotiating International Copyright Protection: The United States and European Community Positions, 14 Loy. L.A. Int'l & Comp. L.J. 301 (1992). –Article Citation.

Anne Moebes, Negotiating International Copyright Protection: The United States and European Community Positions, 14 Loy. L.A. Int'l & Comp. L.J. 301, 310-12 (1992). –Page Citation.

Loyola of Los Angeles Law Review

Ab.: Loy. L.A. L. Rev.

Ex.: Richard L. Antognini, When Will My Troubles End? The Loss in Progress Defense in Progressive Loss Insurance Cases, 25 Loy. L.A. L. Rev. 419 (1992). –Article Citation.

Richard L. Antognini, When Will My Troubles End? The Loss in Progress Defense in Progressive Loss Insurance Cases, 25 Loy. L.A. L. Rev. 419, 431 (1992). –Page Citation.

Loyola University of Chicago Law Journal

Ab.: Loy. U. Chi. L.J.

Ex.: Candace M. Zierdt, Compensation for Birth Mothers: A Challenge to the Adoption Laws, 23 Loy. U. Chi. L.J. 25 (1991). –Article Citation.

Candace M. Zierdt, Compensation for Birth Mothers: A Challenge to the Adoption Laws, 23 Loy. U. Chi. L.J. 25, 27-31 (1991). –Page Citation.

In citing cases in law review footnotes, abbreviate any word listed in table T.6; the names of "states, countries, and other geographical units" unless they are named parties; and any other words of eight or more letters "if substantial space is thereby saved and the result is unambiguous." Bluebook rule 10.2.2. On the other hand, in citing cases in text, abbreviate only widely known acronyms and the following words: "&," "Ass'n," "Bros.," "Co.," "Corp.," "Inc.," "Ltd.," and "No." Bluebook rule 10.2.1(c).

M

Madden & Owen on Products Liability, by David G. Owen, M. Stuart Madden, and Mary J. Davis
–Do not abbreviate the title.

Ex.: 3 David G. Owen et al., <u>Madden & Owen on Products Liability</u>, § 2301 (3d ed. 2000) –Section Citation.

3 David G. Owen et al., <u>Madden & Owen on Products Liability</u>, § 2301, at 168. (3d ed. 2000) –Page Citation.

Madras Law Journal
Ab.: Madras L.J.

Ex.: R. Govindarajan, <u>"Burden of Proof" Under the Tamil Nadu Debt Relief Acts</u>, Madras L.J., July-Dec. 1983, at 28. –Article Citation.

R. Govindarajan, <u>"Burden of Proof" Under the Tamil Nadu Debt Relief Acts</u>, Madras L.J., July-Dec. 1983, at 28, 29-30. –Page Citation.

Magistrate
Ab.: Mag.

Maine Bar Journal
Ab.: Me. B.J.

Ex.: James H. Young, II, <u>Medicaid Eligibility</u>, 5 Me. B.J. 214 (1990). –Article Citation.

James H. Young, II, <u>Medicaid Eligibility</u>, 5 Me. B.J. 214, 215 (1990). –Page Citation.

Maine Constitution
Ab.: Me. Const. art.   , pt.   , §   .
–Not all articles are subdivided into parts.

Ex.: Me. Const. art. I, § 4. –"Cite constitutional provisions currently in force without a date." <u>Bluebook</u> rule 11.

Me. Const. art. XI, § 2 (amended 1988).

Me. Const. art. XI, § 2, <u>amended by</u> Me. Const. Amend. CLVIII. –"When citing a provision that has been subsequently amended, either indicate parenthetically the fact and date of amendment or cite the amending provision in full." <u>Bluebook</u> rule 11.

In law review footnotes, the titles of books and the names of cases, except for procedural phrases, are not underlined. <u>See</u> <u>Bluebook</u> rule 2.1(a) & (b). Further, the following are in large and small capitals: codes, restatements, standards, constitutions, periodicals, authors of books, titles of books, the abbreviated names of codes, most legislative materials except for bills and resolutions, codified ordinances, model codes, court rules, and sentencing guidelines. Refer to <u>The Bluebook</u>.

Maine Government Register (Weil)
    Ab.:   issue no. Me. Gov't Reg. page no. (Weil month year)
    Ex.:   157 Me. Gov't Reg. 9 (Weil Feb. 2004)

Maine Law Review
    Ab.:   Me. L. Rev.
    Ex.:   Dennis M. Doiron, <u>A Better Interpretation of the Wrongful Death Act</u>, 43 Me. L. Rev. 449 (1991). –Article Citation.

           Dennis M. Doiron, <u>A Better Interpretation of the Wrongful Death Act</u>, 43 Me. L. Rev. 449, 455-57 (1991). –Page Citation.

Maine Legislative Service (West)
    Ab.:   year Me. Legis. Serv. page no. (West)
    Ex.:   Act of Mar. 25, 1996, ch. 565, 1996 Me. Legis. Serv. 380 (West) –Citation to an entire session law.

           Act of Mar. 25, 1996, ch. 565, sec. 1, § 1603, 1996 Me. Legis Serv. 380, 380-81 (West) –Citation to a section of a session law amending prior act.

           –<u>See</u> <u>Bluebook</u> rule 12.4.

           –"Cite to Me. Laws, if therein." <u>Bluebook</u> table T.1, p. 212.

Maine Revised Statutes Annotated (West)
    Ab.:   Me. Rev. Stat. Ann. tit. x, § x (year)
    Ex.:   Me. Rev. Stat. Ann. tit. 24, § 2332-B (2000).

           Me. Rev. Stat. Ann. tit. 25, § 1547 (Supp. 1999).

           For proper citation form in papers submitted to Maine state courts, see prefatory pages to Me. Rev. Stat. volumes and <u>Uniform Maine Citations</u> 13 (Michael D. Seitzinger et al. eds, 3d ed. 2003).

Maine Session Laws
    See Acts, Resolves and Constitutional Resolutions of the State of Maine, Laws of the State of Maine, and Maine Legislative Service (West).

Maine Supreme Judicial Court
    Ab.:   Me.

           –Cite to A. or A.2d, if therein; otherwise, cite to Me. Give public domain citation if available. Otherwise, give parallel citations only in documents submitted to Maine state courts.

           –Through 161 Me. 541 (1965), cite as follows:

           In documents submitted to Maine state courts:

                <u>Porter v. Porter</u>, 138 Me. 1, 20 A.2d 465 (1941). –Case Citation.

                <u>Porter v. Porter</u>, 138 Me. 1, 8, 20 A.2d 465, 468 (1941). –Page Citation.

In citing cases in law review footnotes, abbreviate any word listed in table T.6; the names of "states, countries, and other geographical units" unless they are named parties; and any other words of eight or more letters "if <u>substantial</u> space is thereby saved and the result is unambiguous." <u>Bluebook</u> rule 10.2.2. On the other hand, in citing cases in text, abbreviate only widely known acronyms and the following words: "&," "Ass'n," "Bros.," "Co.," "Corp.," "Inc.," "Ltd.," and "No." <u>Bluebook</u> rule 10.2.1(c).

See <u>Uniform Maine Citations</u> § II B (Michael D. Seitzinger et al. eds., 3d ed. 2003), which requires a parallel citation.

In all other documents:

<u>Porter v. Porter</u>, 20 A.2d 465 (Me. 1941). –Case Citation.

<u>Porter v. Porter</u>, 20 A.2d 465, 468 (Me. 1941). –Page Citation.

–After 161 Me. 541 (1965), and until January 1, 1997, when a public domain format was adopted, cite as follows:

In all documents:

<u>Feinerman v. Barrett</u>, 673 A.2d 1341 (Me. 1996). –Case Citation.

<u>Feinerman v. Barrett</u>, 673 A.2d 1341, 1343 (Me. 1996). –Page Citation.

–After January 1, 1997, cite as follows:

In all documents:

<u>Holland v. Sebunya</u>, 2000 ME 160, 759 A.2d 205. –Case Citation.

<u>Holland v. Sebunya</u>, 2000 ME 160, ¶ 24, 759 A.2d 205, 213. –Pinpoint Citation.

See <u>Bluebook</u> rules 10.3.1, 10.3.3, B5.1.3, and table T.1; <u>see also</u> Me. Admin. Order, No. SJC-216 (Aug. 20, 1996) and <u>Uniform Maine Citations</u> § II B (Michael D. Seitzinger et al. eds., 3d ed. 2003).

Major Tax Planning

Ab.:   Major Tax Plan.

Ex.:   William P. Wasserman & Terence F. Cuff, <u>Helping the Kids</u> Buy a <u>House</u>, 47 Major Tax Plan. ¶ 2202.2 (1995). –Section Citation.

William P. Wasserman & Terence F. Cuff, <u>Helping the Kids Buy a House</u>, 47 Major Tax Plan. ¶ 2202.2, at 22-6 (1995). –Page Citation.

Malaya Law Review

Ab.:   Malaya L.R.

Ex.:   Tan C. Han, <u>The General Exception of Necessity Under the Singapore Penal Code</u>, 1990 Malaya L.R. 271. –Article Citation.

Tan C. Han, <u>The General Exception of Necessity Under the Singapore Penal Code</u>, 1990 Malaya L.R. 271, 279-80. –Page Citation.

Malayan Law Journal

Ab.:   Malayan L.J.

Ex.:   <u>Lee Wah Bank Ltd. v. National Union Bank of Employees</u>, [1981] 1 Malayan L.J. 169 (Sup. Ct. 1981).

Manitoba & Saskatchewan Tax Reporter (Commerce Clearing House)

Ab.:   Man. & Sask. Tax Rep. (CCH)

In law review footnotes, the titles of books and the names of cases, except for procedural phrases, are not underlined. <u>See</u> <u>Bluebook</u> rule 2.1(a) & (b). Further, the following are in large and small capitals: codes, restatements, standards, constitutions, periodicals, authors of books, titles of books, the abbreviated names of codes, most legislative materials except for bills and resolutions, codified ordinances, model codes, court rules, and sentencing guidelines. Refer to <u>The Bluebook</u>.

Manitoba Gazette
    Ab.:   M. Gaz.

Manitoba Law Journal
    Ab.:   Man. L.J.
    Ex.:   Humar Foster, <u>Forgotten Arguments: Aboriginal Title and Sovereignty in Canada Jurisdiction Act Cases</u>, 21 Man. L.J. 343 (1992). –Article Citation.
           Humar Foster, <u>Forgotten Arguments: Aboriginal Title and Sovereignty in Canada Jurisdiction Act Cases</u>, 21 Man. L.J. 343, 346 (1992). –Page Citation.

Manitoba Law Reports (Canada) (1875-1883)
    See <u>Bluebook</u> table T.2.
    Ab.:   Man. L.R.
    Ex.:   <u>Onofriechuk v. Burlacu</u>, [1959] 67 Man. L.R. 223 (Ct. App.) (Can.). –Case Citation.
           <u>Onofriechuk v. Burlacu</u>, [1959] 67 Man. L.R. 223, 224 (Ct. App.) (Can.). –Page Citation.

Manitoba Reports (Canada) (1883-1961)
    See <u>Bluebook</u> table T.2.
    Ab.:   Man. R.

Manitoba Reports (2d) (Canada) (1979 - Date)
    See <u>Bluebook</u> table T.2.
    Ab.:   Man. R.2d

manuscript
    Ab.:   ms.

Maritime Law Reporter (Commerce Clearing House)
    Ab.:   Maritime L. Rep. (CCH)

Maritime Lawyer, The
    Ab.:   Mar. Law.
    Ex.:   Curtis G. Pew et al., <u>Maritime Courts in the Middle Kingdom: China's Great Leap Seaward</u>, 11 Mar. Law. 237 (1986). –Article Citation.
           Curtis G. Pew et al., <u>Maritime Courts in the Middle Kingdom: China's Great Leap Seaward</u>, 11 Mar. Law. 237, 249-53 (1986). –Page Citation.

Marquette Law Review
    Ab.:   Marq. L. Rev.
    Ex.:   Ronald R. Hofer, <u>Standards of Review - Looking Beyond the Labels</u>, 74 Marq. L. Rev. 231 (1991). –Article Citation.
           Ronald R. Hofer, <u>Standards of Review - Looking Beyond the Labels</u>, 74 Marq. L. Rev. 231, 233 (1991). –Page Citation.

In citing cases in law review footnotes, abbreviate any word listed in table T.6; the names of "states, countries, and other geographical units" unless they are named parties; and any other words of eight or more letters "if <u>substantial</u> space is thereby saved and the result is unambiguous." <u>Bluebook</u> rule 10.2.2. On the other hand, in citing cases in text, abbreviate only widely known acronyms and the following words: "&.," "Ass'n," "Bros.," "Co.," "Corp.," "Inc.," "Ltd.," and "No." <u>Bluebook</u> rule 10.2.1(c).

Maryland, Annotated Code of the Public General Laws
See Annotated Code of Maryland.

Maryland, Annual Report and Official Opinions of the Attorney General
See Annual Report and Official Opinions of the Attorney General of Maryland.

Maryland Appellate Reports
Ab.:   Md. App.

–Cite to A.2d, if therein; otherwise, cite to Md. App.

–Give parallel citations, if at all, only in documents submitted to
Maryland state courts. See Bluebook rules 10.3.1 and B5.1.3; see also
Md. R. App. Rev. 8-504(a)(1), which requires only a citation to Md.
App.

In documents submitted to Maryland state courts, cite as follows:
Lebac v. Lebac, 109 Md. App. 396, 675 A.2d 131 (1996). –Case
Citation.

Lebac v. Lebac, 109 Md. App. 396, 397, 675 A.2d 131, 132
(1996). –Page Citation.

In all other documents, cite as follows:
Lebac v. Lebac, 675 A.2d 131 (Md. Ct. Spec. App. 1996). –Case
Citation.

Lebac v. Lebac, 675 A.2d 131, 132 (Md. Ct. Spec. App. 1996).
–Page Citation.

Maryland Bar Journal
Ab.:   Md. B.J.

Ex.:   Gary I. Strausberg, Punitive Damages: Another View, Md. B.J., Jan.-
Feb. 1992, at 8. –Article Citation.

Gary I. Strausberg, Punitive Damages: Another View, Md. B.J., Jan.-
Feb. 1992, at 8, 9. –Page Citation.

Maryland Code of Regulations
See Code of Maryland Regulations.

Maryland Constitution
Ab.:   Md. Const. art.   , §   .

Ex.:   Md. Const. art. III, § 38. –"Cite constitutional provisions currently in
force without a date." Bluebook rule 11.

Md. Const. art. XI, § 3 (repealed 1956). –"If the cited provision has
been repealed, either indicate parenthetically the fact and date of repeal
or cite the repealing provision in full." Bluebook rule 11.

In law review footnotes, the titles of books and the names of cases, except for procedural
phrases, are not underlined. See Bluebook rule 2.1(a) & (b). Further, the following are in
large and small capitals: codes, restatements, standards, constitutions, periodicals, authors of
books, titles of books, the abbreviated names of codes, most legislative materials except for
bills and resolutions, codified ordinances, model codes, court rules, and sentencing guidelines.
Refer to The Bluebook.

Md. Const. art. VIII, § 7 (amended 1982). –"When citing a provision that has been subsequently amended, either indicate parenthetically the fact and date of amendment or cite the amending provision in full." Bluebook rule 11.

–The Declaration of Rights is listed separately from the body of the constitution. The form for the citation is that used by Maryland Law Review.

Maryland Journal of Contemporary Legal Issues
Ab.:   Md. J. Contemp. Legal Issues

Ex.:   Edmund G. Howe, Advanced Directives After Cruzan: Are More Too Many?, 2 Md. J. Contemp. Legal Issues 299 (1991). –Article Citation.

Edmund G. Howe, Advanced Directives After Cruzan: Are More Too Many?, 2 Md. J. Contemp. Legal Issues 299, 316 (1991). –Page Citation.

Maryland Journal of International Law and Trade
Ab.:   Md. J. Int'l L. & Trade

Ex.:   Joseph P. Hornyak, Treatment of Dumped Imports From Nonmarket Economy Countries, 15 Md. J. Int'l L. & Trade 23 (1991). –Article Citation.

Joseph P. Hornyak, Treatment of Dumped Imports From Nonmarket Economy Countries, 15 Md. J. Int'l L. & Trade 23, 25 (1991). –Page Citation.

Maryland Law Review
Ab.:   Md. L. Rev.

Ex.:   Richard H. McNeer, Nontidal Wetlands Protection in Maryland and Virginia, 51 Md. L. Rev. 105 (1992). –Article Citation.

Richard H. McNeer, Nontidal Wetlands Protection in Maryland and Virginia, 51 Md. L. Rev. 105, 131 (1992). –Page Citation.

Maryland Register
Ab.:   vol. no. Md. Reg. page no. (month day, year)

Ex.:   30 Md. Reg. 1665 (Nov. 14, 2003).

Maryland Reports
Ab.:   Md.

–Cite to A. or A.2d, if therein; otherwise, cite to Md.

–Give parallel citations, if at all, only in documents submitted to Maryland state courts. See Bluebook rules 10.3.1 and B5.1.3; see also Md. R. App. Rev. 8-504(a)(1), which requires only a citation to Md.

In documents submitted to Maryland state courts, cite as follows:

Manner v. Stephenson, 342 Md. 461, 677 A.2d 560 (1996). –Case Citation.

In citing cases in law review footnotes, abbreviate any word listed in table T.6; the names of "states, countries, and other geographical units" unless they are named parties; and any other words of eight or more letters "if substantial space is thereby saved and the result is unambiguous." Bluebook rule 10.2.2. On the other hand, in citing cases in text, abbreviate only widely known acronyms and the following words: "&," "Ass'n," "Bros.," "Co.," "Corp.," "Inc.," "Ltd.," and "No." Bluebook rule 10.2.1(c).

<u>Manner v. Stephenson</u>, 342 Md. 461, 463, 677 A.2d 560, 561 (1996). –Page Citation.

In all other documents, cite as follows:

<u>Manner v. Stephenson</u>, 677 A.2d 560 (Md. 1996). –Case Citation.

<u>Manner v. Stephenson</u>, 677 A.2d 560, 561 (Md. 1996). –Page Citation.

Maryland Session Laws

See Laws of Maryland and Michie's Annotated Code of Maryland Advance Legislative Service (LexisNexis).

Massachusetts Advance Legislative Service (LexisNexis)

Ab.: year-pamph. no. Mass. Adv. Legis. Serv. page no. (LexisNexis)

Ex.: Act of June 7, 2005, ch. 29, 2005-2 Mass. Adv. Leg. Serv. 41 (LexisNexis) (concerning sick leave bank). –Citation to an entire session law.

–<u>See</u> <u>Bluebook</u> rule 12.4.

–"Cite to Mass. Acts., if therein." <u>Bluebook</u> table T.1, p. 214.

Massachusetts Annotated Laws

See Annotated Laws of Massachusetts (LexisNexis) and Massachusetts General Laws Annotated (West).

Massachusetts Appeals Court Reports

Ab.: Mass. App. Ct.

–Cite to N.E. or N.E.2d, if therein; otherwise, cite to Mass. App. Ct.

–Give parallel citations, if at all, only in documents submitted to Massachusetts state courts. <u>See</u> <u>Bluebook</u> rules 10.3.1 and B5.1.3; see also Mass. R. App. P. 16(g) and Mass. Dist. & Mun. App. Div. R. 16(g), which require only a citation to Mass. App. Ct.

In documents submitted to Massachusetts state courts, cite as follows:

<u>Cournoyer v. Cournoyer</u>, 40 Mass. App. Ct. 302, 663 N.E.2d 863 (1996). –Case Citation.

<u>Cournoyer v. Cournoyer</u>, 40 Mass. App. Ct. 302, 304, 663 N.E.2d 863, 865 (1996). –Page Citation.

In all other documents, cite as follows:

<u>Cournoyer v. Cournoyer</u>, 663 N.E.2d 863 (Mass. App. Ct. 1996). –Case Citation.

<u>Cournoyer v. Cournoyer</u>, 663 N.E.2d 863, 865 (Mass. App. Ct. 1996). –Page Citation.

In law review footnotes, the titles of books and the names of cases, except for procedural phrases, are not underlined. <u>See</u> <u>Bluebook</u> rule 2.1(a) & (b). Further, the following are in large and small capitals: codes, restatements, standards, constitutions, periodicals, authors of books, titles of books, the abbreviated names of codes, most legislative materials except for bills and resolutions, codified ordinances, model codes, court rules, and sentencing guidelines. Refer to <u>The Bluebook</u>.

Massachusetts Appellate Decisions (1941-1977)
    Ab.:   Mass. App. Dec.
    Ex.:   LaBonte v. Miller, 159 Mass. App. Dec. 128 (1976). –Case Citation.

Massachusetts Appellate Division, Advance Sheets (1975-1979)
    Ab.:   year Mass. App. Div. Adv. Sh. page no.

Massachusetts Appellate Division Reports
    Ab.:   Mass. App. Div.
    Ex.:   Oyegbola v. Desimone, 1995 Mass. App. Div. 91 (Dist. Ct.). –Case Citation.

           Oyegbola v. Desimone, 1995 Mass. App. Div. 91, 93 (Dist. Ct.). –Page Citation.

Massachusetts Code of Regulations
    See Code of Massachusetts Regulations.

Massachusetts Constitution
    Ab.:   Mass. Const. pt. , ch. , § , art. .

           Mass. Const. amend. art. . –Citing to amendments.

    Ex.:   Mass. Const. pt. 2, ch. 1, § 1, art. IV. –"Cite constitutional provisions currently in force without a date." Bluebook rule 11.

           –"If the cited provision has been repealed, either indicate parenthetically the fact and date of repeal or cite the repealing provision in full." Bluebook rule 11.

           Mass. Const. pt. 1, art. XXVI (amended 1982).

           Mass. Const. pt. 1, art. XXVI, amended by Mass. Const. amend. art. CXVI. –"When citing a provision that has been subsequently amended, either indicate parenthetically the fact and date of amendment or cite the amending provision in full." Bluebook rule 11.

Massachusetts General Laws
    See General Laws of Massachusetts (Mass. Bar Ass'n/West), Massachusetts General Laws Annotated (West), and Annotated Laws of Massachusetts (LexisNexis).

Massachusetts General Laws Annotated (West)
    Ab.:   Mass. Gen. Laws Ann. ch. x, § x (West year)
    Ex.:   Mass. Gen. Laws Ann. ch. 231, § 108 (West 2000).
           Mass. Gen. Laws Ann. ch. 244, § 14 (West Supp. 2000).
           –"Cite to Mass. Gen. Laws, if therein." Bluebook table T.1, p. 214.
           –For proper citation form in papers submitted to Massachusetts courts, see Mass. R. App. P. 16(g) and Mass. Dist. & Mun. App. Div. R. 16(g).

In citing cases in law review footnotes, abbreviate any word listed in table T.6; the names of "states, countries, and other geographical units" unless they are named parties; and any other words of eight or more letters "if substantial space is thereby saved and the result is unambiguous." Bluebook rule 10.2.2. On the other hand, in citing cases in text, abbreviate only widely known acronyms and the following words: "&," "Ass'n," "Bros.," "Co.," "Corp.," "Inc.," "Ltd.," and "No." Bluebook rule 10.2.1(c).

Massachusetts Law Review
Ab.:   Mass. L. Rev.

Ex.:   Michael D. Weisman & Ben T. Clements, <u>Protecting Reasonable</u>
<u>Expectations: Proof of Lost Profits for New Businesses</u>, 76 Mass. L.
Rev. 186 (1991). –Article Citation.

Michael D. Weisman & Ben T. Clements, <u>Protecting Reasonable</u>
<u>Expectations: Proof of Lost Profits for New Businesses</u>, 76 Mass. L.
Rev. 186, 188 (1991). –Page Citation.

Massachusetts Legislative Service (West)
Ab.:   year Mass. Legis. Serv. page no. (West)

Ex.:   Act of Aug. 9, 1995, ch. 296, 1996 Mass. Legis. Serv. 971 (West) (use
of firearms during hunting season). –Citation to an entire session law.

Act of Aug. 9, 1995, ch. 297, sec. 2, ch. 175 § 108, 1996 Mass. Legis.
Serv. 972, 972 (West) (health insurance). –Citation to a session law
amending prior act.

–<u>See</u> <u>Bluebook</u> rule 12.4.

–"Cite to Mass. Acts, if therein." <u>Bluebook</u> table T.1, p. 214.

Massachusetts Register
Ab.:   issue no. Mass. Reg. page no. (month day, year)

Ex.:   952 Mass. Reg. 54 (July 19, 2003).

Massachusetts Reports
Ab.:   Mass.

–Cite to N.E. or N.E.2d, if therein; otherwise, cite to Mass.

–Give parallel citations, if at all, only in documents submitted to
Massachusetts state courts. <u>See</u> <u>Bluebook</u> rules 10.3.1 and B5.1.3; see
also Mass. R. App. P. 16(g) and Mass. Dist. & Mun. App. Div. R.
16(g), which require only a citation to Mass.

In documents submitted to Massachusetts state courts, cite as follows:
<u>Moakley v. Eastwick</u>, 423 Mass. 52, 666 N.E.2d 505 (1996).
–Case Citation.

<u>Moakley v. Eastwick</u>, 423 Mass. 52, 54, 666 N.E.2d 505, 506
(1996). –Page Citation.

In all other documents, cite as follows:
<u>Moakley v. Eastwick</u>, 666 N.E.2d 505 (Mass. 1996). –Case
Citation.

<u>Moakley v. Eastwick</u>, 666 N.E.2d 505, 506 (Mass. 1996). –Page
Citation.

Massachusetts Session Laws
See Acts and Resolves of Massachusetts, Massachusetts Legislative Service
(West), and Massachusetts Advance Legislative Service (LexisNexis).

In law review footnotes, the titles of books and the names of cases, except for procedural
phrases, are not underlined. <u>See</u> <u>Bluebook</u> rule 2.1(a) & (b). Further, the following are in
large and small capitals: codes, restatements, standards, constitutions, periodicals, authors of
books, titles of books, the abbreviated names of codes, most legislative materials except for
bills and resolutions, codified ordinances, model codes, court rules, and sentencing guidelines.
Refer to <u>The Bluebook</u>.

Massachusetts Supplement
    Ab.:   Mass. Supp.

Master of the Rolls
    Ab.:   M.R.

Matthew Bender
    Ab.:   MB

McCormick on Evidence
    –Do not abbreviate the title.

    Ex.:   2 McCormick on Evidence § 217 (John W. Strong ed., 5th ed. 1999). –Section Citation.

        2 McCormick on Evidence § 217, at 30 (John W. Strong ed., 5th ed. 1999). –Page Citation.

        2 McCormick on Evidence § 217, at 30 n.8 (John W. Strong ed., 5th ed. 1999). –Footnote Citation.

McGeorge Law Review
    Ab.:   McGeorge L. Rev.

    Ex.:   Harrison C. Dunning, California Instream Flow Protection Law: Then and Now, 36 McGeorge L. Rev. 363 (2005). –Article Citation.

        Harrison C. Dunning, California Instream Flow Protection Law: Then and Now, 36 McGeorge L. Rev. 363, 384 (2005). –Page Citation.

McGill Law Journal
    Ab.:   McGill L.J.

    Ex.:   Brian R. Cheffins, European Community Company and Securities Law: A Canadian Perspective, 36 McGill L.J. 1282 (1991). –Article Citation.

        Brian R. Cheffins, European Community Company and Securities Law: A Canadian Perspective, 36 McGill L.J. 1282, 1292 (1991). –Page Citation.

McKinney's Consolidated Laws of New York Annotated (West)
    Ab.:   N.Y. [subject] Law § (McKinney year)

        See Bluebook table T.1, pp. 222-24, for the abbreviation of each subject.

    Ex.:   N.Y. Educ. § 1718 (McKinney 2000).

        N.Y. C.P.L.R. § 2310 (McKinney Supp. 2000).

        –For proper citation form in papers submitted to New York courts, see prefatory pages to McKinney's Consolidated Laws of New York Annotated volumes and New York Law Reports Style Manual, § 3.1 (2002), available at http://www.courts.state.ny.us/reporter/2002_style_manual.pdf.

In citing cases in law review footnotes, abbreviate any word listed in table T.6; the names of "states, countries, and other geographical units" unless they are named parties; and any other words of eight or more letters "if substantial space is thereby saved and the result is unambiguous." Bluebook rule 10.2.2. On the other hand, in citing cases in text, abbreviate only widely known acronyms and the following words: "&," "Ass'n," "Bros.," "Co.," "Corp.," "Inc.," "Ltd.," and "No." Bluebook rule 10.2.1(c).

McKinney's New York Session Law News (West)
Ab.: year N.Y. Sess. Laws page no. (McKinney)
Ex.: Act of June 7, 2005, ch. 91, 2005 N.Y. Sess. Laws 645 (McKinney) (relating to tax law). –Citation to an entire session law.

Act of June 7, 2005, ch. 91, sec. 2, § 1262-n, 2005 N.Y. Sess. Laws 645, 645 (McKinney) (relating to tax law). –Citation to a section of a session law amending prior act.

–See Bluebook rule 12.4.

–"Cite to N.Y. Laws, if therein." Bluebook table T.1, p. 224.

Media Law Reporter (Bureau of National Affairs)
Ab.: Media L. Rep. (BNA)
Ex.: Cable News Network, Inc. v. Video Monitoring Servs. of Am., [Decisions] Media L. Rep. (BNA) (19 Media L. Rep.) 1289 (11th Cir. Sept. 4, 1991). –Cite to looseleaf material.

Moffatt v. Brown, 15 Media L. Rep. (BNA) 1601 (Alaska 1988). –Cite to bound material.

–The above examples are proper if the case is not yet available in, or is not reported in, an official or West reporter, a public domain citation, or in a widely used computer database.

Mediator
Ab.: Med.

Medical Trial Technique Quarterly
Ab.: Med. Trial Tech. Q.
Ex.: Carol Docan, Risk & Responsibility: The Working Woman Makes the Choice, Not the Employer, 38 Med. Trial Tech. Q. 145 (1991). –Article Citation.

Carol Docan, Risk & Responsibility: The Working Woman Makes the Choice, Not the Employer, 38 Med. Trial Tech. Q. 145, 148 (1991). –Page Citation.

Medicare and Medicaid Guide (Commerce Clearing House)
Ab.: Medicare & Medicaid Guide (CCH)
Ex.: Sutphin Pharmacy, Inc. v. Rhodes, 5 Medicare & Medicaid Guide (CCH) ¶ 39,496 (S.D.N.Y. July, 26, 1991). –Cite to looseleaf material.
Westchester Gen. Hosp. v. HEW, [1979-1 Transfer Binder] Medicare & Medicaid Guide (CCH) ¶ 29,526 (M.D. Fla. 1979). –Cite to transfer binder material.

–The above examples are proper if the case is not yet available in, or is not reported in, an official or West reporter, a public domain citation, or in a widely used computer database.

In law review footnotes, the titles of books and the names of cases, except for procedural phrases, are not underlined. See Bluebook rule 2.1(a) & (b). Further, the following are in large and small capitals: codes, restatements, standards, constitutions, periodicals, authors of books, titles of books, the abbreviated names of codes, most legislative materials except for bills and resolutions, codified ordinances, model codes, court rules, and sentencing guidelines. Refer to The Bluebook.

Medicine and Law
Ab.:   Med. & L.

Ex.:   Arie Scholosberg, <u>Issues in Psychiatric Prevention and Enforcement of Treatment</u>, 10 Med. & L. 483 (1991). –Article Citation.

        Arie Scholosberg, <u>Issues in Psychiatric Prevention and Enforcement of Treatment</u>, 10 Med. & L. 483, 484 (1991). –Page Citation.

Medicine, Science, and the Law
Ab.:   Med. Sci. & L.

Ex.:   Alec Samuels, <u>Informed Consent: The Law</u>, 32 Med. Sci & L. 35 (1992). –Article Citation.

        Alec Samuels, <u>Informed Consent: The Law</u>, 32 Med. Sci & L. 35, 38 (1992). –Page Citation.

Medico-Legal Journal
Ab.:   Medico-Legal J.

Ex.:   Michael Kirby, <u>Aids and Prisons in Australia</u>, 59 Medico-Legal J. 252 (1991). –Ariticle Citation.

        Michael Kirby, <u>Aids and Prisons in Australia</u>, 59 Medico-Legal J. 252, 253 (1991). –Page Citation.

medium neutral citations
See public domain citations.

Melanesian Law Journal
Ab.:   Melanesian L.J.

Ex.:   Isikeli Mataitoga, <u>Constitution-Making in Fiji: The Search for a Practical Solution</u>, 19 Melanesian L.J. 43 (1991). –Article Citation.

        Isikeli Mataitoga, <u>Constitution-Making in Fiji: The Search for a Practical Solution</u>, 19 Melanesian L.J. 43, 45-46 (1991). –Page Citation.

Melbourne University Law Review
Ab.:   Melb. U. L. Rev.

Ex.:   Richard G. Fox, <u>The Meaning of Proportionality in Sentencing</u>, 19 Melb. U. L. Rev. 489 (1994). –Article Citation.

        Richard G. Fox, <u>The Meaning of Proportionality in Sentencing</u>, 19 Melb. U. L. Rev. 489, 497 (1994). –Page Citation.

memoranda, basic citation forms
See examples included on the facing page next to the inside back cover and on the inside back cover of <u>The Bluebook</u>.

memoranda, typeface conventions for legal memoranda
See <u>Bluebook</u> rules B13 and 7.

In citing cases in law review footnotes, abbreviate any word listed in table T.6; the names of "states, countries, and other geographical units" unless they are named parties; and any other words of eight or more letters "if <u>substantial</u> space is thereby saved and the result is unambiguous." <u>Bluebook</u> rule 10.2.2. On the other hand, in citing cases in text, abbreviate only widely known acronyms and the following words: "&," "Ass'n," "Bros.," "Co.," "Corp.," "Inc.," "Ltd.," and "No." <u>Bluebook</u> rule 10.2.1(c).

Memorandum, citation to
> Ab.:   Mem.
>
> Ex.:   (Pl.'s Reply Mem. 4).

See Bluebook rule B10 and table BT.1.

Note: See Bluebook rule 10.8.3 for citing litigation materials from another case.

memorandum decision
> Ab.:   mem.
>
> Ex.:   Farlow v. Hardin, 61 F.3d 30 (11th Cir. 1995) (mem.).

Memphis State University Law Review
> Ab.:   Mem. St. U. L. Rev.
>
> Ex.:   Robert Banks, Jr. & Elizabeth T. Collins, Judicial Notice in Tennessee, 21 Mem. St. U. L. Rev. 431 (1991). –Article Citation.
>
> Robert Banks, Jr. & Elizabeth T. Collins, Judicial Notice in Tennessee, 21 Mem. St. U. L. Rev. 431, 435 (1991). –Page Citation.

See University of Memphis Law Review.

Mercer Law Review
> Ab.:   Mercer L. Rev.
>
> Ex.:   Robert M. Travis & Edward C. Brewer, III, Products Liability Law in Georgia Including Recent Developments, 43 Mercer L. Rev. 27 (1991). –Article Citation.
>
> Robert M. Travis & Edward C. Brewer, III, Products Liability Law in Georgia Including Recent Developments, 43 Mercer L. Rev. 27, 33-34 (1991). –Page Citation.

Merit Systems Protection Board Reporter (U.S.)
> Ab.:   M.S.P.B.
>
> Ex.:   Gometz v. Office of Pers. Mgmt., 69 M.S.P.B. 115 (1995).

Metropolitan
> Ab.:   Metro.

Michie's Alabama Code Advance Legislative Service
> Ab.:   year-pamph. no. Ala. Adv. Legis. Serv. page no. (LexisNexis)
>
> Ex.:   Act effective Apr. 13, 2005, No. 73, 2005-2 Ala. Legis. Serv. 37 (West) (relating to the Ala. Sunset Law). –Citation to an entire session law.
>
> Act effective Apr. 13, 2005, No. 73, sec. 7, 2005-2 Ala. Legis. Serv. 37, 38 (West) (relating to the Ala. Sunset Law). –Citation to a section of a session law.
>
> –See Bluebook rule 12.4.
>
> –"Cite to Ala. Laws, if therein." Bluebook table T.1, p.198.

In law review footnotes, the titles of books and the names of cases, except for procedural phrases, are not underlined. See Bluebook rule 2.1(a) & (b). Further, the following are in large and small capitals: codes, restatements, standards, constitutions, periodicals, authors of books, titles of books, the abbreviated names of codes, most legislative materials except for bills and resolutions, codified ordinances, model codes, court rules, and sentencing guidelines. Refer to The Bluebook.

Michie's Alabama Code (LexisNexis)
    Ab.:   Ala. Code § x-x-x (year)
    Ex.:   Ala. Code § 36-19-12 (2002)
             Ala. Code § 40-21-11 (Supp. 2005)

Michie's Annotated Code of Maryland (LexisNexis)
    Ab.:   Md. Code Ann., [subject] § x-x (LexisNexis year)
    Ex.:   Md. Code Ann., Pub. Util. Cos. § 7-512 (LexisNexis 2003)
             Md. Code Ann., Tax-Prop. § 6-301 (LexisNexis Supp. 2004)
See <u>Bluebook</u> table T.1, p. 213, for the abbreviation of each subject matter.

Michie's Annotated Code of Maryland Advance Legislative Service (LexisNexis)
    Ab.:   year-pamph. no. Md. Code Ann. Adv. Legis. Serv. page no.
             (LexisNexis)
    Ex.:   Act of Apr. 26, 2005, ch. 170, 2005-2 Md. Code Ann. Adv. Legis.
             Serv. 262 (LexisNexis) (concerning vehicle laws). –Citation to an
             entire session law.
             Act of Apr. 26, 2005, ch. 170, sec. 1, § 24-102, 2005-2 Md. Code Ann.
             Adv. Legis. Serv. 262, 262 (LexisNexis). –Citation to a section of a
             session law amending prior act.
  See <u>Bluebook</u> rule 12.4.
          –"Cite to Md. Laws, if therein." <u>Bluebook</u> table T.1, p. 213.

Michie's Annotated Statutes of New Mexico (LexisNexis)
    Ab.:   N.M. Stat. Ann. § x-x-x (LexisNexis year)
    Ex.:   N.M. Stat. Ann. § 50-9-4 (LexisNexis 2003)
             N.M. Stat. Ann. § 52-1-22 (LexisNexis Supp. 2005).
             – "Cite to N.M. Stat., if therein." <u>Bluebook</u> table T.1, p. 220
             –For proper citation form in papers submitted to New Mexico courts,
             see N.M. S. Ct. R. 23-112(E).

Michie's Hawaii Revised Statutes Annotated (LexisNexis)
    Ab.:   Haw. Rev. Stat. Ann. § x-x (LexisNexis)
    Ex.:   Haw. Rev. Stat. Ann. § 334-31 (LexisNexis 2000)
             Haw. Rev. Stat. Ann. § 710-1077 (LexisNexis Supp. 1999)
             –"Cite to Haw. Rev. Stat., if therein." <u>Bluebook</u> table T.1, p. 206.

Michie's Hawaii Revised Statutes Annotated Advance Legislative Service (LexisNexis)
    Ab.:   year-pamph. no. Haw. Rev. Stat. Ann. Adv. Legis. Serv. page no.
             (LexisNexis)

In citing cases in law review footnotes, abbreviate any word listed in table T.6; the names of "states, countries, and other geographical units" unless they are named parties; and any other words of eight or more letters "if <u>substantial</u> space is thereby saved and the result is unambiguous." <u>Bluebook</u> rule 10.2.2. On the other hand, in citing cases in text, abbreviate only widely known acronyms and the following words: "&," "Ass'n," "Bros.," "Co.," "Corp.," "Inc.," "Ltd.," and "No." <u>Bluebook</u> rule 10.2.1(c).

Ex.:   Act of July 10, 2004, No. 201, 2004-3 Haw. Rev. Stat. Ann. Adv. Legis. Serv. 305 (LexisNexis) (relating to transportation). –Citation to an entire session law.

Act of July 10, 2004, No. 201, sec. 3, 2004-3 Haw. Rev. Stat. Ann. Adv. Legis. Serv. 305, 308 (LexisNexis) (relating to transportation). –Citation to a section of a session law.

See Bluebook rule 12.4.

–"Cite to Haw. Sess. Laws, if therein." Bluebook table T.1, p. 207.

Michie's Kentucky Revised Statutes Advance Legislative Service (LexisNexis)
Ad.:   year-pamph. no. Ky. Rev. Stat. Adv. Legis. Serv. page no. (LexisNexis)

Ex.:   Act of Apr. 9, 2002, ch. 300, 2002-2 Ky. Rev. Stat. Adv. Leg. Serv. 444 (LexisNexis). –Citation to an entire session law.

Act of Apr. 9, 2002, ch. 300, sec. 2, § 151B.020, 2002-2 Ky. Rev. Stat. Adv. Leg. Serv. 444, 448 (LexisNexis). –Citation to a section of a session law amending prior act.

See Bluebook rule 12.4.

–"Cite to Ky. Acts, if therein." Bluebook table T.1, p. 210.

Michie's Kentucky Revised Statutes Annotated (LexisNexis)
Ab.:   Ky. Rev. Stat. Ann. § x-x (LexisNexis)

Ex.:   Ky. Rev. Stat. Ann. § 376.110 (LexisNexis 2002)

Ky. Rev. Stat. Ann. § 154.45-020 (LexisNexis Supp. 2005)

–For proper citation form in papers submitted to Kentucky courts, see Ky. R. Civ. P. 76.12(4)(g).

Michie's Virginia Advance Legislative Service (LexisNexis)
Ab.:   year-pamph. no. Va. Adv. Legis. Serv. page no. (LexisNexis)

Ex.:   Act of Mar. 28, 2005, Ch. 862, 2005-4 Va. Adv. Legis. Serv. 187 (LexisNexis) (relating to unpaid bills). –Citation to an entire session law.

Act of Mar. 28, 2005, Ch. 862, sec. 1, § 46.2-819.1, 2005-4 Va. Adv. Legis. Serv. 187, 187 (LexisNexis) (relating to unpaid bills). –Citation to a section of a session law amending prior act.

See Bluebook rule 12.4.

–"Cite to Va. Acts, if therein." Bluebook table T.1, p.237.

Michie's West Virginia Code Advance Legislative Service (LexisNexis)
Ab.:   year-pamph. no. W. Va. Code Adv. Legis. Serv. page no. (LexisNexis)

In law review footnotes, the titles of books and the names of cases, except for procedural phrases, are not underlined. See Bluebook rule 2.1(a) & (b). Further, the following are in large and small capitals: codes, restatements, standards, constitutions, periodicals, authors of books, titles of books, the abbreviated names of codes, most legislative materials except for bills and resolutions, codified ordinances, model codes, court rules, and sentencing guidelines. Refer to The Bluebook.

Ex.:   Act of Apr. 8, 2005, No. 3328, 2005-2 W. Va. Code Adv. Legis. Serv.
         715 (LexisNexis) (relating to Office of Emergency Services). –Citation
         to an entire session law.

         Act of Apr. 8, 2005, No. 3328, sec. 1, § 15-5-13, 2005-2 W. Va. Code
         Adv. Legis. Serv. 715, 719 (LexisNexis) (relating to Office of
         Emergency Services). –Citation to a section of a session law amending
         prior act.

         –"Cite to W.Va. Acts, if therein." Bluebook table T.1, p. 238.

See Bluebook rule 12.4.

Michie's West Virginia Code Annotated (LexisNexis)
Ab.:   W. Va. Code Ann. § x-x-x (LexisNexis)
Ex.:   W. Va. Code Ann. § 22-4-24 (LexisNexis 2002)

         W. Va. Code Ann. § 61-10-11 (LexisNexis Supp. 2004)

         – "Cite to W. Va. Code, if therein." Bluebook table T.1, p.238

Michigan Administrative Code (Conway Greene)
Ab.:   Mich. Admin. Code r. x.x (Year)
Ex.:   Mich. Admin. Code r. 259-801 (2001).

Michigan Advance Legislative Service (LexisNexis)
Ab.:   year-pamph. no. Mich. Adv. Legis. Serv. page no. (LexisNexis)
Ex.:   Act of July 20, 2005, No. 89, sec. 1, § 331.531, 2005-3 Mich. Adv.
         Legis. Serv. 89 (LexisNexis). Citation to a section of a session law
         amending prior act.

See Bluebook rule 12.4.

         – "Cite to Mich. Pub. Acts, if therein." Bluebook table T.1, p. 215.

Michigan Appeals Reports
Ab.:   Mich. App.
         –Cite to N.W. or N.W.2d, if therein; otherwise, cite to Mich. App.
         –Give parallel citations only in documents submitted to Michigan state
           courts. See Bluebook rules 10.3.1 and B5.1.3; see also Michigan
           Uniform System of Citation pt. I(A), available at
           http://www.icle.org/michlaw/rules/ao/1987-2.html, which requires a
           parallel citation.
         In documents submitted to Michigan state courts, cite as follows:
             People v. Sawyer, 215 Mich. App. 183, 545 N.W.2d 6 (1996).
             –Case Citation.
             People v. Sawyer, 215 Mich. App. 183, 185, 545 N.W.2d 6, 8
             (1996). –Page Citation.
         In all other documents, cite as follows:
             People v. Sawyer, 545 N.W.2d 6 (Mich. Ct. App. 1996). –Case
             Citation.

In citing cases in law review footnotes, abbreviate any word listed in table T.6; the names of
"states, countries, and other geographical units" unless they are named parties; and any other
words of eight or more letters "if substantial space is thereby saved and the result is
unambiguous." Bluebook rule 10.2.2. On the other hand, in citing cases in text, abbreviate
only widely known acronyms and the following words: "&," "Ass'n," "Bros.," "Co.," "Corp.,"
"Inc.," "Ltd.," and "No." Bluebook rule 10.2.1(c).

People v. Sawyer, 545 N.W.2d 6, 8 (Mich. Ct. App. 1996). –Page Citation.

Michigan Bar Journal
Ab.:   Mich. B.J.
Ex.:   Steven E. Goren, The Workers' Compensation Exclusive Remedy Rule and Its Exceptions, 71 Mich. Bar J. 59 (1992). –Article Citation.
Steven E. Goren, The Workers' Compensation Exclusive Remedy Rule and Its Exceptions, 71 Mich. Bar J. 59, 60 (1992). –Page Citation.

Michigan, Biennial Report of the Attorney General
See Opinions of the Attorney General of Michigan.

Michigan Business Law Journal
Ab.:   Mich. Bus. L.J.

Michigan Compiled Laws (1979)
Ab.:   Mich. Comp. Laws § x.x (year)
For proper citation form in papers submitted to Michigan courts, see Michigan Uniform System of Citation pt. I(B)(2)(a), available at http://www.icle.org/michlaw/rules/ao/1987-2.html.

Michigan Compiled Laws Annotated (West)
Ab.:   Mich. Comp. Laws Ann. § x.x (West year)
Ex.:   Mich. Comp. Laws Ann. § 331.1 (West 1999).
Mich. Comp. Laws Ann. § 333.5131 (West Supp. 2000).
"Cite to Mich. Comp. Laws, if therein." See Bluebook table T.1, p. 215.
–For proper citation form in papers submitted to Michigan courts, see Michigan Uniform System of Citation pt. I(B)(2)(a), available at http://www.icle.org/michlaw/rules/ao/1987-2.html.

Michigan Compiled Laws Service (LexisNexis)
Ab.:   Mich. Comp. Laws Serv. § x.x (LexisNexis year)
Ex.:   Mich. Comp. Laws Serv. § 125.277 (LexisNexis 2003)
Mich. Comp. Laws Serv. § 801.82 (LexisNexis Supp. 2004)
"Cite to Mich. Comp. Laws, if therein." See Bluebook table T.1, p. 215.
–For proper citation form in papers submitted to Michigan courts, see Michigan Uniform System of Citation pt. I(B)(2)(a), available at http://www.icle.org/michlaw/rules/ao/1987-2.html.

Michigan Constitution
Ab.:   Mich. Const. art.   , §   .

In law review footnotes, the titles of books and the names of cases, except for procedural phrases, are not underlined. See Bluebook rule 2.1(a) & (b). Further, the following are in large and small capitals: codes, restatements, standards, constitutions, periodicals, authors of books, titles of books, the abbreviated names of codes, most legislative materials except for bills and resolutions, codified ordinances, model codes, court rules, and sentencing guidelines. Refer to The Bluebook.

Ex.:   Mich. Const. art. I, § 23. –"Cite constitutional provisions currently in force without a date." <u>Bluebook</u> rule 11.

–"If the cited provision has been repealed, either indicate parenthetically the fact and date of repeal or cite the repealing provision in full." <u>Bluebook</u> rule 11.

Mich. Const. art. I, § 15 (amended 1978). –"When citing a provision that has been subsequently amended, either indicate parenthetically the fact and date of amendment or cite the amending provision in full." <u>Bluebook</u> rule 11.

Mich. Const. of 1908, art. II, § 22 (1963). –"Cite constitutions that have been totally superseded by year of adoption; if the specific provision cited was adopted in a different year, give that year parenthetically." <u>Bluebook</u> rule 11.

Michigan Corporate Finance and Business Law Journal
Ab.:   Mich. Corp. Fin. & Bus. L.J.

Michigan Court of Claims Reports (1938-1942)
Ab.:   Mich. Ct. Cl.

Michigan Journal of International Law
Ab.:   Mich. J. Int'l L.

Ex.:   Gerald L. Neuman, <u>"We Are the People": Alien Suffrage in German and American Perspective</u>, 13 Mich. J. Int'l L. 259 (1992). –Article Citation.

Gerald L. Neuman, <u>"We Are the People": Alien Suffrage in German and American Perspective</u>, 13 Mich. J. Int'l L. 259, 261 (1992). –Page Citation.

Michigan Journal of Race & Law
Ab.:   Mich. J. Race & L.

Ex.:   George H. Taylor, <u>Racism as "The Nation's Crucial Sin": Theology and Derrick Bell</u>, 9 Mich. J. Race & L. 269 (2004). –Article Citation.

George H. Taylor, <u>Racism as "The Nation's Crucial Sin": Theology and Derrick Bell</u>, 9 Mich. J. Race & L. 269, 306-08 (2004). –Page Citation.

Michigan Law Review
Ab.:   Mich. L. Rev.

Ex.:   James A. Gardner, <u>The Failed Discourse of State Constitutionalism</u>, 90 Mich. L. Rev. 761 (1992). –Article Citation.

James A. Gardner, <u>The Failed Discourse of State Constitutionalism</u>, 90 Mich. L. Rev. 761, 767-68 (1992). –Page Citation.

Michigan Legislative Service (West)
Ab.:   year Mich. Legis. Serv. page no. (West).

In citing cases in law review footnotes, abbreviate any word listed in table T.6; the names of "states, countries, and other geographical units" unless they are named parties; and any other words of eight or more letters "if <u>substantial</u> space is thereby saved and the result is unambiguous." <u>Bluebook</u> rule 10.2.2. On the other hand, in citing cases in text, abbreviate only widely known acronyms and the following words: "&," "Ass'n," "Bros.," "Co.," "Corp.," "Inc.," "Ltd.," and "No." <u>Bluebook</u> rule 10.2.1(c).

Ex.:   Act of June 26, 1996, No. 335, 1996 Mich. Legis. Serv. 912 (West) (relating to education of children of veterans). –Citation to an entire session law.

Act of Feb. 26, 1996, No. 63, sec. 1, § 287-261, 1996 Mich. Legis. Serv. 130, 130-31 (West) (relating to dogs and the protection of livestock and poultry from damage by dogs). –Citation to a session law amending prior act.

See Bluebook rule 12.4.

–"Cite to Mich. Pub. Acts, if therein." Bluebook table T.1, p. 215.

Michigan Register
Ab.:   issue no. Mich. Reg. page no. (month day, year)

Ex.:   22 Mich. Reg. 18 (Dec. 15, 2003)

Michigan Reports
Ab.:   Mich.

–Cite to N.W. or N.W.2d, if therein; otherwise, cite to Mich.

–Give parallel citations only in documents submitted to Michigan state courts. See Bluebook rules 10.3.1 and B5.1.3; see also Michigan Uniform System of Citation pt. I(A), available at http://www.icle.org/michlaw/rules/ao/1987-2.html, which requires a parallel citation.

In documents submitted to Michigan state courts, cite as follows:

Meatte v. Meatte, 450 Mich. 987, 548 N.W.2d 638 (1996). –Case Citation.

Meatte v. Meatte, 450 Mich. 987, 988, 548 N.W.2d 638, 639 (1996). –Page Citation.

In all other documents, cite as follows:

Meatte v. Meatte, 548 N.W.2d 638 (Mich. 1996). –Case Citation.

Meatte v. Meatte, 548 N.W.2d 638, 639 (Mich. 1996). –Page Citation.

Michigan Session Laws
See Public and Local Acts of the Legislature of the State of Michigan, Michigan Advance Legislative Service (LexisNexis), and Michigan Legislative Service (West).

Michigan State Law Review
Ab.:   Mich. St. L. Rev.

In law review footnotes, the titles of books and the names of cases, except for procedural phrases, are not underlined. See Bluebook rule 2.1(a) & (b). Further, the following are in large and small capitals: codes, restatements, standards, constitutions, periodicals, authors of books, titles of books, the abbreviated names of codes, most legislative materials except for bills and resolutions, codified ordinances, model codes, court rules, and sentencing guidelines. Refer to The Bluebook.

Ex.:   Samuel T. Morison, <u>The Crooked Timber of Liberal Democracy</u>, 2005
Mich. St. L. Rev. 461. –Article Citation.

Samuel T. Morison, <u>The Crooked Timber of Liberal Democracy</u>, 2005
Mich. St. L. Rev. 461, 479. –Page Citation.

Milbank Quarterly, The
Ab.:   Milbank Q.

Ex.:   Robert A. Aronowitz, <u>Lyme Disease: The Social Construction of a New
Disease and Its Social Consequence</u>, 69 Milbank Q. 79 (1991).
–Article Citation.

Robert A. Aronowitz, <u>Lyme Disease: The Social Construction of a New
Disease and Its Social Consequence</u>, 69 Milbank Q. 79, 82-83 (1991).
–Page Citation.

Military Law Reporter
Ab.:   Mil. L. Rep.

Military Law Review
Ab.:   Mil. L. Rev.

Ex.:   Major David S. Jones, <u>Fraternization: Time for a Rational Department
of Defense Standard</u>, 135 Mil. L. Rev. 37 (1992). –Article Citation.

Major David S. Jones, <u>Fraternization: Time for a Rational Department
of Defense Standard</u>, 135 Mil. L. Rev. 37, 41-43 (1992). –Page
Citation.

Minnesota Constitution
Ab.:   Minn. Const. art.   , §   .

Ex.:   Minn. Const. art. XIII, § 5. –"Cite constitutional provisions currently in
force without a date." <u>Bluebook</u> rule 11.

–"If the cited provision has been repealed, either indicate
parenthetically the fact and date of repeal or cite the repealing provision
in full." <u>Bluebook</u> rule 11.

Minn. Const. art. VIII, § 14 (amended 1990). –"When citing a
provision that has been subsequently amended, either indicate
parenthetically the fact and date of amendment or cite the amending
provision in full." <u>Bluebook</u> rule 11.

Minn. Const. of 1857 art. IX, § 16 (1974). –"Cite constitutions that
have been totally superseded by year of adoption; if the specific
provision cited was adopted in a different year, give that year
parenthetically." <u>Bluebook</u> rule 11.

Minnesota Court of Appeals
–Cite to N.W.2d
Ab.:   Minn. Ct. App.

In citing cases in law review footnotes, abbreviate any word listed in table T.6; the names of
"states, countries, and other geographical units" unless they are named parties; and any other
words of eight or more letters "if <u>substantial</u> space is thereby saved and the result is
unambiguous." <u>Bluebook</u> rule 10.2.2. On the other hand, in citing cases in text, abbreviate
only widely known acronyms and the following words: "&," "Ass'n," "Bros.," "Co.," "Corp.,"
"Inc.," "Ltd.," and "No." <u>Bluebook</u> rule 10.2.1(c).

Ex.: Wenzel v. Mathies, 542 N.W.2d 634 (Minn. Ct. App. 1996). –Case
Citation.

Wenzel v. Mathies, 542 N.W.2d 634, 638 (Minn. Ct. App. 1996).
–Page Citation.

Minnesota Journal of Global Trade
Ab.: Minn. J. Global Trade

Ex.: Paul Frantz, International Employment: Antidiscrimination Law Should
Follow Employees Abroad, 14 Minn. J. Global Trade 227 (2005).
–Article Citation.

Paul Frantz, International Employment: Antidiscrimination Law Should
Follow Employees Abroad, 14 Minn. J. Global Trade 227, 247-48
(2005). –Page Citation.

Minnesota Law Review
Ab.: Minn. L. Rev.

Ex.: Jay L. Westbrook, Two Thoughts About Insider Preferences, 76 Minn.
L. Rev. 73 (1991). –Article Citation.

Jay L. Westbrook, Two Thoughts About Insider Preferences, 76 Minn.
L. Rev. 73, 93 (1991). –Page Citation.

Minnesota, Opinions of the Attorney General
See Opinions of the Attorney General of Minnesota.

Minnesota Reports
Ab.: Minn.

–Discontinued after 312 Minn. 602 (1977).

–Cite to N.W. or N.W.2d, if therein; otherwise, cite to Minn.

–Give parallel citations only in documents submitted to Minnesota state
courts. See Bluebook rules 10.3.1 and B5.1.3. Because Minnesota
Supreme Court opinions provide parallel citations to Minnesota
decisions where they exist, we advise giving a parallel citation in
documents submitted to Minnesota state courts.

–Through 312 Minn. 602 (1977), cite as follows

In documents submitted to Minnesota state courts:

Tyra v. Cheney, 129 Minn. 428, 152 N.W. 835 (1915). –Case
Citation.

Tyra v. Cheney, 129 Minn. 428, 430, 152 N.W. 835, 838 (1915).
–Page Citation.

In all other documents:

Tyra v. Cheney, 152 N.W. 835 (Minn. 1915). –Case Citation.

Tyra v. Cheney, 152 N.W. 835, 838 (Minn. 1915). –Page Citation.

In law review footnotes, the titles of books and the names of cases, except for procedural
phrases, are not underlined. See Bluebook rule 2.1(a) & (b). Further, the following are in
large and small capitals: codes, restatements, standards, constitutions, periodicals, authors of
books, titles of books, the abbreviated names of codes, most legislative materials except for
bills and resolutions, codified ordinances, model codes, court rules, and sentencing guidelines.
Refer to The Bluebook.

–After 312 Minn. 602 (1977), cite as follows:

In all documents:

> In re Jensen, 542 N.W.2d 627 (Minn. 1996). –Case Citation.
>
> In re Jensen, 542 N.W.2d 627, 628 (Minn. 1996). –Page Citation.

Minnesota Rules

Ab.: Minn. R. x.x (year)

Ex.: Minn. R. 1205.0300 (1997).

Minnesota Session Laws

See Laws of Minnesota and Minnesota Session Law Service (West).

Minnesota Session Law Service (West)

Ab.: year Minn. Sess. Law Serv. page no. (West)

Ex.: Act effective Sept. 1, 2000, ch. 488, 2000 Minn. Sess. Law Serv. 1236 (West) (public safety). –Citation to an entire session law.

Act effective Sept. 1, 2000, ch. 488, art. 6, sec. 5, § 169.2151, 2000 Minn. Sess. Law Serv. 1236 (West) (public safety). –Citation to a session law amending a prior act.

–"Cite to Minn. Laws, if therein." Bluebook table T.1, p. 215.

Minnesota State Register

Ab.: vol. no. Minn. Reg. page no. (month day, year)

Ex.: 28 Minn. Reg. 1034 (Feb. 17, 2004)

Minnesota Statutes

Ab.: Minn. Stat. § x.x (year)

Ex.: Minn. Stat. § 611.07 (1978).

Minn. Stat. § 363.01 (Supp. 1979).

–"Cite to Minn. Stat., if therein." Bluebook table T.1, p. 215.

Mississippi Code Annotated 1972 Annotated (LexisNexis)

Ab.: Miss. Code Ann. § x-x-x (LexisNexis year)

Ex.: Miss. Code Ann. § 49-5-31 (LexisNexis 2003).

Miss. Code Ann. § 79-11-519 (LexisNexis Supp. 2004).

Mississippi College Law Review

Ab.: Miss. C. L. Rev.

Ex.: Stephen L. Mikochik, Employment Discrimination Against Americans With Disabilities, 11 Miss. C. L. Rev. 255 (1991). –Article Citation.

Stephen L. Mikochik, Employment Discrimination Against Americans With Disabilities, 11 Miss. C. L. Rev. 255, 256-57 (1991). –Page Citation.

Mississippi Constitution

Ab.: Miss. Const. art.   , §   .

In citing cases in law review footnotes, abbreviate any word listed in table T.6; the names of "states, countries, and other geographical units" unless they are named parties; and any other words of eight or more letters "if substantial space is thereby saved and the result is unambiguous." Bluebook rule 10.2.2. On the other hand, in citing cases in text, abbreviate only widely known acronyms and the following words: "&," "Ass'n," "Bros.," "Co.," "Corp.," "Inc.," "Ltd.," and "No." Bluebook rule 10.2.1(c).

Ex.: Miss. Const. art. 8, § 201. –"Cite constitutional provisions currently in force without a date." Bluebook rule 11.

Miss. Const. art. 2, § 3 (repealed 1990). –"If the cited provision has been repealed, either indicate parenthetically the fact and date of repeal or cite the repealing provision in full." Bluebook rule 11.

Miss. Const. art. 10, § 225 (amended 1990). –"When citing a provision that has been subsequently amended, either indicate parenthetically the fact and date of amendment or cite the amending provision in full." Bluebook rule 11.

Mississippi Court of Appeals
Ab.: Miss. Ct. App.

–Cite to So. or So. 2d, if therein; in addition, give public domain citation if available.

–Until July 1, 1997, when a public domain format was adopted, cite as follows:

In all documents:

Church v. Massey, 697 So. 2d 407 (Miss. Ct. App. 1997). –Case Citation.

Church v. Massey, 697 So. 2d 407, 413 (Miss. Ct. App. 1997). –Page Citation.

–From July 1, 1997, cite as follows:

In all documents:

Woodard v. State, 98-KA-01768-COA, 765 So. 2d 573 (Miss. Ct. App. 2000) –Case Citation.

Woodard v. State, 98-KA-01768-COA, ¶12, 765 So. 2d 573, 575 (Miss. Ct. App. 2000) –Pinpoint Citation.

See Bluebook rules 10.3.1, 10.3.3, B5.1.3, and table T.1; see also Miss. R. App. P. 28(e).

Mississippi General Laws Advance Sheets (LexisNexis)
Ab.: year-pamph. no. Miss. Laws Adv. Sh. page no. (LexisNexis)

Ex.: Act of July 1, 2005, Ch. 483, 2005-2 Miss. Laws Adv. Sh. 78 (LexisNexis) (concerning motor vehicle insurance). –Citation to an entire session law.

Act of July 1, 2005, Ch. 483, sec. 1, § 65-15-3, 2005-2 Miss. Laws Adv. Sh. 78, 78 (LexisNexis) (concerning motor vehicle insurance). –Citation to a section of a session law amending prior act.

–See Bluebook rule 12.4.

–"Cite to Miss. Laws, if therein." Bluebook table T.1, p. 216.

In law review footnotes, the titles of books and the names of cases, except for procedural phrases, are not underlined. See Bluebook rule 2.1(a) & (b). Further, the following are in large and small capitals: codes, restatements, standards, constitutions, periodicals, authors of books, titles of books, the abbreviated names of codes, most legislative materials except for bills and resolutions, codified ordinances, model codes, court rules, and sentencing guidelines. Refer to The Bluebook.

Mississippi Government Register (Weil)
Ab.:   issue no. Miss. Gov't Reg. page no. (Weil month year)

Mississippi Law Journal
Ab.:   Miss. L.J.

Ex.:   George Cochran, <u>Rule 11: The Road To Amendment</u>, 61 Miss. L.J. 5 (1991). –Article Citation.

George Cochran, <u>Rule 11: The Road To Amendment</u>, 61 Miss. L.J. 5, 19 (1991). –Page Citation.

Mississippi Session Laws
See General Laws of Mississippi.

Mississippi Supreme Court
Ab.:   Miss.

–Cite to So. or So. 2d, if therein; otherwise, cite to Miss. Give public domain citation if available. Otherwise, give parallel citations only in documents submitted to Mississippi state courts as required by Miss. R. App. P. 28(e).

–Through 254 Miss. 944 (1966), cite as follows:

In documents submitted to Mississippi state courts:

<u>Carter v. Witherspoon</u>, 156 Miss. 597, 126 So. 388 (1930). –Case Citation.

<u>Carter v. Witherspoon</u>, 156 Miss. 597, 603, 126 So. 388, 389 (1930). –Page Citation.

In all other documents:

<u>Carter v. Witherspoon</u>, 126 So. 388 (Miss. 1930). –Case Citation.

<u>Carter v. Witherspoon</u>, 126 So. 388, 389 (Miss. 1930). –Page Citation.

–After 254 Miss. 944 (1966), and until July 1, 1997, when a public domain format was adopted, cite as follows:

In all documents:

<u>Bumpers v. Carruth</u>, 669 So. 2d 83 (Miss. 1996). –Case Citation.

<u>Bumpers v. Carruth</u>, 669 So. 2d 83, 84 (Miss. 1996). –Page Citation.

–From July 1, 1997, cite as follows:

In all documents:

<u>Grant v. Grant</u>, 99-CA-00736-SCT, 765 So. 2d 1263 (Miss. 2000). –Case Citation.

In citing cases in law review footnotes, abbreviate any word listed in table T.6; the names of "states, countries, and other geographical units" unless they are named parties; and any other words of eight or more letters "if <u>substantial</u> space is thereby saved and the result is unambiguous." <u>Bluebook</u> rule 10.2.2. On the other hand, in citing cases in text, abbreviate only widely known acronyms and the following words: "&," "Ass'n," "Bros.," "Co.," "Corp.," "Inc.," "Ltd.," and "No." <u>Bluebook</u> rule 10.2.1(c).

Grant v. Grant, 99-CA-00736-SCT, ¶ 6, 765 So. 2d 1263, 1266 (Miss. 2000). –Pinpoint Citation.

See Bluebook rules 10.3.1, 10.3.3, B5.1.3, and table T.1; see also Miss. R. App. P. 28(e).

Missouri Annotated Statutes, Vernon's
See Vernon's Annotated Missouri Statutes (West).

Missouri Appeals Reports
Ab.:   Mo. App.

–Discontinued after 241 Mo. App. 1244 (1952).

–Cite to S.W., S.W.2d, or S.W.3d, if therein; otherwise, cite to Mo. App.

–Give parallel citations only in documents submitted to Missouri state courts. See Bluebook rules 10.3.1 and B5.1.3. Because Missouri Supreme Court opinions provide parallel citations to Missouri decisions where they exist, we advise giving a parallel citation in documents submitted to Missouri state courts.

–Through 241 Mo. App. 1244 (1952), cite as follows:

In documents submitted to Missouri state courts:

Williams v. Williams, 240 Mo. App. 336, 205 S.W.2d 949 (1947). –Case Citation.

Williams v. Williams, 240 Mo. App. 336, 342-43, 205 S.W.2d 949, 953-54 (1947). –Page Citation.

In all other documents:

Williams v. Williams, 205 S.W.2d 949 (Mo. Ct. App. 1947). –Case Citation.

Williams v. Williams, 205 S.W.2d 949, 953-54 (Mo. Ct. App. 1947). –Page Citation.

–After 241 Mo. 1244 (1952), cite as follows:

In all documents:

Rhodes v. Blair, 919 S.W.2d 561 (Mo. Ct. App. 1996). –Case Citation.

Rhodes v. Blair, 919 S.W.2d 561, 562 (Mo. Ct. App. 1996). –Page Citation.

Missouri Code of State Regulations Annotated
Ab.:   Mo. Code Regs. Ann. tit. , § x-x.x (year)

Ex.:   Mo. Code Regs. Ann. tit. 1, § 15-1.204 (1995).

Missouri Constitution
Ab.:   Mo. Const. art.   , §   .

In law review footnotes, the titles of books and the names of cases, except for procedural phrases, are not underlined. See Bluebook rule 2.1(a) & (b). Further, the following are in large and small capitals: codes, restatements, standards, constitutions, periodicals, authors of books, titles of books, the abbreviated names of codes, most legislative materials except for bills and resolutions, codified ordinances, model codes, court rules, and sentencing guidelines. Refer to The Bluebook.

Ex.:   Mo. Const. art. IX, § 1(a). –"Cite constitutional provisions currently in
          force without a date." Bluebook rule 11.

          Mo. Const. art. XI, § 5 (repealed 1988) –"If the cited provision has
          been repealed, either indicate parenthetically the fact and date of repeal
          or cite the repealing provision in full." Bluebook rule 11.

          Mo. Const. art. IV, § 12 (amended 1990). –"When citing a provision
          that has been subsequently amended, either indicate parenthetically the
          fact and date of amendment or cite the amending provision in full."
          Bluebook rule 11.

          Mo. Const. of 1875 art. V, § 25. –"Cite constitutions that have been
          totally superseded by year of adoption; if the specific provision cited
          was adopted in a different year, give that year parenthetically."
          Bluebook rule 11.

Missouri Law Review
Ab.:   Mo. L. Rev.

Ex.:   Marvin Hill, Jr. & Emily Delacenserie, Procrustean Beds and
          Draconian Choices: Lifestyle Regulations and Officious Intermeddlers–
          Bosses, Workers, Courts and Labor Arbitrators, 57 Mo. L. Rev. 51
          (1992). –Article Citation.

          Marvin Hill, Jr. & Emily Delacenserie, Procrustean Beds and
          Draconian Choices: Lifestyle Regulations and Officious Intermeddlers–
          Bosses, Workers, Courts and Labor Arbitrators, 57 Mo. L. Rev. 51,
          55-56 (1992). –Page Citation.

Missouri Legislative Service (West)
Ab.:   year Mo. Legis. Serv. page no. (West)

Ex.:   Act of July 10, 1996, No. 145, 1996 Mo. Legis. Serv. 704 (West)
          (unemployment compensation income tax). —Citation to an entire
          session law.

          Act of July 10, 1996, No. 145, Sec. A, ch. 288.379, 1996 Mo. Legis.
          Serv. 704, 704 (West) (unemployment compensation income tax).
          –Citation to a section of a session law amending prior act.

          –See Bluebook rule 12.4.

          –"Cite to Mo. Laws, if therein." Bluebook table T.1, p. 217.

Missouri Register
Ab.:   vol. no. Mo. Reg. page no. (month day, year)
Ex.:   29 Mo. Reg. 282 (Feb. 17, 2004).

Missouri Reports
Ab.:   Mo.

          –Discontinued after 365 Mo. 1238 (1956).

          –Cite to S.W., S.W.2d, or S.W.3d, if therein; otherwise, cite to Mo.

In citing cases in law review footnotes, abbreviate any word listed in table T.6; the names of
"states, countries, and other geographical units" unless they are named parties; and any other
words of eight or more letters "if substantial space is thereby saved and the result is
unambiguous." Bluebook rule 10.2.2. On the other hand, in citing cases in text, abbreviate
only widely known acronyms and the following words: "&," "Ass'n," "Bros.," "Co.," "Corp.,"
"Inc.," "Ltd.," and "No." Bluebook rule 10.2.1(c).

–Give parallel citations only in documents submitted to Missouri state courts. See Bluebook rules 10.3.1 and B5.1.3. Because Missouri Supreme Court opinions provide parallel citations to Missouri decisions where they exist, we advise giving a parallel citation in documents submitted to Missouri state courts.

–Through 365 Mo. 1238 (1956), cite as follows:

In documents submitted to Missouri state courts:

> State v. Anderson, 252 Mo. 83, 158 S.W. 817 (1913). –Case Citation.
>
> State v. Anderson, 252 Mo. 83, 87, 158 S.W. 817, 821 (1913). –Page Citation.

In all other documents:

> State v. Anderson, 158 S.W. 817 (Mo. 1913). –Case Citation.
>
> State v. Anderson, 158 S.W. 817, 821 (Mo. 1913). –Page Citation.

–After 365 Mo. 1238 (1956), cite as follows:

In all documents:

> Hollis v. Blevins, 926 S.W.2d 683 (Mo. 1996). –Case Citation.
>
> Hollis v. Blevins, 926 S.W.2d 683, 684 (Mo. 1996). –Page Citation.

Missouri Revised Statutes

Ab.: Mo. Rev. Stat. § x.x (year)

Ex.: Mo. Rev. Stat. § 506.500 (1978).

Missouri Session Laws

See Laws of Missouri and Missouri Legislative Service.

Model Business Corporation Act Annotated

Ex.: 2 Model Bus. Corp. Act Ann. § 8.09 (1994). –Citation to a section of the act.

2 Model Bus. Corp. Act Ann. § 8.09, at 8-83 (1994). –Citation to a page within the act.

See Bluebook rule 12.8.5.

Model Code of Evidence

See American Law Institute Model Code of Evidence.

Model Code of Professional Responsibility (ABA)

See American Bar Association Model Code of Professional Responsibility.

Model Land Development Code

See American Law Institute Model Land Development Code.

In law review footnotes, the titles of books and the names of cases, except for procedural phrases, are not underlined. See Bluebook rule 2.1(a) & (b). Further, the following are in large and small capitals: codes, restatements, standards, constitutions, periodicals, authors of books, titles of books, the abbreviated names of codes, most legislative materials except for bills and resolutions, codified ordinances, model codes, court rules, and sentencing guidelines. Refer to The Bluebook.

Model Penal Code (ALI)
    See American Law Institute Model Penal Code.

Modern Child Custody Practice, 2d ed., by Jeff Atkinson
    –Do not abbreviate the title.
    Ex.:   2 Jeff Atkinson, Child Custody Practice, § 10-8 (2d ed. 2000).
            –Section Citation.
            2 Jeff Atkinson, Child Custody Practice, § 10-8, at 10-17 (2d ed. 2000).
            –Page Citation.

Model Rules of Professional Conduct (ABA)
    See American Bar Association Model Rules of Professional Conduct.

Modern Law Review
    Ab.:   Mod. L. Rev.
            M.L.R. [U.K.]
    Ex.:   Yves Dezalay, Territorial Battles and Tribal Disputes, 54 Mod. L. Rev.
            792 (1991). –Article Citation.
            Yves Dezalay, Territorial Battles and Tribal Disputes, 54 Mod. L. Rev.
            792, 794 (1991). –Page Citation.

Modern Legal Systems Cyclopedia, by Kenneth R. Redden
    –Do not abbreviate the title.
    Ex.:   3 Kenneth R. Redden, Modern Legal Systems Cyclopedia 3.250.31
            (1994). –Page Citation.
            3 Kenneth R. Redden, Modern Legal Systems Cyclopedia 3.250.31
            n.106 (1994). –Footnote Citation.

Modern Trials, by Melvin M. Belli, Sr.
    –Do not abbreviate the title.
    Ex.:   3 Melvin M. Belli, Sr., Modern Trials § 50.33 (2d ed. 1982). –Section
            Citation.
            3 Melvin M. Belli, Sr., Modern Trials § 50.33, at 316 (2d ed. 1982).
            –Page Citation.

modified
    Ab.:   Do not abbreviate title.
    Ex.:   Bonner v. Coughlin, 517 F.2d 1311 (7th Cir. 1975), modified en banc,
            545 F.2d 565 (7th Cir. 1976).

Monash University Law Review
    Ab.:   Monash U. L. Rev.

In citing cases in law review footnotes, abbreviate any word listed in table T.6; the names of "states, countries, and other geographical units" unless they are named parties; and any other words of eight or more letters "if substantial space is thereby saved and the result is unambiguous." Bluebook rule 10.2.2. On the other hand, in citing cases in text, abbreviate only widely known acronyms and the following words: "&," "Ass'n," "Bros.," "Co.," "Corp.," "Inc.," "Ltd.," and "No." Bluebook rule 10.2.1(c).

Ex.: Dennis Rose, <u>Judicial Reasonings and Responsibilities in Constitutional Cases</u>, 20 Monash U. L. Rev. 195 (1994). –Article Citation.

Dennis Rose, <u>Judicial Reasonings and Responsibilities in Constitutional Cases</u>, 20 Monash U. L. Rev. 195, 205 (1994). –Page Citation.

Montana Administrative Register
Ab.: issue no. Mont. Admin. Reg. page no. (month day, year)

Ex.: 3 Mont. Admin. Reg. 339 (Feb. 12, 2004).

Montana Administrative Rules
See Administrative Rules of Montana.

Montana Code Annotated
Ab.: Mont. Code Ann. § x-x-x (year)

Ex.: Mont. Code Ann. § 16-11-101 (1999).

–For proper citation form in papers submitted to Montana courts, see preface to vol. 1, Mont. Code Ann. (2004).

Montana Constitution
Ab.: Mont. Const. art.   , §   .

Ex.: Mont. Const. art. IX, § 1. –"Cite constitutional provisions currently in force without a date." <u>Bluebook</u> rule 11.

–"If the cited provision has been repealed, either indicate parenthetically the fact and date of repeal or cite the repealing provision in full." <u>Bluebook</u> rule 11.

Mont. Const. art. XI, § 5 (amended 1978). –"When citing a provision that has been subsequently amended, either indicate parenthetically the fact and date of amendment or cite the amending provision in full." <u>Bluebook</u> rule 11.

Montana Law Review
Ab.: Mont. L. Rev.

Ex.: Scot Schermerhorn, <u>Efficiency vs. Equity in Close Corporations</u>, 52 Mont. L. Rev. 73 (1991). –Article Citation.

Scot Schermerhorn, <u>Efficiency vs. Equity in Close Corporations</u>, 52 Mont. L. Rev. 73, 78-80 (1991). –Page Citation.

Montana Session Laws
See Laws of Montana.

Montana Supreme Court
Ab.: Mont.

In law review footnotes, the titles of books and the names of cases, except for procedural phrases, are not underlined. See <u>Bluebook</u> rule 2.1(a) & (b). Further, the following are in large and small capitals: codes, restatements, standards, constitutions, periodicals, authors of books, titles of books, the abbreviated names of codes, most legislative materials except for bills and resolutions, codified ordinances, model codes, court rules, and sentencing guidelines. Refer to <u>The Bluebook</u>.

–Cite to P., P.2d, or P.3d, if therein; otherwise, cite to Mont. Give public domain citation if available. Otherwise, give parallel citations only in documents submitted to Montana state courts.

–Until January 1, 1998, when a public domain format was adopted, cite as follows:

In all documents submitted to Montana state courts:

Berlin v. Boedecker, 268 Mont. 444, 887 P.2d 1180 (1994). –Case Citation.

Berlin v. Boedecker, 268 Mont. 444, 445, 887 P.2d 1180, 1181 (1994). –Page Citation.

In all other documents:

Berlin v. Boedecker, 887 P.2d 1180 (Mont. 1994). –Case Citation.

Berlin v. Boedecker, 887 P.2d 1180, 1181 (Mont. 1994). –Page Citation.

–After January 1, 1998, cite as follows:

In documents submitted to Montana state courts:

Benjamin v. Torgerson, 1999 MT 216, 295 Mont. 528, 985 P.2d 734 –Case Citation.

Benjamin v. Torgerson, 1999 MT 216, ¶ 15, 295 Mont. 528, ¶ 15, 985 P.2d 734, ¶ 15 –Pinpoint Citation.

In all other documents:

Benjamin v. Torgerson, 1999 MT 216, 985 P.2d 734. –Case Citation.

Benjamin v. Torgerson, 1999 MT 216, ¶ 15, 985 P.2d 734, 737. –Pinpoint Citation.

See Bluebook rules 10.3.1, 10.3.3, B5.1.3, and table T.1; see also Order in re Opinion Forms & Citation Standards of the Sup. Ct. of Mont. (Dec. 16, 1997).

Monthly Labor Review
Ab.:   Monthly Lab. Rev.

Ex.:   Craig Hukill, Labor and the Supreme Court: Significant Issues of 1991-92, Monthly Lab. Rev., Jan. 1992, at 34. –Article Citation.

Craig Hukill, Labor and the Supreme Court: Significant Issues of 1991-92, Monthly Lab. Rev., Jan. 1992, at 34, 35. –Page Citation.

Moore on International Law
See Digest of International Law, by John B. Moore.

Moore's Federal Practice and Procedure
–Do not abbreviate the title.

In citing cases in law review footnotes, abbreviate any word listed in table T.6; the names of "states, countries, and other geographical units" unless they are named parties; and any other words of eight or more letters "if substantial space is thereby saved and the result is unambiguous." Bluebook rule 10.2.2. On the other hand, in citing cases in text, abbreviate only widely known acronyms and the following words: "&," "Ass'n," "Bros.," "Co.," "Corp.," "Inc.," "Ltd.," and "No." Bluebook rule 10.2.1(c).

Ex.: 7 James Wm. Moore et al., <u>Moore's Federal Practice and Procedure</u> § 60.26[4] (2d ed. 1990). –Section Citation.

7 James Wm. Moore et al., <u>Moore's Federal Practice and Procedure</u> § 60.26[4], at 60-252 (2d ed. 1990). –Page Citation.

12 James Wm. Moore et al., <u>Moore's Federal Practice and Procedure</u> § 350.01[2], at 3-7 n.8 (2d ed. 1990). –Footnote Citation.

6 James Wm. Moore et al., <u>Moore's Federal Practice and Procedure</u> § 24.20 (3d ed. 2005). –Section Citation.

Motion, citation to
Ab.: Mot.

Ex.: (Def.'s Mot. Dismiss ¶ 10).

(Def.'s Mot. Summ. J. 2).

<u>See</u> <u>Bluebook</u> rule B10 and table BT.1.

Note: See <u>Bluebook</u> rule 10.8.3 for citing litigation materials from another case.

Motor Carrier Cases Reports (1936-1986)
See Interstate Commerce Commission Reports, Motor Carrier Cases.

Multistate and Multinational Estate Planning, by Jeffrey A. Schoenblum.
–Do not abbreviate the title

Ex.: 1 Jeffrey A. Schoenblum, <u>Multistate and Multinational Estate Planning</u> § 9.06 (1999). –Section Citation.

1 Jeffrey A. Schoenblum, <u>Multistate and Multinational Estate Planning</u> § 9.06, at 409 (1999). –Page Citation.

1 Jeffrey A. Schoenblum, <u>Multistate and Multinational Estate Planning</u> § 9.06, at 409 n.185 (1999). –Footnote Citation.

1 Jeffrey A. Schoenblum, <u>Multistate and Multinational Estate Planning</u> § 6.02[D], at 11 n.27 (Cum. Supp. 2001). –Footnote Citation in Supplement.

Municipal Finance Journal
Ab.: Mun. Fin. J.

Ex.: Amy V. Puelz, <u>Call Provisions and the Cost Effectiveness of Bond Insurance</u>, 12 Mun. Fin. J., at 23 (1991). –Article Citation.

Amy V. Puelz, <u>Call Provisions and the Cost Effectiveness of Bond Insurance</u>, 12 Mun. Fin. J., at 23, 25 (1991). –Page Citation.

Mutual Funds Guide (Commerce Clearing House)
Ab.: Mut. Funds Guide (CCH)

In law review footnotes, the titles of books and the names of cases, except for procedural phrases, are not underlined. <u>See</u> <u>Bluebook</u> rule 2.1(a) & (b). Further, the following are in large and small capitals: codes, restatements, standards, constitutions, periodicals, authors of books, titles of books, the abbreviated names of codes, most legislative materials except for bills and resolutions, codified ordinances, model codes, court rules, and sentencing guidelines. Refer to <u>The Bluebook</u>.

N

NARAS Journal
Ab.: NARAS J.
Ex.: Stephen F. Rhode, <u>The Power of Suggestion: Does the First Amendment Protect Subliminal Rock Lyrics?</u>, NARAS J., Spring 1991, at 21. –Article Citation.

Stephen F. Rhode, <u>The Power of Suggestion: Does the First Amendment Protect Subliminal Rock Lyrics?</u>, NARAS J., Spring 1991, at 21, 27. –Page Citation.

National Black Law Journal
Ab.: Nat'l Black L.J.
Ex.: Joseph E. Broadus, <u>No Disparate Impact: Gunther's Significant But Ignored Limitation on Sex-Based Pay Disparity Claims Under Title VII</u>, 12 Nat'l Black L.J. 10 (1990). –Article Citation.

Joseph E. Broadus, <u>No Disparate Impact: Gunther's Significant But Ignored Limitation on Sex-Based Pay Disparity Claims Under Title VII</u>, 12 Nat'l Black L.J. 10, 14 (1990). –Page Citation.

National Civic Review
Ab.: Nat'l Civic Rev.
Ex.: Bruce H. Kirschner, <u>Electronic Democracy in the 21st Century</u>, 80 Nat'l Civic Rev. 406 (1991). –Article Citation.

Bruce H. Kirschner, <u>Electronic Democracy in the 21st Century</u>, 80 Nat'l Civic Rev. 406, 408 (1991). –Page Citation.

National Jewish Law Review
Ab.: Nat'l Jewish L. Rev.
Ex.: Moshe Tendler, <u>Confidentiality: A Biblical Perspective on Rights In Conflict</u>, 4 Nat'l Jewish L. Rev. 1 (1989). –Article Citation.

Moshe Tendler, <u>Confidentiality: A Biblical Perspective on Rights In Conflict</u>, 4 Nat'l Jewish L. Rev. 1, 4 (1989). –Page Citation.

National Labor Relations Board Annual Report
Ab.: NLRB Ann. Rep. (year)
Ex.: 45 NLRB Ann. Rep. 20 (1980).

National Labor Relations Board, Decisions and Orders of the (U.S.) (1935-date)
Ab.: N.L.R.B.

In law review footnotes, the titles of books and the names of cases, except for procedural phrases, are not underlined. <u>See</u> <u>Bluebook</u> rule 2.1(a) & (b). Further, the following are in large and small capitals: codes, restatements, standards, constitutions, periodicals, authors of books, titles of books, the abbreviated names of codes, most legislative materials except for bills and resolutions, codified ordinances, model codes, court rules, and sentencing guidelines. Refer to <u>The Bluebook</u>.

Ex.:   Transport America, Inc., 320 N.L.R.B. 882 (1996).

National Law Journal, The
Ab.:   Nat'l L.J.

Ex.:   Randall Samborn, Case Holds Key to U.S. Competitiveness, Nat'l L.J.,
         Apr. 6, 1992, at 1. –Article Citation.

         Phone Records Are Held to be Not Privileged, Nat'l L.J., Apr. 6, 1992,
         at 6. –News Report.

National Public Employment Reporter
Ab.:   Nat'l Pub. Empl. Rep. (Labor Rel. Press)

National Railroad Adjustment Board 1st-3d Div. (U.S.) (1936-1972)
Ab.:   N.R.A.B. (x Div.)

Ex.:   Order of Ry. Conductors, 15 N.R.A.B. (1st Div.) 198 (1938).

National Tax Journal
Ab.:   Nat'l Tax J.

Ex.:   George R. Zodrow, On the "Traditional" and "New" Views of
         Dividend Taxation, 44 Nat'l Tax J. 497 (1991). –Article Citation.

         George R. Zodrow, On the "Traditional" and "New" Views of
         Dividend Taxation, 44 Nat'l Tax J. 497, 498 (1991). –Page Citation.

National Transportation Safety Board Decisions (U.S.) (1967-date)
Ab.:   N.T.S.B.

Ex.:   Metro Air Sys., 2 N.T.S.B. 285 (1973).

Natural Gas Lawyer's Journal, The
Ab.:   Nat. Gas Law. J.

Ex.:   Bernard J. Kennedy, Utilities and Insurance, Nat. Gas Law. J., Feb.
         1987, at 39. –Article Citation.

         Bernard J. Kennedy, Utilities and Insurance, Nat. Gas Law. J., Feb.
         1987, at 39, 43. –Page Citation.

Natural Resources Journal
Ab.:   Nat. Resources J.

Ex.:   Uday Desai, The Politics of Federal State Relations: The Case of
         Surface Mining Regulations, 31 Nat. Resources J. 785 (1991). –Article
         Citation.

         Uday Desai, The Politics of Federal State Relations: The Case of
         Surface Mining Regulations, 31 Nat. Resources J. 785, 791-94 (1991).
         –Page Citation.

In citing cases in law review footnotes, abbreviate any word listed in table T.6;
the names of "states, countries, and other geographical units" unless they are named parties;
and any other words of eight or more letters "if substantial space is thereby saved and the
result is unambiguous." Bluebook rule 10.2.2. On the other hand, in citing cases in text,
abbreviate only widely known acronyms and the following words: "&," "Ass'n," "Bros.,"
"Co.," "Corp.," "Inc.," "Ltd.," and "No." Bluebook rule 10.2.1(c).

Navajo Nation Code (Lamb Studio)
Ab.:   Navajo Nation Code tit. x, § x (year)

Ex.:   Navajo Nation Code tit. 9, § 3 (1993).

Naval Law Review
Ab.:   Naval L. Rev.

Ex.:   Commander D. Michael Hinkley, <u>Protecting American Interests in Antarctica: The Territorial Claims Dilemma</u>, 39 Naval L. Rev. 43 (1990). –Article Citation.

      Commander D. Michael Hinkley, <u>Protecting American Interests in Antarctica: The Territorial Claims Dilemma</u>, 39 Naval L. Rev. 43, 45 (1990). –Page Citation.

Naval War College Review
Ab.:   Naval War C. Rev.

Ex.:   James P. Terry, <u>The Environment and the Laws of War: The Impact of Desert Storm</u>, 1992 Naval War C. Rev. 61. –Article Citation.

      James P. Terry, <u>The Environment and the Laws of War: The Impact of Desert Storm</u>, 1992 Naval War C. Rev. 61, 64-65. –Page Citation.

Nebraska Administrative Code
Ab.:   x Neb. Admin. Code § x-x (year)

Ex.:   23 Neb. Admin. Code § 2-002.03 (1999).

Nebraska Constitution
Ab.:   Neb. Const. art.   , § .

Ex.:   Neb. Const. art. I, § 4. –"Cite constitutional provisions currently in force without a date." <u>Bluebook</u> rule 11.

      Neb. Const. art. IV, § 9 (repealed 1934). –"If the cited provision has been repealed, either indicate parenthetically the fact and date of repeal or cite the repealing provision in full." <u>Bluebook</u> rule 11.

      Neb. Const. art. I, § 6 (amended 1920). –"When citing a provision that has been subsequently amended, either indicate parenthetically the fact and date of amendment or cite the amending provision in full." <u>Bluebook</u> rule 11.

      Neb. Const. of 1866, art. I, § I. –"Cite constitutions that have been totally superseded by year of adoption; if the specific provision cited was adopted in a different year, give that year parenthetically." <u>Bluebook</u> rule 11.

Nebraska Court of Appeals Reports
Ab.:   Neb. App.

      –Cite to N.W. or N.W.2d, if therein; otherwise, cite to Neb. App.

In law review footnotes, the titles of books and the names of cases, except for procedural phrases, are not underlined. <u>See</u> <u>Bluebook</u> rule 2.1(a) & (b). Further, the following are in large and small capitals: codes, restatements, standards, constitutions, periodicals, authors of books, titles of books, the abbreviated names of codes, most legislative materials except for bills and resolutions, codified ordinances, model codes, court rules, and sentencing guidelines. Refer to <u>The Bluebook</u>.

–Give parallel citations only in documents submitted to Nebraska State Courts. See Bluebook rules 10.3.1 and B5.1.3; see also Neb. Unif. Dist. Ct. R. 5(C), which requires a citation to both Neb. App. and the regional reporter, and Neb. Sup. Ct. R. 9(C)(4) and Neb. Worker's Comp. R. 16(B)(4), which expressly permit a parallel citation.

In documents submitted to Nebraska state courts, cite as follows:

Emerson v. Zagurski, 3 Neb. App. 658, 531 N.W.2d 237 (1995). –Case Citation.

Emerson v. Zagurski, 3 Neb. App. 658, 665, 531 N.W.2d 237, 240 (1995). –Page Citation.

In all other documents, cite as follows:

Emerson v. Zagurski, 531 N.W.2d 237 (Neb. Ct. App. 1995). –Case Citation.

Emerson v. Zagurski, 531 N.W.2d 237, 240 (Neb. Ct. App. 1995). –Page Citation.

Nebraska Government Register
Ab.:   issue no. Neb. Gov't Reg. page no. (Weil month year)

Nebraska Law Review
Ab.:   Neb. L. Rev.

Ex.:   Robert F. Schopp, The Psychotherapist's Duty to Protect the Public: The Appropriate Standard and the Foundation in Legal Theory and Empirical Premises, 70 Neb. L. Rev. 327 (1991). –Article Citation.

Robert F. Schopp, The Psychotherapist's Duty to Protect the Public: The Appropriate Standard and the Foundation in Legal Theory and Empirical Premises, 70 Neb. L. Rev. 327, 332-33 (1991). –Page Citation.

Nebraska Laws
See Laws of Nebraska.

Nebraska Reports
Ab.:   Neb.

–Cite to N.W. or N.W.2d, if therein; otherwise, cite to Neb.

–Give parallel citations only in documents submitted to Nebraska state courts. See Bluebook rules 10.3.1 and B5.1.3; see also Neb. Unif. Dist. Ct. R. 5(C), which requires a citation to both Neb. and the regional reporter, and Neb. Sup. Ct. R. 9(C)(4) and Neb. Worker's Comp. R. 16(B)(4), which expressly permit a parallel citation.

In documents submitted to Nebraska state courts, cite as follows:

In citing cases in law review footnotes, abbreviate any word listed in table T.6; the names of "states, countries, and other geographical units" unless they are named parties; and any other words of eight or more letters "if substantial space is thereby saved and the result is unambiguous." Bluebook rule 10.2.2. On the other hand, in citing cases in text, abbreviate only widely known acronyms and the following words: "&," "Ass'n," "Bros.," "Co.," "Corp.," "Inc.," "Ltd.," and "No." Bluebook rule 10.2.1(c).

Venter v. Venter, 249 Neb. 712, 545 N.W.2d 431 (1996). –Case Citation.

Venter v. Venter, 249 Neb. 712, 715, 545 N.W.2d 431, 433 (1996). –Page Citation.

In documents submitted to Nebraska state courts, cite as follows:

Venter v. Venter, 545 N.W.2d 431 (Neb. 1996). –Case Citation.

Venter v. Venter, 545 N.W.2d 431, 433 (Neb. 1996). –Page Citation.

Nebraska Revised Statutes
See Revised Statutes of Nebraska.

Nebraska Session Laws
See Laws of Nebraska.

Negotiation Journal
Ab.:   Negotiation J.

Ex.:   Michael Wheeler, Fighting the Wimp Image: Why Calls for Negotiation Often Fall on Deaf Ears, 8 Negotiation J. 25 (1992). –Article Citation.

Michael Wheeler, Fighting the Wimp Image: Why Calls for Negotiation Often Fall on Deaf Ears, 8 Negotiation J. 25, 28 (1992). –Page Citation.

Netherlands International Law Review
Ab.:   Neth. Int'l L. Rev.

Ex.:   Kofi Otengkufuor, Starvation as a Means of Warfare in the Liberian Conflict, 41 Neth. Int'l L. Rev. 313 (1994). –Article Citation.

Kofi Otengkufuor, Starvation as a Means of Warfare in the Liberian Conflict, 41 Neth. Int'l L. Rev. 313, 315 (1994). –Page Citation.

Nevada Administrative Code
Ab.:   Nev. Admin. Code § x.x (year).

Ex.:   Nev. Admin. Code § 445A.6682 (2003).

Nevada Constitution
Ab.:   Nev. Const. art.   , §   .

Ex.:   Nev. Const. art. 5, § 5. –"Cite constitutional provisions currently in force without a date." Bluebook rule 11.

Nev. Const. art. 2, § 7 (repealed 1966). –"If the cited provision has been repealed, either indicate parenthetically the fact and date of repeal or cite the repealing provision in full." Bluebook rule 11.

Nev. Const. art. 4, § 24 (amended 1990). –"When citing a provision that has been subsequently amended, either indicate parenthetically the fact and date of amendment or cite the amending provision in full." Bluebook rule 11.

In law review footnotes, the titles of books and the names of cases, except for procedural phrases, are not underlined. See Bluebook rule 2.1(a) & (b). Further, the following are in large and small capitals: codes, restatements, standards, constitutions, periodicals, authors of books, titles of books, the abbreviated names of codes, most legislative materials except for bills and resolutions, codified ordinances, model codes, court rules, and sentencing guidelines. Refer to The Bluebook.

Nevada Law Journal
Ab: Nev. L.J.

Ex: Susan Ayres, <u>The Rhetorics of Takings Cases: It's Mine v. Let's Share</u>, 5 Nev. L.J. 615 (2005). –Article Citation.

Susan Ayres, <u>The Rhetorics of Takings Cases: It's Mine v. Let's Share</u>, 5 Nev. L.J. 615, 633 (2005). –Page Citation.

Nevada Register of Administrative Regulations
Ab.:   vol. no. Nev. Reg. Admin. Regs. reg. no. (month day, year)

Ex.:   91 Nev. Reg. Admin. Regs. R049-04A (Mar. 30, 2005).

Nevada Reports
Ab.:   Nev.

–Cite to P., P.2d, or P.3d, if therein; otherwise, cite to Nev.

–Give parallel citations only in documents submitted to Nevada state courts. <u>See</u> <u>Bluebook</u> rules 10.3.1 and B5.1.3. Because Nevada Supreme Court opinions provide parallel citations to Nevada decisions, we advise giving a parallel citation in documents submitted to Nevada state courts.

In documents submitted to Nevada state courts, cite as follows:

<u>Smimrak v. Garcia-Mendoza</u>, 112 Nev. 246, 912 P.2d 822 (1996). –Case Citation.

<u>Smimrak v. Garcia-Mendoza</u>, 112 Nev. 246, 247, 912 P.2d 822, 824 (1996). –Page Citation.

In all other documents, cite as follows:

<u>Smimrak v. Garcia-Mendoza</u>, 912 P.2d 822 (Nev. 1996). –Case Citation.

<u>Smimrak v. Garcia-Mendoza</u>, 912 P.2d 822, 824 (Nev. 1996). –Page Citation.

Nevada Revised Statutes
Ab.:   Nev. Rev. Stat. § x.x (year)

Ex.:   Nev. Rev. Stat. § 81.3435 (1999).

–For proper citation form in papers submitted to Nevada courts, see Nev. Rev. Stat. § 220.170(4) (2000).

Nevada Revised Statutes Annotated (LexisNexis)
Ab.:   Nev. Rev. Stat. Ann. § x.x (LexisNexis year)

Ex.:   Nev. Rev. Stat. Ann. § 393.280 (LexisNexis 2000).

Nev. Rev. Stat. Ann. § 673.377 (LexisNexis Supp. 2005).

–"Cite to Nev. Rev. Stat., if therein." <u>Bluebook</u> table T.1, p. 218.

–For proper citation form in papers submitted to Nevada courts, see Nev. Rev. Stat. § 220.170(4) (2000).

In citing cases in law review footnotes, abbreviate any word listed in table T.6; the names of "states, countries, and other geographical units" unless they are named parties; and any other words of eight or more letters "if <u>substantial</u> space is thereby saved and the result is unambiguous." <u>Bluebook</u> rule 10.2.2. On the other hand, in citing cases in text, abbreviate only widely known acronyms and the following words: "&," "Ass'n," "Bros.," "Co.," "Corp.," "Inc.," "Ltd.," and "No." <u>Bluebook</u> rule 10.2.1(c).

Nevada Session Laws
See Statutes of Nevada.

Nevada State Bar Journal, The
Ab.:   Nev. St. B.J.

Ex.:   Harvey Dickerson, <u>Governor's Power on Board of Pardons Limited by Consitution,</u> Nev. St. B.J., Oct. 1972, at 4. –Article Citation.

Harvey Dickerson, <u>Governor's Power on Board of Pardons Limited by Consitution,</u> Nev. St. B.J., Oct. 1972, at 4, 5-6. –Page Citation.

New Brunswick Reports (Canada)
See <u>Bluebook</u> table T.2.

Ab.:   N.B.R., N.B.R.2d

Ex.:   <u>Johnson v. Barrieau,</u> 54 N.B.R. 429 (1928) (Can.). –Case Citation.

<u>Baniuk v. Carpenter,</u> 112 N.B.R.2d 332 (1990) (Can.). –Case Citation.

New England Journal of Medicine
Ab.:   New Eng. J. Med.

Ex.:   George E. Thibault, <u>Failure to Resolve a Diagnostic Inconsistency,</u> New Eng. J. Med., July 2, 1992, at 36. –Article Citation.

George E. Thibault, <u>Failure to Resolve a Diagnostic Inconsistency,</u> New Eng. J. Med., July 2, 1992, at 36, 37. –Page Citation.

New England Journal on Criminal and Civil Confinement
Ab.:   New Eng. J. on Crim. & Civ. Confinement

Ex.:   Jim Thomas, <u>The "Reality" of Prisoner Litigation: Repacking the Data,</u> 15 New Eng. J. on Crim. & Civ. Confinement 27 (1989). –Article Citation.

Jim Thomas, <u>The "Reality" of Prisoner Litigation: Repacking the Data,</u> 15 New Eng. J. on Crim. & Civ. Confinement 27, 29 (1989). –Page Citation.

New England Law Review
Ab.:   New Eng. L. Rev.

Ex.:   Edward Greer, <u>Rule II: Substantive Bias in Formal Uniformity After the Supreme Court Trilogy,</u> 26 New Eng. L. Rev. 111 (1991). –Article Citation.

Edward Greer, <u>Rule II: Substantive Bias in Formal Uniformity After the Supreme Court Trilogy,</u> 26 New Eng. L. Rev. 111, 120 (1991). –Page Citation.

New Hampshire Bar Journal
Ab.:   N.H. B.J.

In law review footnotes, the titles of books and the names of cases, except for procedural phrases, are not underlined. <u>See</u> <u>Bluebook</u> rule 2.1(a) & (b). Further, the following are in large and small capitals: codes, restatements, standards, constitutions, periodicals, authors of books, titles of books, the abbreviated names of codes, most legislative materials except for bills and resolutions, codified ordinances, model codes, court rules, and sentencing guidelines. Refer to <u>The Bluebook</u>.

Ex.: Maureen D. Smith, <u>The Fleet Factors Rule of Lender Liability for Hazardous Waste Contamination</u>, 32 N.H. B.J. 142 (1991). –Article Citation.

Maureen D. Smith, <u>The Fleet Factors Rule of Lender Liability for Hazardous Waste Contamination</u>, 32 N.H. B.J. 142, 144 (1991). –Page Citation.

New Hampshire Code of Administrative Rules Annotated (LexisNexis)

Ab.: N.H. Code Admin. R. Ann. [department name as abbreviated in rules] x.x (year)

Ex.: N.H. Code Admin. R. Ann. Env-ws 1120.13 (2003).

New Hampshire Constitution

Ab.: N.H. Const. pt.　, art.　.

Ex.: N.H. Const. pt. 2, art. 89. –"Cite constitutional provisions currently in force without a date." <u>Bluebook</u> rule 11.

N.H. Const. pt. 2, art. 99 (repealed 1980). –"If the cited provision has been repealed, either indicate parenthetically the fact and date of repeal or cite the repealing provision in full." <u>Bluebook</u> rule 11.

N.H. Const. pt. 1, art. 6 (amended 1968). –"When citing a provision that has been subsequently amended, either indicate parenthetically the fact and date of amendment or cite the amending provision in full." <u>Bluebook</u> rule 11.

New Hampshire Government Register (Weil)

Ab.: issue no. N.H. Gov't Reg. page no. (Weil month year)

New Hampshire Reports

Ab.: N.H.

–Cite to A. or A.2d, if therein; otherwise, cite to N.H.

–Give parallel citations, if at all, only in documents submitted to New Hampshire state courts. <u>See</u> <u>Bluebook</u> rules 10.3.1 and B5.1.3; see also N.H. Sup. Ct. R. 16(9), which requires a citation only to N.H.

In documents submitted to New Hampshire state courts, cite as follows:

<u>Mason v. Smith</u>, 140 N.H. 696, 672 A.2d 705 (1996). –Case Citation.

<u>Mason v. Smith</u>, 140 N.H. 696, 698, 672 A.2d 705, 707 (1996). –Page Citation.

In all other documents, cite as follows:

<u>Mason v. Smith</u>, 672 A.2d 705 (N.H. 1996). –Case Citation.

<u>Mason v. Smith</u>, 672 A.2d 705, 707 (N.H. 1996). –Page Citation.

New Hampshire Revised Statutes Annotated (West)

Ab.: N.H. Rev. Stat. Ann. § x:x (year).

In citing cases in law review footnotes, abbreviate any word listed in table T.6; the names of "states, countries, and other geographical units" unless they are named parties; and any other words of eight or more letters "if <u>substantial</u> space is thereby saved and the result is unambiguous." <u>Bluebook</u> rule 10.2.2. On the other hand, in citing cases in text, abbreviate only widely known acronyms and the following words: "&," "Ass'n," "Bros.," "Co.," "Corp.," "Inc.," "Ltd.," and "No." <u>Bluebook</u> rule 10.2.1(c).

Ex.: N.H. Rev. Stat. Ann. § 189:49 (1999).

N.H. Rev. Stat. Ann. § 515:7 (Supp. 2000).

–For proper citation form in papers submitted to New Hampshire courts, see prefatory pages to N.H. Rev. Stat. Ann. volumes.

New Hampshire Rulemaking Register
Ab.: vol. no. N.H. Rulemaking Reg. page no. (month day, year)

Ex.: 23 N.H. Rulemaking Reg. 2 (Dec. 26, 2003).

New Hampshire Session Laws
See Laws of the State of New Hampshire.

New Jersey Administrative Code (West)
Ab.: N.J. Admin. Code § x:x-x.x (year)

Ex.: N.J. Admin. Code § 7:28-15.2 (2001).

New Jersey Administrative Reports (1982-date)
Ab.: N.J. Admin., N.J. Admin. 2d

New Jersey Constitution
Ab.: N.J. Const. art.   ,   ¶   .

Ex.: N.J. Const. art. I, ¶ 19. –"Cite constitutional provisions currently in force without a date." Bluebook rule 11.

N.J. Const. art. IV, ¶¶ 1-5 (repealed 1978). –"If the cited provision has been repealed, either indicate parenthetically the fact and date of repeal or cite the repealing provision in full." Bluebook rule 11.

N.J. Const. art. VII, ¶ 2 (amended 1984). –"When citing a provision that has been subsequently amended, either indicate parenthetically the fact and date of amendment or cite the amending provision in full." Bluebook rule 11.

N.J. Const. of 1844, art. I, ¶ 5 (1947). –"Cite constitutions that have been totally superseded by year of adoption, giving parenthetically the year of adoption of the specific provision cited if different." Bluebook rule 11.

New Jersey Equity Reports
Ab.: N.J. Eq.

–Discontinued in 1948.

–Cite to A. or A.2d, if therein; otherwise, cite to N.J. Eq.

–Give parallel citations, if at all, only in documents submitted to New Jersey state courts. See Bluebook rules 10.3.1 and B5.1.3; see also N.J. R. App. Prac. 2:6-2(a)(5), which requires only a citation to N.J. Eq.

In documents submitted to New Jersey state courts, cite as follows:

In law review footnotes, the titles of books and the names of cases, except for procedural phrases, are not underlined. See Bluebook rule 2.1(a) & (b). Further, the following are in large and small capitals: codes, restatements, standards, constitutions, periodicals, authors of books, titles of books, the abbreviated names of codes, most legislative materials except for bills and resolutions, codified ordinances, model codes, court rules, and sentencing guidelines. Refer to The Bluebook.

Temple v. Clinton Trust Co., 142 N.J. Eq. 285, 59 A.2d 590 (Ch. 1948). –Case Citation.

Temple v. Clinton Trust Co., 142 N.J. Eq. 285, 289, 59 A.2d 590, 592 (Ch. 1948). –Page Citation.

In all other documents, cite as follows:

Temple v. Clinton Trust Co., 59 A.2d 590 (N.J. Ch. 1948). –Case Citation.

Temple v. Clinton Trust Co., 59 A.2d 590, 592 (N.J. Ch. 1948). –Page Citation.

New Jersey Law Journal

Ab.:   N.J. L.J.

Ex.:   Alan B. Handler, Taking Better Aim at Judicial Evaluation, N.J. L.J., Mar. 26, 1981, at 1. –Article Citation.

Alan B. Handler, Taking Better Aim at Judicial Evaluation, N.J. L.J., Mar. 26, 1981, at 1, 12. –Page Citation.

New Jersey Law Reports (1790-1948)

Ab.:   N.J.L.

Ex.:   Trade Ins. Co. v. Barracliff, 45 N.J.L. 543 (1883). –Case Citation.

Trade Ins. Co. v. Barracliff, 45 N.J.L. 543, 546 (1883). –Page Citation.

New Jersey Lawyer

Ab.:   N.J. Law.

Ex.:   Deanne M. Wilson, Women in Private Law Firms: An Underdeveloped Asset, N.J. Law., July/Aug. 1991, at 42. –Article Citation.

Deanne M. Wilson, Women in Private Law Firms: An Underdeveloped Asset, N.J. Law., July/Aug. 1991, at 42, 43. –Page Citation.

New Jersey Miscellaneous Reports

Ab.:   N.J. Misc.

–Discontinued in 1949.

–Cite to A. or A.2d, if therein; otherwise, cite to N.J. Misc.

–Give parallel citations, if at all, only in documents submitted to New Jersey state courts. See Bluebook rules 10.3.1 and B5.1.3; see also N.J. R. App. Prac. 2:6-2(a)(5), which requires only a citation to N.J. Misc.

In documents submitted to New Jersey state courts, cite as follows:

Cooper Lumber Co. v. Dammers, 2 N.J. Misc. 289, 125 A. 325 (Sup. Ct. 1924). –Case Citation.

Cooper Lumber Co. v. Dammers, 2 N.J. Misc. 289, 292, 125 A. 325, 326-27 (Sup. Ct. 1924). –Page Citation.

In all other documents, cite as follows:

In citing cases in law review footnotes, abbreviate any word listed in table T.6; the names of "states, countries, and other geographical units" unless they are named parties; and any other words of eight or more letters "if substantial space is thereby saved and the result is unambiguous." Bluebook rule 10.2.2. On the other hand, in citing cases in text, abbreviate only widely known acronyms and the following words: "&," "Ass'n," "Bros.," "Co.," "Corp.," "Inc.," "Ltd.," and "No." Bluebook rule 10.2.1(c).

Cooper Lumber Co. v. Dammers, 125 A. 325 (N.J. Sup. Ct. 1924).
–Case Citation.

Cooper Lumber Co. v. Dammers, 125 A. 325, 326-27 (N.J. Sup.
Ct. 1924). –Page Citation.

New Jersey Register
Ab.: vol. no. N.J. Reg. page no. (month day, year)
Ex.: 35 N.J. Reg. 2165(a) (May 17, 2003).

New Jersey Reports
Ab.: N.J.

–Cite to A. or A.2d, if therein; otherwise, cite to N.J.

–Give parallel citations, if at all, only in documents submitted to New
Jersey state courts. See Bluebook rules 10.3.1 and B5.1.3; see also
N.J. R. App. Prac. 2:6-2(a)(5), which requires only a citation to N.J.

In documents submitted to New Jersey state courts, cite as follows:

State v. Fertig, 143 N.J. 115, 668 A.2d 1076 (1996). –Case
Citation.

State v. Fertig, 143 N.J. 115, 118, 668 A.2d 1076, 1077 (1996).
–Page Citation.

In all other documents, cite as follows:

State v. Fertig, 668 A.2d 1076 (N. J. 1996). –Case Citation.

State v. Fertig, 668 A.2d 1076, 1077 (N.J. 1996). –Page Citation.

New Jersey Revised Statutes (1937)
Ab.: N.J. Rev. Stat. § x:x (year).

–For proper citation form in papers submitted to New Jersey courts, see
New Jersey Manual on Style for Judicial Opinions, § 2(F) (rev. ed.
2004), available at
http://www.judiciary.state.nj.us/appdiv/manualonstyle.pdf.

New Jersey Sessions Laws
See Laws of New Jersey and New Jersey Session Law Service (West).

New Jersey Session Law Service (West)
Ab.: year N.J. Sess. Law Serv. page no. (West)
Ex.: Act of June 28, 1996, ch. 53, 1996 N.J. Sess. Law Serv. 177 (West)
(concerning adoption of building construction codes). –Citation to an
entire session law.

Act of June 28, 1996, ch. 53, § 1, 1996 N.J. Sess. Law Serv. 177, 177
(West) (concerning adoption of building construction codes). –Citation
to a section of a session law.

–See Bluebook rule 12.4.

–"Cite to N.J. Laws, if therein." Bluebook table T.1, p. 219.

In law review footnotes, the titles of books and the names of cases, except for procedural
phrases, are not underlined. See Bluebook rule 2.1(a) & (b). Further, the following are in
large and small capitals: codes, restatements, standards, constitutions, periodicals, authors of
books, titles of books, the abbreviated names of codes, most legislative materials except for
bills and resolutions, codified ordinances, model codes, court rules, and sentencing guidelines.
Refer to The Bluebook.

New Jersey Statutes Annotated (West)
Ab.:   N.J. Stat. Ann. § x:x (West year)

Ex.:   N.J. Stat. Ann. § 19:14-20 (West 1999).

N.J. Stat. Ann. § 39:3-75.3 (West Supp. 2000).

–For proper citation form in papers submitted to New Jersey courts, see prefatory pages to N.J. Stat. Ann. volumes and New Jersey Manual on Style for Judicial Opinions, § 2(F) (rev. ed. 2004), available at http://www.judiciary.state.nj.us/appdiv/manualonstyle.pdf.

New Jersey Superior Court Reports
Ab.:   N.J. Super.

–Cite to A. or A.2d, if therein; otherwise, cite to N.J. Super.

–Give parallel citations, if at all, only in documents submitted to New Jersey state courts. See Bluebook rules 10.3.1 and B5.1.3; see also N.J. R. App. Prac. 2:6-2(a)(5), which requires only a citation to N.J. Super.

In documents submitted to New Jersey state courts, cite as follows:

Rogan Equities, Inc. v. Santini, 289 N.J. Super. 95, 672 A.2d 1281 (App. Div. 1996). –Case Citation.

Rogan Equities, Inc. v. Santini, 289 N.J. Super. 95, 98, 672 A.2d 1281, 1283 (App. Div. 1996). –Page Citation.

In all other documents, cite as follows:

Rogan Equities, Inc. v. Santini, 672 A.2d 1281 (N.J. Super. Ct. App. Div. 1996). –Case Citation.

Rogan Equities, Inc. v. Santini, 672 A.2d 1281, 1283 (N.J. Super. Ct. App. Div. 1996). –Page Citation.

New Jersey Tax Court Reports
Ab.:   N.J. Tax

New Law Journal
Ab.:   New L.J.

N.L.J. [U.K.]

Ex.:   Roger Leng, Imprisonment for Prostitutes, 142 New L.J. 270 (1992). –Article Citation.

Roger Leng, Imprisonment for Prostitutes, 142 New L.J. 270, 271 (1992). –Page Citation.

New Mexico Administrative Code
Ab.:   N.M. Admin. Code tit. , § (year) .

New Mexico Bar Bulletin (Bar Bulletin: State of New Mexico)
See Bar Bulletin: State Bar of New Mexico.

In citing cases in law review footnotes, abbreviate any word listed in table T.6; the names of "states, countries, and other geographical units" unless they are named parties; and any other words of eight or more letters "if substantial space is thereby saved and the result is unambiguous." Bluebook rule 10.2.2. On the other hand, in citing cases in text, abbreviate only widely known acronyms and the following words: "&," "Ass'n," "Bros.," "Co.," "Corp.," "Inc.," "Ltd.," and "No." Bluebook rule 10.2.1(c).

New Mexico Constitution
Ab.:   N.M. Const. art.   , §   .

Ex.:   N.M. Const. art. XX, § 13. –"Cite constitutional provisions currently in force without a date." Bluebook rule 11.

N.M. Const. art. XX, § 17 (repealed 1971). –"If the cited provision has been repealed, either indicate parenthetically the fact and date of repeal or cite the repealing provision in full." Bluebook rule 11.

N.M. Const. art. XII, § 7 (amended 1990). –"When citing a provision that has been subsequently amended, either indicate parenthetically the fact and date of amendment or cite the amending provision in full." Bluebook rule 11.

New Mexico Court of Appeals
Ab.:   N.M. Ct. App.

–Cite to P., P.2d, or P.3d, if therein; otherwise, cite to N.M. Give public domain citation, if available. Otherwise, give parallel citations only in documents submitted to New Mexico state courts.

–Until January 1, 1996, when a public domain format was adopted, cite as follows:

In documents submitted to New Mexico state courts:

Yount v. Johnson, 121 N.M. 585, 915 P.2d 341 (Ct. App. 1996). –Case Citation.

Yount v. Johnson, 121 N.M. 585, 586, 915 P.2d 341, 342 (Ct. App. 1996). –Page Citation.

In all other documents:

Yount v. Johnson, 915 P.2d 341 (N. M. Ct. App. 1996). –Case Citation.

Yount v. Johnson, 915 P.2d 341, 342 (N.M. Ct. App. 1996). –Page Citation.

–From January 1, 1996, cite as follows:

In documents submitted to New Mexico state courts:

State v. Cleave, 2000-NMCA-071, 129 N.M. 355, 8 P.3d 157. –Case Citation.

State v. Cleave, 2000-NMCA-071, ¶ 7, 129 N.M. 355, 358, 8 P.3d 157, 159. –Pinpoint Citation.

In all other documents:

State v. Cleave, 2000-NMCA-071, 8 P.3d 157. –Case Citation.

State v. Cleave, 2000-NMCA-071, ¶ 7, 8 P.3d 157, 159. –Pinpoint Citation.

In law review footnotes, the titles of books and the names of cases, except for procedural phrases, are not underlined. See Bluebook rule 2.1(a) & (b). Further, the following are in large and small capitals: codes, restatements, standards, constitutions, periodicals, authors of books, titles of books, the abbreviated names of codes, most legislative materials except for bills and resolutions, codified ordinances, model codes, court rules, and sentencing guidelines. Refer to The Bluebook.

–See Bluebook rules 10.3.1, 10.3.3, B5.1.3, and table T.1; see also N.M.R. App. P. 12-213(E), N.M. S. Ct. R. 23-112, In re the Adoption of Vendor Neutral Citations (N.M. Jan. 12, 1998), and In re the Amendment of Order Adopting Vendor Neutral Citations (N.M. Nov. 3, 2000). Although there is some conflict among the New Mexico rules, the examples above conform to the form used by the New Mexico Supreme Court in its opinions.

New Mexico Law Review
Ab.: N.M. L. Rev.

Ex.: Richard B. Collins, Justice Scalia and the Elusive Idea of Discrimination Against Interstate Commerce, 20 N.M. L. Rev. 555 (1990). –Article Citation.

Richard B. Collins, Justice Scalia and the Elusive Idea of Discrimination Against Interstate Commerce, 20 N.M. L. Rev. 555, 559-60 (1990). –Page Citation.

New Mexico Legislative Service (West)
Ab.: year N.M. Legis. Serv. page no. (West)

Ex.: Act of Apr. 8, 2005, Ch. 421, sec. 1, § 56-7-1, 2005 N.M. Legis. Serv. 68 (West) (relating to indemnification). –Citation to a section of a session law amending prior act.

See Bluebook rule 12.4.

–"Cite to N.M. Laws, if therein." Bluebook table T.1, p. 220.

New Mexico Register
Ab.: vol. no. N.M. Reg. page no. (month day, year)

Ex.: 14 N.M. Reg. 571 (Aug. 29, 2003).

New Mexico Session Laws
See Laws of the State of New Mexico and New Mexico Legislative Service (West).

New Mexico Statutes 1978
Ab.: N.M. Stat. § x-x-x (year)

Ex.: N.M. Stat. § 5-10-2 (2003)

–For proper citation form in papers submitted to New Mexico courts, see N.M. S. Ct. R. 23-112(E).

New Mexico Supreme Court
Ab.: N.M.

–Cite to P., P.2d, or P.3d, if therein; otherwise, cite to N.M. Give public domain citation if available. Otherwise, give parallel citations only in documents submitted to New Mexico state courts.

In citing cases in law review footnotes, abbreviate any word listed in table T.6; the names of "states, countries, and other geographical units" unless they are named parties; and any other words of eight or more letters "if substantial space is thereby saved and the result is unambiguous." Bluebook rule 10.2.2. On the other hand, in citing cases in text, abbreviate only widely known acronyms and the following words: "&," "Ass'n," "Bros.," "Co.," "Corp.," "Inc.," "Ltd.," and "No." Bluebook rule 10.2.1(c).

–Until January 1, 1996, when a public domain format was adopted, cite as follows:

In documents submitted to New Mexico state courts:

Buffett v. Vargas, 121 N.M. 507, 914 P.2d 1004 (1985). –Case Citation.

Buffett v. Vargas, 121 N.M. 507, 508, 914 P.2d 1004, 1005 (1985). –Page Citation.

In all other documents:

Buffett v. Vargas, 914 P.2d 1004 (N.M. 1985). –Case Citation.

Buffett v. Vargas, 914 P.2d 1004, 1005 (N.M. 1985). –Page Citation.

–After January 1, 1996, cite as follows:

In documents submitted to New Mexico state courts:

In re Dawson, 2000-NMSC-024, 129 N.M. 369, 8 P.3d 856. –Case Citation.

In re Dawson, 2000-NMSC-024, ¶ 11, 129 N.M. 369, 374, 8 P.3d 856, 859. –Pinpoint Citation.

In all other documents:

In re Dawson, 2000-NMSC-024, 8 P.3d 856. –Case Citation.

In re Dawson, 2000-NMSC-024, ¶ 11, 8 P.3d 856, 859. –Pinpoint Citation.

See Bluebook rules 10.3.1, 10.3.3, B5.1.3, and table T.1; see also N.M.R. App. P. 12-213(F), N.M. S. Ct. R. 23-112, In re the Adoption of Vendor Neutral Citations (N.M. Jan. 12, 1998), and In re the Amendment of Order Adopting Vendor Neutral Citations (N.M. Nov. 3, 2000). Although there is some conflict among the New Mexico rules, the examples above conform to the form used by the New Mexico Supreme Court in its opinions.

New South Wales Reports (1960-date)

Ab.: N.S.W.R.

Ex.: Austin v. Royal (1999) 47 N.S.W.R. 27. –Case Citation.

Note: For explanation of Australia's medium-neutral citation, see L.T. Olsson, Guide to Uniform Production of Judgments (2d ed. 1999), available at http://www.aija.org.au/online/judguide.htm.

In law review footnotes, the titles of books and the names of cases, except for procedural phrases, are not underlined. See Bluebook rule 2.1(a) & (b). Further, the following are in large and small capitals: codes, restatements, standards, constitutions, periodicals, authors of books, titles of books, the abbreviated names of codes, most legislative materials except for bills and resolutions, codified ordinances, model codes, court rules, and sentencing guidelines. Refer to The Bluebook.

[The] New Wigmore: A Treatise on Evidence
−Do not abbreviate the title.

Ex.:   Edward J. Imwinkelried, <u>The New Wigmore</u> § 4.2.3 (2002). −Section Citation.

Edward J. Imwinkelried, <u>The New Wigmore</u> § 4.2.3, at 199 (2002). − Page Citation.

New York Appellate Division Reports
Ab.:   A.D., A.D.2d

−Cite to N.Y.S. or N.Y.S.2d, if therein; otherwise, cite to A.D. or A.D.2d.

−Give parallel citations, if at all, only in documents submitted to New York state courts. <u>See</u> <u>Bluebook</u> rules 10.3.1 and B5.1.3; see also N.Y. Ct. App. R. 500.1(a), 500.5(d)(3), 510.1(a), N.Y. Sup. Ct. App. Div. 1st Dep't R. 600.10(a)(11), N.Y. Sup. Ct. App. Div. 4th Dept. R. 1000.4(f)(7), and N.Y. C.P.L.R. 5529(e), which require only a citation to A.D. or A.D.2d.

In documents submitted to New York state courts, cite as follows:

<u>Ferrer v. Dinkins</u>, 218 A.D.2d 89, 635 N.Y.S.2d 965 (1996). −Case Citation.

<u>Ferrer v. Dinkins</u>, 218 A.D.2d 89, 90, 635 N.Y.S.2d 965, 966 (1996). −Page Citation.

In all other documents, cite as follows:

<u>Ferrer v. Dinkins</u>, 635 N.Y.S.2d 965 (App. Div. 1996). −Case Citation.

<u>Ferrer v. Dinkins</u>, 635 N.Y.S.2d 965, 966 (App. Div. 1996). −Page Citation.

New York Codes, Rules and Regulations
See Official Compilation of Codes, Rules and Regulations of the State of New York.

New York Consolidated Laws Service (LexisNexis)
Ab.:   N.Y. [subject] Law § x (Consol. year)

Ex.:   N.Y. Civ. Serv. Law § 61 (Consol. 2005)

N.Y. High Law § 346 (Consol. Supp. 2005)

See <u>Bluebook</u> table T.1, pp. 222-24, for subject abbreviations.

−For proper citation form in papers submitted to New York courts, see <u>New York Law Reports Style Manual</u>, § 3.1 (2002), <u>available at</u> http://www.courts.state.ny.us/reporter/2002_style_manual.pdf.

New York Consolidated Laws Service Advance Legislative Service (LexisNexis)
Ab.:   year-pamph. no. N.Y. Consol. Laws Adv. Legis. Serv. page no. (LexisNexis)

In citing cases in law review footnotes, abbreviate any word listed in table T.6; the names of "states, countries, and other geographical units" unless they are named parties; and any other words of eight or more letters "if <u>substantial</u> space is thereby saved and the result is unambiguous." <u>Bluebook</u> rule 10.2.2. On the other hand, in citing cases in text, abbreviate only widely known acronyms and the following words: "&," "Ass'n," "Bros.," "Co.," "Corp.," "Inc.," "Ltd.," and "No." <u>Bluebook</u> rule 10.2.1(c).

Ex.:   Act of Aug. 9, 2005, ch. 449, sec. 1, § 3061, 2005-7 N.Y. Consol. Laws. Adv. Legis. Serv. 98 (LexisNexis) (concerning trauma centers).

–Citation to a section of a session law amending prior act.

–See Bluebook rule 12.4.

–"Cite to N.Y. Laws, if therein." Bluebook table T.1, p. 224.

New York Constitution
Ab.:   N.Y. Const. art.   , §   .

Ex.:   N.Y. Const. art. I, § 17. –"Cite constitutional provisions currently in force without a date." Bluebook rule 11.

N.Y. Const. art. I, § 10 (repealed 1963). –"If the cited provision has been repealed, either indicate parenthetically the fact and date of repeal or cite the repealing provision in full." Bluebook rule 11.

N.Y. Const. art. XIV, § 1 (amended 1987). –"When citing a provision that has been subsequently amended, either indicate parenthetically the fact and date of amendment or cite the amending provision in full." Bluebook rule 11.

N.Y. Const. of 1894, art. I, § 3 (1938). –"Cite constitutions that have been totally superseded by year of adoption; if the specific provision cited was adopted in a different year–give that year parenthetically." Bluebook rule 11.

New York Court of Appeals
See New York Reports.

New York Law Journal
Ab.:   N.Y. L.J.

Ex.:   Cerisse Anderson, Goldman Widow Gets Disbursement Order, N.Y. L.J., Dec. 31, 1991, at 1. –Article Citation.

Cerisse Anderson, Goldman Widow Gets Disbursement Order, N.Y. L.J., Dec. 31, 1991, at 1, 2. –Page Citation.

New York Law School Journal of Human Rights
Ab.:   N.Y.L. Sch. J. Hum. Rts.

Ex.:   Robert F. Kane & Fred M. Blum, The International Year of Bible Reading: The Unconstitutional Use of the Political Process to Endorse Religion, 8 N.Y.L. Sch. J. Hum. Rts. 333 (1991). –Article Citation.

Robert F. Kane & Fred M. Blum, The International Year of Bible Reading: The Unconstitutional Use of the Political Process to Endorse Religion, 8 N.Y.L. Sch. J. Hum. Rts. 333, 336-37 (1991). –Page Citation.

New York Law School Journal of International and Comparative Law
Ab.:   N.Y.L. Sch. J. Int'l & Comp. L.

In law review footnotes, the titles of books and the names of cases, except for procedural phrases, are not underlined. See Bluebook rule 2.1(a) & (b). Further, the following are in large and small capitals: codes, restatements, standards, constitutions, periodicals, authors of books, titles of books, the abbreviated names of codes, most legislative materials except for bills and resolutions, codified ordinances, model codes, court rules, and sentencing guidelines. Refer to The Bluebook.

Ex.:   Hilary House, <u>The Border That Wouldn't Go Away: Irish Integration in the EC</u>, 11 N.Y.L. Sch. J. Int'l & Comp. L. 229 (1990). –Article Citation.

Hilary House, <u>The Border That Wouldn't Go Away: Irish Integration in the EC</u>, 11 N.Y.L. Sch. J. Int'l & Comp. L. 229, 239 (1990). –Page Citation.

New York Law School Law Review
Ab.:   N.Y.L. Sch. L. Rev.

Ex.:   Howard M. Metzenbaum, <u>Telecommunications Policy: Protecting Consumers by Promoting Diversity</u>, 35 N.Y.L. Sch. L. Rev. 593 (1990). –Article Citation.

Howard M. Metzenbaum, <u>Telecommunications Policy: Protecting Consumers by Promoting Diversity</u>, 35 N.Y.L. Sch. L. Rev. 593, 599 (1990). –Page Citation.

New York, McKinney's Consolidated Laws Annotated
See McKinney's Consolidated Laws of New York Annotated.

New York Miscellaneous Reports
Ab.:   Misc., Misc. 2d

–Cite to N.Y.S. or N.Y.S.2d, if therein; otherwise, cite to Misc. or Misc. 2d.

–Give parallel citations, if at all, only in documents submitted to New York state courts. <u>See</u> <u>Bluebook</u> rules 10.3.1 and B5.1.3; see also N.Y. Ct. App. R. 500.1(a) and 500.5(d)(3), 510.1(a), N.Y. Sup. Ct. App. Div. 1st Dep't R. 600.10(a)(11), N.Y. Sup. Ct. App. Div. 4th Dept. R. 1000.4(f)(7), and N.Y. C.P.L.R. 5529(e), which require only a citation to Misc. or Misc..2d.

In documents submitted to New York state courts, cite as follows:

<u>Okebiyi v. Cortines</u>, 167 Misc. 2d 1008, 641 N.Y.S.2d 791 (Sup. Ct. 1984). –Case Citation.

<u>Okebiyi v. Cortines</u>, 167 Misc. 2d 1008, 1009, 641 N.Y.S.2d 791, 792 (Sup. Ct. 1984). –Page Citation.

In all other documents, cite as follows:

<u>Okebiyi v. Cortines</u>, 641 N.Y.S.2d 791 (Sup. Ct. 1996). –Case Citation.

<u>Okebiyi v. Cortines</u>, 641 N.Y.S.2d 791, 792 (Sup. Ct. 1996). –Page Citation.

New York Opinions of Attorney General
See Opinions of Attorney General of New York.

New York Reports
Ab.:   N.Y., N.Y.2d

In citing cases in law review footnotes, abbreviate any word listed in table T.6; the names of "states, countries, and other geographical units" unless they are named parties; and any other words of eight or more letters "if <u>substantial</u> space is thereby saved and the result is unambiguous." <u>Bluebook</u> rule 10.2.2. On the other hand, in citing cases in text, abbreviate only widely known acronyms and the following words: "&," "Ass'n," "Bros.," "Co.," "Corp.," "Inc.," "Ltd.," and "No." <u>Bluebook</u> rule 10.2.1(c).

–Cite to N.E. or N.E.2d, if therein; otherwise, cite to N.Y., N.Y.2d, or N.Y.S.2d.

–Give parallel citations only in documents submitted to New York state courts. See Bluebook rules 10.3.1 and B5.1.3; see also N.Y. Ct. App. R. 500.1(a) and 500.5(d)(3), 510.1(a), N.Y. Sup. Ct. App. Div. 1st Dep't R. 600.10(a)(11), N.Y. Sup. Ct. App. Div. 4th Dept. R. 1000.4(f)(7), and N.Y. C.P.L.R. 5529(e), which require only a citation to N.Y. or N.Y.2d.

In documents submitted to New York state courts, cite as follows:

Beckman v. Greentree Sec., Inc., 87 N.Y.2d 566, 663 N.E.2d 886, 640 N.Y.S.2d 845 (1996). –Case Citation.

Beckman v. Greentree Sec., Inc., 87 N.Y.2d 566, 569, 663 N.E.2d 886, 887, 640 N.Y.S.2d 845, 847 (1996). –Page Citation.

In all other documents, cite as follows:

Beckman v. Greentree Sec., Inc., 663 N.E.2d 886 (N.Y. 1996). –Case Citation.

Beckman v. Greentree Sec., Inc., 663 N.E.2d 886, 887 (N.Y. 1996). –Page Citation.

New York Session Laws
See McKinney's New York Session Law News.

New York State Bar Journal
Ab.:   N.Y. St. B.J.

Ex.:   Michael E. O'Connor, U.S. Sav. Bonds in the Estate, N.Y. St. B.J., Feb. 1992, at 39. –Article Citation.

Michael E. O'Connor, U.S. Sav. Bonds in the Estate, N.Y. St. B.J., Feb. 1992, at 39, 41. –Page Citation.

New York State Register
Ab.:   vol. no. N.Y. Reg. page no. (month day, year)

Ex.:   26 N.Y. Reg. 72 (Feb. 11, 2004).

New York Stock Exchange Guide (Commerce Clearing House)
Ab.:   N.Y.S.E. Guide (CCH)

New York Supplement and New York Supplement, second series
See West's New York Supplement.

New York Times
Ab.:   N.Y. Times

Ex.:   Seth Mydans, Gates Threatens to Delay Leaving, N.Y. Times, June 8, 1992, at A7. –Signed article.

Chicago Police Kill Boy, 12, Who Pointed a Gun, N.Y. Times, June 8, 1992, at A7. –Unsigned news report.

In law review footnotes, the titles of books and the names of cases, except for procedural phrases, are not underlined. See Bluebook rule 2.1(a) & (b). Further, the following are in large and small capitals: codes, restatements, standards, constitutions, periodicals, authors of books, titles of books, the abbreviated names of codes, most legislative materials except for bills and resolutions, codified ordinances, model codes, court rules, and sentencing guidelines. Refer to The Bluebook.

New York University Annual Survey of American Law
Ab: N.Y.U. Ann. Surv. Am. L.
Ex: Stacey L. Dogan & Joseph P. Liu, <u>Copyright Law and Subject Matter</u>
        <u>Specificity: The Case of Computer Software</u>, 61 N.Y.U. Ann. Surv.
        Am. L. 203 (2005). –Article Citation.
        Stacey L. Dogan & Joseph P. Liu, <u>Copyright Law and Subject Matter</u>
        <u>Specificity: The Case of Computer Software</u>, 61 N.Y.U. Ann. Surv.
        Am. L. 203, 233 (2005). –Page Citation.

New York University Institute on Federal Taxation
Ab.:   Inst. on Fed. Tax'n
Ex.:   Michael F. Klein, Jr. & David K. Grevengoed, <u>Individual Alternative</u>
        <u>Minimum Tax</u>, 48 Inst. on Fed. Tax'n § 6.0, at 6-14 (1990).

New York University Journal of International Law and Politics
Ab.:   N.Y.U. J. Int'l L. & Pol.
Ex.:   Timothy A. Gelatt, <u>Lawyers in China: The Past Decade and Beyond</u>, 23
        N.Y.U. J. Int'l L. & Pol. 751 (1991). –Article Citation.
        Timothy A. Gelatt, <u>Lawyers in China: The Past Decade and Beyond</u>, 23
        N.Y.U. J. Int'l L. & Pol. 751, 756 (1991). –Page Citation.

New York University Law Review
Ab.:   N.Y.U. L. Rev.
Ex.:   Robert Cooter & Bradley J. Freedman, <u>The Fiduciary Relationship: Its</u>
        <u>Economic Character and Legal Consequences</u>, 66 N.Y.U. L. Rev. 1045
        (1991). –Article Citation.
        Robert Cooter & Bradley J. Freedman, <u>The Fiduciary Relationship: Its</u>
        <u>Economic Character and Legal Consequences</u>, 66 N.Y.U. L. Rev. 1045,
        1050 (1991). –Page Citation.

New York University Review of Law and Social Change
Ab.:   N.Y.U. Rev. L. & Soc. Change
Ex.:   Allan H. Macurdy, <u>Classical Nostalgia: Racism, Contract Ideology and</u>
        <u>Formalist Legal Reasoning in Patterson v. McLean Credit Union</u>, 18
        N.Y.U. Rev. L. & Soc. Change 987 (1990-91). –Article Citation.
        Allan H. Macurdy, <u>Classical Nostalgia: Racism, Contract Ideology and</u>
        <u>Formalist Legal Reasoning in Patterson v. McLean Credit Union</u>, 18
        N.Y.U. Rev. L. & Soc. Change 987, 991 (1990-91). –Page Citation.

In citing cases in law review footnotes, abbreviate any word listed in table T.6;
the names of "states, countries, and other geographical units" unless they are named parties;
and any other words of eight or more letters "if <u>substantial</u> space is thereby saved and the
result is unambiguous." <u>Bluebook</u> rule 10.2.2. On the other hand, in citing cases in text,
abbreviate only widely known acronyms and the following words: "&," "Ass'n," "Bros.,"
"Co.," "Corp.," "Inc.," "Ltd.," and "No." <u>Bluebook</u> rule 10.2.1(c).

New Zealand Law Journal, The
    Ab.:   N.Z. L. J.
    Ex.:   J.L. Caldwell, Is Scandalizing the Court a Scandal? 1994 N.Z. L. J.
            442. –Article Citation.

            J.L. Caldwell, Is Scandalizing the Court a Scandal? 1994 N.Z. L. J.
            442, 445. –Page Citation.

New Zealand Law Reports (1883 - date)
    Ab.:   N.Z.L.R.
    Ex.:   R v. Walters, [1989] 2 N.Z.L.R. 33 (C.A.) –Case Citation.
    See Bluebook table T.2. and rule 20.3.1.

New Zealand Universities Law Review
    Ab.:   N.Z.U. L. Rev.
    Ex.:   Gordon R. Walker, A Model of an Initial Public Offering, 15 N.Z.U. L.
            Rev. 396 (1993). –Article Citation.

            Gordon R. Walker, A Model of an Initial Public Offering, 15 N.Z.U. L.
            Rev. 396, 400 (1993). –Page Citation.

Newberg on Class Actions, by Alba Conte and Herbert B. Newberg
    –Do not abbreviate the title.
    Ex.:   6 Alba Conte & Herbert B. Newberg, Newberg on Class Actions § 18:9
            (4th ed. 2002). –Section Citation.

            6 Alba Conte & Herbert B. Newberg, Newberg on Class Actions § 21:1
            (4th ed. Cum. Supp. June 2005) –Supplement citation.

Newfoundland and Prince Edward Island Reports (Canada) (1970-date)
    Ab.:   Nfld. & P.E.I.R.
    Ex.:   Ford Credit Canada Ltd. v. Crosbie Realty Ltd., 90 Nfld. & P.E.I.R.
            191 (1991) (Can.). –Case Citation.
    See Bluebook table T.2.

newsletter
    Ab.:   newsl.

newspapers
    Ex.:   Ruth Marcus, Court Cuts Federal Desegregation Role, Wash. Post,
            Apr.1, 1992, at A1. –Article Citation.

            Judge Drops Juror from Gotti Trial, Wash. Post, Apr. 1, 1992, at A7.
            –News Report Citation.
    See Bluebook rule 16.5.
    –This format also applies to weekly newspapers and magazines.

Nimmer on Copyright, by Melville B. Nimmer and David Nimmer
    –Do not abbreviate the title.

In law review footnotes, the titles of books and the names of cases, except for procedural phrases, are not underlined. See Bluebook rule 2.1(a) & (b). Further, the following are in large and small capitals: codes, restatements, standards, constitutions, periodicals, authors of books, titles of books, the abbreviated names of codes, most legislative materials except for bills and resolutions, codified ordinances, model codes, court rules, and sentencing guidelines. Refer to The Bluebook.

Ex.:   2 Melville B. Nimmer & David Nimmer, <u>Nimmer on Copyright</u> § 7.16[C] (1991). –Section Citation.

2 Melville B. Nimmer & David Nimmer, <u>Nimmer on Copyright</u> § 7.16[C], at 7-169 (1991). –Page Citation.

2 Melville B. Nimmer & David Nimmer, <u>Nimmer on Copyright</u> § 7.16[C], at 17-169 n.135 (1991). –Footnote Citation.

NLRB Decisions
See Labor Law Reporter.

no [introductory] signal
–"Cited authority (i) directly states the proposition, (ii) identifies the source of a quotation, or (iii) identifies an authority referred to in the text." <u>Bluebook</u> rule 1.2(a).

North Carolina Administrative Code (West)
Ab.:   x N.C. Admin. Code x.x (year)

Ex.:   15A N.C. Admin. Code 10B.0118 (1990).

North Carolina Advance Legislative Service (LexisNexis)
Ab.:   year-pamph. no. N.C. Adv. Legis. Serv. page no. (LexisNexis)

Ex.:   Act of July 29, 2004, No. 2004-136, 2004-3 N.C. Adv. Legis. Serv. 67 (LexisNexis) (relating to maximum death benefit). –Citation to an entire session law.

Act of July 29, 2004, No. 2004-136, sec. 1, § 128-27(1), 2004-3 N.C. Adv. Legis. Serv. 67, 67 (LexisNexis) (relating to maximum death benefit). –Citation to a section of a session law amending prior act.

–<u>See</u> <u>Bluebook</u> rule12.4.

–"Cite to N.C. Laws, if therein." <u>Bluebook</u> table T.1, p. 225.

North Carolina Attorney General Reports
Ab.:   N.C. Att'y Gen. Rep.

See Opinions of the Attorney General of North Carolina.

North Carolina Central Law Journal
Ab.:   N.C. Cent. L.J.

Ex.:   Thomas L. Fowler, <u>Filling the Box: Responding to Jury Duty Avoidance</u>, 23 N.C. Cent. L.J. 1 (1997-1998). –Article Citation.

Thomas L. Fowler, <u>Filling the Box: Responding to Jury Duty Avoidance</u>, 23 N.C. Cent. L.J. 1, 13 (1997-1998). –Page Citation.

North Carolina Constitution
Ab.:   N.C. Const. art.   , §   .

In citing cases in law review footnotes, abbreviate any word listed in table T.6; the names of "states, countries, and other geographical units" unless they are named parties; and any other words of eight or more letters "if <u>substantial</u> space is thereby saved and the result is unambiguous." <u>Bluebook</u> rule 10.2.2. On the other hand, in citing cases in text, abbreviate only widely known acronyms and the following words: "&," "Ass'n," "Bros.," "Co.," "Corp.," "Inc.," "Ltd.," and "No." <u>Bluebook</u> rule 10.2.1(c).

Ex.: N.C. Const. art. I, § 20. –"Cite constitutional provisions currently in force without a date." Bluebook rule 11.

N.C. Const. art. IV, § 12 (amended 1982). –"When citing a provision that has been subsequently amended, either indicate parenthetically the fact and date of amendment or cite the amending provision in full." Bluebook rule 11.

N.C. Const. of 1868, art. I, § 15. –"Cite constitutions that have been totally superseded by year of adoption; if the specific provision cited was adopted in a different year, give that year parenthetically." Bluebook rule 11.

North Carolina Court of Appeals Reports

Ab.: N.C. App.

–Cite to S.E. or S.E.2d, if therein; otherwise, cite to N.C. App.

–Give parallel citations only in documents submitted to North Carolina state courts. See Bluebook rules 10.3.1 and B5.1.3; see also N.C. R. App. P. App. B, which requires a parallel citation.

In documents submitted to North Carolina state courts, cite as follows:

Hill v. Hill, 121 N.C. App. 510, 466 S.E.2d 322 (1996). –Case Citation.

Hill v. Hill, 121 N.C. App. 510, 511, 466 S.E.2d 322, 323 (1996). –Page Citation.

In all other documents, cite as follows:

Hill v. Hill, 466 S.E.2d 322 (N.C. Ct. App. 1996). –Case Citation.

Hill v. Hill, 466 S.E.2d 322, 323 (N.C. Ct. App. 1996). –Page Citation.

North Carolina General Statutes

See General Statutes of North Carolina.

North Carolina Journal of International Law and Commercial Regulation

Ab.: N.C. J. Int'l L. & Com. Reg.

Ex.: Ross D. Petty, The U.S. International Trade Commisssion: Import Advertising Arbiter or Artifice?, 17 N.C. J. Int'l L. & Com. Reg. 45 (1992). –Article Citation.

Ross D. Petty, The U.S. International Trade Commisssion: Import Advertising Arbiter or Artifice?, 17 N.C. J. Int'l L. & Com. Reg. 45, 48 (1992). –Page Citation.

North Carolina Law Review

Ab.: N.C. L. Rev.

In law review footnotes, the titles of books and the names of cases, except for procedural phrases, are not underlined. See Bluebook rule 2.1(a) & (b). Further, the following are in large and small capitals: codes, restatements, standards, constitutions, periodicals, authors of books, titles of books, the abbreviated names of codes, most legislative materials except for bills and resolutions, codified ordinances, model codes, court rules, and sentencing guidelines. Refer to The Bluebook.

Ex.: James P. Nehf, <u>A Legislative Framework for Reducing Fraud in the Credit Repair Industry</u>, 70 N.C. L. Rev. 781 (1992). –Article Citation.

James P. Nehf, <u>A Legislative Framework for Reducing Fraud in the Credit Repair Industry</u>, 70 N.C. L. Rev. 781, 786 (1992). –Page Citation.

North Carolina Register
Ab.: vol. no. N.C. Reg. page no. (month day, year)

Ex.: 18 N.C. Reg. 552 (Oct. 15, 2003).

North Carolina Reports
Ab.: N.C.

–Cite to S.E. or S.E.2d, if therein; otherwise, cite to N.C.

–Give parallel citations only in documents submitted to North Carolina state courts. <u>See</u> <u>Bluebook</u> rules 10.3.1 and B5.1.3; see also N.C. R. App. P. App. B, which requires a parallel citation.

In documents submitted to North Carolina state courts, cite as follows:

<u>Grimsley v. Nelson</u>, 342 N.C. 542, 467 S.E.2d 92 (1996). –Case Citation.

<u>Grimsley v. Nelson</u>, 342 N.C. 542, 543, 467 S.E.2d 92, 93 (1996). –Page Citation.

In all other documents, cite as follows:

<u>Grimsley v. Nelson</u>, 467 S.E.2d 92 (N.C. 1996). –Case Citation.

<u>Grimsley v. Nelson</u>, 467 S.E.2d 92, 93 (N.C. 1996). –Page Citation.

North Carolina Session Laws
See Session Laws of North Carolina and North Carolina Advance Legislative Service (LexisNexis).

North Dakota Administrative Code
Ab.: N.D. Admin. Code § x-x-x-x (year).

Ex.: N.D. Admin. Code § 43-02-07-06 (1999).

North Dakota Century Code (LexisNexis)
Ab.: N.D. Cent. Code § x-x-x (year)

Ex.: N.D. Cent. Code § 57-12-06 (2000).

N.D. Cent. Code § 54-03-20 (Supp. 2003).

For proper citation in papers submitted to North Dakota courts, see <u>North Dakota Supreme Court Citation Manual</u> § III (A) (2000), <u>available at</u> http://www.court.state.nd/us/citation.

North Dakota Constitution
Ab.: N.D. Const. art.   , §   .

In citing cases in law review footnotes, abbreviate any word listed in table T.6; the names of "states, countries, and other geographical units" unless they are named parties; and any other words of eight or more letters "if <u>substantial</u> space is thereby saved and the result is unambiguous." <u>Bluebook</u> rule 10.2.2. On the other hand, in citing cases in text, abbreviate only widely known acronyms and the following words: "&," "Ass'n," "Bros.," "Co.," "Corp.," "Inc.," "Ltd.," and "No." <u>Bluebook</u> rule 10.2.1(c).

Ex.:   N.D. Const. art. I, § 7. –"Cite constitutional provisions currently in force without a date." Bluebook rule 11.

N.D. Const. art. II, § 17 (repealed 1984). –"If the cited provision has been repealed, either indicate parenthetically the fact and date of repeal or cite the repealing provision in full." Bluebook rule 11.

N.D. Const. art. IX, § 13 (amended 1982). –"When citing a provision that has been subsequently amended, either indicate parenthetically the fact and date of amendment or cite the amending provision in full." Bluebook rule 11.

North Dakota Court of Appeals
Ab.:   N.D. Ct. App.

–Cite to N.W.2d, if therein; in addition, give public domain citation if available.

–Until January 1, 1997, when a public domain format was adopted, cite as follows:

In all documents:

> State v. Hersch, 467 N.W.2d 463 (N.D. Ct. App. 1991). –Case Citation.
> State v. Hersch, 467 N.W.2d 463, 465 (N.D. Ct. App. 1991). –Page Citation.

–From January 1, 1997, cite as follows:

In all documents:

> City of Bismarck v. Glass, 1998 ND App 1, 581 N.W.2d 474. –Case Citation.
> City of Bismarck v. Glass, 1998 ND App 1, ¶ 7, 581 N.W.2d 474, 475. –Pinpoint Citation.

See Bluebook rules 10.3.1, 10.3.3, B5.1.3, and table T.1; see also N.D. R. Ct. 11.6.

North Dakota Law Review
Ab.:   N.D. L. Rev.

Ex.:   Warren H. Albrecht, Jr., The Changing Face of Employment Law and the Practical Lawyer, 67 N.D. L. Rev. 469 (1992). –Article Citation.

Warren H. Albrecht, Jr., The Changing Face of Employment Law and the Practical Lawyer, 67 N.D. L. Rev. 469, 480 (1992). –Page Citation.

North Dakota, Opinions of the Attorney General
See Opinions of the Attorney General, State of North Dakota.

North Dakota Session Laws
See Laws of North Dakota.

In law review footnotes, the titles of books and the names of cases, except for procedural phrases, are not underlined. See Bluebook rule 2.1(a) & (b). Further, the following are in large and small capitals: codes, restatements, standards, constitutions, periodicals, authors of books, titles of books, the abbreviated names of codes, most legislative materials except for bills and resolutions, codified ordinances, model codes, court rules, and sentencing guidelines. Refer to The Bluebook.

North Dakota Supreme Court
Ab.: N.D.
–Cite to N.W. or N.W.2d, if therein; otherwise, cite to N.D.

Give public domain citation if available. Otherwise, give parallel citations only in documents submitted to North Dakota state courts.

–Through 79 N.D. 865 (1953), cite as follows:

In documents submitted to North Dakota state courts, because North Dakota Supreme Court opinions provide parallel citations to such decisions:

Gunder v. Feeland, 51 N.D. 784, 200 N.W. 909 (1924).
–Case Citation.

Gunder v. Feeland, 51 N.D. 784, 787, 200 N.W. 909, 911 (1924).
–Page Citation.

In all other documents:

Gunder v. Feeland, 200 N.W. 909 (N.D. 1924). –Case Citation.

Gunder v. Feeland, 200 N.W. 909, 911 (N.D. 1924).
–Page Citation.

–After 79 N.D. 865 (1953), and until January 1, 1997, when a public domain format was adopted, cite as follows:

In all documents:

Helmer v. Sortino, 545 N.W.2d 796 (N.D. 1996). –Case Citation.

Helmer v. Sortino, 545 N.W.2d 796, 798 (N.D. 1996).
–Page Citation.

–After January 1, 1997, cite as follows:

In all documents:

Olson v. Olson, 2000 ND 120, 611 N.W.2d 892. –Case Citation.

Olson v. Olson, 2000 ND 120, ¶ 7, 611 N.W.2d 892, 895.
–Pinpoint Citation.

See Bluebook rules 10.3.1, 10.3.3, B5.1.3, and table T.1; see also N.D. R. Ct. 11.6.

North Eastern Reporter
–Do not give a parallel citation unless required by local rule. See Bluebook rules 10.3.1 and B5.1.3. See also the various state court and state reporter entries herein for local rule parallel citation requirements.

Ab.: N.E.

Ex.:

Illinois:

Chance v. Kinsella, 142 N.E. 194 (Ill. 1923). –Case Citation.

Chance v. Kinsella, 142 N.E. 194, 195 (Ill. 1923). –Page Citation.

In citing cases in law review footnotes, abbreviate any word listed in table T.6; the names of "states, countries, and other geographical units" unless they are named parties; and any other words of eight or more letters "if substantial space is thereby saved and the result is unambiguous." Bluebook rule 10.2.2. On the other hand, in citing cases in text, abbreviate only widely known acronyms and the following words: "&," "Ass'n," "Bros.," "Co.," "Corp.," "Inc.," "Ltd.," and "No." Bluebook rule 10.2.1(c).

Indiana:

> Pottenger v. Bond, 142 N.E. 616 (Ind. Ct. App. 1924). –Case Citation.
>
> Pottenger v. Bond, 142 N.E. 616, 619 (Ind. Ct. App. 1924). –Page Citation.

Massachusetts:

> Bagnell v. Boston Elevated Ry. Co., 142 N.E. 63 (Mass. 1924). –Case Citation.
>
> Bagnell v. Boston Elevated Ry. Co., 142 N.E. 63, 64 (Mass. 1924). –Page Citation.

New York:

> Jacobs v. Newman, 172 N.E. 514 (N.Y. 1930). –Case Citation.
>
> Jacobs v. Newman, 172 N.E. 514, 516 (N.Y. 1930). –Page Citation.

Ohio:

> Morris v. Daiker, 172 N.E. 540 (Ohio Ct. App. 1929). –Case Citation.
>
> Morris v. Daiker, 172 N.E. 540, 541 (Ohio Ct. App. 1929). –Page Citation.

North Eastern Reporter, Second Series

> –Do not give a parallel citation unless required by local rule or unless the particular state has a public domain format. See Bluebook rules 10.3.1, 10.3.3, and B5.1.3. See also the various state court and state reporter entries herein for public domain information and local rule parallel citation requirements.
>
> –With volume 514 (1988), North Eastern Reporter, Second Series, became West's North Eastern Reporter, Second Series. Citation form is not affected by this title change.

Ab.: N.E.2d

Ex.:

Illinois:

> Bianchi v. Mikhail, 640 N.E.2d 1370 (Ill. App. Ct. 1994). –Case Citation.
>
> Bianchi v. Mikhail, 640 N.E.2d 1370, 1378 (Ill. App. Ct. 1994). –Page Citation.

Indiana:

> Eyster v. S.A. Birnbaum Contracting, Inc., 662 N.E.2d 201 (Ind. Ct. App. 1996). –Case Citation.
>
> Eyster v. S.A. Birnbaum Contracting, Inc., 662 N.E.2d 201, 203 (Ind. Ct. App. 1996). –Page Citation.

Massachusetts:

> Delk v. Gonzalez, 658 N.E.2d 681 (Mass. 1995). –Case Citation.
>
> Delk v. Gonzalez, 658 N.E.2d 681, 684 (Mass. 1995). –Page Citation.

In law review footnotes, the titles of books and the names of cases, except for procedural phrases, are not underlined. See Bluebook rule 2.1(a) & (b). Further, the following are in large and small capitals: codes, restatements, standards, constitutions, periodicals, authors of books, titles of books, the abbreviated names of codes, most legislative materials except for bills and resolutions, codified ordinances, model codes, court rules, and sentencing guidelines. Refer to The Bluebook.

New York:

> Bartoo v. Buell, 662 N.E.2d 1068 (N.Y. 1996). –Case Citation.
>
> Bartoo v. Buell, 662 N.E.2d 1068, 1070 (N.Y. 1996). –Page Citation.

Ohio:

> Cleveland Bar Ass'n v. Frye, 640 N.E.2d 808 (Ohio 1994).
> –Case Citation.
>
> Cleveland Bar Ass'n v. Frye, 640 N.E.2d 808, 809 (Ohio 1994).
> –Page Citation.

North Western Reporter

> –Do not give a parallel citation unless required by local rule. See
> Bluebook rules 10.3.1 and B5.1.3. See also the various state court
> and state reporter entries herein for local rule parallel citation
> requirements.

Ab.: N.W.

Ex.:

Iowa:

> Farnsworth v. Hazelett, 199 N.W 410 (Iowa 1924). –Case Citation.
>
> Farnsworth v. Hazelett, 199 N.W. 410, 414 (Iowa 1924).
> –Page Citation.

Michigan:

> Garwood v. Burton, 264 N.W. 349 (Mich. 1936). –Case Citation.
>
> Garwood v. Burton, 264 N.W. 349, 351 (Mich. 1936). –Page Citation.

Minnesota:

> Steensland v. W. & S. Life Ins. Co., 264 N.W. 440 (Minn. 1936).
> –Case Citation.
>
> Steensland v. W. & S. Life Ins. Co., 264 N.W. 440, 441 (Minn. 1936).
> –Page Citation.

Nebraska:

> Hilton v. Clements, 291 N.W. 483 (Neb. 1940). –Case Citation.
>
> Hilton v. Clements, 291 N.W. 483, 486 (Neb. 1940). –Page Citation.

North Dakota:

> Patterson Land Co. v. Lynn, 199 N.W. 766 (N.D. 1924).
> –Case Citation.
>
> Patterson Land Co. v. Lynn, 199 N.W. 766, 768 (N.D. 1924).
> –Page Citation.

South Dakota:

> Platt v. Rapid City, 291 N.W. 600 (S.D. 1940). –Case Citation.
>
> Platt v. Rapid City, 291 N.W. 600, 602 (S.D. 1940). –Page Citation.

In citing cases in law review footnotes, abbreviate any word listed in table T.6;
the names of "states, countries, and other geographical units" unless they are named parties;
and any other words of eight or more letters "if substantial space is thereby saved and the
result is unambiguous." Bluebook rule 10.2.2. On the other hand, in citing cases in text,
abbreviate only widely known acronyms and the following words: "&," "Ass'n," "Bros.,"
"Co.," "Corp.," "Inc.," "Ltd.," and "No." Bluebook rule 10.2.1(c).

Wisconsin:

> Stenson v. Schumacher, 290 N.W. 285 (Wis. 1940). –Case Citation.
>
> Stenson v. Schumacher, 290 N.W. 285, 288 (Wis. 1940).
> –Page Citation.

North Western Reporter, Second Series

> –Do not give a parallel citation unless required by local rule or unless the particular state has a public domain citation. See Bluebook rules 10.3.1, 10.3.3, and B5.1.3. See also the various state court and state reporter entries herein for public domain information and local rule parallel citation requirements.
>
> –With volume 414 (1988), North Western Reporter, Second Series, becomes West's North Western Reporter, Second Series. Citation form is not affected by this title change.

Ab.: N.W.2d

Ex.:

Iowa:

> Ahlers v. Emacasco Ins. Co., 548 N.W.2d 892 (Iowa 1996). –Case Citation.
>
> Ahlers v. Emacasco Ins. Co., 548 N.W.2d 892, 894 (Iowa 1996). –Page Citation.

Michigan:

> Halabu v. Behnke, 541 N.W.2d 285 (Mich. Ct. App. 1995). –Case Citation.
>
> Halabu v. Behnke, 541 N.W.2d 285, 288 (Mich. Ct. App. 1995). –Page Citation.

Minnesota:

> State v. Ecker, 524 N.W.2d 712 (Minn. Ct. App. 1994). –Case Citation.
>
> State v. Ecker, 524 N.W.2d 712, 716 (Minn. Ct. App. 1994). –Page Citation.

Nebraska:

> Shuck v. Jacob, 548 N.W.2d 332 (Neb. 1996). –Case Citation.
>
> Shuck v. Jacob, 548 N.W.2d 332, 337 (Neb. 1996). –Page Citation.

North Dakota:

> Bruner v. Hager, 547 N.W.2d 551 (N.D. 1996). –Case Citation.
>
> Bruner v. Hager, 547 N.W.2d 551, 554 (N.D. 1996). –Page Citation.

South Dakota:

> State v. Arguello, 548 N.W.2d 463 (S.D. 1996). –Case Citation.
>
> State v. Arguello, 548 N.W.2d 463, 464 (S.D. 1996). –Page Citation.

In law review footnotes, the titles of books and the names of cases, except for procedural phrases, are not underlined. See Bluebook rule 2.1(a) & (b). Further, the following are in large and small capitals: codes, restatements, standards, constitutions, periodicals, authors of books, titles of books, the abbreviated names of codes, most legislative materials except for bills and resolutions, codified ordinances, model codes, court rules, and sentencing guidelines. Refer to The Bluebook.

Wisconsin:

> Byers v. Labor and Indus. Review Comm'n, 547 N.W.2d 788 (Wis. Ct. App. 1996). –Case Citation.
>
> Byers v. Labor and Indus. Review Comm'n, 547 N.W.2d 788, 791 (Wis. Ct. App. 1996). –Page Citation.

Northern Illinois University Law Review
Ab.: N. Ill. U. L. Rev.

Ex.: Richard S. Wilbur, AIDS and the Federal Bureau of Prisons: A Unique Challenge, 11 N. Ill. U. L. Rev. 275 (1991). –Article Citation.

Richard S. Wilbur, AIDS and the Federal Bureau of Prisons: A Unique Challenge, 11 N. Ill. U. L. Rev. 275, 279 (1991). –Page Citation.

Northern Ireland Law Reports (1925-date)
Ab.: N. Ir. L.R.

Ex.: Conway v. Hannaway, 1988 N. Ir. L.R. 269 (Q.B. 1988). –Case Citation.

See Bluebook rule 20.3.1. See also table T.2, p. 327, concerning medium neutral citation for cases after 2001.

Northern Ireland Legal Quarterly
Ab.: N. Ir. Legal Q.

Ex.: Soli J. Sorabjee, Freedom of Expression and Censorship: Some Aspects of the Indian Experience, 45 N. Ir. Legal Q. 327 (1994). –Article Citation.

Soli J. Sorabjee, Freedom of Expression and Censorship: Some Aspects of the Indian Experience, 45 N. Ir. Legal Q. 327, 337 (1994). –Page Citation.

Northern Kentucky Law Review
Ab.: N. Ky. L. Rev.

Ex.: Michael J. Newman, United States Magistrate Judges: Suggestions to Increase the Efficiency of Their Civil Role, 19 N. Ky. L. Rev. 99 (1991). –Article Citation.

Michael J. Newman, United States Magistrate Judges: Suggestions to Increase the Efficiency of Their Civil Role, 19 N. Ky. L. Rev. 99, 103 (1991). –Page Citation.

Northern Mariana Islands Administrative Code
Ab.: x N. Mar. I. Admin. Code § x (year)

Northern Mariana Islands Commonwealth Code
Ab.: x N. Mar. I. Code § x (year)

In citing cases in law review footnotes, abbreviate any word listed in table T.6; the names of "states, countries, and other geographical units" unless they are named parties; and any other words of eight or more letters "if substantial space is thereby saved and the result is unambiguous." Bluebook rule 10.2.2. On the other hand, in citing cases in text, abbreviate only widely known acronyms and the following words: "&," "Ass'n," "Bros.," "Co.," "Corp.," "Inc.," "Ltd.," and "No." Bluebook rule 10.2.1(c).

Ex.:   2 N. Mar. I. Code § 5319 (2003).

Northern Mariana Islands Commonwealth Register
Ab.:   vol. no. N. Mar. I. Reg. page no. (month day, year)

Ex.:   7 N. Mar. I. Reg. 3774 (July 22, 1985).

Northern Mariana Islands Commonwealth Reporter

See Bluebook rules 10.3.1 and 10.3.3 and table T.1; see also Gen. Order in re Adoption of Universal Citations for App. Opinions, no. 2001-100 (Mar. 13, 2001) and Northern Mariana Island Style Manual for Judicial Decisions (2002), available at http://www. cnmilaw.org/pdf/style_manual/style-manual.pdf. Include a public domain citation, if available.

Ab.: N. Mar. I. Commw.

In all documents:

Ex.:   Weathersbee v. Weathersbee, 1998 MP 14, 5 N. Mar. I Commw. 608
        –Case Citation.

        Weathersbee v. Weathersbee, 1998 MP 14, ¶ 5, 5 N. Mar. I. Commw.
        608, 610. –Pinpoint Citation.

Northern Mariana Islands Session Laws
Ab.:   year N. Mar. I. Pub. L. x-x
        –See Bluebook rule 12.4.

Northrop University Law Journal of Aerospace, Business and Taxation
Ab.:   Northrop U. L.J. Aerospace Bus. & Tax'n

Ex.:   Mark J. Phillips, History and the Law: Judicial Process and the King's Writ, 7 Northrop U. L.J. Aerospace Bus. & Tax'n 77 (1986). –Article Citation.

        Mark J. Phillips, History and the Law: Judicial Process and the King's Writ, 7 Northrop U. L.J. Aerospace Bus. & Tax'n 77, 80-83 (1986). –Page Citation.

Northwest Territories Reports (Canada) (1983-date)
Ab.:   N.W.T.R.

Northwestern Journal of International Law & Business
Ab.:   Nw. J. Int'l L. & Bus.

Ex.:   Frank L. Fine, The Impact of EEC Competition Law on the Music Industry, 12 Nw. J. Int'l L. & Bus. 508 (1992). –Article Citation.

        Frank L. Fine, The Impact of EEC Competition Law on the Music Industry, 12 Nw. J. Int'l L. & Bus. 508, 511-12 (1992). –Page Citation.

Northwestern University Law Review
Ab.:   Nw. U. L. Rev.

In law review footnotes, the titles of books and the names of cases, except for procedural phrases, are not underlined. See Bluebook rule 2.1(a) & (b). Further, the following are in large and small capitals: codes, restatements, standards, constitutions, periodicals, authors of books, titles of books, the abbreviated names of codes, most legislative materials except for bills and resolutions, codified ordinances, model codes, court rules, and sentencing guidelines. Refer to The Bluebook.

Ex.: Roger D. Blair & Jeffrey L. Harrison, <u>Cooperative Buying Monopoly Power, and Antitrust Policy</u>, 86 Nw. U. L. Rev. 331 (1992). –Article Citation.

Roger D. Blair & Jeffrey L. Harrison, <u>Cooperative Buying Monopoly Power, and Antitrust Policy</u>, 86 Nw. U. L. Rev. 331, 342 (1992) –Page Citation.

Norton Bankruptcy Law and Practice 2d, by William L. Norton, Jr.
–Do not abbreviate the title.

Ex.: 2 William L. Norton, Jr., <u>Norton Bankruptcy Law and Practice</u> § 42.14 (2d ed. 1994). –Section Citation.

2 William L. Norton, Jr., <u>Norton Bankruptcy Law and Practice</u> § 42.14, at 42-76 (2d ed. 1994). –Page Citation.

2 William L. Norton, Jr., <u>Norton Bankruptcy Law and Practice</u> § 42.14, at 42-76, n.14 (2d ed. 1994). –Footnote Citation.

Notre Dame Estate Planning Institute Proceedings
Ab.: Notre Dame Est. Plan. Inst. Proc.

Ex.: George Tucker, <u>Estate and Income Tax Planning for Real Property Ownership</u>, 4 Notre Dame Est. Plan. Inst. Proc. 159 (1979). –Article Citation.

George Tucker, <u>Estate and Income Tax Planning for Real Property Ownership</u>, 4 Notre Dame Est. Plan. Inst. Proc. 159, 197-98 (1979). –Page Citation.

Notre Dame Institute on Charitable Giving Foundations and Trusts
Ab.: Notre Dame Inst. on Char. Giving Found. & Tr.

Notre Dame Journal of Law, Ethics & Public Policy
Ab.: Notre Dame J.L. Ethics & Pub. Pol'y

Ex.: Shanto Iyengar, <u>How Television News Affects Voters: From Setting Agendas to Defining Standards</u>, 6 Notre Dame J.L. Ethics & Pub. Pol'y 33 (1992). –Article Citation.

Shanto Iyengar, <u>How Television News Affects Voters: From Setting Agendas to Defining Standards</u>, 6 Notre Dame J.L. Ethics & Pub. Pol'y 33, 41-45 (1992). –Page Citation.

Notre Dame Law Review
Ab.: Notre Dame L. Rev.

In citing cases in law review footnotes, abbreviate any word listed in table T.6; the names of "states, countries, and other geographical units" unless they are named parties; and any other words of eight or more letters "if <u>substantial</u> space is thereby saved and the result is unambiguous." <u>Bluebook</u> rule 10.2.2. On the other hand, in citing cases in text, abbreviate only widely known acronyms and the following words: "&," "Ass'n," "Bros.," "Co.," "Corp.," "Inc.," "Ltd.," and "No." <u>Bluebook</u> rule 10.2.1(c).

Ex.:   Gregory S. Crespi, <u>The Mid-Life Crisis of the Law and Economics Movement: Confronting the Problems of Nonfalsifiability and Normative Bias</u>, 67 Notre Dame L. Rev. 231 (1991). –Article Citation.

Gregory S. Crespi, <u>The Mid-Life Crisis of the Law and Economics Movement: Confronting the Problems of Nonfalsifiability and Normative Bias</u>, 67 Notre Dame L. Rev. 231, 242 (1991). –Page Citation.

Nouveau code de procédure civile (France)
See <u>Bluebook</u> rules 20.2.3 and 20.5.2, and table T.2, p. 267.

Ab.:   N.C.P.C.

Nova Law Review
Ab.:   Nova L. Rev.

Ex.:   Gary A. Poliakoff, <u>The Florida Condominium Act</u>, 16 Nova L. Rev. 471 (1991). –Article Citation.

Gary A. Poliakoff, <u>The Florida Condominium Act</u>, 16 Nova L. Rev. 471, 477-79 (1991). –Page Citation.

Nova Scotia Reports (Canada)
See <u>Bluebook</u> table T.2.

Ab.:   N.S.R., N.S.R.2d

Ex.:   <u>Nuttal v. Vaughan</u>, [1928] 60 N.S.R. 84 (Can.). –Case Citation.

<u>Roberts v. Roberts</u>, [1991] 104 N.S.R.2d 27 (Can.). –Case Citation.

Nuclear Regulation Reports (Commerce Clearing House)
Ab.:   Nuclear Reg. Rep. (CCH)

Ex.:   <u>Kerr-McGee Chem. Corp. v. City of West Chicago</u>, 2 Nuclear Reg. Rep. (CCH) ¶ 20,515 (7th Cir. Sept. 20, 1990). –Cite to looseleaf material.

<u>Ohio Edison Co. v. Zech</u>, [1985-1989 New Developments Transfer Binder] Nuclear Reg. Rep. (CCH) ¶ 20,460 (D.D.C. 1988). –Cite to transfer binder material.

–The above examples are proper if the case is not yet available in, or is not reported in, an official or West reporter, a public domain citation, or in a widely used computer database.

<u>Sacramento Mun. Util. Dist.</u>, 2 Nuclear Reg. Rep. (CCH) ¶ 31,178 (NRC Feb. 6, 1992). –Cite to looseleaf administrative material.

<u>Wrangler Laboratories</u>, [1986-1991 NRC Decisions Transfer Binder] Nuclear Reg. Rep. (CCH) ¶ 33,224.01 (NRC 1991). –Cite to transfer binder administrative material.

In law review footnotes, the titles of books and the names of cases, except for procedural phrases, are not underlined. <u>See</u> <u>Bluebook</u> rule 2.1(a) & (b). Further, the following are in large and small capitals: codes, restatements, standards, constitutions, periodicals, authors of books, titles of books, the abbreviated names of codes, most legislative materials except for bills and resolutions, codified ordinances, model codes, court rules, and sentencing guidelines. Refer to <u>The Bluebook</u>.

Nuclear Regulatory Commission Issuances (1975-date)
    Ab.:   N.R.C.

    Ex.:   Metropolitan Edison Co. (Three Mile Island, Unit 2), 11 N.R.C. 519 (1980).

             Pacific Gas & Elec. Co. (Diablo Canyon Nuclear Power Plant, Unit 1), 14 N.R.C. 950 (1981). –Cite to current unbound material.

Numerals and Symbols
    See Bluebook rule 6.2.

In citing cases in law review footnotes, abbreviate any word listed in table T.6; the names of "states, countries, and other geographical units" unless they are named parties; and any other words of eight or more letters "if substantial space is thereby saved and the result is unambiguous." Bluebook rule 10.2.2. On the other hand, in citing cases in text, abbreviate only widely known acronyms and the following words: "&," "Ass'n," "Bros.," "Co.," "Corp.," "Inc.," "Ltd.," and "No." Bluebook rule 10.2.1(c).

O

Occupational Safety & Health Reporter (Bureau of National Affairs)
–Bound as Occupational Safety & Health Cases (Bureau of National Affairs).

Ab.: O.S.H. Rep. (BNA)
–Bound as O.S.H. Cas. (BNA).

Ex.: Sec'y of Labor v. Sea Sprite Boat Co., [Decisions] O.S.H. Rep. (BNA) (17 O.S.H. Cas.) 1331 (5th Cir. Mar. 17, 1995). –Citation to looseleaf material.

United Crane & Shovel Co. v. Dep't of Labor, 15 O.S.H. Cas. (BNA) 1464 (3d Cir. 1991). –Citation to bound material.

–The above examples are proper only if the case is not yet available in an official or West reporter, or is not reported in an official or West reporter.

Sec'y of Labor v. Newell Recycling Co., [Decisions] O.S.H. Rep. (BNA) (17 O.S.H. Cas.) 1519 (O.S.H. Rev. Comm'n Nov. 13, 1995). –Citation to looseleaf administrative material.

Sec'y of Labor v. Trinity Indus., Inc., 15 O.S.H. Cas. (BNA) 1985 (O.S.H. Rev. Comm'n 1992). –Citation to bound administrative material.

Ocean Development and International Law
Ab.: Ocean Dev. & Int'l L.

Ex.: Ted L. McDorman, Canada and the North Pacific Ocean: Recent Issues, 22 Ocean Dev. & Int'l L. 365 (1991). –Article Citation.

Ted L. McDorman, Canada and the North Pacific Ocean: Recent Issues, 22 Ocean Dev. & Int'l L. 365, 373 (1991). –Page Citation.

Office of Thrift Supervision Journal
Ab.: Off. Thrift Supervision J.

Ex.: Mark Wohar, Should You Abandon the Thrift Charter, Off. Thrift Supervision J., June 1990, at 6. –Article Citation.

Mark Wohar, Should You Abandon the Thrift Charter, Off. Thrift Supervision J., June 1990, at 6, 9. –Page Citation.

Official Code of Georgia Annotated (LexisNexis)
Ab.: Ga. Code Ann. § (year)

In law review footnotes, the titles of books and the names of cases, except for procedural phrases, are not underlined. See Bluebook rule 2.1(a) & (b). Further, the following are in large and small capitals: codes, restatements, standards, constitutions, periodicals, authors of books, titles of books, the abbreviated names of codes, most legislative materials except for bills and resolutions, codified ordinances, model codes, court rules, and sentencing guidelines. Refer to The Bluebook.

Ex.: Ga. Code Ann. § 36-5-21 (2000).

Ga. Code Ann. § 50-13-18 (Supp. 2000).

–For proper citation form in papers submitted to Georgia courts, see Ga. Code Ann. § 1-1-8(e) (2004).

Official Code of Georgia Annotated Advance Legislative Service (LexisNexis)

Ab.: year-pamph. no. Ga. Code Ann. Adv. Legis. Serv. page no. (LexisNexis)

Ex.: H.B. 538, sec. 1, § 48-7-6, 2005-3 Ga. Code Ann. Adv. Legis. Serv. 803 (LexisNexis) (relating to income taxes). –Citation to a section of a session law amending prior act.

See Bluebook rule 12.4.

–"Cite to Ga. Laws, if therein." Bluebook table T.1, p. 206.

Official Compilation of Codes, Rules & Regulations of the State of New York

Ab.: N.Y. Comp. Codes R. & Regs. tit. x, § x (year)

Ex.: N.Y. Comp. Codes R. & Regs. tit. 8, § 50.2 (2001).

Official Compilation Rules & Regulations of the State of Georgia

Ab.: Ga. Comp. R. & Regs. x-x-x.x (year)

Ex.: Ga. Comp. R. & Regs. R. 40-13-9.01 (2003)

Official Compilation Rules and Regulations of the State of Tennessee

Ab.: Tenn. Comp. R. & Regs. x-x-x.x (year)

Ex.: Tenn. Comp. R. & Regs. 0030-1-9-.03 (2000).

Official Journal of the European Community

Ab.: O.J., O.J. Spec. Ed.

Ex.: Commission Regulation 1203/91, 1991 O.J. (L 116) 22, 23.

Commission Proposal for a Council Regulation on Certificates of Specific Character for Foodstuffs, art. 2(2), 1991 O.J. (C 30) 4,5.

–"Cite publications of the Council and of the Commission published beginning January 1, 1994, to the Official Journal of the European Union (O.J). Cite documents published between January 1, 1974, and December 31, 1993, to the Official Journal of the European Communities (also abbreviated O.J.). Cite documents published before January 1, 1974, to the Special Edition of the Official Journal of the European Communities (O.J. Spec. Ed.), if available; otherwise, cite to Journal Officiel des Communautés Européennes (J.O.)." Bluebook rule 21.8.2. See table T.3 for dates which correspond with the abbreviations.

In citing cases in law review footnotes, abbreviate any word listed in table T.6; the names of "states, countries, and other geographical units" unless they are named parties; and any other words of eight or more letters "if substantial space is thereby saved and the result is unambiguous." Bluebook rule 10.2.2. On the other hand, in citing cases in text, abbreviate only widely known acronyms and the following words: "&," "Ass'n," "Bros.," "Co.," "Corp.," "Inc.," "Ltd.," and "No." Bluebook rule 10.2.1(c).

Official Opinions of the Solicitor for the Post Office Department (U.S.) (1873-1951)

Ab.: Op. Solic. P.O. Dep't

Ex.: 1 Op. Solic. P.O. Dep't 671 (1881).

9 Op. Solic. P.O. Dep't 655 (1949).

OHA Law Journal, The

Ab.: OHA L.J.

Ex.: Joyce K. Barlow, <u>Contempt Powers of the Administrative Law Judge</u>, OHA L.J., Fall 1991, at 31. –Article Citation.

Joyce K. Barlow, <u>Contempt Powers of the Administrative Law Judge</u>, OHA L.J., Fall 1991, at 31, 34. –Page Citation.

Ohio Appellate Reports

Ab.: Ohio App., Ohio App. 2d, Ohio App. 3d.

–Cite to N.E. or N.E.2d, if therein; otherwise, cite to Ohio App., Ohio App. 2d, or Ohio App. 3d. Give public domain citation if available. Otherwise, give parallel citations only in documents submitted to Ohio state courts. <u>See</u> <u>Bluebook</u> rules 10.3.1, 10.3.3, and B5.1.3; <u>see also</u> <u>Revisions to the Manual of Citations</u>, 96 Ohio St. 3d CXLIX (2002), <u>available at</u> http://www.sconet.state.oh.us/ROD/pdf/Rev_Manual_Cit_02.pdf.

–For cases decided prior to May 1, 2002, cite as follows:

In documents submitted to Ohio state courts:

<u>State v. Baker</u> (1993), 88 Ohio App.3d 204, 623 N.E.2d 672. –Case Citation.

<u>State v. Baker</u> (1993), 88 Ohio App.3d 204, 206, 623 N.E.2d 672, 675. –Page Citation.

In all other documents:

<u>State v. Baker</u>, 623 N.E.2d 672 (Ohio Ct. App. 1993). –Case Citation.

<u>State v. Baker</u>, 623 N.E. 2d 672, 675 (Ohio Ct. App. 1993). –Page Citation.

–For cases decided after April 30, 2002, cite as follows:

In documents submitted to Ohio state courts:

<u>State v. Goffee</u>, 161 Ohio App.3d 199, 2005-Ohio-2596, 829 N.E.2d 1224. –Case Citation.

<u>State v. Goffee</u>, 161 Ohio App.3d 199, 2005-Ohio-2596, ¶ 12, 204, 829 N.E.2d 1224, 1227. –Pinpoint Citation.

In all other documents:

<u>State v. Goffee</u>, 2005-Ohio-2596, 829 N.E.2d 1224 (Ct. App.).

In law review footnotes, the titles of books and the names of cases, except for procedural phrases, are not underlined. <u>See</u> <u>Bluebook</u> rule 2.1(a) & (b). Further, the following are in large and small capitals: codes, restatements, standards, constitutions, periodicals, authors of books, titles of books, the abbreviated names of codes, most legislative materials except for bills and resolutions, codified ordinances, model codes, court rules, and sentencing guidelines. Refer to <u>The Bluebook</u>.

–Case Citation.

State v. Goffee, 2005-Ohio-2596, ¶ 12, 829 N.E.2d 1224, 1227 (Ct. App.). –Pinpoint Citation.

Ohio Bar Reports
>   Ab.:   Ohio B.

Ohio Circuit Court Decisions
>   –Discontinued in 1923.

>   Ab.:   Ohio C.C. Dec.

Ohio Circuit Court Reports
>   –Discontinued in 1901.

>   Ab.:   Ohio C.C.

Ohio Circuit Court Reports, New Series
>   –Discontinued in 1922.

>   Ab.:   Ohio C.C. (n.s.)

Ohio Circuit Decisions
>   –Discontinued in 1901.

>   Ab.:   Ohio Cir. Dec.

Ohio Constitution
>   Ab.:   Ohio Const. art.   , §   .

>   Ex.:   Ohio Const. art. I, § 7. –"Cite constitutional provisions currently in force without a date." Bluebook rule 11.

>   Ohio Const. art. XV, § 5 (repealed 1976). –"If the cited provision has been repealed, either indicate parenthetically the fact and date of repeal or cite the repealing provision in full." Bluebook rule 11.

>   Ohio Const. art. III, § 17a (amended 1989). –"When citing a provision that has been subsequently amended, either indicate parenthetically the fact and date of amendment or cite the amending provision in full." Bluebook rule 11.

>   Ohio Const. of 1802, art. VIII, § 3 (1851). –"Cite constitutions that have been totally superseded by year of adoption; if the specific provision cited was adopted in a different year, give that year parenthetically." Bluebook rule 11.

Ohio Decisions
>   –Discontinued in 1920.

>   Ab.:   Ohio Dec.

Ohio Decisions, Reprint
>   Ab.:   Ohio Dec. Reprint

In citing cases in law review footnotes, abbreviate any word listed in table T.6; the names of "states, countries, and other geographical units" unless they are named parties; and any other words of eight or more letters "if substantial space is thereby saved and the result is unambiguous." Bluebook rule 10.2.2. On the other hand, in citing cases in text, abbreviate only widely known acronyms and the following words: "&," "Ass'n," "Bros.," "Co.," "Corp.," "Inc.," "Ltd.," and "No." Bluebook rule 10.2.1(c).

Ohio Department Reports
    Ab.:   Ohio Dep't page no. (month day, year)
    Ex.:   Ohio Dep't 295 (Dec. 28, 1964).

Ohio Government Reports
    Ab.:   Ohio Gov't page no. (month day, year)
    Ex.:   Ohio Gov't SC9 (Feb. 25, 1976).

Ohio Legislative Bulletin (LexisNexis)
    Ab.:   Page's Ohio Legislative Bulletin (LexisNexis)

Ohio Legislative Service
See Baldwin's Ohio Legislative Service.

Ohio Miscellaneous Reports
    Ab.:   Ohio Misc., Ohio Misc. 2d

           –Cite to Ohio Misc. or Ohio Misc. 2d, if therein; otherwise, cite to other reporters in order of preference found in Bluebook table T.1. Give public domain citation, if available.

    Ex.:   Travelers Ins. Co. v. Dayton Power & Light Co., 76 Ohio Misc. 2d 17 (C.P. 1996). –Case Citation.

           Travelers Ins. Co. v. Dayton Power & Light Co., 76 Ohio Misc. 2d 17, 19 (C.P. 1996). –Page Citation.

           State v. Underwood, 2005-Ohio-2996, 132 Ohio Misc. 2d 1 (Mun. Ct). –Case Citation

           State v. Underwood, 2005-Ohio-2996, ¶ 11, 132 Ohio Misc. 2d 1, 3 (Mun. Ct.). –Pinpoint Citation.

Ohio Monthly Record (West)
    Ab.:   Ohio Monthly Rec. page no. (month year)
    Ex.:   Ohio Monthly Rec. 158 (Aug. 2005)

Ohio Nisi Prius Reports
    Ab.:   Ohio N.P., Ohio N.P. (n.s.)

           –Discontinued in 1934.

           –Cite to Ohio Misc. or Ohio Misc. 2d, if therein; otherwise, cite to other reporters in order of preference found in Bluebook table T.1.

    Ex.:   Ross v. City of Columbus, 8 Ohio N.P. 420 (C.P. 1892). –Case Citation.

           Ross v. City of Columbus, 8 Ohio N.P. 420, 422 (C.P. 1892). –Page Citation.

           Spencer v. Athletic Ass'n Co., 32 Ohio N.P. (n.s.) 369 (Mun. Ct. 1934). –Case Citation.

           Spencer v. Athletic Ass'n Co., 32 Ohio N.P. (n.s.) 369, 373 (Mun. Ct. 1934). –Page Citation.

In law review footnotes, the titles of books and the names of cases, except for procedural phrases, are not underlined. See Bluebook rule 2.1(a) & (b). Further, the following are in large and small capitals: codes, restatements, standards, constitutions, periodicals, authors of books, titles of books, the abbreviated names of codes, most legislative materials except for bills and resolutions, codified ordinances, model codes, court rules, and sentencing guidelines. Refer to The Bluebook.

Ohio Northern University Law Review
Ab.:   Ohio N.U. L. Rev.

Ex.:   Kenneth W. Thornicroft, The War on Drugs Goes to Work: Employee Drug Testing and the Law, 17 Ohio N.U. L. Rev. 771 (1991). –Article Citation.

Kenneth W. Thornicroft, The War on Drugs Goes to Work: Employee Drug Testing and the Law, 17 Ohio N.U. L. Rev. 771, 778 (1991). –Page Citation.

Ohio Opinions
Ab.:   Ohio Op., Ohio Op. 2d, Ohio Op. 3d

–Discontinued in 1982.

–Cite to Ohio Misc. or Ohio Misc. 2d, if therein; otherwise, cite to other reporters in order of preference found in Bluebook table T.1.

Ex.:   Ohio Edison Co. v. McElrath, 60 Ohio Op. 462 (C.P. 1955). –Case Citation.

Ohio Edison Co. v. McElrath, 60 Ohio Op. 462, 464 (C.P. 1955). –Page Citation.

Whiting v. Roxy Ltd., 66 Ohio Op. 2d 369 (C.P. 1973). –Case Citation.

Whiting v. Roxy Ltd., 66 Ohio Op. 2d 369, 371 (C.P. 1973). –Page Citation.

State v. Ackerman, 19 Ohio Op. 3d 347 (C.P. 1979). –Case Citation.

State v. Ackerman, 19 Ohio Op. 3d 347, 348 (C.P. 1979). –Page Citation.

Ohio, Opinions of the Attorney General
See Opinions of the Attorney General of Ohio.

Ohio Revised Code Annotated
See Page's Ohio Revised Code Annotated and Baldwin's Ohio Revised Code Annotated.

Ohio Session Laws
See State of Ohio: Legislative Acts Passed and Joint Resolutions Adopted and Page's Ohio Legislative Bulletin (LexisNexis).

Ohio State Journal on Dispute Resolution
Ab.:   Ohio St. J. on Disp. Resol.

Ex.:   Roger Richman, Dispute Processing in China During Reform, 7 Ohio St. J. on Disp. Resol. 83 (1991). –Article Citation.

Roger Richman, Dispute Processing in China During Reform, 7 Ohio St. J. on Disp. Resol. 83, 88-91 (1991). –Page Citation.

In citing cases in law review footnotes, abbreviate any word listed in table T.6; the names of "states, countries, and other geographical units" unless they are named parties; and any other words of eight or more letters "if substantial space is thereby saved and the result is unambiguous." Bluebook rule 10.2.2. On the other hand, in citing cases in text, abbreviate only widely known acronyms and the following words: "&," "Ass'n," "Bros.," "Co.," "Corp.," "Inc.," "Ltd.," and "No." Bluebook rule 10.2.1(c).

Ohio State Law Journal
Ab.:   Ohio St. L.J.

Ex.:   Mark A. Hall & John D. Colombo, The Donative Theory of the
         Charitable Tax Exemption, 52 Ohio St. L.J. 1379 (1991).
         –Article Citation.

         Mark A. Hall & John D. Colombo, The Donative Theory of the
         Charitable Tax Exemption, 52 Ohio St. L.J. 1379, 1407 (1991).
         –Page Citation.

Ohio State Reports
Ab.:   Ohio St., Ohio St. 2d, Ohio St. 3d.

         –Cite to N.E. or N.E.2d, if therein; otherwise, cite to Ohio St., Ohio St.
         2d, or Ohio St. 3d. Give public domain citation if available.

         –Otherwise, give parallel citations only in documents submitted to Ohio
         state courts. See Bluebook rules 10.3.1, 10.3.3, and B5.1.3; see also
         Revisions to the Manual of Citations, 96 Ohio St. 3d CXLIX (2002),
         available at
         http://www.sconet.state.oh.us/ROD/pdf/Rev_Manual_Cit_02.pdf.

         –Beginning with 1 Ohio St. 3d (1982), found in Ohio Official Reports.

         –For cases decided prior to May 1, 2002, cite as follows:

         In documents submitted to Ohio state courts:

                 Kostelnik v. Hepler (2002), 96 Ohio St.3d 1, 770 N.E.2d 58. –Case
                 Citation.

                 Kostelnik v. Hepler (2002), 96 Ohio St.3d 1, 3, 770 N.E.2d 58, 60.
                 –Page Citation.

         In all other documents:

                 Kostelnik v. Hepler, 770 N.E.2d 58 (Ohio 2002). –Case
                 Citation.

                 Kostelnik v. Hepler, 770 N.E.2d 58, 60 (Ohio 2002).
                 –Page Citation.

         –For cases decided after April 30, 2002, cite as follows:

         In documents submitted to Ohio state courts:

                 In re S.J., 106 Ohio St.3d 11, 2005-Ohio-3215, 829 N.E.2d 1207
                 –Case Citation.

                 In re S.J., 106 Ohio St.3d 11, 14, 2005-Ohio-3215, ¶ 10, 829
                 N.E.2d 1207, 1209.–Pinpoint Citation.

         In all other documents:

                 In re S.J. 2005-Ohio-3215, 829 N.E.2d 1207 (Ohio).
                 –Case Citation.

                 In re S.J., 2005-Ohio-3215, ¶ 10, 829 N.E.2d 1207, 1209 (Ohio).

In law review footnotes, the titles of books and the names of cases, except for procedural
phrases, are not underlined. See Bluebook rule 2.1(a) & (b). Further, the following are in
large and small capitals: codes, restatements, standards, constitutions, periodicals, authors of
books, titles of books, the abbreviated names of codes, most legislative materials except for
bills and resolutions, codified ordinances, model codes, court rules, and sentencing guidelines.
Refer to The Bluebook.

–Pinpoint Citation.

Oil, Gas & Energy Quarterly
Ab.: Oil Gas & Energy Q.

Ex.: Alan D. Smith, <u>Strategic Management Implications of Domestic Petroleum Reserves</u>, 52 Oil Gas & Energy Q. 731 (2004) –Article Citation.

Alan D. Smith, <u>Strategic Management Implications of Domestic Petroleum Reserves</u>, 52 Oil Gas & Energy Q. 731, 742-43 (2004).

–Page Citation.

Oklahoma Administrative Code
Ab.: Okla Admin. Code § x:x-x-x (year)

Ex.: Ohio Admin. Code § 35:40-17-57 (2000).

Oklahoma City University Law Review
Ab.: Okla. City U. L. Rev.

Ex.: Richard E. Coulson, <u>Is Contractual Arbitration an Unconstitutional Waiver of the Right to Trial by Jury in Oklahoma?</u>, 16 Okla. City U. L. Rev. 1 (1991). –Article Citation.

Richard E. Coulson, <u>Is Contractual Arbitration an Unconstitutional Waiver of the Right to Trial by Jury in Oklahoma?</u>, 16 Okla. City U. L. Rev. 1, 59 (1991). –Page Citation.

Oklahoma Constitution
Ab.: Okla. Const. art.   , § .

Ex.: Okla. Const. art. I, § 3. –"Cite constitutional provisions currently in force without a date." <u>Bluebook</u> rule 11.

Okla. Const. art. IX, § 14 (repealed 1991). –"If the cited provision has been repealed, either indicate parenthetically the fact and date of repeal or cite the repealing provision in full." <u>Bluebook</u> rule 11.

Okla. Const. art. II, § 11 (amended 1914). –"When citing a provision that has been subsequently amended, either indicate parenthetically the fact and date of amendment or cite the amending provision in full." <u>Bluebook</u> rule 11.

Oklahoma Court of Appeals
Ab.: Okla. Ct. App.

–Effective November 1, 1996, Oklahoma Court of Appeals became known as Oklahoma Court of Civil Appeals. <u>See</u> Oklahoma Court of Civil Appeals.

Oklahoma Court of Civil Appeals
Ab.: Okla. Civ. App.

In citing cases in law review footnotes, abbreviate any word listed in table T.6; the names of "states, countries, and other geographical units" unless they are named parties; and any other words of eight or more letters "if <u>substantial</u> space is thereby saved and the result is unambiguous." <u>Bluebook</u> rule 10.2.2. On the other hand, in citing cases in text, abbreviate only widely known acronyms and the following words: "&," "Ass'n," "Bros.," "Co.," "Corp.," "Inc.," "Ltd.," and "No." <u>Bluebook</u> rule 10.2.1(c).

–Cite to P.2d or P.3d, if therein; in addition, give public domain citation, if available.

–For cases promulgated after April 30, 1997:

In all documents, cite as follows:

Brown v. NCI, Inc., 2000 OK CIV APP 78, 8 P.3d 195. –Case citation.

Brown v. NCI, Inc., 2000 OK CIV APP 78, ¶ 5, 8 P.3d 195, 196. –Pinpoint Citation.

–For cases promulgated before May 1, 1997:

In documents submitted to Oklahoma state courts, citation to P.2d or P.3d is required and parallel public domain citation, found at the Oklahoma State Courts' Network Web site, http://www.oscn.net, is encouraged:

Elledge v. Staring, 1996 OK CIV APP 161, 939 P.2d 1163. –Case Citation.

Elledge v. Staring, 1996 OK CIV APP 161, ¶ 7, 939 P.2d 1163, 1165. –Pinpoint Citation.

In all other documents, cite as follows:

Elledge v. Staring, 939 P.2d 1163 (Okla. Civ. App. 1996). –Case Citation.

Elledge v. Staring, 939 P.2d 1163, 1165 (Okla. Civ. App. 1996). –Page Citation.

See Bluebook rules 10.3.1, 10.3.3, B5.1.3, and table T.1; see also Okla. Sup. Ct. R. 1.200(e).

Oklahoma Court of Criminal Appeals

Ab.:   Okla. Crim.

–Cite to P., P.2d, or P.3d, if therein; otherwise, cite to Okla. Crim. Give public domain citation, if available. Otherwise, give parallel citations only in documents submitted to Oklahoma state courts.

–Through 97 Okla. Crim. 415 (1953), cite as follows:

In documents submitted to Oklahoma state courts:

Simmons v. State, 68 Okla. Crim. 337, 98 P.2d 623 (1940). –Case Citation.

Simmons v. State, 68 Okla. Crim. 337, 340, 98 P.2d 623, 624 (1940). –Page Citation.

In all other documents:

Simmons v. State, 98 P.2d 623 (Okla. Crim. App. 1940). –Case Citation.

Simmons v. State, 98 P.2d 623, 624 (Okla. Crim. App. 1940). –Page Citation.

In law review footnotes, the titles of books and the names of cases, except for procedural phrases, are not underlined. See Bluebook rule 2.1(a) & (b). Further, the following are in large and small capitals: codes, restatements, standards, constitutions, periodicals, authors of books, titles of books, the abbreviated names of codes, most legislative materials except for bills and resolutions, codified ordinances, model codes, court rules, and sentencing guidelines. Refer to The Bluebook.

–After 97 Okla. Crim. 415 (1953), and until Jan. 1, 1998, cite as follows:

In documents submitted to Oklahoma state courts:

> Long v. State, 1985 OK CR 119, 706 P.2d 915. –Case Citation.
>
> Long v. State, 1985 OK CR 119, ¶ 6, 706 P.2d 915, 917. –Pinpoint Citation.

In all other documents:

> Long v. State, 706 P.2d 915 (Okla. Crim. App. 1985). –Case Citation.
>
> Long v. State, 706 P. 2d 915, 917 (Okla. Crim. App. 1985). –Page Citation.

–For cases promulgated on or after January 1, 1998, cite as follows:

In all documents:

> State v. McNeal, 2000 OK CR 13, 6 P.3d 1055. –Case Citation
>
> State v. McNeal, 2000 OK CR 13, ¶ 10, 6 P.3d 1055, 1057. –Pinpoint Citation.

See Bluebook rules 10.3.1, 10.3.3, B5.1.3, and table T.1; see also Okla. Crim. App. R. 3.5(C), which strongly encourages a parallel public domain citation for all cases promulgated after 1/1/54. See also, the Oklahoma State Courts network Website, http://www.oscn.net, for parallel public domain citations for cases decided between 1954 and 1998.

Oklahoma Gazette
Ab.: vol. no. Okla. Gaz. page no.
Ex.: 19 Okla. Gaz. 1199 (Dec. 15, 1981).

Oklahoma Law Review
Ab.: Okla. L. Rev.
Ex.: Lawrence Kalevitch, Lien Avoidance on Exemptions: The False Controversy Over Opt-Out, 44 Okla. L. Rev. 443 (1991). –Article Citation.

Lawrence Kalevitch, Lien Avoidance on Exemptions: The False Controversy Over Opt-Out, 44 Okla. L. Rev. 443, 449 (1991). –Page Citation.

Oklahoma Register
Ab.: vol. no. Okla. Reg. page no. (month day, year)
Ex.: 19 Okla. Reg. 2875 (Sept. 3, 2002).

Oklahoma Session Laws (West)
Ab.: year Okla. Sess. Laws page no.
Ex.: Act of May 25, 1995, ch. 287, 1995 Okla. Sess. Laws 1340. –Citation to an entire session law

---

In citing cases in law review footnotes, abbreviate any word listed in table T.6; the names of "states, countries, and other geographical units" unless they are named parties; and any other words of eight or more letters "if substantial space is thereby saved and the result is unambiguous." Bluebook rule 10.2.2. On the other hand, in citing cases in text, abbreviate only widely known acronyms and the following words: "&," "Ass'n," "Bros.," "Co.," "Corp.," "Inc.," "Ltd.," and "No." Bluebook rule 10.2.1(c).

Act of May 25, 1995, ch. 287, § 3, 1995 Okla. Sess. Laws 1340, 1343-44. –Citation to a section of a session law.

See Bluebook rule 12.4.

Oklahoma Session Law Service (West)
Ab.: year Okla. Sess. Law Serv. page no. (West)

Ex.: Act of May 28, 1996, ch. 243, 1996 Okla. Sess. Law Serv. 953 (West) (motor vehicles emission control equipment). –Citation to an entire session law.

Act of May 28, 1996, ch. 243, sec. 1, § 856.1, 1996 Okla. Sess. Law Serv. 953, 953 (West) (motor vehicles emission control equipment). –Citation to a session law amending a prior act.

See Bluebook rule 12.4.

Oklahoma Statutes (West)
Ab.: Okla. Stat. tit. x, § x (year)

Ex.: Okla. Stat. tit. 42, § 141 (1979).

Oklahoma Statutes Annotated (West)
Ab.: Okla. Stat. Ann. tit. x, § x (West year)

Ex.: Okla. Stat. Ann. tit. 19, § 138.4 (West 2000).

Okla. Stat. Ann. tit. 15, § 567 (West Supp. 2000).

–"Cite to Okla. Stat., if therein." Bluebook table T.1, p. 228.

Oklahoma Supreme Court
Ab.: Okla.

–Cite to P., P.2d, or P.3d, if therein; in addition, give public domain citation, if available.

–For cases promulgated after April 30, 1997:

In all documents, cite as follows:

Farrimond v. State ex rel. Fisher, 2000 OK 52, 8 P.3d 872. –Case Citation.

Farrimond v. State ex rel. Fisher, 2000 OK 52, ¶14, 8 P.3d 872, 975.– Pinpoint Citation.

–For cases promulgated before May 1, 1997:

In documents provided to Oklahoma state courts, citation to P., P.2d, or P.3d is required and parallel public domain citation, found at the Oklahoma State Courts Network Web Site, http://www.oscn.net, is encouraged:

Skinner v. Braum's Ice Cream Store, 1995 OK 11, 890 P.2d 922. –Case Citation.

Skinner v. Braum's Ice Cream Store, 1995 OK 11, ¶ 9, 890 P.2d 922, 925. –Pinpoint Citation.

In law review footnotes, the titles of books and the names of cases, except for procedural phrases, are not underlined. See Bluebook rule 2.1(a) & (b). Further, the following are in large and small capitals: codes, restatements, standards, constitutions, periodicals, authors of books, titles of books, the abbreviated names of codes, most legislative materials except for bills and resolutions, codified ordinances, model codes, court rules, and sentencing guidelines. Refer to The Bluebook.

In all other documents, cite as follows:

> Skinner v. Braum's Ice Cream Store, 890 P.2d 922 (Okla. 1995). –Case Citation.

> Skinner v. Braum's Ice Cream Store, 890 P.2d 922, 925 (Okla. 1995). –Page Citation.

See Bluebook rules 10.3.1, 10.3.3, B5.1.3, and table T.1; see also, Okla. Sup. Ct. R. 1.2000(e).

Oklahoma Tribal Court Reports
Ab.: Okla. Trib.

Ex.: Mayes v. Thompson, 5 Okla. Trib. 117 (1996)

O'Neal and Thompson's Close Corporations and LLCs, by Robert B. Thompson
–Do not abbreviate the title.

Ex.: Robert B. Thompson, O'Neal and Thompson's Close Corporations and LLCs § 5.13 (rev. 3d ed. 2004). –Section Citation.

Robert B. Thompson, O'Neal and Thompson's Close Corporations and LLCs § 5.13, at 5-74 (rev. 3d ed. 2004). –Page Citation.

Robert B. Thompson, O'Neal and Thompson's Close Corporations and LLCs § 5.13, at 5-74 n.40 (rev. 3d ed. 2004). –Footnote Citation.

Online Commercial Services
See Electronic media and other nonprint resources.

Ontario Law Reports
See Bluebook table T.2.

Ab.: O.L.R.

Ex.: McLaughlin v. Ont. Iron & Steel Co., [1910] 20 O.L.R. 335, 338 (Can.). –Page Citation.

Ontario Regulations
Ab.: R.O.

Ontario Reports
See Bluebook table T.2.

Ab.: O.R., O.R.2d, O.R.3d

Ex.: Paramount Pictures Corp. v. Howley, [1991] 5 O.R.3d 573, 575 (Can.). –Page Citation.

Jaffe v. Miller, [1990] 75 O.R.2d 133, 137 (Can.). –Page Citation.

Goldex Mines Ltd. v. Revill, [1973] 3 O.R. 869, 872 (Can.). –Page Citation.

Opiniones del Secretario de Justicia de Puerto Rico
Ab.: Op. P.R. Att'y Gen.

In citing cases in law review footnotes, abbreviate any word listed in table T.6; the names of "states, countries, and other geographical units" unless they are named parties; and any other words of eight or more letters "if substantial space is thereby saved and the result is unambiguous." Bluebook rule 10.2.2. On the other hand, in citing cases in text, abbreviate only widely known acronyms and the following words: "&," "Ass'n," "Bros.," "Co.," "Corp.," "Inc.," "Ltd.," and "No." Bluebook rule 10.2.1(c).

See Opinions of the Attorney General of Puerto Rico.

Opinions of the Attorney General (U.S.) (1791-date)
Ab.:   Op. Att'y Gen.

–The name of the opinion may be included in the citation. See Bluebook rule 14.4.

Ex.:   42 Op. Att'y Gen. 301 (1965). –Citation to bound material.

Carriage in United States Vessels of Exports Financed by a Government Agency, 42 Op. Att'y Gen. 301 (1965). –Citation to bound material.

Authority of the United States Olympic Committee to Send American Teams to the 1980 Summer Olympics, 43 Op. Att'y Gen. No. 23 (April 10, 1980). –Citation to separately paginated slip opinion. See Bluebook rule 14.4.

Opinions of the Attorney General and Report to the Governor of Virginia
Ab.:   Op. Va. Att'y Gen.

See Opinions of the Attorney General of Virginia.

Opinions of the Attorney General of Alabama
Ab.:   Op. Ala. Att'y Gen.

Ex.:   Op. Ala. Att'y Gen. No. 94-00089 (Jan. 14, 1994). –Citation to slip opinion.

237 Ala. Q. Rep. Atty. Gen. 43 (1994). –Citation to opinion compiled in the Quarterly Report of the Attorney General.

–If the opinion has a name or title, it may be included before the citation. See Blucbook rule 14.4.

Opinions of the Attorney General of Alaska
Ab.:   Op. Alaska Att'y Gen.

Ex.:   Op. Alaska Att'y Gen. No. 4 (Nov. 8, 1985). –Citation to a formal slip opinion.

Informal Op. Alaska Att'y Gen. No. 663-94-0185 (Jan. 1, 1994). –Citation to an informal slip opinion.

–If the opinion has a name or title, it may be included before the citation. See Bluebook rule 14.4.

Opinions of the Attorney General of Arizona
Ab.:   Op. Ariz. Att'y Gen.

Ex.:   Op. Ariz. Att'y Gen. No. I95-002 (Aug. 30, 1995). –Citation to slip opinion.

–If the opinion has a name or title, it may be included before the citation. See Bluebook rule 14.4.

In law review footnotes, the titles of books and the names of cases, except for procedural phrases, are not underlined. See Bluebook rule 2.1(a) & (b). Further, the following are in large and small capitals: codes, restatements, standards, constitutions, periodicals, authors of books, titles of books, the abbreviated names of codes, most legislative materials except for bills and resolutions, codified ordinances, model codes, court rules, and sentencing guidelines. Refer to The Bluebook.

Opinions of the Attorney General of Arkansas
Ab.:   Op. Ark. Att'y Gen.

Ex.:   Op. Ark. Att'y Gen. No. 94-376 (Jan. 3, 1995). –Citation to slip opinion.

–If the opinion has a name or title, it may be included before the citation. See Bluebook rule 14.4.

Opinions of the Attorney General of California
Ab.:   Op. Cal. Att'y Gen.

Ex.:   Op. Cal. Att'y Gen. No. 94-817 (Jan. 13, 1995). –Citation to slip opinion.

64 Op. Cal. Att'y Gen. 676 (1981). –Citation to compiled opinion.

–If the opinion has a name or title, it may be included before the citation. See Bluebook rule 14.4.

Opinions of the Attorney General of Colorado
Ab.:   Op. Colo. Att'y Gen.

Ex.:   Op. Colo. Att'y Gen. No. 95-1 (Feb. 17, 1995). –Citation to slip opinion.

–If the opinion has a name or title, it may be included before the citation. See Bluebook rule 14.4.

Opinions of the Attorney General of Connecticut
Ab.:   Op. Conn. Att'y Gen.

Ex.:   1989 Op. Conn. Att'y Gen. No. 89-018. –Citation to compiled opinion.

–If the opinion has a name or title, it may be included before the citation. See Bluebook rule 14.4.

Opinions of the Attorney General of Delaware
Ab.:   Op. Del. Att'y Gen.

Ex.:   1982 Op. Del. Att'y Gen. No. 95-IB03 (Jan. 25, 1995). –Citation to slip opinion.

–If the opinion has a name or title, it may be included before the citation. See Bluebook rule 14.4.

Opinions of the Attorney General of Florida
Ab.:   Op. Fla. Att'y Gen.

Ex.:   Fla. Att'y Gen. No. 94-21 (Mar. 16, 1994). –Citation to slip opinion, not yet compiled in the Annual Report of the Florida Attorney General.

1994 Fla. Atty. Gen. Ann. Rep. 51. –Citation to opinion in the Annual Report of the Florida Attorney General.

–If the opinion has a name or title, it may be included before the citation. See Bluebook rule 14.4.

In citing cases in law review footnotes, abbreviate any word listed in table T.6; the names of "states, countries, and other geographical units" unless they are named parties; and any other words of eight or more letters "if substantial space is thereby saved and the result is unambiguous." Bluebook rule 10.2.2. On the other hand, in citing cases in text, abbreviate only widely known acronyms and the following words: "&," "Ass'n," "Bros.," "Co.," "Corp.," "Inc.," "Ltd.," and "No." Bluebook rule 10.2.1(c).

Opinions of the Attorney General of Georgia
Ab.: Op. Ga. Att'y Gen.

Ex.: Op. Ga. Att'y Gen. No. 94-10 (Mar. 14, 1994). –Citation to slip opinion.

1994 Op. Ga. Att'y Gen. 12, No. 94-6. –Citation to compiled opinion.

–If the opinion has a name or title, it may be included before the citation. See Bluebook rule 14.4.

Opinions of the Attorney General of Hawaii
Ab.: Op. Haw. Att'y Gen.

Ex.: Op. Haw. Att'y Gen. No. 94-2 (Oct. 17, 1994). –Citation to slip opinion.

–If the opinion has a name or title, it may be included before the citation. See Bluebook rule 14.4.

Opinions of the Attorney General of Idaho
Ab.: Op. Idaho Att'y Gen.

Ex.: Op. Idaho Att'y Gen. No. 95-06 (Oct. 26, 1995). –Citation to slip opinion.

1995 Idaho Att'y Gen. Ann. Rep. 5, No. 95-01. –Citation to opinion compiled in the Idaho Attorney General's Annual Report.

–If the opinion has a name or title, it may be included before the citation. See Bluebook rule 14.4.

Opinions of the Attorney General of Illinois
Ab.: Op. Ill. Att'y Gen.

Ex.: Op. Ill. Att'y Gen. No. 95-002 (May 25, 1995). –Citation to slip opinion.

–If the opinion has a name or title, it may be included before the citation. See Bluebook rule 14.4.

Opinions of the Attorney General of Indiana
Ab.: Op. Ind. Att'y Gen.

Ex.: Op. Ind. Att'y Gen. No. 95-1 (Mar. 23, 1995). –Citation to slip opinion.

1987-1988 Op. Ind. Att'y Gen. 1, No. 87-1. –Citation to opinion compiled in Official Opinions of the Attorney General of Indiana.

–If the opinion has a name or title, it may be included before the citation. See Bluebook rule 14.4.

Opinions of the Attorney General of Iowa
Ab.: Op. Iowa Att'y Gen.

In law review footnotes, the titles of books and the names of cases, except for procedural phrases, are not underlined. See Bluebook rule 2.1(a) & (b). Further, the following are in large and small capitals: codes, restatements, standards, constitutions, periodicals, authors of books, titles of books, the abbreviated names of codes, most legislative materials except for bills and resolutions, codified ordinances, model codes, court rules, and sentencing guidelines. Refer to The Bluebook.

Ex.:   Op. Iowa Att'y Gen. No. 93-7-5 (July 28, 1993). –Citation to slip opinion.

1993-1994 Iowa Att'y Gen. Biennial Rep. 26, No. 93-7-6 (1993). –Citation to opinion contained in a Biennial Report of the Iowa Attorney General.

–If the opinion has a name or title, it may be included before the citation. See Bluebook rule 14.4.

Opinions of the Attorney General of Kansas
Ab.:   Op. Kan. Att'y Gen.

Ex.:   Op. Kan. Att'y Gen. No. 94-121 (Sept. 20, 1994). –Citation to slip opinion.

29 Op. Kan. Att'y Gen. 34, No. 94-90 (1994). –Citation to compiled opinion.

–If the opinion has a name or title, it may be included before the citation. See Bluebook rule 14.4.

Opinions of the Attorney General of Kentucky
Ab.:   Op. Ky. Att'y Gen.

Ex.:   Op. Ky. Att'y Gen. No. 95-24 (June 16, 1995). –Citation to slip opinion.

1995 Op. Ky. Att'y Gen. 2-111, No. 95-29. –Citation to compiled opinion.

–If the opinion has a name or title, it may be included before the citation. See Bluebook rule 14.4.

Opinions of the Attorney General of Louisiana
Ab.:   Op. La. Att'y Gen.

Ex.:   Op. La. Att'y Gen. No. 92-169 (Dec. 4, 1992). –Citation to slip opinion.

1992-1993 Op. La. Att'y Gen. 18, No. 92-232 (1992). –Citation to compiled opinion.

–If the opinion has a name or title, it may be included before the citation. See Bluebook rule 14.4.

Opinions of the Attorney General of Maine
Ab.:   Op. Me. Att'y Gen.

Ex.:   Op. Me. Att'y Gen. No. 95-12 (July 11, 1995). –Citation to slip opinion.

–If the opinion has a name or title, it may be included before the citation. See Bluebook rule 14.4.

Opinions of the Attorney General of Maryland
Ab.:   Op. Md. Att'y Gen.

In citing cases in law review footnotes, abbreviate any word listed in table T.6; the names of "states, countries, and other geographical units" unless they are named parties; and any other words of eight or more letters "if substantial space is thereby saved and the result is unambiguous." Bluebook rule 10.2.2. On the other hand, in citing cases in text, abbreviate only widely known acronyms and the following words: "&," "Ass'n," "Bros.," "Co.," "Corp.," "Inc.," "Ltd.," and "No." Bluebook rule 10.2.1(c).

Ex.:   74 Op. Md. Att'y Gen. 112 (1989). –Citation to compiled opinion.

–If the opinion has a name or title, it may be included before the citation. See Bluebook rule 14.4.

Opinions of the Attorney General of Massachusetts

Ab.:   Op. Mass. Att'y Gen.

Ex.:   Op. Mass. Att'y Gen. No. 93/94-1 (Aug. 9, 1993). –Citation to slip opinion.

1994 Op. Mass. Att'y Gen. 197, No. 93/94-1 (1993). –Citation to compiled opinion.

–If the opinion has a name or title, it may be included before the citation. See Bluebook rule 14.4.

Opinions of the Attorney General of Michigan

Ab.:   Op. Mich. Att'y Gen.

Ex.:   Op. Mich. Att'y Gen. No. 6750 (Mar. 3, 1993). –Citation to slip opinion.

1993-1994 Op. Mich. Att'y Gen. 12, No. 6750 (1993). –Citation to opinion compiled in the Biennial Report of the Attorney General of the State of Michigan.

–If the opinion has a name or title, it may be included before the citation. See Bluebook rule 14.4.

Opinions of the Attorney General of Minnesota

Ab.:   Op. Minn. Att'y Gen.

Ex.:   Op. Minn. Att'y Gen. No. 627e (Aug. 1, 1994). –Citation to slip opinion.

Op. Minn. Atty. Gen., 27 Minn. Legal Reg. 3 (1994). –Citation to opinion compiled in the Minnesota Legal Register.

–If the opinion has a name or title, it may be included before the citation. See Bluebook rule 14.4.

Opinions of the Attorney General of Mississippi

Ab.:   Op. Miss. Att'y Gen.

Ex.:   1991 Op. Miss. Att'y Gen. No. 237 (May 11, 1995). –Citation to slip opinion.

–If the opinion has a name or title, it may be included before the citation. See Bluebook rule 14.4.

Opinions of the Attorney General of Missouri

Ab.:   Op. Mo. Att'y Gen.

Ex.:   Op. Mo. Att'y Gen. No. 54-95 (Mar. 6, 1995). –Citation to slip opinion.

–If the opinion has a name or title, it may be included before the citation. See Bluebook rule 14.4.

In law review footnotes, the titles of books and the names of cases, except for procedural phrases, are not underlined. See Bluebook rule 2.1(a) & (b). Further, the following are in large and small capitals: codes, restatements, standards, constitutions, periodicals, authors of books, titles of books, the abbreviated names of codes, most legislative materials except for bills and resolutions, codified ordinances, model codes, court rules, and sentencing guidelines. Refer to The Bluebook.

Opinions of the Attorney General of Montana
Ab.:   Op. Mont. Att'y Gen.
Ex.:   43 Op. Mont. Att'y Gen. 288 (1989). –Citation to compiled opinion.
         –If the opinion has a name or title, it may be included before the citation. See Bluebook rule 14.4.

Opinions of the Attorney General of Nebraska
Ab.:   Op. Neb. Att'y Gen.
Ex.:   Op. Neb. Att'y Gen. No. 230 (Oct. 17, 1984). –Citation to a slip opinion.
         –If the opinion has a name or title, it may be included before the citation. See Bluebook rule 14.4.

Opinions of the Attorney General of Nevada
Ab.:   Op. Nev. Att'y Gen.
Ex.:   Op. Nev. Att'y Gen. No. 95-02 (Feb. 23, 1995). –Citation to slip opinion.
         1995 Op. Nev. Att'y Gen. 3. –Citation to opinion compiled in Official Opinions of the Attorney General of Nevada.
         –If the opinion has a name or title, it may be included before the citation. See Bluebook rule 14.4.

Opinions of the Attorney General of New Jersey
Ab.:   Op. N.J. Att'y Gen.
Ex.:   Op. N.J. Att'y Gen. No. 1-1991 (Feb. 19, 1991). –Citation to slip opinion.
         –If the opinion has a name or title, it may be included before the citation. See Bluebook rule 14.4.

Opinions of the Attorney General of New Mexico
Ab.:   Op. N.M. Att'y Gen.
Ex.:   Op. N.M. Att'y Gen. No. 93-1 (Jan. 5, 1993). –Citation to slip opinion.
         –If the opinion has a name or title, it may be included before the citation. See Bluebook rule 14.4.

Opinions of the Attorney General of New York
Ab.:   Op. N.Y. Att'y Gen.
Ex.:   Op. N.Y. Att'y Gen. No. F 95-1 (Mar. 30, 1995). –Citation to formal slip opinion.
         Informal Op. N.Y. Att'y Gen. No. I 95-1 (Jan. 24, 1995). –Citation to informal slip opinion.
         1979 Op. N.Y. Att'y Gen. 31. –Citation to compiled formal opinion.

In citing cases in law review footnotes, abbreviate any word listed in table T.6; the names of "states, countries, and other geographical units" unless they are named parties; and any other words of eight or more letters "if substantial space is thereby saved and the result is unambiguous." Bluebook rule 10.2.2. On the other hand, in citing cases in text, abbreviate only widely known acronyms and the following words: "&," "Ass'n," "Bros.," "Co.," "Corp.," "Inc.," "Ltd.," and "No." Bluebook rule 10.2.1(c).

–If the opinion has a name or title, it may be included before the citation. See Bluebook rule 14.4.

Opinions of the Attorney General of North Carolina
Ab.: Op. N.C. Att'y Gen.

Ex.: 60 N.C. Att'y Gen. Rep. 19 (1990). –Citation to opinion compiled in the North Carolina Attorney General Reports.

–If the opinion has a name or title, it may be included before the citation. See Bluebook rule 14.4.

Opinions of the Attorney General, State of North Dakota
Ab.: Op. N.D. Att'y Gen.

Ex.: Op. N.D. Att'y Gen. No. 95-03 (Feb. 13, 1995). –Citation to slip opinion.

1995 Op. N.D. Att'y Gen. 7. –Citation to compiled opinion.

–If the opinion has a name or title, it may be included before the citation. See Bluebook rule 14.4.

Opinions of the Attorney General of Ohio
Ab.: Op. Ohio Att'y Gen.

Ex.: Op. Ohio Att'y Gen. No. 95-1 (Mar. 28, 1995). –Citation to slip opinion.

1995 Op. Ohio Att'y Gen. 2-1. –Citation to compiled opinion.

–If the opinion has a name or title, it may be included before the citation. See Bluebook rule 14.4.

Opinions of the Attorney General of Oklahoma
Ab.: Op. Okla. Att'y Gen.

Ex.: Op. Okla. Att'y Gen. No. 92-22 (Feb. 3, 1993). –Citation to slip opinion.

24 Op. Okla. Att'y Gen. 34 (1993). –Citation to compiled opinion.

–If the opinion has a name or title, it may be included before the citation. See Bluebook rule 14.4.

Opinions of the Attorney General of Oregon
Ab.: Op. Or. Att'y Gen.

Ex.: Op. Or. Att'y Gen. No. 8227 (Jan. 27, 1994). –Citation to slip opinion

Op. Or. Att'y Gen. 58 (1994). –Citation to compiled opinion.

–If the opinion has a name or title, it may be included before the citation. See Bluebook rule 14.4.

Opinions of the Attorney General of Pennsylvania
Ab.: Op. Pa. Att'y Gen.

In law review footnotes, the titles of books and the names of cases, except for procedural phrases, are not underlined. See Bluebook rule 2.1(a) & (b). Further, the following are in large and small capitals: codes, restatements, standards, constitutions, periodicals, authors of books, titles of books, the abbreviated names of codes, most legislative materials except for bills and resolutions, codified ordinances, model codes, court rules, and sentencing guidelines. Refer to The Bluebook.

Ex.: Op. Pa. Att'y Gen. No. 94-1 (Feb. 4, 1994). –Citation to slip opinion.

1978 Op. Pa. Att'y Gen. 117. –Citation to compiled opinion

–If the opinion has a name or title, it may be included before the citation. See Bluebook rule 14.4.

Opinions of the Attorney General of Puerto Rico

Ab.: Op. P.R. Sec. Just.

Ex.: Op. P.R. Sec. Just. Num. 1991-3 (Feb. 6, 1991). –Citation to slip opinion.

62 Op. P.R. Sec. Just. 8 (1991). –Citation to opinion compiled in the Opiniones del Secretario de Justicia.

–If the opinion has a name or title, it may be included before the citation. See Bluebook rule 14.4.

Opinions of the Attorney General of Rhode Island

Ab.: Op. R.I. Att'y Gen.

Ex.: Op. R.I. Att'y Gen. No. 95-02 (Jan. 11, 1995). –Citation to slip opinion.

–If the opinion has a name or title, it may be included before the citation. See Bluebook rule 14.4.

Opinions of the Attorney General of South Carolina

Ab.: Op. S.C. Att'y Gen.

Ex.: Op. S.C. Att'y Gen. No. 93-8 (Feb. 17, 1993). –Citation to slip opinion.

1993 Op. S.C. Att'y Gen. 31. –Citation to compiled opinion.

–If the opinion has a name or title, it may be included before the citation. See Bluebook rule 14.4.

Opinions of the Attorney General of South Dakota

Ab.: Op. S.D. Att'y Gen.

Ex.: Op. S.D. Att'y Gen. No. 93-12 (Dec. 1, 1993). –Citation to slip opinion.

1993-1994 S.D. Att'y Gen. Biennial Rep. 40 (1993). –Citation to opinion compiled in the Biennial Report of the Attorney General of the State of South Dakota.

–If the opinion has a name or title, it may be included before the citation. See Bluebook rule 14.4.

Opinions of the Attorney General of Tennessee

Ab.: Op. Tenn. Att'y Gen.

In citing cases in law review footnotes, abbreviate any word listed in table T.6; the names of "states, countries, and other geographical units" unless they are named parties; and any other words of eight or more letters "if substantial space is thereby saved and the result is unambiguous." Bluebook rule 10.2.2. On the other hand, in citing cases in text, abbreviate only widely known acronyms and the following words: "&," "Ass'n," "Bros.," "Co.," "Corp.," "Inc.," "Ltd.," and "No." Bluebook rule 10.2.1(c).

Ex.:   10 Op. Tenn. Att'y Gen. 757 (1981). –Cite to bound material. Prior to 1982, opinions are bound in numbered volumes and not separately paginated. See Bluebook rule 14.4.

1989 Op. Tenn. Att'y Gen. No. 89-110. –Cite to bound material. After 1981, opinions are bound in volumes numbered by the year of publication. Opinions are separately paginated. See Bluebook rule 14.4.

Op. Tenn. Att'y Gen. No. 95-008 (Mar. 1, 1995). –Cite to slip opinion that will eventually be included in a volume numbered by the year of publication. See Bluebook rule 14.4.

–If the opinion has a name or title, it may be included before the citation. See Bluebook rule 14.4.

Opinions of the Attorney General of Texas
Ab.:   Op. Tex. Att'y Gen.

Ex.:   Op. Tex. Att'y Gen. DM-317 (June 19, 1995). –Citation to slip formal opinion. (DM are the initials of the Texas Attorney General).

Op. Tex. Att'y Gen. No. LO95-011 (Mar. 17, 1995). –Citation to slip letter opinion.

Op. Tex. Att'y Gen. No. ORD-632 (Mar. 10, 1995). –Citation to slip open records decision.

–If the opinion has a name or title, it may be included before the citation. See Bluebook rule 14.4.

Opinions of the Attorney General of Utah
Ab.:   Op. Utah Att'y Gen.

Ex.:   Op. Utah Att'y Gen. 96-3 Utah Bull. 32 (1995). –Citation to opinion compiled in the Utah State Bulletin.

–If the opinion has a name or title, it may be included before the citation. See Bluebook rule 14.4.

Opinions of the Attorney General of Virgin Islands
Ab.:   Op. V.I. Att'y Gen.

Ex.:   Op. V.I. Att'y Gen. No. 1984-3 (Apr. 24, 1984). –Citation to slip opinion.

10 Op. V.I. Att'y Gen. 16 (1984). –Citation to compiled opinion.

–If the opinion has a name or title, it may be included before the citation. See Bluebook rule 14.4.

Opinions of the Attorney General of Virginia
Ab.:   Op. Va. Att'y Gen.

In law review footnotes, the titles of books and the names of cases, except for procedural phrases, are not underlined. See Bluebook rule 2.1(a) & (b). Further, the following are in large and small capitals: codes, restatements, standards, constitutions, periodicals, authors of books, titles of books, the abbreviated names of codes, most legislative materials except for bills and resolutions, codified ordinances, model codes, court rules, and sentencing guidelines. Refer to The Bluebook.

Ex.: 1995 Op. Va. Att'y Gen. 61. –Citation to opinion compiled in Opinions of the Attorney General and Report to the Governor of Virginia.

–If the opinion has a name or title, it may be included before the citation. See Bluebook rule 14.4.

Opinions of the Attorney General of Washington
Ab.: Op. Wash. Att'y Gen.

Ex.: 1995 Op. Wash. Att'y Gen. No. 1. –Citation to compiled opinion.

–If the opinion has a name or title, it may be included before the citation. See Bluebook rule 14.4.

Opinions of the Attorney General of West Virginia
Ab.: Op. W.Va. Att'y Gen.

Ex.: 1992-1993 Op. W.Va. Att'y Gen. (Feb. 24, 1992). –Citation to slip opinion.

61 Op. W.Va. Att'y Gen. 13 (1985). –Citation to opinion compiled in the Biennial Report and Official Opinions of the Attorney General of the State of West Virginia.

–If the opinion has a name or title, it may be included before the citation. See Bluebook rule 14.4.

Opinions of the Attorney General of Wisconsin
Ab.: Op. Wis. Att'y Gen.

Ex.: Op. Wis. Att'y Gen. No. 1-95 (Feb. 24, 1995). –Citation to slip opinion.

79 Op. Wis. Att'y Gen. 14 (1990). –Citation to compiled opinion.

–If the opinion has a name or title, it may be included before the citation. See Bluebook rule 14.4.

Opinions of the Attorney General of Wyoming
Ab.: Op. Wyo. Att'y Gen.

Ex.: Op. Wyo. Att'y Gen. No. 95-002 (May 22, 1995). –Citation to slip opinion.

1995 Op. Wyo. Att'y Gen. 4. –Citation to compiled opinion.

–If the opinion has a name or title, it may be included before the citation. See Bluebook rule 14.4.

Opinions of the Office of Legal Counsel of the U.S. Department of Justice (1977-date)
Ab.: Op. Off. Legal Counsel

Ex.: 19 Op. Off. Legal Counsel 67 (1992).

–If the opinion has a name or title, it may be included before the citation. See Bluebook rule 14.4.

In citing cases in law review footnotes, abbreviate any word listed in table T.6; the names of "states, countries, and other geographical units" unless they are named parties; and any other words of eight or more letters "if substantial space is thereby saved and the result is unambiguous." Bluebook rule 10.2.2. On the other hand, in citing cases in text, abbreviate only widely known acronyms and the following words: "&," "Ass'n," "Bros.," "Co.," "Corp.," "Inc.," "Ltd.," and "No." Bluebook rule 10.2.1(c).

Order, citation to

> –Do not abbreviate.

Ex.:   (Order Granting Def.'s Mot. Summ. J., May 1, 2005).

See Bluebook rule B10 and table BT.2.

Note: See Bluebook rule 10.8.3 for citing litigation materials from another state.

Order of authorities within each signal
See Bluebook rule 1.4.

Order of signals
See Bluebook rule 1.3.

Ordinals

> –"Unless part of a citation, ordinal numbers appearing in text and footnotes are controlled by rule 6.2(a). If part of a citation, figures are used for all ordinal numbers. Do not use superscripts." Bluebook rule 6.2(b).

Ex.:   92d Cong.

72   51st Leg.

17th ed.

ordinances
Ex.:

> –Citation to uncodified ordinance:

Knoxville, Tenn., Ordinance 0-155-78 (Sept. 8, 1978).

> –Citations to codified ordinances:

Santa Monica, Cal., Mun. Code § 4.16.040 (1964).

Indianapolis, Ind., Rev. Code § 101-4 (1988).

Minneapolis, Minn., Code ch. 2, § 17 (1983).

> –Unified city/county government:

Nashville and Davidson County, Tenn., Metropolitan Code § 3.33.040 (1995).

See Bluebook rule 12.8.2.

Ordinances of the Northwest Territories

Ab.:   O.N.W.T.

Oregon Administrative Rules
Ab.:   Or. Admin. R. x-x-x (year)
Ex.:   Or. Admin. R. 806-001-005 (1997).

Oregon Bulletin
Ab.:   vol. no. Or. Bull. page no. (month day, year)

In law review footnotes, the titles of books and the names of cases, except for procedural phrases, are not underlined. See Bluebook rule 2.1(a) & (b). Further, the following are in large and small capitals: codes, restatements, standards, constitutions, periodicals, authors of books, titles of books, the abbreviated names of codes, most legislative materials except for bills and resolutions, codified ordinances, model codes, court rules, and sentencing guidelines. Refer to The Bluebook.

Ex.:   12 Or. Bull. 78 (Apr. 1, 2005)

Oregon Attorney General Opinions
See Opinions of the Attorney General of Oregon.

Oregon Constitution
Ab.:   Or. Const. art.   , §   .

Ex.:   Or. Const. art. II, § 9. –"Cite constitutional provisions currently in force without a date." Bluebook rule 11.

Or. Const. art. IX, § 1 (amended 1917). –"When citing a provision that has been subsequently amended, either indicate parenthetically the fact and date of amendment or cite the amending provision in full." Bluebook rule 11.

Oregon Law Review
Ab.:   Or. L. Rev.

Ex.:   Joel K. Jacobson, The Collateral Source Rule and the Role of the Jury, 70 Or. L. Rev. 523 (1991). –Article Citation.

Joel K. Jacobson, The Collateral Source Rule and the Role of the Jury, 70 Or. L. Rev. 523, 528 (1991). –Page Citation.

Oregon Laws and Resolutions
Ab.:   year Or. Laws. page no.

year Or. Laws Spec. Sess. page no.
year Or. Laws Adv. Sh. No. x, page no.

Ex.:   Act of Sept. 9, 1995, ch. 616, 1995 Or. Laws 1686. –Citation to an entire session law.

Act of Sept. 9, 1995, ch. 616, § 2, 1995 Or. Laws 1686, 1687. –Citation to a section in a session law.

See Bluebook rule 12.4.

Oregon Reports
Ab.:   Or.

–Cite to P., P.2d , or P.3d, if therein; otherwise, cite to Or.

–Give parallel citations only in documents submitted to Oregon state courts. See Bluebook rules 10.3.1 and B5.1.3; see also Or. Unif. Trial Ct. R. 2.010(13), which requires a citation to Or. and expressly permits a parallel citation.

In documents submitted to Oregon state courts, cite as follows:

Adams v. Kulongoski, 322 Or. 637, 912 P.2d 902 (1996). –Case Citation.

Adams v. Kulongoski, 322 Or. 637, 638, 912 P.2d 902, 903 (1996). –Page Citation.

In citing cases in law review footnotes, abbreviate any word listed in table T.6; the names of "states, countries, and other geographical units" unless they are named parties; and any other words of eight or more letters "if substantial space is thereby saved and the result is unambiguous." Bluebook rule 10.2.2. On the other hand, in citing cases in text, abbreviate only widely known acronyms and the following words: "&," "Ass'n," "Bros.," "Co.," "Corp.," "Inc.," "Ltd.," and "No." Bluebook rule 10.2.1(c).

In all other documents, cite as follows:

> Adams v. Kulongoski, 912 P.2d 902 (Or. 1996). –Case Citation.
>
> Adams v. Kulongoski, 912 P.2d 902, 903 (Or. 1996). –Page Citation.

Oregon Reports, Court of Appeals
Ab.:   Or. App.

–Cite to P.2d or P.3d, if therein; otherwise, cite to Or. App.

–Give parallel citations only in documents submitted to Oregon state courts. See Bluebook rules 10.3.1 and B5.1.3; see also Or. Unif. Trial Ct. R. 2.010(13), which requires a citation to Or. App. and expressly permits a parallel citation.

In documents submitted to Oregon state courts, cite as follows:

> Zell v. Fellner, 140 Or. App. 35, 914 P.2d 23 (1996). –Case Citation.
>
> Zell v. Fellner, 140 Or. App. 35, 37, 914 P.2d 23, 24 (1996). –Page Citation.

In all other documents, cite as follows:

> Zell v. Fellner, 914 P.2d 23 (Or. Ct. App. 1996). –Case Citation.
>
> Zell v. Fellner, 914 P.2d 23, 24 (Or. Ct. App. 1996). –Page Citation.

Oregon Revised Statutes
Ab.:   Or. Rev. Stat. § x.x (year)

Ex.:   Or. Rev. Stat. § 801.365 (1999).

–For proper citation form in papers submitted to Oregon courts, see Preface to vol. 1, Or. Rev. Stat. at x (2003), Or. R. App. P. 5.35(3), and Oregon Appellate Courts Style Manual.

Oregon Session Laws
See Oregon Laws and Resolutions.

Oregon State Bar Bulletin
Ab.:   Or. St. B. Bull.

Ex.:   Philip Yates, ADA Promises Greater Access to Businesses, Or. St. B. Bull., Jan. 1992, at 19. –Article Citation.

Philip Yates, ADA Promises Greater Access to Businesses, Or. St. B. Bull., Jan. 1992, at 19, 20. –Page Citation.

Oregon Tax Reports
Ab.:   Or. Tax

In law review footnotes, the titles of books and the names of cases, except for procedural phrases, are not underlined. See Bluebook rule 2.1(a) & (b). Further, the following are in large and small capitals: codes, restatements, standards, constitutions, periodicals, authors of books, titles of books, the abbreviated names of codes, most legislative materials except for bills and resolutions, codified ordinances, model codes, court rules, and sentencing guidelines. Refer to The Bluebook.

Ex.:   Rogers v. Department of Revenue, 6 Or. Tax. 139, 142 (1975).

Orfield's Criminal Procedure Under the Federal Rules, by Mark S. Rhodes
–Do not abbreviate the title.

Ex.:   5 Mark S. Rhodes, Orfield's Criminal Procedure Under the Federal Rules § 24:4 (2d ed. 1987). –Section Citation.

5 Mark S. Rhodes, Orfield's Criminal Procedure Under the Federal Rules § 33:64, at 368 (2d ed. 1987). –Page Citation.

5 Mark S. Rhodes, Orfield's Criminal Procedure Under the Federal Rules § 33:64, at 368 n.7 (2d ed. 1987). –Footnote Citation.

3 Mark S. Rhodes, Orfield's Criminal Procedure Under the Federal Rules § 24:4 (2d ed. Supp. 2000). –Citation to Supplement Section.

Orphans' Court
Ab.:   Orphans' Ct.

Osaka University Law Review
Ab.:   Osaka U. L. Rev.

Ex.:   Shigenori Matsui, Freedom of Expression in Japan, 38 Osaka U. L. Rev. 13 (1991). –Article Citation.

Shigenori Matsui, Freedom of Expression in Japan, 38 Osaka U. L. Rev. 13, 19-20 (1991). –Page Citation.

Osgoode Hall Law Journal
Ab.:   Osgoode Hall L.J.

Ex.:   David Vaver, Copyright in Legal Documents, 31 Osgoode Hall L.J. 661 (1993). –Article Citation.

David Vaver, Copyright in Legal Documents, 31 Osgoode Hall L.J. 661, 670-73 (1993). –Page Citation.

Otago Law Review
Ab.:   Otago L. Rev.

Ex.:   Graeme Austin, Righting a Child's Right to Refuse Medical Treatment, 7 Otago L. Rev. 578 (1992). –Article Citation.

Graeme Austin, Righting a Child's Right to Refuse Medical Treatment, 7 Otago L. Rev. 578, 583-87 (1992). –Page Citation.

Ottawa Law Review
Ab.:   Ottawa L. Rev.

Ex.:   Denis J.E. Scott, Interception of a Hacker's Computer Communication, 25 Ottawa L. Rev. 525 (1993). –Article Citation.

Denis J.E. Scott, Interception of a Hacker's Computer Communication, 25 Ottawa L. Rev. 525, 529 (1993). –Page Citation.

In citing cases in law review footnotes, abbreviate any word listed in table T.6; the names of "states, countries, and other geographical units" unless they are named parties; and any other words of eight or more letters "if substantial space is thereby saved and the result is unambiguous." Bluebook rule 10.2.2. On the other hand, in citing cases in text, abbreviate only widely known acronyms and the following words: "&," "Ass'n," "Bros.," "Co.," "Corp.," "Inc.," "Ltd.," and "No." Bluebook rule 10.2.1(c).

Oxford Journal of Legal Studies

Ab.:   Oxford J. Legal Stud.

Ex.:   Paul Roberts, <u>Science in the Criminal Process</u>, 14 Oxford J. Legal Stud. 469 (1994). –Article Citation.

Paul Roberts, <u>Science in the Criminal Process</u>, 14 Oxford J. Legal Stud. 469, 472-77 (1994). –Page Citation.

In law review footnotes, the titles of books and the names of cases, except for procedural phrases, are not underlined. <u>See</u> <u>Bluebook</u> rule 2.1(a) & (b). Further, the following are in large and small capitals: codes, restatements, standards, constitutions, periodicals, authors of books, titles of books, the abbreviated names of codes, most legislative materials except for bills and resolutions, codified ordinances, model codes, court rules, and sentencing guidelines. Refer to <u>The Bluebook</u>.

P

Pace Environmental Law Review
    Ab.:   Pace Envtl. L. Rev.

    Ex.:   Ludwik A. Teclaff, The River Basin Concept and Global Climate Change, 8 Pace Envtl. L. Rev. 355 (1991). –Article Citation.

           Ludwik A. Teclaff, The River Basin Concept and Global Climate Change, 8 Pace Envtl. L. Rev. 355, 369-72 (1991). –Page Citation.

Pace Law Review
    Ab.:   Pace L. Rev.

    Ex.:   Vincent M. Bonventre, Court of Appeals - State Constitutional Law Review, 1990, 12 Pace L. Rev. 1 (1992). –Article Citation.

           Vincent M. Bonventre, Court of Appeals - State Constitutional Law Review, 1990, 12 Pace L. Rev. 1, 49-51 (1992). –Page Citation.

Pace Yearbook of International Law
    Ab.:   Pace Y.B. Int'l L.

    Ex.:   Mohammed Bedjaoui, The "Manufacture" of Judgments at the International Court of Justice, 3 Pace Y.B. Int'l L. 29 (1991). –Article Citation.

           Mohammed Bedjaoui, The "Manufacture" of Judgments at the International Court of Justice, 3 Pace Y.B. Int'l L. 29, 49-50 (1991). –Page Citation.

Pacific Law Journal
    Ab.:   Pac. L.J.

    Ex.:   Jeff Brown, Origins and Impact - A Public Defender's Perspective, 23 Pac. L.J. 881 (1992). –Article Citation.

           Jeff Brown, Origins and Impact - A Public Defender's Perspective, 23 Pac. L.J. 881, 899 (1992). –Page Citation.

Pacific Reporter
           –Do not give a parallel citation unless required by local rule. See Bluebook rules 10.3.1 and B5.1.3. See also the various state court and state reporter entries herein for local rule parallel citation requirements.

    Ab.:   P.

In law review footnotes, the titles of books and the names of cases, except for procedural phrases, are not underlined. See Bluebook rule 2.1(a) & (b). Further, the following are in large and small capitals: codes, restatements, standards, constitutions, periodicals, authors of books, titles of books, the abbreviated names of codes, most legislative materials except for bills and resolutions, codified ordinances, model codes, court rules, and sentencing guidelines. Refer to The Bluebook.

Ex.:

Arizona:

> Abbey v. Green, 235 P. 150 (Ariz. 1925). –Case Citation.
>
> Abbey v. Green, 235 P. 150, 153 (Ariz. 1925). –Page Citation.

California:

> Avery v. Peirson, 241 P. 406 (Cal. Dist. Ct. App. 1925).
> –Case Citation.
>
> Avery v. Peirson, 241 P. 406, 407 (Cal. Dist. Ct. App. 1925).
> –Page Citation.

Colorado:

> Estes v. Crann, 216 P. 517 (Colo. 1923). –Case Citation.
>
> Estes v. Crann, 216 P. 517, 518 (Colo. 1923). –Page Citation.

Idaho:

> State v. Main, 216 P. 731 (Idaho 1923). –Case Citation.
>
> State v. Main, 216 P. 731, 734 (Idaho 1923). –Page Citation.

Kansas:

> Indihar v. W. Coal & Mining Co., 241 P. 448 (Kan. 1925).
> –Case Citation.
>
> Indihar v. W. Coal & Mining Co., 241 P. 448, 450 (Kan. 1925). –Page
> Citation.

Montana:

> Weber v. City of Helena, 297 P. 455 (Mont. 1931). –Case Citation.
>
> Weber v. City of Helena, 297 P. 455, 465 (Mont. 1931). –Page
> Citation.

Nevada:

> McCulloch v. Bianchini, 297 P. 503 (Nev. 1931). –Case Citation.
>
> McCulloch v. Bianchini, 297 P. 503, 504 (Nev. 1931). –Page Citation.

New Mexico:

> Epstein v. Waas, 216 P. 506 (N.M. 1923). –Case Citation.
>
> Epstein v. Waas, 216 P. 506, 508 (N.M. 1923). –Page Citation.

Oklahoma:

> Exchange Oil Co. v. Crews, 216 P. 674 (Okla. 1923). –Case Citation.
>
> Exchange Oil Co. v. Crews, 216 P. 674, 675 (Okla. 1923). –Page
> Citation.

Oregon:

> Noble v. Yancey, 241 P. 335 (Or. 1925). –Case Citation.
>
> Noble v. Yancey, 241 P. 335, 338 (Or. 1925). –Page Citation.

In citing cases in law review footnotes, abbreviate any word listed in table T.6;
the names of "states, countries, and other geographical units" unless they are named parties;
and any other words of eight or more letters "if substantial space is thereby saved and the
result is unambiguous." Bluebook rule 10.2.2. On the other hand, in citing cases in text,
abbreviate only widely known acronyms and the following words: "&," "Ass'n," "Bros.,"
"Co.," "Corp.," "Inc.," "Ltd.," and "No." Bluebook rule 10.2.1(c).

Utah:

>Oldroyd v. McCrea, 235 P. 580 (Utah 1925). –Case Citation.
>
>Oldroyd v. McCrea, 235 P. 580, 587 (Utah 1925). –Page Citation.

Washington:

>Trunk v. Wilkes, 297 P. 1091 (Wash. 1931). –Case Citation.
>
>Trunk v. Wilkes, 297 P. 1091, 1092 (Wash. 1931). –Page Citation.

Wyoming:

>Yellowstone Sheep Co. v. Diamond Dot Live Stock Co., 297 P. 1107 (Wyo. 1931). –Case Citation.
>
>Yellowstone Sheep Co. v. Diamond Dot Live Stock Co., 297 P. 1107, 1114 (Wyo. 1931). –Page Citation.

Pacific Reporter, Second Series

>–Do not give a parallel citation unless required by local rule or unless the particular state has a public domain format. See Bluebook rules 10.3.1, 10.3.3, and B5.1.3. See also the various state court and state reporter entries herein for public domain information and local rule parallel citation requirements.
>
>–With volume 744 (1988), Pacific Reporter, Second Series, became West's Pacific Reporter, Second Series. Citation form is not affected by this title change.

Ab.:   P.2d

Ex.:

Alaska:

>Acevedo v. Burley, 994 P.2d 389 (Alaska 1999). –Case Citation.
>
>Acevedo v. Burley, 994 P.2d 389, 392 (Alaska 1999). –Page Citation.

Arizona:

>Randolph v. Groscost, 989 P.2d 751 (Ariz. 1999). –Case Citation.
>
>Randolph v. Groscost, 989 P.2d 751, 753 (Ariz. 1999). –Page Citation.

California:

>Samuels v. Mix, 989 P.2d 701 (Cal. 1999). –Case Citation.
>
>Samuels v. Mix, 989 P.2d 701, 715 (Cal. 1999). –Page Citation.

Colorado:

>People v. Kyler, 991 P.2d 810 (Colo. 1999). –Case Citation.
>
>People v. Kyler, 991 P.2d 810, 818 (Colo. 1999). –Page Citation.

Hawaii:

>State v. White, 990 P.2d 90 (Haw. 1999). –Case Citation.
>
>State v. White, 990 P.2d 90, 95 (Haw. 1999). –Page Citation.

In law review footnotes, the titles of books and the names of cases, except for procedural phrases, are not underlined. See Bluebook rule 2.1(a) & (b). Further, the following are in large and small capitals: codes, restatements, standards, constitutions, periodicals, authors of books, titles of books, the abbreviated names of codes, most legislative materials except for bills and resolutions, codified ordinances, model codes, court rules, and sentencing guidelines. Refer to The Bluebook.

Idaho:

> Clark v. City of Lewiston, 992 P.2d 172 (Idaho 1999). –Case Citation.
>
> Clark v. City of Lewiston, 992 P.2d 172, 174 (Idaho 1999). –Page Citation.

Kansas:

> State v. Johnson, 970 P.2d 990 (Kan. 1998). –Case Citation.
>
> State v. Johnson, 970 P.2d 990, 992 (Kan. 1998). –Page Citation.

Montana:

> Benson v. Heritage Inn, Inc., 971 P.2d 1227 (Mont. 1998). –Case Citation.
>
> Benson v. Heritage Inn, Inc., 971 P.2d 1227, 1231 (Mont. 1998). –Page Citation.

Nevada:

> Goodson v. State, 992 P.2d 472 (Nev. 1999). –Case Citation.
>
> Goodson v. State, 992 P.2d 472, 474 (Nev. 1999). –Page Citation.

New Mexico:

> State v. Lopez, 993 P.2d 727 (N.M.1999). –Case Citation.
>
> State v. Lopez, 993 P.2d 727, 731 (N.M.1999). –Page Citation.

Oklahoma:

> Jackson v. Jackson, 995 P.2d 1109 (Okla. 1999). –Case Citation.
>
> Jackson v. Jackson, 995 P.2d 1109, 1112 (Okla. 1999). –Page Citation.

Oregon:

> Sizemore v. Myers, 994 P.2d 792 (Or. 1999). –Case Citation.
>
> Sizemore v. Myers, 994 P.2d 792, 793 (Or. 1999). –Page Citation.

Utah:

> DeBry v. Godbe, 992 P.2d 979 (Utah 1999). –Case Citation.
>
> DeBry v. Godbe, 992 P.2d 979, 984 (Utah 1999).   –Page Citation.

Washington:

> Phillips v. King County, 968 P.2d 871 (Wash. 1998). –Case Citation.
>
> Phillips v. King County, 968 P.2d 871, 876 (Wash. 1998). –Page Citation.

Wyoming:

> Griswold v. State, 994 P.2d 920 (Wyo. 1999). –Case Citation.
>
> Griswold v. State, 994 P.2d 920, 926 (Wyo. 1999). –Page Citation.

Pacific Reporter, Third Series

> –Do not give a parallel citation unless required by local rule or unless the particular state has a public domain format. See Bluebook rules

---

In citing cases in law review footnotes, abbreviate any word listed in table T.6; the names of "states, countries, and other geographical units" unless they are named parties; and any other words of eight or more letters "if substantial space is thereby saved and the result is unambiguous." Bluebook rule 10.2.2. On the other hand, in citing cases in text, abbreviate only widely known acronyms and the following words: "&," "Ass'n," "Bros.," "Co.," "Corp.," "Inc.," "Ltd.," and "No." Bluebook rule 10.2.1(c).

10.3.1, 10.3.3, and B5.1.3. See also the various state court and state reporter entries herein for public domain information and local rule parallel citation requirements.

Ab.: P.3d

Ex.:

Alaska:

N. Alaska Envtl. Ctr. v. State Dep't of Natural Res., 2 P.3d 629 (Alaska 2000). –Case Citation.

N. Alaska Envtl. Ctr. v. State Dep't of Natural Res., 2 P.3d 629, 634 (Alaska 2000).   –Page Citation.

Arizona:

State v. Bass, 12 P.3d 796 (Ariz. 2000). –Case Citation.

State v. Bass, 12 P.3d 796, 809 (Ariz. 2000). –Page Citation.

California:

People v. Robles, 3 P.3d 311 (Cal. 2000). –Case Citation.

People v. Robles, 3 P.3d 311, 312 (Cal. 2000). –Page Citation.

Colorado:

Corsentino v. Cordova, 4 P.3d 1082 (Colo. 2000). –Case Citation.

Corsentino v. Cordova, 4 P.3d 1082, 1086 (Colo. 2000). –Page Citation.

Hawaii:

State v. Crisostomo, 12 P.3d 873 (Haw. 2000). –Case Citation.

State v. Crisostomo, 12 P.3d 873, 878 (Haw. 2000). –Page Citation.

Idaho:

State v. Daniels, 11 P.3d 1114 (Idaho 2000). –Case Citation.

State v. Daniels, 11 P.3d 1114, 1116 (Idaho 2000). –Page Citation.

Kansas:

In re Kroger Co., 12 P.3d 889 (Kan. 2000). –Case Citation.

In re Kroger Co., 12 P.3d 889, 893 (Kan. 2000). –Page Citation.

Montana:

Kingston v. Ameritrade, Inc., 12 P.3d 929 (Mont. 2000). –Case Citation.

Kingston v. Ameritrade, Inc., 12 P.3d 929, 931 (Mont. 2000). –Page Citation.

Nevada:

Hughes v. State, 12 P.3d 948 (Nev. 2000). –Case Citation.

Hughes v. State, 12 P.3d 948, 953 (Nev. 2000). –Page Citation.

In law review footnotes, the titles of books and the names of cases, except for procedural phrases, are not underlined. See Bluebook rule 2.1(a) & (b). Further, the following are in large and small capitals: codes, restatements, standards, constitutions, periodicals, authors of books, titles of books, the abbreviated names of codes, most legislative materials except for bills and resolutions, codified ordinances, model codes, court rules, and sentencing guidelines. Refer to The Bluebook.

New Mexico:

> State v. Antillon, 2 P.3d 315 (N.M. 1999). –Case Citation.
>
> State v. Antillon, 2 P.3d 315, 316 (N.M. 1999). –Page Citation.

Oklahoma:

> Dixon Property Co. v. Shaw, 2 P.3d 330 (Okla. 1999). –Case Citation.
>
> Dixon Property Co. v. Shaw, 2 P.3d 330, 333 (Okla. 1999). –Page Citation.

Oregon:

> Bruce & Bruce v. City of Hillsboro, 6 P.3d 1097 (Or. 1999).
> –Case Citation.
>
> Bruce & Bruce v. City of Hillsboro, 6 P.3d 1097, 1097 (Or. 1999).
> –Page Citation.

Utah:

> Desert Miriah, Inc. v. B & L Auto, Inc., 12 P.3d 580 (Utah 2000).
> –Case Citation.
>
> Desert Miriah, Inc. v. B & L Auto, Inc., 12 P.3d 580, 581 (Utah 2000).
> –Page Citation.

Washington:

> Haley v. Highland, 12 P.3d 119 (Wash. 2000). –Case Citation.
>
> Haley v. Highland, 12 P.3d 119, 121 (Wash. 2000). –Page Citation.

Wyoming:

> Heinemann v. State, 12 P.3d 692 (Wyo. 2000). –Case Citation.
>
> Heinemann v. State, 12 P.3d 692, 699 (Wyo. 2000). –Page Citation.

Pacific Rim Law & Policy Journal

Ab.:   Pac. Rim L. & Pol'y J.

Ex.:   Yuan Cheng, Legal Protection of Trade Secrets in the Peoples'
        Republic of China, 5 Pac. Rim L. & Pol'y J. 261 (1996). –Article
        Citation.

        Yuan Cheng, Legal Protection of Trade Secrets in the Peoples'
        Republic of China, 5 Pac. Rim L. & Pol'y J. 261, 262 (1996). –Page
        Citation.

page

–Repeat page number when citing to material on the first page of an
article or case.

Ex.:   Rochelle C. Dryfuss & Dorothy Nelkin, The Jurisprudence of Genetics,
        45 Vand L. Rev. 313, 313 (1992).

        –"p." and "pp." are used only for internal cross-reference. See
        Bluebook rule 3.2(a).

In citing cases in law review footnotes, abbreviate any word listed in table T.6;
the names of "states, countries, and other geographical units" unless they are named parties;
and any other words of eight or more letters "if substantial space is thereby saved and the
result is unambiguous." Bluebook rule 10.2.2. On the other hand, in citing cases in text,
abbreviate only widely known acronyms and the following words: "&," "Ass'n," "Bros.,"
"Co.," "Corp.," "Inc.," "Ltd.," and "No." Bluebook rule 10.2.1(c).

Ex.:   See infra p. 41 and n.62.

    –Generally, use "at" with page number only if the page number will be confused with other parts of the citation or after "id."

Ex.:   H.R. Rep. No. 103-403, at 21 (1994).

Ex.:   Id. at 15.

See Bluebook rule 3.2(a).

Page on the Law of Wills, by William J. Bowe and Douglas H. Parker
    –Do not abbreviate the title.

Ex.:   7 William J. Bowe & Douglas H. Parker, Page on the Law of Wills § 63.28 (rev. 1969). –Section Citation.

    7 William J. Bowe & Douglas H. Parker, Page on the Law of Wills § 63.28, at 186 (rev. 1969). –Page Citation.

    7 William J. Bowe & Douglas H. Parker, Page on the Law of Wills § 63.28, (Supp. 1987). –Citation to Supplement Section.

    3 William J. Bowe & Douglas H. Parker, Page on the Law of Wills § 26.9 (rev. ed. 2004). –Section Citation

    3 Jeffrey A. Schoenblum, Page on the Law of Wills § 26.63 (Cum. Supp. 2005). –Citation to Cumulative Supplement Section.

Page's Ohio Legislative Bulletin (LexisNexis)
Ab.:   year Ohio Legis. Bull. page no. (LexisNexis)

Ex.:   Act effective Dec. 14, 2004, File 166, 2004. Ohio Legis. Bull. 2008 (LexisNexis) (requiring students to be immunized against chicken pox). –Citation to an entire session law.

    Act effective Dec. 14, 2004, File 166, sec. 1, § 3701.134, 2004 Ohio Legis. Bull. 2008, 2009 (LexisNexis) (requiring students to be immunized against chicken pox). –Citation to a section of a session law.

    –See Bluebook rule 12.4.

    –"Cite to Ohio Laws, if therein." Bluebook table T.1, page 227.

Page's Ohio Revised Code Annotated (LexisNexis)
Ab.:   Ohio Rev. Code Ann. § x.x (LexisNexis year)

Ex.:   Ohio Rev. Code Ann. § 4701.3 (LexisNexis 2004).

    –For proper citation form in papers submitted to Ohio state courts, see Interim Edition to the Manual of the Forms of Citation used in the Ohio Official Reports, 88 Ohio App. 3d XXVI, XLIV (1992), available at http://www.sconet.state.oh.us/rod/pdf/MANCITEmain.pdf.

Panama Canal Zone Code
See Canal Zone Code.

In law review footnotes, the titles of books and the names of cases, except for procedural phrases, are not underlined. See Bluebook rule 2.1(a) & (b). Further, the following are in large and small capitals: codes, restatements, standards, constitutions, periodicals, authors of books, titles of books, the abbreviated names of codes, most legislative materials except for bills and resolutions, codified ordinances, model codes, court rules, and sentencing guidelines. Refer to The Bluebook.

Pan-American Treaty Series
    Ab.:   Pan-Am. T.S.

paragraph(s)
    Ab.:   ¶, ¶¶ if so in source. Otherwise para., paras.
    Ex.:   2A Richard R. Powell, <u>Powell on Real Property</u> (Patrick J. Rohan ed., 1992) ¶ 269.

           2A Richard R. Powell, <u>Powell on Real Property</u> (Patrick J. Rohan ed., 1992) ¶¶ 269-27.

See <u>Bluebook</u> rules 3.3, 6.2(c), & table T.16.

Parallel citation for state court case
    In documents submitted to state courts, citations to cases decided by the courts of that state should include a parallel citation if there is a public domain citation and if otherwise required by local rule. See <u>Bluebook</u> rules 10.3.1, 10.3.3, and B5.1.3; see also the various state court and state reporter entries herein for public domain information and local rule parallel citation requirements.

parenthetical information and explanatory parenthetical phrases
See <u>Bluebook</u> rules 1.5, 1.6, and 10.6.

Parry's Consolidated Treaty Series (1648-1919)
    Ab.:   Consol. T.S.

Partnership, by Alan R. Bromberg
See Crane and Bromberg on Partnership, by Alan R. Bromberg.

Partnership Taxation, by Arthur B. Willis, John S. Pennell, and Phillip F. Postlewaite
    –Do not abbreviate the title.
    Ex.:   2 Arthur B. Willis et al., <u>Partnership Taxation</u> § 15.06 (6th ed. 1999). –Section Citation.

           2 Arthur B. Willis et al., <u>Partnership Taxation</u> § 15.06, at 15-45 (6th ed. 1999). –Page Citation.

           2 Arthur B. Willis et al., <u>Partnership Taxation</u> § 15.06, at 15-45 n.170 (6th ed. 1999). –Footnote Citation.

Patent Law Annual
    Ab.:   Pat. L. Ann.
    Ex.:   Charles S. Cotropia, <u>The Trademark Law Revision Act of 1988</u>, 26 Pat. L. Ann. 2-1 (1988). –Proceedings Citation.

           Charles S. Cotropia, <u>The Trademark Law Revision Act of 1988</u>, 26 Pat. L. Ann. 2-1, 2-13–2-15 (1988). –Page Citation.

Patents, by Donald S. Chisum
    –Do not abbreviate the title.

In citing cases in law review footnotes, abbreviate any word listed in table T.6; the names of "states, countries, and other geographical units" unless they are named parties; and any other words of eight or more letters "if <u>substantial</u> space is thereby saved and the result is unambiguous." <u>Bluebook</u> rule 10.2.2. On the other hand, in citing cases in text, abbreviate only widely known acronyms and the following words: "&," "Ass'n," "Bros.," "Co.," "Corp.," "Inc.," "Ltd.," and "No." <u>Bluebook</u> rule 10.2.1(c).

Ex.: 6 Donald S. Chisum, <u>Patents</u> § 19.03[3] (2004). –Section Citation.

6 Donald S. Chisum, <u>Patents</u> § 19.03[3], at 19-217 (2004). –Page Citation.

6 Donald S. Chisum, <u>Patents</u> § 19.03[3], at 19-217 n.19 (2004). –Footnote Citation.

Patents, Trademark, & Copyright Journal (Bureau of National Affairs)
Ab.: Pat. Trademark & Copyright J. (BNA)

Ex.: <u>Bernard v. Commerce Drug Co.</u>, [Nov.-Apr.] Pat. Trademark & Copyright J. (BNA) No. 1055, at 10 (E.D.N.Y. Sept 27, 1991). –Citation to looseleaf material.

–The above examples are proper if the case is not yet available in, or is not reported in, an official or West reporter, a public domain citation, or in a widely used computer database.

Patents, United States
Ex.: U.S. Patent No. 6,079,520 (issued June 27, 2000).

See <u>Bluebook</u> rule 14.9.

pending and unreported cases
See also Electronic media and other nonprint resources.

Ex.: <u>United States v. Chen</u>, No. 90-10434 (9th Cir. argued Mar. 11, 1991). –Pending case. See <u>Bluebook</u> rule 10.8.1(a).

<u>United States v. Chen</u>, No. 90-10434, slip op. 6509, 6514 (9th Cir. May 23, 1991). –Unreported case available only in separately printed slip opinion. See <u>Bluebook</u> rule 10.8.1(b).

–An unreported case that is available on a widely used electronic database may be cited to that database. See <u>Bluebook</u> rule 18.1.1.

<u>United States v. Chen</u>, No. 90-10434, 1991 U.S. App. LEXIS 14034, at *2 (9th Cir. May 23, 1991

<u>Tipton v. Ahmad</u>, No. 03A01-9201-CV-16, 1992 WL 91509, at *3 (Tenn. Ct. App. May 6, 1992).

Penn State International Law Review
Ab: Penn St. Int'l L. Rev.

Ex: E. Arcelia Quintana Adriano, <u>Bankruptcy of the Banking System and Guarantees' Regulation in Mexico</u>, 23 Penn St. Int'l L. Rev. 321 (2004). –Article Citation.

E. Arcelia Quintana Adriano, <u>Bankruptcy of the Banking System and Guarantees' Regulation in Mexico</u>, 23 Penn St. Int'l L. Rev. 321, 347 (2004). –Page Citation.

Penn State Law Review
Ab: Penn St. L. Rev.

In law review footnotes, the titles of books and the names of cases, except for procedural phrases, are not underlined. See <u>Bluebook</u> rule 2.1(a) & (b). Further, the following are in large and small capitals: codes, restatements, standards, constitutions, periodicals, authors of books, titles of books, the abbreviated names of codes, most legislative materials except for bills and resolutions, codified ordinances, model codes, court rules, and sentencing guidelines. Refer to <u>The Bluebook</u>.

Ex: Nancy P. Spyke, <u>Heeding the Call: Making Sustainability a Matter of Pennsylvania Law</u>, 109 Penn St. L. Rev. 729 (2005). –Article Citation.

Nancy P. Spyke, <u>Heeding the Call: Making Sustainability a Matter of Pennsylvania Law</u>, 109 Penn St. L. Rev. 729, 756 (2005). –Page Citation.

Pennsylvania Bar Association Quarterly
Ab.: Pa. B. Ass'n. Q.

Ex.: Joyce S. Meyers, <u>A Modest Proposal to Unclog the Courts: The Need for Corrective Legislation to Control the Asbestos Explosion</u>, 53 Pa. B. Ass'n. Q. 20 (1992). –Article Citation.

Joyce S. Meyers, <u>A Modest Proposal to Unclog the Courts: The Need for Corrective Legislation to Control the Asbestos Explosion</u>, 53 Pa. B. Ass'n. Q. 20, 24 (1992). –Page Citation.

Pennsylvania Bulletin (Fry Communications)
Ab.: vol. no. Pa. Bull. page no. (month day, year)

Ex.: 34 Pa. Bull. 951 (Feb. 21, 2004).

Pennsylvania Code (Fry Communications)
Ab.: x Pa. Code § x.x (year)

Ex.: 6 Pa. Code § 21.27 (2000).

Pennsylvania Commonwealth Court Reports
Ab.: Pa. Commw.

–Discontinued after 168 Pa. Commw. 698 (1994).

–Cite to A. or A.2d, if therein; otherwise, cite to Pa. Commw.

–Give parallel citations only in documents submitted to Pennsylvania state courts. <u>See</u> <u>Bluebook</u> rules 10.3.1 and B5.1.3; see also Pa. R. App. P. 2119(b), which requires a parallel citation.

–Through 168 Pa. Commw. 698 (1994), cite as follows:

In documents submitted to Pennsylvania state courts, cite as follows:

<u>Peak v. Petrovitch</u>, 161 Pa. Commw. 261, 636 A.2d 1248 (1994). –Case Citation.

<u>Peak v. Petrovitch</u>, 161 Pa. Commw. 261, 262, 636 A.2d 1248, 1249 (1994). –Page Citation.

In all other documents, cite as follows:

<u>Peak v. Petrovitch</u>, 636 A.2d 1248 (Pa. Commw. Ct. 1994). –Case Citation.

<u>Peak v. Petrovitch</u>, 636 A.2d 1248, 1249 (Pa. Commw. Ct. 1994). –Page Citation.

–After 168 Pa. Commw. 698 (1994), cite as follows:

In citing cases in law review footnotes, abbreviate any word listed in table T.6; the names of "states, countries, and other geographical units" unless they are named parties; and any other words of eight or more letters "if <u>substantial</u> space is thereby saved and the result is unambiguous." <u>Bluebook</u> rule 10.2.2. On the other hand, in citing cases in text, abbreviate only widely known acronyms and the following words: "&," "Ass'n," "Bros.," "Co.," "Corp.," "Inc.," "Ltd.," and "No." <u>Bluebook</u> rule 10.2.1(c).

Gueson v. Reed, 679 A.2d 284 (Pa. Commw. Ct. 1996). –Case Citation.

Gueson v. Reed, 679 A.2d 284, 290 (Pa. Commw. Ct. 1996). –Page Citation.

Pennsylvania Consolidated Statutes
Ab.:   x Pa. Cons. Stat. § x (year)

Ex.:   18 Pa. Cons. Stat. § 4304 (1973 & Supp. 1994).

42 Pa. Cons. Stat. §§ 5984-85 (Supp. 1994).

–At the publication date of this book, Pennsylvania is undertaking its first official codification, Pennsylvania Consolidated Statutes. The old, unofficial compilation is Purdon's Pennsylvania Statutes Annotated, which uses a different numbering system. Purdon is also reprinting the new, official codification as Purdon's Pennsylvania Consolidated Statutes Annotated, which is currently bound with Purdon's Pennsylvania Statutes Annotated. –Cite to Pennsylvania Consolidated Statutes or Purdon's Pennsylvania Consolidated Statutes Annotated, in that order of preference. See Bluebook table T.1, page 229.

–For proper citation form in papers submitted to Pennsylvania courts, see Pa. R. App. P. 2119(b).

Pennsylvania Consolidated Statutes Annotated
See Purdon's Pennsylvania Consolidated Statutes Annotated.

Pennsylvania Constitution
Ab.:   Pa. Const. art. , §

Ex.:   Pa. Const. art. II, § 15. –"Cite constitutional provisions currently in force without a date." Bluebook rule 11.

Pa. Const. art. IV, § 19 (repealed 1967). –"If the cited provision has been repealed, either indicate parenthetically the fact and date of repeal or cite the repealing provision in full." Bluebook rule 11.

Pa. Const. art. I, § 6 (amended 1971). –"When citing a provision that has been subsequently amended, either indicate parenthetically the fact and date of amendment or cite the amending provision in full." Bluebook rule 11.

Pa. Const. of 1838, art. II, § 10 (1874). –"Cite constitutions that have been totally superseded by year of adoption; if the specific provision cited was adopted in a different year, give that year parenthetically." Bluebook rule 11.

Pennsylvania District and County Reports
Ab.:   Pa. D. & C., Pa. D. & C.2d, Pa. D. & C.3d, or Pa. D. & C.4th.

–Cite to the legal reporter for the county, if available, and to Pa. D. & C., Pa. D. & C.2d, Pa. D. & C.3d, or Pa. D. & C.4th.

In law review footnotes, the titles of books and the names of cases, except for procedural phrases, are not underlined. See Bluebook rule 2.1(a) & (b). Further, the following are in large and small capitals: codes, restatements, standards, constitutions, periodicals, authors of books, titles of books, the abbreviated names of codes, most legislative materials except for bills and resolutions, codified ordinances, model codes, court rules, and sentencing guidelines. Refer to The Bluebook.

Ex.: In re Grady's Estate, 34 Pa. D. & C. 143 (Orphan's Ct. 1938). –Case Citation.

In re Grady's Estate, 34 Pa. D. & C. 143, 149 (Orphan's Ct. 1938). –Page Citation.

Acad. of Natural Scis. v. City of Philadelphia, 6 Pa. D. & C.2d 145 (C.P. 1955). –Case Citation.

Acad. of Natural Scis. v. City of Philadelphia, 6 Pa. D. & C.2d 145, 149 (C.P. 1955). –Page Citation.

Hurley v. Inland Fin. Co., 34 Pa. D. & C.3d 336 (C.P. 1984). –Case Citation.

Hurley v. Inland Fin. Co., 34 Pa. D. & C.3d 336, 337 (C.P. 1984). –Page Citation.

Kryeski v. Schott Glass Technicians, Inc., 9 Pa. D. & C.4th 399 (C.P. 1991). –Case Citation.

Kryeski v. Schott Glass Technicians, Inc., 9 Pa. D. & C.4th 399, 402 (C.P. 1991). –Page Citation.

Pennsylvania Fiduciary Reporter
Ab.: Pa. Fiduc., Pa. Fiduc. 2d

Ex.: In re Zappardino Estate, 14 Pa. Fiduc. 212 (Orphan's Ct. 1964). –Case Citation.

In re Zappardino Estate, 14 Pa. Fiduc. 212, 216 (Orphan's Ct. 1964). –Page Citation.

In re Dolinger Estate, 4 Pa. Fiduc. 2d 327 (Orphan's Ct. 1984). –Case Citation.

In re Dolinger Estate, 4 Pa. Fiduc. 2d 327, 330 (Orphan's Ct. 1984). –Page Citation.

–Above examples are correct if case not reported in Pa. D. & C.3d.

Pennsylvania Legislative Service
See Purdon's Pennsylvania Legislative Service.

Pennsylvania Session Laws
See Laws of Pennsylvania and Purdon's Pennsylvania Legislative Service (West).

Pennsylvania State Reports
Ab.: Pa.

–Cite to A. or A.2d, if therein; otherwise, cite to Pa.

–Give parallel citations only in documents submitted to Pennsylvania state courts. See Bluebook rules 10.3.1 and B5.1.3; see also Pa. R. App. P. 2119(b), which requires a parallel citation.

In documents submitted to Pennsylvania state courts, cite as follows:

In citing cases in law review footnotes, abbreviate any word listed in table T.6; the names of "states, countries, and other geographical units" unless they are named parties; and any other words of eight or more letters "if substantial space is thereby saved and the result is unambiguous." Bluebook rule 10.2.2. On the other hand, in citing cases in text, abbreviate only widely known acronyms and the following words: "&," "Ass'n," "Bros.," "Co.," "Corp.," "Inc.," "Ltd.," and "No." Bluebook rule 10.2.1(c).

Commonwealth v. Birdseye, 543 Pa. 251, 670 A.2d 1124 (1996). –Case Citation.

Commonwealth v. Birdseye, 543 Pa. 251, 254, 670 A.2d 1124, 1125 (1996). –Page Citation.

In all other documents, cite as follows:

Commonwealth v. Birdseye, 670 A.2d 1124 (Pa. 1996). –Case Citation.

Commonwealth v. Birdseye, 670 A.2d 1124, 1125 (Pa. 1996). –Page Citation.

Pennsylvania Statutes Annotated (Purdon's)
See Purdon's Pennsylvania Statutes Annotated.

Pennsylvania Superior Court Reports
Ab.:   Pa. Super.

–Discontinued after 456 Pa. Super. 801 (1997).
  –Cite to A. or A.2d, if therein; otherwise, give public domain citation. See Pennsylvania Superior Court, Notice to the Bar, available at http://www.superior.court.state.pa.us/notice_to_the_bar.htm.
  –Give parallel citations only in documents submitted to Pennsylvania state courts. See Bluebook rules 10.3.1 and B5.1.3; see also Pa. R. App. P. 2119(b), which requires a parallel citation.

–Through 456 Pa. Super. 801 (1997), cite as follows:

In documents submitted to Pennsylvania state courts:

Marchetti v. Karpowick, 446 Pa. Super. 509, 667 A.2d 724 (1995). –Case Citation.

Marchetti v. Karpowick, 446 Pa. Super. 509, 512, 667 A.2d 724, 725. –Page Citation.

In all other documents:

Marchetti v. Karpowick, 667 A.2d 724 (Pa. Super. Ct. 1995). –Case Citation.

Marchetti v. Karpowick, 667 A.2d 724, 725 (Pa. Super. Ct. 1995). –Page Citation.

–After 456 Pa. Super. 801 (1997), cite as follows:

In all documents:

Cole v. Czegan, 722 A.2d 686 (Pa. Super Ct. 1998). –Case Citation.

Cole v. Czegan, 722 A.2d 686, 689 (Pa. Super. Ct. 1998) –Page Citation.

–After January 1, 1999, cite as follows to cases not yet published in A.2d:

In law review footnotes, the titles of books and the names of cases, except for procedural phrases, are not underlined. See Bluebook rule 2.1(a) & (b). Further, the following are in large and small capitals: codes, restatements, standards, constitutions, periodicals, authors of books, titles of books, the abbreviated names of codes, most legislative materials except for bills and resolutions, codified ordinances, model codes, court rules, and sentencing guidelines. Refer to The Bluebook.

In all documents:

Taylor v. Solberg, 2000 PA Super 262. –Case Citation.

Taylor v. Solberg, 2000 PA Super 262, ¶ 15. –Pinpoint Citation.

Pension Plan Guide (Commerce Clearing House)
Ab.: Pens. Plan Guide (CCH)

Ex.: Epright v. Envtl. Res. Mgmt., 6 Pens. Plan Guide (CCH) ¶ 23,919D (3d Cir. Feb. 16, 1996). –Citation to looseleaf material.

Delaye v. Agripal, Inc., [1993-1996 Transfer Binder] Pens. Plan Guide (CCH) ¶ 23,904P (9th Cir. 1994). –Citation to transfer binder material.

Pepperdine Law Review
Ab.: Pepp. L. Rev.

Ex.: Jessica L. Darraby, Is Culture a Justiciable Issue?, 18 Pepp. L. Rev. 463 (1991). –Article Citation.

Jessica L. Darraby, Is Culture a Justiciable Issue?, 18 Pepp. L. Rev. 463, 468 (1991). –Page Citation.

per curiam
–Do not abbreviate.

Ex.: Gibbons v. U.S. Dist. Ct., 416 F.2d 14 (9th Cir. 1969) (per curiam).

Anderson v. Gladden, 303 F. Supp. 1134 (D. Or. 1967), aff'd per curiam, 416 F.2d 447 (9th Cir. 1969).

Kent v. Prasse, 385 F.2d 406 (3d Cir. 1967) (per curiam).

See Bluebook rule 10.6(b).

periodicals
See Bluebook rule 16.

NON STUDENT-WRITTEN MATERIALS:

–single law review article

Thomas R. McCoy, Current State Action Theories, the Jackson Nexus Requirement, and Employee Discharges by Semi-Public and State-Aided Institutions, 31 Vand. L. Rev. 785 (1978). –Article Citation.

Thomas R. McCoy, Current State Action Theories, the Jackson Nexus Requirement, and Employee Discharges by Semi-Public and State-Aided Institutions, 31 Vand. L. Rev. 785, 809-13 (1978). –Page Citation.

–multipart law review articles:

Peter L. Costas & Daniel E. Harris, Patents, Trademarks and Copyrights – The Legal Monopolies (pts. 1-2) 36 Conn. B.J. 569 (1963), 37 Conn. B.J. 420 (1963). –For the series.

In citing cases in law review footnotes, abbreviate any word listed in table T.6; the names of "states, countries, and other geographical units" unless they are named parties; and any other words of eight or more letters "if substantial space is thereby saved and the result is unambiguous." Bluebook rule 10.2.2. On the other hand, in citing cases in text, abbreviate only widely known acronyms and the following words: "&," "Ass'n," "Bros.," "Co.," "Corp.," "Inc.," "Ltd.," and "No." Bluebook rule 10.2.1(c).

Peter L. Costas & Daniel E. Harris, <u>Patents, Trademarks and Copyrights – The Legal Monopolies</u> (pt. 2) 37 Conn. B.J. 420 (1963). –For a single part of the series.

–symposium:

Symposium, <u>Transnational Technology Transfer: Current Problems and Solutions for the Corporate Practitioner</u>, 14 Vand. J. Transnat'l L. 249 (1981).   –Symposium as a unit.

Gabriel M. Wilner, <u>The Transfer of Technology to Latin America</u>, 14 Vand. J. Transnat'l L. 269 (1981). –Article within the symposium.

–book review:

Barbara A. Black, Book Review, 90 Yale L.J. 232 (1980). –Citation to untitled book review.

Barbara A. Black, <u>Community and Law in Seventeenth Century Massachusetts</u>, 90 Yale L.J. 232 (1980) (reviewing David T. Konig, <u>Law and Society in Puritan Massachusetts</u> (1979)). –Citation to a titled book review which includes the title of the book reviewed.

Barbara A. Black, <u>Community and Law in Seventeenth Century Massachusetts</u> 90 Yale L.J. 232 (1980) (book review). –Citation to a titled book review when it is not necessary to identify the book under review.

–article in separately paginated issue:

John J. Creedon, <u>Lifetime Gifts of Life Insurance</u>, Prac. Law., Oct. 1974, at 27. –Article Citation.

John J. Creedon, <u>Lifetime Gifts of Life Insurance</u>, Prac. Law., Oct. 1974, at 27, 31-33. –Page Citation.

–When a periodical is paginated only within each issue, the date or period of the issue must be included in the citation. <u>See</u> <u>Bluebook</u> rule 16.4.

–year used as the volume number:

Frank S. Bloch, <u>Cooperative Federalism and the Role of Litigation in the Development of Federal AFDC Eligibility Policy</u>, 1979 Wis. L. Rev. at 1. –Article Citation.

STUDENT-WRITTEN MATERIALS:
–Signed materials

L. Allyn Dixon, Jr., Note, <u>Broadcasters' First Amendment Rights: A New Approach?</u>, 39 Vand. L. Rev. 323 (1986).

Karen Schoen, Comment, <u>Insider Trading: The "Possession Versus Use" Debate</u>, 148 U. Pa. L. Rev. 239, 241 (1999).

Meredith B. Brinegar, Recent Development, <u>Limiting the Application of the Exclusionary Rule: The Good Faith Exception</u>, 34 Vand. L. Rev. 213, 215 n.14 (1981).

In law review footnotes, the titles of books and the names of cases, except for procedural phrases, are not underlined. <u>See</u> <u>Bluebook</u> rule 2.1(a) & (b). Further, the following are in large and small capitals: codes, restatements, standards, constitutions, periodicals, authors of books, titles of books, the abbreviated names of codes, most legislative materials except for bills and resolutions, codified ordinances, model codes, court rules, and sentencing guidelines. Refer to <u>The Bluebook</u>.

–Unsigned materials

Note, <u>The Judicial Role in Attacking Racial Discrimination in Tax-Exempt Private Schools</u>, 93 Harv. L. Rev. 378 (1979).

Case Comment, <u>Antitrust Scrutiny of Monopolists' Innovations: Berkey Photo, Inc. v. Eastman Kodak Co.</u>, 93 Harv. L. Rev. 408, 415-17 (1979).

Recent Case, 25 Vand. L. Rev. 240, 244-45 (1972).

–Book review

Geoffrey C. Rapp, Book Note, <u>DNA's Dark Side</u>, 110 Yale L.J. 163 (2000) (reviewing Jim Duyer, Peter Neufeld & Barry Scheck, <u>Actual Innocence: Five Days to Execution and Other Dispatches from the Wrongly Convicted</u> (2000)). –signed, student-written, titled book review.

Thomas C. Grey, Book Note, 106 Yale L.J. 493 (1996) (reviewing Neil Duxbury, <u>Patterns of American Jurisprudence</u> (1995)). –signed, student-written, untitled book review.

Book Note, <u>Translating Truth</u>, 114 Harv. L. Rev. 640 (2000) (reviewing Peter Brooks, <u>Troubling Confessions: Speaking Guilt in Law and Literature</u> (2000)). –unsigned, student-written book review.

permanent
Ab.:   perm.

Permanent Court of International Justice Advisory Opinions and Cases
Ab.:   P.C.I.J.

Ex.:   <u>Mavromattis Palestine Concessions Case</u> (Greece v. U.K.), 1924 P.C.I.J. (Ser. A) No. 2, at 12 (Aug. 30).

<u>Treatment of Polish Nationals and Other Persons of Polish Origin or Speech in the Danzig Territories</u>, Advisory Opinion, 1932 P.C.I.J. (ser. A/B) No. 44, at 24 (Feb. 4).

<u>See</u> <u>Bluebook</u> rule 21.5.1 and table T.3.

Permanent Court of International Justice Annual Reports
Ab.:   P.C.I.J. Ann. Rep.

Ex.:   <u>Rules for Financial Administration</u>, 1929-1930 P.C.I.J. Ann. Rep. (ser. E) No. 6, at 339 (1930).

<u>See</u> <u>Bluebook</u> rule 21.10 and cite according to rule 16 (periodicals).

–Note: Decisions and other documents of the P.C.I.J. were published in six series (A through F).

Personnel Management
Ab.:   Personnel Mgmt. (BNA)

Peters (United States Reports)
See United States Reports.

In citing cases in law review footnotes, abbreviate any word listed in table T.6; the names of "states, countries, and other geographical units" unless they are named parties; and any other words of eight or more letters "if <u>substantial</u> space is thereby saved and the result is unambiguous." <u>Bluebook</u> rule 10.2.2. On the other hand, in citing cases in text, abbreviate only widely known acronyms and the following words: "&," "Ass'n," "Bros.," "Co.," "Corp.," "Inc.," "Ltd.," and "No." <u>Bluebook</u> rule 10.2.1(c).

petition for certiorari filed
Ab.:   petition for cert. filed

Ex.:   <u>Harbor Tug & Barge Co. v. Papai</u>, 67 F.3d 203 (9th Cir. 1996), <u>petition for cert. filed</u>, 65 U.S.L.W. 3073 (U.S. Apr. 9, 1996) (No. 95-1621).

petition for certiorari granted
Ab.:   cert. granted

Ex.:   <u>Harbor Tug & Barge Co. v. Papai</u>, 67 F.3d 203 (9th Cir. 1996), <u>cert. granted</u>, 65 U.S.L.W. 3254 (U.S. Oct. 1, 1996) (No. 95-1621).

Philippine Law Journal
Ab.:   Philippine L.J.

Ex.:   Evalyn G. Ursua, <u>The Lawyer As Policymaker: A Challenge to Philippine Legal Education</u>, 63 Philippine L.J. 186 (1988). –Article Citation.

Evalyn G. Ursua, <u>The Lawyer As Policymaker: A Challenge to Philippine Legal Education</u>, 63 Philippine L.J. 186, 192 (1988). –Page Citation.

Philosophy & Public Affairs
Ab.:   Phil. & Pub. Aff.

Ex.:   David O. Brink, <u>Mill's Deliberative Utilitarianism</u>, 21 Phil. & Pub. Aff. 67 (1992). –Article Citation.

David O. Brink, <u>Mill's Deliberative Utilitarianism</u>, 21 Phil. & Pub. Aff. 67, 78-79 (1992). –Page Citation.

photoduplicated reprint
Ab.:   photo. reprint

Pike & Fischer
Ab.:   P & F

PLI Course Handbook

Ex.:   John R. Murphy, <u>Life Insurance Fundamentals,</u> <u>in</u> Insurance Law 2003, at 393, 394-95 (PLI Litig. & Admin. Practice, Course Handbook Series No. H-690, 2003).

–<u>See</u> <u>Bluebook</u> rule 15.7.

Police Justice's Court
Ab.:   Police J. Ct.

Political Science Quarterly
Ab.:   Pol. Sci. Q.

In law review footnotes, the titles of books and the names of cases, except for procedural phrases, are not underlined. <u>See</u> <u>Bluebook</u> rule 2.1(a) & (b). Further, the following are in large and small capitals: codes, restatements, standards, constitutions, periodicals, authors of books, titles of books, the abbreviated names of codes, most legislative materials except for bills and resolutions, codified ordinances, model codes, court rules, and sentencing guidelines. Refer to <u>The Bluebook</u>.

Ex.:   Athan Theoharis, <u>FBI Wiretapping: A Case Study of Bureaucratic Autonomy</u>, 107 Pol. Sci. Q. 101 (1992). –Article Citation.

Athan Theoharis, <u>FBI Wiretapping: A Case Study of Bureaucratic Autonomy</u>, 107 Pol. Sci. Q. 101, 119 (1992). –Page Citation.

Powell on Real Property (multivolume edition)
See Law of Real Property, (The) by Richard R. Powell.

Practical Lawyer, The
Ab.:   Prac. Law.

Ex.:   Patricia K. Loop, <u>Accomodating HIV-Positive Employees</u>, Prac. Law., Apr. 1992, at 27. –Article Citation.

Patricia K. Loop, <u>Accomodating HIV-Positive Employees</u>, Prac. Law., Apr. 1992, at 27, 30. –Page Citation.

–When a periodical is paginated only within each issue, the date or period of the issue must be included in the citation (<u>Bluebook</u> rule 16.4).

Practical Real Estate Lawyer, The
Ab.:   Prac. Real Est. Law.

Ex.:   Anthony J. Buonicore, <u>A Guide to Cleanup Jargon</u>, Prac. Real Est. Law., Mar. 1992, at 25. –Article Citation.

Anthony J. Buonicore, <u>A Guide to Cleanup Jargon</u>, Prac. Real Est. Law., Mar. 1992, at 25, 32-35. –Page Citation.

Practical Tax Lawyer, The
Ab.:   Prac. Tax Law.

Ex.:   Kenneth N. Sacks, <u>Choosing the Right Small Business Retirement Plan</u>, Prac. Tax Law., Fall 1991, at 69. –Article Citation.

Kenneth N. Sacks, <u>Choosing the Right Small Business Retirement Plan</u>, Prac. Tax Law., Fall 1991, at 69, 72-75. –Page Citation.

Pravovedenie (Former Soviet Union)
Ab.:   –Do not abbreviate the title.

prefaces and forewords (to books)
Ex.:   William Warren, <u>Preface</u> to Thomas Reed Powell, <u>Vagaries and Varieties in Constitutional Interpretation</u>, at xv (1956).

<u>See</u> <u>Bluebook</u> rule 15.6.

Prentice-Hall, Inc.
Ab.:   P-H

Presidential Papers
Executive Orders
Ab.:   Exec. Order No.

In citing cases in law review footnotes, abbreviate any word listed in table T.6; the names of "states, countries, and other geographical units" unless they are named parties; and any other words of eight or more letters "if <u>substantial</u> space is thereby saved and the result is unambiguous." <u>Bluebook</u> rule 10.2.2. On the other hand, in citing cases in text, abbreviate only widely known acronyms and the following words: "&," "Ass'n," "Bros.," "Co.," "Corp.," "Inc.," "Ltd.," and "No." <u>Bluebook</u> rule 10.2.1(c).

Ex.:   Exec. Order No. 12,375, 47 Fed. Reg. 34,105 (May 1,1982). –Citation
         to material not yet available in the Code of Federal Regulations.

         Exec. Order No. 12,261, 3 C.F.R. 83 (1982).

         Exec. Order No. 11,574, 3 C.F.R. 188 (1970), reprinted in 33 U.S.C.
         § 407 app. at 115 (1976). –Citation if the order is reprinted in U.S.C.,
         U.S.C.A., or U.S.C.S.

         Proclamations

Ab.:   Proclamation No.

Ex.:   Proclamation No. 4957, 47 Fed. Reg. 34,105 (Jan. 21,1982). –Citation
         to material not yet available in the Code of Federal Regulations.

         Proclamation No. 4871, 3 C.F.R. 56 (1982).

         Proclamation No. 4420, 3 C.F.R. 11 (1976), reprinted in 90 Stat. 3081
         (1976).

         –Citation with optional parallel reference to a printing in Statutes at
         Large.

         –Reorganization Plans

         See Reorganization Plans (U.S.).

See Bluebook rule 14.7.

Preview of the United States Supreme Court Cases

Ab.:   Preview U.S. Sup. Ct. Cases

Ex.:   Geoffrey P. Miller, Revisiting the Contingency Factor in Fee-Shifting
         Awards, 1991-92 Preview U.S. Sup. Ct. Cases 327. –Article Citation.

         Geoffrey P. Miller, Revisiting the Contingency Factor in Fee-Shifting
         Awards, 1991-92 Preview U.S. Sup. Ct. Cases 327, 329. –Page
         Citation.

Principles of Bank Regulation, by Michael P. Malloy
         –Do not abbreviate the title.

Ex.:   Michael P. Malloy, Principles of Bank Regulation § 3.5 (2d ed. 2003).
         –Section Citation.

         Michael P. Malloy, Principles of Bank Regulation § 3.5, at 84 (2d ed.
         2003). –Page Citation.

Principles of Evidence, by Irving Younger, Michael Goldsmith, and David A. Sonensheim
         –Do not abbreviate the title.

Ex.:   Irving Younger et al., Principles of Evidence 879 (3d ed. 1997).
         –Page Citation.

         Irving Younger et al., Principles of Evidence 881 n.22 (3d ed. 1997).
         –Footnote Citation.

In law review footnotes, the titles of books and the names of cases, except for procedural
phrases, are not underlined. See Bluebook rule 2.1(a) & (b). Further, the following are in
large and small capitals: codes, restatements, standards, constitutions, periodicals, authors of
books, titles of books, the abbreviated names of codes, most legislative materials except for
bills and resolutions, codified ordinances, model codes, court rules, and sentencing guidelines.
Refer to The Bluebook.

Prior Case History
> –"Give only if significant to the point for which the case is cited or if the disposition cited does not intelligibly describe the issues in the case, as in a Supreme Court 'mem.'" Bluebook rule 10.7.

Ex.: Cornelius v. Nutt, 472 U.S. 648 (1985), rev'g Devine v. Nutt, 718 F.2d 1048 (Fed. Cir. 1983).

Pritchard on the Law of Wills and Administration of Estates Embracing the Law and Practice in Tennessee, by Jack W. Robinson, Sr. and Jeff Mobley
> –Do not abbreviate the title.

Ex. 2 Jack W. Robinson, Sr., & Jeff Mobley, Pritchard on the Law of Wills and Administration of Estates Embracing the Law and Practice in Tennessee § 663 (5th ed. 1994). –Section Citation.

2 Jack W. Robinson, Sr., & Jeff Mobley, Pritchard on the Law of Wills and Administration of Estates Embracing the Law and Practice in Tennessee § 663, at 220 (5th ed. 1994). –Page Citation.

Private Acts of the State of Tennessee
Ab.: year Tenn. Priv. Acts. page no.

Ex.: Act of Mar. 8, 1995, ch. 18, 1995 Tenn. Priv. Acts 40 (to amend charter of Gordonsville relative to the sale of intoxicating liquors). –Citation to an entire session law.

Act of Mar. 8, 1995, ch. 18, § 3, 1995 Tenn. Priv. Acts 40, 40 (to amend charter of Gordonsville relative to the sale of intoxicating liquors). –Citation to a section of a session law.

–See Bluebook rule 12.4.

Private Laws (U.S.)
Ab.: Priv. L. No. x, vol. Stat. page (year)
Ex.: Priv. L. No. 92-23, 85 Stat. 842 (1971).

Private Letter Rulings
Ab.: I.R.S. Priv. Ltr. Rul. or I.R.S. P.L.R.

Ex.: I.R.S. Priv. Ltr. Rul. 97-25-036 (Mar. 24, 1997).

Probate Court
Ab.: Prob. Ct.

Probate Law Journal (National College of Probate Judges and Boston University School of Law)
Ab.: Prob. L.J.

Probate Lawyer, The
Ab.: Prob. Law.

In citing cases in law review footnotes, abbreviate any word listed in table T.6; the names of "states, countries, and other geographical units" unless they are named parties; and any other words of eight or more letters "if substantial space is thereby saved and the result is unambiguous." Bluebook rule 10.2.2. On the other hand, in citing cases in text, abbreviate only widely known acronyms and the following words: "&," "Ass'n," "Bros.," "Co.," "Corp.," "Inc.," "Ltd.," and "No." Bluebook rule 10.2.1(c).

Ex.:   Richard B. Covey, <u>Reflections on Tax Writing and the Regulatory Process as It Affects Trusts and Estates</u>, Prob. Law, Summer 1991, at 1. –Article Citation.

Richard B. Covey, <u>Reflections on Tax Writing and the Regulatory Process as It Affects Trusts and Estates</u>, Prob. Law, Summer 1991, at 1, 8-10. –Page Citation.

Problematics of Moral and Legal Theory, The, by Richard A. Posner
–Do not abbreviate the title.

Ex.:   Richard A. Posner, <u>The Problematics of Moral and Legal Theory</u> 145 (1999). –Page Citation.

Problems of Communism
Ab.:   Probs. Communism

Ex.:   Cole Blasier, <u>Moscow's Retreat From Cuba</u>, Probs. Communism, Nov.- Dec. 1991, at 91. –Article Citation.

Cole Blasier, <u>Moscow's Retreat From Cuba</u>, Probs. Communism, Nov.- Dec. 1991, at 91, 95 (1991). –Page Citation.

Proceedings of the American Society of International Law
Ab.:   Proc. Am. Soc'y Int'l L.

Ex.:   Jeffrey M. Lang, <u>Self-Help in International Trade Disputes</u>, 84 Proc. Am. Soc'y Int'l L. 32 (1990). –Proceedings Citation.

Jeffrey M. Lang, <u>Self-Help in International Trade Disputes</u>, 84 Proc. Am. Soc'y Int'l L. 32, 38-39 (1990). –Page Citation.

Product Safety & Liability Reporter (Bureau of National Affairs)
Ab.:   Prod. Safety & Liab. Rep. (BNA)

Products Liability, by M. Stuart Madden
–Do not abbreviate the title.

Ex.:   1 M. Stuart Madden, <u>Products Liability</u> § 3.7 (2d ed. 1988). –Section Citation.

1 M. Stuart Madden, <u>Products Liability</u> § 3.7, at 68 (2d ed. 1988). –Page Citation.

1 M. Stuart Madden, <u>Products Liability</u> § 3.7, at 68 n.6 (2d ed. 1988). –Footnote Citation.

Products Liability Reports (Commerce Clearing House)
Ab.:   Prod. Liab. Rep. (CCH)

Ex.:   <u>Wood v. Morbank Indus., Inc.</u>, 2 Prod. Liab. Rep. (CCH) ¶ 14,457 (11th Cir. Dec. 18 1995). –Citation to looseleaf material.

<u>Sumner v. General Motors Corp.</u>, [Mar. 1995 - Jan. 1996 Transfer Binder] Prod. Liab. Rep. (CCH) ¶ 14,345 (Mich. Ct. App. Aug. 18, 1995). –Citation to transfer binder material.

In law review footnotes, the titles of books and the names of cases, except for procedural phrases, are not underlined. <u>See</u> Bluebook rule 2.1(a) & (b). Further, the following are in large and small capitals: codes, restatements, standards, constitutions, periodicals, authors of books, titles of books, the abbreviated names of codes, most legislative materials except for bills and resolutions, codified ordinances, model codes, court rules, and sentencing guidelines. Refer to <u>The Bluebook</u>.

–The above examples are proper if the case is not yet available in, or is not reported in, an official or West reporter, a public domain citation, or in a widely used computer database.

Professional Negligence
Ab.:   Prof. Negl.
Ex.:   Steven Fennell, <u>Liability for a Client's Fraud</u>, 7 Prof. Negl. 151 (1991). –Article Citation.

Steven Fennell, <u>Liability for a Client's Fraud</u>, 7 Prof. Negl. 151, 154-55 (1991). –Page Citation.

Prosser and Keeton on the Law of Torts
–Do not abbreviate the title.

Ex.:   W. Page Keeton, <u>Prosser and Keeton on the Law of Torts</u> § 72 (5th ed. 1984). –Section Citation.

W. Page Keeton, <u>Prosser and Keeton on the Law of Torts</u> § 72, at 521 (5th ed. 1984). –Page Citation.

W. Page Keeton, <u>Prosser and Keeton on the Law of Torts</u> § 72, at 521 n.47 (5th ed. 1984). –Footnote Citation.

Psychology, Public Policy, and Law
Ab: Psychol. Pub. Pol'y & L.
Ex: Linda S. Gottfredson, <u>What If the Hereditarian Hypothesis is True?</u>, 11 Psychol. Pub. Pol'y & L. 311 (2005). –Article Citation.

Linda S. Gottfredson, <u>What If the Hereditarian Hypothesis is True?</u>, 11 Psychol. Pub. Pol'y & L. 311, 314-15 (2005). –Page Citation.

Public Acts of the State of Tennessee
Ab.:   year Tenn. Pub. Acts page no.
Ex.:   Act of May 22, 1995, ch. 401, 1995 Tenn. Pub. Acts 678 (relative to collection of delinquent business taxes). –Citation to an entire session law.

Act of May 22, 1995, ch. 401, sec. 1, § 67-4-719, 1995 Tenn. Pub. Acts 678, 678 (relative to collection of delinquent business taxes). –Citation to a section of a session law amending a prior act.

<u>See</u> <u>Bluebook</u> rule 12.4.

Public and Local Acts of the Legislature of the State of Michigan
Ab.:   year Mich. Pub. Acts page no.
Ex.:   Act of Dec. 26, 1994, No. 372, 1994 Mich. Pub. Acts 1821 (relating to Michigan estate tax). –Citation to an entire session law.

Act of Dec. 26, 1994, No. 372, sec. 1 § 202.256, 1994 Mich. Pub. Acts. 1821, 1821-22 (Michigan estate tax additional definitions). –Citation to a section of a session law amending prior act.

In citing cases in law review footnotes, abbreviate any word listed in table T.6; the names of "states, countries, and other geographical units" unless they are named parties; and any other words of eight or more letters "if <u>substantial</u> space is thereby saved and the result is unambiguous." <u>Bluebook</u> rule 10.2.2. On the other hand, in citing cases in text, abbreviate only widely known acronyms and the following words: "&," "Ass'n," "Bros.," "Co.," "Corp.," "Inc.," "Ltd.," and "No." <u>Bluebook</u> rule 10.2.1(c).

See Bluebook rule 12.4.

Public Contract Law Journal
Ab.:　　Pub. Cont. L.J.

Ex.:　　Frank K. Peterson, In-House Counsel and Protective Orders in Bid
　　　　Protests, 21 Pub. Cont. L.J. 53 (1991). –Article Citation.

　　　　Frank K. Peterson, In-House Counsel and Protective Orders in Bid
　　　　Protests, 21 Pub. Cont. L.J. 53, 55 (1991). –Page Citation.

public domain citations
"When citing a decision available in public domain format (also
referred to as medium-neutral format), if the jurisdiction's format can
be cited in the following form (see table T.1), provide the case name,
the year of decision, the state's two-character postal code, the table
T.7 court abbreviation (unless the court is the state's highest court),
the sequential number of the decision, and, if the decision is
unpublished, a capital "U" after the sequential number of the decision.
When referencing specific material within the decision, a pinpoint
citation should be made to the paragraph number at which the material
appears. If available, a parallel citation to the appropriate regional
reporter must be provided." –Bluebook rule 10.3.3.

These examples follow the above Bluebook rule concerning parallel
citations. In papers submitted to the courts of the following
jurisdictions, follow the local rule concerning parallel citations.

The following examples are from jurisdictions which have adopted a
public domain format identical to The Bluebook's:

Maine Supreme Judicial Court

　　Holland v. Sebunya, 2000 ME 160, ¶ 24, 759 A.2d 205, 213.
　　–Pinpoint Citation.

　　See Me. Admin. Order, No. SJC-216 (Aug. 20, 1996).

Montana Supreme Court

　　Benjamin v. Torgerson, 1999 MT 215, ¶ 15, 985 P.2d 734, 737.
　　–Pinpoint Citation.

　　See Order in re Opinion Forms and Citation Standards of the

　　Sup. Ct. of Mont. (Dec. 16, 1997).

North Dakota Supreme Court

　　Olson v. Olson, 2000 ND 120, ¶ 7, 611 N.W.2d 892, 895.
　　–Pinpoint Citation.

　　See N.D. R. Ct. 11.6(b).

In law review footnotes, the titles of books and the names of cases, except for procedural
phrases, are not underlined. See Bluebook rule 2.1(a) & (b). Further, the following are in
large and small capitals: codes, restatements, standards, constitutions, periodicals, authors of
books, titles of books, the abbreviated names of codes, most legislative materials except for
bills and resolutions, codified ordinances, model codes, court rules, and sentencing guidelines.
Refer to The Bluebook.

Oklahoma Supreme Court

> Farrimond v. State ex rel. Fisher, 2000 OK 52 ,¶ 14, 8 P.3d 872, 875. –Pinpoint Citation.
>
> See Okla. Sup. Ct. R. 1.200(e).

South Dakota Supreme Court

> Price v. Price, 2000 SD 64, ¶ 12, 611 N.W.2d 425, 429. –Pinpoint Citation
>
> See S.D. R. App. P. § 15-26A-69.1(2).

Utah Supreme Court

> State v. Reed, 2000 UT 68, ¶11, 8 P.3d 1025, 1027. –Pinpoint Citation.
>
> –Pinpoint Citation.
>
> See Utah Supreme Court Standing Order No. 4 (Jan. 15, 2000).

Vermont Court of Appeals

> Doe v. Forrest, 2004 VT 37, ¶ 16, 853 A.2d 48, 52.
>
> –Pinpoint Citation.
>
> See Vt. R. App. P. 28.2(b).

Wisconsin Supreme Court

> Rumage v. Gullberg, 2000 WI 53, ¶ 8, 611 N.W.2d 458, 461. –Pinpoint Citation.
>
> See Wis. Sup. Ct. R. 80.02.

Wyoming Supreme Court

> Crabtree v. State, 2005 WY 62, ¶ 14, 112 P.3d 618, 621.
>
> –Pinpoint Citation.
>
> See Order Adopting a Public Domain or Neutral-Format Citation (Oct. 2, 2000) and Order Amending Citation Format (Aug. 19, 2005).

United States District Court for the District of South Dakota

> United States v. Swift Hawk, 2000 DSD 52, ¶ 17, 125 F. Supp. 2d 384, 389. –Pinpoint Citation.
>
> See Standing Order in re Citation of District Court Opinions (Oct. 1, 1996).

-When citing cases from a jurisdiction which has adopted a public domain format different from The Bluebook's, observe the jurisdiction's format. See Bluebook rule 10.3.3.

The following examples are from jurisdictions which have adopted a public domain format slightly different from The Bluebook's:

In citing cases in law review footnotes, abbreviate any word listed in table T.6; the names of "states, countries, and other geographical units" unless they are named parties; and any other words of eight or more letters "if substantial space is thereby saved and the result is unambiguous." Bluebook rule 10.2.2. On the other hand, in citing cases in text, abbreviate only widely known acronyms and the following words: "&," "Ass'n," "Bros.," "Co.," "Corp.," "Inc.," "Ltd.," and "No." Bluebook rule 10.2.1(c).

North Dakota Court of Appeals

City of Bismark v. Glass, 1998 ND App 1, ¶ 7, 581 N.W.2d 474, 475. –Pinpoint Citation.

See N.D. R. Ct. 11.6(b).

Oklahoma Court of Civil Appeals

Brown v. NCI, Inc., 2000 OK CIV APP 78, ¶ 5, 8 P.3d 195, 196. –Pinpoint Citation.

See Okla. Sup. Ct. R. 1.200(e).

Oklahoma Court of Criminal Appeals

State v. McNeal, 2000 OK CR 13, ¶ 10, 6 P.3d 1055,1057. –Pinpoint Citation.

See Okla. Ct. Crim. App. R. 3.5(c).

Pennsylvania Superior Court

Taylor v. Solberg, 2000 PA Super 262, ¶ 15, 740 A.2d 735, 737. –Pinpoint Citation.

See Pa. Superior Court, Notice to the Bar, available at http://www.superior.court.state.pa.us/notice_to_the_bar.htm.

Utah Court of Appeals

State v. Tryba, 2000 UT App 230, ¶ 8, P.3d 274, 277. –Pinpoint Citation.

See Utah Supreme Court Standing Order No. 4 (effective Jan. 18, 2000).

Wisconsin Court of Appeals

State v. Phillips, 2000 WI App 184, ¶ 10, 617 N.W.2d 522, 525. –Pinpoint Citation.

See Wis. Sup. Ct. R. 80.02.

Supreme Court of Puerto Rico

Spanish: Mendez v. Kelly Servs., Inc., 2005 TSPR 4.

English: Mendez v. Kelly Servs., Inc., 2005 PRSC 4.

See Resolution of the P.R. Sup. Ct. (June 11, 1999).

Supreme Court of the Commonwealth of the Northern Mariana Islands

Weathersbee v. Weathersbee, 1998 MP 14.

See Gen. Order in re Adoption of Universal Citations for App. Opinions, no. 2001-100 (Mar. 13, 2001).

The following examples are from jurisdictions which have adopted a public domain format markedly different from The Bluebook's:

In law review footnotes, the titles of books and the names of cases, except for procedural phrases, are not underlined. See Bluebook rule 2.1(a) & (b). Further, the following are in large and small capitals: codes, restatements, standards, constitutions, periodicals, authors of books, titles of books, the abbreviated names of codes, most legislative materials except for bills and resolutions, codified ordinances, model codes, court rules, and sentencing guidelines. Refer to The Bluebook.

Louisiana

> Taylor v. Sider, 99-2521, p. 3 (La. App. 4 Cir. 5/31/00); 765 So. 2d 416, 419. –Page Citation.
>
> In re Carreras, 2000-1094, p. 3 (La. 6/16/00); 765 So. 2d 321, 323. –Page Citation.
>
> See La. Sup. Ct. Gen Admin. R. Pt. G. § 8.

Mississippi

> Woodard v. State, 98-KA-01768-COA (¶ 12), 765 So. 2d 573, 575 (Miss. Ct. App. 2000). –Pinpoint Citation.
>
> Grant v. Grant, 99-CA-00736-SCT (¶ 6), 765 So. 2d 1263,1266 (Miss. 2000). –Pinpoint Citation.
>
> See Miss. R. App. P. 28(e).

New Mexico

> State v. Cleave, 2000-NMCA-071, ¶ 7, 8 P.3d 157, 159. –Pinpoint Citation.
>
> In re Dawson, 2000-NMSC-024, ¶ 11, 8 P.3d 856, 859. –Pinpoint Citation.
>
> See N.M. S. Ct. R. 23-112.

Ohio

> State v. Guidugli, 2004-Ohio-2871, ¶ 15, 811 N.E.2d 567, 569 (Ct. App.). –Pinpoint Citation.
>
> See Revisions to the Manual of Citations, 96 Ohio St. 3d CXLIX (2002).

Public Interest, The
> Ab.:   Pub. Int.
>
> Ex.:   Irwin M. Stelzer, What Thatcher Wrought, Pub. Int., Spring 1992, at 18. –Article Citation.
>
> Irwin M. Stelzer, What Thatcher Wrought, Pub. Int., Spring 1992, at 18, 39-40. –Page Citation.

Public Land Law Review
> Ab.:   Pub. Land L. Rev.
>
> Ex.:   Matthew J. McKinney, Instream Flow Policy in Montana: A History and Blueprint for the Future, 11 Pub. Land L. Rev. 81 (1990). –Article Citation.
>
> Matthew J. McKinney, Instream Flow Policy in Montana: A History and Blueprint for the Future, 11 Pub. Land L. Rev. 81, 98-99 (1990). –Page Citation.

In citing cases in law review footnotes, abbreviate any word listed in table T.6; the names of "states, countries, and other geographical units" unless they are named parties; and any other words of eight or more letters "if substantial space is thereby saved and the result is unambiguous." Bluebook rule 10.2.2. On the other hand, in citing cases in text, abbreviate only widely known acronyms and the following words: "&," "Ass'n," "Bros.," "Co.," "Corp.," "Inc.," "Ltd.," and "No." Bluebook rule 10.2.1(c).

Public Law
Ab.: Pub. L.

Ex.: Itzhak Zamir, <u>Courts and Politics in Israel</u>, Pub. L., 1991, at 523. –Article Citation.

Itzhak Zamir, <u>Courts and Politics in Israel</u>, Pub. L., 1991, at 523, 529-30. –Page Citation.

Public Laws (U.S.)
Ab.: Pub. L.

Ex.: Clean Air Act Amendments of 1990, Pub. L. No. 101-549, 1014 Stat. 2399 (codified as amended at 42 U.S.C. §§ 7401-767q (1994 & Supp. II 1996)). –Act Citation.

Pub. L. No. 104-170, 110 Stat. 1489 (codified as amended in scattered sections of 7 U.S.C. and 21 U.S.C). –Act Citation.

Pub. L. No. 101-508, §§ 6601-6610, 104 Stat. 1388, 1388-321 to 1388-327 (codified at 42 U.S.C. §§ 13,101-13,109 (1994)). –Section Citation.

Public Laws of Rhode Island and Providence Plantations
Ab.: year R.I. Pub. Laws

Ex.: Act of July 11, 1994, ch. 303, 1994-3 R.I. Pub. Laws 1247. –Citation to an entire session law.

Act of July 11, 1994, ch. 303, sec. 1, § 11-34-8.1, 1994-3 R.I. Pub. Laws 1247, 1247. –Citation to a section of a session law.

–<u>See</u> <u>Bluebook</u> rule 12.4.

Public Utilities Fortnightly
Ab.: Pub. Util. Fort.

Ex.: Robert D. Rosenberg, <u>Reducing Coal Transportation Costs</u>, Pub. Util. Fort., Oct. 11, 1990, at 31. –Article Citation.

Robert D. Rosenberg, <u>Reducing Coal Transportation Costs</u>, Pub. Util. Fort., Oct. 11, 1990, at 31, 35. –Page Citation.

Public Utilities Reports (PUR)
Ab.: Pub. Util. Rep.

Ex.: <u>Re Transition to Competition in the Local Exchange Market</u>, 171 Pub. Util. Rep. 4th 30 (N.Y. Pub. Serv. Comm'n 1996).

Publishing, Entertainment, Advertising and Allied Fields Law Quarterly
Ab.: Pub. Ent. Advert. & Allied Fields L.Q.

In law review footnotes, the titles of books and the names of cases, except for procedural phrases, are not underlined. <u>See</u> <u>Bluebook</u> rule 2.1(a) & (b). Further, the following are in large and small capitals: codes, restatements, standards, constitutions, periodicals, authors of books, titles of books, the abbreviated names of codes, most legislative materials except for bills and resolutions, codified ordinances, model codes, court rules, and sentencing guidelines. Refer to <u>The Bluebook</u>.

Ex.:   Andrew E. Clark, <u>The Trouble With T-Shirts: Merchandise Bootlegging in the Music Industry</u>, 21 Pub. Ent. Advert. & Allied Fields L.Q. 323 (1983). –Article Citation.

Andrew E. Clark, <u>The Trouble With T-Shirts: Merchandise Bootlegging in the Music Industry</u>, 21 Pub. Ent. Advert. & Allied Fields L.Q. 323, 327-330 (1983). –Page Citation.

Puerto Rico Constitution
Ab.:   P.R. Const. art. , § .

Ex.:   P.R. Const. art. II, § 14. –"Cite constitutional provisions currently in force without a date." <u>Bluebook</u> rule 11.

P.R. Const. art. VII, § 3 (amended 1953). –"When citing a provision that has been subsequently amended, either indicate parenthetically the fact and date of amendment or cite the amending provision in full." <u>Bluebook</u> rule 11.

Puerto Rico Laws
See Laws of Puerto Rico.

Puerto Rico Supreme Court
Ab.:   P.R.

–Cite to P.R. (to 1978) or P.R. Offic. Trans. (from 1978), if therein; cite also to P.R. Dec. or P.R. Sent., in that order of preference:

<u>Ortiz v. Valdejully</u>, 20 P.R. Offic. Trans. 1, 120 P.R. Dec. 1 (1987). –Case Citation.

<u>Ortiz v. Valdejully</u>, 20 P.R. Offic. Trans. 1, 4, 120 P.R. Dec. 1, 4 (1987). –Page Citation.

–The Puerto Rico Supreme Court also began assigning a public domain citation for its decisions effective January 1, 1998, which is the proper citation of the case until published in P.R. Dec., Puerto Rico's official reporter.

<u>Reyes v. Estado Libre Asociado de P.R.</u>, 2000 TSPR 49. –Case Citation. (in Spanish)

<u>Reyes v. Estado Libre Asociado de P.R.</u>, 2000 PRSC 49. –Case Citation. (in English)

<u>See</u> Resolution of the Puerto Rico Supreme Court, June 11, 1999.

Purdon's Pennsylvania Consolidated Statutes Annotated
Ab.:   x Pa. Cons. Stat. Ann. § x (West year)

Ex.:   35 Pa. Cons. Stat. Ann. § 7312 (West 1993).

35 Pa. Cons. Stat. Ann. § 7312 (West Supp. 1996).

–At the publication date of this book, Pennsylvania is undertaking its first official codification, Pennsylvania Consolidated Statutes. The old, unofficial compilation is Purdon's Pennsylvania Statutes

---

In citing cases in law review footnotes, abbreviate any word listed in table T.6; the names of "states, countries, and other geographical units" unless they are named parties; and any other words of eight or more letters "if <u>substantial</u> space is thereby saved and the result is unambiguous." <u>Bluebook</u> rule 10.2.2. On the other hand, in citing cases in text, abbreviate only widely known acronyms and the following words: "&," "Ass'n," "Bros.," "Co.," "Corp.," "Inc.," "Ltd.," and "No." <u>Bluebook</u> rule 10.2.1(c).

Annotated, which uses a different numbering system. Purdon is also reprinting the new, official codification as Purdon's Pennsylvania Consolidated Statutes Annotated, which is currently bound with Purdon's Pennsylvania Statutes Annotated. Cite to Pennsylvania Consolidated Statutes or Purdon's Pennsylvania Consolidated Statutes Annotated, in that order of preference. See Bluebook table T.1, p. 229.

–For proper citation form in papers submitted to Pennsylvania courts, see Pa. R. App. P. 2119(b).

Purdon's Pennsylvania Legislative Service (West)

Ab.:   year Pa. Legis. Serv. page no. (West)

Ex.:   Health Security Act, No. 85, 1996 Pa. Legis. Serv. 366 (West) (providing for certain health insurance benefits following the birth of a child). –Citation to an entire session law with a popular name.

Health Security Act, No. 85, sec. 2, 1996 Pa. Legis. Serv. 366, 370 (West). –Citation to a section of a session law with a popular name.

See Bluebook rule 12.4.

–"Cite to Pa. Laws, if therein." Bluebook table T.1, p. 230.

Purdon's Pennsylvania Statutes Annotated (West)

Ab: x Pa. Stat. Ann. § x (West year)

Ex.:   40 Pa. Stat. Ann. § 72 (West 1999).

63 Pa. Stat. Ann. § 456.04 (West Supp. 2000).

– At the publication date of this book, Pennsylvania is undertaking its first official codification, Pennsylvania Consolidated Statutes, the old, unofficial compilation entitled Purdon's Pennsylvania Statutes Annotated, which uses a different numbering system. Purdon is also reprinting the new, official codification as Pennsylvania's Consolidated Statutes Annotated, which is currently bound with Pennsylvania Statutes Annotated. Cite to Pennsylvania Consolidated Statutes or Pennsylvania Statutes Annotated, in that order of preference. See Bluebook table T.1, p. 229.

–For proper citation form in papers submitted to Pennsylvania courts, see Pa. R. App. P. 2119(b).

In law review footnotes, the titles of books and the names of cases, except for procedural phrases, are not underlined. See Bluebook rule 2.1(a) & (b). Further, the following are in large and small capitals: codes, restatements, standards, constitutions, periodicals, authors of books, titles of books, the abbreviated names of codes, most legislative materials except for bills and resolutions, codified ordinances, model codes, court rules, and sentencing guidelines. Refer to The Bluebook.

Q

Quarterly Journal
Ab.:   Q. J.

Ex.:   Ballard C. Gilmore, <u>Recent Corporate Decisions</u>, 11 Q.J. 43 (1991).
        –Article Citation.

        Ballard C. Gilmore, <u>Recent Corporate Decisions</u>, 11 Q.J. 43, 44 (1991).
        –Page Citation.

Quarterly Report of the Attorney General (Alabama)
Ab.:   Ala. Q. Rep. Att'y Gen.

See Opinions of the Attorney General of Alabama.

Queen's Law Journal
Ab.:   Queen's L.J.

Ex.:   Nicholas Bala, <u>Double Victims: Child Sexual Abuse and the Canadian
        Criminal Justice System</u>, 15 Queen's L.J. 3 (1990). –Article Citation.

        Nicholas Bala, <u>Double Victims: Child Sexual Abuse and the Canadian
        Criminal Justice System</u>, 15 Queen's L.J. 3, 22 (1990). –Page Citation.

Queensland Lawyer (Australia) (1973-date)
Ab.:   Q. Law.

Ex.:   <u>Jameson v. Smith</u>, 11 Q. Law. 47, (1989).

Queensland Reports (Australia) (1958-date)
Ab.:   Q.R.

Ex.:   <u>Sprenger v. Sanderson</u>, [1992] 1 Q.R. 580, 581 (1991) (Austl.).

        Note: For explanation of Australia's medium-neutral citation, see L.T.
        Olsson, <u>Guide to Uniform Production of Judgments</u> (2d ed. 1999),
        <u>available at</u> http://www.aija.org.au/online/judguide.htm.

Queensland State Reports (Australia) (1902-1957)
Ab.:   Q. St. R.

Ex.:   <u>Horton v. Byrne</u>, 1957 Q. St. R. 1, 7-9 (Austl.).

Queensland Supreme Court Reports (Australia) (1860-date)
Ab.:   Q.S. Ct. R.

Ex.:   <u>Miskin v. Hutchinson</u>, 5 Q.S. Ct. R. 85, 89 (1868) (Austl.).

        Note: For explanation of Australia's medium-neutral citation, see L.T.
        Olsson, <u>Guide to Uniform Production of Judgments</u> (2d ed. 1999),
        <u>available at</u> http://www.aija.org.au/online/judguide.htm.

In law review footnotes, the titles of books and the names of cases, except for procedural
phrases, are not underlined. <u>See</u> <u>Bluebook</u> rule 2.1(a) & (b). Further, the following are in
large and small capitals: codes, restatements, standards, constitutions, periodicals, authors of
books, titles of books, the abbreviated names of codes, most legislative materials except for
bills and resolutions, codified ordinances, model codes, court rules, and sentencing guidelines.
Refer to <u>The Bluebook</u>.

Quinnipiac Law Review
Ab: Quinnipiac L. Rev.

Ex: R. George Wright, <u>Personhood 2.0: Enhanced and Unenhanced Persons and the Equal Protection of the Laws</u>, 23 Quinnipiac L. Rev. 1047 (2005). –Article Citation.

R. George Wright, <u>Personhood 2.0: Enhanced and Unenhanced Persons and the Equal Protection of the Laws</u>, 23 Quinnipiac L. Rev. 1047, 1065-67 (2005). –Page Citation.

quotations

–Details for quotations are explained and illustrated in <u>Bluebook</u> rule 5.

quoted in
Ex.:

"As Wigmore notes sequestration 'already had in English practice an independent and continuous existence, even in the time of those earlier modes of trial which preceded the jury and were a part of our inheritance of the common Germanic law.' VI <u>Wigmore on Evidence</u> § 1837 at 348 (3rd 1940), <u>quoted in</u> <u>Geders v. United States</u>, 425 U.S. 80, 87, 96 S. Ct. 1330, 1334, 47 L. Ed. 2d 592 (1976). The rule serves two salutary purposes: (1) it prevents witnesses from tailoring testimony . . . ." –Taken from 675 F.2d 825, 835 (1982).

quoting
Ex.:

Ted J. Fiflis, <u>Soft Information: The SEC's Former Exogeneous Zone</u>, 26 UCLA L. Rev. 95, 116, n.71 (1978) ("A fact is material if there is a substantial likelihood that a reasonable shareholder would consider it important in deciding how to vote.")
(quoting <u>TSC Indus. v. Northway</u>, 426 U.S. 438, 449 (1976)).

In citing cases in law review footnotes, abbreviate any word listed in table T.6; the names of "states, countries, and other geographical units" unless they are named parties; and any other words of eight or more letters "if <u>substantial</u> space is thereby saved and the result is unambiguous." <u>Bluebook</u> rule 10.2.2. On the other hand, in citing cases in text, abbreviate only widely known acronyms and the following words: "&," "Ass'n," "Bros.," "Co.," "Corp.," "Inc.," "Ltd.," and "No." <u>Bluebook</u> rule 10.2.1(c).

R

RAND Journal of Economics, The
    Ab.:   RAND J. Econ.
    Ex.:   E. Nosal, <u>Renegotiating Incomplete Contracts</u>, 23 RAND J. Econ. 20 (1992). −Article Citation.

            E. Nosal, <u>Renegotiating Incomplete Contracts</u>, 23 RAND J. Econ. 20, 21 (1992). −Page Citation.

Real Estate Commission
    Ab.:   Real Est. Comm'n

Real Estate Law Journal
    Ab.:   Real Est. L.J.
    Ex.:   Harvey Boneparth, <u>Taking a Deed in Lieu of Foreclosure: Pitfalls for the Lender</u>, 19 Real Est. L.J. 338 (1991). −Article Citation.

            Harvey Boneparth, <u>Taking a Deed in Lieu of Foreclosure: Pitfalls for the Lender</u>, 19 Real Est. L.J. 338, 340-41 (1991). −Page Citation.

Real Property, Probate and Trust Journal
    Ab.:   Real Prop. Prob. & Tr. J.
    Ex.:   Jean A. Mortland, <u>Attorneys as Real Estate Brokers: Ethical Considerations</u>, 25 Real Prop. Prob. & Tr. J. 755 (1991).
            −Article Citation.

            Jean A. Mortland, <u>Attorneys as Real Estate Brokers: Ethical Considerations</u>, 25 Real Prop. Prob. & Tr. J. 755, 759-63 (1991).
            −Page Citation.

Record (court), citation to
    Ab.:   R.
    Ex.:   (R. at 7).

    <u>See</u> <u>Bluebook</u> rule B10 and table BT.1.

    Note: See <u>Bluebook</u> rule 10.8.3 for citing litigation materials from another case.

Recueil Dalloz, Jurisprudence (France) (1945-64)
    Ab.:   D. Jur.
    Ex.:   Cass. 2e civ. Mar. 6, 1961, Recueil Dalloz, Jurisprudence [D. Jur.], 1961, 322 (Fr.).

<u>See</u> <u>Bluebook</u> rule 20.2.3 and table T.2.

In law review footnotes, the titles of books and the names of cases, except for procedural phrases, are not underlined. <u>See</u> <u>Bluebook</u> rule 2.1(a) & (b). Further, the following are in large and small capitals: codes, restatements, standards, constitutions, periodicals, authors of books, titles of books, the abbreviated names of codes, most legislative materials except for bills and resolutions, codified ordinances, model codes, court rules, and sentencing guidelines. Refer to <u>The Bluebook</u>.

Recueil Dalloz-Sirey, Jurisprudence (France)
Ab.:   D.
Ex.:   Cass. 3e civ., Apr. 17, 1984, Recueil Dalloz-Sirey, Jurisprudence [D.]
1985, 234, note Najjar (Fr.).
See Bluebook rule 20.2.3 and table T.2.

Referee
Ab.:   Ref.

Regent University Law Review
Ab.:   Regent U. L. Rev.
Ex.:   Herbert W. Titus, Public School Chaplains: Constitutional Solution to
the School Prayer Controversy, 1 Regent U. L. Rev. 19 (1991).
–Article Citation.

Herbert W. Titus, Public School Chaplains: Constitutional Solution to
the School Prayer Controversy, 1 Regent U. L. Rev. 19, 21-23 (1991).
–Page Citation.

Regulations of Connecticut State Agencies
Ab.:   Conn. Agencies Regs. § x-x-x   (year)
Ex.:   Conn. Agencies Regs. § 21a-29-2 (2004)

related authority
See   cited in
construed in
quoted in
quoting
reprinted in

Reports from the Secretary-General (U.N.)
Ex.:   The Secretary-General, Report on the Situation of Human Rights in
Cambodia, ¶ 20, delivered to the General Assembly, U.N. Doc.
A/52/489 (June 1, 1997).

Reorganization Plans (U.S.)
Ab.:   Reorganization Plan No. # of year
Ex.:   Reorganization Plan No. 1 of 1978, 43 Fed. Reg. 19,807 (May 9,
1978). –Citation to material not yet available in the Code of Federal
Regulations.

Reorganization Plan No. 3 of 1970, 3 C.F.R. 199 (1970).

Reorganization Plan No. 1 of 1967, 3 C.F.R. 220 (1969), reprinted in 5
U.S.C. app. at 822 (1976) (repealed 1978). –Citation if the plan is
reprinted in U.S.C., U.S.C.A., or U.S.C.S. In this example, the repeal
of the plan is noted parenthetically.

In citing cases in law review footnotes, abbreviate any word listed in table T.6;
the names of "states, countries, and other geographical units" unless they are named parties;
and any other words of eight or more letters "if substantial space is thereby saved and the
result is unambiguous." Bluebook rule 10.2.2. On the other hand, in citing cases in text,
abbreviate only widely known acronyms and the following words: "&," "Ass'n," "Bros.,"
"Co.," "Corp.," "Inc.," "Ltd.," and "No." Bluebook rule 10.2.1(c).

Reorganization Plan No. 4 of 1978, 3 C.F.R. 332 (1979), reprinted in 5 U.S.C. app. at 412 (Supp. IV 1980) and in 92 Stat. 3790 (1978).
–Citation with optional parallel reference to a printing in Statutes at Large.

replacement
Ab.:   repl.

Report of Cases before the Court of Justice of the European Communities
Ab.:   E.C.R.

Ex.:   Case C-244/89, Comm'n v. France, 1991 E.C.R. I-163. –Case Citation.

See Bluebook rule 21.5.2 and table T.3.

Reports, Congressional
See Congressional Reports.

Reports of International Arbitral Awards

Ab.:   Int'l Arb. Awards

Ex.:   Trail Smelter Case (U.S. v. Can.), 3 R. Int'l Arb. Awards (1911) (Perm. Ct. Arb. 1938).

Reports of Patent Cases (England) (1884-1885)
See Reports of Patent, Design and Trademark cases and table T.2.

Ab.:   R.P.C.

Ex.:   Lister v. Norton Bros. & Co., 2 R.P.C. 68 (Ch. 1885) (Eng.).
         –Case Citation.

Reports of Patent, Design, and Trade Mark Cases (England) (1884-date)
Ab.:   R.P.D.T.M.C./R.P.C.

Ex.:   Duracell Int'l, Inc. v. Ever Ready Ltd., 106 R.P.D.T.M.C./R.P.C. 731 (Ch. 1989) (Eng.).

         –Note: These reporters are still designated "Reports of Patent Cases" on the outside cover.

See Bluebook table T.2 concerning neutral citation for cases after 2001.

Reports of the United States Board of Tax Appeals
Ab.:   B.T.A.

Ex.:   Boeing v. Comm'r, 46 B.T.A. 492 (1942).

Reports of the United States Tax Court
Ab.:   T.C.

Ex.:   Miller v. Comm'r, 104 T.C. 330 (1995).

Representative
Ab.:   Rep.

In law review footnotes, the titles of books and the names of cases, except for procedural phrases, are not underlined. See Bluebook rule 2.1(a) & (b). Further, the following are in large and small capitals: codes, restatements, standards, constitutions, periodicals, authors of books, titles of books, the abbreviated names of codes, most legislative materials except for bills and resolutions, codified ordinances, model codes, court rules, and sentencing guidelines. Refer to The Bluebook.

reprint

Ex.: 1 William Blackstone, <u>Commentaries</u> *35 (photo reprint 1979) (1765-1769).

reprinted in

Ex.: <u>United States Policy on Nonrecognition of Communist China</u>, 39 Dep't St. Bull. 385 (1958), <u>reprinted in</u> William W. Bishop, <u>International Law Cases and Materials</u> 351-54 (3d ed. 1962).

S. Rep. No. 368, 96th Cong., 1st Sess. 4-5, <u>reprinted in</u> 1980 U.S.C.C.A.N. 236, 239-41.

Note: "Reprinted in" indicates a full reprinting rather than an excerpt, which is indicated by "as reprinted in." <u>See</u> <u>Bluebook</u> rule 1.6(a)(iii) (3d prtg. 2006).

Res Gestae

Ab.: Do not abbreviate title.

Ex.: Donald P. Bogard & Kenneth R. Yahne, <u>Corporate Pro Bono: Models for Replication</u>, 35 Res Gestae 508 (1992). −Article Citation.

Donald P. Bogard & Kenneth R. Yahne, <u>Corporate Pro Bono: Models for Replication</u>, 35 Res Gestae 508, 512 (1992). −Page Citation.

Research in Law and Economics

Ab.: Res. L. & Econ.

Ex.: Victor P. Goldberg, <u>The International Salt Puzzle</u>, 14 Res. L. & Econ. 31 (1991). −Article Citation.

Victor P. Goldberg, <u>The International Salt Puzzle</u>, 14 Res. L. & Econ. 31, 45-47 (1991). −Page Citation.

Resolutions, Congressional

See Congressional Resolutions.

Response (article designation)

Ex.: Omri Ben-Shahar, Response, <u>Mutual Assent Versus Gradual Ascent: The Debate Over the Right to Retract</u>, 152 U. Pa. L. Rev. 1947 (2004).

See <u>Bluebook</u> rule 16.6.4.

Response, citation to

Ab.: Resp.

Ex.: (Def.'s Resp. Pl.'s Mot. Summ. J. 7).

See <u>Bluebook</u> rule B10 and table BT.2.

Note: See <u>Bluebook</u> rule 10.8.3 for citing litigation materials from another case.

Restatement (Second) of Agency (ALI)

Ab.: Restatement (Second) of Agency § ___ (year)

In citing cases in law review footnotes, abbreviate any word listed in table T.6; the names of "states, countries, and other geographical units" unless they are named parties; and any other words of eight or more letters "if <u>substantial</u> space is thereby saved and the result is unambiguous." <u>Bluebook</u> rule 10.2.2. On the other hand, in citing cases in text, abbreviate only widely known acronyms and the following words: "&," "Ass'n," "Bros.," "Co.," "Corp.," "Inc.," "Ltd.," and "No." <u>Bluebook</u> rule 10.2.1(c).

Ex.:   Restatement (Second) of Agency § 84 cmt. b & c (1957).

Restatement (Second) of Agency § 15 app. (2000).

Restatement (Third) of Agency (ALI)
Ab.:   Restatement (Third) of Agency § ___ (Tentative Draft No. ____, year)

Ex.:   Restatement (Third) of Agency § 1.03 (Tentative Draft No. 1, 2000).

Restatement of Conflict of Laws (ALI)
Ab.:   Restatement of Conflict of Laws § ___ (year)

Ex.:   Restatement of Conflict of Laws § 168 (1934).

Restatement of Conflict of Laws § 288 reporter's note (1971).

Restatement of Conflict of Laws § 115 cmt. e, illus. 4 (1969).

Restatement (Second) of Conflict of Laws (ALI)
Ab.:   Restatement (Second) of Conflict of Laws § ___ (year)

Ex.:   Restatement (Second) of Conflict of Laws § 103 (1969).

Restatement (Second) of Conflict of Laws § 288 reporter's note (1971).

Restatement (Second) of Conflict of Laws § 115 cmt. e, illus. 4 (1969).

Restatement of Contracts (ALI)
Ab.:   Restatement of Contracts § ___ (year)

Ex.:   Restatement of Contracts § 405(1) (1932).

Restatement (Second) of Contracts (ALI)
Ab.:   Restatement (Second) of Contracts § ___ (year)

Ex.:   Restatement (Second) of Contracts § 272(1) & cmt. a (1979).

Restatement (Second) of Contracts § 1 app. (1997).

Restatement of Foreign Relations Law of the United States (ALI)
Ab.:   Restatement of Foreign Relations Law of the United States § ___ (year)

Restatement (Second) of Foreign Relations Law of the United States (ALI)
Ab.:   Restatement (Second) of Foreign Relations Law of the United States § ___ (year)

Ex.:   Restatement (Second) of Foreign Relations Law of the United States § 41 (1965).

Restatement (Third) of Foreign Relations Law of the United States (ALI)
Ab.:   Restatement (Third) of Foreign Relations Law of the United States § ___ (year)

Ex.:   Restatement (Third) of Foreign Relations Law of the United States § 210 (1986).

Restatement (Third) of Foreign Relations Law of the United States § 210 reporter's note 3 (1986).

In law review footnotes, the titles of books and the names of cases, except for procedural phrases, are not underlined. See Bluebook rule 2.1(a) & (b). Further, the following are in large and small capitals: codes, restatements, standards, constitutions, periodicals, authors of books, titles of books, the abbreviated names of codes, most legislative materials except for bills and resolutions, codified ordinances, model codes, court rules, and sentencing guidelines. Refer to The Bluebook.

Restatement (Third) of Foreign Relations Law of the United States § 223 (Supp. 2000).

Restatement (Second) of Judgments (ALI)
Ab.: Restatement (Second) of Judgments § ___ (year)
Ex.: Restatement (Second) of Judgments § 4 (1980).
Restatement (Second) of Judgments § 28 (Supp. 2000).

Restatement (Third) of The Law Governing Lawyers(ALI)
Ab.: Restatement (Third) of The Law Governing Lawyers § ___ (year)
Ex.: Restatement (Third) of The Law Governing Lawyers § 1 (1998).
Restatement (Third) of The Law Governing Lawyers § 1 cmt. h (1998).

Restatement of Property (ALI)
Ab.: Restatement of Prop. § ___ (year)
Ex.: Restatement of Prop. § 154 cmt. dd (Supp. 1992).

Restatement (Second) of Property (ALI)
Ab.: Restatement (Second) of Prop.: subdivision § ___ (year)
Ex.: Restatement (Second) of Prop.: Donative Transfers § 25.2 (1987).
Restatement (Second) of Prop.: Donative Transfers § 34.7 (1991).
Restatement (Second) of Prop.: Landlord & Tenant § 4.4 (Supp. 2000).

Restatement (Third) of Property (ALI)
Ab.: Restatement (Third) of Prop.: subdivision § ___ (year)
Ex.: Restatement (Third) of Prop.: Donative Transfers § 2.2 (1996).

Restatement (Third) of Property (ALI, Tentative Draft)
Ab.: Restatement (Third) of Prop.: subdivision § ___ (Tentative Draft No. __, year)
Ex.: Restatement (Third) of Prop.: Mortgages § 1.6 (Tentative Draft No. 5, 1996).

Restatement of Restitution (ALI)
Ab.: Restatement of Restitution § ___ (year)
Ex.: Restatement of Restitution § 189 cmt. a (1936).

Restatement (Second) of Restitution (ALI)
Ab.: Restatement (Second) of Restitution § ___ (year)
Ex.: Restatement (Second) of Restitution § 3 (Supp. 2000).

Restatement (Second) of Restitution (ALI, Tentative Draft)
Ab.: Restatement (Second) of Restitution § ___ (Tentative Draft No.___, year)

In citing cases in law review footnotes, abbreviate any word listed in table T.6; the names of "states, countries, and other geographical units" unless they are named parties; and any other words of eight or more letters "if substantial space is thereby saved and the result is unambiguous." Bluebook rule 10.2.2. On the other hand, in citing cases in text, abbreviate only widely known acronyms and the following words: "&," "Ass'n," "Bros.," "Co.," "Corp.," "Inc.," "Ltd.," and "No." Bluebook rule 10.2.1(c).

Ex.: Restatement (Second) of Restitution § 31 (Tentative Draft No. 2, 1984).

Restatement (Second) of Restitution § 46 cmt. a (Preliminary Draft No. 4, 1985).

Restatement (Third) of Restitution and Unjust Enrichment (ALI, Discussion Draft)
Ab.: Restatement (Third) of Restitution and Unjust Enrichment § ___ (Discussion Draft No.___, year)
Ex.: Restatement (Third) of Restitution and Unjust Enrichment § 16 (Discussion Draft, 1988).

Restatement of Security (ALI)
Ab.: Restatement of Security § ___ (year)
Ex.: Restatement of Security § 50 (1996).

Restatement of Security § 25 (Supp. 2000).

Restatement (Third) of Suretyship (ALI, Tentative Draft)
Ab.: Restatement (Third) of Suretyship and Guar. § ___ (year)
Ex.: Restatement (Third) of Suretyship and Guar. § 24 (1995).

Restatement (Third) of Suretyship and Guar. § 65 reporter's note (1995).

Restatement (Third) of Suretyship and Guar. § 60 cmt. a, illus. 4 (1995).

Restatement of Torts (ALI)
Ab.: Restatement of Torts § ___ (year)
Ex.: Restatement of Torts § 282 (1934).

Restatement (Second) of Torts (ALI)
Ab.: Restatement (Second) of Torts § _____ (year)
Ex.: Restatement (Second) of Torts § 402 (Supp. 2000).

Restatement (Second) of Torts § 481 app. (Supp. 1995)

Restatement (Third) of Torts: Products Liability (ALI, Tentative Draft)
Ab.: Restatement (Third) of Torts: Products Liability § ___ (Tentative Draft No. ___, year)
Ex.: Restatement (Third) of Torts: Products Liability § 2 (Tentative Draft No. 1, 1994).

Restatement (Third) of Torts: Products Liability § 4 cmt. a (Tentative Draft No. 1, 1994).

Restatement (Third) of Torts: Products Liability (ALI)
Ab.: Restatement (Third) of Torts: Products Liability § ___ (year)

In law review footnotes, the titles of books and the names of cases, except for procedural phrases, are not underlined. See Bluebook rule 2.1(a) & (b). Further, the following are in large and small capitals: codes, restatements, standards, constitutions, periodicals, authors of books, titles of books, the abbreviated names of codes, most legislative materials except for bills and resolutions, codified ordinances, model codes, court rules, and sentencing guidelines. Refer to The Bluebook.

Ex.:   Restatement (Third) of Torts: Products Liability § 19 (1997).

Restatement (Third) of Torts: Products Liability § 20 cmt. g (1997).

Restatement (Second) of Trusts (ALI)

Ab.:   Restatement (Second) of Trusts § ___ (year)

Ex.:   Restatement (Second) of Trusts § 158 (1957).

Restatement (Second) of Trusts § 2 app. (1987).

Restatement (Second) of Trusts § 1 app. (Supp. 2000).

Restatement (Third) of Trusts (ALI, Tentative Draft)

Ab.:   Restatement (Third) of Trusts § ___ (Tentative Draft No. ____, year)

Ex.:   Restatement (Third) of Trusts § 12 (Tentative Draft No. 1, 1996).

Restatement (Third) of Unfair Competition (ALI)

Ab.:   Restatement (Third) of Unfair Competition § ____ (year)

Ex.:   Restatement (Third) of Unfair Competition § 36 (1995).

Restatement (Third) of Unfair Competition § 27 cmt. c, illus. 1 (1995).

Restatement (Third) of Unfair Competition § 742 (Supp. 2000).

Revenue Procedures

Ab.:   Rev. Proc.

Ex.:   Rev. Proc. 92-43, 1992-23 I.R.B. 23. −Citation to a Revenue Proceeding not yet available in bound form.

Rev. Proc. 91-11, 1991-1 C.B. 470. −Bound.

Revenue Rulings

Ab.:   Rev. Rul.

Ex.:   Rev. Rul. 96-33, 1996-27 I.R.B. 4. −Citation to a Revenue Ruling not yet available in bound form.

Rev. Rul. 95-45, 1995-1 C.B. 53. −Bound.

reversed

Ab.:   rev'd

Ex.:   Young v. Edgcomb Steel Co., 363 F. Supp. 961 (M.D.N.C. 1973), rev'd, 499 F.2d 97 (4th Cir. 1974).

Griggs v. Duke Power Co., 420 F.2d 1225 (4th Cir. 1970), rev'd in part, 401 U.S. 424 (1971).

Karlen v. Harris, 590 F.2d 39 (2d Cir. 1978), rev'd sub nom. Stryker's Bay Neighborhood Council v. Karlen, 444 U.S. 223 (1980). −Citation if the case has a different name on appeal.

Review of Litigation, The

Ab.:   Rev. Litig.

In citing cases in law review footnotes, abbreviate any word listed in table T.6; the names of "states, countries, and other geographical units" unless they are named parties; and any other words of eight or more letters "if substantial space is thereby saved and the result is unambiguous." Bluebook rule 10.2.2. On the other hand, in citing cases in text, abbreviate only widely known acronyms and the following words: "&," "Ass'n," "Bros.," "Co.," "Corp.," "Inc.," "Ltd.," and "No." Bluebook rule 10.2.1(c).

Ex.:   Alan B. Rich, <u>Certified Pleadings: Interpreting Texas Rule 13 in Light of Federal Rule 11</u>, 11 Rev. Litig. 59 (1991). –Article Citation.

Alan B. Rich, <u>Certified Pleadings: Interpreting Texas Rule 13 in Light of Federal Rule 11</u>, 11 Rev. Litig. 59, 69-72 (1991). –Page Citation.

Review of Socialist Law
Ab.:   Rev. Socialist L.

Ex.:   George Ginsburgs, <u>The USSR and the Socialist Model of International Cooperation in Criminal Matters</u>, 17 Rev. Socialist L. 199 (1991). –Article Citation.

George Ginsburgs, <u>The USSR and the Socialist Model of International Cooperation in Criminal Matters</u>, 17 Rev. Socialist L. 199, 250-54 (1991). –Page Citation.

Review of Taxation of Individuals, The
Ab.:   Rev. Tax'n Individuals

Ex.:   Rolf Auster, <u>Tax Accounting</u>, 16 Rev. Tax'n Individuals 274 (1992). –Article Citation.

Rolf Auster, <u>Tax Accounting</u>, 16 Rev. Tax'n Individuals 274, 275-77 (1992). –Page Citation.

revised
Ab.:   rev.

Revised Code of Washington
Ab.:   Wash. Rev. Code § x.x.x (year)

Ex.:   Wash. Rev. Code § 26.33.120(1) (1996).

Revised Code of Washington Annotated (West)
Ab.:   Wash. Rev. Code Ann. § x.x.x (West year)

Ex.:   Wash. Rev. Code Ann. § 9A.52.070 (West 2000).

Wash. Rev. Code Ann. § 25.05.125 (West Supp. 2000).

–"Cite to Wash. Rev. Code, if therein." <u>Bluebook</u> table T.1, p. 238.

Revised Model Business Corporation Act (ABA)
See American Bar Association Revised Model Business Corporation Act.

Revised Ordinances of the Northwest Territories (Canada)
Ab.:   R.O.N.W.T.

Ex.:   Sale of Goods Ordinance, R.O.N.W.T., ch. S, § 45(1) (1974) (Can.).

<u>See</u> <u>Bluebook</u> rule 12.8.2.

In law review footnotes, the titles of books and the names of cases, except for procedural phrases, are not underlined. <u>See</u> <u>Bluebook</u> rule 2.1(a) & (b). Further, the following are in large and small capitals: codes, restatements, standards, constitutions, periodicals, authors of books, titles of books, the abbreviated names of codes, most legislative materials except for bills and resolutions, codified ordinances, model codes, court rules, and sentencing guidelines. Refer to <u>The Bluebook</u>.

Revised Regulations of Ontario
Ab.: R.R.O.

Revised Regulations of Prince Edward Island
Ab.: R.R.P.E.I.

Revised Regulations of Quebec
Ab.: R.R.Q.

Revised Reports (England) (1785-1866)
Ab.: Rev. Rep.
Ex.: Markwell v. Markwell, 145 Rev. Rep. 417 (Ch. 1864) (Eng.).
–Case Citation.
Parker v. Tootal, 145 Rev. Rep. 91 (1865) (Eng.). –Case Citation.
–"Cite to English Reports (Eng. Rep.), if therein; otherwise, cite to Revised Reports (Rev. Rep.)." Bluebook table T.2, p. 324.

Revised Statutes of Alberta (Canada)
Ab.: R.S.A.
Ex.: Notaries Public Act, R.S.A., ch. N-11, § 8(2) (1980) (Can.).
See Bluebook rule 20.5.1 and table T.2.

Revised Statutes of British Columbia (Canada)
Ab.: R.S.B.C.
Ex.: Power of Attorney Act, R.S.B.C., ch. 334 (1979) (Can.).
See Bluebook rule 20.5.1 and table T.2.

Revised Statutes of Canada
Ab.: R.S.C.
Ex.: Bank Act, R.S.C., ch. B-1, § 21(b) (1989) (Can.).
See Bluebook rule 20.5.1 and table T.2.

Revised Statutes of Manitoba (Canada)
Ab.: R.S.M.
Ex.: The Condominium Act, R.S.M., ch. C-170, § 5(1) (1987) (Can.).
See Bluebook rule 20.5.1 and table T.2.

Revised Statutes of Nebraska
Ab.: Neb. Rev. Stat. § x-x (year).
Ex.: Neb. Rev. Stat. § 81-3435 (1999).
Neb. Rev. Stat. § 60-3002 (Supp. 2004).
–For proper citation form in papers submitted to Nebraska courts, see prefatory pages to Nev. Rev. Stat. volumes.

In citing cases in law review footnotes, abbreviate any word listed in table T.6; the names of "states, countries, and other geographical units" unless they are named parties; and any other words of eight or more letters "if substantial space is thereby saved and the result is unambiguous." Bluebook rule 10.2.2. On the other hand, in citing cases in text, abbreviate only widely known acronyms and the following words: "&," "Ass'n," "Bros.," "Co.," "Corp.," "Inc.," "Ltd.," and "No." Bluebook rule 10.2.1(c).

Revised Statutes of Nebraska Annotated (LexisNexis)
Ab.:   Neb. Rev. Stat. Ann. § x-x (LexisNexis year).

Ex.:   Neb. Rev. Stat. Ann. § 19-915 (LexisNexis 2004).

Neb. Rev. Stat. Ann. § 81-159 (LexisNexis Supp. 2005).

–"Cite to Neb. Rev. Stat., if therein." Bluebook table T.1, p. 218.

–For proper citation form in papers submitted to Nebraska courts, see prefatory pages to Nev. Rev. Stat. volumes.

Revised Statutes of New Brunswick (Canada)
Ab.:   R.S.N.B.

Ex.:   Marine Insurance Act, R.S.N.B., ch. M-1, § 21(6) (1973) (Can.).

See Bluebook rule 20.5.1 and table T.2.

Revised Statutes of Newfoundland (Canada)
Ab.:   NFld. R.S.

Ex.:   Newfoundland Human Rights Code, Nfld. R.S., ch. 262, § 17(2) (1970) (Can.).

See Bluebook rule 20.5.1 and table T.2.

Revised Statutes of Nova Scotia (Canada)
Ab.:   R.S.N.S.

Ex.:   Accountant General of the Supreme Court Act, R.S.N.S., ch. 1, § 30(1) (1989) (Can.).

See Bluebook rule 20.5.1 and table T.2.

Revised Statutes of Ontario (Canada)
Ab.:   R.S.O.

Ex.:   Ontario Place Corporation Act, R.S.O., ch. 353, § 10(a) (1980) (Can.).

See Bluebook rule 20.5.1 and table T.2.

Revised Statutes of Prince Edward Island (Canada)
Ab.:   R.S.P.E.I.

Ex.:   Lotteries Commission Act, R.S.P.E.I., ch. L-17, § 4(1) (1988) (Can.).

See Bluebook rule 20.5.1 and table T.2.

Revised Statutes of Québec (Canada)
Ab.:   R.S.Q.

Ex.:   Lightning Rods Act, R.S.Q., ch. P-6, § 21 (1977) (Can.).

See Bluebook rule 20.5.1 and table T.2.

Revista de Derecho Puertorriqueño
Ab.:   Rev. D.P.

In law review footnotes, the titles of books and the names of cases, except for procedural phrases, are not underlined. See Bluebook rule 2.1(a) & (b). Further, the following are in large and small capitals: codes, restatements, standards, constitutions, periodicals, authors of books, titles of books, the abbreviated names of codes, most legislative materials except for bills and resolutions, codified ordinances, model codes, court rules, and sentencing guidelines. Refer to The Bluebook.

Ex.: José A. Cuevas Segarra, La Ley de Ventas Condicionales de Puerto Rico, Jurisprudencia, 106 Revista de Derecho Puertorriqueño [Rev. D.P.] 185 (1989-90) (P.R.) –Article Citation.

–See Bluebook rules 20.2.3 and 20.6

Revista del Colegio de Abogados de Puerto Rico
Ab.: Rev. Col. Ab. P.R.

Ex.: Fuster, La misión de la Universidad Católica de Puerto Rico y la situación actual del pais, 21 Revista de Derecho del Colegio de Abogados de Puerto Rico [Rev. Col. Ab. P.R.] 147 (1981). –Article Citation.

–See Bluebook rules 20.2.3 and 20.6.

Revue Critique de Droit International Privé
Ab.: R.C.D.I.P.

Ex.: Pierre-Yves Gautier, Les couples internationaux de concubins, 80 Revue Critique de Droit International Privé [R.C.D.I.P.] 525 (1991) (Fr.). –Article Citation.

–See Bluebook rules 20.2.3 and 20.6.

Revue de Droit (Université de Sherbrooke)
Ab.: R.D.U.S.

Ex.: Pierre F. Mercure, Principes de droit international applicables au phénomène des pluies acides, 21 Revue de Droit (Université de Sherbrooke) [R.D.U.S.] 373 (1991) (Fr.). –Article Citation.

–See Bluebook rules 20.2.3 and 20.6

Revue de Droit International et de Droit Comparé
Ab.: R.D. Int'l & D. Comp.

Ex.: D.H. Bliesener, La compétence du CIRDI dans la pratique arbitrale, 68 Revue de Droit International et de Droit Comparé [R.D. Int'l & D. Comp.] 95 (1991) (Fr.). –Article Citation.

–See Bluebook rules 20.2.3 and 20.6.

Revue Francaise de Droit Adminstratif
Ab.: R. Fr. D. Admin.

Revue Générale de Droit
Ab.: Rev. Gén.

Ex.: Gil Rémillard, Présentation du projet de Code civil du Québec, 22 Revue Générale de Droit [Rev. Gén.] 5 (1991) (Fr.). –Article Citation.

–See Bluebook rules 20.2.3 and 20.6.

Revue Internationale de Droit Comparé
Ab.: R.I.D.C.

In citing cases in law review footnotes, abbreviate any word listed in table T.6; the names of "states, countries, and other geographical units" unless they are named parties; and any other words of eight or more letters "if substantial space is thereby saved and the result is unambiguous." Bluebook rule 10.2.2. On the other hand, in citing cases in text, abbreviate only widely known acronyms and the following words: "&," "Ass'n," "Bros.," "Co.," "Corp.," "Inc.," "Ltd.," and "No." Bluebook rule 10.2.1(c).

Ex.: Francois Rigaux, La liberté de la vie privée, 43 Revue Internationale de Droit Comparé [R.I.D.C.] 539 (1991) (Fr.). –Article Citation.

–See Bluebook rules 20.2.3 and 20.6.

Revue Juridique Thémis
Ab.: R.J.T.

Ex.: Diane L. Demers, Maladies professionnelles et plausibilité biologique, 25 Revue Juridique Thémis [R.J.T.] 29 (1991) (Fr.). –Article Citation.

–See Bluebook rules 20.2.3 and 20.6.

RFE/RL Research Report
Ab.: RFE/RL Res. Rep.

Ex.: Jan Obrman, Slovak Politician Accused of Secret Police Ties, RFE/RL Res. Rep., April 10, 1992, at 13. –Article Citation.

Jan Obrman, Slovak Politician Accused of Secret Police Ties, RFE/RL Res. Rep., April 10, 1992, at 13, 15-16. –Page Citation.

Rhode Island Bar Journal
Ab.: R.I. B.J.

Ex.: Raymond A. Marcaccio, Decisions from the First Circuit: A Crisis for Victims of Age Discrimination, R.I. B.J., May 1992, at 7.

–Article Citation.

Raymond A. Marcaccio, Decisions from the First Circuit: A Crisis for Victims of Age Discrimination, R.I. B.J., May 1992, at 7, 9-10.

Page Citation.

Rhode Island Constitution
Ab.: R.I. Const. art.   , §   .

Ex.: R.I. Const. art. XII, § 1. –"Cite constitutional provisions currently in force without a date." Bluebook rule 11.

R.I. Const. art. I, § 9 (amended 1988). –"When citing a provision that has been subsequently amended, either indicate parenthetically the fact and date of amendment or cite the amending provision in full." Bluebook rule 11.

Rhode Island General Laws
See General Laws of Rhode Island.

Rhode Island General Laws Advance Legislative Service (LexisNexis)
Ab.: year-pamph. no. R.I. Gen. Laws Adv. Legis. Serv. page no. (LexisNexis)

In law review footnotes, the titles of books and the names of cases, except for procedural phrases, are not underlined. See Bluebook rule 2.1(a) & (b). Further, the following are in large and small capitals: codes, restatements, standards, constitutions, periodicals, authors of books, titles of books, the abbreviated names of codes, most legislative materials except for bills and resolutions, codified ordinances, model codes, court rules, and sentencing guidelines. Refer to The Bluebook.

Ex.: Act of July 30, 2004, Ch. 596, 2004-4 R.I. Gen. Laws Adv. Legis. Serv. 674 (LexisNexis) (relating to Human Services). –Citation to an entire session law.

Act of July 30, 2004, Ch. 596, sec. 6, 2004-4 R.I. Gen. Laws Adv. Legis. Serv. 674, 690 (LexisNexis) (relating to Human Services). –Citation to a section of a session law.

–See Bluebook rule 12.4.

–"Cite to R.I. Pub. Laws, if therein." Bluebook table T.1, p. 230.

Rhode Island Government Register (Weil)
Ab.: issue no. R.I. Gov't Reg. page no. (Weil month year)

Rhode Island Reports
Ab.: R.I.

–Discontinued in 1980 after 122 R.I. 923 (1980).

–Cite to A. or A.2d, if therein; otherwise, cite to R.I.

–Give parallel citations only in documents submitted to Rhode Island state courts. Because Rhode Island Supreme Court opinions provide parallel citations to Rhode Island decisions where available, we advise giving a parallel citation in documents submitted to Rhode Island state courts. See Bluebook rules 10.3.1and B5.1.3

–Through 122 R.I. 923 (1980) cite as follows:

In documents submitted to Rhode Island courts:

Morgan v. Thomas, 98 R.I. 204, 200 A.2d 696 (1964).

–Case Citation.

Morgan v. Thomas, 98 R.I. 204, 210, 200 A.2d 696, 699 (1964).
–Page Citation.

In all other documents:

Morgan v. Thomas, 200 A.2d 696 (R.I. 1964). –Case Citation.

Morgan v. Thomas, 200 A.2d 696, 699 (R.I. 1964).

–Page Citation.

–After 122 R.I. 923 (1980) cite as follows:

In all documents:

Gushlaw v. Rohrbaugh, 673 A.2d 63 (R.I. 1996). –Case Citation.

Gushlaw v. Rohrbaugh, 673 A.2d 63, 64 (R.I. 1996). –Page Citation.

Rhode Island Session Laws
See Public Laws of Rhode Island and Providence Plantations.

In citing cases in law review footnotes, abbreviate any word listed in table T.6; the names of "states, countries, and other geographical units" unless they are named parties; and any other words of eight or more letters "if substantial space is thereby saved and the result is unambiguous." Bluebook rule 10.2.2. On the other hand, in citing cases in text, abbreviate only widely known acronyms and the following words: "&," "Ass'n," "Bros.," "Co.," "Corp.," "Inc.," "Ltd.," and "No." Bluebook rule 10.2.1(c).

Richmond Journal of Law & Technology
    Ab.:   Rich. J.L. & Tech.

    Ex.:   John LaBarre & Xavier Goméz-Velasco, <u>Ready, Set, Mark Your Patented Software</u>!, 12 Rich. J.L. & Tech. 1, ¶ 5 (2005), http://law.richmond.edu/jolt/v12i1/article3.pdf.

Rocky Mountain Mineral Law Institute
    Ab.:   Rocky Mtn. Min. L. Inst.

    Ex.:   Thomas F. Cope, <u>Environmental Liabilities of Non-Operating Parties</u>, 37 Rocky Mtn. Min. L. Inst. 1-1 (1991). –Article Citation.

           Thomas F. Cope, <u>Environmental Liabilities of Non-Operating Parties</u>, 37 Rocky Mtn. Min. L. Inst. 1-1, 1-27 (1991). –Page Citation.

Roger Williams University Law Review
    Ab: Roger Williams U. L. Rev.

    Ex: Thomas R. Bender, <u>For a More Vigorous State Constitutionalism</u>, 10 Roger Williams U. L. Rev. 621 (2005). –Article Citation.

           Thomas R. Bender, <u>For a More Vigorous State Constitutionalism</u>, 10 Roger Williams U. L. Rev. 621, 635-36 (2005).–Page Citation.

Rules of Evidence and Procedure
    –Use abbreviations such as those listed in <u>Bluebook</u> rule 12.8.3 or those abbreviations suggested by the rules themselves.

    Ex.:   Fed. R. Evid. 403.

           Fed. R. Civ. P. 11.

           Fed. R. Crim. P. 6.

           Sup. Ct. R. 5.

           Fed. R. App. P. 3.

           3d Cir. R. 7(1).

           Tenn. R. App. P. 6.

Rules of Habeas Procedure
    See Federal Rules of Habeas Procedure.

Rules of the Court of Claims of the United States
    See Court of Claims Rules.

Rules of the Supreme Court of the United States
    See Supreme Court Rules.

Rules of the United States Customs Court
    See Customs Court Rules.

Rutgers Computer and Technology Law Journal
    Ab.:   Rutgers Computer & Tech. L.J.

In law review footnotes, the titles of books and the names of cases, except for procedural phrases, are not underlined. <u>See</u> <u>Bluebook</u> rule 2.1(a) & (b). Further, the following are in large and small capitals: codes, restatements, standards, constitutions, periodicals, authors of books, titles of books, the abbreviated names of codes, most legislative materials except for bills and resolutions, codified ordinances, model codes, court rules, and sentencing guidelines. Refer to <u>The Bluebook</u>.

Ex.:   Richard H. Stern, <u>Copyright in Computer Programming Languages</u>,
         17 Rutgers Computer & Tech. L.J. 321 (1991). –Article Citation.

         Richard H. Stern, <u>Copyright in Computer Programming Languages</u>, 17
         Rutgers Computer & Tech. L.J. 321, 349-53 (1991). –Page Citation.

Rutgers Law Journal
Ab.:   Rutgers L.J.

Ex.:   Robert H.A. Ashford, <u>The Binary Economics of Louis Kelso: The</u>
         <u>Promise of Universal Capitalism</u>, 22 Rutgers L.J. 3 (1990). –Article
         Citation.

         Robert H.A. Ashford, <u>The Binary Economics of Louis Kelso: The</u>
         <u>Promise of Universal Capitalism</u>, 22 Rutgers L.J. 3, 5-7 (1990). –Page
         Citation.

Rutgers Law Review
Ab.:   Rutgers L. Rev.

Ex.:   William G. Ross, <u>The Ethics of Hourly Billing by Attorneys</u>,
         44 Rutgers L. Rev. 1 (1991). –Article Citation.

         William G. Ross, <u>The Ethics of Hourly Billing by Attorneys</u>,
         44 Rutgers L. Rev. 1, 59-62 (1991). –Page Citation.

In citing cases in law review footnotes, abbreviate any word listed in table T.6;
the names of "states, countries, and other geographical units" unless they are named parties;
and any other words of eight or more letters "if <u>substantial</u> space is thereby saved and the
result is unambiguous." <u>Bluebook</u> rule 10.2.2. On the other hand, in citing cases in text,
abbreviate only widely known acronyms and the following words: "&," "Ass'n," "Bros.,"
"Co.," "Corp.," "Inc.," "Ltd.," and "No." <u>Bluebook</u> rule 10.2.1(c).

S

St. John's Journal of Legal Commentary
Ab.:   St. John's J. Legal Comment.

Ex.:   John A. Maher & Kathryn C. Hoefer, <u>Federal Superlien: An Alternative to Lender Liability Under CERCLA</u>, 6 St. John's J. Legal Comment. 41 (1990). –Article Citation.

John A. Maher & Kathryn C. Hoefer, <u>Federal Superlien: An Alternative to Lender Liability Under CERCLA</u>, 6 St. John's J. Legal Comment. 41, 49-50 (1990). –Page Citation.

St. John's Law Review
Ab.:   St. John's L. Rev.

Ex.:   Peter Linzer, <u>White Liberal Looks at Racist Speech</u>, 65 St. John's L. Rev. 187 (1991). –Article Citation.

Peter Linzer, <u>White Liberal Looks at Racist Speech</u>, 65 St. John's L. Rev. 187, 188 (1991). –Page Citation.

St. Louis Bar Journal
Ab.:   St. Louis B.J.

Ex.:   Stephen H. Ringkamp, <u>Uninsured and Underinsured Motor Vehicle Coverage</u>, St. Louis B.J., Spring 1992, at 26. –Article Citation.

Stephen H. Ringkamp, <u>Uninsured and Underinsured Motor Vehicle Coverage</u>, St. Louis B.J., Spring 1992, at 26, 29-31. –Page Citation.

Saint Louis University Law Journal
Ab.:   St. Louis U. L.J.

Ex.:   Michael I. Krauss, <u>Tort Law and Private Ordering</u>, 35 St. Louis U. L.J. 623 (1991). –Article Citation.

Michael I. Krauss, <u>Tort Law and Private Ordering</u>, 35 St. Louis U. L.J. 623, 645-47 (1991). –Page Citation.

Saint Louis University Public Law Review
Ab.:   St. Louis U. Pub. L. Rev.

Ex.:   Mathew Staver, <u>Injunctive Relief and the Madsen Test</u>, 140 St. Louis U. Pub. L. Rev. 465 (1995). –Article Citation.

Mathew Staver, <u>Injunctive Relief and the Madsen Test</u>, 140 St. Louis U. Pub. L. Rev. 465, 467 (1995). –Page Citation.

St. Mary's Law Journal
Ab.:   St. Mary's L.J.

In law review footnotes, the titles of books and the names of cases, except for procedural phrases, are not underlined. <u>See</u> <u>Bluebook</u> rule 2.1(a) & (b). Further, the following are in large and small capitals: codes, restatements, standards, constitutions, periodicals, authors of books, titles of books, the abbreviated names of codes, most legislative materials except for bills and resolutions, codified ordinances, model codes, court rules, and sentencing guidelines. Refer to <u>The Bluebook</u>.

Ex.: H.N. Cunningham III, <u>Transborder-Road Transportation</u>, 23 St. Mary's L.J. 801 (1992). –Article Citation.

H.N. Cunningham III, <u>Transborder-Road Transportation</u>, 23 St. Mary's L.J. 801, 810-11 (1992). –Page Citation.

St. Thomas Law Review
Ab.: St. Thomas L. Rev.

Ex.: Frank Nussbaum, <u>The Economic Loss Rule and Intentional Torts: A Shield or a Sword?</u>, 8 St. Thomas L. Rev. 473 (1996). –Article Citation.

Frank Nussbaum, <u>The Economic Loss Rule and Intentional Torts: A Shield or a Sword?</u>, 8 St. Thomas L. Rev. 473, 480 (1996). –Page Citation.

Samford University (Cumberland School of Law) Law Review
See Cumberland Law Review.

San Diego Law Review
Ab.: San Diego L. Rev.

Ex.: Girard Fisher, <u>Design Immunity for Public Entities</u>, 28 San Diego L. Rev. 214 (1991). –Article Citation.

Girard Fisher, <u>Design Immunity for Public Entities</u>, 28 San Diego L. Rev. 214, 249-50 (1991). –Page Citation.

Santa Clara Computer and High Technology Law Journal
Ab.: Santa Clara Computer & High Tech. L.J.

Ex.: Evan Finkel, <u>Copyright Protection for Computer Software in the Nineties</u>, 7 Santa Clara Computer & High Tech. L.J. 201 (1991). –Article Citation.

Evan Finkel, <u>Copyright Protection for Computer Software in the Nineties</u>, 7 Santa Clara Computer & High Tech. L.J. 201, 203-05 (1991). –Page Citation.

Santa Clara Law Review
Ab.: Santa Clara L. Rev.

Ex.: Russell W. Galloway, <u>The Free Exercise Clause After Smith II</u>, 31 Santa Clara L. Rev. 597 (1991). –Article Citation.

Russell W. Galloway, <u>The Free Exercise Clause After Smith II</u>, 31 Santa Clara L. Rev. 597, 599 (1991). –Page Citation.

Saskatchewan Gazette
Ab.: S. Gaz.

Saskatchewan Law Review
Ab.: Sask. L. Rev.

In citing cases in law review footnotes, abbreviate any word listed in table T.6; the names of "states, countries, and other geographical units" unless they are named parties; and any other words of eight or more letters "if <u>substantial</u> space is thereby saved and the result is unambiguous." <u>Bluebook</u> rule 10.2.2. On the other hand, in citing cases in text, abbreviate only widely known acronyms and the following words: "&," "Ass'n," "Bros.," "Co.," "Corp.," "Inc.," "Ltd.," and "No." <u>Bluebook</u> rule 10.2.1(c).

Ex.:   Tim Quigley, <u>Battered Women and the Defence of Provocation</u>,
         55 Sask. L. Rev. 223 (1991). –Article Citation.

         Tim Quigley, <u>Battered Women and the Defence of Provocation</u>,
         55 Sask. L. Rev. 223, 229-30 (1991). –Page Citation.

School Law Reporter
   Ab.:   Sch. L. Rep. (Nat'l Org. on Legal Problems in Educ.)
   Ex.:   Patricia F. First & Lawrence F. Rossow, <u>The Spring of Race Riots and
          the Retreat from School Desegregation</u>, Sch. L. Rep., June 1992, at 1.
          –Article Citation.

          Patricia F. First & Lawrence F. Rossow, <u>The Spring of Race Riots and
          the Retreat from School Desegregation</u>, Sch. L. Rep., June 1992, at 1,
          2-3. –Page Citation.

Scribes Journal of Legal Writing, The
   Ab.:   Scribes J. Legal Writing
   Ex.:   Albert P. Blaustein, <u>Constitutional Drafting</u>, 2 Scribes J. Legal Writing
          49 (1991). –Article Citation.

          Albert P. Blaustein, <u>Constitutional Drafting</u>, 2 Scribes J. Legal Writing
          49, 53 (1991). –Page Citation.

Search and Seizure, by Wayne L. LaFave
          –Do not abbreviate the title.
   Ex.:   4 Wayne L. LaFave, <u>Search and Seizure</u> § 8.2(g) (4th ed. 2004).
          –Section Citation.

          4 Wayne L. LaFave, <u>Search and Seizure</u> § 8.2(g), at 103 (4th ed. 2004).
          –Page Citation.

          4 Wayne L. LaFave, <u>Search and Seizure</u> § 8.2(g), at 103 n.227 (4th ed.
          2004). –Footnote Citation.

Seattle University Law Review
   Ab.:   Seattle U. L. Rev.
   Ex.:   Sherman Joyce, <u>Product Liability Law in the Federal Arena</u>, 19 Seattle
          U. L. Rev. 421 (1996). –Article Citation.

          Sherman Joyce, <u>Product Liability Law in the Federal Arena</u>, 19 Seattle
          U. L. Rev. 421, 430 (1996). –Page Citation.

SEC Accounting Rules (Commerce Clearing House)
   Ab.:   SEC Accounting R. (CCH)

SEC Docket (Commerce Clearing House)
   Ab.:   SEC Docket
   Ex.:   <u>Michael N. Karp, Esq.</u>, 60 SEC Docket 2731 (1996).

section(s)
   Ab.:   §

In law review footnotes, the titles of books and the names of cases, except for procedural
phrases, are not underlined. <u>See</u> <u>Bluebook</u> rule 2.1(a) & (b). Further, the following are in
large and small capitals: codes, restatements, standards, constitutions, periodicals, authors of
books, titles of books, the abbreviated names of codes, most legislative materials except for
bills and resolutions, codified ordinances, model codes, court rules, and sentencing guidelines.
Refer to <u>The Bluebook</u>.

Ex.:   George G. Bogert, <u>Trusts</u> § 36 (6th ed. 1987).

George G. Bogert, <u>Trusts</u> §§ 106-108 (6th ed. 1987).

<u>See</u> <u>Bluebook</u> rules 3.3 and 6.2(c).

Secured Transactions Guide (Commerce Clearing House)
Ab.:   Secured Transactions Guide (CCH)

Ex.:   <u>Havins v. First Nat'l Bank</u>, 5 Secured Transactions Guide (CCH) ¶ 55,534 (Tex. Ct. App. Mar. 27, 1996). –Citation to looseleaf material.

<u>Hampton Bank v. River City Yachts, Inc.</u>, [1987-1996 Decisions Transfer Binder] Secured Transactions Guide (CCH) ¶ 55,510 (Minn. Ct. App. Feb. 28, 1995).
–Citation to bound material material.

–The above examples are proper if the case is not yet available in, or is not reported in, an official or West reporter, a public domain citation, or in a widely used computer database.

Securities and Exchange Commission Decisions and Reports (1934-date)
Ab.:   S.E.C.

Ex.:   <u>First Independence Group, Inc.</u>, 51 S.E.C. 662 (1993).

<u>Commonwealth Bond Corp.</u>, 1 S.E.C. 13 (FTC 1934). –Citation to an early decision rendered by the FTC.

<u>Lewis Airways, Inc.</u>, 1 S.E.C. 330 (1936).

Securities and Exchange Commission No-Action Letters
Ab.:   SEC No-Action Letter

Ex.:   SML Commercial Mortgage Trust 1994 C-1 SEC No-Action Letter, [1995-1996 Transfer Binder] Fed. Sec. L. Rep. (CCH) ¶ 77,107 (July 21, 1995).

Securities and Exchange Commission Releases
Ab.:   (act) Release No.

Ex.:   Adoption of Form D. Amendments, Exchange Act Release No. 6663, [1986-1987 Transfer Binder] Fed. Sec. L. Rep. (CCH) ¶ 84,032 (Oct. 2, 1986).). –Citation to a release.

<u>Thomas v. Kocherhans</u>, Exchange Act Release No. 36556, [1995-1996 Transfer Binder] Fed. Sec. L. Rep. (CCH) ¶ 85,728 (Dec. 6, 1995).
–Citation to a release that is an adjudication.

<u>See</u> <u>Bluebook</u> rules 14.1 and 14.6(b).

Securities & Federal Corporate Law Report (West)
Ab.:   Sec. & Fed. Corp. L. Rep. (West)

Securities Law Review
Ab.:   Sec. L. Rev.

In citing cases in law review footnotes, abbreviate any word listed in table T.6; the names of "states, countries, and other geographical units" unless they are named parties; and any other words of eight or more letters "if <u>substantial</u> space is thereby saved and the result is unambiguous." <u>Bluebook</u> rule 10.2.2. On the other hand, in citing cases in text, abbreviate only widely known acronyms and the following words: "&," "Ass'n," "Bros.," "Co.," "Corp.," "Inc.," "Ltd.," and "No." <u>Bluebook</u> rule 10.2.1(c).

Ex.:   James D. Gordon, III, <u>Interplanetary Intelligence About Promissory Notes as Securities</u>, 1992 Sec. L. Rev. 3. –Article Citation.

James D. Gordon, III, <u>Interplanetary Intelligence About Promissory Notes as Securities</u>, 1992 Sec. L. Rev. 3, 28-29. –Page Citation.

See Bluebook rule 16.3.

Securities Regulation & Law Report (Bureau of National Affairs)
Ab.:   Sec. Reg. & L. Rep. (BNA)

Ex.:   <u>Armstrong v. CFTC</u>, [Jan.-June] Sec. Reg. & L. Rep. (BNA) (28 Sec. Reg. & L. Rep.) No. 24, at 769 (U.S. June 10, 1996). –Citation to looseleaf material.

<u>United States v. Daiwa Bank Ltd.</u>, 27 Sec. Reg. & L. Rep. 1767 (S.D.N.Y. Nov. 2, 1995). –Citation to bound material.

–The above examples are proper if the case is not yet available in, or is not reported in, an official or West reporter, a public domain citation, or in a widely used computer database.

Securities Regulation Law Journal
Ab.:   Sec. Reg. L.J.

Ex.:   Mark A. Sargent, <u>Blue Sky Law</u>, 20 Sec. Reg. L.J. 96 (1992). –Article Citation.

Mark A. Sargent, <u>Blue Sky Law</u>, 20 Sec. Reg. L.J. 96, 97-98 (1992). –Page Citation.

See

"<u>See</u>" is used when the "cited authority clearly supports the proposition. '<u>See</u>' is used instead of '[no signal]' when the proposition is not directly stated by the cited authority but obviously follows from it; there is an inferential step between the authority cited and the proposition it supports." Bluebook rule 1.2(a).

Ex.:   "Given the wide gap between the sentence imposed and the sentence available under other similar guidelines, and the absence of any other explanation or basis for the discrepancy, I conclude the sentence was unreasonable. See <u>Pearson</u>, 911 F.2d at 191; <u>Landry</u>, 903 F.2d at 341." –Taken from 941 F.2d 745, 753 (9th Cir. 1991).

See also

"<u>See also</u>" is used when the "cited authority constitutes additional source material that supports the proposition. '<u>See also</u>' is commonly used to cite an authority supporting a proposition when authorities that state or directly support the proposition already have been cited or discussed." Bluebook rule 1.2(a).

In law review footnotes, the titles of books and the names of cases, except for procedural phrases, are not underlined. See Bluebook rule 2.1(a) & (b). Further, the following are in large and small capitals: codes, restatements, standards, constitutions, periodicals, authors of books, titles of books, the abbreviated names of codes, most legislative materials except for bills and resolutions, codified ordinances, model codes, court rules, and sentencing guidelines. Refer to <u>The Bluebook</u>.

Ex.:   "If the government granted Mr. Plummer use and derivative use immunity, it would be required to have derived all the information on which the subsequent prosecution was based from a source wholly independent of the statements made in the interview. See Katsinger, 406 U.S. at 453, 92 S. Ct. at 1661; see also 18 U.S.C. § 6002." –Taken from 941 F.2d 799, 803 (9th Cir. 1991).

See generally

"See generally" is used when the "[c]ited authority presents helpful background material related to the proposition." Bluebook rule 1.2(d).

Ex.:   "When, however, a rule 59(e) motion seeks reconsideration of a grant of summary judgment, we conduct a de novo review. See id. at 122-23 n.5. See generally Dole v. Elliott Travel & Tours, Inc., 942 F.2d 962, 965 (6th Cir. 1991) (explaining procedure for district court's determination of summary judgment motion)." –Taken from 951 F.2d 110, 112 (6th Cir. 1991).

Selections from Williston's Treatise on the Law of Contracts, by Samuel Williston and George J. Thompson

–Do not abbreviate the title.

Ex.:   Samuel Williston & George J. Thompson, Selections from Williston's Treatise on the Law of Contracts § 102A (rev. ed. 1938). –Section Citation.

Samuel Williston & George J. Thompson, Selections from Williston's Treatise on the Law of Contracts § 102A, at 131 (rev. ed. 1938). –Page Citation.

Samuel Williston & George J. Thompson, Selections from Williston's Treatise on the Law of Contracts § 102A, at 131 n.15 (rev. ed. 1938). –Footnote Citation.

Senate Bill (U.S. Congress)

See Congressional Bills.

Senate Concurrent Resolution

See Congressional Resolutions.

Senate Conference Report

Ex.:   S. Conf. Rep. No. 99-302, at 97 (1986).

Senate Executive Document

Ab.:   S. Exec. Doc. No.

Senate Joint Resolution

See Congressional Resolutions.

Senate Resolution

See Congressional Resolutions.

In citing cases in law review footnotes, abbreviate any word listed in table T.6; the names of "states, countries, and other geographical units" unless they are named parties; and any other words of eight or more letters "if substantial space is thereby saved and the result is unambiguous." Bluebook rule 10.2.2. On the other hand, in citing cases in text, abbreviate only widely known acronyms and the following words: "&," "Ass'n," "Bros.," "Co.," "Corp.," "Inc.," "Ltd.," and "No." Bluebook rule 10.2.1(c).

Senate Treaty Documents
    Ab.:   S. Treaty Doc. No.
    Ex.:

Senator
    Ab.:   Sen.

series, serial(s)
    Ab.:   ser.

Services
    See Looseleaf services.

Session Cases (Scotland)
    Court of Session:

Ab.:	Session Cases, 1850-date (House of Lords)	S.C. (H.L).
	Sections:	
	Fifth Series, 1898 -1906 (edited by Fraser)	F.
	Fourth Series, 1873-1898 (edited by Rettie)	R.
	Third Series, 1862-1873 (edited by MacPherson)	M.
	Second Series, 1838-1862 (edited by Dunlop)	D.
	First Series, 1821-1838 (edited by Shaw)	S.

    Ex.:   Sowman v. Glasgow Dist. Council, 1984 S.C. (H.L.) 91 (Scot.).
          –Case Citation.
          Killin v. Weir, [1904-05] 7 F. 526 (Sess. 1905) (Scot.).
          –Case Citation.
          Macpherson v. Brown, [1897-98] 25 R. 945 (Sess. 1898) (Scot.).
          –Case Citation.
          Cook v. North British Ry. Co., [1871-72] 10 M. 513 (Sess. 1872)
          (Scot.). –Case Citation.
          Forrest v. Magistrates of Leith, [1860-61] 23 D. 592 (Sess. 1861)
          (Scot.). –Case Citation.
          Cameron v. Chapman, [1837-38] 16 S. 907 (Sess. 1838) (Scot.).
          –Case Citation.
          Note: For information concerning neutral citation for judgments after
          2001, see table T.2, p. 330.

    High Court of Justiciary:

Ab.:	Justiciary Cases, 1917-date:	J.C.
	Session Cases, High Court of Justiciary	Sess. Cas. (J.)
	Fifth Series, 1898-1906 (edited by Fraser)	F. (J.)
	Fourth Series, 1873-1898 (edited by Rettie)	R. (J.)

In law review footnotes, the titles of books and the names of cases, except for procedural phrases, are not underlined. See Bluebook rule 2.1(a) & (b). Further, the following are in large and small capitals: codes, restatements, standards, constitutions, periodicals, authors of books, titles of books, the abbreviated names of codes, most legislative materials except for bills and resolutions, codified ordinances, model codes, court rules, and sentencing guidelines. Refer to The Bluebook.

Ex.:   Smith v. Macdonald, 1984 J.C. 73 (H.C.J.) (Scot.).
           –Case Citation.

           Pollok v. McCabe, [1909-10] 3B Sess. Cas. (J.) 23 (H.C.J. 1909) (Scot.). –Case Citation.

           Peters v. Olson, [1904-1905] 7 F. (J.) 86 (H.C.J. 1905) (Scot.). –Case Citation.

           Wildridge v. Anderson, [1897-98] 25 R. (J.) 27 (H.C.J. 1897) (Scot.). –Case Citation.

           See Bluebook table T.2, p. 329.

           Note: For information concerning neutral citation for judgments after 2001, see table T.2, p. 330.

Session Laws of Alaska

Ab.:   year Alaska Sess. Laws page no.

Ex.:   Act effective Sept. 4, 1995, ch. 75, 1995 Alaska Sess. Laws 1 (relating to workers' compensation insurance rate filing). –Citation to an entire session law.

           Act effective Sept. 4, 1995, ch. 75, sec. 3, § 23.30.017, 1995 Alaska Sess. Laws 1, 3. –Citation to a section of a session law amending prior act.

See Bluebook rule 12.4.

Session Laws, Arizona

Ab.:   year Ariz. Sess. Laws page no.

Ex.:   Act of Apr. 19, 1995, ch. 186, 1995 Ariz. Sess. Laws 1328 (relating to alcoholic beverages - driver's license suspensions). –Citation to an entire session law.

           Act of Apr. 19, 1995, ch. 186, sec. 27, § 4-222, 1995 Ariz. Sess. Laws 1328, 1331. –Citation to a section of a session law amending prior act.

See Bluebook rule 12.4.

Session Laws of Colorado (LexisNexis)

Ab.:   year Colo. Sess. Laws page no.

Ex.:   Act of Apr. 8, 1996, ch. 54, 1996 Colo. Sess. Laws 174. –Citation to an entire session law.

           Act of Apr. 8, 1996, ch. 54, sec. 1, § 10-3-541, 1996 Colo. Sess. Laws 174, 174-77. –Citation to a section of a session law amending prior act.

See Bluebook rule 12.4.

Session Laws of Hawaii

Ab.:   year Haw. Sess. Laws page no.

Ex.:   Act of Apr. 25, 1995, No. 59, 1995 Haw. Sess. Laws 90. –Citation to an entire session law.

           Act of Apr. 25, 1995, No. 59, sec. 1, § 309-1.5, 1995 Haw. Sess. Laws 90, 90-91. –Citation to a section of a session law amending a prior act.

In citing cases in law review footnotes, abbreviate any word listed in table T.6; the names of "states, countries, and other geographical units" unless they are named parties; and any other words of eight or more letters "if substantial space is thereby saved and the result is unambiguous." Bluebook rule 10.2.2. On the other hand, in citing cases in text, abbreviate only widely known acronyms and the following words: "&," "Ass'n," "Bros.," "Co.," "Corp.," "Inc.," "Ltd.," and "No." Bluebook rule 10.2.1(c).

See Bluebook rule 12.4.

Session Laws of Kansas
Ab.:   year Kan. Sess. Laws page no.
Ex.:   Act of Mar. 22, 1996, ch. 60, 1996 Kan. Sess. Laws 174. –Citation to a
        section of a session law.

        Act of Mar. 22, 1996, ch. 60, sec. 2, § 76-12b11, 1996 Kan. Sess. Laws
        174, 175-76. –Citation to a section of a session law amending a prior
        act.

See Bluebook rule 12.4.

Session Laws of North Carolina
Ab.:   year N.C. Sess. Laws page no.
Ex.:   Act of July 20, 2003, No. 337, 2003 N.C. Sess. Laws 953 (clarifying
        legal deadlines falling on holidays). –Citation to an entire session law.

        Act of July 20, 2003, No. 337, sec. 9, § 7B-506(e), 2003 N.C. Sess.
        Laws 953, 955 (clarifying legal deadlines falling on holidays). –
        Citation to a section of a session law amending a prior act.

See Bluebook rule 12.4.

Session Laws of South Dakota
Ab.:   year S.D. Sess. Laws page no.
Ex.:   Act of Feb. 14, 1996, ch. 40, 1996 S.D. Laws 85. –Citation to an entire
        session law.

        Act of Feb. 14, 1996, ch. 40, sec. 1, § 5-14-23, 1996 S.D. Laws 85, 85.
        –Citation to a section of a session law amending a prior act.

See Bluebook rule 12.4.

Session Laws of the Virgin Islands
Ab.:   year V.I. Sess. Laws page no.
Ex.:   Act of May 2, 1994, No. 5972, 1994 V.I. Sess. Laws 53 (creating the
        crime of stalking). –Citation to an entire session law.

        Act of May 2, 1994, No. 5972, § 1, 1994 V.I. Sess. Laws 53, 53-54
        (creating the crime of stalking). –Citation to a section of a session law.

See Bluebook rule 12.4.

Session Laws of Washington
Ab.:   year Wash. Sess. Laws page no.
Ex.:   Act of Mar. 11, 2004, ch. 202, 2004 Wash. Sess. Laws 825 (relating to
        Wash. Rev. Code 57.08.005). –Citation to an entire session law
        amending prior act.

        Act of Mar. 11, 2004, ch. 202, 2004 Wash. Sess. Laws 825, 830
        (relating to Wash. Rev. Code 57.08.005). –Citation to a section of a
        session law amending a prior act.

See Bluebook rule 12.4

In law review footnotes, the titles of books and the names of cases, except for procedural
phrases, are not underlined. See Bluebook rule 2.1(a) & (b). Further, the following are in
large and small capitals: codes, restatements, standards, constitutions, periodicals, authors of
books, titles of books, the abbreviated names of codes, most legislative materials except for
bills and resolutions, codified ordinances, model codes, court rules, and sentencing guidelines.
Refer to The Bluebook.

Session Laws of Wyoming
 Ab.: year Wyo. Sess. Laws page no.
 Ex.: Act of July 1, 1998, ch. 3, 1998 Wyo. Laws 4. —Citation to an entire session law.
    Act of July 1, 1998, ch. 3, sec. 104, § 21-13-102, 1998 Wyo. Laws 4, 8 (an act relating to public schools). —Citation to a section of a session law amending a prior act.
 See Bluebook rule 12.4.

Seton Hall Law Review
 Ab.: Seton Hall L. Rev.
 Ex.: Channing E. Brackey, Choices of Capital: Reducing Their Impact on Taxpayers and the Government, 22 Seton Hall L. Rev. 320 (1992). —Article Citation.
    Channing E. Brackey, Choices of Capital: Reducing Their Impact on Taxpayers and the Government, 22 Seton Hall L. Rev. 320, 335 (1992). —Page Citation.

Seton Hall Legislative Journal
 Ab.: Seton Hall Legis. J.
 Ex.: Robert J. Araujo, Suggestions for a Foundation Course in Legislation, 15 Seton Hall Legis. J. 17 (1991). —Article Citation.
    Robert J. Araujo, Suggestions for a Foundation Course in Legislation, 15 Seton Hall Legis. J. 17, 19-20 (1991). —Page Citation.

Shipping Regulation
 Ab.: Shipping Reg. (P & F)

short forms
 See subsequent citation to legal authority.

shorter works in collection
 Ex.: Henry M. Hart, Jr. & Albert M. Sacks, The Legal Process: Basic Problems, in The Marking and Application of Law 1345-63 (William N. Eskridge, Jr. & Philip P. Frickey eds., 1994).

sic
    —Use "[sic]" to indicate significant mistakes in the original text. See Bluebook rule 5.2(c).
 Ex.: "George Bush and Dan Quayle was [sic] the favorites to win the 1992 election."
 See Bluebook rule 15.5.

signals
 See Bluebook rules 1.2, 1.3, & 1.4.
 See, herein, entries for Accord, But cf., But see, Cf., Compare, Contra, E.g., See, See also, and See generally.

In citing cases in law review footnotes, abbreviate any word listed in table T.6; the names of "states, countries, and other geographical units" unless they are named parties; and any other words of eight or more letters "if substantial space is thereby saved and the result is unambiguous." Bluebook rule 10.2.2. On the other hand, in citing cases in text, abbreviate only widely known acronyms and the following words: "&," "Ass'n," "Bros.," "Co.," "Corp.," "Inc.," "Ltd.," and "No." Bluebook rule 10.2.1(c).

The absence of a signal, according to <u>Bluebook</u> rule 1.2(a), means that the "[c]ited authority (i) directly states the proposition, (ii) identifies the source of a quotation, or (iii) identifies an authority referred to in the text."

signals, order of

See <u>Bluebook</u> rule 1.3.

Singapore Law Review

Ab.: Sing. L. Rev.

Ex.: Chung Wei Han, <u>Japanese and Western Attitudes Towards Law</u>, 12 Sing. L. Rev. 69 (1991). —Article Citation.

Chung Wei Han, <u>Japanese and Western Attitudes Towards Law</u>, 12 Sing. L. Rev. 69, 72 (1991). —Page Citation.

slip opinions

Ab.: slip op.

Ex.: <u>United States v. Cutler</u>, No. 86-3058, slip op. at 3 (9th Cir. Dec. 19, 1986). —Separately paginated.

<u>Freeman v. Rideout</u>, No. 86-2153, slip op. 6801, 6812 (2d Cir. Dec. 20, 1986). —Not separately paginated.

Social Justice

Ab.: Soc. Just.

Ex.: Rosa del Olmo, <u>The Hidden Face of Drugs</u>, Soc. Just., Winter 1991, at 10. —Article Citation.

Rosa del Olmo, <u>The Hidden Face of Drugs</u>, Soc. Just., Winter 1991, at 10, 15-20. —Page Citation.

Social Responsibility: Business, Journalism, Law Medicine

Ab.: Soc. Resp.

Ex.: Robert P. Clark, <u>The Founding Fathers and the Bottom Line</u>, 17 Soc. Resp. 28 (1991). —Article Citation.

Robert P. Clark, <u>The Founding Fathers and the Bottom Line</u>, 17 Soc. Resp. 28, 29-32 (1991). —Page Citation.

Social Sciences

Ab.: Soc. Sci.

Ex.: E. Batalov, <u>Unity in Multiformity</u>, Soc. Sci. 1991 No. 4, at 91. —Article Citation.

E. Batalov, <u>Unity in Multiformity</u>, Soc. Sci. 1991 No. 4, at 91, 99-100. —Page Citation.

Social Security Bulletin

Ab.: Soc. Security Bull.

In law review footnotes, the titles of books and the names of cases, except for procedural phrases, are not underlined. <u>See</u> <u>Bluebook</u> rule 2.1(a) & (b). Further, the following are in large and small capitals: codes, restatements, standards, constitutions, periodicals, authors of books, titles of books, the abbreviated names of codes, most legislative materials except for bills and resolutions, codified ordinances, model codes, court rules, and sentencing guidelines. Refer to <u>The Bluebook</u>.

Ex.: Daniel B. Radner, <u>Changes in the Incomes of Age Groups</u>, Soc. Security Bull., Dec. 1991, at 2. –Article Citation.

Daniel B. Radner, <u>Changes in the Incomes of Age Groups</u>, Soc. Security Bull., Dec. 1991, at 2, 16-18. –Page Citation.

Social Security Claims and Procedures, by Harvey L. McCormick
–Do not abbreviate the title.

Ex.: 1 Harvey L. McCormick, <u>Social Security Claims and Procedures</u> § 4:53 (5th ed. 1998). –Section Citation.

Social Security Rulings, Cumulative Edition (1960-date)
Ab.: year S.S.R. (Cum. Ed.)

Ex.: <u>Rahman v. Harris</u>, 49 S.S.R. (Cum. Ed. 1988)

Software Law Journal
Ab.: Software L.J.

Ex.: Ann C. Keays, <u>Software Trade Secret Protection</u>, 4 Software L.J. 577 (1991). –Article Citation.

Ann C. Keays, <u>Software Trade Secret Protection</u>, 4 Software L.J. 577, 589-90 (1991). –Page Citation.

South Australia State Reports (1922-date)
Ab.: S.A. St. R.

Ex.: <u>Tanner v. South Australia</u>, (1988) 53 S.A. St. R. 307 (Austl.). See <u>Bluebook</u> table T.2.

South Carolina, administrative compilation
See Code of Laws of South Carolina 1976 Annotated (West), Code of Regulations.

South Carolina Code Annotated
See Code of Laws of South Carolina 1976 Annotated.

South Carolina Constitution
Ab.: S.C. Const. art. , § .

Ex.: S.C. Const. art. III, § 33. –"Cite constitutional provisions currently in force without a date." <u>Bluebook</u> rule 11.

S.C. Const. art. III, § 24 (amended 1989). –"When citing a provision that has been subsequently amended, either indicate parenthetically the fact and date of amendment or cite the amending provision in full." <u>Bluebook</u> rule 11.

S.C. Const. of 1868, art. I, § 4 (1895). –"Cite constitutions that have been totally superseded by year of adoption; if the specific provision cited was adopted in a different year, give that year parenthetically." <u>Bluebook</u> rule 11.

South Carolina Court of Appeals
Ab.: S.C. Ct. App.

In citing cases in law review footnotes, abbreviate any word listed in table T.6; the names of "states, countries, and other geographical units" unless they are named parties; and any other words of eight or more letters "if <u>substantial</u> space is thereby saved and the result is unambiguous." <u>Bluebook</u> rule 10.2.2. On the other hand, in citing cases in text, abbreviate only widely known acronyms and the following words: "&," "Ass'n," "Bros.," "Co.," "Corp.," "Inc.," "Ltd.," and "No." <u>Bluebook</u> rule 10.2.1(c).

–Cite to S.E. or S.E.2d, if therein; otherwise, cite to S.C.

–Give parallel citations only in documents submitted to South Carolina state courts. See Bluebook rules 10.3.1 and B5.1.3; see also S.C. App. Ct. R. 239(d), which requires a parallel citation.

In documents submitted to South Carolina state courts, cite as follows:

Patterson v. Reid, 318 S.C. 183, 456 S.E.2d 436 (Ct. App. 1995). –Case Citation.

Patterson v. Reid, 318 S.C. 183, 184, 456 S.E.2d 436, 437 (Ct. App. 1995). –Page Citation.

In all other documents, cite as follows:

Patterson v. Reid, 456 S.E.2d 436 (S.C. Ct. App. 1995). –Case Citation.

Patterson v. Reid, 456 S.E.2d 436, 437 (S.C. Ct. App. 1995). –Page Citation.

South Carolina Law Review
Ab.:   S.C. L. Rev.

Ex.:   Ellen S. Podgor, Mail Fraud: Opening Letters, 43 S.C. L. Rev. 223 (1992). –Article Citation.

Ellen S. Podgor, Mail Fraud: Opening Letters, 43 S.C. L. Rev. 223, 249-54 (1992). –Page Citation.

South Carolina Lawyer
Ab.:   S.C. Law.

Ex.:   W. Keith Shannon, Tips for Lawyers on Dealing with the News Media, S.C. Law., Jan.-Feb. 1992, at 15. –Article Citation.

W. Keith Shannon, Tips for Lawyers on Dealing with the News Media, S.C. Law., Jan.-Feb. 1992, at 15, 16. –Page Citation.

South Carolina Session Laws
See Acts and Joint Resolutions of South Carolina.

South Carolina State Register
Ab.:   vol. no. S.C. Reg. page no. (month day, year)

Ex.:   29 S.C. Reg. 95 (Apr. 1, 2005)

South Carolina Supreme Court
Ab.:   S.C.

–Cite to S.E. or S.E.2d, if therein; otherwise, cite to S.C.

–Give parallel citations only in documents submitted to South Carolina state courts. See Bluebook rules 10.3.1 and B5.1.3; see also S.C. App. Ct. R. 239(d), which requires a parallel citation.

In documents submitted to South Carolina state courts, cite as follows:

Thomas v. Grayson, 318 S.C. 82, 456 S.E.2d 377 (1995). –Case Citation.

In law review footnotes, the titles of books and the names of cases, except for procedural phrases, are not underlined. See Bluebook rule 2.1(a) & (b). Further, the following are in large and small capitals: codes, restatements, standards, constitutions, periodicals, authors of books, titles of books, the abbreviated names of codes, most legislative materials except for bills and resolutions, codified ordinances, model codes, court rules, and sentencing guidelines. Refer to The Bluebook.

Thomas v. Grayson, 318 S.C. 82, 84, 456 S.E.2d 377, 378 (1995).
–Page Citation.

In all other documents, cite as follows:

Thomas v. Grayson, 456 S.E.2d 377 (S.C. 1995). –Case Citation.

Thomas v. Grayson, 456 S.E.2d 377, 378 (S.C. 1995). –Page
Citation.

South Dakota Administrative Rules
See Administrative Rules of South Dakota.

South Dakota Codified Laws (West)
Ab.:   S.D. Codified Laws, § x-x-x (year)

Ex.:   S.D. Codified Laws § 36-15-29 (2004).

S.D. Codified Laws § 16-16-73 (Supp. 2005).

–For proper citation form in papers submitted to South Dakota courts,
see title pages to S.D. Codified Laws volumes.

South Dakota Constitution
Ab.:   S.D. Const. art. , §   .

Ex.:   S.D. Const. art. XXI, § 8. –"Cite constitutional provisions currently in
force without a date." Bluebook rule 11.

S.D. Const. art. XXIV (repealed 1934). "If the cited provision has been
repealed, either indicate parenthetically the fact and date of repeal or
cite the repealing provision in full." Bluebook rule 11.

S.D. Const. art. XIV, § 1 (amended 1988). –"When citing a provision
that has been subsequently amended, either indicate parenthetically the
fact and date of amendment or cite the amending provision in full."
Bluebook rule 11.

South Dakota Law Review
Ab.:   S.D. L. Rev.

Ex.:   Randall P. Bezanson, The Future First Amendment, 37 S.D. L. Rev. 11
(1992). –Article Citation.

Randall P. Bezanson, The Future First Amendment, 37 S.D. L. Rev. 11,
12-13 (1992). –Page Citation.

South Dakota Register
Ab.:   vol. no. S.D. Reg. page no. (month day, year)

Ex.:   30 S.D. Reg. 109 (Dec. 29, 2003).

South Dakota Session Laws
See Session Laws of South Dakota.

South Dakota Supreme Court
Ab.:   S.D.

In citing cases in law review footnotes, abbreviate any word listed in table T.6;
the names of "states, countries, and other geographical units" unless they are named parties;
and any other words of eight or more letters "if substantial space is thereby saved and the
result is unambiguous." Bluebook rule 10.2.2. On the other hand, in citing cases in text,
abbreviate only widely known acronyms and the following words: "&," "Ass'n," "Bros.,"
"Co.," "Corp.," "Inc.," "Ltd.," and "No." Bluebook rule 10.2.1(c).

–Cite to N.W. or N.W.2d, if therein; otherwise cite to S.D. In addition, give public domain citation if available.

–Through 90 S.D. 692 (1976), cite as follows:

In documents submitted to South Dakota state courts:

Dunham v. First Nat'l Bank, 86 S.D. 727 (1972). –Case Citation.

Dunham v. First Nat'l Bank, 86 S.D. 727, 733 (1972). –Page Citation.

Or:

Dunham v. First Nat'l Bank, 201 N.W.2d 227 (1972). –Case Citation.

Dunham v. First Nat'l Bank, 201 N.W.2d 227, 230 (1972). –Page Citation.

In all other documents:

Dunham v. First Nat'l Bank, 201 N.W.2d 227 (S.D. 1972). –Case Citation.

Dunham v. First Nat'l Bank, 201 N.W.2d 227, 230 (S.D. 1972). –Page Citation.

–After 90 S.D. 692 (1976) and until January 1, 1996, when a public domain format was adopted, cite as follows:

In all documents:

Swenson v. Swenson, 529 N.W.2d 901 (S.D. 1995). –Case Citation.

Swenson v. Swenson, 529 N.W.2d 901, 903 (S.D. 1995). –Page Citation.

–After January 1, 1996, cite as follows:

In all documents:

Price v. Price, 2000 SD 64, 611 N.W.2d 425. –Case Citation.

Price v. Price, 2000 SD 64, ¶ 12, 611 N.W.2d 425, 429. –Pinpoint Citation.

See Bluebook rules 10.3.1, 10.3.3, and B5.1.3; see also S.D. R. App. P. § 15-26A-69.1.

South Eastern Reporter

–Do not give a parallel citation unless required by local rule. See Bluebook rules 10.3.1 and B5.1.3. See also the various state court and state reporter entries herein for local rule parallel citation requirements.

Ab.: S.E.

Ex.:

Georgia:

Pollard v. Kent, 200 S.E. 542 (Ga. Ct. App. 1938). –Case Citation.

In law review footnotes, the titles of books and the names of cases, except for procedural phrases, are not underlined. See Bluebook rule 2.1(a) & (b). Further, the following are in large and small capitals: codes, restatements, standards, constitutions, periodicals, authors of books, titles of books, the abbreviated names of codes, most legislative materials except for bills and resolutions, codified ordinances, model codes, court rules, and sentencing guidelines. Refer to The Bluebook.

Pollard v. Kent, 200 S.E. 542, 545 (Ga. Ct. App. 1938). –Page Citation.

North Carolina:

Wilson v. City of Charlotte, 175 S.E. 306 (N.C. 1934). –Case Citation.

Wilson v. City of Charlotte, 175 S.E. 306, 307 (N.C. 1934). –Page Citation.

South Carolina:

Craig v. Clearwater Mfg., 200 S.E. 765 (S.C. 1938). –Case Citation.

Craig v. Clearwater Mfg., 200 S.E. 765, 769 (S.C. 1938). –Page Citation.

Virginia:

Simpson v. Simpson, 175 S.E. 320 (Va. 1934). –Case Citation.

Simpson v. Simpson, 175 S.E. 320, 325 (Va. 1934). –Page Citation.

West Virginia:

Buckland v. State Comp. Comm'r, 175 S.E. 785 (W. Va. 1934). –Case Citation.

Buckland v. State Comp. Comm'r, 175 S.E. 785, 786 (W. Va. 1934). –Page Citation.

South Eastern Reporter, Second Series

–Do not give a parallel citation unless required by local rule. See Bluebook rules 10.3.1, and B5.1.3. See also the various state court and state reporter entries herein for local rule parallel citation requirements.

–With volume 361 (1988), South Eastern Reporter, Second Series, became West's South Eastern Reporter, Second Series. Citation form is not affected by this title change.

Ab.: S.E.2d

Ex.:

Georgia:

King v. State, 509 S.E.2d 32 (Ga. 1998). –Case Citation.

King v. State, 509 S.E.2d 32, 36 (Ga. 1998). –Page Citation.

North Carolina:

Stafford v. Stafford, 520 S.E.2d 785 (N.C. 1999). –Case Citation.

Stafford v. Stafford, 520 S.E.2d 785, 786 (N.C. 1999). –Page Citation.

South Carolina:

State v. Kennerly, 524 S.E.2d 837 (S.C. 1999). –Case Citation.

State v. Kennerly, 524 S.E.2d 837, 839 (S.C. 1999). –Page Citation.

Virginia:

Rivera v. Nedrich, 529 S.E.2d 310 (Va. 1999). –Case Citation.

Rivera v. Nedrich, 529 S.E.2d 310, 313 (Va. 1999). –Page Citation.

In citing cases in law review footnotes, abbreviate any word listed in table T.6; the names of "states, countries, and other geographical units" unless they are named parties; and any other words of eight or more letters "if substantial space is thereby saved and the result is unambiguous." Bluebook rule 10.2.2. On the other hand, in citing cases in text, abbreviate only widely known acronyms and the following words: "&," "Ass'n," "Bros.," "Co.," "Corp.," "Inc.," "Ltd.," and "No." Bluebook rule 10.2.1(c).

West Virginia:

> State v. Calloway, 528 S.E.2d 490 (W. Va. 1999). –Case Citation.
>
> State v. Calloway, 528 S.E.2d 490, 499 (W. Va. 1999). –Page Citation.

South Texas Law Review

Ab.:   S. Tex. L. Rev.

Ex.:   Kenneth G. Engerrand, Seaman Status Reconstructed, 32 S. Tex. L. Rev. 169 (1991). –Article Citation.

> Kenneth G. Engerrand, Seaman Status Reconstructed, 32 S. Tex. L. Rev. 169, 170-72 (1991). –Page Citation.

South Western Reporter

> –Do not give a parallel citation unless required by local rule. See Bluebook rules 10.3.1 and B5.1.3. See also the various state court and state reporter entries herein for local rule parallel citation requirements.

Ab.: S.W.

Ex.:

Arkansas:

> Hart v. State, 257 S.W. 354 (Ark. 1924). –Case Citation.
>
> Hart v. State, 257 S.W. 354, 356 (Ark. 1924). –Page Citation.

Kentucky:

> Varney v. Orinoco Mining Co., 257 S.W. 1016 (Ky. 1924). –Case Citation.
>
> Varney v. Orinoco Mining Co., 257 S.W. 1016, 1018 (Ky. 1924). –Page Citation.

Missouri:

> State v. Mullinix, 257 S.W. 121 (Mo. 1923). –Case Citation.
>
> State v. Mullinix, 257 S.W. 121, 123 (Mo. 1923). –Page Citation.

Tennessee:

> Edwards v. Davis, 244 S.W. 359 (Tenn. 1922). –Case Citation.
>
> Edwards v. Davis, 244 S.W. 359, 361 (Tenn. 1922). –Page Citation.

Texas:

> Empire Gas & Fuel Co. v. Pendar, 244 S.W. 184 (Tex. Civ. App. 1922). –Case Citation.
>
> Empire Gas & Fuel Co. v. Pendar, 244 S.W. 184, 187 (Tex. Civ. App. 1922). –Page Citation.

In law review footnotes, the titles of books and the names of cases, except for procedural phrases, are not underlined. See Bluebook rule 2.1(a) & (b). Further, the following are in large and small capitals: codes, restatements, standards, constitutions, periodicals, authors of books, titles of books, the abbreviated names of codes, most legislative materials except for bills and resolutions, codified ordinances, model codes, court rules, and sentencing guidelines. Refer to The Bluebook.

South Western Reporter, Second Series

–Do not give a parallel citation unless required by local rule. See Bluebook rules 10.3.1, and B5.1.3. See also the various state court and state reporter entries herein for local rule parallel citation requirements.

–With volume 738 (1988), South Western Reporter, Second Series, became West's South Western Reporter, Second Series. Citation form is not affected by this title change.

Ab.: S.W.2d

Ex.:

Arkansas:

Huffman v. Alderson, 983 S.W.2d 899 (Ark. 1998). –Case Citation.

Huffman v. Alderson, 983 S.W.2d 899, 900 (Ark. 1998). –Page Citation.

Kentucky:

Cavender v. Miller, 984 S.W.2d 848 (Ky. 1998). –Case Citation.

Cavender v. Miller, 984 S.W.2d 848, 849 (Ky. 1998). –Page Citation.

Missouri:

Spradlin v. City of Fulton, 982 S.W.2d 255 (Mo. 1998). –Case Citation.

Spradlin v. City of Fulton, 982 S.W.2d 255, 265 (Mo. 1998). –Page Citation.

Tennessee:

State v. Blackmon, 984 S.W.2d 589 (Tenn. 1998). –Case Citation.

State v. Blackmon, 984 S.W.2d 589, 593 (Tenn. 1998). –Page Citation.

Texas:

Boyette v. State, 982 S.W.2d 428 (Tex. Crim. App. 1998). –Case Citation.

Boyette v. State, 982 S.W.2d 428, 429 (Tex. Crim. App. 1998). –Page Citation.

South Western Reporter, Third Series

–Do not give a parallel citation unless required by local rule. See Bluebook rules 10.3.1, and B5.1.3. See also the various state court and state reporter entries herein for local rule parallel citation requirements.

Ab.: S.W.3d

Ex.:

Arkansas:

Thetford v. State, 5 S.W.3d 478 (Ark. 1999). –Case Citation.

Thetford v. State, 5 S.W.3d 478, 479 (Ark. 1999). –Page Citation.

In citing cases in law review footnotes, abbreviate any word listed in table T.6; the names of "states, countries, and other geographical units" unless they are named parties; and any other words of eight or more letters "if substantial space is thereby saved and the result is unambiguous." Bluebook rule 10.2.2. On the other hand, in citing cases in text, abbreviate only widely known acronyms and the following words: "&," "Ass'n," "Bros.," "Co.," "Corp.," "Inc.," "Ltd.," and "No." Bluebook rule 10.2.1(c).

Kentucky:
> Comm'r v. Davis, 14 S.W.3d 9 (Ky. 1999). –Case Citation.
>
> Comm'r v. Davis, 14 S.W.3d 9, 14 (Ky. 1999). –Page Citation.

Missouri:
> State v. Armentrout, 8 S.W.3d 99 (Mo. 1999). –Case Citation.
>
> State v. Armentrout, 8 S.W.3d 99, 109 (Mo. 1999). –Page Citation.

Tennessee:
> Ashe v. Radiation Oncology Ass'n, 9 S.W.3d 119 (Tenn. 1999). –Case Citation.
>
> Ashe v. Radiation Oncology Ass'n, 9 S.W.3d 119, 123 (Tenn. 1999). –Page Citation.

Texas:
> Garza v. State, 7 S.W.3d 164 (Tex. Crim. App. 1999). –Case Citation.
>
> Garza v. State, 7 S.W.3d 164, 167 (Tex. Crim. App. 1999). –Page Citation.

Southern California Interdisciplinary Law Journal
Ab: S. Cal. Interdisc. L.J.

Ex: Tawia Ansah, Genocide and the Eroticization of Death: Law, Violence, and Moral Purity, 14 S. Cal. Interdisc. L.J. 181 (2005). –Article Citation.

Tawia Ansah, Genocide and the Eroticization of Death: Law, Violence, and Moral Purity, 14 S. Cal. Interdisc. L.J. 181, 197-99 (2005).–Page Citation.

Southern California Law Review
Ab.: S. Cal. L. Rev.

Ex.: Marion Crain, Feminism, Labor and Power, 65 S. Cal. L. Rev. 1819 (1992). –Article Citation.

Marion Crain, Feminism, Labor and Power, 65 S. Cal. L. Rev. 1819, 1883-85 (1992). –Page Citation.

Southern California Review of Law & Women's Studies
Ab.: S. Cal. Rev. L. & Women's Stud.

Southern Illinois University Law Journal
Ab.: S. Ill. U. L.J.

Ex.: Daniel R. Gordon, The Demise of American Constitutionalism: Death by Legal Education, 1991 S. Ill. U. L.J. 39. –Article Citation.

Daniel R. Gordon, The Demise of American Constitutionalism: Death by Legal Education, 1991 S. Ill. U. L.J. 39, 95. –Page Citation.

Southern Methodist University Law Review
Ab: SMU L. Rev.

In law review footnotes, the titles of books and the names of cases, except for procedural phrases, are not underlined. See Bluebook rule 2.1(a) & (b). Further, the following are in large and small capitals: codes, restatements, standards, constitutions, periodicals, authors of books, titles of books, the abbreviated names of codes, most legislative materials except for bills and resolutions, codified ordinances, model codes, court rules, and sentencing guidelines. Refer to The Bluebook.

Ex: Ralph C. Brashier, <u>Consanguinity, Sibling Relationships, and the</u>
           <u>Default Rules of Inheritance Law: Reshaping Half-blood Statutes to</u>
           <u>Reflect the Evolving Family</u>, 58 SMU L. Rev. 137 (2005). –Article
           Citation.
           Ralph C. Brashier, <u>Consanguinity, Sibling Relationships, and the</u>
           <u>Default Rules of Inheritance Law: Reshaping Half-blood Statutes to</u>
           <u>Reflect the Evolving Family</u>, 58 SMU L. Rev. 137, 175 (2005). –Page
           Citation.

Southern Reporter

–Do not give a parallel citation unless required by local rule. <u>See</u>
<u>Bluebook</u> rules 10.3.1 and B5.1.3. See also the various state court
and state reporter entries herein for local rule parallel citation
requirements.

Ab.: So.

Ex.:

Alabama:

<u>Slaughter v. Green</u>, 87 So. 358 (Ala. 1921). –Case Citation.

<u>Slaughter v. Green</u>, 87 So. 358, 361 (Ala. 1921). –Page Citation.

Florida:

<u>Kennerly v. Hennessy</u>, 66 So. 729 (Fla. 1914). –Case Citation.

<u>Kennerly v. Hennessy</u>, 66 So. 729, 730 (Fla. 1914). –Page Citation.

Louisiana:

<u>Reynaud v. C.J. Walton & Son, Inc.</u>, 66 So. 549 (La. 1914). –Case
Citation.

<u>Reynaud v. C.J. Walton & Son, Inc.</u>, 66 So. 549, 550 (La. 1914).
–Page Citation.

Mississippi:

<u>Dedeaux v. State</u>, 87 So. 664 (Miss. 1921). –Case Citation.

<u>Dedeaux v. State</u>, 87 So. 664, 666 (Miss. 1921). –Page Citation.

Southern Reporter, Second Series

–Do not give a parallel citation unless required by local rule or unless
the particular state has a public domain format. <u>See</u> <u>Bluebook</u> rules
10.3.1, 10.3.3, and B5.1.3. See also the various state court and state
reporter entries herein for public domain information and local rule
parallel citation requirements.

–With volume 513 (1988), Southern Reporter, Second Series, became
West's Southern Reporter, Second Series. Citation form is not
affected by this title change.

Ab.: So. 2d

In citing cases in law review footnotes, abbreviate any word listed in table T.6;
the names of "states, countries, and other geographical units" unless they are named parties;
and any other words of eight or more letters "if <u>substantial</u> space is thereby saved and the
result is unambiguous." <u>Bluebook</u> rule 10.2.2. On the other hand, in citing cases in text,
abbreviate only widely known acronyms and the following words: "&," "Ass'n," "Bros.,"
"Co.," "Corp.," "Inc.," "Ltd.," and "No." <u>Bluebook</u> rule 10.2.1(c).

Ex.:
Alabama:

>Ex parte Panell, 756 So. 2d 862 (Ala. 1999). –Case Citation.
>
>Ex parte Panell, 756 So. 2d 862, 872 (Ala. 1999). –Page Citation.

Florida:

>State v. Thompson, 750 So. 2d 643 (Fla. 1999). –Case Citation.
>
>State v. Thompson, 750 So. 2d 643, 647 (Fla. 1999). –Page Citation.

Louisiana:

>Tardiff v. Valley Forge Ins. Co., 751 So. 2d 867 (La. 1999). –Case Citation.
>
>Tardiff v. Valley Forge Ins. Co., 751 So. 2d 867, 869 (La. 1999). –Page Citation.

Mississippi:

>Theobald v. Nosser, 752 So. 2d 1036 (Miss. 1999). –Case Citation.
>
>Theobald v. Nosser, 752 So. 2d 1036, 1038 (Miss. 1999). –Page Citation.

Southern University Law Review
Ab.: S.U. L. Rev.

Ex.: Evelyn L. Wilson, Federal Habeas Corpus: An Avenue of Relief for State Prisoners, 18 S.U. L. Rev. 1 (1991). –Article Citation.

Evelyn L. Wilson, Federal Habeas Corpus: An Avenue of Relief for State Prisoners, 18 S.U. L. Rev. 1, 18 (1991). –Page Citation.

Southwestern Legal Foundation Institute on Oil and Gas Law and Taxation
See Institute on Oil and Gas Law and Taxation.

Southwestern University Law Review
Ab.: Sw. U. L. Rev.

Ex.: Timothy A. Tosta et al., Environmental Review After Goleta, 21 Sw. U. L. Rev. 1079 (1992). –Article Citation.

Timothy A. Tosta et al., Environmental Review After Goleta, 21 Sw. U. L. Rev. 1079, 1080-81 (1992). –Page Citation.

Soviet Law and Government
Ab.: Soviet L. & Gov't

Ex.: B.M. Lazarev, President of the USSR, Soviet L. & Gov't, Summer 1991, at 7. –Article Citation.

B.M. Lazarev, President of the USSR, Soviet L. & Gov't, Summer 1991, at 7, 19-20. –Page Citation.

special
Ab.: spec.

In law review footnotes, the titles of books and the names of cases, except for procedural phrases, are not underlined. See Bluebook rule 2.1(a) & (b). Further, the following are in large and small capitals: codes, restatements, standards, constitutions, periodicals, authors of books, titles of books, the abbreviated names of codes, most legislative materials except for bills and resolutions, codified ordinances, model codes, court rules, and sentencing guidelines. Refer to The Bluebook.

Standard Federal Tax Reports (Commerce Clearing House)
  –Bound as U.S. Tax Cases (Commerce Clearing House)
  Ab.:   Stand. Fed. Tax Rep. (CCH)
  –Bound as U.S. Tax Cas.(CCH)
  Ex.:   <u>Dotson v. United States</u>, [U.S. Tax Cases Advance Sheets] Stand. Fed. Tax Rep. (CCH) (96-2 U.S. Tax Cas.) ¶ 50,359 (5th Cir. June 27, 1996). –Citation to looseleaf material.
          <u>Black Hills Corp. v. Comm'r</u>, 96-1 U.S. Tax Cas. (CCH) ¶ 50,036 (8th Cir. Jan. 10, 1996). –Citation to bound material.
          –The above examples are proper if the case is not yet available in, or is not reported in, an official or West reporter, a public domain citation, or in a widely used computer database.

Standards for Traffic Justice
  Ab.:   Standards for Traffic Justice §   (year)
  Ex.:   Standards for Traffic Justice § 1.2 (1975).
          Standards for Traffic Justice § 3.1 cmt. at 5 (1975).

Standards, Generally Accepted
  Ex.:   <u>ABA Standards for Criminal Justice Prosecution Function and Defense Function</u>, Standard 3-2.4 cmt. at 30 (1993).
          <u>Accounting for the Costs of Computer Software to be Sold, Leased or Otherwise Marketed</u>, Statement of Financial Accounting Standards No. 86, § 16 (Financial Accounting Standards Bd. 1985).
  <u>See</u> <u>Bluebook</u> rule 12.8.5.

Standards Relating to Appellate Delay Reduction
  Ex.:   Standards Relating to Appellate Delay Reduction § 3.53 (1988).

Standards Relating to Court Organization and Administration (American Bar Association)
  Ab.:   Standards Relating to Court Org. & Admin. §   (year)
  Ex.:   Standards Relating to Court Org. § 2.1 (1980).

Standards Relating to the Function of the Trial Judge
  Ab.:   Standards Relating to the Function of the Trial Judge § (status if necessary year)
  Ex.:   Standards Relating to the Function of the Trial Judge § 2.4 (Tentative Draft 1972).

Stanford Environmental Law Journal
  Ab.:   Stan. Envtl. L.J.

In citing cases in law review footnotes, abbreviate any word listed in table T.6; the names of "states, countries, and other geographical units" unless they are named parties; and any other words of eight or more letters "if <u>substantial</u> space is thereby saved and the result is unambiguous." <u>Bluebook</u> rule 10.2.2. On the other hand, in citing cases in text, abbreviate only widely known acronyms and the following words: "&," "Ass'n," "Bros.," "Co.," "Corp.," "Inc.," "Ltd.," and "No." <u>Bluebook</u> rule 10.2.1(c).

Ex.: Renee Stone, <u>Wetlands Protection and Development: The Advantages of Retaining Federal Control</u>, 10 Stan. Envtl. L.J. 137 (1991). –Article Citation.

Renee Stone, <u>Wetlands Protection and Development: The Advantages of Retaining Federal Control</u>, 10 Stan. Envtl. L.J. 137, 149-52 (1991). –Page Citation.

Stanford Journal of International Law
Ab.: Stan. J. Int'l L.

Ex.: Robert E. Lutz, <u>The World Court in a Changing World: An Agenda for Expanding the Court's Role from a U.S. Perspective</u>, 27 Stan. J. Int'l L. 247 (1990). –Article Citation.

Robert E. Lutz, <u>The World Court in a Changing World: An Agenda for Expanding the Court's Role from a U.S. Perspective</u>, 27 Stan. J. Int'l L. 247, 249-51 (1990). –Page Citation.

Stanford Journal of International Studies
Ab.: Stan. J. Int'l Stud.

Ex.: John H. Barton, <u>Tacit Political Restraints as a Way to Control Conventional Arms</u>, 14 Stan. J. Int'l Stud. 29 (1979). –Article Citation.

John H. Barton, <u>Tacit Political Restraints as a Way to Control Conventional Arms</u>, 14 Stan. J. Int'l Stud. 29, 40-45 (1979). –Page Citation.

Stanford Journal of Law, Business & Finance
Ab: Stan. J.L. Bus. & Fin.

Ex: Daniel W. Park, <u>Trade Secrets, the First Amendment, and Patent Law: A Collision on the Information Superhighway</u>, Stan. J.L. Bus. & Fin., Autumn 2004, at 46. –Article Citation.

Stanford Law & Policy Review
Ab.: Stan. L. & Pol'y Rev.

Ex.: Doug Bandow, <u>War on Drugs or War on America?</u>, 3 Stan. L. & Pol'y Rev. 242 (1991). –Article Citation.

Doug Bandow, <u>War on Drugs or War on America?</u>, 3 Stan. L. & Pol'y Rev. 242, 244 (1991). –Page Citation.

Stanford Law Review
Ab.: Stan. L. Rev.

Ex.: James M. O'Fallon, <u>Marbury</u>, 44 Stan. L. Rev. 219 (1992). –Article Citation.

James M. O'Fallon, <u>Marbury</u>, 44 Stan. L. Rev. 219, 249-55 (1992). –Page Citation.

State and Local Tax Service (RIA)
Ab.: St. & Loc. Tax Serv. (RIA)

In law review footnotes, the titles of books and the names of cases, except for procedural phrases, are not underlined. <u>See</u> <u>Bluebook</u> rule 2.1(a) & (b). Further, the following are in large and small capitals: codes, restatements, standards, constitutions, periodicals, authors of books, titles of books, the abbreviated names of codes, most legislative materials except for bills and resolutions, codified ordinances, model codes, court rules, and sentencing guidelines. Refer to <u>The Bluebook</u>.

State Constitutional Commentaries and Notes
Ab.: State Const. Commentaries & Notes

Ex.: Anthony Champagne, The Role of Personality in Judicial Reform, 2 State Const. Commentaries & Notes, Winter 1991, at 5. —Article Citation.

Anthony Champagne, The Role of Personality in Judicial Reform, 2 State Const. Commentaries & Notes, Winter 1991, at 5, 6-7. —Page Citation.

State Court Journal
Ab.: State Ct. J.

Ex.: David Prager, The Road to More Effective Judicial System: The Kansas Experience, State Ct. J., Summer 1991, at 20. —Article Citation.

David Prager, The Road to More Effective Judicial System: The Kansas Experience, State Ct. J., Summer 1991, at 20, 25-26. —Page Citation.

State of Louisiana: Acts of the Legislature
Ab.: year La. Acts page no.

Ex.: Act of July 19, 1995, No. 593, 1995 La. Acts 1532. —Citation to an entire session law.

Act of July 19, 1995, No. 593, § 1, 1995 La. Acts 1532, 1532-35. —Citation to a section of a session law.

—See Bluebook rule 12.4.

State of Ohio: Legislative Acts Passed and Joint Resolutions Adopted
Ab.: year Ohio Laws page no.

Ex.: Act of Apr. 12, 1994, No. 590, 1993-1994 Ohio Laws 6546. —Citation to an entire session law.

Act of Apr. 12, 1994, No. 590, sec. 2, 1993-1994 Ohio Laws 6546, 6548-50. —Citation to a section of a session law.

—See Bluebook rule 12.4.

State of Utah Bulletin
Ab.: Utah Bull.

State Tax Guide (Commerce Clearing House)
Ab.: St. Tax Guide (CCH)

State Tax Reporter (Commerce Clearing House)
Ab.: St. Tax Rep. (CCH)

State Tax Reporter -- Tennessee (Commerce Clearing House)
Ab.: St. Tax Rep. (CCH) (Designate volume by state in brackets preceding service abbreviation)

In citing cases in law review footnotes, abbreviate any word listed in table T.6; the names of "states, countries, and other geographical units" unless they are named parties; and any other words of eight or more letters "if substantial space is thereby saved and the result is unambiguous." Bluebook rule 10.2.2. On the other hand, in citing cases in text, abbreviate only widely known acronyms and the following words: "&," "Ass'n," "Bros.," "Co.," "Corp.," "Inc.," "Ltd.," and "No." Bluebook rule 10.2.1(c).

Ex.:   Lowe's Cos. v. Cardwell, [Tennessee] St. Tax Rep. (CCH)   ¶ 400-263 (Tenn. July 22, 1991). –Cite to looseleaf material.

–The above example is proper if the case is not yet available in, or is not reported in, an official or West reporter, a public domain citation, or in a widely used computer database.

State University of New York at Buffalo Law Review
See Buffalo Law Review.

statutes and legislative materials
See specific entries for examples. See also Bluebook rules 12.1 to 12.9 and 13.1 to 13.7.

Statutes and Statutory Construction, by Norman J. Singer
–Do not abbreviate the title.

Ex.:   2A Norman J. Singer, Statutes and Statutory Construction § 48A:05 (6th ed. 2000). –Section Citation.

Statutes at Large
Ab.:   Stat.   (year)

Ex.:   Act of June 15, 1933, ch. 86, 48 Stat. 152. –Citation to pre-1957 session law. The citation is to a chapter in Statutes at Large.

Act of May 24, 1982, Pub. L. No. 97-179, 96 Stat. 90. –Citation to a post-1956 session law.

National Monument Act, ch. 3060, 34 Stat. 225 (1906) (codified at 16 U.S.C. §§ 431-433). –Citation to a pre-1957 session law with a popular name. The citation is to a chapter in Statutes at Large.

Northern Pacific Halibut Act of 1982, Pub. L. No. 97-176, 97 Stat. 78 (codified at 16 U.S.C. §§ 773-773k). –Citation to a post-1956 session law with a popular name.

Economic Recovery Tax Act of 1981, Pub. L. No. 97-34, § 403, 95 Stat. 172, 301-05 (codified in scattered sections in the I.R.C.).

–Citation to a section within a session law.

Tennessee Valley Authority Act, ch. 32, 48 Stat. 58 (1933) (codified as amended at 16 U.S.C. §§ 831a-831dd (1982)). –Illustration of a citation when a session law has been codified and the code location is known. Some of the examples above also illustrate this situation.

The Bankruptcy Act, ch. 541, 30 Stat. 544 (1898) (repealed 1978). –Citation to a repealed statute.

National Industrial Recovery Act, ch. 90, § 3, 48 Stat. 195, 196-97 (1933), repealed by Act of June 14, 1935, ch. 246, 49 Stat. 375. – Citation to a repealed statute with a complete citation to the repealing statute.

In law review footnotes, the titles of books and the names of cases, except for procedural phrases, are not underlined. See Bluebook rule 2.1(a) & (b). Further, the following are in large and small capitals: codes, restatements, standards, constitutions, periodicals, authors of books, titles of books, the abbreviated names of codes, most legislative materials except for bills and resolutions, codified ordinances, model codes, court rules, and sentencing guidelines. Refer to The Bluebook.

Securities Act of 1933, ch. 38, § 2, 48 Stat. 74, 74 (current version at 15 U.S.C. § 77(b) (1976 & Supp. IV 1980)). –Citation to a version of a statute no longer in force. The current version is indicated parenthetically.

Securities Act of 1933, 15 U.S.C. § 77(b) (1976 & Supp. IV 1980) (original version at ch. 38, § 2, 48 Stat. 74, 74 (1933)). –Citation to a code provision's prior history.

Treaty of Alliance, U.S.-Fr., Feb. 6, 1778, 8 Stat. 6, T.S. No. 82.

–Citation to treaties dated prior to 1945 to which the U.S. is a party. See Bluebook rule 21.4.5.

Agreement Respecting Mutual Aid, U.S.-S. Afr., Apr. 17, 1945, 60 Stat. 1576, T.I.A.S. No. 15ll. –Citation to treaties from 1945 to the present to which the U.S. is a party. See Bluebook rule 21.4.5.

Statutes - citing to secondary sources

Act of Feb. 2, 1995, Pub. L. No. 113-95, 1995 U.S.C.C.A.N. (113 Stat.) 166.

See Bluebook rule 12.5(b).

Statutes - Electronic Databases

See Electronic media and other nonprint resources.

Statutes of Alberta (Canada)

Ab.:   S.A.

Ex.:   Legal Profession Act, ch. 9.1, 1990 S.A. 205 (Can.).

Statutes of British Columbia

See British Columbia Statutes.

Statutes of California

Ab.:   year Cal. Stat.

Ex.:   Act of Sept. 29, 1990, ch. 1580, 1990 Cal. Stat. 7553. –Citation to an entire session law.

Act of Sept. 29, 1990, ch. 1580, sec. 2, § 4573, 1990 Cal. Stat 7553, 7554-55. –Citation to a section of a session law amending prior act.

See Bluebook rule 12.4.

Statutes of Canada

Ab.:   S.C.

Canadian Space Agency Act, ch.13, 1990 S.C. 223 (Can.).

Statutes of Manitoba

Ab.:   S.M.

Statutes of Nevada

Ab.:   year Nev. Stat. page no.

In citing cases in law review footnotes, abbreviate any word listed in table T.6; the names of "states, countries, and other geographical units" unless they are named parties; and any other words of eight or more letters "if substantial space is thereby saved and the result is unambiguous." Bluebook rule 10.2.2. On the other hand, in citing cases in text, abbreviate only widely known acronyms and the following words: "&," "Ass'n," "Bros.," "Co.," "Corp.," "Inc.," "Ltd.," and "No." Bluebook rule 10.2.1(c).

Ex.: Act of July 1, 1999, ch. 355, 1999 Nev. Stat. 1557. –Citation to an entire session law.

Act of July 1, 1999, ch. 355, sec. 1, § 931.180, 1999 Nev. Stat. 1557, 1557 (act relating to education personnel). –Citation to a section of a session law.

–See Bluebook rule 12.4.

Statutes of Newfoundland (Canada)
Ab.: S. Nfld.

Ex.: The International Trusts Act, ch. 28, 1989 S. Nfld. 264 (Can.).

Statutes of Nova Scotia (Canada)
Ab.: S.N.S.

Ex.: School Boards Act, ch. 6, 1991 S.N.S. 61 (Can.).

Statutes of Nunavut
Ab.: S.Nu.

Statutes of Ontario (Canada)
Ab.: S.O.

Ex.: Ontario Loan Act of 1990, ch. 21, 1990 S.O. 380 (Can.).

Statutes of Québec (Canada)
Ab.: S.Q.

Ex.: Act of Sept. 4, 1990, ch. 34, 1990 S.Q. 761 (Can.).

Statutes of Saskatchewan (Canada)
Ab.: S.S.

Ex.: Saskatchewan Gaming Comm'n Act, S.S., ch. S-18.1, 1989-1990 S.S. 625 (Can.). –Session law.

Saskatchewan Embalmers Act, S.S., ch. S-15, § 3 (1978) (Can.). – Statutory compilation.

See Bluebook rule 20.5.1 and table T.2.

Statutes of the Yukon Territory (Canada)
Ab.: S.Y.T.

Ex.: Fifth Appropriation Act, ch. 1, 1984-85 S.Y.T. 1 (Can.). –Session law.

Occupational Health and Safety Act, S.Y.T., ch. 123, § 43 (1) (1986) (Can.). –Statutory compilation.

See Bluebook rule 20.5.1 and table T.2.

statutes, subsequent citation to
See subsequent citation to legal authority.

Stetson Law Review
Ab.: Stetson L. Rev.

In law review footnotes, the titles of books and the names of cases, except for procedural phrases, are not underlined. See Bluebook rule 2.1(a) & (b). Further, the following are in large and small capitals: codes, restatements, standards, constitutions, periodicals, authors of books, titles of books, the abbreviated names of codes, most legislative materials except for bills and resolutions, codified ordinances, model codes, court rules, and sentencing guidelines. Refer to The Bluebook.

Ex.:   Morey W. McDaniel, <u>Stockholders and Stakeholders</u>, 21 Stetson L.
          Rev. 121 (1991). −Article Citation.

          Morey W. McDaniel, <u>Stockholders and Stakeholders</u>, 21 Stetson L.
          Rev. 121, 135-37 (1991). −Page Citation.

Stipulation, citation to

Ab.:   Stip.

Ex.:   (Pl.'s Proposed Stip. No. 2).

          (Jt. Stips. ¶ 4).

<u>See</u> <u>Bluebook</u> rule B10 and table BT.1.

Note: See <u>Bluebook</u> rule 10.8.3 for citing litigation materials from another case.

sub nom.

Ex.:   <u>United Jewish Org. v. Wilson</u>, 510 F.2d 512 (2d Cir. 1975), <u>cert.</u>
          <u>granted sub nom.</u> <u>United Jewish Org. v. Carey</u>, 430 U.S. 144 (1977).

          <u>Graves v. Barnes</u>, 378 F. Supp. 640 (W.D. Tex. 1974), <u>vacated as moot</u>
          <u>sub nom.</u> <u>White v. Regester</u>, 422 U.S. 935 (1975). <u>See</u> <u>Bluebook</u> rule
          10.7.2.

subsequent case history

          −"Whenever a decision is cited in full, give the entire <u>subsequent</u>
          history of the case, but omit denials of certiorari or denials of similar
          discretionary appeals, unless the decision is less than two years old or
          the denial is particularly relevant. Omit also the history on remand or
          any denial of a rehearing, unless relevant to the point for which the
          case is cited. Finally, omit any disposition withdrawn by the deciding
          authority, such as an affirmance followed by reversal or rehearing."
          <u>Bluebook</u> rule 10.7.

Ex.:   <u>Shultz v. Consolidation Coal Co.</u>, 475 S.E.2d 467 (W. Va. 1996), <u>cert.</u>
          <u>denied</u>, 65 U.S.L.W. 3505 (U.S. Jan. 21, 1997) (No. 96-731).

          <u>Pacemaker Diagnostic Clinic of Am., Inc. v. Instromedix, Inc.</u>, 725
          F.2d 537 (9th Cir.), <u>cert. denied</u>, 469 U.S. 824 (1984).

          <u>Devine v. Nutt</u>, 718 F.2d 1048 (Fed. Cir. 1983), <u>rev'd sub nom.</u>
          <u>Cornelius v. Nutt</u>, 472 U.S. 648 (1985).

          <u>Blizard v. Fielding</u>, 454 F.Supp. 318 (D. Mass. 1978), <u>aff'd</u> 601 F.2d.
          1217 (1st Cir. 1979).

subsequent citation to legal authority

Ex.:   <u>DeFunis</u>, 416 U.S. at 334. −Subsequent citation for <u>DeFunis v.</u>
          <u>Odegaard</u>, 416 U.S. 312 (1974).

          15 U.S.C. § 2 or § 2. −Subsequent citation for 15 U.S.C. § 2 (1994).

          <u>Id.</u> −citation for material in preceding footnote or text.

          <u>Id.</u> at 470. −citation for page 470 of material in preceding footnote or
          text.

In citing cases in law review footnotes, abbreviate any word listed in table T.6;
the names of "states, countries, and other geographical units" unless they are named parties;
and any other words of eight or more letters "if <u>substantial</u> space is thereby saved and the
result is unambiguous." <u>Bluebook</u> rule 10.2.2. On the other hand, in citing cases in text,
abbreviate only widely known acronyms and the following words: "&," "Ass'n," "Bros.,"
"Co.," "Corp.," "Inc.," "Ltd.," and "No." <u>Bluebook</u> rule 10.2.1(c).

Waller, <u>supra</u> note 11, at 180-82.

Commercial Electronic Databases

Ex.: <u>Reed v. Hamilton,</u> No. W1999-00440-COA-R3-CV, 2000 WL 558613, at *4 (Tenn. Ct. App. May 4, 2000)

becomes

<u>Reed,</u> 2000 WL 558613, at *3.

<u>Ashley v. ITT Hartford,</u> No. C 97-3226 TEH, 1998 U.S. Dist. LEXIS 1228, at *3 (N.D. Cal. Jan. 20, 1998)

becomes

<u>Ashley,</u> 1998 U.S. Dist. LEXIS 1228, at *5.

H.R. 1390, 106th Cong. § 3(c) (1999), 1999 Cong US HR 1390 (Westlaw).

becomes

HR 1390 § 3(c), 1999 Cong US HR 1390 (Westlaw).

Regulation D, 12 C.F.R. § 204.1 (2000), 12 CRF s 204.1 (Westlaw).

becomes

12 C.F.R. § 204.1, 12 CFR s 204.1 (Westlaw) *or* 12 CFR s 204.1 (Westlaw).

<u>See</u> <u>Bluebook</u> rules B5.2, B8.2, 4.1, 4.2, 10.9, 12.9, 13.7, 14.10, 15.9, 16.7, 18.7, and 19.2. See also the rules for the particular authority.

Substantive Criminal Law, by Wayne R. LaFave
–Do not abbreviate the title.

Ex.: 1 Wayne R. LaFave, <u>Substantive Criminal Law</u> § 2.6(d) (2d ed. 2003). –Section Citation

1 Wayne R. LaFave, <u>Substantive Criminal Law</u> § 2.6(d), at 180 (2d ed. 2003). –Page Citation

1 Wayne R. LaFave, <u>Substantive Criminal Law</u> § 2.6(d), at 180 n.42 (2d ed. 2003). –Footnote Citation

Suffolk Transnational Law Journal
Ab.: Suffolk Transnat'l L.J.

Ex.: Claudia M. Pardinas, <u>The Enigma of the Legal Liability of Transnational Corporations</u>, 14 Suffolk Transnat'l L.J. 405 (1991). –Article Citation.

Claudia M. Pardinas, <u>The Enigma of the Legal Liability of Transnational Corporations</u>, 14 Suffolk Transnat'l L.J. 405, 435-47 (1991). –Page Citation.

In law review footnotes, the titles of books and the names of cases, except for procedural phrases, are not underlined. <u>See</u> <u>Bluebook</u> rule 2.1(a) & (b). Further, the following are in large and small capitals: codes, restatements, standards, constitutions, periodicals, authors of books, titles of books, the abbreviated names of codes, most legislative materials except for bills and resolutions, codified ordinances, model codes, court rules, and sentencing guidelines. Refer to <u>The Bluebook</u>.

Suffolk University Law Review
Ab.: Suffolk U. L. Rev.

Ex.: Mark D. Robins, The Resurgence and Limits of the Demurrer, 27 Suffolk U. L. Rev. 637 (1993). –Article Citation.

Mark D. Robins, The Resurgence and Limits of the Demurrer, 27 Suffolk U. L. Rev. 637, 650-52 (1993). –Page Citation.

Superior Court
Ab.: Super. Ct.

supplement
See the various title entries in this work and Bluebook rule 3.1.

supra

–"Portions of text, footnotes, and groups of authorities within the piece may be cited using 'supra' or 'infra.' Use supra to refer back to material that has already appeared within the piece." Bluebook rule 3.5.

Ex.: See cases cited supra note 15.

See supra notes 8-9 and accompanying text.

–"When an authority has been fully cited previously, the supra form may be used (unless 'id.' is appropriate or 'supra' is inappropriate for that authority)." Bluebook rule 4.2. See also rule B8.2.

Ex.: Waller, supra note 11, at 180-82.

Supreme Court (federal)
Ab.: U.S.

Supreme Court (other)
Ab.: Sup. Ct.

Supreme Court, Appellate Division
Ab.: App. Div.

Supreme Court, Appellate Term
Ab.: App. Term

Supreme Court Historical Society Yearbook
Ab.: Sup. Ct. Hist. Soc'y Y.B.

Supreme Court Practice, by Robert L. Stern, Eugene Gressman, Stephen M. Shapiro, and Kenneth S. Geller
–Do not abbreviate this title.

In citing cases in law review footnotes, abbreviate any word listed in table T.6; the names of "states, countries, and other geographical units" unless they are named parties; and any other words of eight or more letters "if substantial space is thereby saved and the result is unambiguous." Bluebook rule 10.2.2. On the other hand, in citing cases in text, abbreviate only widely known acronyms and the following words: "&," "Ass'n," "Bros.," "Co.," "Corp.," "Inc.," "Ltd.," and "No." Bluebook rule 10.2.1(c).

Ex.:   Robert L. Stein et al., <u>Supreme Court Practice</u> § 4.28, at 279 (8th ed. 2002). –Page Citation.

Supreme Court Reporter

–With volume 106 (1985), Supreme Court Reporter became West's Supreme Court Reporter. Citation form is not affected by this title change.

–Cite to U.S., if therein; otherwise, cite to S. Ct., L. Ed., or U.S.L.W., in that order of preference. <u>See</u> <u>Bluebook</u>, table T.1.

Ab.:   S. Ct.

Ex.:   <u>Bush v. Vera</u>, 116 S. Ct. 1941 (1996). –Case Citation.

<u>Bush v. Vera</u>, 116 S. Ct. 1941, 1961 (1996). –Page Citation.

Supreme Court Reports (Canada) (1876-date)

Ab.:   S.C.R.

Ex.:   <u>Canson Enters. v. Broughton & Co.</u>, [1991] 3 S.C.R. 534 (Can.).

–Provide neutral citation, if available. <u>See</u> <u>Bluebook</u> table T.2, p. 254 (3d prtg. 2006).

<u>R. v. Perrier</u>, [2004] 3 S.C.R. 228, 2004 SCC 56 (Can.). –Case with neutral citation.

Note: For information on Canada's neutral citation, see <u>A Neutral Citation Standard for Case Law</u> (2000), <u>available</u> at http://www.lexum.umontreal.ca/ccc-ccr/neutr/neutr.jur_en.html.

Supreme Court Review

Ab.:   Sup. Ct. Rev.

Ex.:   John M. Langbein, <u>The Supreme Court Flunks Trusts</u>, 1990 Sup. Ct. Rev. 207. –Article Citation.

John M. Langbein, <u>The Supreme Court Flunks</u> Trusts, 1990 Sup. Ct. Rev. 207, 210-12. –Page Citation.

Supreme Court Rules (rules of the Supreme Court of the United States).

Ab.:   Sup. Ct. R.

Ex.:   Sup. Ct. R. 5.

<u>See also</u> Rules of Evidence and Procedure and <u>Bluebook</u> rule 12.8.3.

Supreme Judicial Court

Ab.:   Sup. Jud. Ct.

Surrogate's Court

Ab.:   Sur. Ct.

Swedish and International Arbitration

Ab.:   Swed. & Int'l Arb.

In law review footnotes, the titles of books and the names of cases, except for procedural phrases, are not underlined. <u>See</u> <u>Bluebook</u> rule 2.1(a) & (b). Further, the following are in large and small capitals: codes, restatements, standards, constitutions, periodicals, authors of books, titles of books, the abbreviated names of codes, most legislative materials except for bills and resolutions, codified ordinances, model codes, court rules, and sentencing guidelines. Refer to <u>The Bluebook</u>.

Ex.:   Sigvard Jarvin, <u>The Place of Arbitration</u>, 1990 Swed. & Int'l Arb. 85. –Article Citation.

Sigvard Jarvin, <u>The Place of Arbitration</u>, 1990 Swed. & Int'l Arb. 85, 86. –Page Citation.

Sydney Law Review
Ab.:   Sydney L. Rev.

Ex.:   John Gava, <u>Scholarship and Community</u>, 16 Sydney L. Rev. 443 (1994). –Article Citation.

John Gava, <u>Scholarship and Community</u>, 16 Sydney L. Rev. 443, 444-52 (1994). –Page Citation.

symposia
Ex.:   Symposium, <u>A Reevaluation of the Canons of Statutory Interpretation</u>, 45 Vand. L. Rev. 529 (1992). –When citing a symposium as a unit, cite to the first page of the first piece. <u>See</u> <u>Bluebook</u> rule 16.6.3.

Jonathan R. Macey & Geoffrey P. Miller, <u>The Canons of Statutory Construction and Judicial Preferences</u>, 45 Vand. L. Rev. 647 (1992). –Individual articles within a symposium are cited in the same manner as any other article. <u>See</u> <u>Bluebook</u> rule 16.6.3.

Syracuse Journal of International Law and Commerce
Ab.:   Syracuse J. Int'l L. & Com.

Ex.:   Eugene T. Rossides, <u>Cyprus and the Rule of Law</u>, 17 Syracuse J. Int'l L. & Com. 21 (1991). –Article Citation.

Eugene T. Rossides, <u>Cyprus and the Rule of Law</u>, 17 Syracuse J. Int'l L. & Com. 21, 55-67 (1991). –Page Citation.

Syracuse Law Review
Ab.:   Syracuse L. Rev.

Ex.:   Daniel Kramer, <u>Torts</u>, 42 Syracuse L. Rev. 737 (1991). –Article Citation.

Daniel Kramer, <u>Torts</u>, 42 Syracuse L. Rev. 737, 749-50 (1991). –Page Citation.

In citing cases in law review footnotes, abbreviate any word listed in table T.6; the names of "states, countries, and other geographical units" unless they are named parties; and any other words of eight or more letters "if <u>substantial</u> space is thereby saved and the result is unambiguous." <u>Bluebook</u> rule 10.2.2. On the other hand, in citing cases in text, abbreviate only widely known acronyms and the following words: "&," "Ass'n," "Bros.," "Co.," "Corp.," "Inc.," "Ltd.," and "No." <u>Bluebook</u> rule 10.2.1(c).

T

Tasmanian Reports (Australia)
Ab.:   T.R.

Ex.:   <u>Tasmania v. Brett</u>, [2002] TASSC 33; (2002) 10 T.R. 401 (Austl.).

Note: For explanation of Australia's medium-neutral citation, see L.T. Olsson, <u>Guide to Uniform Production of Judgments</u> (2d ed. 1999), <u>available at</u> http://www.aija.org.au/online/judguide.htm.

Tax Adviser, The
Ab.:   Tax Adviser

Ex.:   Lorin D. Luchs, <u>New Rules for Estimated Tax Payments</u>, 23 Tax Adviser 203 (1992). –Article Citation.

Lorin D. Luchs, <u>New Rules for Estimated Tax Payments</u>, 23 Tax Adviser 203, 206 (1992). –Page Citation.

Tax Court
Ab.:   T.C.

Tax Court Memorandum Decisions (Commerce Clearing House)
Ab.:   T.C.M. (CCH)

Ex.:   <u>Kosman v. Comm'r</u>, 71 T.C.M. (CCH) ¶ 51, 219(M) (1995).

–The above example is proper if the case is not yet available in the Reports of the United States Tax Court (TC).

Tax Court Memorandum Decisions (Research Institute of America)
Ab.:   T.C.M. (RIA)

Ex.:   <u>Peterson v. Comm'r</u>, 1997 T.C.M. (RIA) ¶ 97,018 (Jan. 8, 1997). –Citation to looseleaf materials.

<u>Ballard v. Comm'r</u>, 1996 T.C.M. (RIA) ¶ 96,068. –Citation to bound volume.

Tax Court of the United Reports
Ab.:   T.C.

Ex.:   <u>Hager v. Comm'r</u>, 76 T.C. 66 (1981).

Tax Court Reported Decisions (Research Institute of America)
Ab.:   Tax Ct. Rep. Dec. (RIA)

In law review footnotes, the titles of books and the names of cases, except for procedural phrases, are not underlined. <u>See</u> <u>Bluebook</u> rule 2.1(a) & (b). Further, the following are in large and small capitals: codes, restatements, standards, constitutions, periodicals, authors of books, titles of books, the abbreviated names of codes, most legislative materials except for bills and resolutions, codified ordinances, model codes, court rules, and sentencing guidelines. Refer to <u>The Bluebook</u>.

Ex.:   Brookes v. Comm'r, 108 Tax Ct. Rep. Dec. (RIA) ¶ 108.1 (Jan 2, 1997). –Citation to looseleaf material.

P&X Markets, Inc. v. Comm'r, 106 Tax. Ct. Rep. Dec. (RIA) ¶ 106.26 (1996). –Citation to bound volume.

Tax Court Reports (Commerce Clearing House)
Ab.:   Tax Ct. Rep. (CCH)

Ex.:   Thompson v. Comm'r, [Current Memo Decisions] Tax Ct. Rep. (CCH) (72 T.C.M.) Dec. 51,605(M) (Oct. 17, 1996). –Citation to looseleaf material.

Cochrane v. Comm'r, [Current Regular Decisions] Tax Ct. Rep. (CCH) Dec. 51,490 (Aug. 7, 1996). –Citation to looseleaf material.

Brotman v. Comm'r, [1995 Transfer Binder] Tax Ct. Rep. (CCH) Dec. 50,860 (Aug. 24, 1995). –Transfer binder material.

–The above examples are proper if the case is not yet available in, or is not reported in, an official or West reporter, a public domain citation, or in a widely used computer database.

Tax Executive, The
Ab.:   Tax Executive

Ex.:   Leonard F. Francis, IRS Offset Program: A Case Study, 43 Tax Executive 389 (1991). –Article Citation.

Leonard F. Francis, IRS Offset Program: A Case Study, 43 Tax Executive 389, 389-90 (1991). –Page Citation.

Tax Law Review
Ab.:   Tax L. Rev.

Ex.:   William A. Klein, Tax Effects of Nonpayment of Child Support, 45 Tax L. Rev. 177 (1990). –Article Citation.

William A. Klein, Tax Effects of Nonpayment of Child Support, 45 Tax L. Rev. 177, 180-85 (1990). –Page Citation.

Tax Lawyer, The
Ab.:   Tax Law.

Ex.:   David S. Hudson, The Tax Concept of Research or Experimentation, 45 Tax Law. 85 (1991). –Article Citation.

David S. Hudson, The Tax Concept of Research or Experimentation, 45 Tax Law. 85, 89-90 (1991). –Page Citation.

Tax Management International Journal
Ab.:   Tax Mgm't Int'l J.

In citing cases in law review footnotes, abbreviate any word listed in table T.6; the names of "states, countries, and other geographical units" unless they are named parties; and any other words of eight or more letters "if substantial space is thereby saved and the result is unambiguous." Bluebook rule 10.2.2. On the other hand, in citing cases in text, abbreviate only widely known acronyms and the following words: "&," "Ass'n," "Bros.," "Co.," "Corp.," "Inc.," "Ltd.," and "No." Bluebook rule 10.2.1(c).

Ex.:   Brian Hornsby, <u>The United Kingdom Budget Statement 1991 - Some Implications for U.S. Investors</u>, 20 Tax Mgm't Int'l J. 302 (1991). – Article Citation.

Brian Hornsby, <u>The United Kingdom Budget Statement 1991 - Some Implications for U.S. Investors</u>, 20 Tax Mgm't Int'l J. 302, 304-05 (1991). –Page Citation.

Tax Notes
Ab.:   Tax Notes

Ex.:   Donald W. Kiefer, <u>Tax Policy: What Happened? What Next?</u>, 55 Tax Notes 1675 (1992). –Article Citation.

Donald W. Kiefer, <u>Tax Policy: What Happened? What Next?</u>, 55 Tax Notes 1675, 1679 (1992). –Page Citation.

Tax Treaties (Commerce Clearing House)
Ab.:   Tax Treaties (CCH)

Taxation for Accountants
Ab.:   Tax'n for Acct.

Ex.:   Jerome Mauer, <u>Partners Can Control Tax Effects of Retirement Payouts</u>, 49 Tax'n for Acct. 201 (1992). –Article Citation.

Jerome Mauer, <u>Partners Can Control Tax Effects of Retirement Payouts</u>, 49 Tax'n for Acct. 201, 206-07 (1992). –Page Citation.

Taxation for Lawyers
Ab.:   Tax'n for Law.

Ex.:   Eric J. Selter, <u>Leasing Employees May Ease Benefit Compliance</u>, 20 Tax'n for Law. 270 (1992). –Article Citation.

Eric J. Selter, <u>Leasing Employees May Ease Benefit Compliance</u>, 20 Tax'n for Law. 270, 272 (1992). –Page Citation.

Taxation of the Closely Held Corporation, by Theodore Ness and Eugene L. Vogel
–Do not abbreviate the title.

Ex.:   Theodore Ness & Eugene L. Vogel, <u>Taxation of the Closely Held Corporation</u> ¶ 8.14[2][f] (5th ed. 1991). –Section Citation.

Theodore Ness & Eugene L. Vogel, <u>Taxation of the Closely Held Corporation</u> ¶ 8.14[2][f], at 8-40 (5th ed. 1991). –Page Citation.

Theodore Ness & Eugene L. Vogel, <u>Taxation of the Closely Held Corporation</u> ¶ 8.14[2][f], at 8-40 n.62 (5th ed. 1991). –Footnote Citation.

Taxes–The Tax Magazine
Ab.:   Taxes

In law review footnotes, the titles of books and the names of cases, except for procedural phrases, are not underlined. <u>See</u> Bluebook rule 2.1(a) & (b). Further, the following are in large and small capitals: codes, restatements, standards, constitutions, periodicals, authors of books, titles of books, the abbreviated names of codes, most legislative materials except for bills and resolutions, codified ordinances, model codes, court rules, and sentencing guidelines. Refer to <u>The Bluebook</u>.

Ex.:   Orrin Tilevitz, "Condopping" A Co-op, 69 Taxes 558 (1991). –Article Citation.

Orrin Tilevitz, "Condopping" A Co-op, 69 Taxes 558, 560-61 (1991). –Page Citation.

Technical Advice Memoranda
Ab.:   I.R.S. Tech. Adv. Mem.

Ex.:   I.R.S. Tech. Adv. Mem. 199922055 (Aug. 5, 1998).

television broadcasts
Ex.:   ABC World News Tonight (ABC television broadcast, Dec. 9, 1996).

Temple Environmental Law & Technology Journal
Ab.:   Temp. Int'l & Comp. L.J.

Ex.:   Charles H. Montague, Conserving Rail Corridors, 10 Temp. Envtl. L. & Tech. J. 139 (1991). –Article Citation.

Charles H. Montague, Conserving Rail Corridors, 10 Temp. Envtl. L. & Tech. J. 139, 149-52 (1991). –Page Citation.

Temple International and Comparative Law Journal
Ab.:   Temp. Int'l & Comp. L.J.

Ex.:   Donna E. Arzt, Soviet Anti-Semitism: Legal Responses in an Age of Glasnost, 4 Temp. Int'l & Comp. L.J. 163 (1990). –Article Citation.

Donna E. Arzt, Soviet Anti-Semitism: Legal Responses in an Age of Glasnost, 4 Temp. Int'l & Comp. L.J. 163, 172-73 (1990). –Page Citation.

Temple Law Quarterly
Ab.:   Temp. L.Q.

Temple Law Review
Ab.:   Temp. L. Rev.

Ex.:   Laura E. Little, An Excursion into the Uncharted Waters of the Seventeenth Amendment, 64 Temp. L. Rev. 629 (1991). –Article Citation.

Laura E. Little, An Excursion into the Uncharted Waters of the Seventeenth Amendment, 64 Temp. L. Rev. 629, 630-35 (1991). –Page Citation.

temporary
Ab.:   temp.

Temporary Treasury Regulation (Federal)
Ab.:   Temp. Treas. Reg.

In citing cases in law review footnotes, abbreviate any word listed in table T.6; the names of "states, countries, and other geographical units" unless they are named parties; and any other words of eight or more letters "if substantial space is thereby saved and the result is unambiguous." Bluebook rule 10.2.2. On the other hand, in citing cases in text, abbreviate only widely known acronyms and the following words: "&," "Ass'n," "Bros.," "Co.," "Corp.," "Inc.," "Ltd.," and "No." Bluebook rule 10.2.1(c).

Ex.:   Temp. Treas. Reg. § 1.897-6T(a)(2) (1985).

Tennessee Administrative Code
See Official Compilation Rules and Regulations of the State of Tennessee.

Tennessee Administrative Register
Ab.:   vol. no. Tenn. Admin. Reg. page no. (month year)

Ex.:   15 Tenn. Admin. Reg. 12 (Dec. 1989).

Tennessee Appeals Reports
Ab.:   Tenn. App.

–Discontinued in 1972 after 63 Tenn. App. 732 (1972).

–Cite to S.W., S.W.2d, or S.W.3d, if therein; otherwise, cite to Tenn. App.

–Give parallel citations only in documents submitted to Tennessee state courts. See Bluebook rules 10.3.1 and B5.1.3; see also Tenn. R. App. P. 27(h), which permits citation to either the official or South Western Reporter or both.

–Through 63 Tenn. App. 732 (1972), cite as follows:

In documents submitted to Tennessee state courts:

Stevens v. Moore, 24 Tenn. App. 61, 139 S.W.2d 710 (1940). –Case Citation.

Stevens v. Moore, 24 Tenn. App. 61, 67, 139 S.W.2d 710, 713 (1940). –Page Citation.

In all other documents:

Stevens v. Moore, 139 S.W.2d 710 (Tenn. Ct. App. 1940). –Case Citation.

Stevens v. Moore, 139 S.W.2d 710, 713 (Tenn. Ct. App. 1940). –Page Citation.

–After 63 Tenn. App. 732 (1972), cite as follows:

In all documents:

Peaver v. Hunt, 924 S.W.2d 114 (Tenn. Ct. App. 1996). –Case Citation.

Peaver v. Hunt, 924 S.W.2d 114, 115 (Tenn. Ct. App. 1996). –Page Citation.

Tennessee Bar Journal
Ab.:   Tenn. B.J.

Ex.:   Lucian T. Pera, Rule 11 Comes to Tennessee: The Emerging State Law of Sanctions, Tenn. B.J., Jan.-Feb. 1992, at 24. –Article Citation.

Lucian T. Pera, Rule 11 Comes to Tennessee: The Emerging State Law of Sanctions, Tenn. B.J., Jan.-Feb. 1992, at 24, 26. –Article Citation.

In law review footnotes, the titles of books and the names of cases, except for procedural phrases, are not underlined. See Bluebook rule 2.1(a) & (b). Further, the following are in large and small capitals: codes, restatements, standards, constitutions, periodicals, authors of books, titles of books, the abbreviated names of codes, most legislative materials except for bills and resolutions, codified ordinances, model codes, court rules, and sentencing guidelines. Refer to The Bluebook.

Tennessee Circuit Court Practice, by Lawrence A. Pivnick
–Do not abbreviate the title.

Ex.: Lawrence A. Pivnick, Tennessee Circuit Court Practice § 3-16 (2000).
–Section Citation.

Lawrence A. Pivnick, Tennessee Circuit Court Practice § 3-16, at 255 (2000). –Page Citation.

Tennessee Code Annotated (LexisNexis)
Ab.: Tenn. Code Ann. § x-x-x (year)

Ex.: Tenn. Code Ann. § 13-21-107 (1999).

Tenn. Code Ann. § 47-8-105 (Supp. 2004).

–For proper citation form in papers submitted to Tennessee courts, see Tenn. Code Ann. § 1-2-1-1(a) (2003).

Tennessee Code Annotated Advance Legislative Service (LexisNexis)
Ab.: year-pamph. no. Tenn. Code Ann. Adv. Legis. Serv. page no. (LexisNexis)

Ex.: Act effective May 9, 2005, ch. 151, 2005-1 Tenn. Code Ann. Adv. Legis. Serv. 211 (LexisNexis) (relative to child care). –Citation to an entire session law.

Act effective May 9, 2005, ch. 151, sec. 9, § 71-3-503(a), 2005-1 Tenn. Code Ann. Adv. Legis. Serv. 211, 213 (LexisNexis) (relative to child care). –Citation to a section of a session law amending prior act.

See Bluebook rule 12.4.

–"Cite to Tenn. Pub. Acts or Tenn. Priv. Acts, if therein." Bluebook table T.1, p. 233.

Tennessee Constitution
Ab.: Tenn. Const. art.   , §   .

Ex.: Tenn. Const. art. IX, §§ 1,2. –"Cite constitutional provisions currently in force without a date." Bluebook rule 11.

Tenn. Const. art. XI,. § 14 (repealed 1978). –"If the cited provision has been repealed, either indicate parenthetically the fact and date of repeal or cite the repealing provision in full." Bluebook rule 11.

Tenn. Const. art. XI, § 28 (amended 1982). –"When citing a provision that has been subsequently amended, either indicate parenthetically the fact and date of amendment or cite the amending provision in full." Bluebook rule 11.

Tenn. Const. of 1834, art. I, § 29 (1870), –"Cite constitutions that have been totally superseded by year of adoption; if the specific provision cited was adopted in a different year, give that year parenthetically." Bluebook rule 11.

Tennessee Corporations, by Ronald L. Gilman

In citing cases in law review footnotes, abbreviate any word listed in table T.6; the names of "states, countries, and other geographical units" unless they are named parties; and any other words of eight or more letters "if substantial space is thereby saved and the result is unambiguous." Bluebook rule 10.2.2. On the other hand, in citing cases in text, abbreviate only widely known acronyms and the following words: "&," "Ass'n," "Bros.," "Co.," "Corp.," "Inc.," "Ltd.," and "No." Bluebook rule 10.2.1(c).

–Do not abbreviate this title.

Ex.: Ronald L. Gilman, <u>Tennessee Corporations</u> Form 19, at 117 (1991).
      –Page Citation.

      Ronald L. Gilman, <u>Tennessee Corporations</u> § 11.4, at 92 (1991).
      –Page Citation.

Tennessee Criminal Appeals Reports
Ab.: Tenn. Crim. App.

      –Discontinued after 4 Tenn. Crim. App. 723 (1971).

      –Cite to S.W., S.W.2d, or S.W.3d, if therein; otherwise, cite to Tenn.
      Crim. App.

      –Give parallel citations only in documents submitted to Tennessee state
      courts. <u>See</u> <u>Bluebook</u> rules 10.3.1 and B5.1.3; see also Tenn. R. App.
      P. 27(h), which permits citation to either the official or South Western
      Reporter or both.

      –From 1 Tenn. Crim. App. 1 through 4 Tenn. Crim. App. 723, cite as
      follows:

      In documents submitted to Tennessee state courts:

          <u>Stokely v. State</u>, 4 Tenn. Crim. App. 241, 470 S.W.2d 37 (1971).
          –Case Citation.

          <u>Stokely v. State</u>, 4 Tenn. Crim. App. 241, 245, 470 S.W.2d 37, 39
          (1971). –Page Citation.

      In all other documents:

          <u>Stokely v. State</u>, 470 S.W.2d 37 (Tenn. Crim. App. 1971). –Case
          Citation.

          <u>Stokely v. State</u>, 470 S.W.2d 37, 39 (Tenn.. Crim. App. 1971).
          –Page Citation.

      –After 4 Tenn. Crim. App. 723, cite as follows:

      In all documents:

          <u>State v. Forbes</u>, 918 S.W.2d 431 (Tenn. Crim. App. 1995). –Case
          Citation.

          <u>State v. Forbes</u>, 918 S.W.2d 431, 450 (Tenn.. Crim. App. 1995).
          –Page Citation.

Tennessee Jurisprudence
Ab.: vol. no. Tenn. Jur. <u>article's name</u> § (year)

Ex.: 26 Tenn. Jur. <u>Working Contracts</u> § 5 (1985).

Tennessee Law Review
Ab.: Tenn. L. Rev.

In law review footnotes, the titles of books and the names of cases, except for procedural
phrases, are not underlined. <u>See</u> <u>Bluebook</u> rule 2.1(a) & (b). Further, the following are in
large and small capitals: codes, restatements, standards, constitutions, periodicals, authors of
books, titles of books, the abbreviated names of codes, most legislative materials except for
bills and resolutions, codified ordinances, model codes, court rules, and sentencing guidelines.
Refer to <u>The Bluebook</u>.

Ex.:   T. Maxfield Bahner, <u>Tennessee Law of Evidence</u>, 58 Tenn. L. Rev.
        709 (1991). –Article Citation.

        T. Maxfield Bahner, <u>Tennessee Law of Evidence</u>, 58 Tenn. L. Rev.
        709, 710 (1991). –Page Citation.

Tennessee Private Acts
See Private Acts of the State of Tennessee.

Tennessee Public Acts
See Public Acts of the State of Tennessee.

Tennessee Reports
Ab.:   Tenn.

–Discontinued in 1972 after 225 Tenn. 727 (1972).

–Cite to S.W., S.W.2d, or S.W.3d, if therein; otherwise, cite to Tenn.

–Give parallel citations only in documents submitted to Tennessee state
courts. <u>See</u> <u>Bluebook</u> rules 10.3.1 and B5.1.3; see also Tenn. R. App.
P. 27(h), which permits citation to either the official or South Western
Reporter or both.

–Through 225 Tenn. 727 (1972), cite as follows:

In documents submitted to Tennessee state courts:

<u>Cultra v. Cultra</u>, 188 Tenn. 506, 221 S.W.2d 533 (1959). –Case
Citation.

<u>Cultra v. Cultra</u>, 188 Tenn. 506, 509, 221 S.W.2d 533, 535 (1959).
–Page Citation.

In all other documents:

<u>Cultra v. Cultra</u>, 221 S.W.2d 533 (Tenn. 1959). –Case Citation.

<u>Cultra v. Cultra</u>, 221 S.W.2d 533, 535 (Tenn. 1959). –Page
Citation.

–After 225 Tenn. 727 (1972), cite as follows:

In all documents:

<u>State v. Ricci</u>, 914 S.W.2d 475 (Tenn. 1996). –Case Citation.

<u>State v. Ricci</u>, 914 S.W.2d 475, 476 (Tenn. 1996).   –Page
Citation.

Tennessee Rules and Regulations
See Official Compilation Rules and Regulations of the State of Tennessee.

Tennessee Session Laws
See Public Acts of the State of Tennessee and Private Acts of the State of
Tennessee.

Territorial Sea Journal
Ab.:   Terr. Sea J.

In citing cases in law review footnotes, abbreviate any word listed in table T.6;
the names of "states, countries, and other geographical units" unless they are named parties;
and any other words of eight or more letters "if <u>substantial</u> space is thereby saved and the
result is unambiguous." <u>Bluebook</u> rule 10.2.2. On the other hand, in citing cases in text,
abbreviate only widely known acronyms and the following words: "&," "Ass'n," "Bros.,"
"Co.," "Corp.," "Inc.," "Ltd.," and "No." <u>Bluebook</u> rule 10.2.1(c).

Territories Law Reports (Canada) (1885-1907)
  Ab.: Terr. L.R.

Texas Administrative Code
  Ab.: x Tex. Admin. Code § x.x (year)
  Ex.: 37 Tex. Admin. Code § 81.1 (2000).

Texas Bar Journal
  Ab.: Tex. B.J.
  Ex.: Russell Weintraub, <u>The Need for Forum Non Conveniens Legislation in Texas</u>, 55 Tex. B.J. 346 (1992). –Article Citation.
  Russell Weintraub, <u>The Need for Forum Non Conveniens Legislation in Texas</u>, 55 Tex. B.J. 346, 347 (1992). –Page Citation.

Texas Codes Annotated (Vernon)
  See Vernon's Texas Codes Annotated.

Texas Constitution
  Ab.: Tex. Const. Art.   , §   .
  Ex.: Tex. Const. art. XVI, § 22. –"Cite constitutional provisions currently in force without a date." <u>Bluebook</u> rule 11.
  Tex. Const. art. III, § 42 (repealed 1962). –"If the cited provision has been repealed, either indicate parenthetically the fact and date of repeal or cite the repealing provision in full." <u>Bluebook</u> rule 11.
  Tex. Const. art. XI, § 3 (amended 1989). –"When citing a provision that has been subsequently amended, either indicate parenthetically the fact and date of amendment or cite the amending provision in full." <u>Bluebook</u> rule 11.
  Tex. Const. of 1869, art. I, § 4 (1876). –"Cite constitutions that have been totally superseded by year of adoption; if the specific provision cited was adopted in a different year, give that year parenthetically." <u>Bluebook</u> rule 11.

Texas Court of Civil Appeals
  Ab.: Tex. Civ. App.
  See Texas Courts of Appeals.

Texas Court of Criminal Appeals
  Ab.: Tex. Crim. App.
  –Cite to S.W., S.W.2d, or S.W.3d, if therein; otherwise, cite to Tex. Crim.

In law review footnotes, the titles of books and the names of cases, except for procedural phrases, are not underlined. <u>See</u> <u>Bluebook</u> rule 2.1(a) & (b). Further, the following are in large and small capitals: codes, restatements, standards, constitutions, periodicals, authors of books, titles of books, the abbreviated names of codes, most legislative materials except for bills and resolutions, codified ordinances, model codes, court rules, and sentencing guidelines. Refer to <u>The Bluebook</u>.

–Give parallel citations only in documents submitted to Texas state courts. See Bluebook rules 10.3.1 and B5.1.3; see also Tex. Loc. R. 8th Ct. App. 38.1(b), requiring use of Bluebook or Texas Rules of Form, Tex. Loc. R. 10th Ct. App. 13(b), concerning citation of cases, Tex. Loc. R. 13th Ct. App. IV, which does not require parallel Texas Report citations, and Texas Rules of Form (Texas Law Review Ass'n ed., 10th ed. 2003), which requires a parallel citation and which may be obtained from the Texas Law Review Business Office.

–Through 172 Tex. Crim. 655 (1962), when Texas Criminal Reports were discontinued, cite as follows:

In documents submitted to Texas state courts:

> Ex parte Burnett, 85 Tex. Crim. 315, 211 S.W. 934 (1919).
> –Case Citation.

> Ex parte Burnett, 85 Tex. Crim. 315, 319, 211 S.W. 934, 935 (1919). –Page Citation.

In all other documents:

> Ex parte Burnett, 211 S.W. 934 (Tex. Crim. App. 1919). –Case Citation.

> Ex parte Burnett, 211 S.W. 934, 935 (Tex. Crim. App.1919). –Page Citation.

–After 172 Tex. Crim. 655 (1962), cite as follows:

In all documents:

> Robbins v. State, 914 S.W.2d 582 (Tex. Crim. App. 1996). –Case Citation.

> Robbins v. State, 914 S.W.2d 582, 584 (Tex. Crim. App. 1996). –Page Citation.

Texas Courts of Appeals
Ab.:   Tex. App.

–In 1981, the Texas Courts of Appeals (Tex. App.) replaced the Texas Court of Civil Appeals (Tex. Civ. App.), appeal still lying to the Texas Supreme Court (Tex.). At the same time the Texas Courts of Appeals became the intermediate appellate court for criminal cases, from whence appeal lies to the Texas Court of Criminal Appeals (Tex. Crim. App.).

–Give parallel citations only in documents submitted to Texas state courts, for any cases reported in Tex. Civ. App. between 1892 and 1911. See Bluebook rules 10.3.1 and B5.1.3; see also Tex. Loc. R. 8th Ct. App. 38.1(b), requiring use of Bluebook or Texas Rules of Form, Tex. Loc. R. 10th Ct. App. 13(b), concerning citation of cases, Tex. Loc. R. 13th Ct. App. IV, which does not require parallel Texas Report citations, and Texas Rules of Form (Texas Law Review Ass'n ed., 10th ed. 2003), which requires a parallel citation and which may

---

In citing cases in law review footnotes, abbreviate any word listed in table T.6; the names of "states, countries, and other geographical units" unless they are named parties; and any other words of eight or more letters "if substantial space is thereby saved and the result is unambiguous." Bluebook rule 10.2.2. On the other hand, in citing cases in text, abbreviate only widely known acronyms and the following words: "&," "Ass'n," "Bros.," "Co.," "Corp.," "Inc.," "Ltd.," and "No." Bluebook rule 10.2.1(c).

be obtained from the Texas Law Review Business Office.

–In documents submitted to Texas state courts, identify the particular court of appeals:

–Houston [1st Dist.] (formerly Galveston until June 1957), Fort Worth, Austin, San Antonio, Dallas, Texarkana, Amarillo, El Paso, Beaumont, Waco, Eastland, Tyler, Corpus Christi and Houston [14th Dist.].

In addition, Texas state courts also require writ history (for civil cases before September 1, 1997) or petition history (for civil cases on or after September 1, 1997, and for criminal cases), as follows:

–For civil cases before September 1, 1997:

(1) no writ; (2) writ dism'd by agr; (3) writ dism'd; (4) writ dism'd w.o.j. [writ dismissed for want of jurisdiction]; (5) writ dism'd judgm't cor. [writ dismissed, judgment correct]; (6) writ ref'd w.o.m. [writ refused for want of merit]; (7) writ ref'd n.r.e. [writ refused, no reversible error]; (8) writ denied; (9) writ ref'd; (10) writ granted w.r.m. [writ granted without reference to the merits]; (11) writ granted.

–For civil cases on or after September 1, 1997:

(1) no pet. h. [no petition history]; (2) no pet.; (3) pet. filed; (4) pet. dism'd by agr.; (5) pet. withdrawn; (6) pet. dism'd w.o.j. [petition dismissed for want of jurisdiction]; (7) pet. denied; (8) pet. ref'd [petition refused]; (9) pet. struck; (10) pet. dism'd; (11) pet. granted, judgm't vacated w.r.m. [petition granted, judgment vacated without reference to the merits]; (12) pet. granted; (13) pet. abated.

–For criminal cases:

(1) no pet. h. [no petition history]; (2) no pet.; (3) pet. filed; (4) pet. dism'd; (5) pet. ref'd, untimely filed; (6)pet. ref'd [petition refused]; (7) pet. granted; (8) rev. granted, without pet. [review granted, without petititon].

See Texas Rules of Form (Texas Law Review Ass'n ed., 10th ed. 2003).

–In documents submitted to Texas state courts, cite as follows:

Tate v. State Bar, 920 S.W.2d 727(Tex. App. - Houston [1st Dist.] 1996, writ denied). –Case citation.

Tate v. State Bar, 920 S.W.2d 727, 728 (Tex. App. - Houston [1st Dist.] 1996, writ denied). –Page citation.

Johnson v. State, 919 S.W.2d 473 (Tex. App. - Fort Worth 1996, pet. ref'd). –Case Citation.

Johnson v. State, 919 S.W.2d 473, 480 (Tex. App. - Fort Worth 1996, pet. ref'd). –Page Citation.

In law review footnotes, the titles of books and the names of cases, except for procedural phrases, are not underlined. See Bluebook rule 2.1(a) & (b). Further, the following are in large and small capitals: codes, restatements, standards, constitutions, periodicals, authors of books, titles of books, the abbreviated names of codes, most legislative materials except for bills and resolutions, codified ordinances, model codes, court rules, and sentencing guidelines. Refer to The Bluebook.

Brightwell v. Rabeck, 430 S.W.2d 252 (Tex. Civ. App. - Fort
Worth 1968, writ ref'd n.r.e.). –Case Citation.

Brightwell v. Rabeck, 430 S.W.2d 252, 255 (Tex. Civ. App. - Fort
Worth 1968, writ ref'd n.r.e.). –Page Citation.

Outlaw v. Mayor, 999 S.W.2d 252 (Tex. App.-Waco 1999, no pet.)
–Case Citation.

Outlaw v. Mayor, 999 S.W.2d 252, 254 (Tex. App.-Waco 1999, no
pet.) –Page Citation.

–In all other documents, cite as follows:

Tate v. State Bar, 920 S.W.2d 727 (Tex. App. 1996) –Case
Citation.

Tate v. State Bar, 920 S.W.2d 727, 728 (Tex. App. 1996) –Page
Citation.

Johnson v. State, 919 S.W.2d 473 (Tex. App. 1996) –Case
Citation.

Johnson v. State, 919 S.W.2d 473, 480 (Tex. App. 1996) –Page
Citation.

Brightwell v. Rabeck, 430 S.W.2d 252 (Tex. Civ. App. 1968)
–Case Citation.

Brightwell v. Rabeck, 430 S.W.2d 252, 254 (Tex. Civ. App. 1968)
–Page Citation.

Outlaw v. Mayor, 999 S.W.2d 252 (Tex. App. 1999) –Case
Citation.

Outlaw v. Mayor, 999 S.W.2d 252, 254 (Tex. App.1999) –Page
Citation.

Texas Digest of Opinions of the Attorney General
See Opinions of the Attorney General of Texas.

Texas International Law Journal
Ab.:   Tex. Int'l L.J.

Texas Law Review
Ab.:   Tex. L. Rev.

Ex.:   Alex W. Albright, The Texas Discovery Privileges: A Fool's Game?,
70 Tex. L. Rev. 781 (1992). –Article Citation.

Alex W. Albright, The Texas Discovery Privileges: A Fool's Game?,
70 Tex. L. Rev. 781, 833-35 (1992). –Page Citation.

Texas Register
Ab.:   vol. no. Tex. Reg. page no. (month day, year)

In citing cases in law review footnotes, abbreviate any word listed in table T.6;
the names of "states, countries, and other geographical units" unless they are named parties;
and any other words of eight or more letters "if substantial space is thereby saved and the
result is unambiguous." Bluebook rule 10.2.2. On the other hand, in citing cases in text,
abbreviate only widely known acronyms and the following words: "&," "Ass'n," "Bros.,"
"Co.," "Corp.," "Inc.," "Ltd.," and "No." Bluebook rule 10.2.1(c).

Ex.:   29 Tex. Reg. 1479 (Feb. 20, 2004).

Texas Review of Law and Politics
Ab: Tex. Rev. L. & Pol.

Ex: Greg Abbott, <u>Acknowledgement Without Endorsement: Defending the Ten Commandments</u>, 9 Tex. Rev. L. & Pol. 229 (2005). –Article Citation.

Greg Abbott, <u>Acknowledgement Without Endorsement: Defending the Ten Commandments</u>, 9 Tex. Rev. L. & Pol. 229, 245-46 (2005). –Page Citation.

Texas Revised Civil Statutes Annotated
See Vernon's Texas Revised Civil Statutes Annotated.

Texas Session Laws
See General and Special Laws of the State of Texas and Vernon's Texas Session Law Service (West).

Texas Supreme Court
Ab.:   Tex.

Ex.:   –Cite to S.W., S.W.2d, or S.W.3d, if therein; otherwise, cite to Tex.

–Give parallel citations only in documents submitted to Texas state courts. <u>See</u> <u>Bluebook</u> rules 10.3.1 and B5.1.3; see also Tex. Loc. R. 8th Ct. App. 38.1(b), requiring use of <u>Bluebook</u> or <u>Texas Rules of Form</u>, Tex. Loc. R. 10th Ct. App. 13(b), concerning citation of cases, Tex. Loc. R. 13th Ct. App. IV, which does not require parallel Texas Report citations; see also <u>Texas Rules of Form</u> (Texas Law Review Ass'n ed., 10th ed. 2003), which requires a parallel citation and which may be obtained from the Texas Law Review Business Office.

–Through 163 Tex. 638 (1962), cite as follows:

In documents submitted to Texas state courts:

<u>Gleich v. Bongio</u>, 128 Tex. 606, 99 S.W.2d 881 (1937). –Case Citation.

<u>Gleich v. Bongio</u>, 128 Tex. 606, 611-12, 99 S.W.2d 881, 884 (1937). –Page Citation.

In all other documents:

<u>Gleich v. Bongio</u>, 99 S.W.2d 881 (Tex. 1937). –Case Citation.

<u>Gleich v. Bongio</u>, 99 S.W.2d 881, 884 (Tex. 1937). –Page Citation.

–After 163 Tex. 638 (1962), cite as follows:

In all documents:

<u>Felts v. Harris County</u>, 915 S.W.2d 482 (Tex. 1996). –Case Citation.

In law review footnotes, the titles of books and the names of cases, except for procedural phrases, are not underlined. <u>See</u> <u>Bluebook</u> rule 2.1(a) & (b). Further, the following are in large and small capitals: codes, restatements, standards, constitutions, periodicals, authors of books, titles of books, the abbreviated names of codes, most legislative materials except for bills and resolutions, codified ordinances, model codes, court rules, and sentencing guidelines. Refer to <u>The Bluebook</u>.

Felts v. Harris County, 915 S.W.2d 482, 483 (Tex. 1996). –Page
Citation.

Texas Tech Law Review

Ab.:   Tex. Tech L. Rev.

Ex.:   George Anastaplo, <u>The Constitution at Two Hundred: Explorations</u>,
22 Tex. Tech L. Rev. 967 (1991). –Article Citation.

George Anastaplo, <u>The Constitution at Two Hundred: Explorations</u>,
22 Tex. Tech L. Rev. 967, 969-75 (1991). –Page Citation.

Texas Wesleyan Law Review

Ab: Tex. Wesleyan L. Rev.

Ex: Sarah Sargent, <u>Suspended Animation: The Implementation of the Hague
Convention on Intercountry Adoption in the United States and Romania</u>, 10
Tex. Wesleyan L. Rev. 351 (2004). –Article Citation.

Sarah Sargent, <u>Suspended Animation: The Implementation of the Hague
Convention on Intercountry Adoption in the United States and Romania</u>, 10
Tex. Wesleyan L. Rev. 351, 375 (2004). –Page Citation.

Third World Legal Studies

Ab.:   Third World Legal Stud.

Ex.:   Beverly M. Carl, <u>Peanuts, Law Professors and Third World Lawyers</u>,
1986 Third World Legal Stud. 1. –Article Citation.

Beverly M. Carl, <u>Peanuts, Law Professors and Third World Lawyers</u>,
1986 Third World Legal Stud. 1, 8-9. –Page Citation.

Thomas Jefferson Law Review

Ab: T. Jefferson L. Rev.

Ex: Daniel F. Tritter, <u>In the Defense of Fred Korematsu, Vox Clamantis In
Deserto Curiarum</u>, 27 T. Jefferson L. Rev. 255 (2005). –Article
Citation.

Daniel F. Tritter, <u>In the Defense of Fred Korematsu, Vox Clamantis In
Deserto Curiarum</u>, 27 T. Jefferson L. Rev. 255, 290-92 (2005).
–Page Citation.

Thomas M. Cooley Law Review

Ab.:   T.M. Cooley L. Rev.

Ex.:   Joseph Kimble, <u>Plain English: A Charter for Clear Writing</u>, 9 T.M.
Cooley L. Rev. 1 (1992). –Article Citation.

Joseph Kimble, <u>Plain English: A Charter for Clear Writing</u>, 9 T.M.
Cooley L. Rev. 1, 25-26 (1992). –Page Citation.

Thurgood Marshall Law Review

Ab.:   T. Marshall L. Rev.

In citing cases in law review footnotes, abbreviate any word listed in table T.6;
the names of "states, countries, and other geographical units" unless they are named parties;
and any other words of eight or more letters "if <u>substantial</u> space is thereby saved and the
result is unambiguous." <u>Bluebook</u> rule 10.2.2. On the other hand, in citing cases in text,
abbreviate only widely known acronyms and the following words: "&," "Ass'n," "Bros.,"
"Co.," "Corp.," "Inc.," "Ltd.," and "No." <u>Bluebook</u> rule 10.2.1(c).

Ex.:　　Placido G. Gomez, <u>White People Think Differently</u>, 16 T. Marshall L. Rev. 543 (1991). –Article Citation.

　　　　Placido G. Gomez, <u>White People Think Differently</u>, 16 T. Marshall L. Rev. 543, 543-44 (1991). –Page Citation.

Times Law Reports, The (England) (1884-1952)
See <u>Bluebook</u> table T.2.

Ab.:　　T.L.R.

Ex.:　　<u>Beck v. Newbold</u>, [1952] 2 T.L.R. 332 (C.A.) (Eng.). –Case Citation.

title(s)
Ab.:　　tit., tits.

Title News
Ab.:　　Title News

Ex.:　　Burton J. Rain, <u>The Changing Partnership</u>, Title News, Dec. 1989, at 5. –Article Citation.

　　　　Burton J. Rain, <u>The Changing Partnership</u>, Title News, Dec. 1989, at 5, 6. –Page Citation.

Tort & Insurance Law Journal
Ab.:　　Tort & Ins. L.J.

Ex.:　　James M. Fischer, <u>Enforcement of Settlements: A Survey</u>, 27 Tort & Ins. L.J. 82 (1991). –Article Citation.

　　　　James M. Fischer, <u>Enforcement of Settlements: A Survey</u>, 27 Tort & Ins. L.J. 82, 98-99 (1991). –Page Citation.

Tort Trial & Insurance Practice Law Journal
Ab:　　Tort Trial & Ins. Prac. L.J.

Ex:　　Gregory J. May, <u>Successors' Rights to Insurance Coverage for Predecessors' Preacquisitions Activities: Recent Developments</u>, 40 Tort Trial & Ins. Prac. L.J. 911 (2005). –Article Citation.

　　　　Gregory J. May, <u>Successors' Rights to Insurance Coverage for Predecessors' Preacquisitions Activities: Recent Developments</u>, 40 Tort Trial & Ins. Prac. L.J. 911, 930-31 (2005). –Page Citation.

Touro Journal of Transnational Law
Ab.:　　Touro J. Transnat'l L.

Ex.:　　Yoram Dinstein, <u>The Parameters and Content of International Criminal Law</u>, 1 Touro J. Transnat'l L. 315 (1990). –Article Citation.

　　　　Yoram Dinstein, <u>The Parameters and Content of International Criminal Law</u>, 1 Touro J. Transnat'l L. 315, 332-34 (1990). –Page Citation.

Touro Law Review
Ab.:　　Touro L. Rev.

In law review footnotes, the titles of books and the names of cases, except for procedural phrases, are not underlined. <u>See</u> <u>Bluebook</u> rule 2.1(a) & (b). Further, the following are in large and small capitals: codes, restatements, standards, constitutions, periodicals, authors of books, titles of books, the abbreviated names of codes, most legislative materials except for bills and resolutions, codified ordinances, model codes, court rules, and sentencing guidelines. Refer to <u>The Bluebook</u>.

Ex.: William M. Brooks, <u>A Comparison of a Mentally Ill Individual's Right to Refuse Medication Under the United States and the New York State Constitutions</u>, 8 Touro L. Rev. 1 (1991). –Article Citation.

William M. Brooks, <u>A Comparison of a Mentally Ill Individual's Right to Refuse Medication Under the United States and the New York State Constitutions</u>, 8 Touro L. Rev. 1, 45-46 (1991). –Page Citation.

Trade Regulation Reporter (Commerce Clearing House)
–Bound as Trade Cases (Commerce Clearing House)

Ab.: Trade Reg. Rep. (CCH)

Ex.: <u>United States v. Motorola, Inc.</u>, 7 Trade Reg. Rep. (CCH) (1996-1 Trade Cas.) ¶ 71,402 (D.D.C. July 25, 1995). –Citation to looseleaf material.

<u>Florida Seed Co. v. Monsanto Co.</u>, 1995-2 Trade Cas. (CCH) ¶ 71,240 (N.D. Ala. 1995). –Citation to bound material.

–The above examples are proper if the case is not yet available in, or is not reported in, an official or West reporter, a public domain citation, or in a widely used computer database.

Trademark Protection and Practice, by Jerome Gilson & Jeffrey M. Samuels
–Do not abbreviate the title.

Ex.: Jerome Gilson & Jeffrey M. Samuels, <u>Trademark Protection and Practice</u> 400 (1997). –Page Citation.

Trademark Reporter, The
Ab.: Trademark Rep.

Ex.: J. Joseph Bainton, <u>Reflections on the Trademark Counterfeiting Act of 1984: Score a Few for the Good Guys</u>, 82 Trademark Rep. 1 (1992). –Article Citation.

J. Joseph Bainton, <u>Reflections on the Trademark Counterfeiting Act of 1984: Score a Few for the Good Guys</u>, 82 Trademark Rep. 1, 4-5 (1992). –Page Citation.

translation
Ab.: trans.

translator
Ab.: trans.

Transnational Law & Contemporary Problems
Ab.: Transnat'l L. & Contemp. Probs.

In citing cases in law review footnotes, abbreviate any word listed in table T.6; the names of "states, countries, and other geographical units" unless they are named parties; and any other words of eight or more letters "if <u>substantial</u> space is thereby saved and the result is unambiguous." <u>Bluebook</u> rule 10.2.2. On the other hand, in citing cases in text, abbreviate only widely known acronyms and the following words: "&," "Ass'n," "Bros.," "Co.," "Corp.," "Inc.," "Ltd.," and "No." <u>Bluebook</u> rule 10.2.1(c).

Ex.:   Richard A. Falk, <u>Making Foreign Policy Lawful: A Citizen's</u>
<u>Imperative</u>, 1 Transnat'l L. & Contemp. Probs. 225 (1991). –Article
Citation.

Richard A. Falk, <u>Making Foreign Policy Lawful: A Citizen's</u>
<u>Imperative</u>, 1 Transnat'l L. & Contemp. Probs. 225, 230-31 (1991).
–Page Citation.

Transnational Lawyer, The
Ab.:   Transnat'l Law.

Ex.:   Medim P. Vogt, <u>Defensive Measures Against Public Offers Under</u>
<u>Swiss Law</u>, 4 Transnat'l Law. 53 (1991). –Article Citation.

Medim P. Vogt, <u>Defensive Measures Against Public Offers Under</u>
<u>Swiss Law</u>, 4 Transnat'l Law. 53, 69-73 (1991). –Page Citation.

Transportation Journal
Ab.:   Transp. J.

Ex.:   Terence A. Brown, <u>Property Brokers: A Pilot Study of Shippers</u>
<u>Perspectives</u>, Transp. J., Fall 1991, at 45. –Article Citation.

Terence A. Brown, <u>Property Brokers: A Pilot Study of Shippers</u>
<u>Perspectives</u>, Transp. J., Fall 1991, at 45, 47. –Page Citation.

Transportation Law Journal
Ab.:   Transp. L.J.

Ex.:   Melanie B. Daly, <u>America - On the Road to Mass Transit</u>, 19 Transp.
L.J. 357 (1991). –Article Citation.

Melanie B. Daly, <u>America - On the Road to Mass Transit</u>, 19 Transp.
L.J. 357, 369-75 (1991). –Page Citation.

Transportation Practitioners Journal
Ab.:   Transp. Prac. J.

Ex.:   William B. Tye & A. Lawrence Kolbe, <u>Optimal Time Structures for</u>
<u>Rates in Regulated Industries</u>, 59 Transp. Prac. J. 176 (1992). –Article
Citation.

William B. Tye & A. Lawrence Kolbe, <u>Optimal Time Structures for</u>
<u>Rates in Regulated Industries</u>, 59 Transp. Prac. J. 176, 179 (1992).
–Page Citation.

Treasury Decision as published in Internal Revenue Bulletin and Cumulative Bulletin
Ab.:   T.D.

Ex.:   T.D. 8323, 1991-1 C.B. 199. –Citation to bound cases.

T.D. 8414, 1992-93 I.R.B. 18. –Citation to unbound cases.

Treasury Decisions Under Internal Revenue Laws (1898-1942)
Ab.:   Treas. Dec. Int. Rev.

In law review footnotes, the titles of books and the names of cases, except for procedural
phrases, are not underlined. <u>See</u> <u>Bluebook</u> rule 2.1(a) & (b). Further, the following are in
large and small capitals: codes, restatements, standards, constitutions, periodicals, authors of
books, titles of books, the abbreviated names of codes, most legislative materials except for
bills and resolutions, codified ordinances, model codes, court rules, and sentencing guidelines.
Refer to <u>The Bluebook</u>.

    Ex.:   T.D. 5072, 36 Treas. Dec. Int. Rev. 265 (1941).

                T.D. 20,459, 1 Treas. Dec. Int. Rev. 7 (1898).

Treasury Delegation Orders
    Ab.:   I.R.S. Deleg. Order

    Ex.:   I.R.S. Deleg. Order No. 213, 1985-46 I.R.B. 35. –Unbound

                I.R.S. Deleg. Order No. 11 (Rev. 15), 1985-1 C.B. 423. –Bound

Treasury Department Orders
    Ab.:   Treas. Dep't Order

    Ex.:   Treas. Dep't Order 150-02, 1986-19 I.R.B. 12. –Unbound.

                Treas. Dep't Order 150-106, 1985 C.B. 758. –Bound.

Treasury Regulations (Federal)
    Ab.:   Treas. Reg. § (year)

    Ex.:   Treas. Reg. § 1.401(m)-1 (1991). –Unamended regulation.

                Treas. Reg. § 1.401(m)-1 (as amended in 1995). –Amended regulation.

See Bluebook rule 14.5.1

treaties (specific treaties)
    Ex.:   Definitive Treaty of Peace, U.S.-Gr. Brit., Sept. 3, 1783, 8 Stat. 80, T.S. No. 104.

                Treaty of Ghent, U.S.-Gr. Brit., Dec. 24, 1814, 8 Stat. 218, T.S. No. 109. –Citation to a treaty with a widely known popular name.

                Treaty of Ghent, U.S.-Gr. Brit., Dec. 24, 1814, art. 10, at 7. –Citation to a subdivision of a treaty.

                Moscow Agreement, U.S.-U.K.-U.S.S.R., May 1, 1945, 60 Stat. 1899, T.I.A.S. No. 1555. –Citation to a treaty with three or more parties.

                Convention Respecting Sanitary Aerial Navigation, opened for signature Dec. 15, 1944, 59 Stat. 991, T.S No. 992. –Citation to multilateral treaty which is not signed on a single date.

                Instrument for the Amendment of the Constitution of the International Labor Organization, Apr. 20, 1948, 62 Stat. 3485, T.I.A.S. No. 1868, 15 U.N.T.S. 35. –Agreement among three or more parties to which the United States is a party.

                Constitution of the United Nations Educational, Scientific and Cultural Organization, Nov. 16, 1945, 4 U.N.T.S. 275. –Agreement among three or more parties to which the United States is not a party. If only two parties, give their names.

See generally Bluebook rule 21.4.

Treaties and Other International Acts Series (U.S.)
    Ab.:   T.I.A.S. No.

In citing cases in law review footnotes, abbreviate any word listed in table T.6; the names of "states, countries, and other geographical units" unless they are named parties; and any other words of eight or more letters "if substantial space is thereby saved and the result is unambiguous." Bluebook rule 10.2.2. On the other hand, in citing cases in text, abbreviate only widely known acronyms and the following words: "&," "Ass'n," "Bros.," "Co.," "Corp.," "Inc.," "Ltd.," and "No." Bluebook rule 10.2.1(c).

Ex.:   Security of Military Information, U.S.-Ecuador, at 2, July 12, 1985, T.I.A.S. No. 11,257. –Example of treaty between United States and one other country.

Ex.:   General Agreement on Tariffs and Trade, art. III, Oct. 30, 1947, 61 Stat. A-11, T.I.A.S. no. 1700. –Example of treaty among four or more parties, including the United States.

–Give U.S.T. or Stat. citation, if available. See Bluebook rule 21.4.5(a).

Treatise on Constitutional Law, by Ronald D. Rotunda & John E. Nowak
–Do not abbreviate the title.

Ex.:   3 Ronald D. Rotunda & John E. Nowak, Treatise on Constitutional Law § 18.3 (3d ed. 1999). –Section Citation.

3 Ronald D. Rotunda & John E. Nowak, Treatise on Constitutional Law § 18.3, at 253 (3d ed. 1999). –Page Citation.

3 Ronald D. Rotunda & John E. Nowak, Treatise on Constitutional Law § 18.3, at 253 n.104 (3d ed. 1999). –Footnote Citation.

Treatise on Environmental Law, by Frank P. Grad
–Do not abbreviate the title.

Ex.:   2 Frank P. Grad, Treatise on Environmental Law § 9.01[c] (1990). –Section Citation.

2 Frank P. Grad, Treatise on Environmental Law § 9.01[c], at 9-22 (1990). –Page Citation.

2 Frank P. Grad, Treatise on Environmental Law § 9.01[c], at 9-22 n.47 (1990). –Footnote Citation.

Treatise on the Law of Contracts, by Samuel Williston
–Do not abbreviate the title.

Ex.:   8 Samuel Williston, Treatise on the Law of Contracts § 949C (Walter H. Jaeger ed., 3d ed. 1964). –Section Citation to Third Edition.

8 Samuel Williston, Treatise on the Law of Contracts § 949C, at 175 (Walter H. Jaeger ed., 3d ed. 1964). –Page Citation to Third Edition.

8 Samuel Williston, Treatise on the Law of Contracts § 949C, at 175 n.8 (Walter H. Jaeger ed., 3d ed. 1964). –Footnote Citation to Third Edition.

3 Samuel Williston, Treatise on the Law of Contracts § 7.24 (Richard A. Lord ed., 4th ed. 1992). –Section Citation to Fourth Edition.

3 Samuel Williston, Treatise on the Law of Contracts § 7.24, at 449 (Richard A. Lord ed., 4th ed. 1992). –Page Citation to Fourth Edition.

3 Samuel Williston, Treatise on the Law of Contracts § 7.24, at 449 n.13 (Richard A. Lord ed., 4th ed. 1992). –Footnote Citation to Fourth Edition.

In law review footnotes, the titles of books and the names of cases, except for procedural phrases, are not underlined. See Bluebook rule 2.1(a) & (b). Further, the following are in large and small capitals: codes, restatements, standards, constitutions, periodicals, authors of books, titles of books, the abbreviated names of codes, most legislative materials except for bills and resolutions, codified ordinances, model codes, court rules, and sentencing guidelines. Refer to The Bluebook.

Treatise on the Law of Securities Regulation, by Thomas L. Hazen
  –Do not abbreviate the title.
  Ex.:   4 Thomas L. Hazen, Treatise on the Law of Securities Regulation
          § 14.6 (5th Practitioner's ed. 2005). –Section Citation.
          4 Thomas L. Hazen, Treatise on the Law of Securities Regulation
          § 14.6[1], at 221 (5th Practitioner's ed. 2005). –Page Citation.
          4 Thomas L. Hazen, Treatise on the Law of Securities Regulation
          § 14.6[1], at 221 n.54 (5th Practitioner's ed. 2005). –Footnote Citation.

treatises
  Ex.:   5A A. James Corbin, Corbin on Contracts § 1157 (1964).
          A. James Casner, Estate Planning § 6.8.10 (5th ed. Supp. 1987).
          See also author(s).

Treaty Series (U.S.)
  Ab.:   T.S. No.
  Ex.:   Definitive Treaty of Peace, U.S.-Gr. Brit., Sept. 3, 1783, 8 Stat. 80,
          T.S. No. 104. –Agreement between United States and Great Britain.
          Montevideo Convention on the Rights and Duties of States, art. 1, Dec.
          26, 1933, T.S. No. 881, 165 L.N.T.S. 18. –Example of multilateral
          agreement.
          See Bluebook rule 21.4.5.

Treaty Sources
  See Bluebook rule 21.4.5 and table T.4.

Trent Law Journal
  Ab.:   Trent L.J.
  Ex.:   Peter Jones, Equal Pay, 11 Trent L.J. 37 (1987). –Article Citation.
          Peter Jones, Equal Pay, 11 Trent L.J. 37, 38-39 (1987). –Page Citation.

Trial
  Ab.:   Trial
  Ex.:   Alba Conte, Class Action: Remedy for the Hostile Environment, Trial,
          July 1992, at 18. –Article Citation.
          Alba Conte, Class Action: Remedy for the Hostile Environment, Trial,
          July 1992, at 18, 23. –Page Citation.

Trial Lawyer's Guide, The
  Ab.:   Trial Law. Guide
  Ex.:   Angel L. Rodriguez, Attorney's Fees in Class Actions, 35 Trial Law.
          Guide 76 (1991). –Article Citation.
          Angel L. Rodriguez, Attorney's Fees in Class Actions, 35 Trial Law.
          Guide 76, 79-83 (1991). –Page Citation.

In citing cases in law review footnotes, abbreviate any word listed in table T.6;
the names of "states, countries, and other geographical units" unless they are named parties;
and any other words of eight or more letters "if substantial space is thereby saved and the
result is unambiguous." Bluebook rule 10.2.2. On the other hand, in citing cases in text,
abbreviate only widely known acronyms and the following words: "&," "Ass'n," "Bros.,"
"Co.," "Corp.," "Inc.," "Ltd.," and "No." Bluebook rule 10.2.1(c).

Trial Lawyers Quarterly
  Ab.:   Trial Law. Q.
  Ex.:   Michael P. Koskoff, <u>Forum Non Conveniens</u>, Trial Law. Q., Fall 1991,
           at 15. –Article Citation.

           Michael P. Koskoff, <u>Forum Non Conveniens</u>, Trial Law. Q., Fall 1991,
           at 15, 19-20. –Page Citation.

Trial Transcript, citation to
  Ab.:   Trial Tr.

  Ex.:   (Trial Tr. vol. 1, 10-15, May 1, 2005).

  See <u>Bluebook</u> rule B10 and table BT.1.

  Note: See <u>Bluebook</u> rule 10.8.3 for citing litigation materials from another case.

Tribe on American Constitutional Law
  See American Constitutional Law, by Laurence H. Tribe.

Tribunax Arbitraux Mixtes
  Ab.:   Trib. Arb. Mixtes

Tribute (article designation)

  Ex.:   Tribute, <u>Dean John W. Wade</u>, 48 Vand. L. Rev. 571 (1995).
  See <u>Bluebook</u> rule 16.6.4.

Trusts and Estates
  Ab.:   Tr. & Est.
  Ex.:   Judith McCue, <u>The States Are Acting to Reform Their Guardianship
           Statutes</u>, Tr. & Est., July 1992, at 32. –Article Citation.

           Judith McCue, <u>The States Are Acting to Reform Their Guardianship
           Statutes</u>, Tr. & Est., July 1992, at 32, 37. –Page Citation.

Tulane Environmental Law Journal
  Ab.:   Tul. Envtl. L.J.
  Ex.:   Anthony R. Chase, <u>The Lender Liability Paradox: A Fresh Approach</u>,
           5 Tul. Envtl. L.J. 1 (1991). –Article Citation.

           Anthony R. Chase, <u>The Lender Liability Paradox: A Fresh Approach</u>,
           5 Tul. Envtl. L.J. 1, 10-11 (1991). –Page Citation.

Tulane Law Review
  Ab.:   Tul. L. Rev.
  Ex.:   Jonathan R. Cohen, <u>The Immorality of Denial</u>, 79 Tul. L. Rev. 903
           (2005). –Article Citation.

           Jonathan R. Cohen, <u>The Immorality of Denial</u>, 79 Tul. L. Rev. 903,
           945-46 (2005). –Page Citation.

In law review footnotes, the titles of books and the names of cases, except for procedural
phrases, are not underlined. <u>See</u> <u>Bluebook</u> rule 2.1(a) & (b). Further, the following are in
large and small capitals: codes, restatements, standards, constitutions, periodicals, authors of
books, titles of books, the abbreviated names of codes, most legislative materials except for
bills and resolutions, codified ordinances, model codes, court rules, and sentencing guidelines.
Refer to <u>The Bluebook</u>.

Tulane Maritime Law Journal

Ab.: Tul. Mar. L.J.

Ex.: Geoffrey Brice, <u>Unexplained Losses in Maritime Insurance</u>, 16 Tul. Mar. L.J. 105 (1991). –Article Citation.

Geoffrey Brice, <u>Unexplained Losses in Maritime Insurance</u>, 16 Tul. Mar. L.J. 105, 110-111 (1991). –Page Citation.

Tulsa Law Review

Ab: Tulsa L. Rev.

Ex: Phyllis G. Bossin, <u>Same-Sex Unions: The New Civil Rights Struggle or an Assault on Traditional Marriage?</u>, 40 Tulsa L. Rev. 381 (2005). –Article Citation.

Phyllis G. Bossin, <u>Same-Sex Unions: The New Civil Rights Struggle or an Assault on Traditional Marriage?</u>, 40 Tulsa L. Rev. 381 (2005). –Page Citation.

typeface conventions for briefs

See <u>Bluebook</u> rules B13 and 7. See also the examples on the facing pages on the inside back cover of <u>The Bluebook</u>.

typeface conventions for law review footnotes

See <u>Bluebook</u> rules 2.1 and 7. See also the examples on the facing pages on the inside front cover of <u>The Bluebook</u>.

typeface conventions for law review texts

See <u>Bluebook</u> rules 2.2. and 7.

typeface conventions for legal memoranda

See <u>Bluebook</u> rules B13 and 7. See also the examples on the facing pages on the inside back cover of <u>The Bluebook</u>.

In citing cases in law review footnotes, abbreviate any word listed in table T.6; the names of "states, countries, and other geographical units" unless they are named parties; and any other words of eight or more letters "if <u>substantial</u> space is thereby saved and the result is unambiguous." <u>Bluebook</u> rule 10.2.2. On the other hand, in citing cases in text, abbreviate only widely known acronyms and the following words: "&," "Ass'n," "Bros.," "Co.," "Corp.," "Inc.," "Ltd.," and "No." <u>Bluebook</u> rule 10.2.1(c).

U

U.C. Davis Law Review
Ab.: U.C. Davis L. Rev.

Ex.: Elyn R. Saks, <u>Multiple Personality Disorder and Criminal Responsibility</u>, 25 U.C. Davis L. Rev. 383 (1992). –Article Citation.

Elyn R. Saks, <u>Multiple Personality Disorder and Criminal Responsibility</u>, 25 U.C. Davis L. Rev. 383, 385-87 (1992). –Page Citation.

UCLA Journal of Environmental Law and Policy
Ab.: UCLA J. Envtl. L. & Pol'y

Ex.: Linda A. Malone, <u>The Necessary Interrelationship Between Land Use and Preservation of Groundwater Resources</u>, 9 UCLA J. Env't L. & Pol'y 1 (1990). –Article Citation.

Linda A. Malone, <u>The Necessary Interrelationship Between Land Use and Preservation of Groundwater Resources</u>, 9 UCLA J. Env't L. & Pol'y 1, 55-67 (1990). –Page Citation.

UCLA Journal of International Law and Foreign Affairs
Ab: UCLA J. Int'l L. & Foreign Aff.

Ex: Connie de la Vega, <u>Human Rights and Trade: Inconsistent Application of Treaty Law in the United States</u>, 9 UCLA J. Int'l L. & Foreign Aff. 1 (2004). –Article Citation.

Connie de la Vega, <u>Human Rights and Trade: Inconsistent Application of Treaty Law in the United States</u>, 9 UCLA J. Int'l L. & Foreign Aff. 1, 23-24 (2004). –Page Citation.

UCLA Law Review
Ab.: UCLA L. Rev.

Ex.: Marc M. Arkin, <u>Rethinking the Constitutional Right to a Criminal Appeal</u>, 39 UCLA L. Rev. 503 (1992). –Article Citation.

Marc M. Arkin, <u>Rethinking the Constitutional Right to a Criminal Appeal</u>, 39 UCLA L. Rev. 503, 505 (1992). –Page Citation.

UCLA Pacific Basin Law Journal
Ab.: UCLA Pac. Basin L.J.

In law review footnotes, the titles of books and the names of cases, except for procedural phrases, are not underlined. <u>See</u> Bluebook rule 2.1(a) & (b). Further, the following are in large and small capitals: codes, restatements, standards, constitutions, periodicals, authors of books, titles of books, the abbreviated names of codes, most legislative materials except for bills and resolutions, codified ordinances, model codes, court rules, and sentencing guidelines. Refer to <u>The Bluebook</u>.

Ex.: Edward G. Eurney, <u>Protection of Computer Programs Under Japanese Copyright Law</u>, 9 UCLA Pac. Basin L.J. 1 (1991). –Article Citation.

Edward G. Eurney, <u>Protection of Computer Programs Under Japanese Copyright Law</u>, 9 UCLA Pac. Basin L.J. 1, 11-12 (1991). –Page Citation.

UMKC Law Review
Ab.: UMKC L. Rev.

Ex.: Robert J. Gregory, <u>The Clearly Expressed Intent and the Doctrine of Congressional Acquiescence</u>, 60 UMKC L. Rev. 27 (1991). –Article Citation.

Robert J. Gregory, <u>The Clearly Expressed Intent and the Doctrine of Congressional Acquiescence</u>, 60 UMKC L. Rev. 27, 55-61 (1991). –Page Citation.

Unemployment Insurance Reports (Commerce Clearing House)
Ab.: Unempl. Ins. Rep. (CCH)

uniform acts
Ex.: U.C.C. § 9-312(5)(b) (1994).

Unif. P'ship Act § 103 (1994).

Unif. Common Interest Ownership Act § 1-104 (1994).

Unif. Probate Code § 6-107 (1989).

Unif. R. of Crim. P. 432 (amended 1991).

<u>See</u> <u>Bluebook</u> rule 12.8.4.

Uniform Commercial Code
Ab.: U.C.C. § (year U.C.C. last amended)

Ex.: U.C.C. § 9-312(5)(b) (1994).

Uniform Commercial Code, by James J. White and Robert S. Summers
–Do not abbreviate this title.

Ex.: James J. White & Robert S. Summers, <u>Uniform Commercial Code</u> § 9-2 (5th ed. 2000). –Section Citation.

James J. White & Robert S. Summers, <u>Uniform Commercial Code</u> § 9-2, at 343 (5th ed. 2000). –Page Citation.

James J. White & Robert S. Summers, <u>Uniform Commercial Code</u> § 9-2, at 343 n.2 (5th ed. 2000). –Footnote Citation.

Uniform Commercial Code, by Ronald A. Anderson
–Do not abbreviate this title.

Ex.: 9A Ronald A. Anderson, <u>Uniform Commercial Code</u> § 9-504:157 (3d ed. 1994). –Section Citation.

9A Ronald A. Anderson, <u>Uniform Commercial Code</u> § 9-504:157, at 545 (3d ed. 1994). –Page Citation.

In citing cases in law review footnotes, abbreviate any word listed in table T.6; the names of "states, countries, and other geographical units" unless they are named parties; and any other words of eight or more letters "if <u>substantial</u> space is thereby saved and the result is unambiguous." <u>Bluebook</u> rule 10.2.2. On the other hand, in citing cases in text, abbreviate only widely known acronyms and the following words: "&," "Ass'n," "Bros.," "Co.," "Corp.," "Inc.," "Ltd.," and "No." <u>Bluebook</u> rule 10.2.1(c).

9A Ronald A. Anderson, <u>Uniform Commercial Code</u> § 9-504:157, at 545 n.1064 (3d ed. 1994). –Footnote Citation.

9A Ronald A. Anderson, <u>Uniform Commercial Code</u> § 9-504:157 (3d ed. Supp. 1996). –Section Citation to Supplement.

Uniform Commercial Code Law Journal
Ab.: UCC L.J.

Ex.: John M. Norwood, <u>Punitive Damages for Wrongful Dishonour of a Check</u>, 64 UCC L.J. 64 (1991). –Article Citation.

John M. Norwood, <u>Punitive Damages for Wrongful Dishonour of a Check</u>, 64 UCC L.J. 64, 69-70 (1991). –Page Citation.

Uniform Commercial Code Reporting Service (CBC)
Ab.: U.C.C. Rep. Serv. (CBC)

Ex.: <u>All Am. Auto Salvage v. Camp's Auto Wreckers</u>, [Current Materials] U.C.C. Rep. Serv. 2d (CBC) (30 U.C.C. Rep. Serv. 2d) 1 (N.J. Super. Aug. 1, 1996). –Citation to looseleaf material.

<u>Kultura, Inc. v. S. Leasing Corp.</u>, 29 U.C.C. Rep. Serv. 2d (CBC) 1046 (Tenn. Mar. 25, 1996). –Citation to bound material.

–The above examples are proper if the case is not yet available in, or is not reported in, an official or West reporter, a public domain citation, or in a widely used computer database.

Uniform Commercial Code Series, by William D. Hawkland
–Do not abbreviate this title.

Ex.: 9 William D. Hawkland et al., <u>Uniform Commercial Code Series</u> § 9-309:1 (2001). –Section Citation.

9 William D. Hawkland et al., <u>Uniform Commercial Code</u> Series § 9-309:1, at 9-333 n.6 (2001). –Footnote Citation.

Uniform Laws Annotated
Ab.: U.L.A.

Ex.: Unif. Partnership Act § 302, 6 U.L.A. 35-36 (1994).

<u>See</u> <u>Bluebook</u> rule 12.8.4.

Union Labor Report
Ab.: Union Lab. Rep. (BNA)

United Kingdom Statutes
Ex.: Channel Tunnel Act, 1987, c. 53, § 2 (Eng.).

<u>See</u> <u>Bluebook</u> rule 20.5.1 and table T.2, p. 320.

United Nations Charter
See Charter of the United Nations.

In law review footnotes, the titles of books and the names of cases, except for procedural phrases, are not underlined. <u>See</u> <u>Bluebook</u> rule 2.1(a) & (b). Further, the following are in large and small capitals: codes, restatements, standards, constitutions, periodicals, authors of books, titles of books, the abbreviated names of codes, most legislative materials except for bills and resolutions, codified ordinances, model codes, court rules, and sentencing guidelines. Refer to <u>The Bluebook</u>.

United Nations Documents
Ab.: U.N. Doc.

See <u>Bluebook</u> rule 21.7.2.

United Nations Juridical Yearbook
Ab.: U.N. Jurid. Y.B.

Ex.: 1991 U.N. Jurid. Y.B. 276, U.N. Doc. ST/LEG/SER.C.29.

See <u>Bluebook</u> rule 21.7.9.

United Nations Official Records:
Economic and Social Council Official Records:

Ab.: U.N. ESCOR

See <u>Bluebook</u> rules 21.7.1, 21.7.2, and table T.3.

General Assembly Official Records:

Ab.: U.N. GAOR

Ex.: G.A. Res. 56/204, ¶ 5, U.N. GAOR, 56th Sess., Supp. No. 49, 90th plen. mtg., U.N. Doc. A/56/49 (2001).

See <u>Bluebook</u> rules 21.7.1, 21.7.2, and table T.3.

Security Council Official Records:

Ab.: U.N. SCOR

Ex.: S.C. Res. 1181, U.N. SCOR, 53d Sess., 3902d mtg., U.N. Doc. S/RES/1181 (1998).

See <u>Bluebook</u> rules 21.7.1, 21.7.2, and table T.3.

Trusteeship Council Official Records:

Ab.: U.N. TCOR

See <u>Bluebook</u> rules 21.7.1, 21.7.2, and table T.3.

Trade and Development Board Official Records:

Ab.: U.N. TDBOR

See <u>Bluebook</u> rules 21.7.1, 21.7.2, and table T.3.

Note: All of the aforementioned documents may have an Annex or Supplement.

United Nations Reports
See <u>Bluebook</u> rule 21.7.3.

United Nations Reports of International Arbitral Awards
Ab.: R.I.A.A.

Ex.: <u>Revaluation of German Mark</u>, 19 R.I.A.A. 67 (U.N. 1980).

United Nations Resolutions in General Assembly Official Records
Ab.: G.A. Res.

In citing cases in law review footnotes, abbreviate any word listed in table T.6; the names of "states, countries, and other geographical units" unless they are named parties; and any other words of eight or more letters "if <u>substantial</u> space is thereby saved and the result is unambiguous." <u>Bluebook</u> rule 10.2.2. On the other hand, in citing cases in text, abbreviate only widely known acronyms and the following words: "&," "Ass'n," "Bros.," "Co.," "Corp.," "Inc.," "Ltd.," and "No." <u>Bluebook</u> rule 10.2.1(c).

Ex.:   G.A. Res. 1068, U.N. GAOR, ¶ 8, 11th Sess., Supp. No. 17, U.N. Doc.
            A/3572 (Mar. 1, 1957).

            Respect for Human Rights in Armed Conflicts, G.A. Res. 2444, U.N.
            GAOR, 23d Sess., Supp. No. 18, U.N. Doc. A/7218 (Dec. 19, 1968).

            See Bluebook rule 21.7.2.

United Nations Treaty Series
Ab.:   U.N.T.S.

Ex.:   Agreement on the Abolition of the Visa Requirement, Hung.-Malta, art.
            5, Feb. 4, 1983, 1351 U.N.T.S. 166. –Agreement to which United
            States is not a party.

            Geneva Convention Relative to the Treatment of Prisoners of War,

            Aug. 12, 1948, 6 U.S.T. 3316, 75, U.N.T.S. 135. –Agreement to which
            the United States is a party.

See Bluebook rule 21.4.5.

United Nations Yearbook
Ab.:   U.N.Y.B.

Ex.:   Legal Aspects of International Political Relations, 1986 U.N.Y.B. 986,
            U.N. Sales No. E.90.I.1.

United States Agricultural Decisions
See Agriculture Decisions (U.S.).

United States Atomic Energy Commission Reports
See Atomic Energy Commission Reports (U.S.).

United States Civil Aeronautics Board Reports (vol. 1 by C.A.A.)
See Civil Aeronautics Board Reports (U.S.).

United States Claims Court
See Claims Court.

United States Claims Court Reporter
See Claims Court Reporter.

United States Code
Ab.:   U.S.C.

Ex.:   42 U.S.C. § 7706(a) (2000).

            5 U.S.C. app. § 103(a) (1994). –Citation to appendix.

            23 U.S.C. § 101 (2000 & Supp. II 2002). –Citation to both main
            volume and the supplement.

            42 U.S.C. §§ 677(a) - 677(b) (2000).

            42 U.S.C. § 1320a-8 - 10 (2000). –Citations to consecutive
            subsections.

In law review footnotes, the titles of books and the names of cases, except for procedural
phrases, are not underlined. See Bluebook rule 2.1(a) & (b). Further, the following are in
large and small capitals: codes, restatements, standards, constitutions, periodicals, authors of
books, titles of books, the abbreviated names of codes, most legislative materials except for
bills and resolutions, codified ordinances, model codes, court rules, and sentencing guidelines.
Refer to The Bluebook.

Sherman Act § 2, 15 U.S.C. § 2 (2000). –Citation to a section which is part of an act known by a popular name.

37 U.S.C. § 312 (1982), amended by 37 U.S.C. § 312 (Supp. III 1985). –Citation to a non-current version of a code section with a complete citation to the amending statute.

37 U.S.C. § 312 (Supp. III 1985) (amending 37 U.S.C. 312 (1982)). –Citation to a statute giving prior history parenthetically.

1 U.S.C. § 108 (1994) (originally enacted as Act of July 30, 1947, ch. 388, § 108, 61 Stat. 634, 635). –Citation to a statute giving prior history parenthetically.

2 U.S.C. § 25 (1994) (corresponds to Act of June 1, 1789, ch. 1, § 2, 1 Stat. 23, 23). –Citation to a statute giving prior history parenthetically.

United States Code Annotated
Ab.:   U.S.C.A. §   (West year)

Ex.:   5 U.S.C.A. § 8332 (West 1996).

19 U.S.C.A. § 1673 (West Supp. 1981-1995). –Citation to a statute found in a supplemental volume.

7 U.S.C.A. § 1309 (West Supp. 1996). –Citation to a statute found in a pocket part.

United States Code Congressional and Administrative News
Ab.:   U.S.C.C.A.N.

Ex.:   Personal Responsibility and Work Opportunity Act of 1996, Pub. L. No. 104-193, 1996 U.S.C.C.A.N. (110 Stat.) 2105.

H.R. Rep. No. 104-311, at 96 (1995), as reprinted in 1995 U.S.C.C.A.N. 793, 808.

United States Code Service (LexisNexis)
Ab.:   U.S.C.S. §   (LexisNexis)

Ex.:   49 U.S.C.S. § 506 (LexisNexis 2004).

49 U.S.C.S. § 5301 (Lexis 2004 & Supp. 2005). –Citation to a statute found in both the main body and supplement of the code.

United States Comptroller General's Opinions
See Decisions of the Comptroller General of the United States.

United States Comptroller Treasury Decisions
See Decisions of the Comptroller General of the United States.

United States Constitution
Ab.:   U.S. Const.

Ex.:   U.S. Const. art. II, § 2.

U.S. Const. amend. XIV, § 1.

In citing cases in law review footnotes, abbreviate any word listed in table T.6; the names of "states, countries, and other geographical units" unless they are named parties; and any other words of eight or more letters "if substantial space is thereby saved and the result is unambiguous." Bluebook rule 10.2.2. On the other hand, in citing cases in text, abbreviate only widely known acronyms and the following words: "&," "Ass'n," "Bros.," "Co.," "Corp.," "Inc.," "Ltd.," and "No." Bluebook rule 10.2.1(c).

–"Cite constitutional provisions currently in force without date. If the cited provision has been repealed, either indicate parenthetically the fact and date of repeal or cite the repealing provision in full." Bluebook rule 11.

U.S. Const. art. IV, § 2, cl. 3, repealed by U.S. Const. amend. XIII.

–"When citing a provision that has been subsequently amended, either indicate parenthetically the fact and date of amendment or cite the amending provision in full." Bluebook rule 11.

U.S. Const. art. I, § 2, cl. 3 (amended 1868).

U.S. Const. art. II, § 1, cl. 3, amended by U.S. Const. amend. XIV, § 2.

See Bluebook rule 11.

United States Copyright Decisions
See Copyright Decisions (U.S).

United States Court Martial Reports
See Court Martial Reports.

United States Court of Appeals for the Armed Forces
Ab.:   C.A.A.F.

Ex.:   United States v. Melanson, 53 M.J. 1 (C.A.A.F. 2000).

Court Rules:

Ab.:   C.A.A.F.

Ex.:   C.A.A.F. R. 43

United States Court of Appeals for the First Circuit
Cases:

Ab.:   (1st Cir. year)

Ex.:   Montilla Records, Inc. v. Morales, 575 F.2d 324 (1st Cir. 1978).

Court Rules:

Ab.:   1st Cir. R.

Ex.:   1st Cir. R. 11.

United States Court of Appeals for the Second Circuit
Cases:

Ab.:   (2d Cir. year)

Ex.:   Cent. Hanover Bank & Trust Co. v. Herbst, 93 F.2d 510 (2d Cir. 1937).

Court Rules:

Ab.:   2d Cir. R.

Ex.:   2d Cir. R. 4(b).

United States Court of Appeals for the Third Circuit
Cases:

In law review footnotes, the titles of books and the names of cases, except for procedural phrases, are not underlined. See Bluebook rule 2.1(a) & (b). Further, the following are in large and small capitals: codes, restatements, standards, constitutions, periodicals, authors of books, titles of books, the abbreviated names of codes, most legislative materials except for bills and resolutions, codified ordinances, model codes, court rules, and sentencing guidelines. Refer to The Bluebook.

Ab.:   (3d Cir. year)

Ex.:   United States v. Anderskow, 88 F.3d 245 (3d Cir. 1996).

Court Rules:

Ab.:   3d Cir. R.

Ex.:   3d Cir. R. 15.1.

United States Court of Appeals for the Fourth Circuit
Cases:

Ab.:   (4th Cir. year)

Ex.:   Fennell v. Monongahela Power Co., 350 F.2d 867 (4th Cir. 1965).

Court Rules:

Ab.:   4th Cir. R.

Ex.:   4th Cir. R. 11.

United States Court of Appeals for the Fifth Circuit
Cases:

Ab.:   (5th Cir. year)

Ex.:   John P. McGuire Co. v. Herzog, 421 F.2d 419 (5th Cir. 1970).

Court Rules:

Ab.:   5th Cir. R.

Ex.:   5th Cir. R. 8.2.

United States Court of Appeals for Fifth Circuit (Fifth Circuit split)
–Decisions rendered in 1981, labeled as "5th Cir.":

Ex.:   Lewis v. Reagan, 660 F.2d 124 (5th Cir. Oct. 1981).

–Decisions with unit information:

Ex.:   United States v. Wright, 661 F.2d 60 (5th Cir. Unit A 1981).

–Decisions rendered after September 30, 1981, labeled as Former Fifth Circuit judgment:

Ex.:   Helms v. Jones, 660 F.2d 120 (Former 5th Cir. 1981).

See Bluebook rule 10.8.2.

United States Court of Appeals for the Sixth Circuit
Cases:

Ab.:   (6th Cir. year)

Ex.:   Johnson v. Heffron, 88 F.3d 404 (6th Cir. 1996).

Court Rules:

Ab.:   6th Cir. R.

Ex.:   6th Cir. R. 6(a).

United States Court of Appeals for the Seventh Circuit
Cases:

In citing cases in law review footnotes, abbreviate any word listed in table T.6; the names of "states, countries, and other geographical units" unless they are named parties; and any other words of eight or more letters "if substantial space is thereby saved and the result is unambiguous." Bluebook rule 10.2.2. On the other hand, in citing cases in text, abbreviate only widely known acronyms and the following words: "&," "Ass'n," "Bros.," "Co.," "Corp.," "Inc.," "Ltd.," and "No." Bluebook rule 10.2.1(c).

Ab.: (7th Cir. year)
Ex.: <u>Booker v. Ward</u>, 94 F.3d 1052 (7th Cir. 1996).
Court Rules:
Ab.: 7th Cir. R.
Ex.: 7th Cir. R. 10(b).

United States Court of Appeals for the Eighth Circuit
Cases:
Ab.: (8th Cir. year)
Ex.: <u>NLRB v. Skelly Oil Co.</u>, 473 F.2d 1079 (8th Cir. 1973).
Court Rules:
Ab.: 8th Cir. R.
Ex.: 8th Cir. R. 11A.

United States Court of Appeals for the Ninth Circuit
Cases:
Ab.: (9th Cir. year)
Ex.: <u>United States v. Neff</u>, 615 F.2d 1235 (9th Cir. 1980).
Court Rules:
Ab.: 9th Cir. R.
Ex.: 9th Cir. R. 6-1.

United States Court of Appeals for the Tenth Circuit
Cases:
Ab.: (10th Cir. year)
Ex.: <u>United States Fid. & Guar. Co. v. Sidwell</u>, 525 F.2d 472 (10th Cir. 1975).
Court Rules:
Ab.: 10th Cir. R.
Ex.: 10th Cir. R. 2.1.

United States Court of Appeals for the Eleventh Circuit
Cases:
Ab.: (11th Cir. year)
Ex.: <u>Profitt v. Wainwright</u>, 685 F.2d 1227 (11th Cir. 1982).
Court Rules:
Ab.: 11th Cir. R.
Ex.: 11th Cir. R. 11-2.

United States Court of Appeals for the District of Columbia Circuit
Cases:

In law review footnotes, the titles of books and the names of cases, except for procedural phrases, are not underlined. <u>See</u> <u>Bluebook</u> rule 2.1(a) & (b). Further, the following are in large and small capitals: codes, restatements, standards, constitutions, periodicals, authors of books, titles of books, the abbreviated names of codes, most legislative materials except for bills and resolutions, codified ordinances, model codes, court rules, and sentencing guidelines. Refer to <u>The Bluebook</u>.

Ab.: (D.C. Cir. year)

Ex.: <u>Mountain States Legal Found. v. Glickman</u>, 484 F.2d 820 (D.C. Cir. 1973).

Court Rules:

Ab.: D.C. Cir. R.

Ex.: D.C. Cir. R. 9(a).

United States Court of Appeals for the Federal Circuit
Cases:

Ab.: (Fed. Cir. year)

Ex.: <u>Medtronic, Inc. v. Intermedics, Inc.</u>, 799 F.2d 734 (Fed. Cir. 1986).

Court Rules:

Ab.: Fed. Cir. R.

Ex.: Fed. Cir. R. 11(a).

–Succeeded United States Court of Customs and Patent Appeals and the appellate jurisdiction of the Court of Claims.

–If not in F., F.2d, or F.3d, cite to the official reporter (Court of Claims Reports or Court of Customs and Patent Appeals Reports).

United States Court of Appeals for Veterans Claims

Ab.: Vet. App.

Ex.: <u>Dillon v. Brown</u>, 8 Vet. App. 165 (1955).

Court Rules:

Ab.: Vet. App. R.

Ex.: Vet. App. R. 4(a)

United States Court of Claims
See Court of Claims.

United States Court of Claims Reports
See Court of Claims Reports.

United States Court of Customs and Patent Appeals Reports
See Court of Customs and Patent Appeals Reports.

United States Court of Federal Claims

Ab.: Fed. Cl.

–Created 1992, formerly United States Claims Court (Cl. Ct., created 1982), which was in turn successor to the Court of Claims (Ct. Cl.).

–<u>See</u> Bluebook table T.1, p. 194.

United States Court of International Trade

Ab.: Ct. Int'l Trade

In citing cases in law review footnotes, abbreviate any word listed in table T.6; the names of "states, countries, and other geographical units" unless they are named parties; and any other words of eight or more letters "if <u>substantial</u> space is thereby saved and the result is unambiguous." Bluebook rule 10.2.2. On the other hand, in citing cases in text, abbreviate only widely known acronyms and the following words: "&," "Ass'n," "Bros.," "Co.," "Corp.," "Inc.," "Ltd.," and "No." Bluebook rule 10.2.1(c).

–Created 1980, successor to the United States Customs Court (Cust. Ct.), which was created in 1926.

–Cite to Court of International Trade in the following order of preference: Reports (Ct. Int'l Trade), if therein, otherwise to F. Supp., F. Supp. 2d., Customs Bulletin and Decisions (Cust. B. & Dec.), or to International Trade Reporter Decisions (I.T.R.D. (BNA)).

Ex.:   S.I. Stud, Inc. v. United States, 17 Ct. Int'l Trade 661 (1993).

Federal-Mogul Corp. v. United States, 918 F. Supp. 386 (Ct. Int'l Trade 1996).

Wolfe Shoe Co. v. United States, 30 Cust B. & Dec. No. 36, at 118 (Ct. Int'l Trade 1996).

Item Co. v. United States, 18 I.T.R.D. (BNA) 1769 (Ct. Int'l Trade 1996).

United States Court of Military Appeals
See Court of Military Appeals.

United States Cumulative Bulletin
See Cumulative Bulletin (U.S.).

United States Customs Bulletin and Decisions
See Customs Bulletin and Decisions (U.S.).

United States Customs Court
Ab.:   Cust. Ct.

Created 1926 and succeeded in 1980 by the United States Court of International Trade (Ct. Int'l Trade).

–Cite to Customs Court Reports (Cust. Ct.), if therein.

Ex.:   Connors Steel Co. v. United States, 85 Cust. Ct. 132 (1980).

United States Decisions of the Comptroller General
See Decisions of the Comptroller General (U.S.).

United States Decisions of the Department of the Interior
See Decisions of the United States Department of the Interior (U.S.).

United States Decisions of the Employees' Compensation Appeals Board
See Decisions of the Employees' Compensation Appeals Board (U.S.).

United States Decisions of the Federal Maritime Commission
See Decisions of the Federal Maritime Commission (U.S).

United States Decisions of the United States Maritime Commission
See Decisions of the United States Maritime Commission.

United States Department of Justice
Ab.:   U.S. Dep't of Justice

In law review footnotes, the titles of books and the names of cases, except for procedural phrases, are not underlined. See Bluebook rule 2.1(a) & (b). Further, the following are in large and small capitals: codes, restatements, standards, constitutions, periodicals, authors of books, titles of books, the abbreviated names of codes, most legislative materials except for bills and resolutions, codified ordinances, model codes, court rules, and sentencing guidelines. Refer to The Bluebook.

Ex.:   Bureau of Justice Statistics, U.S. Dep't of Justice, <u>Tracking Offenders:</u> <u>The Child Victim</u> 1-2 (1984).

         –For citations to works by institutional authors, <u>See</u> <u>Bluebook</u> rule 15.1(c).

United States Department of State
Ab.:   U.S. Dep't of State

Ex.:   U.S. Dep't of State, <u>Documents on Germany 1944-1985,</u> at 348 (1985).

         –For citations to works by institutional authors, <u>See</u> <u>Bluebook</u> rule 15.1(c).

United States Department of State Bulletin
See Department of State Bulletin (U.S.).

United States Department of State Dispatch
Ab.:   U.S. Dep't St. Dispatch

United States District Court for the Middle District of Alabama
Ab.:   (M.D. Ala. year)

United States District Court for the Northern District of Alabama
Ab.:   (N.D. Ala. year)

United States District Court for the Southern District of Alabama
Ab.:   (S.D. Ala. year)

United States District Court for the District of Alaska
Ab.:   (D. Alaska year)

United States District Court for the District of Arizona
Ab.:   (D. Ariz. year)

United States District Court for the Eastern District of Arkansas
Ab.:   (E.D. Ark. year)

United States District Court for the Western District of Arkansas
Ab.:   (W.D. Ark. year)

United States District Court for the Central District of California
Ab.:   (C.D. Cal. year)

United States District Court for the Eastern District of California
Ab.:   (E.D. Cal. year)

United States District Court for the Northern District of California
Ab.:   (N.D. Cal. year)

United States District Court for the Southern District of California
Ab.:   (S.D. Cal. year)

In citing cases in law review footnotes, abbreviate any word listed in table T.6; the names of "states, countries, and other geographical units" unless they are named parties; and any other words of eight or more letters "if <u>substantial</u> space is thereby saved and the result is unambiguous." <u>Bluebook</u> rule 10.2.2. On the other hand, in citing cases in text, abbreviate only widely known acronyms and the following words: "&," "Ass'n," "Bros.," "Co.," "Corp.," "Inc.," "Ltd.," and "No." <u>Bluebook</u> rule 10.2.1(c).

United States District Court for the District of Colorado
    Ab.:   (D. Colo. year)

United States District Court for the District of Connecticut
    Ab.:   (D. Conn. year)

United States District Court for the District of Delaware
    Ab.:   (D. Del. year)

United States District Court for the District of Columbia
    Ab.:   (D.D.C. year)

United States District Court for the Middle District of Florida
    Ab.:   (M.D. Fla. year)

United States District Court for the Northern District of Florida
    Ab.:   (N.D. Fla. year)

United States District Court for the Southern District of Florida
    Ab.:   (S.D. Fla. year)

United States District Court for the Middle District of Georgia
    Ab.:   (M.D. Ga. year)

United States District Court for the Northern District of Georgia
    Ab.:   (N.D. Ga. year)

United States District Court for the Southern District of Georgia
    Ab.:   (S.D. Ga. year)

United States District Court for the District of Guam
    Ab.:   (D. Guam year)

United States District Court for the District of Hawaii
    Ab.:   (D. Haw. year)

United States District Court for the District of Idaho
    Ab.:   (D. Idaho year)

United States District Court for the Central District of Illinois
    Ab.:   (C.D. Ill. year)

United States District Court for the Northern District of Illinois
    Ab.:   (N.D. Ill. year)

United States District Court for the Southern District of Illinois
    Ab.:   (S.D. Ill. year)

United States District Court for the Northern District of Indiana
    Ab.:   (N.D. Ind. year)

In law review footnotes, the titles of books and the names of cases, except for procedural phrases, are not underlined. See Bluebook rule 2.1(a) & (b). Further, the following are in large and small capitals: codes, restatements, standards, constitutions, periodicals, authors of books, titles of books, the abbreviated names of codes, most legislative materials except for bills and resolutions, codified ordinances, model codes, court rules, and sentencing guidelines. Refer to The Bluebook.

United States District Court for the Southern District of Indiana
    Ab.:   (S.D. Ind. year)

United States District Court for the Northern District of Iowa
    Ab.:   (N.D. Iowa year)

United States District Court for the Southern District of Iowa
    Ab.:   (S.D. Iowa year)

United States District Court for the District of Kansas
    Ab.:   (D. Kan. year)

United States District Court for the Eastern District of Kentucky
    Ab.:   (E.D. Ky. year)

United States District Court for the Western District of Kentucky
    Ab.:   (W.D. Ky. year)

United States District Court for the Eastern District of Louisiana
    Ab.:   (E.D. La. year)

United States District Court for the Middle District of Louisiana
    Ab.:   (M.D. La. year)

United States District Court for the Western District of Louisiana
    Ab.:   (W.D. La. year)

United States District Court for the District of Maine
    Ab.:   (D. Me. year)

United States District Court for the District of Maryland
    Ab.:   (D. Md. year)

United States District Court for the District of Massachusetts
    Ab.:   (D. Mass. year)

United States District Court for the Eastern District of Michigan
    Ab.:   (E.D. Mich. year)

United States District Court for the Western District of Michigan
    Ab.:   (W.D. Mich. year)

United States District Court for the District of Minnesota
    Ab.:   (D. Minn. year)

United States District Court for the Northern District of Mississippi
    Ab.:   (N.D. Miss. year)

United States District Court for the Southern District of Mississippi
    Ab.:   (S.D. Miss. year)

In citing cases in law review footnotes, abbreviate any word listed in table T.6; the names of "states, countries, and other geographical units" unless they are named parties; and any other words of eight or more letters "if <u>substantial</u> space is thereby saved and the result is unambiguous." <u>Bluebook</u> rule 10.2.2. On the other hand, in citing cases in text, abbreviate only widely known acronyms and the following words: "&," "Ass'n," "Bros.," "Co.," "Corp.," "Inc.," "Ltd.," and "No." <u>Bluebook</u> rule 10.2.1(c).

United States District Court for the Eastern District of Missouri
    Ab.:   (E.D. Mo. year)

United States District Court for the Western District of Missouri
    Ab.:   (W.D. Mo. year)

United States District Court for the District of Montana
    Ab.:   (D. Mont. year)

United States District Court for the District of Nebraska
    Ab.:   (D. Neb. year)

United States District Court for the District of Nevada
    Ab.:   (D. Nev. year)

United States District Court for the District of New Hampshire
    Ab.:   (D.N.H. year)

United States District Court for the District of New Jersey
    Ab.:   (D.N.J. year)

United States District Court for the District of New Mexico
    Ab.:   (D.N.M. year)

United States District Court for the Eastern District of New York
    Ab.:   (E.D.N.Y. year)

United States District Court for the Northern District of New York
    Ab.:   (N.D.N.Y. year)

United States District Court for the Southern District of New York
    Ab.:   (S.D.N.Y. year)

United States District Court for the Western District of New York
    Ab.:   (W.D.N.Y. year)

United States District Court for the Eastern District of North Carolina
    Ab.:   (E.D.N.C. year)

United States District Court for the Middle District of North Carolina
    Ab.:   (M.D.N.C. year)

United States District Court for the Western District of North Carolina
    Ab.:   (W.D.N.C. year)

United States District Court for the District of North Dakota
    Ab.:   (D.N.D. year)

United States District Court for the Northern Mariana Islands
    Ab.:   (D. N. Mar. I. year)

In law review footnotes, the titles of books and the names of cases, except for procedural phrases, are not underlined. See Bluebook rule 2.1(a) & (b). Further, the following are in large and small capitals: codes, restatements, standards, constitutions, periodicals, authors of books, titles of books, the abbreviated names of codes, most legislative materials except for bills and resolutions, codified ordinances, model codes, court rules, and sentencing guidelines. Refer to The Bluebook.

United States District Court for the Northern District of Ohio
    Ab.:   (N.D. Ohio year)

United States District Court for the Southern District of Ohio
    Ab.:   (S.D. Ohio year)

United States District Court for the Eastern District of Oklahoma
    Ab.:   (E.D. Okla. year)

United States District Court for the Northern District of Oklahoma
    Ab.:   (N.D. Okla. year)

United States District Court for the Western District of Oklahoma
    Ab.:   (W.D. Okla. year)

United States District Court for the District of Oregon
    Ab.:   (D. Or. year)

United States District Court for the Eastern District of Pennsylvania
    Ab.:   (E.D. Pa. year)

United States District Court for the Middle District of Pennsylvania
    Ab.:   (M.D. Pa. year)

United States District Court for the Western District of Pennsylvania
    Ab.:   (W.D. Pa. year)

United States District Court for the District of Puerto Rico
    Ab.:   (D.P.R. year)

United States District Court for the District of Rhode Island
    Ab.:   (D.R.I. year)

United States District Court for the District of South Carolina
    Ab.:   (D.S.C. year)

United States District Court for the District of South Dakota
See public domain citations.
    Ab.:   (D.S.D. year)

United States District Court for the Eastern District of Tennessee
    Ab.:   (E.D. Tenn. year)

United States District Court for the Middle District of Tennessee
    Ab.:   (M.D. Tenn. year)

United States District Court for the Western District of Tennessee
    Ab.:   (W.D. Tenn. year)

United States District Court for the Eastern District of Texas
    Ab.:   (E.D. Tex. year)

In citing cases in law review footnotes, abbreviate any word listed in table T.6; the names of "states, countries, and other geographical units" unless they are named parties; and any other words of eight or more letters "if substantial space is thereby saved and the result is unambiguous." Bluebook rule 10.2.2. On the other hand, in citing cases in text, abbreviate only widely known acronyms and the following words: "&," "Ass'n," "Bros.," "Co.," "Corp.," "Inc.," "Ltd.," and "No." Bluebook rule 10.2.1(c).

United States District Court for the Northern District of Texas
    Ab.:   (N.D. Tex. year)

United States District Court for the Southern District of Texas
    Ab.:   (S.D. Tex. year)

United States District Court for the Western District of Texas
    Ab.:   (W.D. Tex. year)

United States District Court for the District of Utah
    Ab.:   (D. Utah year)

United States District Court for the District of Vermont
    Ab.:   (D. Vt. year)

United States District Court for the District of the Virgin Islands
    Ab.:   (D.V.I. year)

United States District Court for the Eastern District of Virginia
    Ab.:   (E.D. Va. year)

United States District Court for the Western District of Virginia
    Ab.:   (W.D. Va. year)

United States District Court for the Eastern District of Washington
    Ab.:   (E.D. Wash. year)

United States District Court for the Western District of Washington
    Ab.:   (W.D. Wash. year)

United States District Court for the Northern District of West Virginia
    Ab.:   (N.D. W. Va. year)

United States District Court for the Southern District of West Virginia
    Ab.:   (S.D. W. Va. year)

United States District Court for the Eastern District of Wisconsin
    Ab.:   (E.D. Wis. year)

United States District Court for the Western District of Wisconsin
    Ab.:   (W.D. Wis. year)

United States District Court for the District of Wyoming
    Ab.:   (D. Wyo. year)

United States Federal Communications Commission Reports
    See Federal Communications Commission Reports.

United States Federal Power Commission Reports
    See Federal Power Commission Reports.

In law review footnotes, the titles of books and the names of cases, except for procedural phrases, are not underlined. See Bluebook rule 2.1(a) & (b). Further, the following are in large and small capitals: codes, restatements, standards, constitutions, periodicals, authors of books, titles of books, the abbreviated names of codes, most legislative materials except for bills and resolutions, codified ordinances, model codes, court rules, and sentencing guidelines. Refer to The Bluebook.

United States Federal Reserve Bulletin
See Federal Reserve Bulletin.

United States Federal Trade Commission Decisions
See Federal Trade Commission Decisions.

United States Interstate Commerce Commission Reports, Second Series
See Interstate Commerce Commission Reports, Second Series.

United States Law Week (Bureau of National Affairs)
Ab.: U.S.L.W. (BNA - publisher need not be indicated.)

Ex.: Immigration and Naturalization Serv. v. Yueh-Shaio Yang,
      65 U.S.L.W. 4009 (U.S. Nov. 13, 1996). –Citation to looseleaf
      material.

      –Cite only until case is available in an official or unofficial reporter.

United States Merit Systems Protection Board
See Merit Systems Protection Board Reporter (U.S.).

United States Motor Carrier Cases
See Interstate Commerce Commission Motor Carrier Cases (U.S.).

United States National Labor Relations Board Decisions and Orders
See National Labor Relations Board, Decisions and Orders of the (U.S.).

United States National Railroad Adjustment Board, 1st-3rd Div.
See National Railroad Adjustment Board, 1st-3rd Div. (U.S.) (1936-1972).

United States National Transportation Safety Board Decisions
See National Transportation Safety Board Decisions (U.S.) (1967-1977).

United States Official Opinions of the Solicitor for the Post Office Department
See Official Opinions of the Solicitor for the Post Office Department (1873-
      1951).

United States Opinions of the Attorney General
See Opinions of the Attorney General (U.S.) (1791-date).

United States Patents Quarterly, The (Bureau of National Affairs)
Ab.: U.S.P.Q. (BNA)

Ex.: Henkel Corp. v. Coral, Inc., [Advance Sheets] U.S.P.Q. (BNA) (21
      U.S.P.Q. 2d) 1081 (N.D. Ill. Dec. 28, 1990). –Citation to looseleaf
      material.

      Solomon v. Greco, 18 U.S.P.Q. 2d (BNA) 1917 (E.D.N.Y. Oct. 2,
      1990). –Citation to bound material.

      –The above examples are proper if the case is not yet available in, or is
      not reported in, an official or West reporter, a public domain citation,
      or in a widely used computer database.

In citing cases in law review footnotes, abbreviate any word listed in table T.6;
the names of "states, countries, and other geographical units" unless they are named parties;
and any other words of eight or more letters "if substantial space is thereby saved and the
result is unambiguous." Bluebook rule 10.2.2. On the other hand, in citing cases in text,
abbreviate only widely known acronyms and the following words: "&," "Ass'n," "Bros.,"
"Co.," "Corp.," "Inc.," "Ltd.," and "No." Bluebook rule 10.2.1(c).

United States Public Laws
See Public Laws (U.S.).

United States Reports
(91 U.S., 1875 to date)

Ab.: U.S.

Ex.: Willy v. Coastal Corp., 503 U.S. 131 (1992). –Case Citation.

Willy v. Coastal Corp., 503 U.S. 131, 135 (1992). –Page Citation.

O'Hare Truck Serv., Inc. v. City of Northlake, No. 95-191, slip op. at 3 (U.S. June 28, 1996). –Slip Opinion.

United States Reports
–Cite to U.S., if therein; otherwise, cite to S. Ct., L. Ed., or U.S.L.W., in that order of preference. See Bluebook table T.1.

(1 U.S. - 90 U.S., pre-1875)

Dallas (1790-1800):

Ab.: Dall.

Ex.: The Eliza, 4 U.S. (4 Dall.) 32 (1800). –Case Citation.

The Eliza, 4 U.S. (4 Dall.) 32, 38-39 (1800). –Page Citation.

Cranch (1801-1815):

Ab.: Cranch

Ex.: Finley v. Williams, 13 U.S. (9 Cranch) 164 (1815). –Case Citation.

Finley v. Williams, 13 U.S. (9 Cranch) 164, 167 (1815). –Page Citation.

Wheaton (1816-1827):

Ab.: Wheat.

Ex.: Janney v. Columbian Ins. Co., 23 U.S. (10 Wheat.) 409 (1825). –Case Citation.

Janney v. Columbian Ins. Co., 23 U.S. (10 Wheat.) 409, 416 (1825). –Page Citation.

Peters (1828-1842):

Ab.: Pet.

Ex.: United States v. One Hundred Twelve Casks of Sugar, 33 U.S. (8 Pet.) 275 (1834). –Case Citation.

United States v. One Hundred Twelve Casks of Sugar, 33 U.S. (8 Pet.) 275, 279-80 (1834). –Page Citation.

Howard (1843-1860):

Ab.: How.

Ex.: Taylor v. Doe, 54 U.S. (13 How.) 287 (1851). –Case Citation.

Taylor v. Doe, 54 U.S. (13 How.) 287, 291 (1851). –Page Citation.

In law review footnotes, the titles of books and the names of cases, except for procedural phrases, are not underlined. See Bluebook rule 2.1(a) & (b). Further, the following are in large and small capitals: codes, restatements, standards, constitutions, periodicals, authors of books, titles of books, the abbreviated names of codes, most legislative materials except for bills and resolutions, codified ordinances, model codes, court rules, and sentencing guidelines. Refer to The Bluebook.

Black (1861-1862):

Ab.: Black

Ex.: Chicago City v. Robbins, 67 U.S. (2 Black) 418 (1862). –Case Citation.

Chicago City v. Robbins, 67 U.S. (2 Black) 418, 423 (1862). –Page Citation.

Wallace (1863-1874):

Ab.: Wall.

Ex.: Gaines v. Thompson, 74 U.S. (7 Wall.) 347 (1868). –Case Citation.

Gaines v. Thompson, 74 U.S. (7 Wall.) 347, 353 (1868). –Page Citation.

United States Securities and Exchange Commission Decisions and Reports
See Securities and Exchange Commission Decisions and Reports.

United States Sentencing Guidelines Manual
Ab.: U.S. Sentencing Guidelines Manual

Ex.: U.S. Sentencing Guidelines Manual § 2K2.4 (1998).

See Bluebook rules B6.1.3 and 12.8.5.

United States Statutes at Large
See Statutes at Large.

United States Supreme Court Reports
See Supreme Court Reporter.

United States Supreme Court Reports, Lawyers' Edition
–Cite to U.S., if therein; otherwise, cite to S. Ct., L. Ed., or U.S.L.W., in that order of preference. See Bluebook table T.1.

Ab.: L. Ed., L. Ed. 2d

Ex.: United States v. Di Re, 92 L. Ed. 210 (1948). –Case Citation.

United States v. Di Re, 92 L. Ed. 210, 219 (1948). –Page Citation.

ICC v. Transcon Lines, 130 L. Ed. 2d 562 (1995). –Case Citation.

ICC v. Transcon Lines, 130 L. Ed. 2d 562, 567 (1995). –Page Citation.

United States Supreme Court Rules
Ab.: Sup. Ct. R.

Ex.: Sup. Ct. R. 6.

United States Tax Cases (Commerce Clearing House)
Ab.: U.S. Tax Cas. (CCH)

See Federal Estate and Gift Tax Reporter (Commerce Clearing House).

United States Tax Court Reports
Ab.: T.C.

In citing cases in law review footnotes, abbreviate any word listed in table T.6; the names of "states, countries, and other geographical units" unless they are named parties; and any other words of eight or more letters "if substantial space is thereby saved and the result is unambiguous." Bluebook rule 10.2.2. On the other hand, in citing cases in text, abbreviate only widely known acronyms and the following words: "&," "Ass'n," "Bros.," "Co.," "Corp.," "Inc.," "Ltd.," and "No." Bluebook rule 10.2.1(c).

Ex.: Estate of Young v. C.I.R., 110 T.C. 297 (1998).

United States Treasury Decisions Under Internal Revenue Laws (1898-1942)
See Treasury Decisions Under Internal Revenue Laws (1898-1942).

United States Treasury Department, Comptroller General's Opinion
See Decisions of the Comptroller General of the United States.

United States Treasury Regulations
See Treasury Regulations (Federal).

United States Treaties and Other International Acts Series
See Treaties and Other International Acts Series (U.S.).

United States Treaties and Other International Agreements
Ab.: U.S.T.
Ex.: Treaty of Friendship, Commerce and Navigation, U.S.-F.R.G., art. I,
Oct. 29, 1954, 7 U.S.T. 1839. –Example of treaty between United
States and one other party.

International Convention for the Safety of Life at Sea, Ch. XI, Nov. 1,
1974, 32 U.S.T. 47, 1184 U.N.T.S. 278. –Example of treaty among
four or more parties, including the United States.

See Bluebook rule 21.4.5(a).

United States Treaty Series
See Treaty Series (U.S.).

University of Akron Law Review
See Akron Law Review.

University of Alabama Law Review
See Alabama Law Review.

University of Arizona Law Review
See Arizona Law Review.

University of Arkansas Law Review
See Arkansas Law Review.

University of Arkansas at Little Rock Law Journal
Ab.: U. Ark. Little Rock L.J.
Ex.: Vincene Verdun, Postdated Checks: An Old Problem with a New
Solution in the Revised U.C.C., 14 U. Ark. Little Rock L.J. 37 (1991).
–Article Citation.

Vincene Verdun, Postdated Checks: An Old Problem with a New
Solution in the Revised U.C.C., 14 U. Ark. Little Rock L.J. 37, 59-60
(1991). –Page Citation.

In law review footnotes, the titles of books and the names of cases, except for procedural
phrases, are not underlined. See Bluebook rule 2.1(a) & (b). Further, the following are in
large and small capitals: codes, restatements, standards, constitutions, periodicals, authors of
books, titles of books, the abbreviated names of codes, most legislative materials except for
bills and resolutions, codified ordinances, model codes, court rules, and sentencing guidelines.
Refer to The Bluebook.

University of Arkansas at Little Rock Law Review
    Ab.:   U. Ark. Little Rock L. Rev.

    Ex.:   Honorable Terry Crabtree, <u>Abstracting the Record</u>, 21 U. Ark. Little Rock L. Rev. 1 (1998). –Article Citation.

            Honorable Terry Crabtree, <u>Abstracting the Record</u>, 21 U. Ark. Little Rock L. Rev. 1, 7 n.27 (1998). –Footnote Citation.

University of Baltimore Journal of Environmental Law
    Ab.:   U. Balt. J. Envtl. L.

    Ex.:   John C. Buckley, <u>Considering Environmental Law</u>, 1 U. Balt. J. Envtl. L. 1 (1991). –Article Citation.

            John C. Buckley, <u>Considering Environmental Law</u>, 1 U. Balt. J. Envtl. L. 1, 1 (1991). –Page Citation.

University of Baltimore Law Review
    Ab.:   U. Balt. L. Rev.

    Ex.:   Ralph S. Brown, <u>Copyright-Like Protection for Designs</u>, 19 U. Balt. L. Rev. 308 (1989-1990). –Article Citation.

            Ralph S. Brown, <u>Copyright-Like Protection for Designs</u>, 19 U. Balt. L. Rev. 308, 319-20 (1989-1990). –Page Citation.

University of Bridgeport Law Review
    Ab.:   U. Bridgeport L. Rev.

    Ex.:   Steven M. Spaeth, <u>The Deregulation of Transportation and Natural Gas Production in the United States and its Relevance to the Soviet Union and Eastern Europe in the 1990's</u>, U. Bridgeport L. Rev. 43 (1991). –Article Citation.

            Steven M. Spaeth, <u>The Deregulation of Transportation and Natural Gas Production in the United States and its Relevance to the Soviet Union and Eastern Europe in the 1990's</u>, U. Bridgeport L. Rev. 43, 89-91 (1991). –Page Citation.

University of British Columbia Law Review
    Ab.:   U. Brit. Colum. L. Rev.

    Ex.:   Benjamin Van Primmeler, <u>The Missing Lynx: Trapping Logging and Compensation</u>, 25 U. Brit. Colum. L. Rev. 335 (1991). –Article Citation.

            Benjamin Van Primmeler, <u>The Missing Lynx: Trapping Logging and Compensation</u>, 25 U. Brit. Colum. L. Rev. 335, 340 (1991). –Page Citation.

University of California Law Review
    See California Law Review.

University of Chicago Law Review
    Ab.:   U. Chi. L. Rev.

In citing cases in law review footnotes, abbreviate any word listed in table T.6; the names of "states, countries, and other geographical units" unless they are named parties; and any other words of eight or more letters "if <u>substantial</u> space is thereby saved and the result is unambiguous." <u>Bluebook</u> rule 10.2.2. On the other hand, in citing cases in text, abbreviate only widely known acronyms and the following words: "&," "Ass'n," "Bros.," "Co.," "Corp.," "Inc.," "Ltd.," and "No." <u>Bluebook</u> rule 10.2.1(c).

Ex.:   James Q. Whitman, <u>Why Did the Revolutionary Lawyers Confuse Custom and Reason?</u>, 58 U. Chi. L. Rev. 1321 (1991). –Article Citation.

James Q. Whitman, <u>Why Did the Revolutionary Lawyers Confuse Custom and Reason?</u>, 58 U. Chi. L. Rev. 1321, 1329-31 (1991). –Page Citation.

University of Chicago Legal Forum
Ab.:   U. Chi. Legal F.

Ex.:   Robert K. Fullinwider, <u>Multicultural Education</u>, 1991 U. Chi. Legal F. 75. –Article Citation.

Robert K. Fullinwider, <u>Multicultural Education</u>, 1991 U. Chi. Legal F. 75, 79-83. –Page Citation.

University of Cincinnati Law Review
Ab.:   U. Cin. L. Rev.

Ex.:   Nicholas Wolfson, <u>Free Speech Theory and Hateful Words</u>, 60 U. Cin. L. Rev. 1 (1991). –Article Citation.

Nicholas Wolfson, <u>Free Speech Theory and Hateful Words</u>, 60 U. Cin. L. Rev. 1, 2 (1991). –Page Citation.

University of Colorado Law Review
Ab.:   U. Colo. L. Rev.

Ex.:   Alessandra Lippucci, <u>Surprised by Fish</u>, 63 U. Colo. L. Rev. 1 (1992). –Article Citation.

Alessandra Lippucci, <u>Surprised by Fish</u>, 63 U. Colo. L. Rev. 1, 69-70 (1992). –Page Citation.

University of Connecticut Law Review
See Connecticut Law Review.

University of Dayton Law Review
Ab.:   U. Dayton L. Rev.

Ex.:   Terry A. Bethel, <u>Recent Supreme Court Employment Law Decisions, 1990-91</u>, 17 U. Dayton L. Rev. 33 (1991). –Article Citation.

Terry A. Bethel, <u>Recent Supreme Court Employment Law Decisions, 1990-91</u>, 17 U. Dayton L. Rev. 33, 39-42 (1991). –Page Citation.

University of Detroit Law Review
Ab.:   U. Det. L. Rev.

In law review footnotes, the titles of books and the names of cases, except for procedural phrases, are not underlined. <u>See</u> Bluebook rule 2.1(a) & (b). Further, the following are in large and small capitals: codes, restatements, standards, constitutions, periodicals, authors of books, titles of books, the abbreviated names of codes, most legislative materials except for bills and resolutions, codified ordinances, model codes, court rules, and sentencing guidelines. Refer to <u>The Bluebook</u>.

Ex.:   Lawrence C. Mann, <u>Mediation of Civil Cases: Neither Panacea nor Anathema (A Prescription for Change in Procedural Rules)</u>, 67 U. Det. L. Rev. 531 (1990). –Article Citation.

Lawrence C. Mann, <u>Mediation of Civil Cases: Neither Panacea nor Anathema (A Prescription for Change in Procedural Rules)</u>, 67 U. Det. L. Rev. 531, 564-70 (1990). –Page Citation.

University of Detroit Mercy Law Review
Ab.:   U. Det. Mercy L. Rev.

Ex.:   Luis Kutner, <u>Jesus Before the Sanhedrin</u>, 69 U. Det. Mercy L. Rev. 1 (1991). –Article Citation.

Luis Kutner, <u>Jesus Before the Sanhedrin</u>, 69 U. Det. Mercy L. Rev. 1, 8-9 (1991). –Page Citation.

University of Florida Journal of Law and Public Policy
Ab.:   U. Fla. J.L. & Pub. Pol'y

Ex.:   Michael I. Meyerson, <u>Impending Legal Issues for Integrated Broadband Networks</u>, 3 U. Fla. J.L. & Pub. Pol'y 49 (1990). –Article Citation.

Michael I. Meyerson, <u>Impending Legal Issues for Integrated Broadband Networks</u>, 3 U. Fla. J.L. & Pub. Pol'y 49, 53-54 (1990).   –Page Citation.

University of Florida Law Review
Ab.:   U. Fla. L. Rev.

Ex.:   Donna D. Adler, <u>Master Limited Partnerships</u>, 40 U. Fla. L. Rev. 755 (1988). –Article Citation.

Donna D. Adler, <u>Master Limited Partnerships</u>, 40 U. Fla. L. Rev. 755, 778-80 (1988). –Page Citation.

University of Georgia Law Review
See Georgia Law Review.

University of Hawaii Law Review
Ab.:   U. Haw. L. Rev.

Ex.:   Stanley K. Laughlin, Jr., <u>The Constitutional Structure of the Courts of the United States Territories: The Case of American Samoa</u>, 13 U. Haw. L. Rev. 379 (1991). –Article Citation.

Stanley K. Laughlin, Jr., <u>The Constitutional Structure of the Courts of the United States Territories: The Case of American Samoa</u>, 13 U. Haw. L. Rev. 379, 440-42 (1991). –Page Citation.

University of Houston Law Review
See Houston Law Review.

University of Idaho Law Review
See Idaho Law Review.

In citing cases in law review footnotes, abbreviate any word listed in table T.6; the names of "states, countries, and other geographical units" unless they are named parties; and any other words of eight or more letters "if <u>substantial</u> space is thereby saved and the result is unambiguous." <u>Bluebook</u> rule 10.2.2. On the other hand, in citing cases in text, abbreviate only widely known acronyms and the following words: "&," "Ass'n," "Bros.," "Co.," "Corp.," "Inc.," "Ltd.," and "No." <u>Bluebook</u> rule 10.2.1(c).

University of Illinois Law Review
Ab.: U. Ill. L. Rev.

Ex.: Martha G. Duncan, <u>"A Strange Liking": Our Admiration for Criminals</u>, 1991 U. Ill. L. Rev. 1. –Article Citation.

Martha G. Duncan, <u>"A Strange Liking": Our Admiration for Criminals</u>, 1991 U. Ill. L. Rev. 1, 49-52. –Page Citation.

University of Iowa Law Review
See Iowa Law Review.

University of Kansas Law Review, The
Ab.: U. Kan. L. Rev.

Ex.: Thomas E. Baker, <u>The Impropriety of Expert Witness Testimony on the Law</u>, 40 U. Kan. L. Rev. 325 (1992). –Article Citation.

Thomas E. Baker, <u>The Impropriety of Expert Witness Testimony on the Law</u>, 40 U. Kan. L. Rev. 325, 249-52 (1992). –Page Citation.

University of Kentucky Law Review
See Kentucky Law Journal.

University of Louisville Journal of Family Law
See Journal of Family Law.

University of Maine Law Review
See Maine Law Review.

University of Maryland Law Review
Scc Maryland Law Review.

University of Memphis Law Review
Ab.: U. Mem. L. Rev.

Ex.: Neil D. Hamilton, <u>State Regulation of Agricultural Production Contracts</u>, 25 U. Mem. L. Rev. 1051 (1995). –Article Citation.

Neil D. Hamilton, <u>State Regulation of Agricultural Production Contracts</u>, 25 U. Mem. L. Rev. 1051, 1055 (1995). –Page Citation.

University of Miami Entertainment and Sports Law Review
Ab.: U. Miami Ent. & Sports L. Rev.

Ex.: Terrill L. Johnson, <u>The Antitrust Implications of the Divisional Structure of the National Collegiate Athletic Association</u>, 8 U. Miami Ent. & Sports L. Rev. 97 (1991). –Article Citation.

Terrill L. Johnson, <u>The Antitrust Implications of the Divisional Structure of the National Collegiate Athletic Association</u>, 8 U. Miami Ent. & Sports L. Rev. 97, 111-12 (1991). –Page Citation.

University of Miami Inter-American Law Review
Ab.: U. Miami Inter-Am. L. Rev.

In law review footnotes, the titles of books and the names of cases, except for procedural phrases, are not underlined. <u>See</u> Bluebook rule 2.1(a) & (b). Further, the following are in large and small capitals: codes, restatements, standards, constitutions, periodicals, authors of books, titles of books, the abbreviated names of codes, most legislative materials except for bills and resolutions, codified ordinances, model codes, court rules, and sentencing guidelines. Refer to <u>The Bluebook</u>.

Ex.: Rudy Sandoval, <u>Mexico's Path Towards the Free Trade Agreement with the U.S.</u>, 23 U. Miami Inter-Am. L. Rev. 133 (1991). –Article Citation.

Rudy Sandoval, <u>Mexico's Path Towards the Free Trade Agreement with the U.S.</u>, 23 U. Miami Inter-Am. L. Rev. 133, 149-52 (1991). –Page Citation.

University of Miami Law Review
Ab.: U. Miami L. Rev.

Ex.: Keith N. Hylton, <u>Litigation Costs and the Economic Theory of Tort Law</u>, 46 U. Miami L. Rev. 111 (1991). –Article Citation.

Keith N. Hylton, <u>Litigation Costs and the Economic Theory of Tort Law</u>, 46 U. Miami L. Rev. 111, 119-22 (1991). –Page Citation.

University of Michigan Journal of Law Reform
Ab.: U. Mich. J.L. Reform

Ex.: Mark R. Brown, <u>Accountability in Government and Section 1983</u>, 25 U. Mich. J.L. Reform 53 (1991). –Article Citation.

Mark R. Brown, <u>Accountability in Government and Section 1983</u>, 25 U. Mich. J.L. Reform 53, 99 (1991). –Page Citation.

University of Michigan Law Review
See Michigan Law Review.

University of Minnesota Law Review
See Minnesota Law Review.

University of Mississippi Law Journal
See Mississippi Law Journal.

University of Missouri-Kansas City Law Review
See UMKC Law Review.

University of Missouri Law Review
See Missouri Law Review.

University of Montana Law Review
See Montana Law Review.

University of Nebraska Law Review
See Nebraska Law Review.

University of New Brunswick Law Journal
Ab.: U.N.B. L.J.

Ex.: Dale Gibson, <u>Equality for Some</u>, 40 U.N.B. L.J. 2 (1991). –Article Citation.

Dale Gibson, <u>Equality for Some</u>, 40 U.N.B. L.J. 2, 15 (1991). –Page Citation.

In citing cases in law review footnotes, abbreviate any word listed in table T.6; the names of "states, countries, and other geographical units" unless they are named parties; and any other words of eight or more letters "if <u>substantial</u> space is thereby saved and the result is unambiguous." <u>Bluebook</u> rule 10.2.2. On the other hand, in citing cases in text, abbreviate only widely known acronyms and the following words: "&," "Ass'n," "Bros.," "Co.," "Corp.," "Inc.," "Ltd.," and "No." <u>Bluebook</u> rule 10.2.1(c).

University of New Mexico Law Review
See New Mexico Law Review.

University of New South Wales Law Journal, The
Ab.:   U.N.S.W. L.J.
Ex.:   Neil F. Douglas, <u>Freedom of Expression Under The Australian Constitution</u>, 16 U.N.S.W. L.J. 315 (1993). –Article Citation.

Neil F. Douglas, <u>Freedom of Expression Under The Australian Constitution</u>, 16 U.N.S.W. L.J. 315, 318-21 (1993). –Page Citation.

University of North Carolina Law Review
See North Carolina Law Review.

University of North Dakota Law Review
See North Dakota Law Review.

University of Oklahoma Law Review
See Oklahoma Law Review.

University of Oregon Law Review
See Oregon Law Review.

University of Pennsylvania Journal of Constitutional Law
Ab.:   U. Pa. J. Const. L.
Ex.:   Mark Tushnet, <u>Returning with Interest; Observations on Some Putative Benefits of Studying Comparative Constitutional Law</u>, 1 U. Pa. J. Const. L. 325 (1998). –Article Citation.

University of Pennsylvania Journal of International Business Law
Ab.:   U. Pa. J. Int'l Bus. L.
Ex.:   Zipora Cohen, <u>Fiduciary Duties of Controlling Shareholders: A Comparative View</u>, 12 U. Pa. J. Int'l Bus. L. 379 (1991). –Article Citation.

Zipora Cohen, <u>Fiduciary Duties of Controlling Shareholders: A Comparative View</u>, 12 U. Pa. J. Int'l Bus. L. 379, 389-92 (1991). –Page Citation.

University of Pennsylvania Journal of International Economic Law
Ab.:   U. Pa. J. Int'l Econ. L.
Ex.:   Christopher T. Curtis, <u>The Status of Foreign Deposits Under the Federal Depositor - Preference Law</u>, 21 U. Pa. J. Int'l Econ. L. 237 (2000). –Article Citation.

Christopher T. Curtis, <u>The Status of Foreign Deposits Under the Federal Depositor - Preference Law</u>, 21 U. Pa. J. Int'l Econ. L. 237, 241 n.19 (2000). –Footnote Citation.

In law review footnotes, the titles of books and the names of cases, except for procedural phrases, are not underlined. <u>See</u> Bluebook rule 2.1(a) & (b). Further, the following are in large and small capitals: codes, restatements, standards, constitutions, periodicals, authors of books, titles of books, the abbreviated names of codes, most legislative materials except for bills and resolutions, codified ordinances, model codes, court rules, and sentencing guidelines. Refer to <u>The Bluebook</u>.

University of Pennsylvania Journal of Labor and Employment Law
Ab.:   U. Pa. J. Lab. & Emp. L.

Ex.:   Clyde W. Summers, <u>Employment at Will in the United States: The Divine Right of Employers</u>, 3 U. Pa. J. Lab. & Emp. L. 65 (2000). –Article Citation.

Clyde W. Summers, <u>Employment at Will in the United States: The Divine Right of Employers</u>, 3 U. Pa. J. Lab. & Emp. L. 65, 65 (2000). –Page Citation.

University of Pennsylvania Law Review
Ab.:   U. Pa. L. Rev.

Ex.:   Harold S. Lewis, Jr. & Theodore Y. Blumoff, <u>Reshaping Section 1983's Asymmetry</u>, 140 U. Pa. L. Rev. 755 (1992). –Article Citation.

Harold S. Lewis, Jr. & Theodore Y. Blumoff, <u>Reshaping Section 1983's Asymmetry</u>, 140 U. Pa. L. Rev. 755, 793-96 (1992). –Page Citation.

University of Pittsburgh Law Review
Ab.:   U. Pitt. L. Rev.

Ex.:   Stephen A. Newman, <u>Euthanasia: Orchestrating "The Last Syllable of. . . Time"</u>, 53 U. Pitt. L. Rev. 153 (1991). –Article Citation.

Stephen A. Newman, <u>Euthanasia: Orchestrating "The Last Syllable of. . . Time"</u>, 53 U. Pitt. L. Rev. 153, 169-70 (1991). –Page Citation.

University of Puget Sound Law Review
Ab.:   U. Puget Sound L. Rev.

Ex.:   Earle A. Partington, <u>RICO, Merger, and Double Jeopardy</u>, 15 U. Puget Sound L. Rev. 1 (1991). –Article Citation.

Earle A. Partington, <u>RICO, Merger, and Double Jeopardy</u>, 15 U. Puget Sound L. Rev. 1, 29-30 (1991). –Page Citation.

University of Queensland Law Journal
Ab.:   U.Q. L.J.

Ex.:   Peter McDermott, <u>External Affairs and Treaties - The Founding Fathers' Perspective</u>, 16 U.Q. L.J. 123 (1990). –Article Citation.

Peter McDermott, <u>External Affairs and Treaties - The Founding Fathers' Perspective</u>, 16 U.Q. L.J. 123, 129-31 (1990). –Page Citation.

University of Richmond Law Review
Ab.:   U. Rich. L. Rev.

Ex.:   Harriette H. Shivers, <u>Guardianship Laws: Reform Efforts in Virginia</u>, 26 U. Rich. L. Rev. 325 (1992). –Article Citation.

Harriette H. Shivers, <u>Guardianship Laws: Reform Efforts in Virginia</u>, 26 U. Rich. L. Rev. 325, 329-32 (1992). –Page Citation.

In citing cases in law review footnotes, abbreviate any word listed in table T.6; the names of "states, countries, and other geographical units" unless they are named parties; and any other words of eight or more letters "if <u>substantial</u> space is thereby saved and the result is unambiguous." <u>Bluebook</u> rule 10.2.2. On the other hand, in citing cases in text, abbreviate only widely known acronyms and the following words: "&," "Ass'n," "Bros.," "Co.," "Corp.," "Inc.," "Ltd.," and "No." <u>Bluebook</u> rule 10.2.1(c).

University of San Diego Law Review
See San Diego Law Review.

University of San Francisco Law Review
Ab.:   U.S.F. L. Rev.

Ex.:   John E. Rumel, <u>The Hourglass and Due Process: The Propriety of Time Limits on Civil Trials</u>, 26 U.S.F. L. Rev. 237 (1992). –Article Citation.

John E. Rumel, <u>The Hourglass and Due Process: The Propriety of Time Limits on Civil Trials</u>, 26 U.S.F. L. Rev. 237, 249-52 (1992). –Page Citation.

University of Santa Clara Law Review
See Santa Clara Law Review.

University of South Carolina Law Review
See South Carolina Law Review.

University of South Dakota Law Review
See South Dakota Law Review.

University of Southern California Annual Tax Institute
See Major Tax Planning.

University of Tasmania Law Review
Ab.:   U. Tas. L. Rev.

Ex.:   George Winterton, <u>Reserve Powers in an Australian Republic</u>, 12 U. Tas. L. Rev. 249 (1993). –Article Citation.

George Winterton, <u>Reserve Powers in an Australian Republic</u>, 12 U. Tas. L. Rev. 249, 256 (1993). –Page Citation.

University of Tennessee Law Review
See Tennessee Law Review.

University of Texas Law Review
See Texas Law Review.

University of the District of Columbia David Clarke School of Law Law Review
Ab: UDC/DCSL L. Rev.

Ex: Mary M. Cheh, <u>Demonstrations, Security Zones, and First Amendment Protection of Special Places</u>, 8 UDC/DCSL L. Rev. 53 (2004). –Article Citation.

Mary M. Cheh, <u>Demonstrations, Security Zones, and First Amendment Protection of Special Places</u>, 8 UDC/DCSL L. Rev. 53, 60-61 (2004). –Page Citation.

University of the Pacific Law Journal
See Pacific Law Journal.

In law review footnotes, the titles of books and the names of cases, except for procedural phrases, are not underlined. <u>See</u> <u>Bluebook</u> rule 2.1(a) & (b). Further, the following are in large and small capitals: codes, restatements, standards, constitutions, periodicals, authors of books, titles of books, the abbreviated names of codes, most legislative materials except for bills and resolutions, codified ordinances, model codes, court rules, and sentencing guidelines. Refer to <u>The Bluebook</u>.

University of Toledo Law Review
Ab.: U. Tol. L. Rev.

Ex.: Andrew C. Barrett, <u>The Telecommunications Infrastructure of the Future</u>, 23 U. Tol. L. Rev. 85 (1991). −Article Citation.

Andrew C. Barrett, <u>The Telecommunications Infrastructure of the Future</u>, 23 U. Tol. L. Rev. 85, 89-90 (1991). −Page Citation.

University of Toronto Faculty of Law Review
Ab.: U. Toronto Fac. L. Rev.

Ex.: Jacqueline R. Castel, <u>Women's Sexual Exploitation in Therapy</u>, 49 U. Toronto Fac. L. Rev. 42 (1991). −Article Citation.

Jacqueline R. Castel, <u>Women's Sexual Exploitation in Therapy</u>, 49 U. Toronto Fac. L. Rev. 42, 59-61 (1991). −Page Citation.

University of Toronto Law Journal
Ab.: U. Toronto L.J.

Ex.: Jamie Cameron, <u>The Charter and Remedial Choice</u>, 45 U. Toronto L.J. 525 (1995). −Article Citation.

Jamie Cameron, <u>The Charter and Remedial Choice</u>, 45 U. Toronto L.J. 525, 530 (1995). −Page Citation.

University of Tulsa Law Journal
See Tulsa Law Journal.

University of Utah Law Review
See Utah Law Review.

University of Virginia Law Review
See Virginia Law Review.

University of Washington Law Quarterly
See Washington University Law Quarterly.

University of West Los Angeles Law Review
Ab.: UWLA L. Rev.

Ex.: Tyron J. Sheppard & Richard Nevirs, <u>Constitutional Equity - Reparations at Last</u>, 22 UWLA L. Rev. 105 (1991). −Article Citation.

Tyron J. Sheppard & Richard Nevirs, <u>Constitutional Equity - Reparations at Last</u>, 22 UWLA L. Rev. 105, 109-11 (1991). −Page Citation.

University of Western Australia Law Review
Ab.: U. W. Austl. L. Rev.

In citing cases in law review footnotes, abbreviate any word listed in table T.6; the names of "states, countries, and other geographical units" unless they are named parties; and any other words of eight or more letters "if <u>substantial</u> space is thereby saved and the result is unambiguous." <u>Bluebook</u> rule 10.2.2. On the other hand, in citing cases in text, abbreviate only widely known acronyms and the following words: "&," "Ass'n," "Bros.," "Co.," "Corp.," "Inc.," "Ltd.," and "No." <u>Bluebook</u> rule 10.2.1(c).

Ex.:   Lakshman Marasinghe, <u>Choice of Forum in International Litigation</u>, 23 U. of W. Austl. L. Rev. 264 (1993). –Article Citation.

Lakshman Marasinghe, <u>Choice of Forum in International Litigation</u>, 23 U. of W. Austl. L. Rev. 264, 267-71 (1993). –Page Citation.

University of Wisconsin Law Review
See Wisconsin Law Review.

University of Wyoming Law Review
See Land and Water Law Review and Wyoming Law Review.

unpublished materials
–Explained and illustrated in <u>Bluebook</u> rule 17.

Ex.:   Daniel Sipe, A Moment of the State: The Enactment of the National Labor Relations Act, 1935, at 110 (May 1, 1981) (unpublished Ph.D. dissertation, University of Pennsylvania) (on file with author). –unpublished dissertation.

Robert Smith, URESA and Mexican Family Law (November 17, 1996) (unpublished manuscript, on file with Vanderbilt Journal of Transnational Law). –unpublished manuscript.

Letter from Kurt Grasinger, Film Critic, The New Yorker, to Jean Winter, Editor, Vanderbilt Law School Brief (Feb. 26, 1996) (on file with author). –unpublished letter.

See <u>Bluebook</u> rule 17.1.4.

Interview with Pam Malone, President of the National Association for Legal Placement, in Nashville, Tenn. (Dec. 10, 1996). –author conducted interview.

Interview by Stephen Teel with Don Welch, Associate Dean, Vanderbilt University Law School, in Nashville, Tenn. (Jan 2, 1997). –author did not conduct interview.

–unpublished interviews

unreported cases
See pending and unreported cases and any local rules concerning citing unreported opinions.

unreported decisions
See pending and unreported cases and any local rules concerning citing unreported opinions.

Urban Lawyer
Ab.:   Urb. Law.

In law review footnotes, the titles of books and the names of cases, except for procedural phrases, are not underlined. <u>See</u> <u>Bluebook</u> rule 2.1(a) & (b). Further, the following are in large and small capitals: codes, restatements, standards, constitutions, periodicals, authors of books, titles of books, the abbreviated names of codes, most legislative materials except for bills and resolutions, codified ordinances, model codes, court rules, and sentencing guidelines. Refer to <u>The Bluebook</u>.

Ex.:   Daniel R. Mandelker & A. Dan Tarlock, <u>Shifting the Presumption of Constitutionality in Land Use Law</u>, 24 Urb. Law. 1 (1992). –Article Citation.

Daniel R. Mandelker & A. Dan Tarlock, <u>Shifting the Presumption of Constitutionality in Land Use Law</u>, 24 Urb. Law. 1, 39-40 (1992). –Page Citation.

Utah Administrative Code (LexisNexis)
Ab.:   Utah Admin. Code r. x-x-x (year)

Ex.:   Utah Admin. Code r. 81-4A-1 (2000).

Utah Bar Journal
Ab.:   Utah B.J.

Utah Code Annotated (LexisNexis)
Ab.:   Utah Code Ann. § x-x-x (year)

Ex.:   Utah Code Ann. § 72-10-404 (2004).

Utah Code Ann. § 71-8-4 (Supp. 2005).

Utah Constitution
Ab.:   Utah Const. art.   , §   .

Ex.:   Utah Const. art. XII, § 19. –"Cite constitutional provisions currently in force without a date." <u>Bluebook</u> rule 11.

Utah Const. art. VI, § 23 (repealed 1982). –"If the cited provision has been repealed, either indicate parenthetically the fact and date of repeal or cite the repealing provision in full ." <u>Bluebook</u> rule 11.

Utah Const. art. I, § 8 (amended 1988). –"When citing a provision that has been subsequently amended, either indicate parenthetically the fact and date of amendment or cite the amending provision in full." <u>Bluebook</u> rule 11.

Utah Court of Appeals
Ab.:   Utah Ct. App.

–Cite to P.2d. or P.3d, if therein; in addition, give public domain citation if available.

–Until January 1, 1999, when a public domain format was adopted, cite as follows:

In all documents:

<u>Eyring v. Fairbanks</u>, 918 P.2d 489 (Utah Ct. App. 1996). –Case Citation.

<u>Eyring v. Fairbanks</u>, 918 P.2d 489, 492 (Utah Ct. App. 1996). –Page Citation.

–From January 1, 1999, cite as follows:

In all documents:

In citing cases in law review footnotes, abbreviate any word listed in table T.6; the names of "states, countries, and other geographical units" unless they are named parties; and any other words of eight or more letters "if <u>substantial</u> space is thereby saved and the result is unambiguous." <u>Bluebook</u> rule 10.2.2. On the other hand, in citing cases in text, abbreviate only widely known acronyms and the following words: "&," "Ass'n," "Bros.," "Co.," "Corp.," "Inc.," "Ltd.," and "No." <u>Bluebook</u> rule 10.2.1(c).

State v. Tryba, 2000 UT App 230, 8 P.3d 274. –Case Citation.

State v. Tryba, 2000 UT App 230, ¶ 8, 8 P.3d 274, 277. –Pinpoint Citation.

See Bluebook rules 10.3.1, 10.3.3, and B5.1.3; see also Utah Supreme Court Standing Order No. 4 (effective Jan. 18, 2000).

Utah Law Review
Ab.:   Utah L. Rev.

Ex.:   Allan J. Samansky, <u>Nonstandard Thoughts About the Standard Deduction</u>, 1991 Utah L. Rev. 531. –Article Citation.

Allan J. Samansky, <u>Nonstandard Thoughts About the Standard Deduction</u>, 1991 Utah L. Rev. 531, 534. –Page Citation.

Utah Session Laws
See Laws of Utah.

Utah State Bulletin
Ab.:   issue no. Utah Bull. page no. (month day, year)

Ex.:   2005-12 Utah Bull. 47 (June 15, 2005).

See also Opinions of the Attorney General of Utah.

Utah Supreme Court
–Cite to P., P.2d, or P.3d, if therein; otherwise, cite to Vt. Give public domain citation if available. Otherwise, give parallel citations only in documents submitted to Utah state courts.

–Through 30 Utah 2d 462 (1974), cite as follows:

In documents submitted to Utah state courts:

Hobbs v. Fenton, 25 Utah 2d 206, 479 P.2d 472 (1971). –Case Citation.

Hobbs v. Fenton, 25 Utah 2d 206, 209, 479 P.2d 472, 473-74 (1971). –Page Citation.

In all other documents:

Hobbs v. Fenton, 479 P.2d 472 (Utah 1971). –Case Citation.

Hobbs v. Fenton, 479 P.2d 472, 473-74 (Utah 1971). –Page Citation.

(Note: Because Utah Supreme Court opinions provide parallel citations to Utah cases until 1974, we advise giving a parallel citation in documents submitted to Utah state courts. See Bluebook rules 10.3.1 and B5.1.3.)

–After 30 Utah 2d 462 (1974) and until January 1, 1996, when a public domain format was adopted, cite as follows:

In all documents:

Tucker v. Tucker, 910 P.2d 1209 (Utah 1996). –Case Citation.

In law review footnotes, the titles of books and the names of cases, except for procedural phrases, are not underlined. See Bluebook rule 2.1(a) & (b). Further, the following are in large and small capitals: codes, restatements, standards, constitutions, periodicals, authors of books, titles of books, the abbreviated names of codes, most legislative materials except for bills and resolutions, codified ordinances, model codes, court rules, and sentencing guidelines. Refer to <u>The Bluebook</u>.

<u>Tucker v. Tucker</u>, 910 P.2d 1209, 1210 (Utah 1996). –Page Citation.

–After January 1, 1996, cite as follows:

In all documents:

<u>State v. Reed</u>, 2000 UT 68, 8 P.3d 1025. –Case Citation.

<u>State v. Reed</u>, 2000 UT 68, ¶ 11, 8 P.3d 1025, 1027. –Pinpoint Citation.

See <u>Bluebook</u> rules 10.3.1, 10.3.3, and B5.1.3; <u>see also</u> Utah Supreme Court Standing Order No. 4 (effective Jan. 18, 2000).

Utilities Law Reports (Commerce Clearing House)
 Ab.:   Util. L. Rep. (CCH)

In citing cases in law review footnotes, abbreviate any word listed in table T.6; the names of "states, countries, and other geographical units" unless they are named parties; and any other words of eight or more letters "if <u>substantial</u> space is thereby saved and the result is unambiguous." <u>Bluebook</u> rule 10.2.2. On the other hand, in citing cases in text, abbreviate only widely known acronyms and the following words: "&," "Ass'n," "Bros.," "Co.," "Corp.," "Inc.," "Ltd.," and "No." <u>Bluebook</u> rule 10.2.1(c).

V

Valparaiso University Law Review
Ab.:   Val. U. L. Rev.

Ex.:   Laura G. Dooley, <u>Sounds of Silence on the Civil Jury</u>, 26 Val. U. L. Rev. 405 (1991). −Article Citation.

Laura G. Dooley, <u>Sounds of Silence on the Civil Jury</u>, 26 Val. U. L. Rev. 405, 409-11 (1991). −Page Citation.

Vanderbilt Journal of Entertainment Law & Practice
Ab.:   Vand. J. Ent. L. & Prac.

Ex.:   S. E. Oross, <u>Fighting the Phantom Menace; The Motion Picture Industry's Struggle to Protect Itself Against Digital Piracy</u>, 2 Vand. J. Ent. L. & Prac. 149, 152 (2000). −Page Citation.

Vanderbilt Journal of Transnational Law
Ab.:   Vand. J. Transnat'l L.

Ex.:   James D. Harmon, Jr., <u>RICO Meets Keiretsu: A Response to Predatory Transfer Pricing</u>, 25 Vand. J. Transnat'l L. 3 (1992). −Article Citation.

James D. Harmon, Jr., <u>RICO Meets Keiretsu: A Response to Predatory Transfer Pricing</u>, 25 Vand. J. Transnat'l L. 3, 35-36 (1992). −Page Citation.

Vanderbilt Law Review
Ab.:   Vand. L. Rev.

Ex.:   Barry Friedman, <u>Habeas and Hubris</u>, 45 Vand. L. Rev. 797 (1992). −Article Citation.

Barry Friedman, <u>Habeas and Hubris</u>, 45 Vand. L. Rev. 797, 823-25 (1992). −Page Citation.

Vanderbilt Lawyer, The
Ab.:   Vand. Law.

Ex.:   Thomas R. McCoy, <u>A Doctrinal Dilemma</u>, Vand. Law., Spring 1991, at 20. −Article Citation.

Thomas R. McCoy, <u>A Doctrinal Dilemma</u>, Vand. Law., Spring 1991, at 20, 21-23. −Page Citation.

vendor neutral citations
See public domain citations.

In law review footnotes, the titles of books and the names of cases, except for procedural phrases, are not underlined. <u>See</u> <u>Bluebook</u> rule 2.1(a) & (b). Further, the following are in large and small capitals: codes, restatements, standards, constitutions, periodicals, authors of books, titles of books, the abbreviated names of codes, most legislative materials except for bills and resolutions, codified ordinances, model codes, court rules, and sentencing guidelines. Refer to <u>The Bluebook</u>.

Vermont Advance Legislative Service (LexisNexis)

Ab.: year-pamph. no. Vt. Adv. Legis. Serv. page no. (LexisNexis)

Ex.: Act of May 3, 2005, No. 13, 2005-2 Vt. Adv. Legis. Serv. 69 (LexisNexis) (relating to exposure to mercury). –Citation to an entire session law.

Act of May 3, 2005, No. 13, sec. 1, § 7105, 2005-2 Vt. Adv. Legis. Serv. 69, 73 (LexisNexis) (relating to exposure to mercury). –Citation to a section of a session law amending prior act.

–See Bluebook rule 12.4.

–"Cite to Vt. Acts & Resolves, if therein." Bluebook table T.1, p. 236.

Vermont Bar Journal and Law Digest

Ab.: Vt. B.J. & L. Dig.

Ex.: John M. Hall, The Ethical Duty to Assure a Client's Competency When Preparing Powers of Attorney, Vt. B.J. & L. Dig., Feb. 1992, at 34. –Article Citation.

John M. Hall, The Ethical Duty to Assure a Client's Competency When Preparing Powers of Attorney, Vt. B.J. & L. Dig., Feb. 1992, at 34, 35. –Page Citation.

Vermont Constitution

Ab.: Vt. Const. ch.   , §   .

Ex.: Vt. Const. ch. II , art. 67. –"Cite constitutional provisions currently in force without a date." Bluebook rule 11.

–"If the cited provision has been repealed, either indicate parenthetically the fact and date of repeal or cite the repealing provision in full." Bluebook rule 11.

Vt. Const. ch. II, art. 68 (amended 1964). –"When citing a provision that has been subsequently amended, either indicate parenthetically the fact and date of amendment or cite the amending provision in full." Bluebook rule 11.

Vt. Const. of 1786, ch. I, art. 7 (1793). –"Cite constitutions that have been totally superseded by year of adoption; if the specific provision cited was adopted in a different year, give that year parenthetically." Bluebook rule 11.

Vermont Government Register (Weil)

Ab.: issue no. Vt. Gov't Reg. page no. (Weil month year)

Ex.: 107 Vt. Gov't Reg. 8 (Weil Dec. 1999)

Vermont Law Review

Ab.: Vt. L. Rev.

In citing cases in law review footnotes, abbreviate any word listed in table T.6; the names of "states, countries, and other geographical units" unless they are named parties; and any other words of eight or more letters "if substantial space is thereby saved and the result is unambiguous." Bluebook rule 10.2.2. On the other hand, in citing cases in text, abbreviate only widely known acronyms and the following words: "&," "Ass'n," "Bros.," "Co.," "Corp.," "Inc.," "Ltd.," and "No." Bluebook rule 10.2.1(c).

Ex.:   Kevin J. Greene, <u>Terrorism as Impermissible Political Violence: An International Law Framework</u>, 16 Vt. L. Rev. 461 (1992). –Article Citation.

Kevin J. Greene, <u>Terrorism as Impermissible Political Violence: An International Law Framework</u>, 16 Vt. L. Rev. 461, 488 (1992). –Page Citation.

Vermont Reports
Ab.:   Vt.

–Cite to A. or A.2d, if therein; otherwise, cite to Vt. Give public domain citation if available. Otherwise, give parallel citations only in documents submitted to Vermont state courts. <u>See</u> <u>Bluebook</u> rules 10.3.1, 10.3.3, and B5.1.3; see also Vt. R. App. P. 28.2(b), which requires parallel citation

–Until January 1, 2003, cite as follows:

In documents submitted to Vermont state courts, cite as follows:

<u>Godino v. Cleanthes</u>, 163 Vt. 237, 656 A.2d 991 (1996). –Case Citation.

<u>Godino v. Cleanthes</u>, 163 Vt. 237, 240, 656 A.2d 991, 993 (1996). –Page Citation.

In all other documents, cite as follows:

<u>Godino v. Cleanthes</u>, 656 A.2d 991 (Vt. 1996). –Case Citation.

<u>Godino v. Cleanthes</u>, 656 A.2d 991, 993 (Vt. 1996). –Page Citation.

–After January 1, 2003, cite as follows:

In documents submitted to Vermont state courts:

<u>Doe v. Forrest</u>, 2004 VT 37, 176 Vt. 476, 853 A.2d 48. –Case Citation.

<u>Doe v. Forrest</u>, 2004 VT 37, ¶ 9, 176 Vt. 476, 853 A.2d 48. –Pinpoint Citation.

In all other documents:

<u>Doe v. Forrest</u>, 2004 VT 37, 853 A.2d 48. –Case Citation

<u>Doe v. Forrest</u>, 2004 VT 37, ¶ 9, 853 A.2d 48, 53. –Pinpoint Citation.

Vermont Session Laws
See Acts and Resolves of Vermont.

Vermont Statutes Annotated (LexisNexis)
Ab.:   Vt. Stat. Ann. tit. x, § x (year)
Ex.:   Vt. Stat. Ann. tit. 30, § 112 (2000).
          Vt. Stat. Ann. tit. 32, § 10105 (Supp. 2000).

In law review footnotes, the titles of books and the names of cases, except for procedural phrases, are not underlined. <u>See</u> <u>Bluebook</u> rule 2.1(a) & (b). Further, the following are in large and small capitals: codes, restatements, standards, constitutions, periodicals, authors of books, titles of books, the abbreviated names of codes, most legislative materials except for bills and resolutions, codified ordinances, model codes, court rules, and sentencing guidelines. Refer to <u>The Bluebook</u>.

–For proper citation forms in papers submitted to Vermont courts, see prefatory pages of Vt. Stat. Ann. volumes.

Vernon's Annotated Missouri Statutes (West)

Ab.: Mo. Ann. Stat. § x.x (West year)

Ex.: Mo. Ann. Stat. § 163.191 (West 2000).

Mo. Ann. Stat. § 316.233 (West Supp. 2000).

–"Cite to Mo. Rev. Stat., if therein." Bluebook table T.1, p. 217.

Vernon's Kansas Statutes Annotated

Ab.: Kan. subject Ann. § x-x (West year)

See Bluebook table T.1, p. 209, for the abbreviation of each subject.

Ex.: Kan. U.C.C. Ann. § 84-6-102 (West 1968).

Kan. U.C.C. Ann. § 84-6-106 (West Supp. 1986).

– "Cite to Kan. Stat. Ann., if therein." Bluebook table T.1, p. 209.

–For proper citation form in papers submitted to Kansas courts, see title pages to Kansas Statutes Annotated volumes.

Vernon's Texas Business Corporation Act Annotated (West)

Ab.: Tex. Bus. Corp. Act. Ann. art. x (Vernon year)

Ex.: Tex. Bus. Corp. Act Ann. art 7.04 (Vernon 2004).

Vernon's Texas Code of Criminal Procedure Annotated (West)

Ab.: Tex. Code Crim. P. Ann. art. (Vernon year)

Ex.: Tex. Code Crim. P. Ann. art. 21.03 (Vernon 1989).

Vernon's Texas Insurance Code Annotated (West)

Ab.: Tex. Ins. Code Ann. art. x (Vernon year)

Ex.: Tex. Ins. Code Ann. art. 21.14-1 (Vernon 2002).

Vernon's Texas Probate Code Annotated (West)

Ab.: Tex. Prob. Code Ann. § x (Vernon year)

Ex.: Tex. Prob. Code Ann. § 279 (Vernon 1980).

Vernon's Texas Revised Civil Statutes Annotated

Ab.: Tex. Rev. Civ. Stat. Ann. art. x, § x (Vernon year)

Ex: Tex. Rev. Civ. Stat. Ann. art. 37.07, § 3(c) (Vernon 1981).

Tex. Rev. Civ. Stat. Ann. art. 21.80 (Vernon Supp. 2000).

Vernon's Texas Session Law Service (West)

Ab.: year Tex. Sess. Law Serv. page no. (West)

Ex.: Act of Apr. 8, 1992, ch. 1, 1992 Tex. Sess. Law Serv. 1 (West) (senatorial district boundaries). –Citation to an entire session law.

Act of Apr. 8, 1992, ch. 1, § 2, 1992 Tex. Sess. Law Serv. 1, 2 (West) (senatorial district boundaries). –Citation to a section of a session law.

In citing cases in law review footnotes, abbreviate any word listed in table T.6; the names of "states, countries, and other geographical units" unless they are named parties; and any other words of eight or more letters "if substantial space is thereby saved and the result is unambiguous." Bluebook rule 10.2.2. On the other hand, in citing cases in text, abbreviate only widely known acronyms and the following words: "&," "Ass'n," "Bros.," "Co.," "Corp.," "Inc.," "Ltd.," and "No." Bluebook rule 10.2.1(c).

–See Bluebook rule 12.4.

–"Cite to Tex. Gen. Laws, if therein." Bluebook table T.1, p. 235.

Vernon's Texas Statutes and Codes Annotated
Form: Tex. [subject] Code Ann. § (Vernon year)

Ex.:   Tex. Loc. Gov't Code Ann. § 153.003 (Vernon 1999).

Tex. Util. Code Ann. § 121.505 (Vernon Supp. 2000).

See Bluebook table T.1, pp. 234-35.

–For proper citation form in papers submitted to Texas courts, see Texas Rules of Form 40 (Texas Law Review Ass'n ed., 10th ed. 2003).

Verträge der Bundesrepublik Deutschland
Ab.:   Vol. Verträge der Bundesrepublik Deutschland (ser. A), No.

Ex.:   68 Verträge der Bundesrepublik Deutschland (ser. A), No. 847.

Veterans Appeals Reporter
See West's Veterans Appeals Reporter.

Vice Chancellor
Ab.:   V.C.

Victorian Reports
Ab.:   V.R.

Ex.:   Saunders v. Nash, [1991] 2 V.R. 63 (Austl.).

Note: For explanation of Australia's medium-neutral citation, see L.T. Olsson, Guide to Uniform Production of Judgments (2d ed. 1999), available at http://www.aija.org.au/online/judguide.htm.

Victoria University of Wellington Law Review
Ab.:   Vict. U. Wellington L. Rev.

Ex.:   Malcolm Luey, Proprietary Remedies in Insurance Subrogation, 25 Vict. U. Wellington L. Rev. 449 (1995). –Article Citation.

Malcolm Luey, Proprietary Remedies in Insurance Subrogation, 25 Vict. U. Wellington L. Rev. 449, 452-54 (1995). –Page Citation.

videotapes, noncommercial
Ex.   Videotape: The Call to Practice (Shyster Enterprises, Inc. 2001) (on file with the Vanderbilt Univ. Law School Library).

See Bluebook rule 18.5.

Villanova Environmental Law Journal
Ab.:   Vill. Envtl. L.J.

In law review footnotes, the titles of books and the names of cases, except for procedural phrases, are not underlined. See Bluebook rule 2.1(a) & (b). Further, the following are in large and small capitals: codes, restatements, standards, constitutions, periodicals, authors of books, titles of books, the abbreviated names of codes, most legislative materials except for bills and resolutions, codified ordinances, model codes, court rules, and sentencing guidelines. Refer to The Bluebook.

Ex.:   Jerome B. Simandle, <u>Resolving Multi-Party Hazardous Waste Litigation</u>, 2 Vill. Envtl. L.J. 111 (1991). –Article Citation.

Jerome B. Simandle, <u>Resolving Multi-Party Hazardous Waste Litigation</u>, 2 Vill. Envtl. L.J. 111, 115-16 (1991). –Page Citation.

Villanova Law Review
Ab.:   Vill. L. Rev.

Ex.:   David Chang, <u>A Critique of Judicial Supremacy</u>, 36 Vill. L. Rev. 281 (1991). –Article Citation.

David Chang, <u>A Critique of Judicial Supremacy</u>, 36 Vill. L. Rev. 281, 333-35 (1991). –Page Citation.

Virgin Islands Code Annotated (LexisNexis)
Ab.:   V.I. Code Ann. tit. x § x-x (year)

Ex.:   V.I. Code Ann. tit. 11A § 9-301 (2003)

V.I. Code Ann. tit. 12 § 670 (Supp. 2004)

–For proper citation form in papers submitted to Virgin Islands courts, see V.I. Code Ann. § 1(b) (2003).

Virgin Islands Code Annotated Advance Legislative Service (LexisNexis)
Ab.:   year-pamph. no. V.I. Code Ann. Adv. Legis. Serv. page no. (LexisNexis)

Ex.:   Act of June 18, 2003, No. 6585, 2003-1 V.I. Code Ann. Adv. Legis. Serv. 30 (LexisNexis) (relating to banking institutions license fees). –Citation to an entire session law.

Act of June 18, 2003, No. 6585, sec. 6, § 33-4A, 2003-1 V.I. Code Ann. Adv. Legis. Serv. 30, 31 (LexisNexis) (relating to banking institution license fees). –Citation to a section of a session law amending prior act.

–<u>See</u> <u>Bluebook</u> rule 12.4.

–"Cite to V.I. Sess. Laws, if therein." <u>Bluebook</u> table T.1, p. 242.

Virgin Islands Government Register (Weil)
Ab.:   issue no. V.I. Gov't Reg. page no. (Weil month year)

Virgin Islands Reports
Ab.:   V.I.

Ex.:   <u>Vidal v. Virgin Islands Hous. Auth.</u>, 20 V.I. 3 (Terr. Ct. 1983). –Case Citation.

<u>Vidal v. Virgin Islands Hous. Auth.</u>, 20 V.I. 3, 5 (Terr. Ct. 1983). –Page Citation.

<u>See</u> V.I. R. App. P. 15(b).

Virginia Administrative Code
Ab.:   x Va. Admin. Code § x-x-x (year).

In citing cases in law review footnotes, abbreviate any word listed in table T.6; the names of "states, countries, and other geographical units" unless they are named parties; and any other words of eight or more letters "if <u>substantial</u> space is thereby saved and the result is unambiguous." <u>Bluebook</u> rule 10.2.2. On the other hand, in citing cases in text, abbreviate only widely known acronyms and the following words: "&," "Ass'n," "Bros.," "Co.," "Corp.," "Inc.," "Ltd.," and "No." <u>Bluebook</u> rule 10.2.1(c).

Ex.: 8 Va. Admin. Code § 85-10-50 (2000).

Virginia Bar Association Journal
Ab.: Va. B. Ass'n J.

Ex.: J.R. Zepkin, Increasing the Litigator's Risk, Va. B. Ass'n J., Spring 1992, at 16. –Article Citation.

J.R. Zepkin, Increasing the Litigator's Risk, Va. B. Ass'n J., Spring 1992, at 16, 18. –Page Citation.

Virginia Code
See Code of Virginia 1950 Annotated.

Virginia Constitution
Ab.: Va. Const. art. , § .

Ex.: Va. Const. art. XI, § 3. –"Cite constitutional provisions currently in force without a date." Bluebook rule 11.

Va. Const. art. VIII, § 8 (amended 1990). –"When citing a provision that has been subsequently amended, either indicate parenthetically the fact and date of amendment or cite the amending provision in full." Bluebook rule 11.

Virginia Court of Appeals Reports
Ab.: Va. App.

–Cite to S.E. or S.E.2d, if therein; otherwise, cite to Va. App.

–Give parallel citations only in documents submitted to Virginia state courts. See Bluebook rules 10.3.1 and B5.1.3; see also Va. Sup. Ct. R. 5:17(c)(1), 5:28(a), 5A:20(a), and 5A:21(a), which require a parallel citation.

In documents submitted to Virginia state courts, cite as follows:

Rocco Turkeys, Inc. v. Lemus, 21 Va. App. 503, 465 S.E.2d 156 (1996). –Case Citation.

Rocco Turkeys, Inc. v. Lemus, 21 Va. App. 503, 504, 465 S.E.2d 156, 157 (1996). –Page Citation.

In all other documents, cite as follows:

Rocco Turkeys, Inc. v. Lemus, 465 S.E.2d 156 (Va. Ct. App. 1996). –Case Citation.

Rocco Turkeys, Inc. v. Lemus, 465 S.E.2d 156, 157 (Va. Ct. App. 1996). –Page Citation.

Virginia Environmental Law Journal
Ab.: Va. Envtl. L.J.

In law review footnotes, the titles of books and the names of cases, except for procedural phrases, are not underlined. See Bluebook rule 2.1(a) & (b). Further, the following are in large and small capitals: codes, restatements, standards, constitutions, periodicals, authors of books, titles of books, the abbreviated names of codes, most legislative materials except for bills and resolutions, codified ordinances, model codes, court rules, and sentencing guidelines. Refer to The Bluebook.

Ex.: Steven F. Ferrey, <u>Shaping American Power: Federal Preemption and Technological Change</u>, 11 Va. Envtl. L.J. 47 (1991). –Article Citation.

Steven F. Ferrey, <u>Shaping American Power: Federal Preemption and Technological Change</u>, 11 Va. Envtl. L.J. 47, 55-56 (1991). –Page Citation.

Virginia Journal of International Law
Ab.: Va. J. Int'l L.

Ex.: Lawrence R. Helfer, <u>Lesbian and Gay Rights as Human Rights: Strategies for a United Europe</u>, 32 Va. J. Int'l L. 157 (1991). –Article Citation.

Lawrence R. Helfer, <u>Lesbian and Gay Rights as Human Rights: Strategies for a United Europe</u>, 32 Va. J. Int'l L. 157, 158 (1991). –Page Citation.

Virginia Journal of Social Policy and the Law
Ab.: Va. J. Soc. Pol'y & L.

Ex.: James A. Armstrong, Jr., <u>From the Inside</u>, 3 Va. J. Soc. Pol'y & L. 331 (1996). –Article Citation.

James A. Armstrong, Jr., <u>From the Inside</u>, 3 Va. J. Soc. Pol'y & L. 331, 333 (1996). –Page Citation.

Virginia Law Review
Ab.: Va. L. Rev.

Ex.: Paul G. Mahoney, <u>Precaution Cost and the Law of Fraud in Impersonal Markets</u>, 78 Va. L. Rev. 623 (1992). –Article Citation.

Paul G. Mahoney, <u>Precaution Cost and the Law of Fraud in Impersonal Markets</u>, 78 Va. L. Rev. 623, 659-60 (1992). –Page Citation.

Virginia Lawyer
-alternates with Virginia Lawyer Register

Ab.: Va. Law.

Ex.: Hon. Frank J. Ceresi, <u>The Drug Crisis in Family Court</u>, Va. Law., Jan., 1992, at 18. –Article Citation.

Hon. Frank J. Ceresi, <u>The Drug Crisis in Family Court</u>, Va. Law., Jan., 1992, at 18, 19. –Page Citation.

Virginia Lawyer Register
See Virginia Lawyer.

Virginia Opinions of the Attorney General and Report to the Governor
See Opinions of the Attorney General and Report to the Governor of Virginia.

Virginia Register of Regulations (Weil)
Ab.: vol. no. Va. Regs. Reg. page no. (month day, year)

In citing cases in law review footnotes, abbreviate any word listed in table T.6; the names of "states, countries, and other geographical units" unless they are named parties; and any other words of eight or more letters "if <u>substantial</u> space is thereby saved and the result is unambiguous." <u>Bluebook</u> rule 10.2.2. On the other hand, in citing cases in text, abbreviate only widely known acronyms and the following words: "&," "Ass'n," "Bros.," "Co.," "Corp.," "Inc.," "Ltd.," and "No." <u>Bluebook</u> rule 10.2.1(c).

Ex.: 20 Va. Regs. Reg. 1100 (Feb. 19, 2004).

Virginia Reports
Ab.: Va.

–Cite to S.E. or S.E.2d, if therein; otherwise, cite to Va.

–Give parallel citations only in documents submitted to Virginia state courts. See Bluebook rules 10.3.1 and B5.1.3; see also Va. Sup. Ct. R. 5:17(c)(1), 5:28(a), 5A:20(a), and 5A:21(a), which require a parallel citation.

In documents submitted to Virginia state courts, cite as follows:

Ware v. Jensen, 251 Va. 116, 465 S.E.2d 809 (1996).
–Case Citation.

Ware v. Jensen, 251 Va. 116, 117, 465 S.E.2d 809, 810 (1996).
–Page Citation.

In all other documents, cite as follows:

Ware v. Jensen, 465 S.E.2d 809 (Va. 1996). –Case Citation.

Ware v. Jensen, 465 S.E.2d 809, 810 (Va. 1996). –Page Citation.

Virginia Session Laws
See Acts of the General Assembly of the Commonwealth of Virginia.

Virginia Tax Review
Ab.: Va. Tax Rev.

Ex.: Walter D. Schwidetzky, Is it Time to Give the S Corporation a Proper Burial?, 15 Va. Tax Rev. 591 (1996). –Article Citation.

Walter D. Schwidetzky, Is it Time to Give the S Corporation a Proper Burial?, 15 Va. Tax Rev. 591, 601 (1996). –Page Citation.

volume(s)
Ab.: vol., vols.

In law review footnotes, the titles of books and the names of cases, except for procedural phrases, are not underlined. See Bluebook rule 2.1(a) & (b). Further, the following are in large and small capitals: codes, restatements, standards, constitutions, periodicals, authors of books, titles of books, the abbreviated names of codes, most legislative materials except for bills and resolutions, codified ordinances, model codes, court rules, and sentencing guidelines. Refer to The Bluebook.

W

Wage and Hour Cases (Bureau of National Affairs)
See Labor Relations Reporter (BNA).

Wage-Price Law and Economics Review
Ab.: Wage-Price L. & Econ. Rev.

Wake Forest Law Review
Ab.: Wake Forest L. Rev.

Ex.: John L. Douglas, Deposit Insurance Reform, 27 Wake Forest L. Rev. 11 (1992). –Article Citation.

John L. Douglas, Deposit Insurance Reform, 27 Wake Forest L. Rev. 11, 19-20 (1992). –Page Citation.

Wallace (United States Reports)
See United States Reports.

Washburn Law Journal
Ab.: Washburn L.J.

Ex.: Paul B. Rasor, A Law Teacher Looks at the Good Samaritan Story, 31 Washburn L.J. 71 (1991). –Article Citation.

Paul B. Rasor, A Law Teacher Looks at the Good Samaritan Story, 31 Washburn L.J. 71, 77 (1991). –Page Citation.

Washington Administrative Code
Ab.: Wash. Admin. Code x-x-x (year)

Ex.: Wash. Admin. Code 60-12-005 (2000).

Washington and Lee Law Review
Ab.: Wash. & Lee L. Rev.

Ex.: Edward Dumbauld, Thomas Jefferson's Equity Commonplace Book, 48 Wash. & Lee L. Rev. 1257 (1991). –Article Citation.

Edward Dumbauld, Thomas Jefferson's Equity Commonplace Book, 48 Wash. & Lee L. Rev. 1257, 1270 (1991). –Page Citation.

Washington Appellate Reports
Ab.: Wash. App.

–Cite to P., P.2d, or P.3d, if therein; otherwise, cite to Wash. App.

–Give parallel citations only in documents submitted to Washington state courts. See Bluebook rules 10.3.1 and B5.1.3; see also Wash. Gen. Application Ct. R. 14, which requires a parallel citation.

In law review footnotes, the titles of books and the names of cases, except for procedural phrases, are not underlined. See Bluebook rule 2.1(a) & (b). Further, the following are in large and small capitals: codes, restatements, standards, constitutions, periodicals, authors of books, titles of books, the abbreviated names of codes, most legislative materials except for bills and resolutions, codified ordinances, model codes, court rules, and sentencing guidelines. Refer to The Bluebook.

In documents submitted to Washington state courts, cite as follows:

Riss v. Angel, 80 Wn. App. 553, 912 P.2d 1028 (1996). –Case Citation.

Riss v. Angel, 80 Wn. App. 553, 556, 912 P.2d 1028, 1031 (1996). –Page Citation.

In all other documents, cite as follows:

Riss v. Angel, 912 P.2d 1028 (Wash. Ct. App. 1996). –Case Citation.

Riss v. Angel, 912 P.2d 1028, 1031 (Wash. Ct. App. 1996). –Page Citation.

Washington Constitution

Ab.: Wash. Const. art. , § .

Ex.: Wash. Const. art. X, § 1. –"Cite constitutional provisions currently in force without a date." Bluebook rule 11.

Wash. Const. art. II, § 33 (repealed 1966).
Wash. Const. art. II, § 33, repealed by Wash. Const. amend. 42. –"If the cited provision has been repealed, either indicate parenthetically the fact and date of repeal or cite the repealing provision in full." Bluebook rule 11.

Wash. Const. art. IV, § 31 (amended 1989).
Wash. Const. art. IV, § 3, amended by Wash. Const. amend. 85. –"When citing a provision that has been subsequently amended, either indicate parenthetically the fact and date of amendment or cite the amending provision in full." Bluebook rule 11.

Washington Law Review

Ab.: Wash. L. Rev.

Ex.: Jule A. Davies, Direct Actions for Emotional Harm: Is Compromise Possible?, 67 Wash. L. Rev. 1 (1992). –Article Citation.

Jule A. Davies, Direct Actions for Emotional Harm: Is Compromise Possible?, 67 Wash. L. Rev. 1, 39-40 (1992). –Page Citation.

Washington Lawyer, The

Ab.: Wash. Law.

Ex.: Susan L. Crowley & Ann Charnley, Watchword for the '90s: Client Service, Wash. Law., Jan./Feb. 1992, at 22. –Article Citation.

Susan L. Crowley & Ann Charnley, Watchword for the '90s: Client Service, Wash. Law., Jan./Feb. 1992, at 22, 23. –Page Citation.

Washington Reports

Ab.: Wash. or Wash. 2d

–Cite to P., P.2d, or P.3d, if therein; otherwise, cite to Wash. or Wash. 2d.

In citing cases in law review footnotes, abbreviate any word listed in table T.6; the names of "states, countries, and other geographical units" unless they are named parties; and any other words of eight or more letters "if substantial space is thereby saved and the result is unambiguous." Bluebook rule 10.2.2. On the other hand, in citing cases in text, abbreviate only widely known acronyms and the following words: "&," "Ass'n," "Bros.," "Co.," "Corp.," "Inc.," "Ltd.," and "No." Bluebook rule 10.2.1(c).

–Give parallel citations only in documents submitted to Washington state courts. See Bluebook rule 10.3.1 and B5.1.3; see also Wash. Gen. Application Ct. R 14, which requires a parallel citation.

In documents submitted to Washington state courts, cite as follows:

State v. Johnson, 128 Wn. 2d 431, 909 P.2d 293 (1996). –Case Citation.

State v. Johnson, 128 Wn. 2d 431, 434, 909 P.2d 293, 296 (1996). –Page Citation.

In all other documents, cite as follows:

State v. Johnson, 909 P.2d 293 (Wash. 1996). –Case Citation.

State v. Johnson, 909 P.2d 293, 296 (Wash. 1996). –Page Citation.

Washington Revised Code Annotated
See Revised Code of Washington Annotated (West).

Washington Session Laws
See Session Laws of Washington and West's Washington Legislative Service.

Washington State Register
Ab.:   issue no. Wash. St. Reg. page no. (month day, year)
Ex.:   98-18 Wash. St. Reg. 300 (Sept. 16, 1998)

Washington Territory Reports (1854-1888)
Ab.:   Wash. Terr.

Washington University Journal of Urban and Contemporary Law
Ab.:   Wash. U. J. Urb. & Contemp. L.
Ex.:   Marc R. Buljon, Off-Site Mitigation and the EIS Threshold: NEPA is Faulty Framework, 41 Wash. U. J. Urb. & Contemp. L. 101 (1992). –Article Citation.

Marc R. Buljon, Off-Site Mitigation and the EIS Threshold: NEPA is Faulty Framework, 41 Wash. U. J. Urb. & Contemp. L. 101, 105-06 (1992). –Page Citation.

Washington University Law Quarterly
Ab.:   Wash. U. L.Q.
Ex.:   Andrew Kull, Unilateral Mistake: The Baseball Card Case, 70 Wash. U. L.Q. 57 (1992). –Article Citation.

Andrew Kull, Unilateral Mistake: The Baseball Card Case, 70 Wash. U. L.Q. 57, 59-63 (1992). –Page Citation.

Wayne Law Review
Ab.:   Wayne L. Rev.

In law review footnotes, the titles of books and the names of cases, except for procedural phrases, are not underlined. See Bluebook rule 2.1(a) & (b). Further, the following are in large and small capitals: codes, restatements, standards, constitutions, periodicals, authors of books, titles of books, the abbreviated names of codes, most legislative materials except for bills and resolutions, codified ordinances, model codes, court rules, and sentencing guidelines. Refer to The Bluebook.

Ex.: Kenneth R. Thomas, <u>Public Courts and Private Litigation: Proposed Changes to the Use of Confidentiality and Sealing Orders in Civil Cases</u>, 37 Wayne L. Rev. 1761 (1991). –Article Citation.

Kenneth R. Thomas, <u>Public Courts and Private Litigation: Proposed Changes to the Use of Confidentiality and Sealing Orders in Civil Cases</u>, 37 Wayne L. Rev. 1761, 1764 (1991). –Page Citation.

Weekly Compilation of Presidential Documents
Ab.: Weekly Comp. Pres. Doc.

Ex.: Remarks at the 53d Annual Awards Presentation Ceremonies, 17 Weekly Comp. Pres. Doc. 377 (Mar. 31, 1981).

Weekly Law Reports (England) (1953-date)
See <u>Bluebook</u> table T.2.

Ab.: W.L.R.

Ex.: <u>Reed v. Madon</u>, [1989] 2 W.L.R. 553 (ch. 1988) (Eng.). –Case Citation.

<u>Bellinger v. Bellinger</u>, [2003] UKHL 21, [2003] 2 W.L.R. 1174 (Eng.). –Case with neutral citation.

<u>Douglas v. Hello! Ltd</u>, [2005] EWCA (Civ) 595, [2005] 3 W.L.R. 881 (Eng.). –Case with neutral citation.

Weekly Notes (England) (1866-1952)
See <u>Bluebook</u> table T.2.

Ab.: W.N.

Ex.: <u>Westminster Bank, Ltd. v. Imperial Airways, Ltd.</u>, 1936 W.N. 238 (K.B. 1936) (Eng.). –Case Citation.

Weil's Arkansas Government Register
Ab.: issue no. Ark. Reg. page no. (Weil month year)

Weil's Code of Hawaii Rules
Ab.: Haw. Code R. § x-x-x (Weil year)

Ex.: Haw. Code R. § 13-167-6 (Weil 2003).

Weil's Code of Louisiana Rules (Weil)
Ab.: La. Code R. tit. x § x (Weil year)

Ex.: La. Code R. tit. 33 § 4201 (Weil 2004).

Weil's Code of Massachusetts Regulations
Ab.: x Mass. Code Regs. x.x (Weil year)

Ex.: 102 Mass. Code Regs. 201.309 (Weil year).

Weil's Code of Wyoming Rules
Ab.: x-x-x Weil's Code Wyo. R. § x. (Weil year)

In citing cases in law review footnotes, abbreviate any word listed in table T.6; the names of "states, countries, and other geographical units" unless they are named parties; and any other words of eight or more letters "if <u>substantial</u> space is thereby saved and the result is unambiguous." <u>Bluebook</u> rule 10.2.2. On the other hand, in citing cases in text, abbreviate only widely known acronyms and the following words: "&," "Ass'n," "Bros.," "Co.," "Corp.," "Inc.," "Ltd.," and "No." <u>Bluebook</u> rule 10.2.1(c).

Ex.:   005-000-024 Weil's Code Wyo. R. § 4 (Weil 2003).

Weil's Connecticut Government Register
Ab.:   issue no. Conn. Gov't Reg. page no. (Weil month year)

Weil's Georgia Government Register
Ab.:   issue no. Ga. Gov't Reg. page no. (Weil month year)

Weil's Hawaii Government Register
Ab.:   issue no. Haw. Gov't Reg. page no. (Weil month year)

Weil's Wyoming Government Register
Ab.:   issue no. Wyo. Gov't Reg. page no. (Weil month year)

Weinstein's Federal Evidence, by Jack B. Weinstein and Margaret A. Berger
          –Do not abbreviate the title.

Ex.:   5 Jack B. Weinstein & Margaret A. Berger, <u>Weinstein's Federal</u>
          <u>Evidence</u> § 803.08[8][a] (Joseph M. McLaughlin ed., 2d ed. 2005).
          –Section Citation.

West Indian Law Journal
Ab.:   W. Indian L.J.

Ex.:   M.C. Jozanna, <u>The Proposed South African Bill of Rights - A</u>
          <u>Prescription for Equality or Neo-Apartheid</u>, 15 W. Indian L.J. 1 (1991).
          –Article Citation.

          M.C. Jozanna, <u>The Proposed South African Bill of Rights - A</u>
          <u>Prescription for Equality or Neo-Apartheid</u>, 15 W. Indian L.J. 1, 29-32
          (1991). –Page Citation.

West Indian Reports
Ab.:   W.I.R.

West Virginia, Biennial Report & Official Opinions of the Attorney General
          See Biennial Report & Official Opinions of the Attorney General of the State of
          West Virginia.

West Virginia Code
Ab.:   W. Va. Code § x-x-x (year)
Ex.:   W. Va. Code § 20-5-5 (1996).
          W. Va. Code § 20-2-5d (Supp. 1996).

West Virginia Code of State Rules
Ab.:   W. Va. Code St. R. § x-x-x (year)
Ex.:   W. Va. Code St. R. § 47-10-4.1.b. (2000).

West Virginia Constitution
Ab.:   W. Va. Const. art.   , §   .

In law review footnotes, the titles of books and the names of cases, except for procedural
phrases, are not underlined. <u>See</u> <u>Bluebook</u> rule 2.1(a) & (b). Further, the following are in
large and small capitals: codes, restatements, standards, constitutions, periodicals, authors of
books, titles of books, the abbreviated names of codes, most legislative materials except for
bills and resolutions, codified ordinances, model codes, court rules, and sentencing guidelines.
Refer to <u>The Bluebook</u>.

Ex.:   W. Va. Const. art. XII, § 1. –"Cite constitutional provisions currently in force without a date." <u>Bluebook</u> rule 11.

W. Va. Const. art. X, § 2 (repealed 1970). –"If the cited provision has been repealed, either indicate parenthetically the fact and date of repeal or cite the repealing provision in full." <u>Bluebook</u> rule 11.

W. Va. Const. art. VI, § 36 (amended 1984). –"When citing a provision that has been subsequently amended, either indicate parenthetically the fact and date of amendment or cite the amending provision in full." <u>Bluebook</u> rule 11.

West Virginia Criminal Justice Review
Ab.:   W. Va. Crim. Just. Rev.

West Virginia Law Review
Ab.:   W. Va. L. Rev.

Ex.:   Archibald Cox, <u>Ethics in Government: The Cornerstone of Public Trust</u>, 94 W. Va. L. Rev. 281 (1991-92). –Article Citation.

Archibald Cox, <u>Ethics in Government: The Cornerstone of Public Trust</u>, 94 W. Va. L. Rev. 281, 297-98 (1991-92). –Page Citation.

West Virginia Register
Ab.:   vol. no. W. Va. Reg. page no. (month day, year)

Ex.:   21 W. Va. Reg. 353 (Feb. 20, 2004).

West Virginia Reports
Ab.:   W. Va.

–Cite to S.E. or S.E.2d, if therein; otherwise, cite to W. Va.

–Give parallel citations only in documents submitted to West Virginia state courts. <u>See</u> <u>Bluebook</u> rules 10.3.1 and B5.1.3. Because West Virginia Supreme Court opinions provide a parallel citation to West Virginia decisions, we advise giving a parallel citation in documents submitted to West Virginia state courts.

In documents submitted to West Virginia state courts, cite as follows:

<u>Buckler v. Buckler</u>, 195 W. Va. 705, 466 S.E.2d 556 (1995). –Case Citation.

<u>Buckler v. Buckler</u>, 195 W. Va. 705, 707, 466 S.E.2d 556, 558 (1995). –Page Citation.

In all other documents, cite as follows:

<u>Buckler v. Buckler</u>, 466 S.E.2d 556 (W.Va. 1995). –Case Citation.

<u>Buckler v. Buckler</u>, 466 S.E.2d 556, 558 (W.Va. 1995). –Page Citation.

West Virginia Session Laws
See Acts of the Legislature of West Virginia.

In citing cases in law review footnotes, abbreviate any word listed in table T.6; the names of "states, countries, and other geographical units" unless they are named parties; and any other words of eight or more letters "if <u>substantial</u> space is thereby saved and the result is unambiguous." <u>Bluebook</u> rule 10.2.2. On the other hand, in citing cases in text, abbreviate only widely known acronyms and the following words: "&," "Ass'n," "Bros.," "Co.," "Corp.," "Inc.," "Ltd.," and "No." <u>Bluebook</u> rule 10.2.1(c).

Western Legal History
  Ab.:   W. Legal Hist.
  Ex.:   Kent D. Richards, <u>Historical Antecedents to the Boldt Decision</u>,
        4 W. Legal Hist. 69 (1991). –Article Citation.

        Kent D. Richards, <u>Historical Antecedents to the Boldt Decision</u>,
        4 W. Legal Hist. 69, 79-81 (1991). –Page Citation.

Western New England Law Review
  Ab.:   W. New Eng. L. Rev.
  Ex.:   Francis J. Mootz, <u>Principles of Insurance Coverage: A Guide for the</u>
        <u>Employment Lawyer</u>, 18 W. New Eng. L. Rev. 5 (1996). –Article
        Citation.

        Francis J. Mootz, <u>Principles of Insurance Coverage: A Guide for the</u>
        <u>Employment Lawyer</u>, 18 W. New Eng. L. Rev. 5, 11 (1996). –Page
        Citation.

Western State University Law Review
  Ab.:   W. St. U. L. Rev.
  Ex.:   Bruce I. Shapiro, <u>The Heavy Burden of Establishing Weight as a</u>
        <u>Handicap Under Anti-Discrimination Statutes</u>, 18 W. St. U. L. Rev.
        565 (1991). –Article Citation.

        Bruce I. Shapiro, <u>The Heavy Burden of Establishing Weight as a</u>
        <u>Handicap</u> Under Anti-Discrimination Statutes, 18 W. St. U. L. Rev.
        565, 569-72 (1991). –Page Citation.

Western Weekly Reports (Canada)
        –Cite provincial reporters, if therein, in the order of preference shown
        in <u>Bluebook</u> table T.2, pp. 255-56; otherwise, cite D.L.R., W.W.R.,
        A.P.R., E.L.R., M.P.R., or W.L.R. <u>See</u> <u>Bluebook</u> table T.2, p. 255.
  Ab.:   W.W.R.
  Ex.:   <u>Livaditis v. Calgary</u>, [1992] 1 W.W.R. 53 (Alta. C.A. 1991) (Can.).

Westlaw
    See pending and unreported cases, electronic media and other nonprint
      resources, and <u>Bluebook</u> rule 18.1.

West's Alabama Legislative Service
  Ab.:   year Ala. Legis. Serv. page no. (West)
  Ex.:   Act effective Oct. 1, 2005, No. 172, 2005 Ala. Legis. Serv. 1390
        (West) –Citation to an entire session law.
    –<u>See</u> <u>Bluebook</u> rule 12.4.

In law review footnotes, the titles of books and the names of cases, except for procedural phrases, are not underlined. <u>See</u> <u>Bluebook</u> rule 2.1(a) & (b). Further, the following are in large and small capitals: codes, restatements, standards, constitutions, periodicals, authors of books, titles of books, the abbreviated names of codes, most legislative materials except for bills and resolutions, codified ordinances, model codes, court rules, and sentencing guidelines. Refer to <u>The Bluebook</u>.

– "Cite to Ala. Laws, if therein." <u>Bluebook</u> table T.1, p. 198.

West's Annotated California Code
Ab.:   Cal. [subject] Code §   (West year)

          See <u>Bluebook</u> table T.1, p.201, for the abbreviation of each subject.

Ex.:   Cal. Welf. & Inst. Code § 4689.2 (West 1998).

          Cal. Gov't Code § 21419 (West Supp. 2000).

          – "Cite to either the West or the Deering subject-matter code, if therein." <u>Bluebook</u> table T.1, p. 201.

          –For proper citation form in papers submitted to California courts, see Cal. R. Ct. 313(g) and <u>California Style Manual</u>.

West's Annotated Code of Maryland
Ab.:   Md. Code Ann., [subject] § x-x (West year)

Ex.:   Md. Code Ann., Lab. & Empl. § 99-1105 (West 2004).

          Md. Code Ann., Lab. & Empl. § 8-911 (West Supp. 2004).

See <u>Bluebook</u> table T.1, p. 213, for the abbreviation of each subject matter.

West's Annotated Code of Virginia
Ab.:   Va. Code Ann. § x-x (West year)

Ex.:   Va. Code Ann. § 8.01-53 (West 2005).

          Va. Code Ann. § 30-106 (West Supp. 2005).

          – "Cite to Va. Code Ann., if therein." <u>Bluebook</u> table T.1, p.237.

West's Annotated Code of West Virginia
Ab.:   W. Va. Code Ann. § x-x-x (West year)

Ex.:   W. Va. Code Ann. § 7-20-4 (West 2004).

          W. Va. Code Ann. § 51-9-3 (West Supp. 2005).

          – "Cite to W. Va. Code, if therein." <u>Bluebook</u> table T.1, p.238.

West's Annotated Indiana Code
Ab.:   Ind. Code Ann. § x-x-x-x (West year)

Ex.:   Ind. Code Ann. § 28-1-23-3 (West 2000).

          Ind. Code Ann. § 36-9-37-12 (West Supp. 2004).

          – "Cite to Ind. Code, if therein." <u>Bluebook</u> table T.1, p. 208.

          –For proper citation form in papers submitted to Indiana courts, see Ind. Code § 1-1-1-1 (2002) and Ind. R. App. P. 22.

West's Annotated Mississippi Code
Ab.:   Miss. Code Ann. § x-x-x (West year)

Ex.:   Miss. Code Ann. § 61-7-13 (West 2004).

          Miss. Code Ann. § 49-17-44 (West Supp. 2004).

In citing cases in law review footnotes, abbreviate any word listed in table T.6; the names of "states, countries, and other geographical units" unless they are named parties; and any other words of eight or more letters "if <u>substantial</u> space is thereby saved and the result is unambiguous." <u>Bluebook</u> rule 10.2.2. On the other hand, in citing cases in text, abbreviate only widely known acronyms and the following words: "&," "Ass'n," "Bros.," "Co.," "Corp.," "Inc.," "Ltd.," and "No." <u>Bluebook</u> rule 10.2.1(c).

– "Cite to Miss. Code Ann., if therein." <u>Bluebook</u> table T.1, p.216.

West's Arkansas Code Annotated
Ab.: Ark. Code Ann. § x-x-x (West year)

Ex.: Ark. Code Ann. § 2-33-207 (West 2004).

Ark. Code Ann. § 4-22-101 (West Supp. 2005).

– "Cite to Ark. Code Ann. (published by LexisNexis), if therein." <u>Bluebook</u> table T.1, p. 200.

–For proper citation form in papers submitted to Arkansas courts, see Ark. Code Ann. § 1-2-113(c) (1996).

West's Arkansas Legislative Service
Ab.: year Ark. Legis. Serv. page no. (West)

Ex.: Act of Apr. 13, 2005, No. 2147, 2005 Ark. Legis. Serv. 4176 (West) (relating to junkyard visibility). –Citation to an entire session law.

Act. of Apr. 13, 2005, No. 2147, sec. 4, § 27-74-409(a), 2005 Ark. Legis. Serv. 4176, 4177 (West) (relating to junkyard visibility). –Citation to a section of a session law amending prior act.

<u>See</u> <u>Bluebook</u> rule 12.4.

– "Cite to Ark. Acts, if therein." <u>Bluebook</u> table T.1, p. 200.

West's Bankruptcy Reporter
See Bankruptcy Reporter.

West's California Jurisprudence, third edition
Ab.: Cal. Jur. 3d

Ex.: 58 Cal. Jur. 3d <u>Specific Performance</u> § 43 (2004).

West's California Reporter
Ab.: Cal. Rptr.

-Give parallel citations, if at all, only in documents submitted to California state courts. <u>See</u> <u>Bluebook</u> rules 10.3.1 and B5.1.3. See also Cal. R. Ct. 313(c), which requires citation only to the official reporters, Cal., Cal. 2d, Cal. 3d, or Cal. 4th, Cal. App., Cal. App. 2d, Cal App. 3d, or Cal. App. 4th, or Cal. App. Supp., Cal. App. 2d Supp., Cal. App. 3d Supp., or Cal. App. 4th Supp., Cal. R. Ct. 313(g), which requires adherence to either <u>The Bluebook</u> or to the <u>California Style Manual</u>, and the <u>California Style Manual</u> § 1.12 (4th ed. 2000), which encourages one or more parallel citations. Therefore, in documents submitted to California state courts, you may cite as follows:

<u>Mangini v. Aerojet-Gen. Corp.</u>, 12 Cal. 4th 1087, 912 P.2d 1220, 51 Cal. Rptr. 2d 272 (1996). –Case Citation.

In law review footnotes, the titles of books and the names of cases, except for procedural phrases, are not underlined. <u>See</u> <u>Bluebook</u> rule 2.1(a) & (b). Further, the following are in large and small capitals: codes, restatements, standards, constitutions, periodicals, authors of books, titles of books, the abbreviated names of codes, most legislative materials except for bills and resolutions, codified ordinances, model codes, court rules, and sentencing guidelines. Refer to <u>The Bluebook</u>.

Mangini v. Aerojet-Gen. Corp., 12 Cal. 4th 1087, 1088, 912 P.2d 1220, 1222, 51 Cal. Rptr. 2d 272, 273 (1996). –Page Citation.

Brantley v. Pisaro, 42 Cal. App. 4th 1591, 50 Cal. Rptr. 2d 431 (Ct. App. 1996). –Case Citation.

Brantley v. Pisaro, 42 Cal. App. 4th 1591, 1593, 50 Cal Rptr. 2d 431, 433 (Ct. App. 1996). –Page Citation.

People v. Studley, 44 Cal. App. 4th Supp. 1, 52 Cal Rptr. 2d 461 (App. Dep't Super. Ct. 1996). –Case Citation.

People v. Studley, 44 Cal. App. 4th Supp. 1, 5, 52 Cal. Rptr. 2d 461, 463 (App. Dep't Super. Ct.1996). –Page Citation.

In all other documents, cite as follows:

Mangini v. Aerojet-Gen. Corp., 912 P.2d 1220 (Cal. 1996). –Case Citation.

Mangini v. Aerojet-Gen. Corp., 912 P.2d 1220, 1222 (Cal. 1996) –Page Citation.

Brantley v. Pisaro, 50 Cal. Rptr. 2d 431 (Ct. App 1996). –Case Citation.

Brantley v. Pisaro, 50 Cal. Rptr. 2d 431, 433 (Ct. App. 1996). –Page Citation.

People v. Studley, 52 Cal. Rptr. 2d 461 (App. Dep't Super. Ct. 1996). –Case Citation.

People v. Studley, 52 Cal. Rptr. 2d 461, 463 (App. Dep't Super. Ct. 1996). – Page Citation.

West's Code of Georgia Annotated
Ab.:   Ga. Code Ann. § x-x-x (West year)

Ex.:   Ga. Code Ann. § 36-67-5 (West 2004).

Ga. Code Ann. § 47-2-299 (West Supp. 2005).

– "Cite to the official version of Ga. Code Ann. (published by LexisNexis), if therein." Bluebook table T.1, p. 206.

–For proper citation form in papers submitted to Georgia courts, see Ga. Code Ann. § 1-1-8(e) (2004).

West's Colorado Revised Statutes Annotated
Ab.:   Colo. Rev. Stat. Ann. § x-x-x (West year)

Ex.:   Colo. Rev. Stat. Ann. § 39-22-621 (West 2000).

Colo. Rev. Stat. Ann. § 39-22-508 (West Supp. 2005).

– "Cite to Colo. Rev. Stat., if therein." Bluebook table T.1, p.202.

In citing cases in law review footnotes, abbreviate any word listed in table T.6; the names of "states, countries, and other geographical units" unless they are named parties; and any other words of eight or more letters "if substantial space is thereby saved and the result is unambiguous." Bluebook rule 10.2.2. On the other hand, in citing cases in text, abbreviate only widely known acronyms and the following words: "&," "Ass'n," "Bros.," "Co.," "Corp.," "Inc.," "Ltd.," and "No." Bluebook rule 10.2.1(c).

West's Florida Session Law Service
Ab.:   year Fla. Sess. Law. Serv. page no. (West)

Ex.:   Act of June 20, 2005, No. 272, 2005 Fla. Sess. Law. Serv. 1894 (West) (to be codified at Fla. Stat. § 768 1382). –Citation to an entire session law.

See Bluebook rule 12.4.

– "Cite to Fla. Laws, if therein." Bluebook table T.1, p. 205.

West's Florida Statutes Annotated
Ab.:   Fla. Stat. Ann. § x.x (West year)

Ex.:   Fla. Stat. Ann. § 794.011 (West 2004).

Fla. Stat. Ann. § 985.215 (West Supp. 2004).

–"Cite to Fla. Stat., if therein." Bluebook table T.1, p. 205.

–For proper citation form in papers submitted to Florida courts, see Fla. R. App. P. 9.800(g).

West's Hawaii Reports
See Hawaii Reports, West's.

West's Indiana Legislative Service
Ab.:   year Ind. Legis. Serv. page no. (West)

Ex.:   Act effective Jan. 1, 2006, No. 571, sec. 7, § 36-1-7-15, 2005 Ind. Legis. Serv. 2079 (West). –Citation to a section of a session law amending a prior act.

See Bluebook rule 12.4.

–"Cite to Ind. Acts, if therein." Bluebook table T.1, p. 208.

West's Iowa Code Annotated
Ab.:   Iowa Code Ann. § x.x (West year)

Ex.:   Iowa Code Ann. § 476.15 (West 1999).

Iowa Code Ann. § 809A.12 (West Supp. 2000).

–"Cite to Iowa Code, if therein." Bluebook table T.1, p. 209.

West's Louisiana Children's Code Annotated
Ab.:   La. Child. Code Ann. art. x (West year)

Ex.:   La. Child. Code Ann. art. 114 (West 1995).

La. Child. Code Ann. art. 601 (West Supp. 2001).

West's Louisiana Civil Code Annotated
Ab.:   La. Civ. Code Ann. art. x (West year)

Ex.:   La. Civ. Code Ann. art. 218 (West 1993).

La. Civ. Code Ann. art. 245 (West Supp. 1996).

In law review footnotes, the titles of books and the names of cases, except for procedural phrases, are not underlined. See Bluebook rule 2.1(a) & (b). Further, the following are in large and small capitals: codes, restatements, standards, constitutions, periodicals, authors of books, titles of books, the abbreviated names of codes, most legislative materials except for bills and resolutions, codified ordinances, model codes, court rules, and sentencing guidelines. Refer to The Bluebook.

West's Louisiana Code of Civil Procedure Annotated
Ab.: La. Code Civ. Proc. Ann. art. x (West year)

Ex.: La. Code Civ. Proc. Ann. art. 2122 (West 1961).

West's Louisiana Code of Criminal Procedure Annotated
Ab.: La. Code Crim. Proc. Ann. art. x (West year)

Ex.: La. Code Crim. Proc. Ann. art. 404 (West 1991).

La. Code Crim. Proc. Ann. art. 230.2 (West Supp. 1996).

West's Louisiana Code of Evidence Annotated
Ab.: La. Code Evid. Ann. art. x (West year)

Ex.: La. Code Evid. Ann. art. 613 (West 1995).

La. Code Evid. Ann. art. 608 (West Supp. 1996)

West's Louisiana Revised Statutes Annotated
Ab.: La. Rev. Stat. Ann. § x:x (West year)

Ex.: La. Rev. Stat. Ann. § 51:1723 (West 2003).

La. Rev. Stat. Ann. § 49:1822 (West Supp. 2004).

For proper citation form in papers submitted to Louisiana courts, see prefatory pages to La. Rev. Stat. volumes

West's Louisiana Session Law Service
Ab.: year La. Sess. Law Serv. page no. (West)

Ex.: Act of July 12, 2005, No. 482, sec. 1, § 54, 2005 La. Sess. Law Serv. 1345 (West) (concerning public school superintendents). –Citation to a section of a session law amending prior act.

See Bluebook rule 12.4.

–"Cite to La Acts, if therein." Bluebook table T.1, p. 211.

West's Military Justice Reporter
Ab.: M.J.

Ex.: United States v. Dickens, 30 M.J. 986 (A.C.M.R. 1990). –Case Citation.

United States v. Dickens, 30 M.J. 986, 988 (A.C.M.R. 1990). –Page Citation.

United States v. Brown, 30 M.J. 839, 841 (N-M.C.M.R. 1990). –Page Citation.

United States v. Givens, 30 M.J. 294, 297 (C.M.A. 1990). –Page Citation.

United States v. Smith, 30 M.J. 1022, 1026 (A.F.C.M.R. 1990). –Page Citation.

West's Mississippi Legislative Service
Ab.: year Miss. Legis. Serv. page no.

In citing cases in law review footnotes, abbreviate any word listed in table T.6; the names of "states, countries, and other geographical units" unless they are named parties; and any other words of eight or more letters "if substantial space is thereby saved and the result is unambiguous." Bluebook rule 10.2.2. On the other hand, in citing cases in text, abbreviate only widely known acronyms and the following words: "&," "Ass'n," "Bros.," "Co.," "Corp.," "Inc.," "Ltd.," and "No." Bluebook rule 10.2.1(c).

Ex.: Act effective April 17, 2000, ch. 392, 2000 Miss. Legis. Serv. 191 (West) (garbage disposal). –Citation to an entire session law.

Act effective April 17, 2000, ch. 392, sec. 1, § 17-17-5, 2000 Miss. Legis. Serv. 191, 191 (West). –Citation to a section of a session law amending a prior act.

See Bluebook rule 12.4.

–"Cite to Miss. Laws, if therein." Bluebook table T.1, p. 216.

West's Nevada Revised Statutes Annotated
Ab.: Nev. Rev. Stat. Ann. § x.x (West year)

Ex.: Nev. Rev. Stat. Ann. § 599B.005 (West 2004).

Nev. Rev. Stat. Ann. § 11.060 (West Supp. 2005).

– "Cite to Nev. Rev. Stat., if therein." Bluebook table T.1 p. 218.

–For proper citation form in papers submitted to Nevada courts, see Nev. Rev. Stat. § 220.170(4) (2000).

West's New Mexico Statutes Annotated
Ab.: N.M. Stat. Ann. § x-x-x (West year)

Ex.: N.M. Stat. Ann. § 76-6A-6 (West 2004).

N.M. Stat. Ann. § 19-31-9 (West Supp. 2005).

– "Cite to N.M. Stat., if therein." Bluebook table T.1, p. 220.

–For proper citation form in papers submitted to New Mexico Courts, see N.M. S. Ct. R. 23-112(E).

West's New York Supplement
Ab.: N.Y.S., N.Y.S.2d

–Give parallel citations, if at all, only in documents submitted to New York state courts. See Bluebook rules 10.3.1 and B5.1.3; see also N.Y. Ct. App. R. 500.1(a), 500.5(d)(3), 510.1(a), N.Y. Sup. Ct. App. Div. 1st Dept. R. 600.10(a)(11), N.Y. Sup. Ct. App. Div. 4th Dept. R. 1000.4(f)(7), and N.Y. C.P.L.R. 5529(e), which require only a citation to A.D. or A.D.2d.

In documents submitted to New York state courts, cite as follows:

Ferrer v. Dinkins, 218 A.D.2d 89, 635 N.Y.S.2d 965 (1996). –Case Citation.

Ferrer v. Dinkins, 218 A.D.2d 89, 90, 635 N.Y.S.2d 965, 966 (1996). –Page Citation.

Okebivi v. Cortines, 167 Misc. 2d 1008, 641 N.Y.S.2d 791 (Sup. Ct. 1984). –Case Citation.

Okebivi v. Cortines, 167 Misc. 2d 1008, 1009, 641 N.Y.S.2d 791, 792 (Sup. Ct. 1984). –Page Citation.

In law review footnotes, the titles of books and the names of cases, except for procedural phrases, are not underlined. See Bluebook rule 2.1(a) & (b). Further, the following are in large and small capitals: codes, restatements, standards, constitutions, periodicals, authors of books, titles of books, the abbreviated names of codes, most legislative materials except for bills and resolutions, codified ordinances, model codes, court rules, and sentencing guidelines. Refer to The Bluebook.

Beckman v. Greentree Sec., Inc., 87 N.Y.2d 566, 663 N.E.2d 886, 640 N.Y.S.2d 845 (1996). –Case Citation.

Beckman v. Greentree Sec., Inc., 87 N.Y.2d 566, 569, 663 N.E.2d 886, 887, 640 N.Y.S.2d 845, 847 (1996). –Page Citation.

In all other documents cite as follows:

Ferrer v. Dinkins, 635 N.Y.S.2d 965 (App. Div. 1996). –Case Citation.

Ferrer v. Dinkins, 635 N.Y.S.2d 965, 966 (App. Div. 1996). –Page Citation.

Okebiyi v. Cortines, 641 N.Y.S.2d 791 (Sup. Ct. 1996). –Case Citation.

Okebiyi v. Cortines, 641 N.Y.S.2d 791, 792 (Sup. Ct. 1996). –Page Citation.

Beckman v. Greentree Sec., Inc., 663 N.E.2d 886 (N.Y. 1996). –Case Citation.

Beckman v. Greentree Sec., Inc., 663 N.E.2d 886, 887 (N.Y. 1996). –Page Citation.

West's North Carolina General Statutes Annotated
Ab.:   N. C. Gen. Stat. Ann. § x-x (West year)

Ex.:   N. C. Gen. Stat. Ann. § 90-21.31 (West 2004).

N. C. Gen. Stat. Ann. § 158-33 (West Supp. 2005).

"Cite to N.C. Gen Stat. (published by LexisNexis), if therein." Bluebook table T.1, p. 225.

–For proper form in papers submitted to North Carolina courts, see N.C. R. App. P. app. B.

West's Oregon Revised Statutes Annotated
Ab.:   Or. Rev. Stat. Ann. § x.x (West year)

Ex.:   Or. Rev. Stat. Ann. § 70.020 (West 2003).

Or. Rev. Stat. Ann. § 52.670 (West Supp. 2004).

"Cite to Or. Rev. Stat., if therein." Bluebook table T.1, p. 228.

–For proper citation form in papers submitted to Oregon courts, see Preface to vol. 1, Or. Rev. Stat. at x (2003), Or. R. App. P. 5.35(3), and Oregon Appellate Courts Style Manual.

West's Smith-Hurd Illinois Compiled Statutes Annotated
Ab.:   x Ill. Comp. Stat. Ann. x/x-x (West year)

Ex.:   815 Ill. Comp. Stat. Ann. 307/10-30.5 (West 1999).

815 Ill. Comp. Stat. Ann. 307/10-80 (West Supp. 2000).

"Cite to Ill. Comp. Stat., if therein." Bluebook table T.1 p. 208.

–For proper citation form in papers submitted to Illinois courts, see

---

In citing cases in law review footnotes, abbreviate any word listed in table T.6; the names of "states, countries, and other geographical units" unless they are named parties; and any other words of eight or more letters "if substantial space is thereby saved and the result is unambiguous." Bluebook rule 10.2.2. On the other hand, in citing cases in text, abbreviate only widely known acronyms and the following words: "&," "Ass'n," "Bros.," "Co.," "Corp.," "Inc.," "Ltd.," and "No." Bluebook rule 10.2.1(c).

Ill. Sup. Ct. R. 6.

West's Tennessee Code Annotated
Ab.: Tenn. Code Ann. § x-x-x (West year)

Ex.: Tenn. Code Ann. § 12-6-107 (West 2004).

Tenn. Code Ann. § 47-6-102 (West Supp. 2005).

– "Cite to Tenn. Code Ann. (published by LexisNexis), if therein." Bluebook table T.1, p. 233.

–For proper citation form in papers submitted to Tennessee courts, see Tenn. Code Ann. § 1-2-1-1(a) (2003).

West's Tennessee Legislative Service
Ab.: year Tenn. Legis. Serv. page no. (West)

Ex.: Act effective July 1, 2005, ch. 185, sec. 2, § 37-1-403, 2005 Tenn. Legis. Serv. 87 (West) (concerning child abuse reporting). –Citation to a section of a session law amending prior act.

See Bluebook rule 12.4.

–"Cite to Tenn. Pub. Acts or Tenn. Priv. Acts, if therein." Bluebook table T.1, p. 233.

West's Utah Code Annotated
Ab.: Utah Code Ann. § x-x-x (West year)

Ex.: Utah Code Ann. § 72-10-404 (West 2004).

Utah Code Ann. § 71-3-1 (West Supp. 2005).

– "Cite to Utah Code Ann. (published by LexisNexis), if therein." Bluebook table T.1, p.236.

West's Veterans Appeals Reporter
Ab.: Vet. App.

Ex.: Dillon v. Brown, 8 Vet. App. 165 (1995).

West's Virginia Legislative Service
Ab.: year Va. Legis. Serv. page no. (West)

Ex.: Act of Mar. 28, 2005, ch. 878, sec. 1, § 251.204, 2005 Va. Legis. Serv. 1179 (West) (relating to eminent domain proceedings). –Citation to a section of a session law amending prior act.

See Bluebook rule 12.4.

–"Cite to Va. Acts, if therein." Bluebook table T.1, p. 237.

West's Washington Legislative Service
Ab.: year Wash. Legis. Serv. page no. (West)

In law review footnotes, the titles of books and the names of cases, except for procedural phrases, are not underlined. See Bluebook rule 2.1(a) & (b). Further, the following are in large and small capitals: codes, restatements, standards, constitutions, periodicals, authors of books, titles of books, the abbreviated names of codes, most legislative materials except for bills and resolutions, codified ordinances, model codes, court rules, and sentencing guidelines. Refer to The Bluebook.

Ex.: Act of Mar. 29, 1996, Ch. 277, 1996 Wash. Legis. Serv. 926 (West) (relating to offender debts, correctional facilities). –Citation to an entire session law.

Act of Mar. 29, 1996, Ch. 277, sec. 1, § 72.109.450, 1996 Wash. Legis. Serv. 926, 926-27 (West) (relating to offender debts, correctional facilities). –Citation to a session law amending a prior act.

See Bluebook rule 12.4.

–"Cite to Wash. Laws, if therein." Bluebook table T.1, p. 238.

West's Wisconsin Legislative Service

Ab.: Year Wis. Legis. Serv. page no. (West)

Ex.: Act of June 27, 1996, Act 460, 1996 Wis. Legis. Serv. 3706 (West) (fruit and vegetable produce security). –Citation to an entire session law.

Act of June 27, 1996, Act 460, sec. 1, § 20.115, 1996 Wis. Legis. Serv. 3706, 3706 (West) (fruit and vegetable produce security). –Citation to a section of a session law amending a prior act.

See Bluebook rule 12.4.

–"Cite to Wis. Laws, if therein." Bluebook table T.1, p. 239.

West's Wisconsin Statutes Annotated

Ab.: Wis. Stat. Ann. § x.x (West year)

Ex.: Wis. Stat. Ann. § 81.15 (West 2000).

Wis. Stat. Ann. § 442.12 (West Supp. 2005).

"Cite to Wis. Stat., if therein." Bluebook table T.1, p. 239.

Wharton's Criminal Procedure, by Charles E. Torcia

–Do not abbreviate the title.

Ex.: 1 Charles E. Torcia, Wharton's Criminal Procedure § 144 (13th ed. 1989). –Section Citation.

1 Charles E. Torcia, Wharton's Criminal Procedure § 144, at 509 (13th ed. 1989). –Page Citation.

1 Charles E. Torcia, Wharton's Criminal Procedure § 144, at 509 n.39 (13th ed. 1989). –Footnote Citation.

Wheaton (United States Reports)

See United States Reports.

White and Summers on the UCC

See Uniform Commercial Code, by James J. White & Robert S. Summers.

Whiteman Digest

See Digest of International Law, by Marjorie M. Whiteman.

In citing cases in law review footnotes, abbreviate any word listed in table T.6; the names of "states, countries, and other geographical units" unless they are named parties; and any other words of eight or more letters "if substantial space is thereby saved and the result is unambiguous." Bluebook rule 10.2.2. On the other hand, in citing cases in text, abbreviate only widely known acronyms and the following words: "&," "Ass'n," "Bros.," "Co.," "Corp.," "Inc.," "Ltd.," and "No." Bluebook rule 10.2.1(c).

Whittier Law Review
    Ab.:   Whittier L. Rev.

    Ex.:   Matthew Lippman, <u>Civil Resistance: Revitalizing International Law in the Nuclear Age</u>, 13 Whittier L. Rev. 17 (1992). –Article Citation.

            Matthew Lippman, <u>Civil Resistance: Revitalizing International Law in the Nuclear Age</u>, 13 Whittier L. Rev. 17, 33 (1992). –Page Citation.

Widener Law Review
    Ab: Widener L. Rev.

    Ex: Erin Daly, <u>The New Liberty</u>, 11 Widener L. Rev. 221 (2005). –Article Citation.

         Erin Daly, <u>The New Liberty</u>, 11 Widener L. Rev. 221, 235-36 (2005). –Page Citation.

Wigmore on Evidence
         –Do not abbreviate the title.

    Ex.:   I John H. Wigmore, <u>Evidence</u> § 6.4 (Tillers rev. 1983). –Citation to Volume One.

         IA John H. Wigmore, <u>Evidence</u> § 62.2 (Tillers rev. 1983). –Citation to Volume One A.

         II John H. Wigmore, <u>Evidence</u> § 290 (Chadbourne rev. 1979). –Citation to Volume Two.

         III John H. Wigmore, <u>Evidence</u> § 769 (Chadbourne rev. 1970). –Citation to Volume Three.

         IIIA John H. Wigmore, <u>Evidence</u> § 982 (Chadbourne rev. 1970). –Citation to Volume Three A.

         IV John H. Wigmore, <u>Evidence</u> § 1151 (Chadbourne rev. 1972). –Citation to Volume Four.

         V John II. Wigmore, <u>Evidence</u> § 1484 (Chadbourne rev. 1974). –Citation to Volume Five.

         VI John H. Wigmore, <u>Evidence</u> § 1773 (Chadbourne rev. 1976). –Citation to Volume Six.

         VII John H. Wigmore, <u>Evidence</u> § 2042 (Chadbourne rev. 1978). –Citation to Volume Seven.

         VIII John H. Wigmore, <u>Evidence</u> § 2251 (McNaughton rev. 1961). –Citation to Volume Eight.

         IX John H. Wigmore, <u>Evidence</u> § 2501 (Chadbourne rev. 1981). –Citation to Volume Nine.

         IX John H. Wigmore, <u>Evidence</u> § 2501 (Supp. 1999). –Citation to Supplement.

Willamette Law Review
    Ab.:   Willamette L. Rev.

In law review footnotes, the titles of books and the names of cases, except for procedural phrases, are not underlined. <u>See</u> <u>Bluebook</u> rule 2.1(a) & (b). Further, the following are in large and small capitals: codes, restatements, standards, constitutions, periodicals, authors of books, titles of books, the abbreviated names of codes, most legislative materials except for bills and resolutions, codified ordinances, model codes, court rules, and sentencing guidelines. Refer to <u>The Bluebook</u>.

Ex.: Alfred L. Brophy, <u>Law and Indentured Servitude in Mid-Eighteenth Century Pennsylvania</u>, 28 Willamette L. Rev. 69 (1991). –Article Citation.

Alfred L. Brophy, <u>Law and Indentured Servitude in Mid-Eighteenth Century Pennsylvania</u>, 28 Willamette L. Rev. 69, 81-83 (1991). –Page Citation.

William and Mary Bill of Rights Journal
Ab: Wm. & Mary Bill Rts. J.

Ex: Randolph N. Jonakait, <u>Rasul v. Bush: Unanswered Questions</u>, 13 Wm. & Mary Bill Rts. J. 1103 (2005). –Article Citation.

Randolph N. Jonakait, <u>Rasul v. Bush: Unanswered Questions</u>, 13 Wm. & Mary Bill Rts. J. 1103, 1114 (2005). –Page Citation.

William and Mary Law Review
Ab.: Wm. & Mary L. Rev.

Ex.: Frederick Schauer, <u>The First Amendment as Ideology</u>, 33 Wm. & Mary L. Rev. 853 (1992). –Article Citation.

Frederick Schauer, <u>The First Amendment as Ideology</u>, 33 Wm. & Mary L. Rev. 853, 859-63 (1992). –Page Citation.

William Mitchell Law Review
Ab.: Wm. Mitchell L. Rev.

Ex.: Rita C. DeMeules, <u>Minnesota's Variable Approach to State Constitutional Claims</u>, 17 Wm. Mitchell L. Rev. 163 (1991). –Article Citation.

Rita C. DeMeules, <u>Minnesota's Variable Approach to State Constitutional Claims</u>, 17 Wm. Mitchell L. Rev. 163, 178-81 (1991). –Page Citation.

Williams and Taylor American Land Planning Law
–Do not abbreviate the title.

Ex.: 6 Norman Williams, Jr. & John M. Taylor, <u>Williams and Taylor American Land Planning Law</u> § 118.2 (rev. ed. 2003). –Section Citation.

6 Norman Williams, Jr. & John M. Taylor, <u>Williams and Taylor American Land Planning Law</u> § 118.2, at 105 (rev. ed. 2003). –Page Citation.

Williston on Contracts (multi-volume treatise)
See Treatise on the Law of Contracts, by Samuel Williston.

Williston on Contracts Student Edition
See Selections from Williston's Treatise on the Law of Contracts, by Samuel Williston and George J. Thompson.

In citing cases in law review footnotes, abbreviate any word listed in table T.6; the names of "states, countries, and other geographical units" unless they are named parties; and any other words of eight or more letters "if <u>substantial</u> space is thereby saved and the result is unambiguous." <u>Bluebook</u> rule 10.2.2. On the other hand, in citing cases in text, abbreviate only widely known acronyms and the following words: "&," "Ass'n," "Bros.," "Co.," "Corp.," "Inc.," "Ltd.," and "No." <u>Bluebook</u> rule 10.2.1(c).

Wisconsin Administrative Code
    Ab.:   Wis. Admin. Code [agency abbreviation] § x.x (year)
    Ex.:   Wis. Admin. Code ATCP § 3.01(2) (2003).

Wisconsin Administrative Register
    Ab.:   issue no. Wis. Admin. Reg. page no. (month day, year)
    Ex.:   594 Wis. Admin. Reg. 9 (June 15, 2005)

Wisconsin Bar Bulletin
    Ab.:   Wis. B. Bull.
    Ex.:   William M. Gabler, Isn't That Motion Frivolous, Counsel?, Wis. B. Bul., Dec. 1988, at 17. –Article Citation.

         William M. Gabler, Isn't That Motion Frivolous, Counsel?, Wis. B. Bul., Dec. 1988, at 17, 61-62. –Page Citation.

Wisconsin Board of Tax Appeals Reports
    Ab.:   Wis. B.T.A.

Wisconsin Constitution
    Ab.:   Wis. Const. art. , §   .
    Ex.:   Wis. Const. art. I, § 22. –"Cite constitutional provisions currently in force without a date." Bluebook rule 11.

         Wis. Const. art. III, §§ 4-6 (repealed 1986). –"If the cited provision has been repealed, either indicate parenthetically the fact and date of repeal or cite the repealing provision in full." Bluebook rule 11.

         Wis. Const. art. V, § 1 (amended 1990). –"When citing a provision that has been subsequently amended, either indicate parenthetically the fact and date of amendment or cite the amending provision in full." Bluebook rule 11.

Wisconsin Court of Appeals
    Ab.:   Wis. Ct. App.
         –Cite to N.W. or N.W.2d, if therein; otherwise, cite to Wis. Give public domain citation if available. Otherwise, give parallel citations only in documents submitted to Wisconsin state courts.
         –Until January 1, 2000, when public domain format was adopted, cite as follows:
        In documents submitted to Wisconsin state courts:
            Huffman v. Altec Int'l, Inc., 200 Wis. 2d 78, 546 N.W.2d 162 (Ct. App. 1996). –Case Citation.
            Huffman v. Altec Int'l, Inc., 200 Wis. 2d 78, 80, 546 N.W.2d 162, 164 (Ct. App. 1996). –Case Citation.
        In all other documents:

In law review footnotes, the titles of books and the names of cases, except for procedural phrases, are not underlined. See Bluebook rule 2.1(a) & (b). Further, the following are in large and small capitals: codes, restatements, standards, constitutions, periodicals, authors of books, titles of books, the abbreviated names of codes, most legislative materials except for bills and resolutions, codified ordinances, model codes, court rules, and sentencing guidelines. Refer to The Bluebook.

Huffman v. Altec Int'l, Inc., 546 N.W.2d 162 (Wis. Ct. App. 1996). –Case Citation.

Huffman v. Altec Int'l, Inc., 546 N.W.2d 162, 164 (Wis. Ct. App. 1996). –Page Citation.

–After January 1, 2000, cite as follows:

In documents submitted to Wisconsin state courts:

State v. Phillips, 2000 WI App 184, 238 Wis. 2d 279, 617 N.W. 2d 522. –Case Citation.

State v. Phillips, 2000 WI App 184, ¶ 10, 238 Wis. 2d 279, 284, 617 N.W. 2d 522, 525. –Pinpoint Citation.

In all other documents:

State v. Phillips, 2000 WI App 184, 617 N.W.2d 522. –Case Citation.

State v. Phillips, 2000 WI App 184, ¶ 10, 617 N.W.2d 522, 525. –Pinpoint Citation.

See Bluebook rules 10.3.1, 10.3.3, and B5.1.3; see also Wis. App. P. R. 809.19(1)(e) and Wis. Sup. Ct. R. 80.02.

Wisconsin International Law Journal
Ab.: Wis. Int'l L.J.

Ex.: Donna E. Arzt, Religious Freedom in a Religious State: The Case of Israel in Comparative Constitutional Perspective, 9 Wis. Int'l L.J. 1 (1990). –Article Citation.

Donna E. Arzt, Religious Freedom in a Religious State: The Case of Israel in Comparative Constitutional Perspective, 9 Wis. Int'l L.J. 1, 49-53 (1990). –Page Citation.

Wisconsin Law Review
Ab.: Wis. L. Rev.

Ex.: Ann Althouse, Saying What Rights Are - In and Out of Context, 1991 Wis. L. Rev. 929. –Article Citation.

Ann Althouse, Saying What Rights Are - In and Out of Context, 1991 Wis. L. Rev. 929, 929. –Page Citation.

Wisconsin Lawyer
Ab.: Wisc. Law.

Ex.: Christopher J. Johnson, The Civil Rights Act of 1991, Wisc. Law., Feb. 1992, at 12. –Article Citation.

Christopher J. Johnson, The Civil Rights Act of 1991, Wisc. Law., Feb. 1992, at 12, 13. –Page Citation.

Wisconsin Legislative Service (West)
See West's Wisconsin Legislative Service.

In citing cases in law review footnotes, abbreviate any word listed in table T.6; the names of "states, countries, and other geographical units" unless they are named parties; and any other words of eight or more letters "if substantial space is thereby saved and the result is unambiguous." Bluebook rule 10.2.2. On the other hand, in citing cases in text, abbreviate only widely known acronyms and the following words: "&," "Ass'n," "Bros.," "Co.," "Corp.," "Inc.," "Ltd.," and "No." Bluebook rule 10.2.1(c).

Wisconsin Session Laws

Ab.: year Wis. Sess. Laws page no.

Ex.: Act of Dec. 11, 2003, No. 101, 2003 Wis. Sess. Laws 588 (relating to a health benefit project). –Citation to an entire session law.

Act of Dec. 11, 2003, No. 101, 2003 Wis. Sess. Laws 588, 589 (relating to a health benefit project). –Citation to a section of a session law.

See Bluebook rule 12.4.

Wisconsin Statutes

Ab.: Wis. Stat. § x.x (year)

Ex.: Wis. Stat. § 757.295 (1977).

Wis. Stat. § 939.62 (Supp. 1980).

Wisconsin Statutes Annotated, West's

See West's Wisconsin Statutes Annotated.

Wisconsin Supreme Court

Ab.: Wis. or Wis. 2d

–Cite to N.W. or N.W.2d, if therein; otherwise, cite to Wis. or Wis. 2d. Give public domain citation if available. Otherwise, give parallel citations only in documents submitted to Wisconsin state courts.

–Until January 1, 2000, when a public domain format was adopted, cite as follows:

In documents submitted to Wisconsin state courts:

Nowatske v. Osterloh, 198 Wis. 2d 419, 543 N.W.2d 265 (1996). –Case Citation.

Nowatske v. Osterloh, 198 Wis. 2d 419, 421, 543 N.W.2d 265, 268 (1996). –Page Citation.

In all other documents:

Nowatske v. Osterloh, 543 N.W.2d 265 (Wis. 1996). –Case Citation.

Nowatske v. Osterloh, 543 N.W.2d 265, 268 (Wis. 1996). –Page Citation.

–After January 1, 2000, cite as follows:

In documents submitted to Wisconsin state courts:

Rumager v. Gullberg, 2000 WI 53, 235 Wis. 2d 279, 611 N.W.2d 458. –Case Citation.

Rumager v. Gullberg, 2000 WI 53, ¶ 8, 235 Wis. 2d 279, 285, 611 N.W.2d 458, 461. –Pinpoint Citation.

In all other documents:

In law review footnotes, the titles of books and the names of cases, except for procedural phrases, are not underlined. See Bluebook rule 2.1(a) & (b). Further, the following are in large and small capitals: codes, restatements, standards, constitutions, periodicals, authors of books, titles of books, the abbreviated names of codes, most legislative materials except for bills and resolutions, codified ordinances, model codes, court rules, and sentencing guidelines. Refer to The Bluebook.

> Rumager v. Gullberg, 2000 WI 53, 611 N.W.2d 458. –Case Citation.
>
> Rumager v. Gullberg, 2000 WI 53, ¶ 8, 611 N.W.2d 458, 461. –Pinpoint Citation.

See Bluebook rules 10.3.1, 10.3.3, and B5.1.3; see also Wis. App. P. R. 809.19(1)(e) and Wis. Sup. Ct. R. 80.02.

Women Lawyers Journal
Ab.:   Women Law. J.

Ex.:   James R. Giddings, Mandatory Sentences: Why Can't We Trust Our Judges?, Women Law. J., Summer 1991, at 6. –Article Citation.

James R. Giddings, Mandatory Sentences: Why Can't We Trust Our Judges?, Women Law. J., Summer 1991, at 6, 7. –Page Citation.

Women's Rights Law Reporter
Ab.:   Women's Rts. L. Rep.

Ex.:   Norma J. Wikler & Lynn H. Schafran, Learning from the New Jersey Supreme Court Task Force on Women in the Courts: Evaluation, Recommendations and Implications for Other States, 12 Women's Rts. L. Rep. 313 (1991). –Article Citation.

Norma J. Wikler & Lynn H. Schafran, Learning from the New Jersey Supreme Court Task Force on Women in the Courts: Evaluation, Recommendations and Implications for Other States, 12 Women's Rts. L. Rep. 313, 351-55 (1991). –Page Citation.

worker's compensation
Ab.:   worker's comp.

Working Papers

Ex.:   Carol Anne Heimer, Remodeling the Garbage Can: Implications of the Causal Origins of Items in Decision Streams 31-35 (Am. B. Found., Working Paper No. 9805, 1999).

See Bluebook rule 17.3.

World Arbitration Reporter
Ab.:   World Arb. Rep.

World Competition, Law and Economics Review
Ab.:   World Competition L. & Econ. Rev.

Ex.:   Piet Eeckhout, The External Dimension of the EC Internal Market - A Portrait, World Competition L. & Econ. Rev., Dec. 1991, at 5. –Article Citation.

Piet Eeckhout, The External Dimension of the EC Internal Market - A Portrait, World Competition L. & Econ. Rev., Dec. 1991, at 5, 19-21. –Page Citation.

In citing cases in law review footnotes, abbreviate any word listed in table T.6; the names of "states, countries, and other geographical units" unless they are named parties; and any other words of eight or more letters "if substantial space is thereby saved and the result is unambiguous." Bluebook rule 10.2.2. On the other hand, in citing cases in text, abbreviate only widely known acronyms and the following words: "&," "Ass'n," "Bros.," "Co.," "Corp.," "Inc.," "Ltd.," and "No." Bluebook rule 10.2.1(c).

World Trade Organization

Ab.: WTO

Ex.: Appellate Body Report, <u>Korea–Measures Affecting Imports of Fresh, Chilled, and Frozen Beef</u>, ¶ 137, WT/DS161/AB/R (Dec. 11, 2000). –Appellate Body Decision.

Panel Report, <u>Japan–Measures Affecting Consumer Photographic Film and Paper</u>, ¶ 8, WT/DS44/R (Mar. 31, 1998) [hereinafter Film Panel Report]. –Panel Decision.

See <u>Bluebook</u> rule 21.8.4.

World Wide Web (WWW) Sites

See Electronic media and other nonprint resources.

Wright & Miller on Federal Practice and Procedure

See Federal Practice and Procedure, by Charles A. Wright & Arthur R. Miller.

Wyoming Constitution

Ab.: Wyo. Const. art. , § .

Ex.: Wyo. Const. art. 7, § 16. –"Cite constitutional provisions currently in force without a date." <u>Bluebook</u> rule 11.

Wyo. Const. art. 9, § 6 (repealed 1990). –"If the cited provision has been repealed, either indicate parenthetically the fact and date of repeal or cite the repealing provision in full." <u>Bluebook</u> rule 11.

Wyo. Const. art. 9, § 15 (amended 1990). –"When citing a provision that has been subsequently amended, either indicate parenthetically the fact and date of amendment or cite the amending provision in full." <u>Bluebook</u> rule 11.

Wyoming Law Review

Ab: Wyo. L. Rev.

Ex: John M. Burman, <u>Wyoming Attorneys' Pro Bono "Obligation"</u>, 5 Wyo. L. Rev. 421 (2005). –Article Citation.

John M. Burman, <u>Wyoming Attorneys' Pro Bono "Obligation"</u>, 5 Wyo. L. Rev. 421, 444 (2005). –Page Citation.

Wyoming Reports

Ab.: Wyo.

–Discontinued in 1959 after 80 Wyo. 492 (1959).

–Cite to P., P.2d, or P.3d, if therein; otherwise, cite to Wyo. Give public domain citation, if available. Otherwise, give parallel citations only in documents submitted to Wyoming state courts.

–Through 80 Wyo. 492 (1959), cite as follows:

In documents submitted to Wyoming state courts:

In law review footnotes, the titles of books and the names of cases, except for procedural phrases, are not underlined. See <u>Bluebook</u> rule 2.1(a) & (b). Further, the following are in large and small capitals: codes, restatements, standards, constitutions, periodicals, authors of books, titles of books, the abbreviated names of codes, most legislative materials except for bills and resolutions, codified ordinances, model codes, court rules, and sentencing guidelines. Refer to <u>The Bluebook</u>.

Lucksinger v. Salisbury, 72 Wyo. 164, 262 P.2d 396 (1953). –Case Citation.

Lucksinger v. Salisbury, 72 Wyo. 164, 173, 262 P.2d 396, 398-99 (1953). –Page Citation.

(Note: Because Wyoming Supreme Court opinions provide parallel citations to such decisions, we advise giving a parallel citation in documents submitted to Wyoming state courts.)

In all other documents:

Lucksinger v. Salisbury, 262 P.2d 396 (Wyo. 1953). –Case Citation.

Lucksinger v. Salisbury, 262 P.2d 396, 398-99 (Wyo. 1953). –Page Citation.

–After 80 Wyo. 492 (1959) and until January 1, 2001, cite as follows:

In all documents:

Carrar v. Bourke, 910 P.2d 572 (Wyo. 1996). –Case Citation.

Carrar v. Bourke, 910 P.2d 572, 573 (Wyo. 1996). –Page Citation.

–For cases decided Jan. 1, 2001, to date, cite as follows:

In all documents:

Steele v. Steele, 2005 WY 33, 108 P.3d 844 (Wyo. 2005). –Case Citation.

Steele v. Steele, 2006 WY 33, ¶ 17, 108 P.3d 844, 851 (Wyo. 2005) –Pinpoint Citation.

See Bluebook rules 10.3.1, 10.3.3, and B5.1.3; see also Order Amending Citation Format (Aug. 19, 2005).

Wyoming Rules and Regulations
See Weil's Code of Wyoming Rules.

Wyoming Session Laws
See Session Laws of Wyoming.

Wyoming Statutes Annotated (LexisNexis)
Ab.:   Wyo. Stat. Ann. § x-x-x (year)

Ex.:   Wyo. Stat. Ann. § 35-7-1404 (2001).

Wyo. Stat. Ann. § 14-3-302 (Supp. 2005).

In citing cases in law review footnotes, abbreviate any word listed in table T.6; the names of "states, countries, and other geographical units" unless they are named parties; and any other words of eight or more letters "if substantial space is thereby saved and the result is unambiguous." Bluebook rule 10.2.2. On the other hand, in citing cases in text, abbreviate only widely known acronyms and the following words: "&," "Ass'n," "Bros.," "Co.," "Corp.," "Inc.," "Ltd.," and "No." Bluebook rule 10.2.1(c).

Y

Yale Journal of Health Policy, Law, and Ethics
Ab: Yale J. Health Pol'y L. & Ethics
Ex: Dean M. Hashimoto, <u>The Proposed Patients' Bill of Rights: The Case of the Missing Equal Protection Clause</u>, 1 Yale J. Health Pol'y L. & Ethics 77 (2001). –Article Citation.

Dean M. Hashimoto, <u>The Proposed Patients' Bill of Rights: The Case of the Missing Equal Protection Clause</u>, 1 Yale J. Health Pol'y L. & Ethics 77, 82 (2001). –Page Citation.

Yale Journal of International Law
Ab.: Yale J. Int'l L.
Ex.: Geoffrey R. Watson, <u>Offenders Abroad: The Case for Nationality-Based Criminal Jurisdiction</u>, 17 Yale J. Int'l L. 41 (1992). –Article Citation.

Geoffrey R. Watson, <u>Offenders Abroad: The Case for Nationality-Based Criminal Jurisdiction</u>, 17 Yale J. Int'l L. 41, 57-64 (1992). –Page Citation.

Yale Journal of Law and Feminism
Ab.: Yale J.L. & Feminism
Ex.: Ruth Colker, <u>Marriage</u>, 3 Yale J.L. & Feminism 321 (1991). –Article Citation.

Ruth Colker, <u>Marriage</u>, 3 Yale J.L. & Feminism 321, 325 (1991). –Page Citation.

Yale Journal of Law and the Humanities
Ab.: Yale J.L. & Human.
Ex.: John M. Fischer, <u>The Trolley and the Sorites</u>, 4 Yale J.L. & Human. 105 (1992). –Article Citation.

John M. Fischer, <u>The Trolley and the Sorites</u>, 4 Yale J.L. & Human. 105, 109-15 (1992). –Page Citation.

Yale Journal of Law and Liberation
Ab.: Yale J.L. & Lib.

Yale Journal of World Public Order
Ab.: Yale J. World Pub. Ord.

In law review footnotes, the titles of books and the names of cases, except for procedural phrases, are not underlined. <u>See</u> <u>Bluebook</u> rule 2.1(a) & (b). Further, the following are in large and small capitals: codes, restatements, standards, constitutions, periodicals, authors of books, titles of books, the abbreviated names of codes, most legislative materials except for bills and resolutions, codified ordinances, model codes, court rules, and sentencing guidelines. Refer to <u>The Bluebook</u>.

Ex.: Siegfried Wiessner, <u>The Public Order of the Geostationary Orbit:</u> <u>Blueprints for the Future</u>, 9 Yale J. World Pub. Ord. 217 (1983). –Article Citation.

Siegfried Wiessner, <u>The Public Order of the Geostationary Orbit:</u> <u>Blueprints for the Future</u>, 9 Yale J. World Pub. Ord. 217, 231-32 (1983). –Page Citation.

Yale Journal on Regulation
Ab.: Yale J. on Reg.

Ex.: George L. Priest, <u>Can Absolute Manufacturer Liability be Defended?</u>, 9 Yale J. on Reg. 237 (1992). –Article Citation.

George L. Priest, <u>Can Absolute Manufacturer Liability be Defended?</u>, 9 Yale J. on Reg. 237, 249-52 (1992). –Page Citation.

Yale Law and Policy Review
Ab.: Yale L. & Pol'y Rev.

Ex.: David Cole, <u>First Amendment Antitrust: The End of Laissez-Faire in</u> <u>Campaign Finance</u>, 9 Yale L. & Pol'y Rev. 236 (1991). –Article Citation.

David Cole, <u>First Amendment Antitrust: The End of Laissez-Faire in</u> <u>Campaign Finance</u>, 9 Yale L. & Pol'y Rev. 236, 259-60 (1991). –Page Citation.

Yale Law Journal
Ab.: Yale L.J.

Ex.: Heidi M. Hurd, <u>Challenging Authority</u>, 100 Yale L.J. 1611 (1991). –Article Citation.

Heidi M. Hurd, <u>Challenging Authority</u>, 100 Yale L.J. 1611, 1639-45 (1991). –Page Citation.

Yearbook Commercial Arbitration
Ab.: Y.B. Com. Arb.

Ex.: Neil Kaplan, <u>Hong Kong</u>, 16 Y.B. Com. Arb. 391 (1991). –Article Citation.

Neil Kaplan, <u>Hong Kong</u>, 16 Y.B. Com. Arb. 391, 392 (1991). –Page Citation.

Yearbook of the European Convention on Human Rights
Ab.: Y.B. Eur. Conv. on H.R.

Ex.: <u>Farrell v. United Kingdom</u>, 1982 Y.B. Eur. Conv. on H.R. (Eur. Comm'n on H.R.) 124.

–When citing, note in a parenthetical whether the case was before the Court or the Commission. <u>See</u> <u>Bluebook</u> rule 21.5.3.

In citing cases in law review footnotes, abbreviate any word listed in table T.6; the names of "states, countries, and other geographical units" unless they are named parties; and any other words of eight or more letters "if <u>substantial</u> space is thereby saved and the result is unambiguous." <u>Bluebook</u> rule 10.2.2. On the other hand, in citing cases in text, abbreviate only widely known acronyms and the following words: "&," "Ass'n," "Bros.," "Co.," "Corp.," "Inc.," "Ltd.," and "No." <u>Bluebook</u> rule 10.2.1(c).

Yearbook of the International Law Commission
    Ab.:   Y.B. Int'l L. Comm'n

    Ex.:   <u>Summary Records of the Meetings of the Forty-Sixth Session 2 May --</u>
           <u>22 July 1994</u>, [1994] 1 Y.B. Int'l L. Comm'n 19, U.N. Doc.
           A/CN.4/SER.A/1994.

Yearbook of the United Nations
    Ab.:   U.N.Y.B.

    Ex.:   1986 U.N.Y.B. 672, U.N. Sales No. E.90.I.1.

           <u>See</u> <u>Bluebook</u> rule 21.7.9.

Yearbook (or Year Book)
    Ab.:   Y.B.

Youth Court
    Ab.:   Youth Ct.

In law review footnotes, the titles of books and the names of cases, except for procedural phrases, are not underlined. <u>See</u> <u>Bluebook</u> rule 2.1(a) & (b). Further, the following are in large and small capitals: codes, restatements, standards, constitutions, periodicals, authors of books, titles of books, the abbreviated names of codes, most legislative materials except for bills and resolutions, codified ordinances, model codes, court rules, and sentencing guidelines. Refer to <u>The Bluebook</u>.

Z

Zoning and Planning Law Report
   Ab.:   Zoning & Plan. L. Rep.

   Ex.:   Edith M. Netter, <u>Using Medication to Resolve Land Use Disputes</u>, 15 Zoning & Plan. L. Rep. 25 (1992). –Article Citation.

           Edith M. Netter, <u>Using Medication to Resolve Land Use Disputes</u>, 15 Zoning & Plan. L. Rep. 25, 27-28 (1992). –Page Citation.

In law review footnotes, the titles of books and the names of cases, except for procedural phrases, are not underlined. <u>See</u> <u>Bluebook</u> rule 2.1(a) & (b). Further, the following are in large and small capitals: codes, restatements, standards, constitutions, periodicals, authors of books, titles of books, the abbreviated names of codes, most legislative materials except for bills and resolutions, codified ordinances, model codes, court rules, and sentencing guidelines. Refer to <u>The Bluebook</u>.

Tables

All information provided in the Tables was contributed by
Bernard J. Sussman, J.D., M.L.S., C.P., Law Librarian,
United States Court of Appeals for Veterans Claims.

Table 1

States' Highest Courts

A state's highest court is called "the Supreme Court," except in the following instances:

Court of Appeals

    District of Columbia
    Maryland
    New York

Supreme Judicial Court

    Maine
    Massachusetts

Supreme Court of Appeals

    West Virginia

Court of Criminal Appeals (co-exists with non-criminal Supreme Court)

    Oklahoma
    Texas

TABLE 2

Discontinued State Reporters
(Since circa 1950)

Arranged by State, the volume number of the last state volume and the parallel West regional reporter, and the year.

last volume	West parallel	year
295 Ala.	325 So. 2d	1976
57 Ala. App.	326 So. 2d	1974
17 Alaska	348 P.2d	1958
27 Ariz. App.	558 P.2d	1977
200 Colo.	618 P.2d	1980
44 Colo. App.	620 P.2d	1980
6 Conn. Cir. Ct.	360 A.2d	1976
59 Del. (9 Story)	219 A.2d	1966
43 Del. Ch.	240 A.2d	1968
160 Fla.	40 So. 2d	1948
10 Haw. App.	880 P.2d	1994
275 Ind.	419 N.E.2d	1981
182 Ind. App.	396 N.E.2d	1979
261 Iowa	159 N.W.2d	1968
314 Ky.	238 S.W.2d	1951
263 La.	270 So. 2d	1972
161 Me.	215 A.2d	1965
312 Minn.	253 N.W.2d	1977
254 Miss.	183 S.W.2d	1966
364 Mo.	295 S.W.2d	1956
241 Mo. App.	252 S.W.2d	1955
79 N.D.	60 N.W.2d	1953
208 Okla.	285 P.2d	1953
122 R.I.	413 A.2d	1980
90 S.D.	245 N.W.2d	1976
225 Tenn.	476 S.W.2d	1972
63 Tenn. App.	480 S.W.2d	1972
4 Tenn. Crim. App.	475 S.W.2d	1972
163 Tex.	359 S.W.2d	1962
172 Tex. Crim.	362 S.W.2d	1963
30 Utah	519 P.2d	1974
80 Wyo.	345 P.2d	1959

Fla. Supp. discontinued in 1992, and Ohio Op. discontinued in 1982. −No West parallel for either reporter.

Table 3

Year, Congress & Session, Volume Number

Year	Congress	Session	Fed Reg.	Cong. Rec.	Statutes at Large
1931	72	1	--	75	47
1932	72	2	--	76	47
1933	73	1	--	77	48
1934	73	2	--	78	48
1935	74	1	--	79	49
1936	74	2	1 (see note)	80	49
1937	75	1-2	2	81-82	50-51 (see note)
1938	75	3	3	83	52
1939	76	1	4	84	53 (see note)
1940	76	3	5	86	54
1941	77	1	6	87	55 (see note)
1942	77	2	7	88	56
1943	78	1	8	89	57
1944	78	2	9	90	58
1945	79	1	10	91	59 (see note)
1946	79	1	11	92	60
1947	80	1	12	93	61
1948	80	2	13	94	62
1949	81	1	14	95	63 (see note)
1950	81	2	15	96	64
1951	82	1	16	97	65
1952	82	2	17	98	66
1953	83	1	18	99	67
1954	83	2	19	100	68
1955	84	1	20	101	69
1956	84	2	21	102	70 (see note)
1957	85	1	22	103	71 (see note)
1958	85	1	23	104	72
1959	86	1	24	105	73
1960	86	2	25	106	74
1961	87	1	26	107	75
1962	87	2	27	108	76
1963	88	1	28	109	77
1964	88	2	29	110	78
1965	89	1	30	111	79 (see note)
1966	89	2	31	112	80
1967	90	1	32	113	81
1968	90	2	33	114	82
1969	91	1	34	115	83
1970	91	2	35	116	84
1971	92	1	36	117	85
1972	92	2	37	118	86

1973	93	1	38	119	87
1974	93	2	39	120	88
1975	94	1	40	121	89
1976	94	2	41	122	90
1977	95	1	42	123	91
1978	95	2	43	124	92
1979	96	1	44	125	93
1980	96	2	45	126	94
1981	97	1	46	127	95
1982	97	2	47	128	96
1983	98	1	48	129	97
1984	98	2	49	130	98
1985	99	1	50	131	99
1986	99	2	51	132	100
1987	100	1	52	133	101
1988	100	2	53	134	102
1989	101	1	54	135	103
1990	101	2	55	136	104
1991	102	1	56	137	105
1992	102	2	57	138	106
1993	103	1	58	139	107
1994	103	2	59	140	108
1995	104	1	60	141	109
1996	104	2	62	142	110
1997	105	1	63	143	111
1998	105	2	64	144	112
1999	106	1	65	145	113
2000	106	2	66	146	114
2001	107	1	67	147	115
2002	107	2	68	148	116
2003	108	1	69	149	117
2004	108	2	70	150	118
2005	109	1	70	151	119

Notes:

1936: Federal Register first issue is Saturday, March 14, 1936. Volume two begins in January 1937. Originally the Federal Register was issued daily, Tuesday thru Saturday. In January 1973, volume thirty-eight changed to Monday thru Friday.

1937: 75th Congress, second session (November-December 1937) is 51 Statutes at Large pages three thru five, the rest of the volume is treaties of 1937. The third session (January-June 1938) is 52 Statutes at Large.

1939: 76th Congress, second session (October-November 1939) begins 54 Statutes at Large page three. The third session (January 1940 – January 1941) begins on page thirteen.

1941: West's US Code Congressional & Administrative News (USCCAN) begins coverage, with the beginning of the 77th Congress, 1st Session, 1941, with its own typesetting of the public laws in 55 Statutes at Large (therefore, USCCAN page numbers do not correspond to Stat. page numbers).

1945: The National Archives's occasional volume of Codification of Presidential Proclamations & Executive Orders begins its coverage with President Truman's first day in office, April 13, 1945 (Exec. Order No. 9538, Proclamation No. 648).

1949: The Second Edition of the Code of Federal Regulations (CFR) is published. The first edition was published in 1939 as a set of hardcover volumes with annual supplementary hardcover volumes. The 1949 Second Edition was similarly hardcover volumes with supplementary volumes. The Revised Edition of 1956 was hardcover with pocket parts. In 1964, the annual paperback volume format was begun.

1956: Code of Federal Regulations (CFR) changes format slightly, from hardcover main volumes with hardcover supplement volumes to a "revised edition" of hardcover volumes with annual pocket parts.

1957: The numbering system of the Acts of Congress changes. Previously, from 1902 through the end of 1956, both the chapter number (which began with each session) and the Public Law number (which began with each Congress) were assigned to Acts—although most citation manuals and the United States Code only gave the chapter numbers. Starting with the beginning of the 57th Congress, 1st session, 1957, 71 Statutes at Large, chapter numbers are no longer used, the number of the Congress is added as a prefix to the Public Law number, and only Public Law numbers are used.

1964: Code of Federal Regulations (CFR) adopts its present format of annual paperback volumes, replaced annually.

1975: Congress changes the format of the slip editions of the new laws, and of the Statutes at Large. Previously, new laws were published in separate booklets, called slip editions, with temporary and unofficial page numbers and page breaks. The official and permanent pagination of Statutes at Large did not appear until the Statutes at Large volumes were printed, as much as a year or two after the enactment. Starting with the beginning of the 95th Congress, 1st session, 1975, 89 Stat., a printing format was adopted so that the slip editions could immediately show the page numbers and page breaks which would appear in the Statutes at Large volumes. West's US Code Congressional & Administration News thereupon ceased its own typesetting of the laws and began photographically reproducing the slip editions of the public laws with the Statutes at Large page numbers.

Table 4

Numbering Acts of Congress

CHAPTER numbers were used from the 1st Congress, 1789, 1 <u>United States Statutes at Large</u> (hereinafter <u>Statutes at Large</u>), through the 84th Congress, 1956, 70 <u>Statutes at Large</u>. The chapter numbers began with a new series each *session* of Congress (there are at least two sessions per two-year Congress).

PUBLIC LAW numbers are in a single series for the entire two-year Congress. Public Law numbers were used in two stages.

First, Public Law numbers without the number of the Congress, were used simultaneously with the chapter numbers, from the first session of the 56th Congress, 1902, 32 <u>Statutes at Large</u>, through the second session of the 84th Congress, 1956, 70 <u>Statutes at Large</u> (<u>U.S. Code</u> source notes, and many citation manuals for Acts during that period mention only the chapter number, but not the Public Law number).

Then, with the start of the 85th Congress, 1957, 71 <u>Statutes at Large</u>, chapter numbers ceased and Public Law numbers were used exclusively. Now the Public Law number included a prefix with the number of the Congress (e.g., Public Law 85-1).

Until 1975, it was the practice of <u>Statutes at Large</u> to try to conserve space by following the end of one statutes with the beginning of another on the same page in <u>Statutes at Large</u> (this sometimes got even three or more statutes on one page). Shortly after laws were enacted, a copy of the text was available in an individual slip edition with its own unofficial page numbers, and a year might elapse before the final and official United States <u>Statutes at Large</u> page numbers became available. But starting with the first session of the 94th Congress in 1975, 89 <u>Statutes at Large</u>, each statute began at the top of a new page. This change enabled the slip editions of each statute to reflect the permanent and official Statutes at Large page numbers almost immediately. This change also enabled West's <u>United States Code Congressional and Administrative News</u>, which previously had reset the <u>Acts of Congress</u> in its own typeface with its own unofficial page breaks, to photographically reproduce the <u>Statutes at Large</u> pages, with the official page numbering, for its advance sheets and its permanent volumes (starting with the U.S.C.C.A.N. for 1975).

West's <u>United States Code Congressional and Administrative News</u> began as the <u>U.S. Code Congressional Service</u>, 77th Congress, 1st Session, 1941 (55 <u>Statutes at Large</u>). It was renamed the <u>United States Code Congressional and Administrative Service</u>, 82nd Congress, 1st Session, 1951 (65 <u>Statutes at Large</u>). It was given its present name of the <u>United States Code Congressional and Administrative News</u>, 82d Congress, 2d Session, 1952 (66 <u>Statutes at Large</u>). Starting in 1975, 94th Congress, 1st Session (89 <u>Statutes at Large</u>), it began reproducing the official pages and page numbers of <u>Statutes at Large</u> photographically, instead of doing its own typesetting of the statutes into its own unofficial page numbers.

Table 5

Dates and Coverage of United States Code Editions

Although most people use a commercial edition such as the United States Code Annotated (U.S.C.A.) or United States Code Service (U.S.C.S.), because The Bluebook calls for citation to the official editions and supplements of the United States Code, this table is provided showing the dates and coverage of the various official editions over the years.

The United States Code was worked up during the early 1920s by the House Committee on the Revision of the Laws, which had retained professional editors from West Publishing Company for this purpose. In June 1926 Congress adopted (as "prima facie evidence of the law") the finished product—a logical, rather than chronological, arrangement of the current general and permanent statutes, as amended—with an "as of" date of December 7, 1925. This was published in 1927 as volume forty-four of the Statutes at Large. In the same year, West Publishing began issuing the United States Code Annotated. As of 2005, the only volume of that first edition still found in current sets of the U.S.C.A. is Title 27 – Intoxicating Liquors.

Another annotated edition, long forgotten, was Mason's United States Code Annotated, published in three volumes in 1927 by the Citer-Digest Company of St. Paul, Minn. This was updated with a few supplementary volumes until 1936, when the Bobbs-Merrill Company bought the series and issued it starting in 1938, initially in thirteen volumes, as Federal Code Annotated (F.C.A.), and updating it more frequently than Mason had. In 1972, the service was bought from Bobbs-Merrill by the Lawyer's Co-operative Publishing Company, which continued it under the name United States Code Service (U.S.C.S.). In the mid-1990s the publication again charged hands, to Lexis Publishing Company, which has continued it according to the style and standards set by Lawyers Co-operative.

The U.S.C.S. is somewhat different from the U.S.C. and West's U.S.C.A. Whereas the text of the U.S.C., reproduced exactly in the U.S.C.A., has been edited (and thereby slightly modified) from the original statutes, U.S.C.S. has examined and reproduced the exact wording of the original statutes, occasionally providing a necessary reference or antecedent in square brackets, reconstructing every section of the U.S.C. (except for those titles which were re-enacted as positive law), to which the publisher added its own cases notes (somewhat different from those of U.S.C.A.).

External to the actual sections, the notes (worked up by the House Legislative Revision Counsel) of Executive Orders and Presidential Proclamations and some other materials (such as court rules and relevant but unassigned sections of statutes) appended to the sections of the official edition of U.S.C. might be re-arranged or re-located in U.S.C.A. and U.S.C.S.

The United States Code began with fifty titles (as the topics were known), in alphabetical order after the first six titles. Over the years a few titles have been renamed so the alphabetic effect has been impaired (e.g., title 38, originally "Pensions," was renamed "Veterans Benefits" in 1958), a few titles have been dropped (e.g., title 6, originally "Official and Penal Bonds," was renamed "Surety Bonds" in 1947, and then was completely repealed in 1982, and was an empty title until November 2002, when title 6 was renamed "Domestic Security" and filled out with legislation relating to the Department of Homeland Security), and several titles have been re-enacted exactly as intended to appear in the U.S.C., thereby becoming "positive law."

Suppl.	As of date	Ending with Stat. vol.
1926 edition (= 44 Stat.)		
Main	12/7/25	43
I	12/5/27	44
II	5/29/28	45 Stat 1008
III	3/4/29	45
IV	7/3/30	46 Stat 1018
V	3/4/31	46
VI	7/16/32	47 Stat 701
VII	6/16/33	48 Stat 311
1934 edition		
Main	1/3/35	48
I	8/31/35	49 Stat 1081
II	7/13/36	49
III	9/2/37	50
IV	6/30/38	52
V	11/4/39	53
1940 edition		
Main	1/3/41	54
I	1/2/42	55
II	12/29/42	56
III	12/23/43	57
IV	1/3/45	58
V	1/13/46	59
1946 edition		
Main	1/2/47	60
I	1/5/48	61
II	1/2/49	62

III	1/2/50	63
IV	1/2/51	64
V	1/7/52	65
1952 edition		
Main	1/2/53	66
I	1/5/54	67
II	1/4/55	68
III	1/2/56	69
IV	1/2/57	70A
V	1/6/58	71

Suppl.	As of date	Ending with Stat. vol.
1958 edition		
Main	1/6/59	72
I	1/5/60	73
II	1/2/61	74
III	1/9/62	75
IV	1/9/63	76
V	1/6/64	77
1964 edition		
Main	1/3/65	78
I	1/9/66	79
II	1/9/67	80
III	1/14/68	81
IV	1/2/69	82
V	1/18/70	83
1970 edition		
Main	1/20/71	84
I	1/17/72	85
II	1/2/73	86
III	1/20/74	87
IV	1/2/75	88
V	1/18/76	89
1976 edition		
Main	1/3/77	90
I	1/18/78	91
II	1/14/79	92
III	1/8/80	93
IV	1/5/81	95

V	1/25/82	95
1982 edition		
Main	1/14/83	96
I	1/22/84	97
II	1/2/85	98
III	1/20/86	99
IV	1/5/87	100
V	2/5/88	101

1988 edition		
Main	1/3/89	102
I	1/22/90	103
II	1/2/91	104
III	1/2/92	105
IV	1/4/93	106
V	1/24/94	107
1994 edition		
Main	1/3/95	108
I	1/16/96	109
II	1/6/97	110
III	1/26/98	111
IV	1/5/99	112
V	1/23/2000	113
2000 edition		
Main	1/2/01	114
I	1/22/02	115
II	1/6/03	116
III	1/19/04	117
IV	1/3/05	118
V	- - -	- -
2006 edition		
Main		

TABLE 6

United States Supreme Court Reporters

Nominatives: The early reports of the United States Supreme Court are frequently identified by the name of the individual responsible for compiling the volumes.   These "nominative" reports constitute the first ninety volumes of the U.S. Reports series, and volumes issued after that are simply known by their volume number as "U.S.".   Those first ninety volumes had titles such as "Reports of Cases Argued and Adjudged in the Supreme Court of the United States by ...," but subsequent to the ninetieth, the reports are cited only by a "U.S." volume number.   The entire set could be cited as "U.S.," but some authorities (e.g., some early style sheets such as Miles O. Price's 1958 manual, and some distinguished jurists such as Associate Justice Felix Frankfurter) preferred to cite the early reports only by the reporters' names. (Some citations early in the Twentieth Century, also referred to volumes 91-107 U.S. by the name of their reporter, W.T. Otto.)

The named reporters, alphabetically, are:

Black (abbreviated: "Black"), 2 vols. = 66-67 U.S. (1861-1862); Jeremiah Sullivan Black (1810 - 1882) previously U.S. Attorney General.

Cranch ("Cranch"), 9 vols. = 5-13 U.S. (1801-1815); William Cranch (1769-1855) judge of the District of Columbia Circuit Court.

Dallas ("Dall."), 4 vols. = 1-4 U.S. (1790-1800); Alexander J. Dallas (1759-1817) U.S. Secretary of State, subsequently U.S. Secretary of the Treasury.

Howard ("How."), 24 vols. = 42-65 U.S. (1843-1860); Benjamin Chew Howard (1791-1872) previously a member of the U.S. House of Representatives from Maryland, and then in the Maryland Senate.

Otto ("Otto"), 17 vols. = 91-107 U.S. (1875-1882) [these usually are cited by their "U.S." number, without mentioning Otto]; William Todd Otto (1816-1905) previously a judge in Indiana and Assistant Secretary of the Interior.

Peters ("Pet."), 16 vols. = 26-41 U.S. (1828-1842); Richard Peters (1780-1848) previously compiler of the decisions of the U.S. Circuit Court for Philadelphia, editor of "Chitty on Bills of Exchange" and "Bushrod Washington's Circuit Court Reports."

Wallace ("Wall."), 23 vols. = 68-90 U.S. (1863-1874); John William Wallace (1815-1884) previously librarian to the Law Association of Philadelphia, compiler of decisions of the US Court of Appeals for the Third Circuit.

Wheaton ("Wheat."), 12 vols. = 14-25 U.S. (1816-1827); Henry Wheaton (1785-1848) previously a judge in Rhode Island, translator of the Napoleonic Code, subsequently diplomat in Denmark and Prussia and authority on international law.

The volumes of the early reporters:

Name	U.S.	L. Ed.	Term	Chief Justice
1 Dallas	1 U.S.	1 L.Ed.	(see note ___)	--
2 Dallas	2 U.S.	1 L.Ed.	Feb. 1790 – Aug. 1793	Jay
3 Dallas	3 U.S.	1 L.Ed.	1894-Feb. 1799	Jay, Rutledge, Ellsworth
4 Dallas	4 U.S.	1 L.Ed.	Aug. 1799-Aug. 1800	Elsworth
1 Cranch	5 U.S.	2 L.Ed.	1801-Feb. 1803	Marshall
2 Cranch	6 U.S.	2 L.Ed.	Feb. 1804-1805	Marshall
3 Cranch	7 U.S.	2 L.Ed.	1805-1806	Marshall
4 Cranch	8 U.S.	2 L.Ed.	1807-1808	Marshall
5 Cranch	9 U.S.	3 L.Ed.	1809	Marshall
6 Cranch	10 U.S.	3 L.Ed.	1810	Marshall
7 Cranch	11 U.S.	3 L.Ed.	1812-1813	Marshall
8 Cranch	12 U.S.	3 L.Ed.	1814	Marshall
9 Cranch	13 U.S.	3 L.Ed.	1815	Marshall
1 Wheat.	14 U.S.	4 L.Ed.	1816	Marshall
2 Wheat.	15 U.S.	4 L.Ed.	1817	Marshall
3 Wheat.	16 U.S.	4 L.Ed.	1818	Marshall
4 Wheat.	17 U.S.	4 L.Ed.	1819	Marshall
5 Wheat.	18 U.S.	5 L.Ed.	1820	Marshall
6 Wheat.	19 U.S.	5 L.Ed.	1821	Marshall
7 Wheat.	20 U.S.	5 L.Ed.	1822	Marshall
8 Wheat.	21 U.S.	5 L.Ed.	1823	Marshall
9 Wheat.	22 U.S.	6 L.Ed.	1824	Marshall
10 Wheat.	23 U.S.	6 L.Ed.	1825	Marshall
11 Wheat.	24 U.S.	6 L.Ed.	1826	Marshall
12 Wheat.	25 U.S.	6 L.Ed.	1827	Marshall
1 Pet.	26 U.S.	7 L.Ed.	1828	Marshall
2 Pet.	27 U.S.	7 L.Ed.	1829	Marshall
3 Pet.	28 U.S.	7 L.Ed.	1830	Marshall
4 Pet.	29 U.S.	7 L.Ed.	1830	Marshall
5 Pet.	30 U.S.	8 L.Ed.	1831	Marshall
6 Pet.	31 U.S.	8 L.Ed.	1832	Marshall
7 Pet.	32 U.S.	8 L.Ed.	1833	Marshall
8 Pet.	33 U.S.	8 L.Ed.	1834	Marshall
9 Pet.	34 U.S.	9 L.Ed.	1835	Marshall
10 Pet.	35 U.S.	9 L.Ed.	1836	Taney
11 Pet.	36 U.S.	9 L.Ed.	1837	Taney
12 Pet.	37 U.S.	9 L.Ed.	1838	Taney
13 Pet.	38 U.S.	10 L.Ed.	1839	Taney

Name	U.S.	L. Ed.	Term	Chief Justice
14 Pet.	39 U.S.	10 L.Ed.	1840	Taney
15 Pet.	40 U.S.	10 L.Ed.	1841	Taney
16 Pet.	41 U.S.	10 L.Ed.	1842	Taney
1 How.	42 U.S.	11 L.Ed.	1843	Taney
2 How.	43 U.S.	11 L.Ed.	1844	Taney
3 How.	44 U.S.	11 L.Ed.	1845	Taney
4 How.	45 U.S.	11 L.Ed.	1846	Taney
5 How.	46 U.S.	12 L.Ed.	1847	Taney
6 How.	47 U.S.	12 L.Ed.	1848	Taney
7 How.	48 U.S.	12 L.Ed.	1849	Taney
8 How.	49 U.S.	12 L.Ed.	1850	Taney
9 How.	50 U.S.	13 L.Ed.	1850	Taney
10 How.	51 U.S.	13 L.Ed.	1850	Taney
11 How.	52 U.S.	13 L.Ed.	1850	Taney
12 How.	53 U.S.	13 L.Ed.	1851	Taney
13 How.	54 U.S.	14 L.Ed.	1851	Taney
14 How.	55 U.S.	14 L.Ed.	1852	Taney
15 How.	56 U.S.	14 L.Ed.	1853	Taney
16 How.	57 U.S.	14 L.Ed.	1853	Taney
17 How.	58 U.S.	15 L.Ed.	1854	Taney (see note)
18 How.	59 U.S.	15 L.Ed.	1855	Taney
19 How.	60 U.S.	15 L.Ed.	1856	Taney
20 How.	61 U.S.	15 L.Ed.	1857	Taney
21 How.	62 U.S.	16 L.Ed.	1858	Taney
22 How.	63 U.S.	16 L.Ed.	1859	Taney
23 How.	64 U.S.	16 L.Ed.	1859	Taney
24 How.	65 U.S.	16 L.Ed.	1860	Taney
1 Black	66 U.S.	17 L.Ed.	1861	Taney
2 Black	67 U.S.	17 L.Ed.	1862	Taney
1 Wall.	68 U.S.	17 L.Ed.	1863	Taney
2 Wall.	69 U.S.	17 L.Ed.	1864	Taney, Chase
3 Wall.	70 U.S.	18 L.Ed.	1865	Chase
4 Wall.	71 U.S.	18 L.Ed.	1866	Chase
5 Wall.	72 U.S.	18 L.Ed.	1866	Chase
6 Wall.	73 U.S.	18 L.Ed.	1867	Chase
7 Wall.	74 U.S.	19 L.Ed.	1868	Chase
8 Wall.	75 U.S.	19 L.Ed.	1869	Chase
9 Wall.	76 U.S.	19 L.Ed.	1869	Chase
10 Wall.	77 U.S.	19 L.Ed.	1869	Chase
11 Wall.	78 U.S.	20 L.Ed.	1870	Chase
12 Wall.	79 U.S.	20 L.Ed.	1870	Chase
13 Wall.	80 U.S.	20 L.Ed.	1871	Chase
14 Wall.	81 U.S.	20 L.Ed.	1871	Chase
15 Wall.	82 U.S.	21 L.Ed.	1872	Chase

Name	U.S.	L. Ed.	Term	Chief Justice
16 Wall.	83 U.S.	21 L.Ed.	1872	Chase
17 Wall.	84 U.S.	21 L.Ed.	Dec. 1872-Oct. 1873	Chase
18 Wall.	85 U.S.	21 L.Ed.	Oct. 1873	Waite
19 Wall.	86 U.S.	22 L.Ed.	1873	Waite
20 Wall.	87 U.S.	22 L.Ed.	1873-1874	Waite
21 Wall.	88 U.S.	22 L.Ed.	1874	Waite
22 Wall.	89 U.S.	22 L.Ed.	1874	Waite
23 Wall.	90 U.S.	23 L.Ed.	1874	Waite
1 Otto	91 U.S.	23 L.Ed.	1875	Waite (see note)
2 Otto	92 U.S.	23 L.Ed.	1875	Waite
3 Otto	93 U.S.	23 L.Ed.	1876	Waite
4 Otto	94 U.S.	24 L.Ed.	1876	Waite
5 Otto	95 U.S.	24 L.Ed.	1877	Waite
6 Otto	96 U.S.	24 L.Ed.	1877	Waite
7 Otto	97 U.S.	24 L.Ed.	1877	Waite
8 Otto	98 U.S.	25 L.Ed.	1878	Waite
9 Otto	99 U.S.	25 L.Ed.	1878	Waite
10 Otto	100 U.S.	25 L.Ed.	1879	Waite
11 Otto	101 U.S.	25 L.Ed.	1879	Waite
12 Otto	102 U.S.	26 L.Ed.	Oct. 1879-Oct. 1880	Waite
13 Otto	103 U.S.	26 L.Ed.	1880	Waite
14 Otto	104 U.S.	26 L.Ed.	1881	Waite
15 Otto	105 U.S.	26 L.Ed.	1881	Waite

{end of the nominatives and beginning of West's Supreme Court Reporter}

Name	U.S.	L. Ed.	S. Ct.	Term	Chief Justice
16 Otto	106 U.S.	27 L.Ed.	1-2 S.Ct.	1881-1882	Waite (see note)
17 Otto	107 U.S.	27 L.Ed.	2 S.Ct.	1882	Waite
--	108 U.S.	27 L.Ed.	2 S.Ct.	1882	Waite
--	109 U.S.	27 L.Ed.	3 S.Ct.	1883	Waite
--	110 U.S.	28 L.Ed.	3-4 S.Ct.	1883	Waite
--	111 U.S.	28 L.Ed.	4 S.Ct.	1884	Waite

{Beginning with the October term of 1884, S.Ct. volume five, West's Supreme Court Reporter commenced issuing one volume to cover an entire annual term. The remainder of this table is, therefore, by October term, listing the volumes at the beginning of that term. An asterisk (*) indicates that part of that volume began in the preceding term;, usually because the one-line dispositions that are issued on the first day of a term are put at the end of the official United States Reports for the preceding term, thereby carrying that volume into the next term, and in

West's <u>Supreme Court Reporter</u> and <u>United States Supreme Court Reports, Lawyers Edition</u> at the beginning of the volume for the new term.}

Oct. term	U.S.	L.Ed.	S.Ct.	Chief Justice
1884	112	28*	5	Waite
1885	115*	29*	6	Waite
1886	118	30	7	Waite
1887	123	31	8	Waite / Fuller
1888	128	32*	9	Fuller
1889	132	33*	10	Fuller
1890	137	34*	11	Fuller
1891	141*	35*	12	Fuller
1892	146	36*	13	Fuller
1893	150	37*	14	Fuller (see note)
1894	155	39*	15	Fuller
1895	159*	40*	16	Fuller
1896	164	41*	17	Fuller
1897	168	42*	18	Fuller
1898	171*	43*	19	Fuller
1899	175	44	20	Fuller
1900	179	45	21	Fuller
1901	183	46	22	Fuller
1902	187	47	23	Fuller
1903	191	48	24	Fuller
1904	195	49	25	Fuller
1905	199	50	26	Fuller
1906	203	51	27	Fuller
1907	207	52	28	Fuller
1908	211	53	29	Fuller
1909	215	54	30	Fuller
1910	218*	54*	31	Fuller /White
1911	222	56	32	White
1912	226	57	33	White
1913	231	58	34	White
1914	235	59	35	White
1915	239	60	36	White
1916	242	61	37	White
1917	245	62	38	White
1918	248	63	39	White
1919	250*	63*	40	White
1920	254	65	41	White / Taft
1921	257	66	42	Taft
1922	260	67	43	Taft
1923	263	68	44	Taft
1924	266	69	45	Taft

Name	U.S.	L. Ed.	Term	Chief Justice
1925	269	70	46	Taft
1926	272	71	47	Taft
1927	275	72	48	Taft
1928	278	73	49	Taft
1929	280	74	50	Taft / Hughes
1930	282	75	51	Hughes
1931	284	76	52	Hughes
1932	287	77	53	Hughes
1933	290	78	54	Hughes
1934	293	79	55	Hughes
1935	296	80	56	Hughes
1936	299	81	57	Hughes
1937	302	82*	58	Hughes
1938	305	83	59	Hughes
1939	308	84	60	Hughes
1940	311	85	61	Hughes
1941	314	86	62	Stone
1942	317	87	63	Stone
1943	320*	88	64	Stone
1944	323	89	65	Stone
1945	325	90	66	Stone
1946	329	91	67	Vinson
1947	332	92	68	Vinson
1948	335*	93	69	Vinson
1949	338*	94	70	Vinson
1950	340	95	71	Vinson
1951	342	96	72	Vinson (see note)
1952	344	97	73	Vinson
1953	346*	98	74	Warren
1954	348	99	75	Warren
1955	350	100	76	Warren

{L.Ed.2d commences with October 1956}

Oct. term	U.S.	L.Ed.	S.Ct.	Chief Justice
1956	352	1 (2nd)	77	Warren (see note)
1957	355	2	78	Warren
1958	358	3	79	Warren
1959	361	4	80	Warren (see note)
1960	364	5	81	Warren
1961	368	7	82	Warren

Name	U.S.	L. Ed.	Term	Chief Justice
1962	371	9	83	Warren
1963	375	11	84	Warren
1964	379	13	85	Warren
1965	382	15	86	Warren
1966	385	17	87	Warren
1967	389	19	88	Warren
1968	393	21	89	Warren
1969	396	24	90	Burger
1970	400	27	91	Burger
1971	404	30	92	Burger (see note)
1972	409	34	93	Burger
1973	414	38	94	Burger
1974	419	42	95	Burger
1975	423	46	96	Burger
1976	429	50	97	Burger
1977	434	54	98	Burger
1978	439	58	99	Burger
1979	444	62	100	Burger
1980	449	66	101	Burger
1981	453	69	102	Burger
1982	459	74	103	Burger
1983	464	77	104	Burger
1984	469	83	105	Burger
1985	474	88	106	Burger
1986	479	93	107	Rehnquist
1987	484	98	108	Rehnquist
1988	488	102	109	Rehnquist
1989	493	107	110	Rehnquist
1990	498	112	111	Rehnquist
1991	501*	116	112	Rehnquist
1992	506	121	113	Rehnquist
1993	510	126	114	Rehnquist
1994	512*	130	115	Rehnquist
1995	516	133	116	Rehnquist
1996	519	136	117	Rehnquist
1997	522	139	118	Rehnquist
1998	525	142	119	Rehnquist
1999	528	145	120	Rehnquist
2000	531	148	121	Rehnquist
2001	534	151	122	Rehnquist
2002	537	154	123	Rehnquist
2003	540	157	124	Rehnquist
2004	- -	160	125	Rehnquist
2005	- -	- -	126	Roberts
2006	- -	- -	127	- -

FOOTNOTES:

1 U.S. = Volume one of <u>United States Reports</u> (=1 Dallas) does not contain anything of the U.S. Supreme Court but is entirely devoted to various Pennsylvania courts, including several pages of decisions issued before Independence. The style for most of these decisions is a lengthy extract or summary of the pleadings by both sides followed by a brief opinion of the court as to which argument won.

2 U.S. (=2 Dallas) continues to present Pennsylvania court decisions, with some decisions of the U.S. Court of Appeals, in Philadelphia, and U.S. Supreme Court decisions do not begin until 2 U.S. 399 (=1 L.Ed. 432), commencing with the February term of 1790 (not until 5 U.S. = 1 Cranch are the reports only of U.S. Supreme Court decisions). In its early decades the U.S. Supreme Court had two or three fairly short terms -- originally February and August, changed in early 1801 to June and December. In March 1802, this changed again to a single, longer term in February, causing the Court to wait until the next year to do business. In 1827, that term moved up to mid-January, moved again in 1845 to mid-December, and finally in 1873 to early October. The term is the only way to date decisions until 1854 (= 54 U.S., q.v.). In its early decades, the style of U. S. Supreme Court opinions as reported in U.S. Reports (described in the note above concerning 1 U.S.) continued for some time, with occasional exceptions similar to the modern style of decision. Only "major" decisions were published. Memo dispositions such as denial of certiorari were not published, and individual opinions, either concurring or dissenting, were almost never mentioned.

15 U.S. (= 2 Wheaton), during the period covered by this volume, Congress provided for the appointment of an official U.S. Supreme Court reporter and for the publication of an official edition of his reports, 3 Stat. 376 (March 3, 1817).

30 U.S. (=17 Howard, 15 L. Ed. 1831), Associate Justice Henry Baldwin joins the Court and distinguishes his short career there by publishing dissenting opinions. Until then, it was the practice of the Justices not to publicize their disagreements.

54 U.S. (= 17 Howard, 15 L. Ed., 1854), decisions dates begin to appear, but only in volume fifteen of Lawyers Edition. The dates do not appear in the official U.S. Reports until 1882 when L. Ed. and S. Ct. begin publishing, namely 108 U.S., 27 L. Ed. West's S. Ct. has the decision dates from the beginning of its coverage, in 1881, 106 U.S.

84 U.S. 9 (=17 Wallace, 21 L. Ed., 1873), by Act of Congress, in January 1873, the Supreme Court will have only one regular term, which will begin the first Monday in October each year.

91 U.S. (= 1 Otto, 1875), until this volume, the reports were financed privately. In 1884, Congress appropriated money for the reports, making them an official government publication and naming it officially the <u>United States Reports,</u> numbering the first volume issued under this title as 91, and numbering previous volumes retroactively with 1 Dallas = 1 U.S. (this scheme clearly indicated that a few volumes issued by former reporters were not counted as official reports). Beginning with 91 U.S., the name of the reporter ceases to be used by most legal writers.

106 US (= 16 Otto, 1882) At this time both West Brothers Publishing Co. and Lawyers Co-operative Publishing Co. begin printing their own editions of Supreme Court decisions. Lawyers Co-op begins producing the Lawyers' Edition (L. Ed.), originally edited by Stephen K. Williams (1819-1916), a former prosecutor, judge, state legislator, and co-founder of the publishing house. The L. Ed goes back to the first volume of Dallas, provides its own header summarizing the decision (this eventually becomes categorized headnotes), star numbers to the pages of the official edition, several essays in each volume on legal issues raised in decisions (originally presented as long footnotes, later as articles following the relevant decisions), and summations of the points and authorities cited by both sides (this last feature is mostly unavailable for cases before 1879 = circa 25 L. Ed = 101 U.S.). West Publishing begins producing the Supreme Court Reporter (S. Ct.), its first volume beginning in mid-1881 (= circa 106 U.S. = 27 L. Ed.), not attempting to reprint earlier decisions (although notes derived from those pre-1881 decisions are included in West's Supreme Court Digest); its particular features are providing headnotes using the West key number system, and one volume of S. Ct. covering an entire annual term of the Supreme Court (this last feature did not become obvious until volume 5 S. Ct. = 112 U.S., 1884).

126 U.S., 1887, contains only one case, a very cumbersome and complicated lawsuit involving several challenges to the patent on the telephone.

131 U.S., 1888, the reporter, J.C. Bancroft Davis, adds to volume 131 U.S. a very bulky appendix containing a brief essay on the history of the U.S. Reports, down to his own appointment in 1883, when he was instructed to publish every opinion of the Court, however brief, and to find and publish hitherto unpublished decisions. This appendix also included his essay summarizing decisions in admiralty or between states made under the Articles of Confederation, and a table of Supreme Court decisions invalidating federal or state laws. Most importantly, this appendix contained about 190 pages of Supreme Court decisions previously unpublished, going back to 1839. These decisions are cited to Appendix pages (using roman numerals) of 131 U.S., but are distributed in various places - not always chronologically appropriate nor promptly, nor always correctly correlated to 131 U.S. - in volumes of L. Ed. up through 76 L. Ed. (1931). In volume 154 U.S., 1894, Davis included another bulky appendix with approximately two hundred more previously unpublished decisions, which are similarly distributed throughout L. Ed.

154 U.S., 1894, the official volume contains an extensive appendix of hitherto unpublished decisions (see note for 131 U.S.).

257 U.S., 1921, the printing of the official edition, previously done by commercial publishers under government contract, is taken over by the U.S. Government Printing Office.

342 U.S. (= 96 L. Ed., 72 S. Ct., 1951), beginning with volume 96 L. Ed., Lawyers Edition begins including West's S. Ct. citation, as well as the official U.S. citation, in the heading of the cases. West's S. Ct. does not return the favor until 1971 (92 S. Ct. = 404 U.S., 30 L. Ed. 2d).

352 U.S. (= 1 L. Ed. 2d, 1956), 100 L. Ed. is followed by 1 L. Ed. 2d. The change in volume numbering includes a stylistic change; the summation of the precedents cited by both sides, which formerly appeared just before the Opinion of the Court, and the occasional editorial annotation on legal topics, which formerly followed the relevant decision, are now both moved to the back of the permanent edition. This enables the advance sheets to publish the decisions

with the permanent L. Ed. 2d pagination, those other items not appearing until the permanent hardcover volume.

362 U.S. (= 80 s. Ct., 4 L. Ed. 2d, 1960), in light of the increasing output of the Supreme Court, West stretches its original scheme of "one volume per year." Beginning with February 1960, volume eight of S. Ct. is followed by a volume with the number 80A on the spine but continuing the page numbers from the previous volume; the letters added on the individual binding are not citable, however. The last case in the second volume would be cited as 80 S. Ct. 1639. This practice continues to this day, when S. Ct. issues three bindings a year.

404 U.S. (= 92 S. Ct., 30 L. Ed. 2d, 1971), beginning with a decisions issued in June 1971, West's S. Ct. includes the L. Ed. 2d citation in the heading of the decisions (see note for 342 U.S.).

406 U.S. (= 32 L. Ed. 2d, 1972), L. Ed. 2d volumes, beginning with 32 L. Ed. 2d, are constructed for annual pocket parts, which correct any errors appearing in the hardcover volume, and update notes on the citation of the decisions in the volume and on the essays. The L. Ed. annual updates for volumes before 32 L. Ed. 2d are usually shelved between 31 L. Ed. 2d and 32 L Ed. 2d. While this information used to be provided in a hardcover volume designed for accommodating an annual pocket part, at present it is provided in two annual softcover volumes.